Communications
in Computer and Information Science 395

Editorial Board

Simone Diniz Junqueira Barbosa
Pontifical Catholic University of Rio de Janeiro (PUC-Rio),
Rio de Janeiro, Brazil

Phoebe Chen
La Trobe University, Melbourne, Australia

Alfredo Cuzzocrea
ICAR-CNR and University of Calabria, Italy

Xiaoyong Du
Renmin University of China, Beijing, China

Joaquim Filipe
Polytechnic Institute of Setúbal, Portugal

Orhun Kara
TÜBİTAK BİLGEM and Middle East Technical University, Turkey

Igor Kotenko
St. Petersburg Institute for Informatics and Automation
of the Russian Academy of Sciences, Russia

Krishna M. Sivalingam
Indian Institute of Technology Madras, India

Dominik Ślęzak
University of Warsaw and Infobright, Poland

Takashi Washio
Osaka University, Japan

Xiaokang Yang
Shanghai Jiao Tong University, China

Jerzy Mikulski (Ed.)

Activities of Transport Telematics

13th International Conference
on Transport Systems Telematics, TST 2013
Katowice-Ustroń, Poland, October 23-26, 2013
Selected Papers

 Springer

Volume Editor

Jerzy Mikulski
Silesian University of Technology
Faculty of Transport
Krasińskiego 8
40-019 Katowice, Poland
E-mail: jerzy.mikulski@polsl.pl

ISSN 1865-0929   e-ISSN 1865-0937
ISBN 978-3-642-41646-0   e-ISBN 978-3-642-41647-7
DOI 10.1007/978-3-642-41647-7
Springer Heidelberg New York Dordrecht London

Library of Congress Control Number: 2013951047

CR Subject Classification (1998): K.4, H.4, I.6, I.2, J.1, J.2, J.7

© Springer-Verlag Berlin Heidelberg 2013
This work is subject to copyright. All rights are reserved by the Publisher, whether the whole or part of
the material is concerned, specifically the rights of translation, reprinting, reuse of illustrations, recitation,
broadcasting, reproduction on microfilms or in any other physical way, and transmission or information
storage and retrieval, electronic adaptation, computer software, or by similar or dissimilar methodology
now known or hereafter developed. Exempted from this legal reservation are brief excerpts in connection
with reviews or scholarly analysis or material supplied specifically for the purpose of being entered and
executed on a computer system, for exclusive use by the purchaser of the work. Duplication of this publication
or parts thereof is permitted only under the provisions of the Copyright Law of the Publisher's location,
in ist current version, and permission for use must always be obtained from Springer. Permissions for use
may be obtained through RightsLink at the Copyright Clearance Center. Violations are liable to prosecution
under the respective Copyright Law.
The use of general descriptive names, registered names, trademarks, service marks, etc. in this publication
does not imply, even in the absence of a specific statement, that such names are exempt from the relevant
protective laws and regulations and therefore free for general use.
While the advice and information in this book are believed to be true and accurate at the date of publication,
neither the authors nor the editors nor the publisher can accept any legal responsibility for any errors or
omissions that may be made. The publisher makes no warranty, express or implied, with respect to the
material contained herein.

Typesetting: Camera-ready by author, data conversion by Scientific Publishing Services, Chennai, India

Printed on acid-free paper

Springer is part of Springer Science+Business Media (www.springer.com)

Preface

Transport plays a vital role in the economic development of any country. It is a well-established fact that a weak transport network hampers economic and social progress. Therefore, in these tough economic times, investments in the transport sector can benefit the whole of society by providing access to markets, jobs, education, healthcare and other services, by lowering the cost of moving goods, and by saving lives and avoiding injuries in unnecessary accidents.

Investments in the transport infrastructure, including investments in Intelligent Transportation Systems (ITS), stimulate economic growth and enhance trade and mobility of people. It can be said that "smart" investments in transport are very effective for running the economy.

A lot remains to be done, particularly since each mode of transport has developed its own solutions, sometimes locally and sometimes globally.

Transport telematics is one of the areas of transport that shows the greatest potential. We hope, therefore, to work closely on the preparation of relevant specifications and concrete implementations of ITS services, which will be fully interoperable and accessible all over the EU.

The Transport Systems Telematics (TST) Conference provides a unique forum for sharing the latest technologies, solutions and best practices. Participants in the 2013 event will exchange knowledge and take it back with them for the benefit of their industry and society.

I will be honoured by your participation in TST 2013 conference.

October 2013   Jerzy Mikulski

Organization

Organizers

Department of Railway Engineering, Faculty of Transport, Silesian University of
  Technology
Polish Academy of Sciences, Transport Committee
Polish Association of Transport Telematics
Association Southern Railway Cluster

Co-organizers

Faculty of Transport and Electrical Engineering, University of Technology and
  Humanities in Radom, Poland
Faculty of Navigation, Gdynia Maritime University, Poland
Faculty of Economics, University of Economics in Katowice, Poland
Faculty of Social and Technical Sciences, Silesian School of Management, Poland
Faculty of Transport, Warsaw University of Technology, Poland
Faculty of Finance and Management, Wroclaw School of Banking, Poland
Regional Centre of Road Traffic, Katowice, Poland
Motor Transport Institute in Warsaw, Poland
Railway Institute, Warsaw, Poland
Civil Aviation Personnel Education Centre of Central and Eastern Europe,
  Poland

Organizing Committee

Chair

J. Młyńczak

Members

A. Białoń
P. Gorczyca
J. Łukasik
S. Surma

Secretary

R. Skowrońska

The conference took place under the patronage of

Minister of Transport, Construction and Maritime Economy
Member of lower house of Polish Parliament Bartłomiej Bodio
Silesian Voivode
Marshal of the Silesian Voivodeship

Scientific Program Committee

J. Mikulski – Chair	Silesian University of Technology, Polish Association of Transport Telematics, Poland
E. Szychta - Vice-chair	University of Technology and Humanities in Radom, Poland
A. Weintrit - Vice-chair	Gdynia Maritime University, Poland
R. Bańczyk	Regional Centre of Road Traffic, Katowice, Poland
A. Bujak	Wroclaw School of Banking, Poland
M. Bukljaš Skočibušić	University of Zagreb, Croatia
M. Dado	University of Zilina, Republic of Slovakia
A. Dewalska-Opitek	Silesian School of Management, Katowice, Poland
J. Dyduch	UTH, Radom, Transport Committee, Polish Academy of Sciences, Poland
A. Fellner	Silesian University of Technology, Poland
M. Franeková	University of Zilina, Republic of Slovakia
V. Gavriluk	Dnipropetrovsk National University of Railway Transport, Ukraine
M. Holec	Gdynia Maritime University, Poland
A. Jabłoński	Southern Railway Cluster, Poland
M. Jabłoński	Southern Railway Cluster, Poland
A. Janota	University of Zilina, Republic of Slovakia
J. Januszewski	Gdynia Maritime University, Poland
Z. Jóźwiak	Maritime University of Szczecin, Poland
U. Jumar	ifak, Magdeburg, Germany
A. Kalašová	University of Zilina, Republic of Slovakia
J. Kisilowski	UTH, Radom, Poland
J. Klamka	Polish Academy of Sciences, Katowice Branch, Poland
K. Kołowrocki	Gdynia Maritime University, Poland
B. Kos	University of Economics, Katowice, Poland
S. Krawiec	Silesian University of Technology, Poland
O. Krettek	RWTH Aachen, Germany
J. Krimmling	TU Dresden, Germany
R. Krystek	Motor Transport Institute, Warsaw, Poland

J. Lewitowicz	Air Force Institute of Technology, Warsaw, Poland
A. Lewiński	UTH, Radom, Poland
M. Luft	UTH, Radom, Poland
B. Lazarz	Silesian University of Technology, Poland
Z. Łukasik	UTH, Radom, Poland
M. Michałowska	University of Economics, Katowice, Poland
G. Nowacki	Military University of Technology, Warsaw, Poland
Z. Pietrzykowski	Maritime University of Szczecin, Poland
B. Piotrowski	Silesian Inspectorate of Road Transport, Katowice, Poland
A. Prokopowicz	Centre for Analyses of Transport and Infrastructure, Poland
K. Rástočný	University of Zilina, Republic of Slovakia
M. Siergiejczyk	Warsaw University of Technology, Poland
M. Sitarz	Silesian University of Technology, Poland
L. Sladkeviciene	Vilnius College of Technologies and Design, Lithuania
J. Spalek	University of Zilina, Republic of Slovakia
Z. Stotsko	Lviv Polytechnic National University, Ukraine
W. Suchorzewski	Warsaw University of Technology, Poland
M. Svítek	Czech Technical University in Prague, ITS&S, Czech Republic
R. Tomanek	University of Economics, Katowice, Poland
A. Tomasik	The Upper Silesian Aviation Group (GTL), Poland
Z. Toš	University of Zagreb, Croatia
R. Wawruch	Gdynia Maritime University, Poland
W. Wawrzyński	Warsaw University of Technology, Poland
B. Wiśniewski	Maritime University of Szczecin, Poland
A. Wojciechowski	Motor Transport Institute, Warsaw, Poland
K. Wydro	University College of Technology and Business, Warsaw, Poland
E. Załoga	University of Szczecin, Poland
J. Ždánsky	University of Zilina, Republic of Slovakia
J. Żurek	Air Force Institute of Technology, Warsaw, Poland

Additional Reviewers

Stanisław Krawiec	Jacek Januszewski	Jerzy Mikulski
Kornel Wydro	Gabriel Nowacki	Zbigniew Pietrzykowski
Piotr Czech	Grzegorz Sierpiński	Ryszard Wawruch
Elżbieta Macioszek	Mirosław Siergiejczyk	Jakub Młyńczak

Tomasz Figlus

Mária Franekova

Stanisłław Iwan

Alica Kalašová

Grzegorz Karoń

Barbara Kos

Tomasz Burdzik

Aleš Janota

Jolanta
    Joszczuk-Januszewska

Mihaele Bukljaš
    Skočibušić

Rafał Bobiński

Andrzej Białoń

Table of Contents

Time Dependencies Modelling in Traffic Control Algorithms

Grzegorz Andrzejewski, Wojciech Zając, and Małgorzata Kołopieńczyk

University of Zielona Góra Licealna 9, 65-417 Zielona Gora, Poland
{g.andrzejewski,w.zajac,m.kolopienczyk}@iie.uz.zgora.pl

Abstract. The paper presents the concept of discrete control systems for traffic control implementation on PLC devices. A transformation of popular finite state machine (FMS) model to the form that allows to represent the time dependencies is presented. An example of lights control on a pedestrian crossing is presented. Two implementation methods that can be a reference for particular real-life traffic control examples are discussed. Results of implementation of the example are shown.

Keywords: time dependencies, algorithms, traffic control.

1 Introduction

An automated traffic control systems design is an important issue. Such systems are implemented on a variety of hardware platforms, from single and autonomous specialised circuits comprising microcontrollers to professional platforms based on Programmable Logic Controllers (PLCs). Regardless of the implementation platform, the design process must involve the following phases: specification, modelling, implementation and verification [1, 4].

The paper presents discrete control systems modelling rules in application to traffic control problems. A methodology of model implementation to the level that it is synthesizable on a PLC platform is also shown.

2 Modelling of Binary Control Algorithms

Efficiency of tools for control systems design highly depends on both the algorithms used and formal models in use. Therefore a formal model should have the following features [2, 3]: uniqueness, capabilities to represent parallelism, semantic consistency with the language specification and implementation, ease of translation, mathematical apparatus, availability of efficient algorithms and independence of the specification and implementation. It is particularly important in the case of describing parallelism, communication, dataflow and control flow specification as well as modelling the time dependencies [5, 6].

J. Mikulski (Ed.): TST 2013, CCIS 395, pp. 1–6, 2013.
© Springer-Verlag Berlin Heidelberg 2013

The readability of specification plays an important role in the efficiency of its use. Graphic specifications may be considered to be more transparent and clear from the text, but many designers prefer the text version. Formally, both versions are complementary.

One of the most popular ways of binary control algorithms modelling is the Finite State Machine (FSM). It is widely used to describe a control system, as the behaviour of such systems in time is simply described by the states and transitions between them. Actions related to states (Moore machine) are also modelled in finite automata, besides the states and transitions between the states.

Let us define a finite state machine with Moore type outputs as in equation (1).

$$FSM = \{S, F, X, Y, \delta, \lambda\} \tag{1}$$

where: $S = \{s_1,...,s_j\}$ is non-empty and finite set of states; F is non-empty set of directed arcs such that $F \subset (S \times S)$; $X = \{x_1,...,x_i\}$ is a finite non-empty set of inputs; $Y = \{y_1,...,y_k\}$ is a finite set of outputs; δ is a function assigning to each arc of a subset of the input δ: $F \rightarrow X$; λ is a function assigning to each state a subset of the output λ: $S \rightarrow Y$.

In it's basic form, FSM model does not allow to use the time parameters as conditions for changing the successive states. Since the engineering practice often requires such a possibility, the FSM definition can be modified to include the time dependencies. It is required, however, to define the concept of additional discrete time scale function and an state activity function.

Let's define the discrete time scale $\mathcal{F}$ as a set of values assigned to the discrete time values, ordered by the ordering relation.

Let's define the state activity as such a function $ac(s) \rightarrow \{true, false\}$ that assigns to the every state the value *true* if the state is active and *false* if the state is inactive.

Let's define the finite state machine with time dependencies representation as in equation (2).

$$FSM = \{S, F, X, Y, \mathcal{F}, \delta, \lambda, \tau\} \tag{2}$$

where: S, F, X, Y, δ and λ are defined as in equation (1); $\mathcal{F}$ – is a discrete time scale; τ: $F \rightarrow \mathcal{F}$ is a time function, assigning a number from discrete time scale to set of arcs F.

Operation of such defined automata can be defined with use of conditions of transition the machine to the next state and actions associated with this transition.

Let the arc f connects two states s and s', wherein the arc is directed from s to s', and let t_0 is the moment of activation of the state $s \in S$. Function $\tau(f)$ at the time t_0 assigns a certain number from discrete time-scale to the arc f: $\tau(f, t_0) = t$ (where $t \in \mathcal{F}$). In the following moments of time this number is decremented and after the time t it reaches the value 0: $\tau(f, t_0+t) = 0$. In the following description the symbol $\tau(f) = 0$ describes the function value at the time at which it is equal to 0

Conditions of transition the machine state from s to s' can be presented as:

1) $ac(s) = true$ – initial state activity;
2) $\delta(f) = true$ – fulfilling the logic condition imposed on the arc;
3) $\tau(f) = 0$ – expiration of activity time for initial state s, associated with the arc f.

Actions related with transition of the machine state from state s to s' can be presented as:

1) $ac(s) := false$ – deactivation of initial state;
2) $\forall$ $(y \in \lambda(s))$: $y := false$ – deactivation of outputs related to initial state s;
3) $ac(s') := true$ – activation of final state s';
4) $\forall$ $(y \in \lambda(s'))$: $y := true$ – activation of the outputs related to final state s';

3   Control Algorithm for a Pedestrian Crossing

Fig. 1. presents an example of a control system, in which there exists a problem of time dependencies.

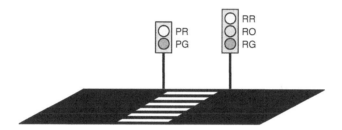

Fig. 1. Control object: a pedestrian crossing

Symbols in Fig. 1 have the following meaning: PR – pedestrian crossing red signal, PG – pedestrian crossing green signal, RR – road red light, RO – road orange light, RG - road green light.

An appropriate sequence of turning the signals on and off may be defined for this control object. Such a sequence is modelled with the use of described above modified FSM graph (Fig. 2).

In the presented algorithm the transition from state S1 to S2 has two conditions: activity of state S1 and expiration of 60 seconds of S1 activity. After this, state S1 changes the state to inactive and S2 becomes active. In addition, RG signal is deactivated and RO is activated.

The presented example representation, in a form understandable for tools for PLC-based control systems programming, can be effectively implemented using a Ladder Diagram (LD or LAD) language. Fig. 3 presents a part of program, responsible for transition from state S1 to S2. The timing operations were implemented with the use of a Timer-On-Delay (TON) block. The OUT output is activated after the delay defined on PT (Preset Time) input, and deactivated after deactivation of IN input.

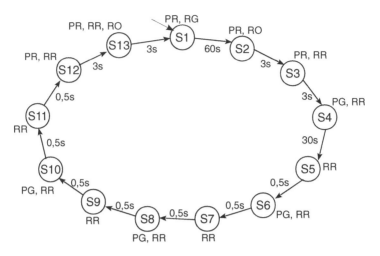

Fig. 2. FSM graph of the control algorithm

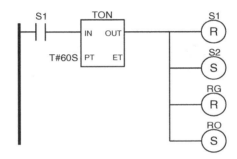

Fig. 3. Example of a transition from S1 to S2 with timing conditions

The other transitions can be implemented in the same way. Although such a solution is easy to understand and implement in LD, it implies usage of numerous timers to model particular timing conditions.

To avoid that, an observation can be used that the control graph is a cyclic one. It gives a possibility to apply in the program only one timer to generate timing in the whole program. To achieve this, it is convenient to use an additional binary variable *tmp*, as in Fig. 4, to reinitialise the timer after completion of a single cycle.

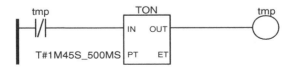

Fig. 4. A single cycle timing mechanism

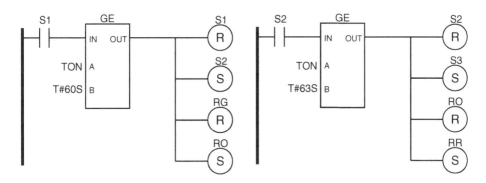

Fig. 5. Modified transitions implementation, transitions S1 to S2 and S2 to S3

The implementation of transitions with the use of a single timer is presented in Fig. 5. A mechanism for comparison of current value of global timer with preset timing values, calculated as a cumulative time of process progress in a single work cycle of algorithm, was used.

Both methods of problem solving, the first with separate timers and the second with a single total-cycle timer were compared. As the algorithm written in LD has to be synthesised into PLC, the resources consumption was the comparison criterion.

Table 1 presents results of research on the quality of presented methods synthesis. The synthesis was realised using Siemens TIA Portal V11 for PLC platform S7-1200 CPU 1214C.

Table 1. Synthesis results comparison in terms of PLC resources consumption

	Total	First method: separate timers			Second method: single timer		
		Used	OB	DB	Used	OB	DB
Load Memory	1MB	24 691B	7 688B	17 003B	8 819B	7 514B	1 305B
Work Memory	51 200B	938B	678B	260B	540B	520B	20B

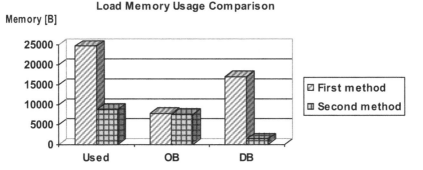

Fig. 6. Graphical comparison of synthesis results – load memory usage

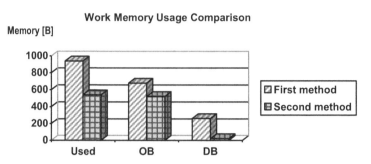

Fig. 7. Graphical comparison of synthesis results – work memory usage

4   Conclusion

The presented method for modelling and synthesis of control algorithm for traffic control problem shows a simple and effective way to save the system resources. The method uses a well-known Finite State Machine model, modified to represent time dependencies. As shown in research results, the method can lead to a significant reduction of system resources consumption.

The control problem was of small complexity. In the case of middle and high complexity control problems the method can allow to fit the synthesised code into a control unit that would not be capable to hold it without such optimisation.

Future work on this method would be to formalise it appropriately to allow modelling and synthesis of parallel processes with time dependencies.

References

1. Bieganowski, J.: Synthesis of microprogram control units oriented toward decreasing the number of macrocells of addressing circuit. University of Zielona Gora Press, Zielona Gora, Poland, Zielona Góra (2011)
2. Adamski, M., Skowroński, Z.: Interpreted Petri Nets – Formal Model for Hardware/Software Co-design. Measurement Automation and Control (Pomiary, Automatyka, Kontrola) (2-3), 17–20 (2003) (in Polish)
3. Małecki, K., Jaszczak, S., Sokołowski, R.: Synthesis of Hardware and Software Traffic Control Simulator for a Particular Area. Measurement Automation and Control (Pomiary, Automatyka, Kontrola) (7), 608–610 (2012) (in Polish)
4. Barkalov, A., Titarenko, L., Hebda, O.: Synthesis of Moore FSM with encoding of collections of microoperations implemented with ASIC. Measurement Automation and Control (Pomiary, Automatyka, Kontrola) 58(6), 514–518 (2012)
5. Iwan, S., Małecki, K.: Data Flows in the Integrated Urban Freight Transport Telematics System. In: Mikulski, J. (ed.) TST 2012. CCIS, vol. 329, pp. 79–86. Springer, Heidelberg (2012)
6. Barkalov, A., Titarenko, L. (eds.): Logic synthesis for compositional microprogram control units. LNEE, vol. 22. Springer, Heidelberg (2008)

Model of Inference Processes in the Automatic Maritime Communication System

Paweł Banaś, Anna Wójcik, and Zbigniew Pietrzykowski

Maritime University of Szczecin,
Wały Chrobrego 1-2, 70-500 Szczecin, Poland
{p.banas,a.wojcik,z.pietrzykowski}@am.szczecin.pl

Abstract. This article presents an inference model for the automatic communication system at sea. Based on an analysis of inference methods used in other fields such as business, inference methods for the automatic communication at sea have been presented in this article. The complexity of communication at sea and specific navigation issues have been taken into account. Part of the process of automatic communication has been shown by making use of the proposed model and automatic inference.

Keywords: automatic communication, negotiation process, inference rules, e-navigation.

1 Introduction

Human errors are one of the major causes of navigational accidents at sea. Among other reasons, these errors may result from a lack of information needed to make the right decision or from misinterpretation of information. Excess information and consequent difficulties in identifying the relevant information also create potential threats. Advancing automation of navigational information acquisition, selection, processing and presentation on ships and in land-based centres to some extent reduces these risks.

In presently used systems communication is executed at two levels:

- low level direct communication between equipment and systems using protocols used in data transmission – electronic data interchange,
- high level communication between computer systems – electronic document interchange.

There is a distinct gap between the two levels. What seems to be lacking is a uniform environment for data exchange between people and machines, enabling acquisition of data, needed in communication between operators, from a variety devices and systems based on one standard. Developed at IMO forum, the concept of e-navigation aims at this issue. The concept is based, among others, on an expanding standardization of navigational information form and exchange.

J. Mikulski (Ed.): TST 2013, CCIS 395, pp. 7–14, 2013.
© Springer-Verlag Berlin Heidelberg 2013

A navigational situation may be complex enough to require navigators concerned to establish communication. They may want to agree on what the actual situation is, or to specify the intentions and manoeuvres. Analyses of marine accidents show that the source of human errors lies in communication difficulties, mainly between navigators steering their ships. Among the causes are a lack of communication, misunderstanding of a received message, or wrong interpretation of exchanged information. One should expect that another step in eliminating potential sources of navigators' errors will be made towards the automation of communication processes, taking place between:

- operators (navigators on ships, land-based centres personnel),
- computer systems on ships and in the centres,
- operators and computer systems, in various combinations and proportions.

It is envisaged that automated communication will comprise, *inter alia*, selective acquisition of information, including intentions, and their automatic interpretation. If ship navigators happen to have divergent purposes, automatic negotiations will be started. This calls for the development of inference model or models, capable of tackling with the complex character of communication at sea and specifics of navigational issues.

2   The Inference Model

From an analysis of the present use of communications systems at sea, which covered processes of communication and inference in other areas (solutions for business), a model of inference processes has been proposed. Two inference processes are distinguished:

- preliminary inference,
- principal inference.

The former uses navigational situation information (coming from shipboard systems – AIS, ARPA, etc.) supplemented with data on possible request of establishing contact, regardless of a navigational situation. Such case occurs when one navigator steering a ship calls another to establish contact, or his/her ship is called by another ship or a coast station. All these data are available in an accurate form that does not require interpretation of imprecise terms.

The latter type of inference is based on the results of preliminary inference, supplemented with information obtained from the navigator and as a result of a ship-ship dialog, which generates new knowledge on a navigational situation. As received messages may contain imprecise information, it has to be accounted for by mathematical tools.

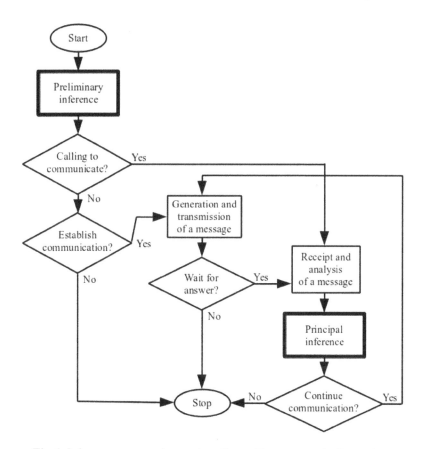

Fig. 1. Inference processes in an automatic maritime communication system

Figure 1 illustrates an executive algorithm used in the process of automatic communication at sea. The following functional blocks are distinguished:

- **Preliminary inference** – responsible for an analysis of current situation (observation) and inference aimed at ascertaining whether communication has to be established and its possible scope [1].
- **Principal inference** – gives a basis to make a decision on further manner of communication. The module "Principal inference" differs from the other in that is has a capability of analyzing imprecise information [2]. After executed inference, new knowledge on a navigational situation is acquired.
- **Generation and transmission of a message** – given the inference outcome, this module prepares and sends a message to another ship or coast station.
- **Receipt and analysis of a message** – this module receives a message sent by another ship or coast station, then transforms it into a symbolic form, used in further stages of communication. The symbolic form will allow to further analyze a message by mathematical methods and tools (e.g. computing with words) [3].

It is expected that the algorithm will operate automatically in a loop. Cyclic calling takes place at preset time intervals, individually selected depending on voyage and vessel parameters.

The first stage in the process of automatic communication at sea is preliminary inference. It is aimed at establishing basic facts essential for the entire process of communication:

- if there is need for communication,
- cause of such communication, that may result from:
  - present navigational situation,
  - navigator's request,
  - outside calling,

  or a combination of the above.

The result of executed preliminary inference determines the manner of further actions:

- if there was an outside calling, a control signal is immediately sent to the message receipt and analysis block,
- if not, the system checks whether it is necessary to establish communication due to navigator's request or because of the current navigational situation. If this is the case, a control signal is sent to the message generation and transmission block.

Need to establish contact is automatically detected when:

- it is required by regulations (COLREGS, local regulations, etc.),
- possessed information is insufficient, imprecise or contradictory,
- it is necessary to undertake negotiations aimed at developing a preventive manoeuvre and its parameters,
- other situations appear that require communication to be established,
- non-standard situations appear for which the knowledge base has no rules. Then communication is maintained at the navigator – navigator level.

If a decision to establish communication is made (automatically or by navigator's calling), the outcome of preliminary inference block constitutes a basis for generating a message sent to another ship or shore-based station. On this basis a decision is made to wait for an answer. The algorithm completes its operation (Fig. 1), if the message sent does not require an answer. If an answer is necessary, (e.g. data transmission is expected), a control signal is sent to the message receipt and analysis block. When an answer comes, the block transforms it into a symbolic form, an input for the principal inference block.

As a result of principal inference, on the basis of a message received, the decision is made whether to continue communication or stop it. If it is to be continued, a control signal is sent to the message generation and transmission block, whose function has herein been described. This module utilizes the results of completed inference to generate a message of relevant content.

3   Information Flow in the Inference Model

Discussing the processes presented in Chapter 2, we should define input and output data. Information flow between particular elements of the model is illustrated in Figure 2.

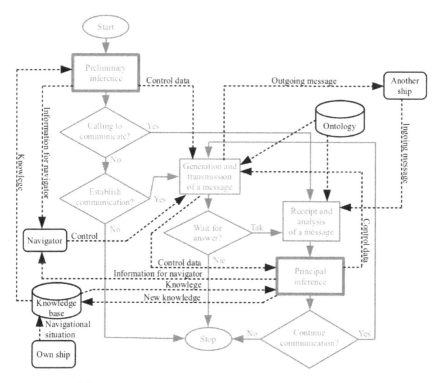

Fig. 2. Information flow in an automatic marine communication system

Information processed in automatic communication can be divided as follows:

- input information (data):
  - possessed data on a given navigational situation from various shipboard systems – such data are currently gathered in a knowledge base; these are accurate data, a basis for preliminary inference.
  - knowledge base – base of rules used during inference; the rules are supplemented with knowledge of current navigational situation from shipboard systems and the knowledge arising in the process of inference,
  - ontology of navigational information [4], used for generating outgoing messages and interpretation of ingoing messages,
  - messages received from another ship or coast station in a text format (natural language) or an XML file.
  - ship navigator's decisions,

- Output data:
  - messages sent to another ship or coast station, as an XML file, with an attached schema enabling understanding of the message by people [5] or as a text in a natural language,
  - new knowledge on a navigational situation created as an outcome of inference,
  - information on inference results intended for the ship's navigator on watch.
- internal control data sent between the modules; these data contain information on worked out conclusions and additional technical knowledge needed for appropriate continuation of communication and inference processes.

Internal data sent between the modules and gathered in the knowledge base are written symbolically, associated with navigational information ontology. The conversion of input data to the symbolic form is presented as an example in Chapter 5.

4   Inference

The presented model (Figs. 1, 2) comprises two inference blocks: preliminary inference and principal inference. Depending on received data, the whole model of communication processes may feature basic inference of the traditional binary logic or, when principal inference has to account for imprecise data, approximate and fuzzy inference will take place. The rules fundamental for the whole model are referred to as modus ponens, modus tollens and, in cases of imprecise or approximate data, equivalents of these rules called rules of approximate inference and rules of fuzzy inference [6]. These rules are composed of three basic elements: premises, implications and a conclusion, which have a formal notation by using the tools of computing with words. Premises are data and other information from ships, defining a navigational situation, and interpreted by means of navigational information sub-ontology. Then the knowledge base is considered, i.e. knowledge, expressed by means of implications, from sea traffic regulations extended with expertise. Inference is performed on the basis of these elements. The rules modus ponens and modus tollens are schematically given in Table 1 below:

Table 1. Schematic inference rules for binary logic

Modus ponens	Modus tollens
A	¬A
A⇒B	B⇒A
B	¬B

Using computing with words and ontology, the premises and implications get this form [7]:

$$X \; is \; A \tag{1}$$

$$If \; A \; then \; B \tag{2}$$

$$If \text{ X } is \text{ A } then \text{ Y } is \text{ B} \tag{3}$$

where X, Y are certain parameters, and A, B are values that these parameters can reach. Further in the article a formal notation of an example ship-to-ship dialog will be described.

5   An Example

An example communication here presented takes place between two ships called Alpha and Beta, proceeding on opposite courses [3]. In compliance with regulations in force, the ships should pass each other port-to-port, while passing starboard-to-starboard is only allowed after agreeing on such manoeuvre, as said in the dialog below:

A: Our CPA is 0.5 nautical mile.
A: Is it possible that we pass starboard to starboard ?
B: I intend to alter my course to starboard for 20 minutes and cross ahead of you at a distance 1.3 nautical miles.
A: Ok, cross ahead of me at a distance more than 1.1 nautical miles.

The dialog, formally written by means of tools derived from computing with words, is shown in Table 2.

Table 2. Formal notations generated in the system

Message	Formal notation
1. Our CPA is 0.5 nautical mile	WARNING(CPA(Alpha, Beta) is 0.5) → W(C(A, B) is 0.5)
2. Is it possible that we pass starboard to starboard?	QUESTION(PASS(Alpha.starboard, Beta.starboard) is possible) → Q(P(A.R, B.R) is F)
3. I intend to alter my course to starboard for 20 minutes and cross ahead of you at a distance 1.3 Nm.	INTENTION((TIME(TURN(B, R)) is 20 minutes and (CROSS(B, A) and (DISTANCE(A, B) is 1.3Nm))) → I((Z(T(B, R)) is 20) and (E(B, A) and (D(A, B) is 1.3))
4. OK, cross ahead of me at a distance more than 1.1Nm.	REQUEST (CROSS(B, A) and ((DISTANCE(A, B) is MORE(1.1Nm))) → F(E(B, A) and (D(A, B) is M(1.1)))

After an analysis of the information stored, the system in its preliminary inference makes a decision on starting communication, and sends messages Nos 1 and 2 to the ship Beta. Then an answer from the ship Beta is awaited. Once the message No 3 is received and interpreted (using the navigational information subontology), principal inference is performed. Data from messages No 1 and 3 are premises in the form as presented above. Implications applied here are derived from regulations. For instance, *If CPA>1.1Nm, then navigational situation is safe (safe manoeuvre).* In the inference block the system generates a piece of information that the suggested passing distance is for the ship Alpha acceptable in terms of manoeuvring safety. The system passes the inference outcome to the navigator and sends a relevant message to the ship Beta.

6   Conclusion

A growing automation of the processes of navigational information acquisition, selection, processing and presentation, both on ships and in land-based centres, offers an increasingly wide access to information and its interchange required in the process of safe ship conduct. This information helps the navigator assess the situation and make decisions accordingly.

If a navigational situation happens to be complex one, navigators may want to communicate verbally, to ensure what in fact the situation is like, and to specify their intentions and planned manoeuvres.

In this connection, one should expect that further marine communication automation will be aimed at information exchanges between operators, systems or operators and systems. It will include, *inter alia,* selective acquisition of information, including navigators' intentions and their automatic interpretation, and if those intentions turn out to be divergent, the system will start negotiations.

A model of inference in an automatic maritime communication system is presented in this article. Besides, inference methods are proposed for such systems. A fragment of possible automatic communication between two ships is given, incorporating automatic inference using the proposed model.

Further work on these issues will be focused on the extension of the present model, particularly the inference modules carrying out negotiation processes.

References

1. Pietrzykowski, Z., Szewczuk, T., Wójcik, A., Banaś, P.: Reasoning Processes in Automatic Marine Communication System, vol. XX. Scientific Papers of Warsaw University of Technology (Transport) Warszawa (in print, 2013) (in Polish)
2. Pietrzykowski, Z., Banaś, P., Wójcik, A., Szewczuk, T.: Information exchange automation in maritime communication. In: International Conference TransNav, Gdynia (2013)
3. Pietrzykowski, Z., Banaś, P., Wójcik, A.: Computing With Words in Communication Processes. Methods of Applied Computer Science (5) (30), 207–214 (2011)
4. Banaś, P.: Using the Protégé environment for building ontology for automated communication system at sea. Scientific Journal (30), 12–17 (2012)
5. Pietrzykowski, Z., Hołowiński, G., Magaj, J., Chomski, J.: Automation of Message Interchange Process in Maritime Transport. TransNav, the International Journal on Marine Navigation and Safety of Sea Transportation 5(2), 175–181 (2011)
6. Kacprzyk, J.: Fuzzy sets in system analysis, Warszawa, pp. 213-215 (1986) (in Polish)
7. Zadeh, L.A.: Fuzzy sets. Information and Control 8(3), 338–353 (1965)

Microscopic Simulation of the Coordinated Signal Controlled Intersections

Ľubomír Černický and Alica Kalašová

University of Žilina, The Faculty of Operation and Economics of Transport
and Communications, Department of Road and Urban Transport,
Univerzitná 1, 01026 Žilina, Slovakia
{Lubomir.Cernicky,Alica.Kalasova}@fpedas.uniza.sk

Abstract. At rest, urban agglomerations are characterized by concentrating a large number of vehicles in a confined space, while usually there is not possible to increase extensively the range of the road communications, but it is necessary to achieve their better utilisation and better quality of transport. The traffic in urban agglomerations is optimised mainly for two groups of users: (1) individual traffic and (2) public transport. Creation of successful management means to integrate and to optimise the quality of transport. When intersection signal control is used, not only the high degree of safety is ensured, but also permeability of the intersection increases. But when there are several signal controlled intersections on the one route, the control of the intersections can act like a brake of the traffic flow. For better and more effective use of the network the coordinated road traffic control and the higher intelligent control of the intersections (central traffic control) is used. In this paper we would like to evaluate on the basis of microscopic simulation the coordination of the signal controlled intersections in the city of Žilina. For the simulation the Aimsun is used.

Keywords: model, traffic light, controlled intersections.

1 Introduction

During the last thirty years there has been tremendous growth in road transport. With the increasing number of vehicles the delay times on the network also increase. There is a significant impact of capacity of nodes on the capacity and permeability of the whole transport network. In the case of road network the capacity of nodes means mainly capacity and permeability of particular junctions. The traffic lights can be an important part when improving traffic conditions at the junction.

Each signal controlled junction has its own control logic where various experimental research techniques of modelling and simulation can be used. These techniques enable assessing the scope of current transport solutions and to verify the functionality and suitability of future transport solutions. Because of still increasing traffic, there is necessary to look for appropriate methods that can be used in practice.

Development of computer technology and increase in computing power enabled to create sophisticated simulation tools. There is possibility to reliable simulate the

J. Mikulski (Ed.): TST 2013, CCIS 395, pp. 15–22, 2013.
© Springer-Verlag Berlin Heidelberg 2013

examined problem in this simulation tools and consequently make a series of simulation experiments. These tools enable for example to assess various traffic solution. The assessment can be executed by changing attributes of the model, particular parts of the model or traffic control of traffic situation on the simulated network. For our study Aimsun was used. Aimsun is specialised in simulation in the field of road transport. With the assistance of the Aimsun there is possibility to assess effectiveness of existing traffic solutions, effectiveness of future solutions and various variants of traffic solutions.

2   Characteristic of the Solved Area

The Veľká Okružná Street with its length of about 1.5 km is one of the most important road communications in the city of Žilina. Currently Veľká Okružná Street consists of two-lane urban roads and junctions at grade. It is distributor road of the urban roads category B1 and it is part of the second ring road of Žilina. In its vicinity are built residential building, amenities, secondary schools, police, companies and Protestant church, which generate a large number of transit relations. Daily over 10,000 of vehicles pass this street, while an hour´s traffic volumes come up to 800 veh/sec. [6] In addition, nearly each public transport line leads on this street or at least crosses the street.

In 2011, there were reconstructed roads around the Aupark Shopping Centre in Žilina. It meant adjustment of roadways and pavements, structural modifications at junctions, and modification of bus bay at the Street Veľká Okružná (V.O.). Traffic signals at the junctions (V.O. – Predmestská – 1. Mája, V.O – Spanyola, V.O. – Komenského, and V.O.- Hálková.)were also changed during this reconstruction There were exchanged poles, semaphores, and controllers, added camera detectors, and calculated new signal plans for these junctions. From that time, signal controlled junction at the V.O. Street are coordinated. The mentioned junctions are marked at the Fig. 1.

Fig. 1. Model of the transport network – chosen part of the Street Veľká Okružná (V.O.) Junctions: 1 - V.O.-Hálková; 2 - V.O. – Komenského; 3 - V.O – Spanyolova; 4 - V.O. – Predmestská

3   Microscopic Simulation of the Solved Area

After the modernization of traffic control at junctions as well as after the structural modification there were expected benefits in the traffic flow in the central part of the city of Žilina. In order to verify this assumption, the microscopic simulation was carried out. For the microscopic simulation Aimsun was used. The inputs data for simulation were traffic volumes at the sections, turnings of vehicles at the junctions, public transport lines, characteristics of individual vehicles, and signal plans of the junctions. Traffic volumes and turnings of vehicles data were obtained from traffic surveys of the University of Žilina in 2010 and 2011. These surveys mean direct traffic counting, where counters during one day (6:00-10:00 and 14:00-18:00) recorded means of conveyance (car, truck, bus, articulated bus, bicycle and motorcycle), and directions (left, right, straight) at each junction entrance. The rush hour during the counting was the time between 15:00 and 16:00. The outputs of the counting during the rush hour are show at the Fig.2.

During the creation of the model there was an attempt to faithfully represent the real traffic situation on the Street [1]. The time period for the simulation was the afternoon rush hour and there were simulated two variants:

(1) the state before reconstruction;
(2) the state after reconstruction - current traffic situation.

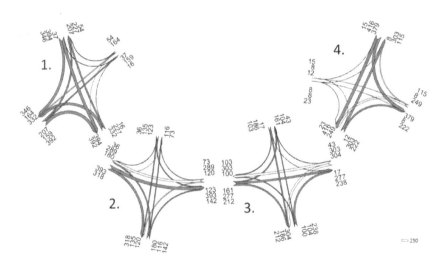

Fig. 2. Traffic volume and turning of vehicles on solved junctions during the rush hour

3.1   Simulation Outputs

Simulation in Aimsun provides various outputs, which are divided into groups: network statistics, section and turn statistics, subpath statistics, O/D matrix statistics and public transport statistics. For the comparison in our study were chosen following outputs [6]:

Delay Time:
- for sections: average delay time per vehicle. This is the difference between the expected travel time (time it would take to traverse the section under ideal conditions) and the travel time. It is calculated as the average of all vehicles,
- for the network: average delay time per vehicle per kilometre. This is the difference between the expected travel time (the time it would take to traverse the system under ideal conditions) and the travel time. It is calculated as the average of all vehicles and then converted into time per kilometre,

Mean Speed:
- for sections: average speed for all vehicles that have traversed the section. This is calculated using the mean speed for the section journey for each vehicle,
- for the network: average speed for all vehicles that have left the system. This is calculated using the mean journey speed for each vehicle,

Number of Stops:
- for sections: average number of stops per vehicle while travelling in the section
- for the network: average number of stops per vehicle per kilometre,

Stop Time:
- for the network: average time at standstill per vehicle per kilometre.

These outputs were studied for individual transport (Car), public transport (Bus), but also for all modes of transport together (All).

3.2   Simulation of the State "Before Reconstruction" and of the State "After Reconstruction"

With the help of microscopic modelling there were obtained values of chosen statistics for the sections, the result of which you can see in the Table 1. In this table are written out only sections that represent junction entrance shoulders. Variant "Before Reconstruction" represents previous traffic situation and variant "After Reconstruction" represents current traffic situation at the Street Veľká Okružná. You can see in this table worsened traffic situation at several junction entrances. Entrances with Delay Times of higher value than 40 sec are marked in grey. You can see also how values changed after reconstruction -"Difference", which represents relative difference between the "After and Before Reconstruction" state.

Namely, according to the simulation, worsened traffic situation were at these junction entrances:

– V.O. – Hálková; where Delay Time for vehicles coming from V.O Street at the Police station (1A) were 50.32 sec for cars and 46.75 sec for buses. Mean speed at this entrance was 23.56 km/h for cars and 22.89 km/h for buses, and these vehicles had to stop at this shoulder in average 1.5 times. After the reconstruction all these characteristic improved and at present Delay Time values are around 25-29 sec, mean speed around 31.5 km/h and vehicles have to stop at this entrance in average 1.08 times.

Table 1. Delay Times at junctions entrances (section statistics)

Entrance	A			B			C			D		
Mode of transport	All	Car	Bus	All	Car	Bus	All	Car	Bus	All	Car	Bus
Veľká Okružná - Hálková												
"Before Rec." (sec)	50.31	50.32	46.75	24.1	23.9	30.52	27.29	27.35	25.89	52.08	51.24	70.95
"After Rec." (sec)	28.46	28.52	25.27	20.51	20.42	27.93	35.12	34.7	43.92	50.13	49.29	67.5
Difference (%)	-43.4	-43.3	-45.9	-14.6	-14.6	-8.5	28.7	26.9	69.6	-3.7	-3.8	-4.9
Veľká Okružná - Komenského												
"Before Rec." (sec)	20.14	20	33.57	26.1	26.3	12.57	23.1	23.25	18.78	18.88	18.92	18.32
"After Rec." (sec)	14.88	14.73	28.78	5.53	5.36	20.6	37.67	37.92	31.73	42.65	42.51	44.56
Difference (%)	-26.1	-26.4	-14.3	-78.8	-79.6	59.6	63.1	63.1	69	125.9	124.7	143.2
Veľká Okružná -Spanyolova												
"Before Rec." (sec)	28.66	28.6	30.2	18.3	18.9	12.86	27.31	27.31	26.28	266.86	267.13	
"After Rec." (sec)	48.18	48.17	51.13	23.34	23.59	3.6	45.01	45.47	28.8	48.22	48.21	
Difference (%)	68.1	68.4	69.3	29.5	30.4	-72	64.8	66.5	9.6	-81.9	-82	
Veľká Okružná – Predmestská												
"Before Rec." (sec)	15.52	15.5	16.81	41.25	41.04	49.02	33.37	33.52	28.33	49.8	49.8	
"After Rec." (sec)	27.72	27.64	30.9	31.73	31.65	35.37	34.81	35.48	14.56	46.96	46.96	
Difference (%)	78.6	78.3	79	-23.1	-22.9	-27.8	4.3	5.8	-48.6	-5.7	-5.7	

— V.O. – Hálková –entrance 1.D; where Delay Time values for cars were around 51 sec and for Buses were higher than 70 sec. (Mean Speed 12.39 km/h for Cars and 10.03 km/h for Buses, number of stops 1.14 times (Cars and 1.49 times Buses). After reconstruction these values slightly improved, but traffic situation stayed worsened (Delay Time 49.29 and 67.5 sec, Mean Speed 12.82 and 9.12 km/h).

— V.O. – Spanyolova, where tended to be large amount of vehicles at Spanyolova Street waiting to entrance to junction (entrance 3.D). This state was caused by many factors; one of them was too short green phase for this entrance (cycle 70 sec and green phase 12 sec) and only one common lane for each direction. This waiting is reflected in Delay Time of 266 sec and Mean Speed of 6.64 sec. In average, cars had to stop at this entrance 3.24 times. After the reconstruction traffic at this shoulder significantly improved, but still there are worsened values (Delay Time of 48.21 sec, Mean Speed of 21.46 km/h and Number of Stops 1.11 times. There are no public transport lines at this shoulder.

— V.O. –Predmestská; where Delay Time for vehicles waiting at the Street 1.Mája (entrance 4.B) was 41.04 for Cars and 49.02 for Buses. Mean Speed was 14.16 and 11.84 km/h, and Number of Stops was 1.41 for Cars and 1.59 for Buses. After the reconstruction values improved – Delay Time is 31.65 and 35.37 sec, Mean Speed is 20.42 and 14.76 km/h and Number of Stops is 1.08 and 1.31 times.

— V.O. – Predmestská, entrance 1.D; where Delay time is higher than 40 sec, but there are only 39 vehicles entering this shoulder during rush hour, so we don´t consider the traffic situation as worsened.

As you can see, in most cases traffic situation at abovementioned "problematic" entrance shoulders was managed to solve. But this solving reflected at other shoulders, where Delay Time worsened. An example of such worsening could be junction V.O-Spanyolova, where entrance shoulder 1.D was solved, but other entrance shoulders now reach higher Delay Time values than before reconstruction.

3.3   Comparison

When comparing microscopic modelling outputs of both variants (before reconstruction and after reconstruction) you can see that permeability of some junction entrances improved, permeability of others worsened (Table 1). You can see increased number of the junction entrances, where delay times are higher than 40 sec. Therefore it may seem that traffic situation at the V.O. Street worsened after the reconstruction. This conjecture can also be based on the fact that network statistics (Table 2) for public transport worsened in the variant "after reconstruction". But network statistics also shows 13.02% decrease in Delay Times of all modes of transport, 14.37% decrease in Number of Stops and nearly 12.5% decrease in Stop Times. Regarding to all these facts we can come to the conclusion that coordination of the examined junction have positive impact on traffic and traffic situation after the reconstruction improved.

Table 2. Network statistics - comparison of investigated variants

Time Series	"Before"	"After"	Total Difference	Units	Relative Difference	
Delay Time All	125.15	108.86	-16.29	sec/km	-13.02	%
Delay Time Car	125.24	108.16	-17.08	sec/km	-13.64	%
Delay Time Bus	120.84	133.02	12.18	sec/km	10.08	%
Mean Speed All	24.64	25.64	1	km/h	4.06	%
Mean Speed Car	24.67	25.72	1.05	km/h	4.26	%
Mean Speed Bus	23.61	22.63	-0.98	km/h	-4.15	%
Number of Stops All	3.34	2.86	-0.48	N/km	-14.37	%
Number of Stops Car	3.34	3.84	0.5	N/km	14.97	%
Number of Stops Bus	3.45	3.33	-0.12	N/km	-3.48	%
Stop Time All	110.09	96.43	-13.66	sec/km	-12.41	%
Stop Time Car	110.34	95.82	-14.52	sec/km	-13.16	%
Stop Time Bus	100.56	118.2	17.64	sec/km	17.54	%

But it is important to note that however the traffic situation improved after the reconstruction, traffic problems in the centre of the city of Žilina are not completely solved. Traffic saturation mainly during rush hour is so high, that any further delay (traffic accidents, maintenance or reparation of roads) results in creation of widespread congestions. Further traffic solution in Žilina should be focused not only on the Street Veľká Okružná, but it is necessary to solve the traffic completely in the entire city - it may happen that solving of the traffic in one area may cause worsening of traffic in other areas. Regarding to the fact that traffic solutions in the form of building of new infrastructure are very limited because of insufficient space within the city, the only possible way is to solve traffic by modern traffic solutions. One of such possible way is higher usage of information and communication technologies the backbone of which are Intelligent Transport Systems. As an example it can be mentioned usage of variable message signs, with the assistance of which part of the traffic could be diverted from overcrowded areas. Another possible way is higher support of public transport system, where public transport priority on the roads as well as at our investigated junctions (Veľká Okružná) could play a key role. In all these cases simulation of alternative traffic solutions could be helpful in selection of appropriate solution, assessing the economic benefits of the investments as well as in eliminating / minimizing of potential problems.

4 Conclusion

As we mentioned, recently there is tremendous growth in road transport, which has great demands on the accessibility of the city. Still increasing traffic results in growth in number of congestion, in increasing idle times and environmental damage. Traffic modelling helps to manage all these problems. Traffic modelling doesn´t include only traffic simulation, but it is wide range of tools ranging from simple application for only one purpose to complex tools which enable to perform complicated analysis of transport networks [3,5]. Then the outputs can be easily understandable models which can be implemented into the real environment and which provide relevant information. One of the disadvantages of traffic modelling is the fact, that traffic model and simulation don't solve the problem. The outputs of the simulation can only indicate the correct way of solving the problem. Traffic modelling can be used to many operations and there is assumption that importance of the traffic modelling will be increasing with increase of transport. In our study traffic modelling confirmed improvement of traffic situation after the coordination of signal controlled junctions in the particular Slovak city and also traffic modelling was shown as convenient tool in creation process of further transport solutions.

Acknowledgements. This contribution is the result of the project implementation: VEGA Project no. 1/0159/13 – KALAŠOVÁ, A. and collective: Basic Research of Telematic Systems, Conditions of Their Development and Necessity of Long-term Strategy. University of Žilina, the Faculty of Operation and Economics of Transport and Communications, 2013-2015.
Centre of Excellence for Systems and Services of Intelligent Transport II.,
ITMS 26220120050 supported by the Research & Development Operational Programme funded by the ERDF.

References

1. Gogola, M.: The Microscopic Modeling of Traffic on Chosen Part of Commercial Area in City of Zilina. Perner's Contacts, 41–46 (2012),
   http://pernerscontacts.upce.cz/25_2011/Gogola.pdf (date of access: July 17, 2013)

2. Kalašová, A., Paľo, J.: Traffic Engineering - Organization and Management. EDIS – editorship ŽU v Žiline, p. 162s (2003) ISBN 80-8070-076-1
3. Park, B., Schneeberger, J.D.: Microscopic Simulation Model Calibration and Validation. Case Study of Vissim Simulation Model for a Coordinated Actuated Signal System. Transportation Research Record, 185–192 (1856),
   http://faculty.virginia.edu/brianpark/SimCalVal/Docs/trb03-microscopic-simulation-cal-val.pdf (date of access: July 17, 2013)
4. Rievaj, V., Hudák, A.: The Road Transport and Safety. In: CONAT 2010: the 11th International Congress on Automotive and Transport Engineering, Brasov, Romania, October 27-29. The Congress Proceedings, pp. S.187-S.192 (2010) ISSN 2069-0428. - [S.l.: s.n.]
5. Šulgan, M., Kubasáková, I., Ivánková, K.: City Logistics and its Solutions. LOGI Scientific Journal on Transport and Logistics 1, 71–78 (2010) ISSN 1804-3216. 6,
   http://www.zilina.sk/docs/2012/upm_zilina/SMERNA_CAST_text.pdf (date of access: July 17, 2013)
6. TSS – Transport Simulation Systems. Aimsun 7 Dynamic Simulators User´s Manual (2012)

Directions and Benefits of Using Traffic Modelling Software in the Urban Public Transport

Grzegorz Dydkowski and Anna Urbanek

University of Economics in Katowice,
40-287 Katowice, Poland
dydkowski@onet.pl, anna.urbanek@ue.katowice.pl

Abstract. The swelling of urbanised areas and separation of areas functions related to housing and at the same time commercial and recreational functions concentration – are the main factors increasing mobility of cities residents and average distance of travelling. Therefore, the transport factor is becoming the main determinant conditioning the development potential of large cities and the quality of life in the city. The public sector, which is responsible for meeting the essential social needs should effectively use available resources and strive for high quality services fulfilling social expectations. It requires using professional tools, especially computer software, which becomes more and more powerful. From this point of view, current and long-term transport offer managing is one of those areas which are essential. Therefore, the article presents costs and benefits of using by public urban transport organisers professional software for traffic modelling and demand forecasting.

Keywords: public urban transport, traffic analyses, traffic models, demand forecasting.

1 Introduction

Urban public transport in Poland and world-wide, with few exceptions, is considered to be a part of public service sector, and – besides the income from sales of services – is financed to a greater or lesser degree by public means. Substantial involvement of public means, in the financing of both current activities, and investments in urban public transport, should in parallel force the implementation of solutions, which assure efficient use of those funds. Many tools can be listed, which enhance and improve the efficiency of service provision [1,2], among the more important ones are innovations, including the implementation and making use of possibilities provided by IT-based management systems [3,4,5].

IT systems cover various spheres of activities, and their application generates various benefits. This paper is going to focus on making use of urban traffic forecasting systems, and mainly upon the costs and benefits of applying those systems.

J. Mikulski (Ed.): TST 2013, CCIS 395, pp. 23–31, 2013.
© Springer-Verlag Berlin Heidelberg 2013

2   Areas Where Traffic Modelling Can Be Used for Public Transport Purposes

Urbanisation ranks among the most important processes, which have been of economic, spatial, political, and social significance over recent years. At present about a half of the world's population lives in towns and cities, whereas some 200 years ago only 3% of the total population lived there. In European Union member states some 76% people live in towns and cities, that is forecasted to increase [6], by 2050, to about 84%. Big cities imply high population density, longer distances to commute, less and less pedestrian traffic, significant conflicts concerning locations.

The increasing number of city and town dwellers, coupled with expectations concerning good living and transport conditions there, is a challenge for urban transport, as transport is one of the factors enabling the development of towns and cities. Thus, along with many other activities, both current functioning and development of transport systems in cities is crucial, mass transit systems included, which in turn requires proper tools. One should depart from quantitative development of transport, especially road transport and individual ownership of vehicles, in which approach the increased demand for transport, increasing number of vehicles and trips by means of private cars entails growing funds targeting the construction and modernisation of roads, as well as financial means in household budgets supporting individual car ownership and use. Transport management systems should have ever increasing application, including also the use of traffic modelling when planning transport network and the offer of transport services.

The history of traffic modelling and forecasting, with the use of formal mathematical models, reaches of few dozen years back in time, however, the practical applications – due to the complexity of the problem and the necessity of making numerous calculations – of traffic models have become more widespread with the development of IT and data processing devices, namely in the 1960s and 1970s.

The methods of developing models and forecasting urban traffic, ending with distribution of traffic into specific sections of the road and street network, are a highly specialised discipline, so far there have been only a few centres dealing with that in Poland, mainly offices dealing with planning of road systems, as well as universities, and publication in that field are far from numerous. Substantial input in the development and popularization of traffic modelling is owed to the Instytut Kształtowania Środowiska (Institute for Development of Environment) in Warszawa later named Instytut Gospodarki Komunalnej i Przestrzennej (Institute of Spatial and Municipal Economy) and Politechnika Warszawska (Warsaw University of Technology) [7,8,9]. Large studies, organized by Biuro Studiów i Projektów Komunikacji in Katowice (Bureau of Studies and Transport Projects), were also conducted in the central part of the Silesian Province in years 1986 – 1988. What is more, the barriers for the universal use of traffic models include limited availability of data, or absence of some data, indispensable for the development of forecasts, or time consuming and costly acquiring of such data. Also the necessity of updating the data in a systematic manner is significant. Generally speaking, traffic models result from human activities, invariably related to movement in order to meet demands and obtain profits from work, and specific passenger preferences concerning ways, distances, and time of travel.

Traffic forecasting in cities may only concern aggregate figures, such as the number of journeys, as well as distribution into means of transport used for making those journeys (in particular the division between private cars and means of public transport), however, such data is not sufficient to manage the offer of transport services. For the purpose of planning transport systems and the offer of public transport services in cities/towns it is necessary to possess knowledge concerning traffic volumes for particular sections of the road and street network at various time ranges. That is why, after the determination of traffic volume, a spatial distribution of the traffic is made (the traffic frame/matrix is determined), then the traffic is divided in accordance with the means of travelling (pedestrian traffic as well as use of various means of transport) and in the end the traffic is distributed on the transport network [10].

The traffic volume is the number of journeys started and ended in a determined time range (e.g. day/24 hours) in specific regions/areas. It depends upon factors, which may be grouped as follows [7,8,9]:

- those which characterise the inhabitants of a given region/area, e.g. the total number of inhabitants, number of professionally active (working) inhabitants, income of a household, profession of the person or persons working in a given household, age, status concerning vehicle ownership,
- those which characterise the infrastructure and environment of the region/area, as well as the entire city/town, e.g. the economic potential of the area, access to transport infrastructure, existence of a service centre, distance to the city/town centre.

On the basis of figures, in which the variables are expressed, it is possible to determine the level of traffic generated and absorbed in specific transport areas.

The next stage concerns determination of the number of travels made between transport areas. Many mathematical models have been developed for that purpose. A popular one is the so-called gravitation based model, which specifies the traffic volume between regions/areas as dependent upon their attraction potentials and distance between the areas. The attraction potential depends mainly upon spatial development of specific regions/areas. The taking into consideration of the distance between regions/areas reflects the behaviour, the principle of which is that people search for destinations for commuting (work, shopping, etc.) relatively near, which generates more traffic between regions/areas that are closer to each other, and less traffic between regions/areas that are farther apart. The result of calculations made in that stage is the so-called journey matrix, containing the number of trips within a region/area and between specific regions/areas.

When dividing traffic into categories, which depend on how people get from one place to another, the fact is taken into consideration, that the share of pedestrian traffic depends upon the distance which people cover, density and availability of public transport networks, the remaining parameters that describe the quality of collective transport, availability of the town/city centre for private cars, car ownership coefficient, etc. By means of coefficients one can also divide the traffic into pedestrian traffic, travelling using own cars, as well as public transport.

The distribution of traffic into specific transport routes (roads) is the last step. We already have at our disposal the data concerning forecasted traffic volume, which will be executed by private cars and means of public transport, between specific transport regions/areas (traffic frame/matrix). Traffic gets distributed between the existing and designed road network. In case there is only one connection (one road) between the selected regions/areas, all the traffic is attributed to that road. However, more often than not, there are several roads between the traffic source and destination. Those roads are used by those who travel between various transport regions/areas. It is thus necessary to allocate traffic to roads connecting any two transport areas, as well as to add the traffic generated from various transport areas, on specific road sections.

Traffic models developed for the purpose of managing urban collective transport may serve first of all the purposes of the present state of affairs analysis, which finds application in the operational short-term management of transport services offer, as well as forecasts, which is planning over a longer time.

Efficient management of the transport services offer, putting the traffic model to use, allows to simulate, assess, and compare different variants of transportation services, and only on the basis of the above to make ongoing changes in the public transport service offer. Various changes are possible – most often they consist of making corrections in the frequency of services, route for a given line, or changing the capacity of rolling stock operating specific lines. IT programmes (software) serving the purpose of traffic modelling enable the introduction of changes into the model developed previously, as well as current assessment and comparison of resultant variants of traffic distribution.

The current management of transport services offer consists mainly of adjusting the offer to present demands and expectations of inhabitants. Changes in the arrangement of urban public transport lines may be divided in accordance with their causes. The first of those causes may be the modifications resulting from repairs and modernisation of line and point infrastructure of transport. These might be minor changes, e.g. diversions for the time of repair of street sections, that remain valid between several days and a few months, they may also be significant changes. An example to be provided here may be the construction of the new railway station in Katowice, and the related reconstruction of the city centre, which – in fact – changed completely the existing arrangement of routes and lines, as well as forced the organiser of urban public transport, the transport union of municipalities, Komunikacyjny Związek Komunalny Górnośląskiego Okręgu Przemysłowego in Katowice (KZK GOP), to design a new arrangement of lines in the centre of Katowice. The second group of changes contains modifications made as a consequence of new housing or shopping projects, which result in a change of sources and destinations of traffic, as well as needs and expectations of inhabitants. Modifications of both types are numerous indeed, they depend – of course – upon the size and type of the area, in which collective transport is managed. For example, in KZK GOP there are some 400 modifications of time table introduced every year, including changes in departure times, routes of public transport lines, as well as changes resulting from inclusion of new stops, or exclusion of some stops. These are mainly changes requested by passengers, NGOs, or municipalities being members of the transport union. Moreover, in the KZK GOP transport union, some 150 changes are introduced every year, which result from repairs of infrastructure and necessary route diversions [11].

An equally important application of traffic models are the long-term – sometimes for the time horizon of several or a few dozen years – forecasts of changes in the functioning of the town's transport system, with which the changes in behaviour are connected, that result from alterations in spatial development, including the execution of new investments in the town/city, e.g. new plants, educational institutions, trade and service centres, housing estates, as well as places of recreation, or other structures that are the sources of and destinations for the traffic. Changes are also exerted by investments in the city's transport infrastructure. Specialized software, which enables traffic modelling, is the basis that allows to obtain data on forecasted traffic loads for the road and street network, as well as occupancy of public transport lines which – in turn – enables preparation of feasibility studies for projects, and comparison of various variants of proposed solutions (among others – line routes, use of various means of public transport), both from the perspective of transport services, costs for the entity providing public transport services, as well as from the point of view of external costs and benefits, e.g. in environmental impact, among others regarding the emission of noxious substances and noise, or road accidents.

3   Identification of the Costs of Implementation of Traffic Modelling System, with the Use of Specialized Software

The purchase of software for traffic modelling and forecasting, its upgrading as well as collection of data, indispensable for the construction of a model, is connected with substantial expenditures – it is a typical investment project. Taking a decision about implementation of traffic modelling system with the use of specialized software requires preparation of indispensable specification of estimated outlays and benefits that may be obtained, and on that basis making the efficiency assessment of such an investment project. Preparation of more or less complex feasibility study is also necessary in the circumstances of applying for external funding, including also EU funding, which does not have to be repaid, or funding offered by other states or institutions.

It should be noted that some of the benefits related to the purchase of such software, obtained in the environment of transport system, both on a local community and on the national scale. It is important to prepare a reliable forecast of outlays, as often in the case of IT projects the costs as well implementation time are underestimated. Oftentimes, when preparing feasibility studies, not all costs are identified, as the study focuses mainly on the purchase of hardware and software, or expenditures that are of investment type [12].

Among the main cost items, related to the implementation and use of traffic modelling programmes, the following should be listed first of all:

1. The cost of purchase of software and computers having suitable computing power.
2. Costs related to the collection of input data for the model. The development of traffic model for a given area is connected with the necessity of collecting and introducing to the programme a definite data package, which contains mainly the following data:
   - data concerning the road network (number of lanes, turning relations, average speed, traffic capacity of road sections),
   - demographic data (population age structure, employment/professional activity, place of residence),
   - data concerning the transport behaviour of inhabitants in the area analysed (sources and destinations of traffic, division of transport tasks/services).
   - data on public transport system (routes of transport lines, time tables, capacity and type of rolling stock, as well as results of occupancy studies).

The traffic model for a given area is constructed on the basis of topographic maps of the area, as well as data from the Geographic Information System (GIS). On that basis, the model of road network is developed, as well as the model of public transport system, functioning in a given area. The division of the analysed area into transport districts requires obtaining demographic data. For that purpose, it is possible to use the database containing PESEL numbers (Powszechny Elektroniczny System Ewidencji Ludności – universal electronic system for citizen records), which is kept by appropriate departments of commune administration, in the form of municipal registration of inhabitants. The PESEL number identifies unequivocally the inhabitants of a given constituency, as it provides information about the sex and age, connected with that number is also the address of residence [13]. For the purpose of model construction, it is not necessary to know the entire number, which is legally protected, but only the first six digits, the number expressing sex, and the address, to which a given number is attached. On that basis it is possible to build a model, where the known values are age and gender structure of the population, as well as distribution of the population in the city/town.

Getting a complex knowledge concerning the traffic generation potential requires, however, collecting the data concerning transport behaviour of inhabitants of the area, for which the model is constructed. It is one of the most expensive stages of the model development, as it requires conducting primary questionnaire studies, by means of standardised questionnaires. The purpose of such studies is, first of all, to obtain knowledge concerning sources and destinations of traffic, the number of trips made, as well as means of transport held and used by households. The results of questionnaire survey form the basis for development of traffic frame/matrix. Depending upon the number of households questioned, a specific error probability is obtained, which will always accompany the construction of a model. The sample size, in turn, determines the costs of data collection [9].

An equally important element, which influences the quality of the constructed model will also be the data concerning the demand for urban public transport services. As a rule, such data is collected by the organisers of public transport, by counting the passengers getting on and getting off the vehicle. Urban transport vehicle occupancy studies are primary studies, which require recruiting a relatively large number of observers and co-ordinators. For example, KZK GOP spends some 350 thousand Polish zloty a year for such studies [11].

3. The remaining costs of implementation, which should include the costs of user training and purchase of suitable training materials.
4. Costs connected with the use of the traffic modelling system, which contains the cost of developing and functioning of one or several work-stations, which will deal with that work on an ongoing basis, as well as the cost of upgrading such software.

It can be seen from the above, that the very cost of purchase and implementation of software is but a part of the cost – paid at the investment stage. The current functioning of the software will generate the cost of software upgrade, as well as update of data, and various other costs, including the cost of personnel, related to the construction of traffic models, in compliance with the demand reported.

4 Identification of Benefits Connected with the Use of Traffic Modelling Systems by Entities Dealing with Collective Transport

Identification of benefits obtained in connection with utilisation of systems of traffic modelling and forecasting is assessed as the benefits obtained by the operator or manager of urban public transport (the so-called financial assessment of the undertaking) as well as external benefits, taking into account the influence upon the surroundings (the so-called economic assessment).

From the operators or managers of local collective transport point of view, the following benefits may be enumerated [15,16]:

1. Reduction of expenditures related to the transport work, as a result of more efficient management of the transport offer (arrangement of routes and lines, which results in a reduced number of vehicle-kilometres, with simultaneous provision of the same quality of transport services, better selection of rolling stock as regards its capacity),
2. Cutting down the travel time, increase in the transport speed, easier transfers, which is related to making the transport offer more attractive, and thus may be translated into higher tariff-related income.
3. Improved image, connected with meeting passengers' needs and expectations in a better way, increased demand for services, and increased tariff-related income.

Making use of systems for traffic modelling and prediction in the course of transport offer management allows also to get some external benefits. Those are related mainly to better adjustment of the services offer to the needs of passengers, improved image of collective transport, and enhanced competitiveness of that transport, in particular in comparison with individual means of transport. Restricting the number of trips made by means of individual transport entails first of all reduction of congestion and of negative environmental impact (reduced emission of noxious substances and noise), as well as improved quality of life in cities and urbanised areas. Moreover, collective transport that is efficient and suited to the needs of passengers [14]:

- increases the demand for services and products in towns/cities and conurbation,
- makes access to jobs easier,
- is of social importance.

Transport systems are requisites for lifestyle and mobility of inhabitants (provision of better quality services influences the demand) [15]. Moreover, they are one of the key factors that matter at decisions concerning location of investment projects, thus being decisive as regards competitiveness of cities/towns regions, in the eye of investors and people considering their settlement decisions. The development of an urban public transport system provides access to new areas, it simplifies access to the place of work and learning, while employers are provided with possibilities to attract employees from a wider area [15]. Thus, external benefits count here, which on the one hand often provide motivation to proceed with a given undertaking – as in the case of external benefits they are not to be obtained by the entity that undertakes a project, by the environment/surroundings – yet on the other hand it creates a chance to obtain financing for system implementation from external sources, such as European Union funds.

5   Conclusion

The implementation of an IT system ranks among investment projects that are connected with costs, but which also give benefits. In the case of an undertaking implemented for public transport, due to the substantial impact upon the environment, besides the internal costs and benefits – identified and important from the point of view of the service provider, also external costs and benefits are important. It is often the case that external costs and benefits are decisive for the implementation of a given solution, or selection of implementation variant.

The entities providing the urban public transport services should, to an ever greater degree, manage the transport offer making use of traffic modelling systems. So far, those systems – due to substantial costs and specialized knowledge – have been used by planning entities, and their use has been substantially limited. The increasing demands concerning the quality of services in public transport, striving to better adjust the transport offer to the needs, lack of spare capacity in road and street systems, as well as increasing environmental demands, all create the requirement to use them more universally in current management of transport offers. Also the benefits obtained through complex computerisation of the entity in question cannot be overestimated, as they entail embracing by an integrated IT system of all spheres of its activity.

References

1. Frączkiewicz–Wronka, A.: Poszukiwanie istoty zarządzania publicznego. In: Frączkiewicz–Wronka, A. (ed.) Zarządzanie Publiczne – Elementy Teorii i Praktyki, pp. 19–49. Wydawnictwo Akademii Ekonomicznej w Katowicach, Katowice (2009)

2. Austen, A.: Efektywność usług publicznych. In: Austen, A., Dydkowski, G. (eds.) Zarządzanie Usługami Użyteczności Publicznej, pp. 21–27. Wydawnictwo Uniwersytetu Ekonomicznego w Katowicach, Katowice (2012)

3. Niedzielski, P.: Polityka innowacyjna w transporcie, Rozprawy i Studia T. 462, Uniwersytet Szczeciński, pp. 89—103, Szczecin (2003)

4. Burnewicz, J.: Spójny i innowacyjny system transportowy Pomorza, pp. 71–89. Wydawnictwo Uniwersytetu Gdańskiego, Gdańsk (2011)

5. Burnewicz, J.: A study of innovative trends in transport. In: Burnewicz, J. (ed.) Innovative Perspective of Transport and Logistics, pp. 74–117. Wydawnictwo Uniwersytetu Gdańskiego, Gdańsk (2009)

6. EU transport in figures. Statistical Pocketbook 2011, European Commission, p. 16. European Union (2011), http://ec.europa.eu (access date July 17, 2013)

7. Lilpop, Z., Sidorenko, A., Waltz, A.: Prognozowanie ruchu miejskiego. Instytut Kształtowania Środowiska, Warszawa (1983)

8. Dybicz, T.: Pakiet oprogramowania Visum jako narzędzie do modelowania ruchu transportu publicznego w Warszawie. In: Conference "Transport Publiczny w Warszawie", 10-11.10.2005 rok. Website of Urząd m. st. Warszawy, Warsaw Town Hall, http://www.um.warszawa.pl (access date July 17, 2013)

9. Suchorzewski, W., et al.: Planowanie systemów transportu w miastach. IGPiK, Warszawa (1992)

10. Gaca, S., Suchorzewski, W., Tracz, M.: Inżynieria ruchu drogowego. Teoria i praktyka. WKiŁ, Warszawa (2008)

11. Internal data of KZK GOP, http://www.kzkgop.com.pl (access date July 17, 2013)

12. Kos, B.: Systemy informatyczne w tworzeniu wartości dodanej w usługach sektora TSL (transport – spedycja – logistyka). In: Marketing przyszłości. Trendy. Strategie. Instrumenty. Uniwersytet Szczeciński, Zeszyty Naukowe No. 595, Ekonomiczne Problemy Usług (55), 49–57 (2010)

13. Act of law of April 10, 1974 on census and identification documents; Official Journal of Law, (Dz.U.), No. 14 item 85, p. 9, with subsequent changes (1974)

14. Tomanek, R.: Integracja komunikacji miejskiej – od porozumienia taryfowego do zarządu transportu. Transport Miejski (10) (1996)

15. Dydkowski, G.: Ocena efektywności działalności oraz przedsięwzięć rozwojowych transportu. In: Michałowska, M. (ed.) Efektywność Transportu w Warunkach Gospodarki Globalnej, pp. 96–119. Prace Naukowe Uniwersytetu Ekonomicznego w Katowicach, Katowice (2012)

16. Kos, B.: Ocena efektów zastosowań rozwiązań telematycznych w organizacjach sektora TSL. In: Michałowska, M. (ed.) Efektywność Transportu w Warunkach Gospodarki Globalnej, pp. 143–149. Prace Naukowe Uniwersytetu Ekonomicznego w Katowicach, Katowice (2012)

17. Mikulski, J.: The possibility of using telematics in urban transportation. In: Mikulski, J. (ed.) TST 2011. CCIS, vol. 239, pp. 54–69. Springer, Heidelberg (2011)

Data Transmission System Architecture for e-Navigation

Damian Filipkowski

Gdynia Maritime University, Faculty of Navigation,
Morska Str. 81-87,81-225 Gdynia, Poland
dfilipkowski@wn.am.gdynia.pl

Abstract. The subject of research is the modeling of data consistent with the objectives of the e-Navigation concept. Author presents general aspects of data transmissions in maritime transportation. He shows possible directions of communication and connection methods and identify the problems arising from the application of specific solutions for individual transmission paths. Author presents also a prototype architecture of the e-Navigation concept tested during the EfficienSea project and an original concept of structure in line with the idea of "OneWindow" contact point.

Keywords: e–Navigation, EfficienSea project, radio-communication.

1 Introduction

Maritime communication and data transmission in maritime transportation are widely discussed at the work on e-Navigation concept. There is a big difference between the technological capabilities available on board the ships (e.g. satellite Internet connection), and the systems required by regulations – Global Maritime Distress Safety System (GMDSS). In addition, the duty officer is burdened with unnecessary sending thousands of kilobytes of data, often available from other sources. On the other hand, most of the solutions used in a communication system is obsolete. Exchange of information between ship and shore is now a natural and necessary procedure to manage vessel in a safe manner. Unfortunately, it is believed that the existing GMDSS is in some ways an archaic system and cannot deal with modern communication requirements. Users have a constant access to new technologies and they are putting pressure on the administration to change regulations when it comes to communication and data transmission at sea. We need to change the rules and create a new data exchange system that will modernize and streamline data transmission in maritime transport. The idea of e-Navigation is a solution that not only improve communication, but also provides a number of useful features for both group of users, this ones on shore and this ones on the ship [9,11].

2 e-Navigation

e-Navigation is a concept developed under the auspices of the International Maritime Organization (IMO) in order to improve the safety of navigation of commercial

J. Mikulski (Ed.): TST 2013, CCIS 395, pp. 32–41, 2013.
© Springer-Verlag Berlin Heidelberg 2013

vessels through better management of data structures on ships and ashore, better exchange of data between ships and authorized land stations (e.g. Vessel Traffic Services, VTS stations) and reliable communications between them. The definition of e-Navigation proposed by International Association of Marine Aids to Navigation and Lighthouse Authorities(IALA), it is generally accepted, the initial definition of the emerging system [4].

"e-Navigation is the harmonized collection, integration, exchange, presentation and analysis of maritime information onboard and ashore by electronic means to enhance berth to berth navigation and related services, for safety and security at sea and protection of the marine environment."

Another identified problem is an enormous amount of information which Officer Of the Watch (OOW) has to process and interpret. The need for standardization and integration is a natural consequence of the introduction of new technologies. An example of the integration of systems can be Integrated Bridge Systems (IBS) or Integrated Navigation Systems (INS). Unfortunately this systems are limited, to devices available on board the vessel. e-Navigation in its assumptions, is a concept that treats maritime transport in a holistic way. That means that one of the goals is to integrate, standardize and automate the exchange of information between ship and shore, between two ships and between shore users as well. e-Navigation is not limited to data concerning only the vessel and sea environment but the scope of the system includes also authorized shore users. It must be remembered that the land is the starting and ending point of each sea voyage and it is obvious that shore structures are important part of maritime industry [2, 10].

3   Data Transmission Directions in Sea Transportation

Radio-communication systems for maritime transport, due to the nature of this brunch of industry, should provide effective and constant connection. There are four directions of the flow of data in shipping [5]:

- ship-shore,
- shore-ship,
- ship-ship,
- shore-shore.

Due to the nature of transmitted data, it have to be chosen a method of communication. It have to be specified how users can establish communications and transmit data. For each of the four directions mentioned above, we can identify three ways of data transmissions [5]:

- pull - request for messages, data is transmitted from sender X to recipient Y but flow is initiated by recipient Y. An example of this type of transmission is communication between a client and server in a typical TCP/IP network,

- push adressed – sending addressed messages, data is sent from sender X to a specified recipient Y. An example would be sending SMS via mobile phone or sending addressed messages via AIS (Automatic Identification System) device,
- push-multicast - data is sent by the sender X to multiple recipients Y. An example would be Navtex, radio and AIS messages. This method sends data to a group of recipients simultaneously in a single transmission. A special case is broadcasting, when a group Y consist of all possible recipients.

Table 1. Directions and methods of data transmissions in maritime transport [5]

	Pull	*Push-addressed*	*Push-multicast*
Ship → Shore	Data pulled from ship on shore initiative.	Data pushed from ship to single component on shore.	Data pushed from ship to multiple components on shore.
Shore→Ship	Data pulled from shore server by ship.	Data pushed from shore to a single ship.	Data pushed from shore to multiple ships.
Ship→Ship	Data pulled from ship on other ships initiative.	Data pushed from ship to another ship.	Data pushed from ship to multiple ships.
Shore →Shore	Data pulled from shore component to other shore component.	Data pushed from shore component to another shore component.	Data pushed from shore component to multiple other shore components.

When creating system to enable the connection in the above mentioned directions and using mentioned methods, there are three aspects which have to be considered. Firstly, communication systems often provide connectivity in several directions, such as by using different protocol (e.g. AIS data can be transmitted in land-to-ship relations, ship-to-ship and ship-to-shore). Secondly, the use of different communication systems often gives different transmission characteristics (e.g. both the Internet and the AIS can be used as a communications system and to provide data from ship to shore, but both of these solutions have very different characteristics in terms of capacity and reliability). Thirdly, there is no communication system that would allow transmission in all directions to all above-mentioned methods. There is a need to create a new system using new techniques of data transmissions or a system that would effectively integrate currently existing transmission techniques [6].

4   Data Transmission System Architecture – EfficienSea Project

EfficienSea is a project of the European Union regarding the safety and vessel traffic in the Baltic Sea. One of the working groups, dealing with the issue of e-Navigation, has developed a prototype of the system architecture. In this chapter there are assumptions of the project and a chart scheme of system architecture. There are also some conclusions which are results of research carried out on the possibility of using different methods of communication in e-Navigation.

4.1   Ship Infrastructure

Facilities on board consists of software that runs in the Windows environment. The program is called an e-Navigation Enhanced INS (ee-INS). This software is free and available with source code. This gives possibility to change or modify software by programmers. In addition, display chart systems is based on the OpenMap license. It is an open platform that is the source of maps (no navigational), which are displayed on the user's monitor. Commercial plug-ins allow to use Electronic Navigational Charts (ENC), but they are not necessary for purpose to test data links. The application has a few basic navigation functions. Personal Computer (PC)is connected to the Internet through Multi-WAN router, but also has a connection to the AIS. The structure of the prototype is consistent with the objectives of the IMO regarding development of e - Navigation, see Fig. 1 [5].

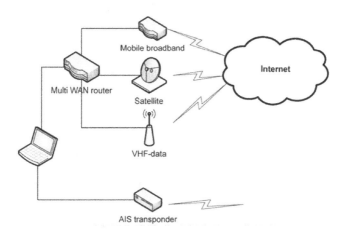

Fig. 1. Ship infrastructure[5]

In this approach, conception of architecture of a new system includes three different Internet connections:

- mobile broadband,
- satellite communication,
- data transmission via VHF

and AIS as a complementary system or back up in the situation of failure of Internet connection.

4.2   Shore Infrastructure

The infrastructure on the land consists of the following components: the e-Navigation server, VTS stations and land based AIS. The elements on the land are connected via Internet. E-Navigation Server provides connectivity compatible with request-response method of connection. This structure allows to use Internet on the ship and VTS stations. The server uses land based AIS network to send and receive AIS messages.

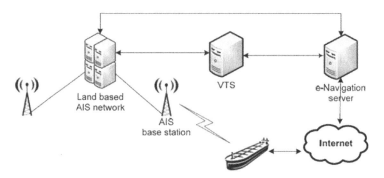

Fig. 2. Shore infrastructure [5]

The structure of the prototype is consistent with the objectives of the IMO regarding the e-Navigation, see Fig. 2 [5].

e-Navigation server in proposed concept allows creators of the system to use the various services that will be available in e-Navigation Fig. 2. Software applications are available through online services and, in some cases, through the Internet overlay (data can be displayed and entered by the user). Computer programs are dependent on multiple data sources, such as hydro-meteorological and oceanographic data, weather forecasts and data from the AIS. Most of these sources are separate and independent services. The acquired data are stored on separate servers, and e-Navigation server is used as a "One Window" contact point for easy access to the data. Thanks to this service regulations may be distributed across multiple physical servers. This is the so-called Service Oriented Architecture (SOA). Distributed server network not only provides faster data access (prevents server overload), but also provides a level of redundancy in case of failure of one of the servers [1].

As a web services protocol were chosen XML-RPC protocol and HTTP protocol. XML-RPC is better suited to SOA because it is simpler and data models (questions and answers) can easily be converted to XSD (XML Schema, Schema Extensible Markup Language) rather than to the WSDL (Web Services Description Language). XML is used to query and response in a client-server relation, and the HTTP protocol is used to transport the data [5].

5   Data Transmission System Architecture – Author's Proposition

There is believe that one of the main tasks of e-Navigation concept is the exchange and storage of data. To ensure effective exchange of information, the structure of the system must be composed of elements on the ship and land based infrastructure. EfficienSea working group dealing with the issue of e-Navigation has created a proposal for the structure of the system (Fig. 1 and Fig. 2). Author creating his own infrastructure diagram tried to use a different approach. Basing on the international regulations and his professional knowledge he tried to identify information that is now transmitted in maritime transport. Later on he created information flow paths between different users and create a project of system structure. In Fig. 3 and Fig. 4. author presents his own vision for the structure of the system. The chart diagrams shows the main elements of both structures on the land and on the ship. There are also symbolically presented directions in which the data will be transmitted. There is also emphasized need for a "One Window" contact point (both on board and on shore).

5.1   Shore Infrastructure

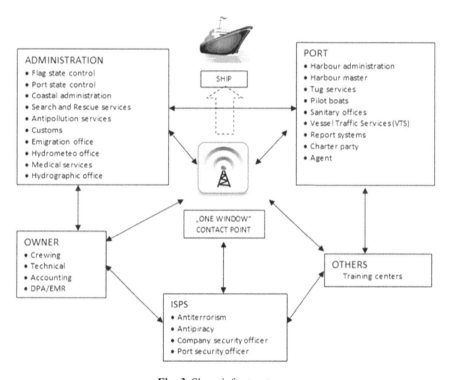

Fig. 3. Shore infrastructure

In Fig.3 there are indicated land users with which a ship currently exchanging data. It is also shown how authorized land users can obtain ship data using "One Window" contact point. That point may be one of the servers on which the data would be collected and archived. As the creators of the EfficienSea project author believes that the distribution of servers allow for better and faster exchange of data and provide a level of redundancy in case of failure of one of them. Currently in Poland there is under construction National System of Maritime Safety(KSBM, Krajowy System Bezpieczeństwa Morskiego). There will be three centers, one for each Maritime Office, which can be treated as a "One Window" contact points. User will have possibility to get information stored on KSBM servers thanks to SWIŻB software (System Wymiany Informacji Bezpieczeństwa Żeglugi, Maritime Safety Information Exchange System) [8]. As shown in Fig. 3 land users are also able to exchange data directly with each other. Because the Internet provides connectivity in shore-shore relation, possibility to exchange information directly between users ashore will reduce the server load, speed up the exchange of data. There is also a risk because data is not verified in "One Window" contact point and may be inaccurate or even false [1].

5.2   Ship Infrastructure

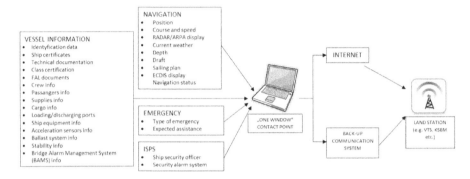

Fig. 4. Ship infrastructure

Figure 4 shows schematically a vessel network which allows easy and fast exchange of information and data. The diagram presents categories of information that ship exchanges with other users. All data is collected in a "One Window" contact point. A point on the vessel may be a ship's server or a VDR device appropriately adapted for this purpose. The data is then sent to the authorized land user (e.g. VTS), where data are collected, archived, reviewed and possibly shared with other authorized users [7].

Transmission is possible through the use of satellite Internet connection. Detailed analysis shows that the Internet offers the possibility of access to a large number of services that have been defined in concept development of e-Navigation. In addition, through the use of diverse Internet software system has ability to adapt to changing conditions and user needs. However, as mentioned earlier, does not provide communications in all directions and to all methods listed in Table 1, which is why it is necessary to use other means of communication such as AIS. This is consistent with EfficienSea project. AIS has in its message structure an empty space which developers assumptions were intended for use in new systems. Such a system could be e-Navigation [3].

6   Evaluation of System Architecture

The following are the conclusions and findings to a large extent on an EfficienSea research. During testing data transmission links as shown in Fig. 1 and Fig.2, there have been identified some problems, and the observations which are presented below. Author basing on the differences and similarities between his concept and EfficienSea project tries to predict what problems may arise in the future, and what solutions can deliver measurable results.

6.1   Assessment of EfficienSea Project

Data Modeling and Coding

The process of describing the data transmitted using UML and transform it into an XML schema definition (XSD) was simple and effective. Using XML protocol for data encoding introduced to increase the amount of data due to the markers and a textual representation of the number as opposed to the binary encoding. The use of compression for HTTP-enabled significantly reduce the amount of transmitted data [5].

Communication via Internet

Internet has proven to be an effective method of communication in relations shore→ ship (push) and shore → ship (pull). Polling is an effective solution in relation shore → ship (push), but it has some significant drawbacks caused by delay for the polling interval, which is not acceptable for some services, such as coordination of SAR (Search and Rescue) action. Delay in communication in distress is also inconsistent with the provisions of Chapter V of SOLAS Convention (Safety of Life at Sea).

The bandwidth of each of the three ways to connect to the Internet used in the test proved to be sufficient for the purposes of testing prototype. Answers to websites and establish the connection did not last longer than 10 seconds. Of course, the question arises whether the connection will be sufficient for large data packets? There is a belief that communication via satellite is too expensive, via VHF is to slow and via mobile phones available only near the shore [5].

Communication via AIS

AIS proved appropriate for periodic transmission of small packets message. For more complex tasks AIS limits reduced communication. It was found that the use of AIS to communications between vessels was quite reliable. Using the base stations to send and receive messages were less reliable because they depend on the distance from the base station, and the characteristics of the station [5].

Ship Infrastructure

Ship devices allow you to connect additional external PC via the pilot plug. Using pilot plug on the bridge of the ship turned out to be more difficult than previously expected. Quite often plug for the pilot was not properly connected or not connected at all. In addition, the challenge was to connect the remote control plugs into the computer. Finally used equipment that connect to Wi-Fi. To connect to the Internet uses a simple router (Multi-WAN router). Failover when one connection becomes inactive, causing problems due to the delay resulting from the switch from one system to another. When the connection is not available, such as mobile broadband connection status can vary considerably over a period of time. At the end of the call is eventually lost. This can lead to frequent changes in the type of calls at the time. It is believed that more advanced routers installed on the ship would operate better [5].

Shore Infrastructure
Using the Internet and standard software components as Web pages, application servers and databases did not cause major problems. Only one server-side land-based infrastructure has been shown that in order to achieve high reliability of the system, individual servers should be avoided in the future [5].

6.2   Conclusion on the Author's System Architecture

Internet well suited as a data transmission system in relation land-land and land-to-ship, ship-to-shore, while the poor ship-to-ship. The author suggests that the communications ship-to-ship can be replaced, to some extent, by communications ship-shore-shore-ship. Data transmission via land based servers (PCs) would not only transfer large data packets, but also allow for their review and possible protection against unauthorized access. Currently, access to information like position, speed and course of the ship can get everyone in Internet. Authorized and properly protected land access to the servers allow control over the outflow of data. Currently, the exchange of data in ship-to-ship is limited to the transmission of AIS and VHF voice. Both systems work in the same frequency and are characterized by a relatively small range of approximately 30 nautical miles. Both systems should remain for fast communication in a range of coastal stations and between vessels.

7   Conclusion

Suitable systems for communication are essential to ensure effective and efficient communication in e-Navigation. There is believe that one method of communication is not enough, because each of the currently existing methods will behave differently depending on what and where is transmitted and what effect you want to achieve. Author and EfficienSea working group, they proposed usage of two transmission methods AIS and Internet. Each of these methods has certain advantages but also limitations. In EfficienSeaproject AIS and Internet are equivalent means of transmission, however, the author believes that the Internet should be the primary way communication and AIS should be considered as a back-up system. Capacity, transmission speed, reliability and topology are some of the parameters that determine the effectiveness of the system in particular transmission. Main goal of tests carried out during the EfficienSea project and research in the Faculty of Navigation of Gdynia Maritime University was to select the communication method and use it in e-Navigation. Second aim was to identify what system may be needed in the future, because there is no doubt that the existing systems (especially the minimum required by regulations) are not sufficient.

References

1. Filipkowski, D., Wawruch, R.: Concept of "One Window" Data Exchange System Fulfilling the Recommendation for e-Navigation System. In: Mikulski, J. (ed.) TST 2010. CCIS, vol. 104, pp. 85–95. Springer, Heidelberg (2010)
2. Filipkowski, D.: eReport – Information Presentation Form Comply with Recommendations of the eNavigation System. Archives of Transport System Telematics IV(1), 37–41 (2011)
3. Filipkowski, D.: Informatyczne elementy systemu e-Nawigacji. Logistyka Issue (6) (2011)
4. IALA e-Navigation Comitee: e-Navigation Frequently Asked Questions (Version 1.5) (2010)
5. IMO Sub-Comitee on Communication Search and Rescue: Development of an e-Navigation Strategy implementation plan - Report from the EfficienSea Project. Sub-Comitee on Communication Search and Rescue (2011)
6. ISO 16425: Ship and marine technology – Installation guideline for ship communication network of improving communication for shipboard equipment and systems (2011)
7. Stupak, T., Wawruch, R.: Data transmission, integration and presentation in Vessel Traffic Management System (VTMS). In: Mikulski, J. (ed.) Advances in Transport Systems Telematics, pp. 267–276. Wydawnictwo Komunikacji i Łączności, Warszawa (2009)
8. Stupak, T.: Global ships monitoring system, Zeszyty Naukowe Akademii Marynarki Wojennej im. Bohaterów Westerplatte (2009)
9. Sub-Committee on Safety of Navigation, Session 85: Strategy for the development and implementation of e-Navigation. IMO, London (2009)
10. Sub-Committee on Safety of Navigation, Sessions 53-55: Development of e-Navigation strategy. IMO, London (2007-2009)
11. Weintrit, A., Wawruch, R., Specht, C., Gucma, L., Pietrzykowski, Z.: An approach to e Navigation, "Coordinates", Delhi, vol. III(6), pp. 15–22 (2007)

Algorithm for Surface Creation from a Cloud of Points

Marián Hruboš and Aleš Janota

University of Žilina, Faculty of Electrical Engineering, Department of Control and Information Systems, Univerzitna 2, 01026 Žilina, Slovak Republic
{marian.hrubos,ales.janota}@fel.uniza.sk

Abstract. The paper presents a designed algorithm which makes possible to create surfaces of scanned objects based on point clouds and thus to provide basis for the following graphical operations. For such created surfaces we may further apply graphical algorithms enabling usage of photographs leading to creation of objects with their own texture. The algorithm is designed as a universal procedure in such a way that point clouds may be loaded from the external file. This feature brings possibility to apply it to processing of point clouds coming from other sources, too.

Keywords: point cloud, surface creation, Matlab, data processing.

1 Introduction

Nowadays people are more and more aware of the need for digitizing the outside world. For example, digitization of historic buildings can help us in the preservation of our cultural heritage for future generations, and on this basis it is also possible to design the procedures for their renovations. Digitization of the surrounding world also gives us many other benefits. Digitized cities may be presented through the virtual tours to potential visitors and thus develop tourism, but digital data may be also helpful in the design of general city plans. So digitization of industrial halls may also make subsequent analysis and optimization of the production process possible.

Current trend of digitization, digital mapping and three-dimensional space imaging offer designers and programmers new chances and reliefs. Applications commonly used to view various graphic formats are also beginning to support the formats that allow three-dimensional imaging. There are also available standards prescribing the internal structure of these files.

Generally, point clouds are acquired with stereo cameras, monocular systems or laser scanners. The aim of the paper is to present an algorithm which was designed, programmed and tested to create object surfaces based on scanned point clouds. There are many methods and approaches available such as e.g. [1], based on extraction of so called "feature points; or [2], which defines the surface as the isosurface of a trivariate volume model, or many others. Our own original solution represents a partial solution of the complex problem of scanning a road surface and its surrounding area for the purpose of identification and classification of selected objects and creating the virtual model of the road utilized in future developed Intelligent Transport System ITS applications.

J. Mikulski (Ed.): TST 2013, CCIS 395, pp. 42–49, 2013.
© Springer-Verlag Berlin Heidelberg 2013

1.1   Getting a Cloud of Points

Input data for the proposed algorithm is in the form of a cloud of points received through the mobile measurement platform. This measurement platform (Fig. 1) is primarily used to monitor the state of the road surface. Its secondary use is to monitor the area around the road. Road surface is measured by the laser scanner LMS-100 produced by the SICK Company. Measurements of the surrounding areas are realized by the 360° scanner LD-OEM 1000 from the same producer. Gathering of visual information about the measured area is provided through cameras installed in the front part of the measurement platform. We use the SPAN CTP navigation system to get precise position of the measurement platform. It is a combination of a classical GPS receiver providing basic position data, corrected with position data received from the OMNISTAR satellites and the inertial navigation system. So the SPAN CTP navigation system evaluates its current location just on the basis of the classical position determined from the GPS with OMNISTAR correction, but this position is also corrected based on real motion sensed by a set of accelerometers and gyroscopes [3].

For points cloud processing we use our own algorithm that incorporates a real position of the measurement equipment and tilts in all axes. To be compatible with various visualization equipment we use *.OBJ format of the output data file.

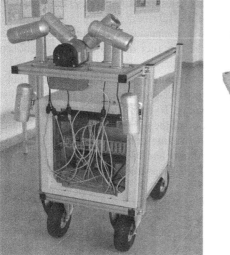

Fig. 1. Photographs of the mobile measurement platform (*left*), the navigation system SPAN-CPT (*right top*) and the laser scanner LD-OEM1000 (*right bottom*)

1.2   Description of the Measurement Unit

The concept of the measurement unit is based on getting data about the measured space and its fast processing. Data are obtained through the laser scanner. The control program is based on the calculation algorithm that depends on the used measurement method and is implemented in the form of evaluation software (Fig. 2). It re-calculates individual values obtained from the laser scanner. Outputs of the measurement unit are in the form of spatial coordinates of measured points, saved into the output file [4].

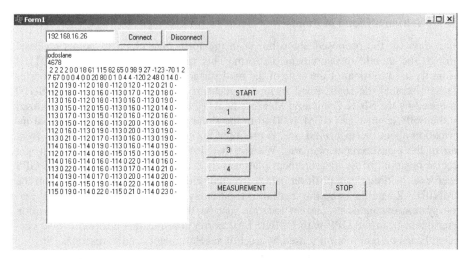

Fig. 2. View of the evaluation software

The measurement unit has been designed with the usage of the laser scanner LD-OEM1000 produced by the SICK Company. The measurement system consists of the laser scanner and evaluation software. The measurement principle is based on Time of Flight of the laser beam. The scanner may be connected to the supervisory system via RS-232, CAN, or Ethernet. In our case the Ethernet interface has been chosen. The laser scanner is then in the role of the TCP/IP server.

The laser scanner provides data about measured points through the initial angle, number of measured points, angle difference between individual points and distances between the laser scanner and measured points. To apply these data we must adapt parametric equations of the circle for calculation of the i-th measured point in the n-th cut.

The angle contained by the axis x and the line containing the measured point is given by sum of the constant, representing mechanical rotation of the laser scanner, initial angle and the sequential number of the measured point in the given cut multiplied by angle difference.

Based on the number of measured points we can set the value of the calculation cycle repeating. Calculation is being repeated so many times, how many measured points we have. The sequential number of the measured point is incremented in each calculation cycle of the given cut.

The value of the z coordinate is incremented for every new measured cut. The adapted parametric equations of the circle used to calculate the i-th measurement point in the n-th cut are given below (1).

$$x_{in} = \cos\left[(\alpha_{0n} + i * \Delta\alpha_n + 90) * \pi * 2 / 360\right] * d_{in},$$

$$y_{in} = -\sin\left[(\alpha_{0n} + i * \Delta\alpha_n + 90) * \pi * 2 / 360\right] * d_{in},$$

(1)

$$z_{in} = n,$$

where:
- x_{in}, y_{in} and z_{in} are coordinates of the i-th measured point in the n-th cut,
- i is the sequence number of the currently calculated point,
- $\Delta\alpha_n$ is the value of angle increment for the given cut,
- d_{in} is the value of distance between the i-th point in the n-th cut and the laser scanner,
- n is the sequence number of the measured cut, while the n value is incremented when measuring a new cut [5].

Evaluation software of the measurement unit is based on on-line processing of measured data. Its realization results from analysis of the packet structure.

Fig. 3. Measured point cloud representing a part of the Žilina university campus

Sample result of the described measurement process is illustrated in Fig. 3 where a part of the university campus was scanned and visualized.

1.3   Description of the Used Output Format

As an output format we have chosen the OBJ format. It is suitable for display of objects in the three-dimensional space. Another advantage of that format is its compatibility with multiple imaging software environments. The internal structure is freely available and the process of data storage is simply algorithmizable.

The internal structure is defined at least by vertices of the object edges. Other parameters are object edges or points and edges of texture applied to the objects. A sample of the cube object displayed by the visualization software MeshLab is shown below.

Fig. 4. The cubes object visualization

To create the visualized object one must start with definition of object vertices. Individual objects are entered using and identifier and a number of coordinates. The role of the identifier is to determine what is being represented: a vertex, edge or surface. Identifier of the vertex is given as „v", followed by the coordinates of the point given in the form X, Y and Z. For example, one of the vertices of the cube could be entered and represented by the form „v 1 1 1". Once all visualized vertices have been defined, we may define surfaces. Surface in the OBJ format may be defined through the identifier and an arbitrary number of vertices, however, at least three. To define an area one must enter at least three vertices not contained on the same line. Then the visualization software is able to interpret them and connect the vertices into one surface. The identifier of the surface is „f" (face). For example, using the data set „f 3 2 1" we define one half-surface of the cube.

2   The Algorithm for Surfaces Creation

This algorithm is used to create surfaces of objects defined by a cloud of points. There are many methods designed for creation of a surface based on known points of individual objects. The method utilized in this algorithm is designed in such way that three points are necessary to create surface. In this way it is possible to reach better interpretation of final objects thanks to smaller dimensions of individual surfaces.

As indicated in the flowchart (Fig. 5) the algorithm processes the points on a mass scale. The first step of the algorithm is reading of the point cloud into the input matrix. Then a cycle is initiated whose number of repetitions depends on the number of points contained in the input matrix. In every step of that cycle another cycle is being initiated hose repeating again depends on the number of points in the input matrix. In that way the algorithm is able to compare each point of the input matrix with each. The comparing process is based on calculation of four parameters. The first one is calculation of a distance between the points to be compared. To do that we use the equation:

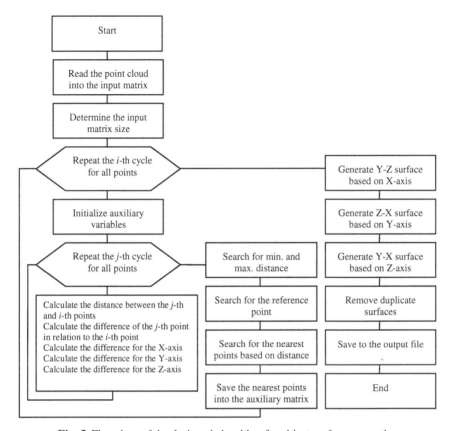

Fig. 5. Flowchart of the designed algorithm for object surface generation

$$r = \sqrt{(x_i - x_j)^2 + (y_i - y_j)^2 + (z_i - z_j)^2}$$ (2)

In Matlab the problem may be solved in the following way:

```
DIF(j,1)=sqrt([X(i,1)-X(j,1)]^2  +  [X(i,2)-X(j,2)]^2  +
[X(i,3)-X(j,3)]^2);
```

Another three parameters are used to determine axes difference – one parameter for one axis. Axis difference determines deviation of points within one axis. To calculate that we use the equation:

$$r = \sqrt{(x_i - x_j)^2}$$ (3)

In Matlab the problem can be solved in the following way:

```
DIF(j,2)=sqrt([X(i,1)-X(j,1)]^2);
DIF(j,3)=sqrt([X(i,2)-X(j,2)]^2);
DIF(j,4)=sqrt([X(i,3)-X(j,3)]^2);
```

Further only those points are being processed whose distance is minimum, i.e. that the value of the first parameter is the lowest. Then based on axis difference we are able to determine, which of the surfaces is described by the given points. The surface is generated in three successive phases. At first the surface Y-Z is generated, then Z-X and finally Y-X. As the algorithm generates all the surfaces, it is necessary to remove those of them that are duplicate, i.e. those where area of the square is described by four triangular surfaces. After removing duplicate surfaces we may save the final matrix, containing the results, into the OBJ type file. Figures show gradual creation of the cube surface. Results are visualized in the MashLab environment, however any other software supporting the OBJ format may be used.

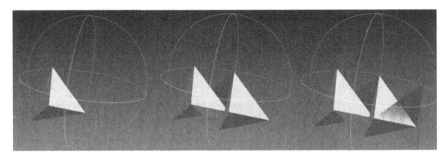

Fig. 6. Generated surface for the 1st point (*left*), 2 (*middle*) and 3 compared points (*right*)

Fig. 7. Generated surface for the 9 (*left*), 17 (*middle*) and 26 (*right*) compared points

3   Conclusion

This work introduced the designed algorithm which makes possible to create surface of measured (scanned) objects based on the given cloud of points and thus provide the basis for the following graphical operations. On these surfaces we are then able to apply graphical algorithms enabling work with photographs and thus to create objects with their own texture.

Acknowledgments. The paper was elaborated with support of the Slovak grant agency VEGA, grant No. 1/0453/12 "Study of interactions of a motor vehicle, traffic flow and road."

References

1. Toll, B., Cheng, F.: Surface Reconstruction from Point Clouds. In: Olling, G.J., Choi, B.K., Jerard, R.B. (eds.) Machining Impossible Shapes. IFIP, vol. 18, pp. 173–178. Springer, Boston (1999)
2. Huang, A., Nielson, G.M.: Surface Approximation to Point Cloud Data Using Volume Modeling. In: Mundici, D., Gottlob, G., Leitsch, A. (eds.) KGC 1993. LNCS, vol. 713, pp. 333–343. Springer, Heidelberg (1993)
3. Halgaš, J., Janota, A.: Technical Devices Cooperation to Obtain Data for 3D Environment Modelling. In: Mikulski, J. (ed.) TST 2011. CCIS, vol. 239, pp. 330–337. Springer, Heidelberg (2011)
4. Hruboš, M.: Nástroj na zistenie stavu degradácie vozovky v čase (A Tool to Detect Status of Road Degradation in Time). MSc. thesis No. 28260220122010, Dept. of Control & Information Systems, University of Žilina, Slovakia, 77 p. (2012)
5. Halgaš, J., Hruboš, M., Pirník, R., Janota, A.: Determination of Formulas for Processing of Measured Points Representing Road Surface Deformations. Archives of Transport System Telematics 5(1), 7–10 (2012)

Impact of Telematics on Efficiency of Urban Freight Transport

Stanisław Iwan[1], Krzysztof Małecki[2], and Jerzy Korczak[3]

[1] Maritime University of Szczecin,
Pobożnego 11, 70-515 Szczecin, Poland
s.iwan@am.szczecin.pl
[2] West Pomeranian University of Technology,
Żołnierska 11, 71-210 Szczecin, Poland
kmalecki@wi.zut.edu.pl
[3] Koszalin University of Technology,
Kwiatkowskiego 6e, 75-343 Koszalin, Poland
korczak1@gazeta.pl

Abstract. The need for telematics solutions to support goods transport and distribution in urban areas is mainly due to the complexity of the processes in urban transport systems and the often conflicting expectations of different groups of road users and other stakeholders of urban freight transport (city administrators, residents, traders, hauliers, etc.). The main objective is optimisation of the freight transport by ensuring adequate availability of the linear and point transport infrastructure, while reducing the negative impact of the transport system on the environment. The usability of the telematics in urban freight transport is manifested by reduced freight distribution costs as well as by increased capacity of urban freight systems. This paper is focused on the key areas of telematics influence on the functioning of urban freight transport systems, as well as its influence on the systems efficiency. The chosen good practices were used for this purpose.

Keywords: urban freight transport, city logistics, telematics systems, efficiency of transport systems.

1   Introduction

Due to the growing demand for transport, more and more importance is given to systems that enable efficient management of traffic flows and the overall functioning of the transportation system. Since they are complex, and in particular considerably susceptible to external impacts and largely dependent on the time factor, the systems must be based on a holistic approach which accounts for the overall structure and the functional interdependencies. Therefore, they rely on solutions based on integrating many different subsystems and, via application of modern technologies, on optimising their functioning. Development of such solutions could not circumvent urban systems. The significance of state-of-the-art technologies has been emphasised in one of the classical definitions of the city logistics, proposed by [6], saying that „city logistics is

J. Mikulski (Ed.): TST 2013, CCIS 395, pp. 50–57, 2013.
© Springer-Verlag Berlin Heidelberg 2013

the process for totally optimising the logistics and transport activities by private companies with the support of advanced information systems in urban areas considering the traffic environment, its congestion, safety and energy savings within the framework of market economy" [5]. Interestingly, in this way the authors verified the earlier version of their definition, complementing it with the aspect of advanced information technologies.

Application of telematics solutions in city transport systems management results from the need to effectively solve the problems found in urban areas. The objective of applying telematics in city logistics is therefore optimising the access to logistic nodes and linear infrastructure, while reducing the adverse impact of human activity on the environment. Telematics systems are capable of supporting all transport areas, vehicles, infrastructure, transport organisation and management, and any intermediary areas between them.

The need for telematics solutions to support goods transport and distribution in urban areas is mainly due to, on the one hand, the complexity of processes taking place in urban transport systems, and on the other hand, the interweaving and often conflicting expectations of the particular groups of road users and other stakeholders of urban freight transport (city administrators, inhabitants, entrepreneurs, hauliers etc.) Here, the main objective is optimisation of transport operations via ensuring adequate availability of linear and point infrastructure, while reducing the adverse impact of the transport system on the environment. Utilization of telematics systems in the area of urban freight transport depends on [4]:

- reducing freight distribution costs
  - increasing productivity of local delivery vehicles;
  - increasing reliability of commercial vehicle operations;
  - increasing safety;
- increasing the capacity of urban freight systems (without providing additional traffic infrastructure).

2   Significance of Integration in Transport Telematics Systems

Due to their intended use and specificity, the telematics systems used in the road transport area integrate many various technologies and require the use of diverse devices and software. The solutions may be divided according to two major criteria [2]:

- **purpose**, into:
  - solutions of **general** purpose, applied universally in different areas and disciplines, which were adapted to the needs of transport telematics;
  - **dedicated** solutions, developed and designed directly for the needs of transport telematics, tailored to its specificity and functional requirements;
- **location of the system main components**, into:
  - **infrastructural**, where the vital, pivotal components are installed within the transport infrastructure;

  - **in-vehicle**, whose operation is based on the solutions installed inside the vehicles;
  - **mixed**, which function based on both the components installed within the infrastructure as well as inside the vehicles.

Table 1 shows the classification of the key solutions of road telematics taking into account the presented criteria.

Table 1. Classification of selected technologies applied in road transport telematics [2]

		Purpose criterion	
		general purpose	dedicated
Component location criterion	infrastructural	• Internet • Radio Data System – RDS • Global System for Mobile Communication (GSM) • Geographical Information System – GIS • Digital road maps	• Urban Traffic Control • Automatic detection of abnormal traffic behaviour • Weather Monitoring and Forecasting Systems • Man Machine Interfaces – MMI • Smart cards • Traffic and Traveller Information Centre – TTIC • Strategic Information Systems – SIS • Dynamic Road Guide – DRG • Variable Message Signs – VMS • Automatic Vehicle Identification – AVI • Traffic detectors and sensors
	in-vehicle		• In-vehicle computers
	mixed	• Global Positioning System – GPS • Radio Frequency Identification – RFID	• Fleet Management Systems • Electronic Toll Collection Systems

Although the solutions themselves already prove effective, their integration very often results in a synergy effect, and integrated systems manifest a number of benefits compared to independent systems. In particular, they are characterised by [3]:

  • integration of technology, applied tools and software, enabling effective information flow;
  • "intelligence" understood as capacity to make decisions autonomously in changing circumstances;
  • flexibility and high adaptivity - the configuration may be adjusted to the needs;
  • effectiveness understood as universal benefits.

One of the significant factors that facilitate integration of individual subsystems is a developed network structure, and in particular availability of fast internet connections. Application of web-based technologies makes it possible to exchange data between them and to transmit the information to road users. Thanks to network technologies, including wireless solutions, all the subsystems may communicate with each other regardless of the spatial arrangement of their individual constituents (detectors, cameras, variable message signs, etc.).

Integrated systems are usually built of modules, which makes it possible to implement the individual elements in stages, and to concentrate on the ones that are the most important in given conditions. Within each system it is possible to distinguish individual functional subsystems (usually corresponding to the modules referred to above), responsible directly for carrying out the specified tasks.

3   Application of Telematics Technologies in Urban Freight Transport

Telematics may support many urban functional areas, and its application has to be considered in various aspects. Defines urban telematics as „(…) a concise specification of various applications of computer and telecommunication techniques – in order to streamline the urban, i.e. in principle local information systems, municipal services, transport or parking systems (see transport telematics), and also the systems that support the functioning of self-governments or implementing elements of electronic democracy (…)" [7]. Its basic task aimed to support effective management of an urban transport system is information management. Its effect is improving the quality of the city logistics system via increasing the possibility of controlling the traffic flows in the whole system.

Telematics systems applied to support urban transport mainly deal with limiting the congestion effect (at present it is probably the most important transport problem in cities, and it generates subsequent problems such as pollution, increased noise level and accident rate, etc.). The increase in congestion is caused on the one hand by the growing number of vehicles and on the other hand by the dynamic lifestyle and the resulting need to transfer persons and goods both often and fast. In order to limit congestion by replacing the dispersed individual transport with collective transport (e.g. public transportation to carry persons, or solutions based on freight consolidation in the case of freight transport), it is necessary to provide adequately prepared technical infrastructure, efficient communication systems and tools for providing a proper safety level. In each of these areas the systems are based on telematics solutions.

Due to the development of information and communication technologies, numerous solutions were created that concentrated directly on supporting the functioning of urban freight transport, based on application of telematics and intelligent transport systems. These can be divided into two basic groups: freight transport management systems (used by hauliers and logistic companies) and road traffic management systems (used by city administrators) - Table 2.

Table 2. Telematics systems in Urban Freight Transport, own wor based on [1]

Freight transport management systems (e.g. fleet management systems and tracking & tracing systems)	• Computerised Vehicle Routing and Scheduling: efficient planning by vehicle operators to plan vehicle loads and journeys • Navigation systems and traffic control: used to provide specific routeing guidance and real-time information about vehicle location, traffic incidents and changes in customers' requirements • In-Cab Communication systems: these allow the driver to communicate with their company planners and also with customer by voice or computer • Slot booking systems: used to co-ordinate and plan goods vehicle arrivals at major sites generating large flows
Traffic management systems (e.g. access control systems, traffic management and information systems)	• Urban traffic management and control (UTMC) systems: – Urban Traffic Control (UTC) systems to co-ordinate traffic signal timings, – Variable message signs (VMS) to communicate information to drivers via roadside signs, – Car park occupancy sensors, – Journey-time measurement systems via automatic number-plate recognition technology • The provision of mapping or route guidance • Automated vehicle access controls

In the functional context, three major categories of solutions are based directly on telematics, and their proper functioning is dependent on application of ICT tools. These include:

- the systems that guide delivery vehicles entering the city centre to the planned routes, e.g. by means of placing special road signs (most often variable message signs and boards) or providing maps showing the planned routes and traffic information relevant for trucks;
- intelligent freight traffic routeing systems, integrating the planned routes and information aimed at delivery vehicles with navigation software, in which the data obtained from trucks in traffic, regarding their location, carried cargo and planned destination, may be connected with the road traffic data in real time;
- integrated logistics tools, being the solutions based first and foremost on web technologies application (mainly the internet and www technology), making it possible to connect and coordinate producers, receivers and logistic operators with regard to order placement, in order to streamline logistic flows.

Apart from that, telematics systems are applied in many other solutions regarding urban freight transport, as additional tools to support and improve their effectiveness.

Over the recent years, more and more significance is gained by the systems based on V2V (Vehicle-to-Vehicle), V2I (Vehicle-to-Infrastructure) and I2V (Infrastructure-to-Vehicle) communication, which are the result of direct implementation of the so-called Cloud Computing concept in road transport systems. As nowadays most fields of life are more and more dominated by information technology, it is expected to see its further expansion also with regard to urban freight transport and further growth of telematics systems significance in that area.

4 Impact of Telematics Technologies on the Urban Freight Transport Functioning

The basic task of telematics solutions being the tools that enable effective support of urban freight transport is managing the information flows generated in its area, and the most important effect of that process is improving the quality of the city logistics system functioning via increasing the possibilities of controlling and influencing the data flows. Application of telematics results in a number of benefits in terms of both improving the urban transport system functioning and of increasing the safety level and limiting the adverse effect on the urban environment. Telematics technologies also play a significant part in supporting the clean last mile solutions. With regard to the selected solutions, the following impacts can be emphasised [1]:

- Computerised Vehicle Routeing and Scheduling – vehicle routeing and scheduling systems can result in journey time savings of 10 to 15%, customers can receive more precise delivery time estimates, the proportion of first time delivery success should increase, operational costs can be reduced.
- GPS-based Route Navigation System – provides new drivers with detailed routeing instructions to travel between deliveries, overcomes lack of local knowledge – increasing speed of deliveries and driver flexibility.
- Real-time Traffic Information – still in its infancy, collection and dissemination of data to help update transport plans to maximise vehicle utilization and first time delivery success.
- Radio Frequency Identification (RFID) – still at an early stage, vehicle and transit unit identification is possible and is under trial at sites in the Ruhr and the Netherlands, transport process updates can be added to basic product information and are another way to give real time supply chain information for customers and operators, early problems of reader sensitivity, standardization of information and application costs still need to be overcome.

Analysing the impact of telematics solutions on urban freight transport effectiveness, it is necessary to take into account four major impact areas:

- social, expressed mainly via the mitigation of the congestion effect and decreasing the number of accidents and limiting their effects;
- economic, including changes in fixed costs and operating costs (in particular in relation to the hauliers and contracting parties);
- environmental, expressed via changes in the demand for energy, including pollution emissions (mainly CO_2 and NO_x) and the impact on the noise level;
- mobility, taking into account, inter alia, urban traffic development, demand for transport, indicators of infrastructure availability, classification of road users, etc.

The social and economic impact depends mainly on the volume of goods flows generated on a given market, being the resultant of customers' individual needs and suppliers' transport decisions. They determine the input/output values for the transport system, which may be reflected using the origin-destination matrix or input-output models.

As for the environmental aspect, specifying the impact of urban freight transport is concentrated mainly on establishing the energy consumption volume and the environmental impact of the transport. The impact may be considered in three main aspects:

- pollutants emission, depending directly on energy (fuel) consumption;
- generated vibrations;
- noise emission level.

In this context, particular importance is given to the fuel consumption issue and the actions aimed at limiting the pollution.

5   Conclusion

As for the effectiveness of telematics solutions for urban freight transport, major difficulties are a result of problems connected with data acquisition. Due to the lack of possibility to acquire them or failing to competently identify their sources, telematics solutions will not have the expected full impact on the effectiveness of transport system management processes, even if they are appropriately planned and implemented.

Please note that the fact that the data source is known does not necessarily mean that they may be accessed. Many a time it is well known what data should be acquired and where from, however, there is no way to know how to do that at the right time, by what means and at what cost, etc. We should emphasise that in most cities there are basic, minimum data resources. The data resources are bigger in cities with some traditions of planning and analysing their urban freight transport, or in cities making efforts aimed at improving the public transport quality and the general effectiveness of the transport system. However, in general the issue of data acquisition for the purposes of urban freight transport telematics systems is a big challenge, unmet so far. Difficulties in this regard result mainly from [6]:

- the fact that it is mainly private companies that are involved in freight transport in cities, and they are reluctant to share their data on transactions, deliveries or transported cargoes with their competitors and the public sector. (By the way, this problem is observed not only in the case of intracity transport, but also with respect to intercity, national or international transport.)
- the lack of standardised methods for researching and analysing freight transport and deliveries in cities.

The former issue is particularly problematic. Private companies, which make the vast majority of transport operation in cities, are not willing to to make available any data on the kind of deliveries, utilization of cargo space, transport routes, etc. This is mainly due to their concerns related to maintaining their competitive market position. A solution to alleviate some, but not all, difficulties in this respect is application of telematics technologies based on traffic detection and vehicle classification. The systems enable non-invasive measurements that are unnoticeable to drivers and require no need to cooperate with transport companies. However, the problem is that, given the specificity of urban deliveries, this would make it necessary to deploy a considerable number of detectors that would enable data acquisition from a wide area.

It must be emphasised that in many cities their authorities take steps to alleviate the aforementioned problems and make efforts to implement solutions enabling data acquisition on a current basis. Nevertheless, the problem remains unsolved and the issue is still being hotly discussed in the fora dealing with with the problems of urban freight transport.

Acknowledgements. This paper was financed under the project "Analysis of information needs of heterogeneous environment in sustainable urban freight transport system" by the Polish National Science Centre, decision number DEC-2012/05/B/HS4/03818.

References

1. Allen, J., Thorne, G., Browne, M.: BESTUFS. Good Practice Guide on Urban Freight Transport (2007)
2. Iwan, S.: Wdrażanie dobrych praktyk w obszarze transport dostawczego w miastach. Wydawnictwo Naukowe Akademii Morskiej w Szczecinie, Szczecin (2013)
3. Mikulski, J., Kwaśny, A.: Role of telematics in reducing the negative environmental impact of transport. In: Mikulski, J. (ed.) TST 2010. CCIS, vol. 104, pp. 11–29. Springer, Heidelberg (2010)
4. Taniguchi, E., Thompson, R.G., Yamada, T., van Duin, R.: City Logistics. Network Modelling and Intelligent Transport Systems. Pergamon, Oxford (2001)
5. Taniguchi, E., Thompson, R.G., Yamada, T.: Recent Advances in Modelling City Logistics. In: Taniguchi, E., Thompson, R.G. (eds.) City Logistics II, pp. 3–34. Institute of Systems Science Research, Kyoto (2001)
6. Taniguchi, E., Thompson, R.G., Yamada, T.: Data Collection for Modelling, Evaluating and Benchmarking City Logistics Schemes. In: Taniguchi, E., Thompson, R.G. (eds.) Recent Advances in City Logistics. Elsevier (2006)
7. Wydro, B.K.: Telematyka – znaczenia i definicje terminu, Telekomunikacja i techniki informacyjne, nr 1-2, Instytut Łączności, Warszawa (2005)
8. Mikulski, J.: Using telematics in transport. In: Mikulski, J. (ed.) TST 2010. CCIS, vol. 104, pp. 175–182. Springer, Heidelberg (2010)
9. Mikulski, J.: The possibility of using telematics in urban transportation. In: Mikulski, J. (ed.) TST 2011. CCIS, vol. 239, pp. 54–69. Springer, Heidelberg (2011)
10. Mikulski, J.: Telematic Technologies in Transportation. In: Janecki, R., Sierpiński, G. (eds.) Contemporary Transportation Systems. Selected Theoretical and Practical Problems. New Culture of Mobility, pp. 131–143. Publishing House of the Silesian University of Technology, Monograph no. 324, Gliwice (2011)

Transfer of Technology in the Field of Rail Transport through Cluster Initiatives Management

Adam Jabłoński and Marek Jabłoński

Southern Railway Cluster Association
Ligocka 103, bud. Nr 7, 40-568 Katowice, Poland
{adam.jablonski,marek.jablonski}@ottima-plus.com.pl

Abstract. The authors have presented the key priorities of technology transfer in the area of rail transport. They have also presented selected elements of building the company technological potential through cluster initiatives as well as practical solutions for building the technology management system in a railway company supporting the development of technology for rail transport in Poland.

Keywords: technology transfer, open innovation, cluster initiatives.

1   Introduction

The current functioning of rail transport in Poland and Europe sets new mechanisms of shaping the market, both in terms of organization and technology. A look at the cause and effect relationship in the railway system allows to build an effective and efficient technology management system covering all its components and affecting each other directly or indirectly. This is particularly important for components that affect the safety of rail transport. Undoubtedly, these are important components of rail transport systems. Because of the fact that the primary responsibility for the consequences of any inconsistencies, incidents, accidents or, in extreme cases, rail disasters is shifted onto a manufacturer or user, the place and role of technology transfer increases, as well as a way of implementing them in practice, appropriate to the solutions used in the rail transport sector.

The paper presents the key priorities of technology transfer in the area of rail transport. It also presents selected elements of building the company technological potential through cluster initiatives as well as practical solutions for building the technology management system in a railway company supporting the development of technology for rail transport systems.

2   Mechanisms for Technology Transferring in Rail Transport

The modern view of the transport system requires that new standards for the technology transfer should be determined. An important question should be asked at this point.

J. Mikulski (Ed.): TST 2013, CCIS 395, pp. 58–66, 2013.
© Springer-Verlag Berlin Heidelberg 2013

How to transfer technology in the rail transport and what necessary criteria must be fulfilled so that the transfer guarantees that measurable results are obtained? These results may apply, among others, to:

- system safety parameters, including the criteria required for safety management systems in the rail transport [1]
- system reliability parameters [2]
- system interoperability parameters (including its consistency, integrity and functionality) [3]
- parameters fulfilling qualitative, ecological and ergonomic criteria.

It is also necessary to ask how will the technological process proceed in the subjective context? How will the knowledge and technological competences be transferred?
It may proceed in three subject streams:

1. Transport Sector 1 - Transport Sector 2 (e.g. air transport – rail transport)
2. Sector n - Transport Sector n (e.g. energy sector – rail sector)
3. Transport Sector n - Sector n (e.g. road transport sector – construction sector)

Presented subjectively, however, it may include the relationships in the Market - Products – Technology system. Figure 1 below presents a classic model of technology transfer, including the defined relationship in a roadmap system.

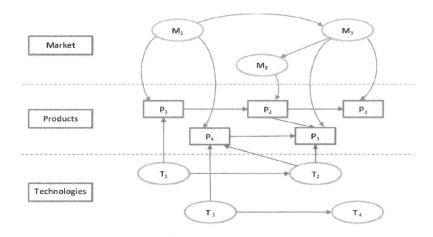

Fig. 1. A model of technology transfer using a roadmap [8]

A change in the approach to designing and implementing transport systems should also be highlighted. For example, the following priorities can be adopted:
Yesterday independent systems – **Today** Inconsistent systems – **Tomorrow** networked systems – **The Day After Tomorrow** - coherent, compact systems.

This leads to an appropriate model of rail innovation development in Poland. This model should be based on the use of three key priorities: Innovation, Competitiveness, Internationalization.

Innovation (according to the OECD, Eurostat, 2008) is the implementation of a new or significantly improved product, service or process in business practice, including the implementation of a new marketing or organizational method concerning the way of working or the relationship with the environment.

Competitiveness of the company can be understood as its ability to efficiently achieve objectives in the competition market arena [1].

These priorities have a significant impact on the management of the entire product lifecycle, so-called "Cradle to cradle". The following is a model of the product life cycle along with a change in technology in the function of time.

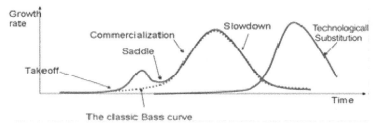

Fig. 2. Turning points in the product life cycle [2]

The classic Bass model starts with a spontaneous adoption by an initial group of adopters but does not provide explanations for the mechanisms that lead to this initial adoption, or take-off. Studies on the take-off focus on this initial stage and explore the market's behaviour and the interface between the adoption and the start of communication interactions [2].

The system of mutual interactions occurring when innovations are created both on a national level and in various railway companies is also important.

On a national level, the institutional support systems need to be aware that the components of a system of innovation include not only private firms and their R&D activities but also public organizations such as universities, public research institutes, science parks, and so on. Another important aspect of policy making according to an evolutionary framework consists, therefore, in supporting and fostering those connections and interactions, which constitute the basic structure defining the properties of a system and its dynamic trajectory over time [3].

3   Selected Aspects of the Network Structures in the Rail Transport

A cluster initiative may be an optimal tool used to effectively and efficiently transfer technology in the field of rail transport. A cluster is a geographic concentration of interconnected companies, specialized suppliers, service providers, companies operating in related industries and associated institutions in various fields (e.g. universities, research institutes, industry associations, supporting bodies), competing with each other, but also supporting each other. A cluster is closely linked with the territory in which it operates, it is region-based. Clusters are a specific form of organization of production, involving the concentration of flexible enterprises conducting complementary businesses in the close area. The entities both cooperate and compete with each other, they also have corporate relationships with other institutions working in the field. A cluster is based on cooperative links between the entities that generate processes of creating specific knowledge and increasing adaptive capacity [4].

A concept of so-called open innovation can be applied here, especially for the SME sector, such as those operating in the rail sector. Open Innovation is a term proposed by a professor and executive director of the Open Innovation Centre at the University of Berkeley, Henry Chesbrough. The most important point of this concept is that in the world of widely spread knowledge, companies cannot rely only on their own research, but they should acquire patents or licenses for inventions and other innovations from other companies. Moreover, companies should make their inventions, which they do not use themselves, available to other entities based on selling licences, establishing consortia or spin-off companies. A concept of closed innovation is opposite to the Open Innovation concept. It refers to the process of limiting the use of internal resources of innovative solutions to their own business and not using resources from outside. It should be noted that the concept of open innovation was already applied in the rail transport when the ETCS ERTMS systems were implemented. Open ETCS is such an attempt to utilize the principles of open standards on various levels including open source software, based on the results provided by the study called "Economic impact of open source software on innovation and the competitiveness of the Information and Communication Technologies sector".

A possible model of open innovation application in the rail transport sector for SMEs is given on fig. 3.

Within their limited resources, SMEs must find ways to achieve production economies of scale, to market their products effectively, and to provide satisfactory support services. Collaboration with other organisations is one method. We have noted that SMEs are flexible and more innovative in new areas, but can lack resources and capabilities [5].

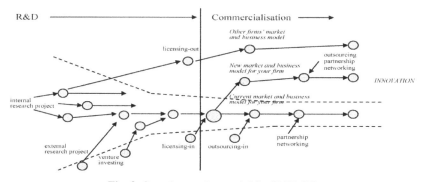

Fig. 3. Open innovation model for SMEs [5]

When the concept of open innovation is combined with the network structure, a strong platform for technological development of railway companies is created. Considering further the network model in the criterion of cooperation and interaction maturity, based on experience and observation of the existing cluster networks, several levels of activity can be distinguished that are based on the criterion of relationships intensity in the cluster initiative.

- Type I - passive participation, lack of activity of cluster members and their formalized participation
- Type II - active participation in the cluster initiative

- level 1: participation in conferences, seminars, meetings, and gaining knowledge on a small scale
- level II: participation in small projects of the cluster with cluster participants, irregular cooperation within the Railway Cluster
- level III: regular participation in the Railway Cluster undertakings and projects
- level IV: Strategic Partnership within the cluster and its members, creating new joint ventures

The cluster relationships should be embedded in the region and they should be favourable to its development. Then a proper dialogue at all levels of relationships and mutual communication takes place Fig. 4.

Fig. 4. Cluster Relationships [Own study]

Such priorities should be the basis for developing a cluster business model.

The cluster business model presented above indicates that the relationships with various stakeholders of the project are built. Major partners of the project, together with the cluster coordinator, are responsible for the project management leading to achieving its objectives and indicators. Potential users, manufacturers, railway infrastructure administrators, railway companies and other entities could be the recipients of value, for example in the rail sector.

This approach to the development of railways, but in general to the entire transport system in Poland, may enable a better absorption of foreign technology, the development of national technologies and organizational solutions and the search for best practices that can be applied in Polish conditions. The cooperation of science and business aimed to increase innovation and competitiveness of railway companies should take place through professional network forms such as clusters.

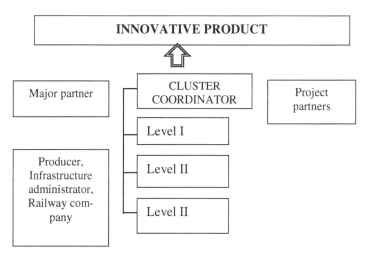

Fig. 5. A cluster business model in the context of building technology platforms in rail transport [Own study]

4   Technology Strategy of a Rail Cluster

A rail cluster should be technologically developed in a systematic way. The optimal solution is to develop a technology strategy, which will be a tool designed to implement the technology management system. It should be noted that Polish railway companies now suffer so called technological gap. This is due to the difference in the level of scientific and technical thinking in relation to those countries in Europe and the world, where the most advanced countries may allocate a higher percentage of national income to scientific research. Although in Poland there are a lot of research centres dealing with the rail transport, their financial strength does not allow them to carry out projects that would bring revolutionary solutions, including patents, which would be widely adopted by the European or global market [6].

Table 1. The range of priority strategic issues and the approach that the Railway Cluster has to them in terms of technology transfer. Strategic priorities of the Railway Cluster activity in the context of technology transfer [Own study]

No	Subject scope	Tasks	
1.	Safety in rail transport	1.	Disseminating knowledge of the best organizational and technological practices relating to safety in rail transport.
		2.	Proposing solutions used to manage risk in rail transport on the basis of foreign experience.
		3.	Creating a platform of railway technologies focused on improving the safety of rail transport.
		4.	Supporting companies in developing technologies aimed to improve the safety of rail transport.
		5.	Consulting safety solutions with the Office of Rail Transport.
		6.	Consulting safety solutions with participants of rail traffic and with the economic environment.
2.	Interoperability	1.	Creating the grounds for understanding the issue of rail interoperability in the context of the role of producer, distributor, notified bodies, the Office of Rail Transport, research institutes and universities.
		2.	Helping the cluster to understand conditions of creating innovation in the context of interoperability processes.
		3.	Using the best foreign practices of interoperability.
3.	Innovation	1.	Creating conditions favourable to creating innovation through a network of companies and institutions in the cluster and to stimulating them to create innovations through meetings, workshops, thematic trips, to indicate the direction of potential innovation by exchanging information between cluster members.
		2.	Promoting the knowledge from abroad about absorption of technology transfer, about innovation and acting as a knowledge broker.
		3.	Building the grounds for contacts favourable to innovation through the platform of national technology.
4.	Energy efficiency	1.	Popularizing and stimulating actions aimed to follow the principle of 3 x 20
		2.	Promoting solutions favourable to energy efficiency in rail transport, regarding power supply, control systems, energy efficiency of the railway rolling stock, etc.
		3.	Creating benchmarking projects in terms of best practices of energy efficiency in rail transport in Europe and the world.
		4.	Implementing partnership projects aimed to identify best practices in this field and promoting these solutions in the rail market.
5.	Internationalization	1.	Creating conditions of companies internationalization, building international relations and international branches by organizing trade missions, building platforms for business relationships and contact networks, and classifying them according to relevant focus groups.
		2.	Disseminating knowledge of international markets through participation in international cluster networks (ERCI) and other partners.

It should be noted that a cluster is a plane which its members use to obtain new opportunities for business development, technology transfer, learning and using the network effect and potential to create business relationships and to develop innovative solutions by creating new business space inherent in the potential of the network. Activity of cluster members in the focus groups should contribute to achieving their competitive advantages and it should increase the chance of creating new and innovative, technological and organizational solutions.

Figure 6 shows the author's way of managing the technology platform supporting activity of a sample cluster network constituting its business model. The presented business model is based on a model by [7].

This model includes the relationship between several areas of activity focused on creating innovation, standardizing descriptions of parameters characterizing the technology and the possibilities of their commercialization.

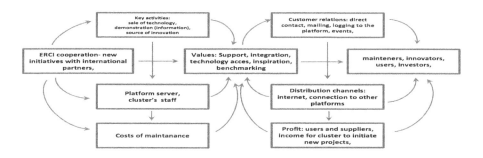

Fig. 6. Technology Platform business model [Own study]

In this model, solutions for the optimal use of the technology management system are accumulated, which generates value for all participants in the rail market. This model shapes the mechanisms of creating new technological solutions, together with the exchange of experience between entities interacting with each other.

5   Conclusion

Technological development in the rail transport poses a challenge for managing directors in terms of management, organization and technology. A technological development model should be built in the network system, where all participants in the rail transport are its users.

The paper has highlighted selected aspects of using the cluster network and its business model to create innovative solutions and technology transfer. It has also presented the key principles of building technology management systems, which have applications in rail transport systems.

References

1. Stankiewicz, M.J.: Company Competitiveness, Building Company Competitiveness in Globalisation Conditions. Wydawnictwo Naukowe PWN, p. 92, Warszawa (2002)
2. Peres, R., Muller, E., Mahajan, V.: Innovation diffusion and new product growth models: A critical review and research directions. Intern. J. of Research in Marketing 27, 91–106 (2010)
3. van Hemert, P., Nijkamp, P.: Knowledge investments, business R&D and innovativeness of countries: A qualitative meta-analytic comparison. Technological Forecasting & Social Change 77, 369–384 (2010)
4. Matusiak, K.B. (ed.): Innovation and Technology Transfer. A Dictionary of Terms, Polish Agency for Enterprise Development, Warszawa (2008)
5. Leea, S., Park, G., Yoonc, B., Park, J.: Open innovation in SMEs—An intermediated network model. Research Policy 39, 290–300 (2010)
6. Jabłoński, A., Jabłoński, M.: Implementation and Managing of Innovation in the Conditions of Legal and Economic Constraints on the Based of Rail Transport. In: Mikulski, J. (ed.) TST 2012. CCIS, vol. 329, pp. 423–432. Springer, Heidelberg (2012)
7. Osterwalder, A., Pigneur, Y.: Aligning Profit and Purpose Through Business Model Innovation. In: Palazzo, G., Wentland, M. (eds.) Responsible Management Practices for the 21st Century, Pearson Education France, Paris (2011)
8. Rinne, M.: Technology roadmaps: Infrastructure for innovation. Technological Forecasting & Social Change 71, 69 (2004)
9. Mikulski, J.: Using telematics in transport. In: Mikulski, J. (ed.) TST 2010. CCIS, vol. 104, pp. 175–182. Springer, Heidelberg (2010)

Forecasts for Technical Variants of ITS Projects – Example of Upper-Silesian Conurbation

Grzegorz Karoń and Jerzy Mikulski

Silesian University of Technology, Faculty of Transport,
Krasińskiego 8, 40-019 Katowice, Poland
{grzegorz.karon,jerzy.mikulski}@polsl.pl

Abstract. Planning of transportation systems with ITS systems and mobility management should have a right reflection in forecasting models [1, 6]. When measuring or estimating the costs of the network and its utilisation, it is essential to draw up a model, which describes the current network status and how ITS can change the situation. It may describe, for example, the changes in the vehicle-kilometres travelled on various streets caused by a park-and-ride system and whether this change will affect the need for investments in the road infrastructure. A scheme of traffic forecasts of technical variants of investment projects for *CBA* (cost-benefit analysis) has been described in this article.

Keywords: transportation modelling, traffic forecasts, technical variants / alternatives of investment projects.

1 Introduction

The ITS investments may affect the functional parameters of the transportation systems such as the travel time, the frequency of transportation services, the travel comfort, the capacity of network elements, the network congestion, the transportation availability of the area and the modal split (between private and public transport as well as between the means of transportation within the public transportation). These impacts are results of main activities of intelligent urban transportation [3]:

- the increase in the interoperability of the ITS (intelligent transportation systems) solutions and the interaction of intelligent vehicles with the intelligent infrastructure,
- gathering and processing of the data on the traffic and travel in order to ensure a dynamic traffic management and to provide the passenger, driver and carrier information,
- a better passenger information improves the passenger mobility as it allows a conscious mode choice and travel time as well as the creation of a multimodal travel option.

In this way the mobility of inhabitants of the region is affected. Transportation system models (travel demand/transportation supply/land use models) are basic traffic analysis tools, applicable both to the current state and to the forecasts, especially in

J. Mikulski (Ed.): TST 2013, CCIS 395, pp. 67–74, 2013.
© Springer-Verlag Berlin Heidelberg 2013

the case of investment projects in transportation, where they can serve as an instrument allowing a comparison and assessment of a few investment variants from the point of view of the transportation system functionality and the users' mobility conditions at different forecast timeframes [1, 6].

2   Traffic Forecasts for Technical Variants of Investment Projects

The traffic analysis is tailored to the type and scope of the investment project influence on the transportation system and on the space within which the system is operational. The traffic analysis and traffic forecasts of investment project are performed for a few predefined technical variants as well as for the base variant constituting the baseline for the CBA (cost-benefit analysis).The methodology for projects of transport systems (including ITS systems), which are implemented in Poland with UE financial resources, was worked out in manuals called The Blue Paper (2008).The methodology for cost-benefit analysis (CBA)is presented there. It is noteworthy that the Blue Paper is a study recommended by Polish Ministry of Regional Development and Ministry of Infrastructure.

The CBA is based on results of analysis of actual traffic state and traffic forecasting: traffic flows, average travel length and average travel times and also haulage work forecasting for a few defined investment variants and the adopted comparative variant. In this case the correctness of the four-stage travel demand model (trip generation, trip distribution: origin-destination (O-D) matrix, mode choice, distribution of traffic flow on transport network) de facto formed the basis of a correctly done CBA. Microscopic simulation models with individual vehicle types and driver behaviours based on car-following and lane-changing models are the best to evaluate ITS solutions. Therefore the four-stage macro model is not good to evaluate travel management and operational strategies, such as intelligent transportation systems (ITS), because of limited capabilities to accurately estimate changes in operational characteristics (such as flow, speed, density, delay, and queuing) and a poor representation of the dynamic nature of traffic.

The variants assessed are the result of a preliminary selection from a number of variants analysed in the pre-project studies such as feasibility studies or another preliminary analysis. The selection is understood as the choice of the most promising solution from the standpoint of technical, legal, environmental, economic and policy constraints. The number and types of technical options selected for the analysis depends on the investments project type.

Examples of variants matrix of four technical variants/alternatives (V1, V2, V3 and V4) differing in a new or modernized infrastructure, a modernized tramway track, the priority on intersections (ITS service) are shown in Fig.1. An additional variant V0 is not a technical variant but it is the situation without the investment project (the status quo). This is the reference "variant" for the CBA analysis.

Technical Variants of Project	Example of elements of technical variants for transportation system				
	New Infrastructure	Modernization of Infrastructure	Modernization of tramway track	Priority on Intersections	Passenger Information System
V0	No	No	No	No	No
V1	Yes/No	Yes/No	Yes/No	Yes/No	Yes/No
V2	Yes/No	Yes/No	Yes/No	Yes/No	Yes/No
V3	Yes/No	Yes/No	Yes/No	Yes/No	Yes/No
V4	Yes/No	Yes/No	Yes/No	Yes/No	Yes/No

Fig. 1. Technical variants matrix for a transport investment project [5]

Each variant should be defined in such a way that it can be assessed from the effectiveness of the project objectives accomplishment point of view. It is recommended that the project objectives in public transportation domain include widely understood improvement to the conditions in the city achieved in particular by means of increasing the mobility of travellers and increasing the mobility conditions within the transportation system (understood as such a transportation offer, which allows making multimodal trips). The project objectives should not be defined as too narrow. For example, the construction of a new train line with specific functional features is not a properly formulated objective as it is in fact just a practical definition of project scope. A very narrow definition of project objectives strongly limits the number of possible technical options, which means that the potential of the CBA will not be properly utilised. Here are some examples of the public transportation project objectives (*Blue Paper – public transport sector* (2008)):

- increase in the travel speed of transportation systems and reduction of travel time,
- improvement to the traffic smoothness in particular in the case of public transportation,
- integration of different transportation systems,
- improvement in the area of accessibility to the transportation system;
- improvement in the availability of the transportation system for elderly and disabled citizens;
- improvement in the traffic safety;
- increased travel comfort;
- reduction of the maintenance and operating cost of the public transportation vehicles;
- reduction of the influence of the traffic on the environment by the reduction of private vehicles' traffic and shift of part of the journeys to the public transportation.

	Base year	Horizons of Forecasts					
Technical Variants of Project	2010	2015	2020	2025	2030	2035	2040
1	2	3	4	5	6	7	8
V0	V0_2010	V0_2015	V0_2020	V0_2025	V0_2030	V0_2035	V0_2040
V1	x	V1_2015	V1_2020	V1_2025	V1_2030	V1_2035	V1_2040
V2	x	V2_2015	V2_2020	V2_2025	V2_2030	V2_2035	V2_2040
V3	x	V3_2015	V3_2020	V3_2025	V3_2030	V3_2035	V3_2040
V4	x	W4_2015	V4_2020	V4_2025	V4_2030	V4_2035	V4_2040

Fig. 2. Variants-forecasts matrix – example [5]

The traffic forecasts apply to the following periods: one year after the investment project commissioning, subsequent five year intervals and the final year of the analysed time frame (for transport infrastructure at least 25 years from the year of commissioning). Technical variants with horizons of forecasts are summarized in the variants-forecasts matrix – the example in Fig. 2.

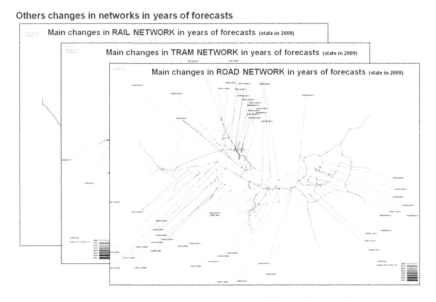

Others changes in networks in years of forecasts

Main changes in RAIL NETWORK in years of forecasts (state in 2009)

Main changes in TRAM NETWORK in years of forecasts (state in 2009)

Main changes in ROAD NETWORK in years of forecasts (state in 2009)

Fig. 3. Example of main changes in transportation systems of Upper-Silesian Conurbation [4, 5]

In order to build and implement the forecasting network and traffic models it is necessary to analyse in detail the development strategy of the studied area (regarding both the network changes and the changes in spatial development). The data sources may comprise strategies, investment plans, development plans, operating programmes, status diagnoses, re-vitalization programmes, city council resolutions, influence studies at the regional, province, city or public transportation organizers' level. An example of identified main changes in the transportation systems of Upper-Silesian Conurbation is shown in Fig. 3.

The forecasting traffic models defining the forecasted demand for the transportation offer require the social, economic and spatial data to be estimated. The factors directly independent of the transportation policy and the mobility management plans and programmes, which are necessary for the development of the forecasting traffic models, include:

- forecasted demographic changes including in particular the age structure (production and post-production) and the education level structure,
- forecasted socio-economic changes, population income, motoring index and the unemployment level taken into account.

The second set of data includes the factors dependent on the transportation policy, mobility management plans and programmes, as well as on the above mentioned demographic and socio-economic factors. These are:

- forecasted changes in spatial development leading to the changes in spatial distribution and traffic production (changes in the traffic generator structure),
- forecasted changes in the modal split.

All elements of forecasting process are shown in Fig. 4.

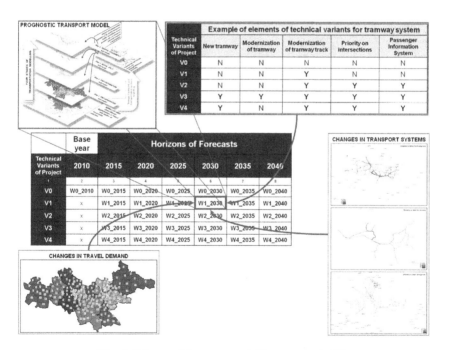

Fig. 4. Scheme of forecasts modelling – example [5]

Results of forecasts for each technical variant and each horizon of forecast consist of traffic flows in the forecasted networks and measures of effectiveness *MOEs*. The complexity and structure of results are shown in Fig. 5 as a scheme of variants-forecasts results in traffic flows. Results depend on:

- time period: AM peak hour, PM peak hour, day and year,
- user class: workers in industrial, service, private, and public sectors, students of primary school, university students, retiree, and others,
- purpose: home-work, work-home, home-school, school-home, home-other, other-home, non-home based, total,
- flows in mode: pedestrians, bus-passengers, tram-passengers, rail-passengers, car-users, total,
- mode: walk, bicycle, bus, tram, rail, car, park&ride, total,
- source of results: surveys, model,
- technical variant: V0, V1, V2, V3, V4,
- forecast horizon: 2010, 2015, 2020, 2025, 2030, 2035, 2040,
- and others.

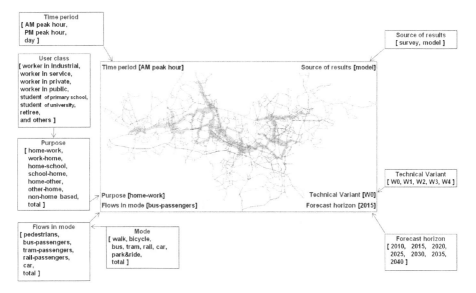

Fig. 5. Scheme of variants-forecasts results in traffic flows – example [4, 5]

Aggregation of all partial results (Fig. 5) and main measures of effectiveness (*MOEs*) are shown in Fig. 6. Main *MOEs* are:

- travel distance/time total,
- changes in modal split,
- average speed,
- average travel distance/time,
- average values of perceived travel time for each mode.

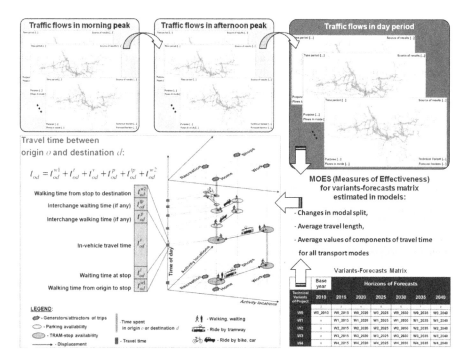

Fig. 6. Scheme of variants-forecasts of measures of effectiveness – example [5]

3 Conclusion

The ITS projects' point of comparison is so-called variant 0, which represents the predicted state of the transport system in the case the project is not implemented. In ITS projects it is important to define the evaluated project and subprojects. Individual subprojects (e.g. monitoring) often do not have impact mechanisms of their own. The impacts are created by a greater whole. On the other hand, a subproject can serve several wholes, thus making the allocation of impacts more difficult. ITS projects are typically heterogeneous [2, 3]. The projects differ from one another insofar as user groups and technical solutions are concerned more than traditional transport infra-structure projects. Some of the ITS functions [3] do not have direct primary impacts on the transport system's end users. These functions include, e.g. traffic monitoring systems and traffic management and information centres. These functions are subsys-tems in the production of services for end users, and their operation is therefore an absolute prerequisite for the implementation of functions that affect the end users. There are two ways to evaluate ITS functions that have no direct impacts on end users:

- evaluating the impacts of a greater group of systems, to which the subsystem belongs,
- assessing how well the subsystem is fulfilling its own role in the system as a whole.

If a project's impacts can be evaluated in terms of money, a cost-benefit analysis should also be drawn up. The objective of a cost-benefit analysis is to investigate how productive a project is, taking into account all of the project's significant socio-economic impacts. A cost-benefit analysis can be used both while deciding on future projects and during the post-evaluation of project's socio-economic impacts.

References

1. Cascetta, E.: Transportation Systems Analysis. Models and Applications, 2nd edn. Springer, Heidelberg (2009)
2. Karoń, G., Mikulski, J.: Transportation Systems Modelling as Planning, Organisation and Management for Solutions Created with ITS. In: Mikulski, J. (ed.) TST 2011. CCIS, vol. 239, pp. 277–290. Springer, Heidelberg (2011)
3. Karoń, G., Mikulski, J.: Problems of ITS Architecture Development and ITS Implementation in Upper-Silesian Conurbation in Poland. In: Mikulski, J. (ed.) TST 2012. CCIS, vol. 329, pp. 183–198. Springer, Heidelberg (2012)
4. Karoń, G., Janecki, R., Sobota, A.: Traffic Modelling in Silesian Area – Public Transport Network Model. In: Zeszyty Naukowe Politechniki Śląskiej, Seria TRANSPORT z. 66. Nr kol. 1825, pp.35-42, Gliwice (2010)
5. Karoń, G., Janecki, R., Sobota, A., et al.: The investment program for the development of tramway infrastructure in 2008 – 2011. Traffic analysis. Silesian University of Technology, Katowice (2009)
6. Ortuzar, J., De, D., Willumsen, L.G.: Modelling Transport, 3rd edn. Wiley, New York (2009)

Block Programming Technique in Traffic Control

Małgorzata Kołopieńczyk, Grzegorz Andrzejewski, and Wojciech Zając

University of Zielona Góra,
Licealna 9, 65-417 Zielona Gora, Poland
{M.Kolopienczyk,G.Andrzejewski,W.Zajac}@iie.uz.zgora.pl

Abstract. In the paper there are discussed benefits of using the block-oriented approach in programming the PLC controller. As an example there is taken a model of traffic junction with multiple traffic flow (including the railway crossing). The model is described and control system structure is presented. There are discussed principles of block-oriented programming approach in Ladder Diagram (LAD) language. Benefits of using this technique are shown and example is discussed.

Keywords: traffic control, PLC programming, block programming technique.

1 Introduction

Traffic control systems are growing in complexity and this tendency does not seem to reduce. The reasons for that are multiple. The obvious one is just simple increase in number of vehicles taking part in the traffic control system. Another but as important as the previous is growing tendency to improve the traffic safety. The other causes are: economical factors in logistics and growing understanding of need to reduce pollution caused by vehicles [1].

Complex control systems require more than simple switching devices, even those with variants of programs, changed depending on the daytime, week day or a season. Effective traffic control requires use of some type of adaptive system, with widely configurable control parameters and communication capabilities. As the control task is based on certain logic, the perfect solution is to apply Programmable Logic Controller (PLC) [2].

PLCs are developed intensely since sixties and today they are very complex microprocessor systems. What's important, the PLCs are classified with regard to the scale of control problem, from simple ones, average class and big and huge systems.

Many available PLC solutions allow to compose a flexible, scalable and parameterized system with safety and security features. In this work there is used a novel PLC product S7-1200 by Siemens, a 1214C model. The controller is equipped with 14 digital inputs and 10 digital outputs. The construction allows to extend the address space maximally up to 142 inputs and 138 outputs, with use of dedicated I/O modules. Such capabilities are sufficient to handle small to average size control problems. In the presented system there were used less than half of this.

J. Mikulski (Ed.): TST 2013, CCIS 395, pp. 75–80, 2013.
© Springer-Verlag Berlin Heidelberg 2013

2   Object of Control

In the research there was used a model of complex traffic junction, with a number of independent traffic flows and a railroad crossing (Fig. 1.). There were used three types of signallers: three colour traffic light S1, two colour railroad traffic light and one colour rail crossing alarm.

The control system comprised of S7-1200 PLC with modules extending the I/O addressing space. There were used four I/O modules with 16 binary inputs and 16 binary outputs each.

The traffic control algorithm was designed to meet the appropriate Polish legal regulations concerning traffic signs and signal devices and procedures [3]. The regulation puts a number of conditions on the signal sequences timing, modes switching and signals order. There are defined operation modes depending on the season of the year, daytime and simplified night-time programs, procedures of modes switching and signalisation shutdown and start-up procedure.

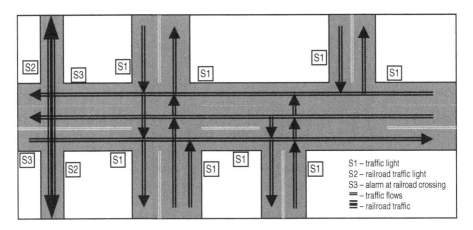

Fig. 1. Scheme of control object

The control algorithm was implemented with use of Siemens TIA Portal V11. The programming environment allows to compose complex algorithms in effective way and provides tools for program testing and diagnosis. Main programming language is Ladder Diagram (LD) and some specific types of modules can be implemented in Function Block Diagram (FBD) and Structured Text (ST) languages.

The programming environment offers a convenient project design interface that allows to organise the program structure into required hierarchy, corresponding to the structure of control task. It allows to design at the high-level of abstraction the control hierarchy and ensure appropriate dataflow structure and to monitor it efficiently in runtime mode. Such a feature helps to avoid design errors, which can be of inexplicit nature [4].

3   Block Programming Approach

In a program structure for the traffic control there can be identified elements of identical or similar structure. If properly designed, such a feature can be used as advantage in program design. To make use of it, it is necessary to declare two types of program elements: Function Blocks (FB elements) and Function (FC elements). Both elements are designed to realise particular sub-tasks of control algorithm and the main difference between them is that the programming environment creates for each FB a separate data block, which is independent from the other program elements. Therefore FC is a plain function, which can be called with a number of parameters, while FB can additionally store own data.

PLC controller operation comprises five elements (Fig. 2.): system initialisation, inputs readout and process image update, program execution, outputs state update according to updated process image state, system testing and communication. Except for the first one, steps are repeated cyclically in the PLC runtime mode until PLC stop or power-down.

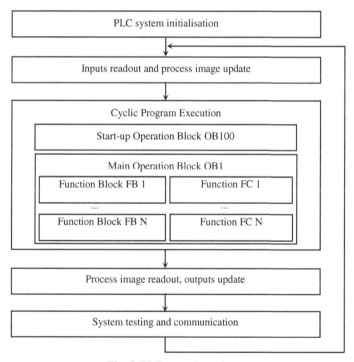

Fig. 2. PLC operation scheme

In the modelled system there can be identified the following operation elements: initialisation of variables, signalisation start-up, regular operation with program modifications and separate control for railroad crossing, signalisation shutdown and a lamp-test functionality. In the Fig. 3. there is presented program structure in a project tree window of TIA Portal. For the CPU of Traffic Control PLC there were defined five program blocks and six program blocks groups (Fig 3., picture to the left). Program blocks are: Start-up Operational Block OB100, which is executed only once when the PLC is started, the Main Operational Block OB1, executed cyclically until PLC stops, Lamp Test function FC5 and Data Block DB1 to store program variables (except for PLC Tags and Markers).

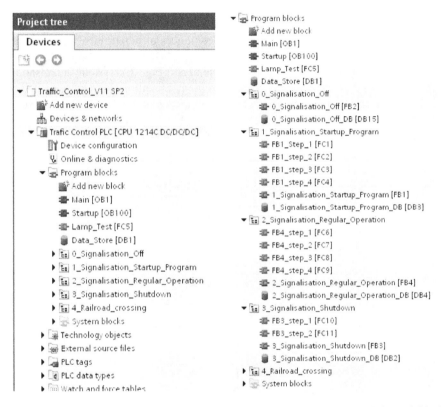

Fig. 3. Program structure in TIA Portal: program blocks structure (to the left) and blocks contents: Functions FC, Function Blocks FB and Data Blocks DB (to the right)

Fig. 3. presents detailed view to the contents of program block groups (picture to the right). Dependently on the group complexity and the operation performed, they contain Function Blocks, Functions and Data Blocks.

Main program is the superior control module and it contains calls to appropriate Function Blocks, Functions and some control logic as well. Fig. 4. presents an example of network with conditional execution of Function Block FB4.

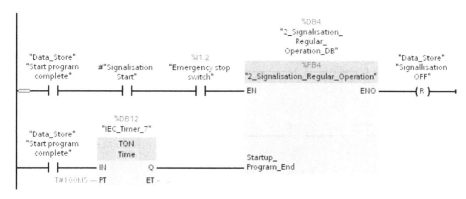

Fig. 4. Example of Function Block call in Main program

Call parameters, defined in function block call, are passed to the FB block and are processed accordingly to the block program definition. Fig. 5. presents a part of an example Function Block with calls of FC functions. There can be observed that FC's pay role of user-defined procedures, called in program as regular blocks in described hierarchy.

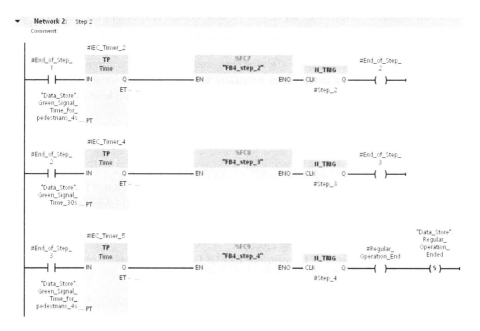

Fig. 5. Example of Function Block with Functions calls

Call parameters are passed to the FC blocks and they are used as input parameters of control and they modify the algorithm performed by the block. An FC example is presented in Fig. 6.

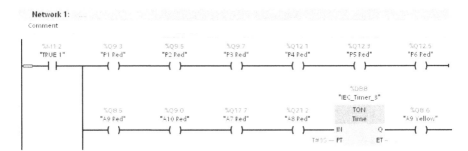

Fig. 6. Example of Function FC

4   Conclusion

In the paper there are presented results of research on applying the modular, hierar-chical approach to the control algorithm design for solving traffic control problem. Use of such a technique proved to produce clear and understandable project. Repre-sentation of control algorithm is easy to comprehend, maintain and modify, despite the modelled problem complexity, which tends to be rather large. What's important, the block-oriented hierarchical algorithm representation can be applied to perform logical system decomposition into state machine components, which allows to apply the Petri net analytic apparatus to ensure the control process safety and reliability [5, 6]. Besides ensuring the program effectiveness, such analysis gives tools to perform minimisation of the system resources necessary to implement the control algorithm. This can be crucial for more complex control problems to be modelled in PLC de-vices with limited resources.

References

1. Małecki, K., Iwan, S.: Development of Cellular Automata for Simulation of the Crossroads Model with a Traffic Detection System. In: Mikulski, J. (ed.) TST 2012. CCIS, vol. 329, pp. 276–283. Springer, Heidelberg (2012)
2. Barkalov, A., Titarenko, L.: Logic synthesis for compositional microprogram control units. LNEE, vol. 22. Springer, Heidelberg (2008)
3. Regulation of the Minister of Infrastructure dated 3 July 2003 of detailed technical specifi-cations for signs and traffic signals and traffic safety equipment and conditions of their plac-ing on the roads, OJ 2003 No. 220, item. 2181 (2003)
4. Iwan, S., Małecki, K.: Data Flows in an Integrated Urban Freight Transport Telematic Sys-tem. In: Mikulski, J. (ed.) TST 2012. CCIS, vol. 329, pp. 79–86. Springer, Heidelberg (2012)
5. Węgrzyn, A., Karatkevich, A., Bieganowski, J.: Detection of deadlocks and traps in Petri nets by means of Thelen's prime implicant method. International Journal of Applied Ma-thematics and Computer Science 14(1) (2004)
6. Adamski, M., Tkacz, J.: Formal reasoning in logic design of reconfigurable controllers. In: Proceedings of 11th IFAC/IEEE International Conference on Programmable Devices and Embedded Systems, PDeS 2012, Brno, Czech Republic (2012)

Modern Tools of Passenger Public Transport Integration

Karolina Lubieniecka - Kocoń, Barbara Kos, Łukasz Kosobucki, and Anna Urbanek

University of Economics in Katowice,
40-287 Katowice, Poland
`lubieniecka@interia.pl,{bkos,anna.urbanek}@ue.katowice.pl,`
`lukasz.kosobucki@gmail.com`

Abstract. The development of IT technologies and data transfer, as well as their greater accessibility, allowed for more popular implementation of modern solutions using, among others, e-card as a tool to present data proving payment or the right to use public transport based on the rule other than paid ticket. Within last few years in Poland there were implemented numerous solutions using such tools as e- tickets. Currently, consumers using public transport service has become more demanding, therefore the companies offering public transport services are constantly forced to introduce innovations in order to satisfy consumers' needs and to improve the quality of public transport itself. Taking advantage of IT tools and solutions it is possible to manage the services better, to improve their quality and to offer passengers more comfortable services use. Most important, however, IT tools are the important instruments of transport integration. In the article there are presented some of the modern solutions concerning public transport in the urban areas.

Keywords: transport integration, urban cards, electronic tickets, urban and regional public transport.

1 Introduction

Public sector may affect transport integration process in various ways. One of the tools that have been more and more popular among public authorities in Poland and abroad are IT and ICT technologies. They are mainly used in fleet management, passenger information systems and in the transport fees processes. Although investment in moderns IT systems requires considerable amounts of money, they do not demand noticeable interference in public space, nor much of transformation or organization changes on the objects present on the market. Their exceptional role is based on quick, reliable and effective information flow among all transport market participants. IT and ICT systems are becoming the elements that merge separate phases of transport process, transport branches and transport offer of various subjects present on the market.

2 Public Passenger Transport Integration Tools

One of the widest and most commonly quoted definition of passenger transport integration, both in Polish and foreign literature is the one required for the report

J. Mikulski (Ed.): TST 2013, CCIS 395, pp. 81–88, 2013.
© Springer-Verlag Berlin Heidelberg 2013

entitled Integration and Regulatory Structures in Public Transport. According to it, passenger transport integration is the organization process, through which the elements of the passenger transport system elements (transport network, infrastructure, ticket tariffs, information and marketing, etc.) of various transport branches and many carriers cooperate closer and in more effective way, which result in the quality increase of public transport services, connected with the elements of individual travels [1].

In foreign scientific literature there is also the term interconnectivity used in case of passenger transport integration [3]. That term is also used in European Commission documents. Its main characteristics is that it focuses on technical aspects of transport integration process. According to European Commission definition from 1998, interconnectivity concerns horizontal integration of transport branches in order to acquire integrated transport services called „from door to door", and such coordination is conditioned with transfer of specific technologies, tools and equipment, advanced supervising systems and directions, as well as appropriately educated and trained personnel [3]. Interconnectivity may then be discussed when two transport systems belonging to the same or two different transport branches are physically and operationally capable to cooperate for the sake of transport uninterrupted with the borders of those systems [4].

The notion of passenger transport integration deal mostly with the issues of public transport integration in cities and agglomerations, where there may be differentiated several levels of such process [5]:

- the integration of public transport services offered by carriers of various transport branches within a city,
- the integration of public transport systems with different range: over- local and local within passenger transfer center,
- the integration public and individual transport, including bicycle and pedestrian ones, which is connected with building appropriate infrastructure and with creating passenger information system as well as traffic management systems.

Urban public transport integration may have various range and concern the chosen element of the whole system, such as common tariff- ticket system, timetables coordination, communication lines cooperation, common information system, standardized technical- exploitation services or standardized transportation services and common transport unit hubs infrastructure [6].

Public authorities, being the transport policy subjects, may stimulate the integration process of transport markets in many ways. The basic integration tools include investment in transport infrastructure, changes in transport markets organization (creating the structures that integrate services selling), investment in IT and ICT systems which support transport management process, integration process and public help, which may supplement creating and maintaining certain integrated solutions [7].

From the perspective of passenger transport, among the basic functions of IT systems supporting transport management and transport integration process, one ought to enumerate [8]:

- locating the vehicles (in fleet management, passenger information, systems supporting vehicle coordination, passengers transfer and information concerning disruptions and deviations from timetables),
- charging the transport using electronic cards, Internet transfers, or a mobile (ticket integration, the possibility for various subjects to calculate costs among each other, prices diversification, public transport competitiveness improvement, facilities in offering services, integration of the device to accept the fees in public transport with devices used for other charges, e.g. in city cards, credit cards or electronic student cards,
- IT systems enabling the identification of passengers flow on specific lines and route parts, which plays significant role in the passengers flow planning process or in calculating the costs for providing the transport units),
- managing production factors in public transport units (assigning vehicles to transport tasks, drivers' working schedules, cost identification of transport services.

3   Integration Role of Electronic Toll Collection Systems

One of the crucial elements in transport integration process is common tariff- ticket system, possible, among others, thanks to implementing electronic toll systems for public transport. Such systems are based on electronic cards, which become the devices to carry appropriate types of tickets or money for their purchasing. Among additional advantages of those systems one ought to enumerate the possibility to use, and pay for, other city services, such as parking fees, taxes payments or even the possibility to purchase the goods not provided by public sector units. However, despite widening the range of functions and services for which one may to pay for, among public services it is payment for urban public transport which is of biggest financial flow [9]. Because of their complexity and, in case of correct assumptions of their creators, the possibility to develop, electronic toll collection systems allow for connecting another applications and solutions, which may be built on the basis of the already existing ones, e.g. dynamic passenger information system. They also enable to control the way public transport functions and facilitate the management of this transport area [10].

The systems described above allow for storing a lot of data. In a typical system, a card may be the storing device for a set period ticket, a number of one way ticket or money for purchasing such. In case of big agglomerations where there exist numerous transport systems and thus many transport organizers and transport operators, there function many tickets and tariffs; that makes passengers have certain knowledge about each of them. In case every of the organizers (operators) mentioned above decided to implement electronic toll system via electronic card, every passenger willing to use the services of more than one transport unit would have to have at least two cards. However, a card may work for more than one operator; the systems automatically collect information concerning the route depending on the vehicle a passenger used and the tariff valid in the vehicle.

This is the way the integration process of activities in the area of transport payment possibilities. Electronic toll collection systems also create the possibility to measure precisely each journey, which helps in building mutual financial calculation system among various passenger transport organizers.

Among additional possibilities of using the cards in passenger transport there are also the options to pay for parking and the possibility to identify and offer discounts for passengers using both individual and public transport system in the *Park and Ride* option.

Many Polish cities have already implemented electronic tickets and electronic urban cards, treating them as a tool to standardize the way to collect fees for services provided by a city (such as public transport), to increase their accessibility and attractiveness and to optimize their costs, as well as for advertisement and city promotion, thus increasing inhabitants satisfaction level. Among such cities there are Białystok, Bydgoszcz, Częstochowa, Elbląg, Gdańsk, Jaworzno, Kielce, Kraków, Lublin, Poznań, Radom, Radomsko, Rybnik, Suwałki, Tarnów, Warszawa, Wrocław, Zielona Góra.

Such ticket may also be bought through a mobile. Such way of purchase can be conducted in any city, equipped with any tariff system. This solution can prove useful, especially in the situation when one forgets or simply does not have time to buy a ticket: it is enough, after entering a vehicle, to sent proper text or call, and in this way to buy a ticket in the same price as a traditional one. The purchase is possible thank to moBilet application, after a single, free of charge registration on www.mobilet.pl, when a passenger gives their personal data and a telephone number, choosing also the payment method (automatic bank payment or via pre-paid system). After registration there is a text sent on a client's mobile, enabling the download of the moBilet application, which should be then installed and, after initiating its work, set a personal password. Electronic ticket should be sent and used directly after the vehicle started and the application opened. Purchase time and ticket validity is downloaded automatically from the server. During ticket control one ought to show their mobile to ticket inspector – they will estimate ticket validity, reading the data and security measures needed [11, 12]. In the same way it is possible to buy a ticket using a mobile with Internet connection in the SkyCash system. SkyCash is an independent, Universal payment-via- mobile system, providing simple, fast and secure cash flow. It works in every GSM network and in every mobile with Internet access. Such solution is used in many Polish cities (among them in Biała Podlaska, Gniezno, Inowrocław, Jelenia Góra, Lublin, Łódź, Rzeszów, Warszawa, Wrocław, Zamość) [12]. Moreover, on 24th October 2011 Municipal Union Of Transport Of The Upper Silesian Industrial Region (KZK GOP) chose yet another form of purchasing a ticket via mobile, using the Call-Pay system. CallPay enables buying single KZK GOP tickets via standard phone calls on specific numbers, which may be found labeled on bus stops and on www.callpay.pl website. Via CallPay, passengers can buy KZK GOP tickets, but also the tickets of regional rail carriers. CallPay operates in every mobile and GSM network without the need to install any application [13,14].

Such solutions as electronic ticket, urban card or the possibility to purchase a ticket via a mobile are considered as service facilities and increase those service accessibility.

4   Passenger Information System Integration

The attractiveness of the provided services is influenced by the completeness and the form of the passing information. From the perspective of quality criteria it is classified as accessibility criterion. Such information may be presented at the bus stop, in the vehicle, via Internet. It is especially important in case of passing concerning traffic disruptions [15]. If a passenger has the possibility to use the service provided by many transport unit sit is advisable such information is passed via standardized system. Electronic information tables, installed at bus stops and transport hubs may be an ex ample of modern solutions enabling the achievement of such goals. In majority of currently operating systems of that type, such as in Public Transport Office in Rybnik (ZTZ Rybnik) the boards show the information concerning real departure time of the vehicles. Less often, such systems present static information included in timetables, like in Fast Regional Rail in Tychy (SKR Tychy). The real departure times is the result of using GPS (Global Positioning System) devices in vehicles, which provide coordinates of a vehicle (longitude and latitude), as well as some algorithms which calculate the real time for the vehicle to reach a chosen bus stop. Presenting the real departure times may work not only at bus stops; similar type of information is possible to share via Internet. The basic rule for them to operate and the necessary equipment are the same as in case of information boards. Transport management has therefore two methods to present the same type of data: at the bus stops and in the Internet. A test portal, enabling such form of presenting data was initiated in 2013 in ZTZ Rybnik.

From the perspective of public urban transport users, information systems at the bus stops may have the following functions [16]:

- supporting the choice where to wait for the transport,
- determining the time needed for the vehicle to come,
- supporting the decision about the possibility to change the means of transport planned to be used as an alternative.

Passenger information system, through appropriate devices, should provide fast and easy information access to the passengers in all accessible places during the journey. Apart from bus stop information boards, buses are also equipped with information and direction boards. Passenger Information System in public transport vehicles mostly consists of [17]:

- front direction board,
- side direction boards,
- back number board,
- internal board,
- speaker,
- a computer or a driver.

Vehicle equipped with information boards make it so much easier for passengers to learn where they are going and what place they are currently in, they also show the route, the line number, start and end stop as well as other important information [18].

In even bigger number of cities in Poland dynamic information boards are implemented, among them there are Białystok, Bydgoszcz, Gliwice, Jaworzno, Katowice, Lublin, Sosnowiec, Poznań, Puławy, Rybnik, Trójmiasto, Warszawa, Wrocław.

The system also provides much information for organizers of public urban transport, facilitating transport management. Such information include [19]:

- present position of the vehicles pictured in the set task,
- transport route,
- route being realized,
- information concerning delays or router realized too quickly,
- realization stage of the chosen system elements, e.g. bus stop boards.

The solutions presented above are the results of implementing modern IT and ICT technologies. For those systems to be of integrating function it is necessary to obtain the cooperation among the organizers (operators) interested in such type of services. Currently, in road transport in cities, the integration understood as presented above has not been used yet. Such solutions functioned only in rail transport where rail infrastructure manager dealt also with passenger information means (apart from the units installed in vehicles). In case of road transport it is necessary to install in the vehicles the appropriate devices to send data crucial for the system to work properly and to analyze it. It is also important to share timetable in electronic form which, as well as vehicle coordinates, should be prepared in form possible to transform and read by dynamic passenger information systems which are or are to be implemented.

Adapting the information to mobile devices create new possibilities for the travelers. Implementing appropriate applications of Java mobile technology provides nonstop access to urban communication timetables in every mobile phone which operates with this application. Timetables in a mobile work well in a situation when there is no present Internet access and there is a need to check departure time of a specific means of transport (bus, tram, etc.). Mobile timetables also offer the possibility to look for and to indentify the connections between any stops in a city during the travel as well as about potential transfer possibilities [20]. Most often, it is possible to access given line through entering its number or specific stop name and choosing from the lines available from there.

Mobile passenger information is available, among others, by the application called myBus online, which is a part of Passenger Information System (SIP) included in the MUNICOM.premium – program made by PZI TARAN company. myBus online, thanks to developed stops search, from the list of all, closest, most favorite stops or from a map allows for quick access to proper timetable. SIP system is installed in many Polish cities (Biała Podlaska, Bolesławiec, Dębica, Elbląg, Gdańsk, Kielce, Kraśnik, Lublin, Mielec, Ostrów Wielkopolski, Płock, Puławy, Stalowa Wola, Suwałki, Świdnica, Świerklaniec, Wałbrzych), and allow a passenger to access following communication information [21]:

- on-line on electric information boards at bus stops or in so called virtual boards (Copie electronic boards state in Internet browser),
- on-line in WWW browsers via GoogleMaps,
- off-line in WWW browsers via classic HTML sites,
- on-line in portable devices working with WAP sites,
- on-line in portable devices serviced by Android system.

Wrocław offered mobile versions of timetables in July 2009, by implementing tables with 2D codes, facilitating the access to actual timetables from the given stop. Thanks to the codes passenger have easier access to web sites with updated timetables. 2D code links a user to the site providing with the information concerning the closest departures from the given stop for each of the lines that service it [22].

5   Conclusion

Companies operating on a competitive market, in order to maintain their position, are forced to constant search for modern solutions for their activity range; that also includes the units providing public passenger transport. The activities, undertaken in this area, are connected with implementing solutions of various kind, which are based on IT Technologies that offer a client better possibilities to use the services, as well as increasing the access to information concerning such offer. There should be noticed the systems and devices facilitating urban transport, such as electronic information devices or information boards. There are also innovative solutions, such as ticket selling systems, mobile timetables etc. such solutions are implemented by cities of various size, which offer public transport services and try to make public communication more attractive and to increase liveability level of their inhabitants.

References

1. Integration and Regulatory Structures in Public Transport. Final Report, Project Leader NEA Transport Research and Training. Study commissioned by European Commission DG TREN, p. 5, Rijswijk (2003)
2. Grzelec, K.: Integracja komunikacji miejskiej w aglomeracjach miejskich. In: Wyszomirski, O. (ed.) Gospodarowanie w komunikacji miejskiej, Wydawnictwo Uniwersytetu Gdańskiego, Gdańsk, pp. 189–190 (2002)
3. Janic, M., Reggiani, A.: Integrated transport systems in the European Union: an overview of some recent developments. Transport Reviews 21(4), 472 (2001)
4. Mulley, C., Nelson, J.D.: Interoperability and transport policy: the impediments to interoperability in the organization of trans – European transport systems. Journal of Transport Geography (7), 94 (1999)
5. Tomanek, R.: Konkurencyjność transportu miejskiego. Prace Naukowe Akademii Ekonomicznej w Katowicach. Wydawnictwo Akademii Ekonomicznej im. K. Adamieckiego w Katowicach, Katowice, pp. 113–114 (2002)

6. Kołodziejski, H.: Integracja transportu miejskiego w aglomeracjach i konurbacjach miejskich. In: Wyszomirski, O. (ed.) Transport Miejski. Ekonomika i organizacja, Wydawnictwo Uniwersytetu Gdańskiego, Gdańsk, p. 249 (2008)
7. Michałowska, M., Tomanek, R.: Integracja systemów transportowych jako przedmiot badań naukowych. Logistyka (2), 11 (2006)
8. Dydkowski, G.: Obszary zastosowań oraz efektywność rozwiązań telematycznych. Badania integracji transportu miejskiego. In: Inteligentny System Zarządzania Transportem Publicznym, Zespół Automatyki w Transporcie, Wydział Transportu, p. 162. Politechnika Śląska (2007)
9. Dydkowski, G.: Koszty i korzyści wynikające z wprowadzania bezgotówkowych systemów płatności za usługi miejskie, (602). Zeszyty Naukowe Uniwersytetu Szczecińskiego, Szczecin (2010)
10. Kos, B., Kosobucki, Ł.: E-karta jako instrument zarządzania transportem miejskim na przykładzie miasta Rybnik, Wydziałowe Zeszyty Naukowe no. 89. Uniwersytet Ekonomiczny w Katowicach, Katowice (2011)
11. MoBilet Website, http://www.mobilet.pl (date of access: July 26, 2013)
12. KZK GOP, http://www.kzkgop.com.pl (date of access: July 26, 2013)
13. SkyCash, http://www.skycash.com/pl (date of access: July 26, 2013)
14. CallPay, http://www.callpay.pl/ (date of access: July 26, 2013)
15. Rudnicki, A.: Kryteria i mierniki oceny miejskiej komunikacji zbiorowej, Izba Gospodarcza Komunikacji Miejskiej, Warszawa (1999)
16. Molecki, B.: Przystankowe tablice dynamicznej informacji pasażerskiej. Transport Miejski i Regionalny (7-8) (2011)
17. Pixel Website, http://pixel.pl (date of access: July 26, 2013)
18. Dysten Website, http://www.dysten.pl (date of access: July 26, 2013)
19. Sims Company, http://sims.pl (date of access: July 26, 2013)
20. MobileMPK, http://www.mmpk.info (date of access: July 26, 2013)
21. Taran Company, http://www.taran.com.pl (date of access: July 26, 2013)
22. Miasto Wrocław, http://www.wroclaw.pl (date of access: July 26, 2013)

Telematic Systems to Aid in Safety in Inland Water Tourism

Zbigniew Łukasik and Tomasz Perzyński

University of Technology and Humanities in Radom,
Faculty of Transport and Electrical Engineering,
26-600 Radom, Malczewskiego 29, Poland
{z.lukasik,t.perzynski}@uthrad.pl

Abstract. The paper presents the solutions used on Polish inland waters which raise safety in water tourism. The presented solutions first and foremost allow limiting dangerous events caused by weather phenomenon and permit to decrease the number of injured people. Aside from contemporary solutions, the article presents an additional, new telematic system, similar to those used in the sea and ocean areas, which allows for faster emergency services reaction (Aquatic Volunteer Emergency Corps) to dangerous events (faster localization of capsized boat).

Keywords: inland water area, telematic systems.

1 Introduction

The Great Masuria Lakes have been for years one of the largest holiday resorts and the largest sailing centre in Poland. In the high season there are even 26 thousand tourists [11]. The popularity of this kind of water sports, including better access to boats, was also influenced by changes in the current legislation, with reference to both sailing boats and motorboats. The changes in the boats design, their equipment and noticeable changes in the infrastructure do not ensure a sufficient level of safety. In August 2007 a white squall (12 on the Beaufort scale, three metre waves, overturned 40 boats, killing 12 people) appeared on the Masuria Lakes [10]. At that time there were no weather phenomena warning systems. This paper presents not only the currently used system of early warning of weather phenomena installed on the route of The Masuria Lakes, but also it proposes a new emergency notification system of events on the water (capsizing yacht). The proposed system is similar to those used in open waters - EPIRB (Emergency Position Indicating Radio Beacon). A typical emergency EPIRB (Emergency Position-Indicating Radio Beacon) transmits a signal and its location is based on the GPS signal. The system proposed in the presented article assumes a A-GPS solution. Thanks to a different form of message sending (action based on the GSM network), in contrast to the EPIRB, it will not require registration with the Office of Civil Aviation [4].

J. Mikulski (Ed.): TST 2013, CCIS 395, pp. 89–96, 2013.
© Springer-Verlag Berlin Heidelberg 2013

2   Basic Legal Requirements for Water Tourism

The Act of 21 December 2000 on Inland Navigation stipulates current legal requirements for water tourism. It was amended on 16 October 2010 by the Act of 25 June 2010 on Sports. The Act on Sports repealed the earlier sports regulations. Polish legislator decided to introduce a distinction between boat users with a qualification document issued by the competent Polish sports federation, and the users who do not have such a document. This distinction was the basis to introduce a ban on the use of sailing boats of hull length exceeding 7.5m or of motorboats with an engine over 10 kW by those without documented skills.

In the last amendment of the Act on Inland Navigation one article has been added (Art. 37a cl. 4) with reference to motorboats, which exempts the users of yachts with engine power up to 75 kW with a hull length up to 13m, where the maximum speed is structurally limited to 15km/h (Fig. 1.) from the requirement of the qualifying document. Such persons must be only trained in the field of safety on the water, where they are tenants of such motorboats. [1, 2, 10, 11].

For the sake of revised legal rules and greater availability of yachts it becomes essential to maintain an appropriate level of safety including the use of modern telematic solutions.

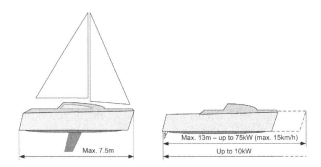

Fig. 1. Polish regulation of water boat and motorboat tourism

3   Technology and Safety in Polish Inland Water Tourism

In order to improve safety on Masuria Lakes, a warning system against dangerous weather phenomena was activated in 2011. It covers all Masuria Lakes area. According to the Minister of Infrastructure Regulation of 28 April 2003 on navigation regulations on inland waterways [1], persons on lakes are informed about weather dangers by light signals placed on appropriate masts, as presented in Fig. 2. The flash signal occurring at a frequency of 40 flashes per minute warn people of the expected storm or high winds, but without specifying the time and place of meteorological phenomena arrival. Imminent danger of storms and strong winds is indicated by 90 flashes per minute [10].

Fig. 2. The warning system with an MSL-50000Y lamp

After receiving the information about weather conditions, the server with the appropriate software interprets the message and, if necessary, sends the information to the masts. The lights turn on automatically. The light signals stop transmitting the light message after cancelling the announcement or its expiry. Currently the system consists of 17 warning masts. LED lamps were installed as light sources. The beacon is visible from a distance of 8 - 9 km. The scheme of the systems is presented in Fig. 3. [11]. The list of masts and their locations are available on the website of the Regional Water Management Authority in Warsaw [6, 10].

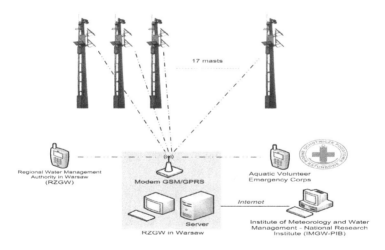

Fig. 3. Diagram of an early warning system against a possibility of meteorological phenomena

Apart from the described system, displays have been installed in most ports, indicating the wind strength as well as current and anticipated conditions in the water area. Additionally, tourists use the information available on the respective websites. Figure 4 presents an example of the window informing about the current weather conditions (weather conditions for Gizycko city – *Kisajno* lake - on 10.05.2013), [8]. Information and parameters such as wind, air pressure and rainfall can prevent many dangerous situations.

In addition to the safety provided by these systems, adequate qualifications of sailors in keeping the boat in rough weather conditions are still the most important.

Time Friday 10.05.13		Temperature (feel)	Rain	Pressure	Speed of wind		Visibility	Humidity
0:00	☁	14.0 (11.0) °C	0.0 mm	998 hPa	5 m/s	◤	1000 m	94%
3:00	☁	13.0 (10.0) °C	0.0 mm	996 hPa	6 m/s	◤	1000 m	91%
6:00	☁	13.0 (10.0) °C	0.0 mm	995 hPa	6 m/s	◤	1000 m	88%
9:00	☁	15.0 (11.0) °C	0.0 mm	994 hPa	6 m/s	◤	1000 m	83%
12:00	☁	14.0 (12.0) °C	0.5 mm	994 hPa	5 m/s	◤	1000 m	90%
15:00	☁	14.0 (12.0) °C	0.0 mm	994 hPa	4 m/s	◤	1000 m	89%
18:00	☁	15.0 (13.0) °C	0.0 mm	995 hPa	4 m/s	◤	1000 m	88%
21:00	☁	14.0 (12.0) °C	0.0 mm	995 hPa	3 m/s	◤	1000 m	91%

Fig. 4. Weather conditions for Gizycko city – *Kisajno* lake

A high board of boat and wind can upset the lateral stability of the boat and its capsizing, what is presented in Fig. 5 [7].

Fig. 5. Boat capsizing

In an emergency situation we can always call an emergency phone *601 100 100* activated in 2003, by the company Polkomtel S.A. This phone operates within the *Integrated Rescue System* on the water [5].

4   Emergency Notification System (ENoS)

Because of the situation shown in Fig. 5 and legal regulations for water tourism (allowing sailing of people with the lack of skills), the authors have proposed to use an additional system on yachts, informing the appropriate emergency services of a breakdown, dangerous events and finally of boat capsizing.

During the yacht sailing the aerodynamic and hydrodynamic forces give rise to a heeling moment of the yacht. From the safety point of view the most important is lateral stability, which depends on the force of gravity and buoyancy. In the event of boat heeling the centre of buoyancy changes and a righting moment arises. The largest righting moment arises at an angle of approximately 40°. Above this angle the righting moment decreases. In the case of 70° tilt the righting moment reaches zero. In this situation only helmsman skills (e.g. proper ballasting) may return the yacht to balance, otherwise the boat will capsize. The forces and the stability of a centreboard yacht is shown in Fig. 6 [9].

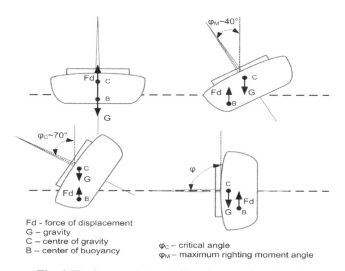

Fd - force of displacement
G – gravity
C – centre of gravity
B – center of buoyancy

φ_C – critical angle
φ_M – maximum righting moment angle

Fig. 6. The forces and the stability of a centreboard yacht

In the event of boat capsizing, in many cases the help of emergency services becomes necessary. The faster the position of capsized boat will be fixed the faster will be the response of emergency services. It is worth to be mentioned that the personal things, phones, are usually below the yacht deck. In the proposed solution the position problem will be solved via an A-GPS system using the GSM network. In the event of an emergency situation a precise measurement of the position is required. In the case of GPS system it is possible if the time scale of the user is synchronized with the GPS system time. For the GPS system, the principle of determining the boat position in three-dimensional space is shown in Fig. 7. (Three satellites to are used determine the location).

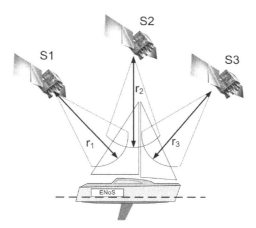

Fig. 7. Principle of determining the boat position in three-dimensional space

In a real system, to eliminate the time shift also the information from the fourth satellite should be used. It means that four pseudo–distances should be determined and the following equation solved:

$$d_i^* = \sqrt{(x_{si} - x_0)^2 + (y_{si} - y_o)^2 + (z_{si} - z_0)^2} + c\Delta\tau \qquad (1)$$

where:

- x_{si}, y_{si}, z_{si} - co-ordinate of satellite in a rectangular geocentric system
- x_0, y_0, z_0 - searching object co-ordinate in a rectangular geocentric system
- $\Delta\tau$ - displacement object time scale in relation to GPS time scale
- c - speed of electromagnetic wave

The most common reason of boat capsizing is a sudden strong wind, accompanied by thunderstorms. Torrential rain and clouds can break the connection with the satellite. Therefore, the disturbed signal from satellites requires using an A-GPS module to locate the boat quickly. In the A-GPS solution, the time to the first fix is below 1min (in the GPS system ~ 2-3min). The proposed system will be located in a hermetic casing with its own power supply. A general scheme of the system is shown in Fig. 8. In the case of exceeding the critical angle, and reaching ~ 90 ° tilt, a tilt sensor will give an impulse to a microcontroller. The microcontroller will switch on the A-GPS module and after gathering relevant information it will send an *sms* message to the Aquatic Volunteer Emergency Corps – mobile phone *601 100 100*. The data on the geographical location of the boat will be in the *sms* message. In difficult weather conditions, using only information from the A-GPS module, the positional accuracy may fall to about tens to hundreds of meters and it will be possible to quickly find the victims and help them.

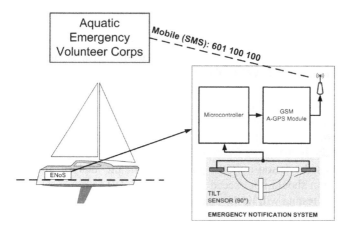

Fig. 8. General scheme of the ENoS system

On the basis of available maps, the authors analysed the availability of signal from the BTS (*Base Transceiver System*) in the Masuria Lakes district. The map of BTS installation is presented in Fig. 9, [3].

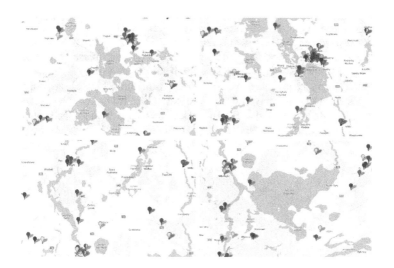

Fig. 9. Map of BTS installation in the Masuria Lakes district

After capsizing of a boat the system may be immersed in water and in such situation a problem may occur how to locate the system in a boat. It is related to the problem of high-frequency attenuation by water. As a last resort the proposed system can be built similarly to the *EPIRP* and will detach during boat capsizing.

5   Conclusion

On open waters the GMDSS system (Global Maritime Distress and Safety System) has been working for many years, which intrinsically contains a number of procedures and equipment used to notify appropriate services of dangerous events. The EPIRB is one of GMDSS elements. Basing on this solution the authors have proposed a similar system for inland water area – ENoS (Emergency Notification System). This proposed solution may be treated as an additional equipment of each yacht, boat on the inland waters. In the future it can be also expanded by additional functions. At this stage the proposed solution is in the phase of economic analysis and it is estimated that such solution should not exceed the amount of 250 Euro. An attempt to build a device ready for testing will be the next step.

References

1. Dz. U. z 2003 r. Nr 212, poz. 2072
2. Dz.U. z 2006 r. Nr 123, poz. 857 - with change
3. http://mapa.btsearch.pl/ (date of access: July 19, 2013)
4. http://www.magazynwiatr.pl/artykul-93 (date of access: July 19, 2013)
5. http://www.polkomtel.com.pl/ (date of access: July 19, 2013)
6. http://www.warszawa.rzgw.gov.pl/gorne_menu-szlaki_zeglowne-system_sygnalizacji_ostrzegawczej.html (date of access: July 19, 2013)
7. http://www.youtube.com/watch?v=IxaSWedN5YM (date of access: July 19, 2013)
8. http://www.zagle.com.pl/pogoda/gizycko/ (date of access: July 19, 2013)
9. Kolaszewski, A., Świdwiński, P.: Żeglarz i sternik jachtowy. Almapress, Warszawa (2011)
10. Perzyński, T.: Turystyka i rekreacja wodna – infrastruktura i bezpieczeństwo, Autobusy, technika, eksploatacja. Systemy Transportowe. Nr. 3/2013 (CD)
11. Perzyński, T., Prokop-Perzyńska, E.: Turystyka i rekreacja wodna – jachting w prawie i praktyce. Logitrans, Logistyka Nr 3/2012, CD (2012)

Analysis of the Effect of Congestion in the Lanes at the Inlet to the Two-Lane Roundabout on Traffic Capacity of the Inlet

Elżbieta Macioszek

Silesian University of Technology, Faculty of Transport,
Krasinskiego 8, 40-019 Katowice, Poland
elzbieta.macioszek@polsl.pl

Abstract. A considerable number of two-lane roundabouts is used in Poland today. Observations of the behaviour of drivers who drive through this type of intersections show that the lanes in the area of the intersection are not equally loaded. Drivers are more willing to use the right traffic lane at the roundabout's inlet, even if traffic intensity is considerably high. With regard to this fact, the paper presents the analysis of the effect of load in the individual lanes at the inlet of a two-lane roundabout on traffic capacity at the inlet. Analysis focused on conventional two-lane roundabouts, without consideration of the cases of traffic organization typical of turbo roundabouts with two lanes at the inlet.

Keywords: circular intersections, two-lane roundabouts, road traffic engineering.

1   Introduction

The number of roundabouts in Poland has considerably increased since the nineties of the 20th century. Initially, the single-lane roundabouts were usually designed, with the external diameter ranging from 14 to 45 m for the roundabouts located in build-up areas and from 30 to 50 m for the roundabouts located outside build-up areas [8]. Single-lane roundabouts turned out to be solutions which function effectively but only below particular traffic intensities in the area of the intersection. The results obtained in empirical studies carried out in Poland and abroad have demonstrated that traffic capacity in the roundabouts ranges from 1500 to 2700 PCU/h [1, 4 - 7, 12, 16, 17]. Thus, if higher values of traffic intensity are estimated, the two-lane roundabouts are sometimes designed.

According to the guidelines [8], two-lane roundabouts are supposed to have external diameter from 37.5 m to over 55 m for the roundabouts located in build-up areas and from 40 m to 65 m for roundabouts situated outside build-up areas.

At present, vast majority of the roundabouts in Poland are single-lane roundabouts, located both in build-up areas and outside them. Two-lane roundabouts are a slightly less numerous group of intersection with roundabout-type traffic. As practice shows, single-lane roundabouts are the solutions which, in Polish conditions, ensure a very high level of safety to the users and high (considering single-lane intersections) traffic

J. Mikulski (Ed.): TST 2013, CCIS 395, pp. 97–104, 2013.
© Springer-Verlag Berlin Heidelberg 2013

capacity. Furthermore, two-lane roundabouts are not entirely perfect solutions since substantial number of drivers use chiefly the right lane, both at the inlets to the roundabouts and on the roadway, even with high values of traffic intensity in the area of the intersection. Uneven load with traffic streams in individual lanes in the inlets to two-lane roundabouts leads consequently to overall decrease in traffic capacity in the inlet and in the whole intersection. With regard to these solutions, the paper presents analysis of the effect of load in the lanes at the inlet of a double-lane roundabout on traffic capacity at the inlet. Analysis focused on conventional two-lane roundabouts, without analysis of the cases of traffic organization typical of turbo roundabouts with two lanes at the inlet.

2   The Use of Traffic Lanes at the Inlets to Multi-lane Roundabouts (Literature Study)

Due to a number of reasons, chiefly traffic capacity and safety in road traffic, it is important that the drivers move on multi-lane roundabouts properly and in a manner that ensures even load to the lanes at the inlets. The literature survey on the use of lanes at the inlets to multi-lane roundabouts, the following can be observed:

- drivers are more willing to use the right lane at the inlet rather than the left one. During the empirical tests carried out in Poland, $62\% \div 87\%$ drivers on average chose the right lane, depending on the traffic intensity. The study found that, with high levels of traffic intensities at the inlets, the use of the left lane rises by ca. 34%-45% [11],
- it was found based on the results obtained in a study [15] that older drivers in the multi-lane roundabouts are more willing to use the right external traffic lane,
- a particular correlation between individual types of vehicles and the use of individual lanes in the roundabouts by drivers is observed (e.g. cyclists prefer right external lanes [9], the drivers in heavy goods vehicles more often choose external lanes in the multi-lane roundabouts [10]). This fact can be confirmed through actual observation of traffic in selected elements of the transport network. Global identification of traffic and modal split is possible through e.g. application of modern GIS, GPS and GSM technologies (more information see [13, 14]),
- R. Akcelik, in his study [2], found uneven use of lanes in multi-lane roundabouts and presented a method which allowed for inclusion of this relationship in calculations of traffic intensity.

3   Analysis of the Effect of Congestion in the Lanes at the Inlet to the Two-Lane Roundabout on Traffic Capacity of the Inlet

Traffic capacity in multi-lane inlets in roundabouts differs depending on e.g. roundabout dimensions, directions and type of traffic, mean velocity of the vehicles, number of vehicles on individual lanes at the inlets and many other characteristics of road traffic. In the case of models of traffic designed specifically for two-lane roundabouts, a simplification is assumed that a single vehicle stream is present on the roadway and at the inlet to the roundabout, without division into individual lanes.

Analysis of the effect of the load to individual lanes at the inlet to roundabouts on traffic capacity at the inlet was presented with the example of the two-lane roundabout with external diameter (D_z) of 45.0 m and width of the roadway (l_{jr}) of 8.0 m. However, similar procedure can be carried out for any two-lane roundabout. Models designed based on the theory of acceptance of headways in the main stream were adopted for calculations of initial traffic capacities for individual lanes at the inlets. These models use the spline function which is composed of the shifted exponential distribution and Cowan's distribution M3 and submodels in the form of functions that characterize individual parameters of these distributions. Therefore, a model used for estimation of initial traffic capacity of the right lane at the inlet of the two-lane roundabout is given by [11]:

$$C_{oP} = \begin{cases} 1{,}01 \cdot 3600 \cdot t_{fP}^{-1} = 1{,}01 \cdot \dfrac{3600}{t_{fP}} \quad [PCU \cdot h^{-1}] \\ \qquad \text{for } Q_{nP} = 0\,[PCU \cdot h^{-1}] \\[2em] \dfrac{1{,}01 \cdot 3600 \cdot e^{-\left(\frac{Q_{jr\_w}}{3600 - Q_{jr\_w} \cdot t_{p1}} + \frac{Q_{jr\_z}}{3600 - Q_{jr\_z} \cdot t_{p2}}\right)(t_{gP} - t_{p1})} \cdot \left(\frac{Q_{jr\_w}}{3600 - Q_{jr\_w} \cdot t_{p1}} + \frac{Q_{jr\_z}}{3600 - Q_{jr\_z} \cdot t_{p2}}\right)}{\left(1 - e^{-t_{fP}\left(\frac{Q_{jr\_w}}{3600 - Q_{jr\_w} \cdot t_{p1}} + \frac{Q_{jr\_z}}{3600 - Q_{jr\_z} \cdot t_{p2}}\right)}\right) \cdot \left(1 + \frac{t_{p1} \cdot Q_{jr\_w}}{3600 - Q_{jr\_w} \cdot t_{p1}}\right)\left(1 + \frac{t_{p2} \cdot Q_{jr\_z}}{3600 - Q_{jr\_z} \cdot t_{p2}}\right)} \quad [PCU \cdot h^{-1}] \\ \qquad \text{for } 1 < Q_{nP} \le 100\,[PCU \cdot h^{-1}] \\[2em] \dfrac{1{,}01 \cdot 3600 \cdot \phi_1 \cdot \phi_2 \cdot e^{-\left[\left(\frac{\phi_1 \cdot Q_{jr\_w}}{3600 - Q_{jr\_w} \cdot t_{p1}} + \frac{\phi_2 \cdot Q_{jr\_z}}{3600 - Q_{jr\_z} \cdot t_{p2}}\right)(t_{gP} - t_{p1})\right]} \cdot \left(\frac{\phi_1 \cdot Q_{jr\_w}}{3600 - Q_{jr\_w} \cdot t_{p1}} + \frac{\phi_2 \cdot Q_{jr\_z}}{3600 - Q_{jr\_z} \cdot t_{p2}}\right)}{\left(1 - e^{-t_{fP}\left(\frac{\phi_1 Q_{jr\_w}}{3600 - Q_{jr\_w} \cdot t_{p1}} + \frac{\phi_2 Q_{jr\_z}}{3600 - Q_{jr\_z} \cdot t_{p2}}\right)}\right) \cdot \left(\phi_1 + \frac{\phi_1 \cdot Q_{jr\_w} \cdot t_{p1}}{3600 - Q_{jr\_w} \cdot t_{p1}}\right)\left(\phi_2 + \frac{\phi_2 \cdot Q_{jr\_z} \cdot t_{p2}}{3600 - Q_{jr\_z} \cdot t_{p2}}\right)} \quad [PCU \cdot h^{-1}] \\ \qquad \text{for } Q_{nP} > 100\,[PCU \cdot h^{-1}] \wedge Q_{nP} < C_{jr} \\[2em] \cong 0\,[PCU \cdot h^{-1}] \\ \qquad \text{for } Q_{nP} \cong C_{jr} \end{cases}$$

$$\tag{1}$$

where:

C_{oP}	- initial traffic capacity of the right lane at the inlet [PCU/h],
C_{jr}	- traffic capacity of the roadway [PCU/h],
t_{fP}	- headway between the vehicles that enter the roundabout from the queue on the right lane at the inlet [s],
t_{p1}, t_{p2}	- minimum headways between the vehicles on the 1st and 2nd lane of the roadway, respectively [s],

t_{gP} - headway limit for the drivers in the vehicles on the right lane at the inlet [s],

Q_{nP} - main traffic intensity for the drivers in the vehicles on the right lane at the inlet [PCU/h],

ϕ_1, ϕ_2 - share of vehicles moving freely on the 1st and 2nd lane of the roadway, respectively [-],

Q_{jr_w}, Q_{jr_z}- traffic intensity for the vehicles on the 1st and 2nd lane of the roadway, respectively [PCU/h].

Furthermore, the model used for estimation of initial traffic capacity of the left lane at the inlet of the two-lane roundabout is given by [11]:

$$C_{oL} = \begin{cases} 1,01 \cdot 3600 \cdot t_{fL}^{-1} = 1,01 \cdot \dfrac{3600}{t_{fL}} \quad [PCU \cdot h^{-1}] \\ \quad for \quad Q_{nL} = 0 \, [PCU \cdot h^{-1}] \\[2mm] 1,01 \cdot 3600 \cdot \dfrac{e^{-\left(\frac{Q_{jr\_w}}{3600 - Q_{jr\_w} \cdot t_{p1}} + \frac{Q_{jr\_z}}{3600 - Q_{jr\_z} \cdot t_{p2}}\right)\left(t_{gL} - t_{p1}\right)} \cdot \left(\frac{Q_{jr\_w}}{3600 - Q_{jr\_w} \cdot t_{p1}} + \frac{Q_{jr\_z}}{3600 - Q_{jr\_z} \cdot t_{p2}}\right)}{\left[1 - e^{-t_{fL}\left(\frac{Q_{jr\_w}}{3600 - Q_{jr\_w} \cdot t_{p1}} + \frac{Q_{jr\_z}}{3600 - Q_{jr\_z} \cdot t_{p2}}\right)}\right] \cdot \left(1 + \frac{t_{p1} \cdot Q_{jr\_w}}{3600 - Q_{jr\_w} \cdot t_{p1}}\right) \cdot \left(1 + \frac{t_{p2} \cdot Q_{jr\_z}}{3600 - Q_{jr\_z} \cdot t_{p2}}\right)} \quad [PCU \cdot h^{-1}] \\ \quad for \quad 1 < Q_{nL} \le 100 \, [PCU \cdot h^{-1}] \\[2mm] 1,01 \cdot 3600 \cdot \phi_1 \cdot \phi_2 \cdot \dfrac{e^{-\left[\left(\frac{\phi_1 \cdot Q_{jr\_w}}{3600 - Q_{jr\_w} \cdot t_{p1}} + \frac{\phi_2 \cdot Q_{jr\_z}}{3600 - Q_{jr\_z} \cdot t_{p2}}\right)\left(t_{gL} - t_{p1}\right)\right]} \cdot \left(\frac{\phi_1 \cdot Q_{jr\_w}}{3600 - Q_{jr\_w} \cdot t_{p1}} + \frac{\phi_2 \cdot Q_{jr\_z}}{3600 - Q_{jr\_z} \cdot t_{p2}}\right)}{1 - e^{-t_{fL}\left(\frac{\phi_1 \cdot Q_{jr\_w}}{3600 - Q_{jr\_w} \cdot t_{p1}} + \frac{\phi_2 \cdot Q_{jr\_z}}{3600 - Q_{jr\_z} \cdot t_{p2}}\right)} \cdot \left(\phi_1 + \frac{\phi_1 \cdot Q_{jr\_w} \cdot t_{p1}}{3600 - Q_{jr\_w} \cdot t_{p1}}\right)\left(\phi_2 + \frac{\phi_2 \cdot Q_{jr\_z} \cdot t_{p2}}{3600 - Q_{jr\_z} \cdot t_{p2}}\right)} \quad [PCU \cdot h^{-1}] \\ \quad for \quad Q_{nL} > 100 \, [PCU \cdot h^{-1}] \quad \wedge \quad Q_{nL} < C_{jr} \\[2mm] \cong 0 \, [PCU \cdot h^{-1}] \\ \quad for \quad Q_{nL} \cong C_{jr} \end{cases}$$

(2)

where:

C_{oL} - initial traffic capacity of the left lane at the inlet [PCU/h],

t_{fL} - headway between the vehicles that enter the roundabout from the queue on the left lane at the inlet [s],

t_{gL} - headway limit for the drivers in the vehicles on the left lane at the inlet [s],

Q_{nL} - main traffic intensity for the drivers in the vehicles on the left lane at the inlet [PCU/h],

The relationship used for calculation of the traffic capacity at the inlet to a two-lane roundabout that takes into consideration the traffic intensity on individual traffic lanes at the inlet (load to the traffic lanes at the inlet) [11]:

$$C_{wl} = \sum_{i=1}^{n} \rho_i \cdot C_i = \frac{\sum_{i=1}^{n} Q_i}{X} = \frac{Q_L + Q_P}{\max\left[\dfrac{Q_L}{C_L} ; \dfrac{Q_P}{C_P}\right]} \ [PCU / h] \tag{3}$$

where:

X - load in an individual lane, determined as a quotient of traffic intensity in a particular lane to its traffic capacity [-],

Q_L - traffic intensity at the inlet to the left lane [PCU/h],

Q_P - traffic intensity at the inlet to the right lane [PCU/h],

C_L - traffic capacity at the inlet to the left lane [PCU/h],

C_P - traffic capacity at the inlet to the right lane [PCU/h].

Fig. 1 illustrates the results of the analysis of traffic capacity at the inlet to a medium two-lane roundabout with variable load to lanes with streams of vehicles at the inlet and the known equal load of traffic streams in individual lanes on the roadway (obviously, these charts can be made with varied load to the lanes on the roadway). The charts show that traffic capacity of the inlet to the two-lane roundabout varies significantly. Accurate estimation of traffic capacity at the inlet is possible through taking into consideration the load to individual lanes at the inlet. Non-consideration of the load to individual lanes at the inlet leads to serious errors. Consequently, these errors result in improper decisions made during planning, designing and using roundabouts.

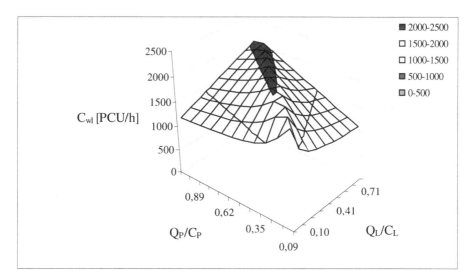

Fig. 1. Two-lane roundabouts inlet capacity in the case of taking into consideration the degree of congestion at the inlet to traffic lanes [Own study]

Comparison of traffic capacity at the inlet of the two-lane roundabout calculated in consideration of the load with traffic streams to individual lanes at the inlet and without taking into consideration the load to the lanes at the inlet is presented in Fig. 2. Fig. 2 shows that, with particular main traffic intensity, the scope of variability of traffic capacity in the case of taking into consideration the load to the lanes at the inlet is considerably higher, which is caused by the fact that, in the process of calculation of traffic capacity at the inlet, another factor which determines traffic capacity is taken into consideration. The model of estimation of the traffic capacity that does not take into consideration the variable load with vehicle streams in individual lanes at the inlet lacks this advantage.

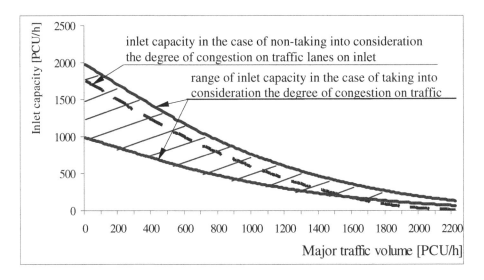

Fig. 2. Comparison of two-lane roundabout inlet capacity [Own study]

Quantitative comparison of the traffic capacity in the two-lane roundabout studied for the traffic intensity at the lanes at the inlet corresponding to the cases of: L=0%, R=100%; L=25%, R=75%; L=50%, R=50%; L=75%, R=25%; L=100%, R=0% (where L denotes left lane at the inlet, R means right lane at the inlet) is illustrated in the table 1. Based on the obtained results it can be concluded that traffic capacity depends on the type of load with the streams of vehicles at the inlet. The highest traffic capacity is obtained when the streams of vehicles at the inlets are characterized by equal load to individual lanes and the lowest traffic capacity occurs with unequal distribution of this load. This conclusion can be also drawn with respect to other inlets to multi-lane roundabouts. However, observation of the traffic on multi-lane roundabouts carried out in empirical studies shows that equal distribution of traffic streams in individual lanes at the inlet is in practice a very rare occurrence.

Table 1. Comparison of initial capacities of two-lane roundabout with different degree of congestion on traffic lanes at the inlet

Major traffic volume [PCU/h]	Initial capacities for major traffic volume = 800 PCU/h; external diameter = 45.0m, main roadway width = 8.0m, (lane width on the main roadway = 4.0m)				
	L= 0%; R= 100%	L= 25%; R= 75%	L= 50%; R= 50%	L= 75%; R= 25%	L= 100%; R= 0%
$Q_n = 100$	920	1226	1839	1406	1054
$Q_n = 200$	851	1135	1702	1298	973
$Q_n = 300$	782	1043	1564	1189	892
$Q_n = 400$	714	952	1429	1083	812
$Q_n = 500$	647	863	1295	980	735
$Q_n = 600$	585	780	1170	884	663
$Q_n = 700$	527	703	1055	796	597
$Q_n = 800$	474	632	948	715	536
$Q_n = 900$	425	567	850	640	480
$Q_n = 1000$	380	507	760	572	429
$Q_n = 1100$	338	451	677	509	382
$Q_n = 1200$	300	400	601	452	339
$Q_n = 1300$	265	354	531	400	300
$Q_n = 1400$	234	311	467	352	264
$Q_n = 1500$	204	273	409	308	231
$Q_n = 1600$	178	238	356	269	202
$Q_n = 1700$	154	206	309	233	175
$Q_n = 1800$	133	177	266	201	151
where: L – left lane on the inlet, R – right lane on the inlet.					

4   Conclusion

The investigations presented in this paper lead to the conclusion that one of the factors which affect the level of traffic capacity at the inlets to two-lane roundabouts is how the traffic lanes are used at these inlets. The highest traffic capacity can be reached for equal load with streams of vehicles to the traffic lanes at the inlet. It should be noted that in two-lane roundabouts, the upper curve (Fig. 2) defines traffic capacity obtained with equal load with vehicle streams to individual lanes at the inlet. In Poland, this case of road traffic is in practice very rare. The traffic lanes at the inlets to two-lane roundabouts are considerably more often loaded with the streams of vehicles with advantage of more intensive use of the right lane.

In the situation when traffic lanes at the inlet are equally used, more vehicles at the inlet are able to enter the circular roadway using the same headways between the vehicles on the roadway. Furthermore, the lowest traffic capacity at the inlet occurs for insignificant load to the left traffic lane at the inlet (lower than 20%). It was also found that the way the lanes on the circular roadway are utilized affects traffic capacity of the inlet. It can be noted that, with particular main traffic intensity, the most favourable (with respect to traffic capacity of the inlet) situation occurs when the vehicles on both lanes of the roadway are moving at the same time.

References

1. Akcelik, R.: Roundabouts: Capacity and Performance Analysis. ARRB Transport Research. Research Report ARR 321, Australia (1998)
2. Akcelik, R.: Lane-by-Lane Modeling of Unequal Lane Use and Flares at Roundabouts and Signalized Intersections: The SIDRA Solution. Traffic Engineering and Control 38(7/8), 388–399 (1997)
3. Mikulski, J.: Using telematics in transport. In: Mikulski, J. (ed.) TST 2010. CCIS, vol. 104, pp. 175–182. Springer, Heidelberg (2010)
4. Brilon, W., Stuwe, B., Bondzio, R.: Kleine Kreisverkehre-Empfehlungen Zum Einsatz und Zur Gestaltung. Ministerium Stadtentwicklung und Verkehr des Landes, Duisburg (1993)
5. Camus, R., Dall'Acqua, M., Longo, G.: Capacity and Queue Modelling in Unsignalized Roundabouts. In: Association for European Transport 2004, 1–34127, Trieste (2004)
6. Chodur, J.: Funkcjonowanie Skrzyżowań Drogowych w Warunkach Zmienności Ruchu. Monografia 347, seria Inżynieria Lądowa, Politechnika Krakowska, Kraków (2007)
7. Generalna Dyrekcja Dróg Krajowych i Autostrad: Metoda Obliczania Przepustowości Rond. Instrukcja obliczania, Warszawa (2004)
8. Generalna Dyrekcja Dróg Publicznych w Warszawie: Wytyczne Projektowania Skrzyżowań Drogowych. Część II. Ronda, Warszawa (2001)
9. Macioszek, E.: The Influence of Motorcycling and Cycling on Small One-Lane Roundabouts Capacity. In: Mikulski, J. (ed.) TST 2011. CCIS, vol. 239, pp. 291–298. Springer, Heidelberg (2011)
10. Macioszek, E.: Geometrical Determinants of Car Equivalents for Heavy Vehicles Crossing Circular Intersections. In: Mikulski, J. (ed.) TST 2012. CCIS, vol. 329, pp. 221–228. Springer, Heidelberg (2012)
11. Macioszek, E.: Modele Przepustowości Wlotów Skrzyżowań Typu Rondo w Warunkach Wzorcowych. Open Access Library, Gliwice (2013)
12. Mauro, R.: Calculation of Roundabouts. Capacity, Waiting Phenomena and Reliability. Springer, Heidelberg (2010)
13. Sierpiński, G.: Theoretical Model and Activities to Change the Modal Split of Traffic. In: Mikulski, J. (ed.) TST 2012. CCIS, vol. 329, pp. 45–51. Springer, Heidelberg (2012)
14. Sierpiński, G.: Travel Behaviour and Alternative Modes of Transportation. In: Mikulski, J. (ed.) TST 2011. CCIS, vol. 239, pp. 86–93. Springer, Heidelberg (2011)
15. Tollazzi, T., Rencelj, M., Rodosek, V., Zalar, B.: Traffic Safety of Older Drivers in Various Types of Road Intersections. Promet 22(3), 193–201 (2010)
16. Tracz, M., Chodur, J., Gaca, S., Gondek, S.: Instrukcja Projektowania Małych Rond. Załącznik do Zarządzenia, vol. (4). Ekodroga, Kraków (1996)
17. Verweij, C.A., et al.: Roundabouts-Application and Design. A Practical Manual. DHV Group and Royal Haskoning. Holandia (2009)

Evaluation of Railway Stations Reliability

Jerzy Mikulski

Silesian University of Technology, Faculty of Transport,
Krasinskiego 8, 40-019 Katowice, Poland
jerzy.mikulski@polsl.pl

Abstract. The paper presents possibilities of studying (checking) the operational reliability of a railway station. A schematic diagram of the station is the basis for such studies. Such studies may be carried out in the form of computer calculations. Reliability (probability) parameters of individual elements of railway traffic control systems are components of such simulations. The results give a possibility to change the layout of a railway station at the stage of designing. Studies on station's reliability (availability) should be obligatory for railway managements.

Keywords: railway station, reliability.

1   Introduction

The railway traffic control is a special case of control and may be considered as a separate area of automatic control.

Railway traffic control systems work in diversified, frequently most critical, operating conditions. The experience from such equipment operation confirms the dependence of proper systems' functioning on the reliability of their components.

All components of railway traffic control systems are required to show an operational certainty. The operational certainty is understood as a probability of fault (device defect) non-occurrence.

The term of a railway traffic control system operation as a technical object is understood as its use according to the purpose.

2   System Reliability

The system reliability is a probability that the system will be properly fulfilling its tasks during a predetermined period in specific environmental conditions. In accordance with the standard „Reliability; service quality" [PN-93/N-50191 /IEC 50 (191)] the term *reliability* should be understood as a set of properties describing the object's *availability*. The *availability* is the object's capability to remain in a condition enabling fulfilment of functional requirements.

J. Mikulski (Ed.): TST 2013, CCIS 395, pp. 105–114, 2013.
© Springer-Verlag Berlin Heidelberg 2013

Each system may be presented in a form of various combinations of its individual components. There are four types of system reliability structures: serial, parallel, mixed (parallel – serial, serial – parallel), and bridge-type.

A serial system of components has a feature that it is reliable, if each of its components is reliable. A failure of one component results in a failure of the whole system.

A system structure is referred to as parallel, if it is enough that one of components is useable to make the system to be in a useable condition.

A system structure is mixed, if the usability of more than one component, but less than all, is the condition for the system usability. Components of a mixed structure system may be divided into sets having a serial or parallel structure, and these sets make then systems connected in series or parallel.

The reliability of system $p(t)$ consisting of n independent components connected in series is equal to a product of those components reliability:

$$p(t) = \prod_{i=1}^{n} p_i(t)$$
(1)

The reliability of a system consisting of k independent components connected parallel is:

$$p(t) = 1 - f(t) = 1 - \prod_{i=1}^{k} f_i(t) = 1 - \prod_{i=1}^{k} [1 - p_i(t)]$$
(2)

The reliability of a serial – parallel system is:

$$p(x) = \left[1 - (1 - p_{11}p_{12} \cdots p_{1n})(1 - p_{21}p_{22} \cdots p_{2n}) \ldots 1 - p_{k1}p_{k2} \cdots p_{kn}) \right] \quad (3)$$

The reliability of a parallel – serial system is:

$$\begin{aligned} p = &\left[1 - (1 - p_{11})(1 - p_{21}) \ldots (1 - p_{k1}) \right] \cdot \\ &\cdot \left[1 - (1 - p_{12})(1 - p_{22}) \ldots (1 - p_{k2}) \right] \\ \ldots \ldots \quad \cdot \\ &\cdot \left[1 - (1 - p_{1n})(1 - p_{2n}) \ldots (1 - p_{kn}) \right] \end{aligned}$$
(4)

To calculate the reliability of a bridge-type structure system may be used a decomposition method (factorisation algorithm).

In this method the component, with respect to which the decomposition is carried out (e.g. component 5 in Fig. 1), is replaced once with an entirely reliable component, obtaining a parallel – serial structure, and then with an entirely unreliable component, obtaining a serial – parallel structure [3, 6].

Case A

If the above decomposition is possible, that is a passage through element no 5 is possible in both directions, then the reliability function is:

$$p = p_s\{[1 - f_1 f_2][1 - f_3 f_4]\} + f_s\{1 - [1 - p_1 p_3][1 - p_2 p_4]\} =$$
$$= p_s\{[1 - (1 - p_1)(1 - p_2)][1 - (1 - p_3)(1 - p_4)]\} + (1 - p_s)\{1 - [1 - p_1 p_3][1 - p_2 p_4]\} = \quad (5)$$
$$= p_s\{[p_1 + p_2 - p_1 p_2][p_3 + p_4 - p_3 p_4]\} + (1 - p_s)\{p_1 p_3 + p_2 p_4 - p_1 p_2 p_3 p_4\}$$

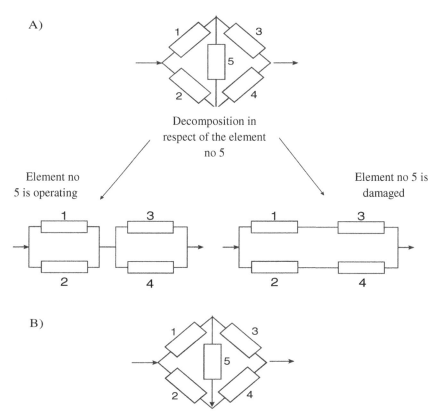

A)

Decomposition in respect of the element no 5

Element no 5 is operating

Element no 5 is damaged

B)

Fig. 1. Example of bridge structure decomposition (with respect to component 5) [3]. A – example of possible decomposition, B – example of impossible decomposition.

Case B

In the case, where a passage through elementnt 5 may occur only in the indicated direction (element 5 may be e.g. a device operating, when the current flows in a strictly defined direction; a unidirectional track may be another example), a bridge-type system decomposition is not possible due to a loss of information on the direction of passage through a reliable component 5 in a parallel – serial system. As a result, a graphical interpretation would present tracks, which are absent in the system. So in such a case the reliability function has a form of:

$$p = p_5\left[(p_1 + p_2 - p_1 p_2)p_4 + p_1 p_3(1 - p_4)\right] + (1 - p_5)\left[p_1 p_3 + p_2 p_4 - p_1 p_2 p_3 p_4\right] \quad (6)$$

The effectiveness of the decomposition method to a large extent depends on the choice of component (group of components), with respect to which a structural function should be decomposed. It should be situated in the system symmetry centre.

3   Railway Station Reliability

An availability structure of a railway station shows how many and which of its components should be capable of executing determined functions to consider that the station, as a whole, is capable of performing the determined tasks. The testing of a railway station availability consists in specifying its reliability.

So a station reliability may be determined based on its components reliability and this could be done in turn examining the station's schematic diagram.

Examples of two stations models will be presented next, together with general formulae, derived to calculate their availability (reliability).

Models of stations occurring on poorly loaded one-track lines were taken as typical in considerations.

The following pieces of equipment were included in station schematic diagrams and in block diagrams:

- signal (marked as e.g. „sem A")
- block system – starting signal release mechanism and home signal release (marked e.g. "Po" and "Ko")
- track insulation (marked e.g. „It1")
- points insulation (marked e.g. „Iz1")
- point detection (marked e.g. "Kn1+" and "Kn1-").

The following symbols for individual devices were taken in station's availability (reliability) calculations:

p_1 – signals reliability
p_2 – block system reliability
p_3 – track insulation reliability
p_4 – points insulation reliability
p_5 – point detection reliability, in normal position "+"
p_6 – point detection reliability, in turnout position "-".

In practice, defects of point detection in position "+" and "-" occur nearly with the same frequency, therefore $p_5 = p_6$ may be assumed in further calculations.

3.1   Model of a Station Example – Case 1

This is a model of a station adjoined by two one-track lines. This station has one running line and three additional tracks. Fig. 2 presents the station's schematic diagram and the block diagram.

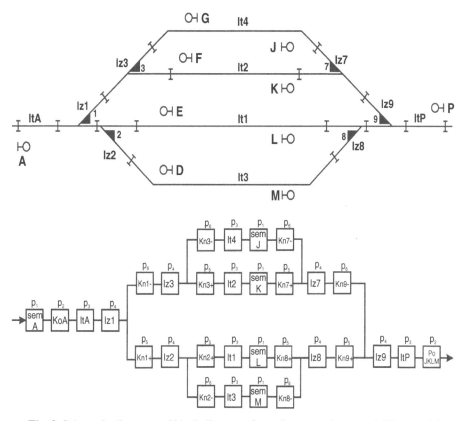

Fig. 2. Schematic diagram and block diagram of a station example – case 1 [Own study]

The station layout allows a stop of three trains and a passage of the fourth train. It is important, how the station reliability is affected by the layout of point switches and the number of station tracks and hence the number of all interconnected and working together devices.

The block diagram shows that this station model has a serial structure at the entry and exit, while the central part has a serial – parallel structure.

The following pieces of equipment (making a serial system) must be in running order to enable a passage through the station:

- signal A
- block: end KoA and starting PoJKLM

- track insulations: ItA and ItP
- points insulations: Iz1 and Iz9.

Then – depending on which devices are in running order – the train can drive on the station track:

- No 1 – when the following are in running order: Kn1+, Iz2, Kn2+, It1, semL, Kn8+, Iz8, Kn9+
- No 2 – when the following are in running order: Kn1-, Iz3, Kn3+, It2, semK, Kn7+, Iz7, Kn9-
- No 3 – when the following are in running order: Kn1+, Iz2, Kn2-, It3, semM, Kn8-, Iz8, Kn9+
- No 4 – when the following are in running order: Kn1-, Iz3, Kn3-, It4, semJ, Kn7-, Iz7, Kn9-.

The number of devices on a station example (case 1) is presented in Table 1.
So a general formula for this station reliability:

$$p_{st} = p_1 (p_2 p_3 p_4)^2 [1 - \{1 - (p_4 p_5)^2 (1 - [1 - p_1 p_3 (p_5)^2]^2)\}^2] \tag{7}$$

Table 1. Number of devices on station 1

Equipment	Number of pieces of equipment	Comments
Signals	5	
Line block systems	2	
Track insulations	6	
Points insulations	6	
Points	6	There are 12 point detection devices

3.2   Model of a Station Example – Case 2

Fig. 3 presents a model of station adjoined by two one-track lines and which has one running line and three additional tracks.

The number of tracks is the same as in case 1, however, the exit from track 3 via point switch 8 in case 1 was continued along point switch 9, while in this model point switch 9 is the last in the course (a train leaves track 3 not through point switch 8).

So the following pieces of equipment (making a serial system) must be in running order to enable a passage through the station:

- signal A
- block: end KoA and starting PoJKLM
- track insulations: ItA and ItP
- points insulations: Iz1 and Iz9

and then, depending on which station track the train will drive, the following must be in running order:

- on track No 1 - Kn1+, Iz2, Kn2+, It1, semL, Kn8+, Iz8, Kn9+
- on track No 2 - Kn1-, Iz3, Kn3+, It2, semK, Kn7+, Iz7, Kn8-, Iz8, Kn9+
- on track No 3 - Kn1+, Iz2, Kn2-, It3, semM, Kn9-
- on track No 4 - Kn1-, Iz3, Kn3-, It4, semJ, Kn7-, Iz7, Kn8-, Iz8, Kn9+.

The number of devices on a station example (case 2) is presented in Table 2.

Table 2. Number of devices on station 2

Equipment	Number of pieces of equipment	Comments
Signals	5	
Line block systems	2	
Track insulations	6	
Points insulations	6	
Points	6	There are 12 point detection devices

It results from the block diagram that this station model has a serial structure at the entry and exit, while the central part has a bridge-type structure with orientation (in Fig. 7 and in the introduced formula the bridge components are marked with digits from 1 to 5, in accordance with Fig. 5), where inside the bridge also serial and serial - parallel structures exist, and hence

$$p_{st} = p_1(p_2p_3)^2 (p_4p_5)^3 [p_1p_3p_5\{p_4[1+ (p_5p_4) \{1-[\ 1 - p_1p_3\,(p_5)^2]^2\}(1-p_5p_4)] + \\ + p_1p_3p_5(1-p_4p_5)\}+(1- p_1p_3\,(p_5)^2) \{p_1p_3 +(p_4)^2\{1- p_1p_3\,p_4(p_5)^3\} \\ \{1- [1 - p_1p_3\,(p_5)^2]^2\}\}] \qquad (8)$$

4   Software Implementation

The possession of a software way of station objects presentation (a computer simulation) allows primarily to use the created station's schematic diagram to analyse its operation (to run the trains traffic it is necessary to present the tracks layout, the traffic situation and the current condition of objects making the station).

Such a software allows also (after some modifications) to analyse the station in terms of other requirements. The testing of station reliability is one of such requirements.

For example Fig. 4 presents a plan of a station fragment (screen dump), while Fig. 5 a reliability diagram of this station obtained on its basis.

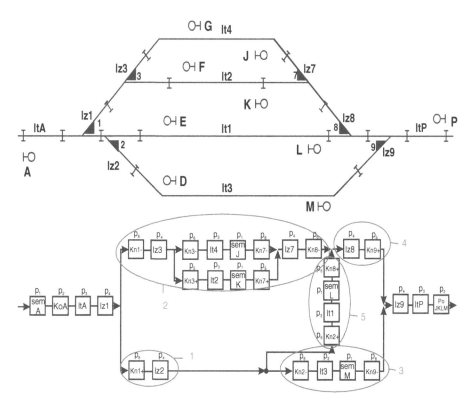

Fig. 3. Schematic diagram and block diagram of a station example – case 2 [Own study]

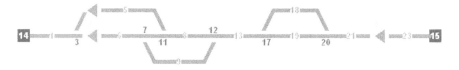

Fig. 4. Example of station's plan [Own study]

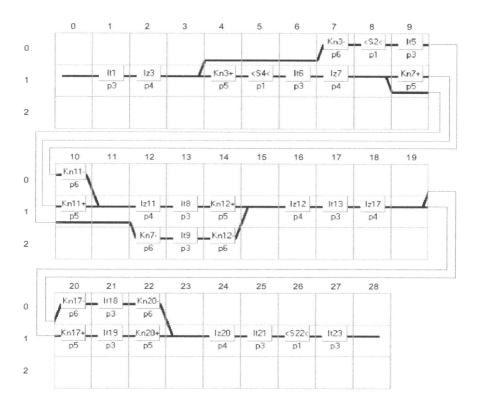

Fig. 5. Station's reliability diagram [Own study]

A reliability graph may be obtained based on the station's reliability diagram (Fig. 6).

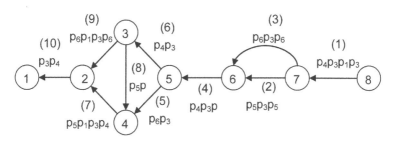

Fig. 6. Station's reliability diagram in the form of a graph [Own study]

5   Conclusion

To determine a station's reliability it is necessary to collect (process) the data from the railway traffic control equipment operation. Having gathered statistics on failure rates of individual components of railway traffic control systems (the size of individual groups and the period of statistics collection remain a separate issue) it is possible to calculate the availability (probability of reliability) of station examples (as well as any other analysed station).

Making use of detailed analyses of railway traffic control equipment service it is possible to determine a railway station's reliability without considering equipment inspections, and also the same availability figures (probabilities) taking into account normal inspections and predictive inspections (maintenance in optimal periods).

The automation of the reliability structure formation based on the existing station's track layout allows a quick comparison of alternative solutions. It also enables a quick answer to the question: in what way it is most favourable to modify or to expand the station's track layout?

A system for unreliability analyses and for forecasting fitness of railway traffic control equipment in railway stations as well as testing, on this basis, of station reliability shall be obligatory introduced on the entire railway network as an operational strategy. Reliability (availability) calculations of the station shall be also the object of interest for investment services prior to making a decision on the "appearance" and size of a future, newly constructed station.

References

1. Dąbrowa–Bajon, M.: Podstawy sterowania ruchem kolejowym, Oficyna Wydawnicza Politechniki Warszawskiej, Warszawa (2002)
2. Gołkowska, G.: Analiza niezawodności urządzeń sterowania ruchem kolejowym, Praca dyplomowa pod kierunkiem J. Mikulskiego, Katowice (2003)
3. Karpiński, J., Korczak, E.: Metody oceny niezawodności dwustanowych systemów technicznych, Wydawnictwo Instytutu Badań Systemowych PAN, Warszawa (1990)
4. Mikulski, J.: Influence of railway traffic control equipment malfunctions on traffic fluidity, Mezinarodni vedecka konference při přiležitosti 50 let założeni Fakulty Strojni, Ostrava (2000)
5. Mikulski, J., Sobański, M.: Niezawodność i bezpieczeństwo urządzeń prowadzenia ruchu kolejowego, Prace Komisji Naukowych PAN, Oddział Katowice 24, 62–63 (2000)
6. Ważyńska–Fiok, K.: Podstawy teorii eksploatacji i niezawodności systemów transportowych, Wydawnictwa Politechniki Warszawskiej, Warszawa (1993)
7. Program Reliability Workbench, Isograph, http://www.isograph.com (date of access May 12, 2013)
8. Lüley, P., Franeková, M., Hudák, M.: Safety and functionality assessment of railway applications in terms of software. In: Mikulski, J. (ed.) TST 2012. CCIS, vol. 329, pp. 396–405. Springer, Heidelberg (2012)
9. Franeková, M., Výrostko, M.: Approaches to a Solution of Key Management System for Cryptography Communications within Railway Applications. In: Mikulski, J. (ed.) TST 2012. CCIS, vol. 329, pp. 301–313. Springer, Heidelberg (2012)

RFID-Based Traffic Signs Recognition System

Krzysztof Małecki and Kamil Kopaczyk

West Pomeranian University of Technology, Dept. of Computer Science,
Żołnierska 52, 71-210 Szczecin, Poland
{kmalecki,kkopaczyk}@wi.zut.edu.pl

Abstract. This paper presents the concept of a traffic sign recognition system based on RFID. Two computer programs are developed. The first allows the encoding of RFID tags, the second one reads the signs and displays them on the screen in such way that the driver had knowledge of the most important traffic signs, under which he or she is. In order to prove proper operation of the model, it was prepared in a micro scale. This solution was compared with other similar and the authors show differences.

Keywords: traffic sign recognition, RFID.

1 Introduction

Rapid technological development, especially that of automatization and informatization, has led to many innovative solutions which support the users, provide comfort and simplify certain aspects of life. This process has not omitted the automotive branch. Cars are used more and more frequently and the manufacturers take part in a technological race aiming to attract customers with brand new useful facilities.

One of the executed ideas is supporting drivers in the process of recognition and memorization of traffic signs in effect on specific roads. A driver is obliged to recognize and abide those signs, and taking into consideration the fact that they are constantly changing, support in this regard has proved to be very helpful. Since 2006, when Siemens announced having created a system (Siemens VDO Traffic Sign Recognition), which among other things recognizes traffic signs, more and more companies have been adapting this solution in their models. Currently, many similar systems exist. Most of them utilize a (sometimes GPS enabled) built in camera inside the vehicle with an on-board computer analyzing the captured picture. Upon detection of a sign, the system may – depending on its functionality – display the sign, make a sound or e.g. alert that the driver is not driving on the correct side of the road. All of this has one aim – to make it easier for the drivers to navigate roads and increase the safety of vehicle users and, indirectly, pedestrians.

Video camera based systems are weather dependent. According to users, in everyday situations, the effectiveness of such systems leaves a lot to be desired. Rain, fog, and insufficient lighting increase the number of incorrect interpretations.

This paper describes a method of traffic sign recognition based on RFID technology. The general concept of such a system has been presented in [1] and focuses on the

J. Mikulski (Ed.): TST 2013, CCIS 395, pp. 115–122, 2013.
© Springer-Verlag Berlin Heidelberg 2013

use of radio waves to identify previously encoded objects (RFID tags). RFID tags placed on a lane store information on the traffic signs situated by this lane, while an RFID reader and system are responsible for the recognition and proper presentation of those signs to the driver. In this paper, the authors present a new traffic sign coding system which allows for a significant decrease in the number of RFID tags.

1.1   RFID Technology

Radio-frequency identification (RFID) [2, 3, 4] is the wireless non-contact use of radio-frequency electromagnetic fields to transfer data, for the purposes of automatically identifying and tracking tags attached to objects. The tags contain electronically stored information. Some tags are powered and read at short ranges (a few meters) via magnetic fields (electromagnetic induction). Others use a local power source such as a battery, or else have no battery but collect energy from the interrogating EM field, and then act as a passive transponder to emit microwaves or UHF radio waves (i.e., electromagnetic radiation at high frequencies). Battery powered tags may operate at hundreds of meters. Unlike a bar code, the tag does not necessarily need to be within line of sight of the reader, and may be embedded in the tracked object.

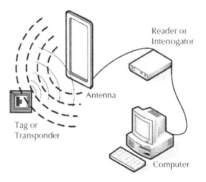

Fig. 1. Concept of the RFID technology [5]

RFID systems vary in many aspects: work frequency and read range, memory type and tag memory capacity, data destination and security. RFID reader is a device responsible for the communication with tags. Generating and receiving waves is possible thanks to one or two integrated antennas which detect tags in their range, decode them and sometimes write to them. The most frequent variant of an RFID system is the cooperation of passive transponders and an active reader with its own (external) power source.

The idea of the object identification process is to send a radio wave via the reader's antenna and await a response from encountered tags. The antenna generates a varying EM wave which induces voltage powering tags' circuits (fig. 1). After accumulating enough energy, the transponder responds by modulating the EM field induced by its coil, sending out the data it contains, which is picked up by the same (or another, if the reader has two) antenna.

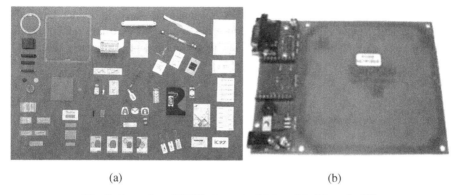

(a)   (b)

Fig. 2. Examples of RFID elements: (a) tags [6], (b) reader [7]

Tags are small circuits with the task of providing communication between their memory, processor, battery and an external reader (via an integrated antenna). Because of the minuscule size, a tag can be of any size (not smaller than the circuit) and integrated with virtually any material (fig. 2a) that does not affect radio communication and allows for correct communication with a reader (fig. 2b).

2   Traffic Sign Recognition

In this chapter, certain technical aspects of the system are described: the idea of the traffic sign recognition (TSR) system, its architecture, modules and their communication as well as user interface of both developed applications.

2.1   Concept of the Traffic Sign Recognition with the Use of RFID Technology

The general idea of traffic sign recognition based on RFID technology is presented in fig. 3 [1].

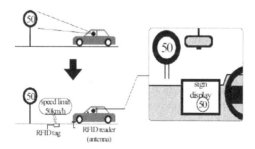

Fig. 3. General concept of the use of RFID technology in the TSR process [1]

The authors of this publication focused on devising a new method of encoding traffic signs in RFID tags which allows to reduce the number of used tags which results in lower costs of the implementation of such a solution. Fig. 4a depicts the RFID encoding method according to [1], and fig. 4b – the new encoding method.

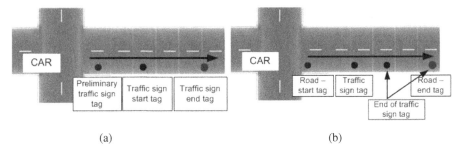

(a)   (b)

Fig. 4. RDIF tags encoding method: (a) according to the authors of [1], (b) presented in this article

In [1] the authors suggested using three tags for each sign. In case of a greater number of signs, such a method is largely ineffective, as presented in table 1. The authors of this publication suggest encoding each road and its end with two tags and each traffic sign with one tag and the end of the range of this sign with another tag. In case of a speed limit, a new sign is also the end of the previous one – there can only be one speed limitation in effect for each type of vehicles at a time. The authors have taken into consideration the fact that at one section of a road various types of vehicles may move with different maximum speeds.

2.2   Assumptions and Aim of the Work

For an information system to work correctly, assumptions and restrictions need to be specified. For this work the authors have developed: a traffic sign encoding mechanism (as the elaboration of the idea presented in [1]), an encoded sign recognition mechanism and a mechanism displaying the signs so that the driver can quickly interpret them. Prepared applications are based on own algorithms. It was assumed that the speed limit signs are very important and the system is supposed to provide constant information on the maximum allowed speed on a set section of a road. In this case the speed limit tags are only overwritten which makes it impossible to revoke a sign without passing another one. To function correctly, the system does not require any additional devices such as cameras or GPS receivers.

Due to the complexity of the topic of the data transmission security, it will not be described in this article.

2.3   System Model and Architecture

To ensure correct work of the system, the functionality has been divided into two main programs (TrafficSignManager and TrafficSignReader), so that they can work independently and the user has access to operations required for a specific application.
A general model of the developed system is presented in fig. 5.

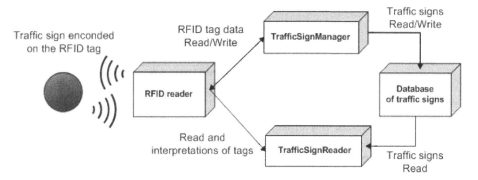

Fig. 5. Architecture of the developed system

TrafficSignManager – allows for adding new signs, deleting existing ones and modification of related metadata.

TrafficSignReader – the task of this application is detecting tags located within the reader's range, reading the stored data and its appropriate interpretation. The program offers additional functions:

- grouping signs (by category: prohibitory, mandatory, warning, information). This introduces a certain convention which allows the user to quickly check the category they are looking for instead of having to search for a certain sign in the entire workspace of the application. There is also an option to select the number of displayed signs of a category and to look up the signs of the chosen type if there are more of them than the number set in the options.
- turning sound on (off) – in case of reading a sign that has not been displayed yet, a sound notification is given (or not). This aims to increase safety and comfort of using the application and reducing the necessity of maintaining eye contact with the device running the application.
- Categorizing traffic signs – displaying only signs from a user-specified set. There are three predefined sets to choose from: car, truck, other. Thanks to this, only signs from a selected collection are displayed on the screen. This allows for optimization of the size of needed workspace and minimizes the amount of information useless for the user.

The project of the graphical interface assumed the clarity and intuitivity of the application. The main aim was for the driver to pay as little attention as possible to the device displaying the signs while receiving all the information they need. Thus, the application's workspace has been divided into six equal parts (2 rows, 3 columns)

Fig. 6. TrafficSignReader application screen

hereinafter called panels. One of the panels has been reserved solely for displaying a speed limit sign and the type of road one travels. Thanks to this, the driver is able to quickly check present speed limit.

Four panels have been designed to display separate types of signs (prohibitory, mandatory, warning, information). The number of signs displayed on these panels depends on the application's settings (available options: 1,2,4). Additionally, if the number of signs of a category exceeds the number selected in the options, there is a possibility to temporary look them up.

Fig. 7. Exemplary tag encoding screen in TrafficSignManager application

The graphical interface of the TrafficSignManager application has been designed to be compact yet clear and easy to use. Fig. 7 presents the application's main window which displays all signs added to the system and allows to modify them, add new ones and write signs to RFID tags.

2.4   Experimental Results

In order to prove that the presented method of encoding signs is more effective than the one suggested in the article [1], a few experiments have been carried out. The first one involved simulating the quantity of tags on a set section of a road. All possible signs have been included. The results are presented in fig. 8 and table 1

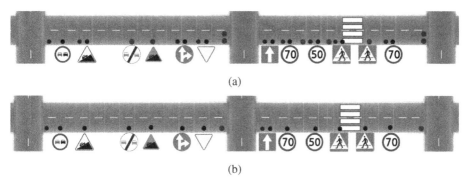

Fig. 8. Example 1 – RFID tags placement on a set section of a road: (a) accordingly to the method presented in [1], (b) accordingly to the method presented in this publication

The second example (fig. 9) depicts a short section of a road with a small number of traffic signs. In this case, the method presented in [1] proved to be better.

Fig. 9. Example 2 – RFID tags placement on a short section of a road: (a) accordingly to the method presented in [1], (b) accordingly to the method presented in this publication

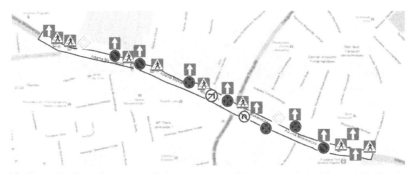

Fig. 10. Example 3 – placement of signs on one of the streets (ul. Adama Mickiewicza) in Szczecin (Poland)

To visualize how important a topic is tackled in this paper, the authors have shown the number of traffic signs on a selected section of a road (fig. 10) in the center of the city of Szczecin (Poland). It is true that many of them are repeated because of intersections. However, many traffic signs distract drivers.

The results of comparison of all described examples are presented in table 1.

Table 1. Comparison of traffic sign encoding methods, by the amount of used RFID tags

Number	Number of RFID tags for [1]	Number of RFID tags (this publication)
Example 1 (fig. 1)	27	16
Example 2 (fig. 2)	6	7
Example 3 (fig. 3)	84	50

The method presented in this paper is the more effective, the more traffic signs are situated on a section of a road.

3   Conclusion

A new method of encoding tags for a general concept of traffic sign recognition with the use of RFID technology has been presented. A comparison has been made and a better adaptation in terms of the number of used tags (the fewer, the better) has been proved. This directly influences the cost of implementation such a system in cities. Two applications have been proposed in the article: TrafficSignManager – for RFID tags management and TrafficSignReader – for RFID reader handling, sign recognition and display. Further research will aim to determine whether a large number of tags and readers will not cause interference of radio waves.

References

1. Sato, Y., Makane, K.: Development and Evaluation of In-Vechicle Signing System Utilizing RFID Tags as Digital Traffic Signals. Int. J. ITS Res. 4, 53–58 (2006)
2. Bhuptani, M., Moradpour, S.: RFID Field Guide: Deploying Radio Frequency Identification Systems. Book (2005)
3. Brown, D.: RFID Implementation. Book (2006)
4. Shepard, S.: RFID: Radio Frequency Identification. McGraw-Hill Networking Professional (2004)
5. http://www.alexan-tech.com (date of access July 26, 2013)
6. http://www.rfidbr.com.br (date of access July 26, 2013)
7. http://www.netronix.pl (date of access July 26, 2013)

Overview of Telematics-Based Prognostics and Health Management Systems for Commercial Vehicles

Mohammad Mesgarpour[1], Dario Landa-Silva[1], and Ian Dickinson[2]

[1] ASAP Research Group, School of Computer Science, University of Nottingham,
Nottingham, NG8 1BB, UK
[2] Microlise Ltd, Eastwood, Nottingham, NG16 3AG, UK
{mohammad.mesgarpour,dario.landasilva}@nottingham.ac.uk,
ian.dickinson@microlise.com

Abstract. Prognostics and Health Management/Monitoring (PHM) are methods to assess the health condition and reliability of systems for the purpose of maximising operational reliability and safety. Recently, PHM systems are emerging in the automotive industry. In the commercial vehicle sector, reducing the maintenance cost and downtime while also improving the reliability of vehicle components can have a major impact on fleet performance and hence business competitiveness. Nowadays, telematics and GPS are used mainly for fleet tracking and diagnostics purposes. Increased numbers of sensors installed on commercial vehicles, advancement of data analytics and computational intelligence methods, increased capabilities for on-board data processing as well as in the cloud, are creating an opportunity for PHM systems to be deployed on commercial vehicles and hence improve the overall operational efficiency.

Keywords: prognostics, health management, telematics.

1 Introduction

Telematics have traditionally been used to track the position of vehicles using the Global Positioning System (GPS), but with the power of cloud data storage and computing, telecommunication and data analytics, various other services such as: fuel saving, fleet performance management, driving behaviour monitoring, dynamic routing, diagnostics and prognostics are being offered by telematics providers. Therefore, the number of fleet operators and Original Equipment Manufacturers (OEM's) that have started to use telematics has increased considerably in recent years. The main aim is to reduce costs and the impact on the environment as well as improving resource productivity, efficiency and asset management.

Moreover, as a result of advances in the automotive industry, commercial vehicles have become more advanced in technology and hence, reliability of individual critical components is an important factor for improving the overall reliability and quality of the vehicle. Commercial vehicle can be defined as "any motorized road vehicle which by its type of construction and equipment is designed for, and capable of, transporting, whether for payment or not: (a) more than nine persons, including the driver; or

J. Mikulski (Ed.): TST 2013, CCIS 395, pp. 123–130, 2013.
© Springer-Verlag Berlin Heidelberg 2013

(b) goods" [6]. Therefore, trucks, coaches, buses, vans and trailers are categorised as commercial vehicles.

Telematics-based on-board tracking systems are comprised of three core parts: a GPS location tracking system, a CAN-bus (controller area network) interface and a supplement data collector. The GPS location tracking system transmits the location of the vehicle at a regular timed interval, distance or after predefined event triggers. The system interface to the CAN-bus is used to read, decode and pre-process the data from the vehicle bus. The supplementary data includes the on-board unit state-of-health, state-of-function data and external information such as ambient temperature.

The server-side of a tracking system is responsible for collecting, processing and storing all data transmitted by the on-board tracking system and displaying the status of the vehicle as well as statistical reports to the users (e.g. fleet managers, fleet operators, and drivers) via a web portal, smart phone apps or in-cab screen. On-board and server side systems can communicate via various networks such as cellular wireless (e.g. 2G/3G/4G) and Wireless LANs.

Recently, Prognostics and Health Management/Monitoring (PHM) is becoming more important to fleet managers because it plays an important role in improving profit margins. PHM systems aim to predict the future behaviour, state-of-health and remaining useful life (RUL) of individual vehicle components based on assessing the current and past health (diagnosis) and future health (prognosis) [26]. The feasibility of designing and implementing PHM systems has increased with the wider availability of low cost and more accurate sensors in commercial vehicles, powerful on-board telematics systems, fast mobile data communication and cloud computing.

PHM systems in commercial vehicles can help to meet several critical goals: eliminate or at least minimise the risk of unexpected breakdowns and unscheduled downtime, minimise unscheduled and/or unnecessary periodic maintenance, reduce maintenance costs (including spare parts and labour), improve the reliability of the fleet, keep the fleet in top performance condition, reduce warranty costs, improve customer service

On-Board Diagnostics (OBD) systems can be used to evaluate the health of vehicle components. Various legislations state that all manufactured HGV's in Europe after the 1st of October 2006 should be equipped with an OBD system [7]. Therefore, OBD became a standard component of modern vehicles.

This paper conducts a brief literature review of PHM systems in commercial vehicles in order to identify key development and challenges. Section 2 makes a review of the main maintenance strategies and then Section 3 discusses the literature on vehicle predictive maintenance. Section 4 discusses some of the key challenges for the further application of PHM in the automotive industry. Finally, Section 5 looks into the future of telematics-based PHM systems for commercial vehicles.

2   Repair and Maintenance Strategies

Several maintenance strategies can be identified in the literature and they can be classified into two main types: corrective and preventive. In a corrective, run-to-failure or reactive maintenance strategy, the equipment is repaired after a breakdown or an obvious fault occurs without performing any scheduled maintenance. Within preventive or proactive maintenance strategies, three categories can be identified: scheduled preventive maintenance, condition-based maintenance (CBM), and predictive maintenance (PdM).

In scheduled preventive maintenance (also known as time-based or periodic), inspections and (possibly) repairs are performed at specific interval times given by a pre-specified schedule. Time intervals are usually calculated based on age, usage or failure distribution [3]. In CBM, the performance of the system is monitored in real time and maintenance tasks are triggered when some reading measurements go beyond a predefined limit (threshold) or tolerance. The PdM strategy is based on collecting measurements about the state of the systems in order to analyse and find trends and patterns. This type of analysis is then used to predict the RUL, and hence the degradation and the failure time of the system [4, 9, 3, 21]. The PdM strategy aims to reduce the risk of unexpected failures, which may occur before the next scheduled maintenance, as well as unnecessary scheduled maintenance activities [17]. In fact, CBM and PdM can be considered maintenance strategies of the same type because both are based on monitoring the system status [9]. However, CBM can be considered mainly a reactive strategy while PdM can be considered as a more proactive strategy.

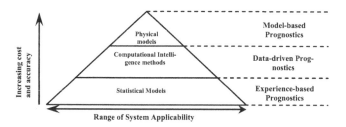

Fig. 1. Hierarchy of prognostic approaches

Prognostics usually refers to a process carried out to prognosticate or predict a failure in advance [11]. There are mainly four categories: experience-based, model-based, data-driven based and hybrid [13], [25]. The experience-based or statistical approach is mainly based on historical service failure data and expert judgment for developing a rule-based model. The model-based or physical degradation approach is based on the physical fundamentals of a system. Although, this approach is highly accurate for a specific system, any minor changes in the component and operating conditions require the model to be updated. The data-driven approach requires large amount of historical failure data to capture the system behaviour using data analytics and machine learning techniques. The main disadvantage of this approach is that it highly depends on quality and quantity of historical data [20].

The hybrid approach is a combination of one or more of the other approaches and seeks to benefit from their respective advantages. One of the main applications of the hybrid approach is in multi-component systems. Figure 1 illustrates the hierarchy of these main types of prognostic approaches [19]. The pyramid in Figure 1 indicates that there is a trade-off between the applicability range of the approach and its accuracy and that as expected, the more accurate the approach the more costly it is.

It is beneficial to note that the e-maintenance concept which has recently been discussed several times in the literature refers to the integration of information and communication technologies within the maintenance strategies [12, 24]. Integrated Vehicle Health Management (IVHM) is another concept which is derived from the Health and Usage Monitoring System (HUMS) developed for helicopters during the 1980s and 1900s. The IVHM system is originally designed to determine, verify and solve the aircraft faults [8].

3   An Overview of PHM System for Vehicle

The amount of literature on prognostics systems for vehicles is much less than on diagnostics systems as many research studies have focused on fault detection in mechanical or electrical components of the vehicle which is mainly of interest to the Original Equipment Manufacturers (OEM's). However, some of the research studies that we have identified in the area of vehicle prognostics systems are discussed in this section.

Grantner et al. [10] introduced a fuzzy model to diagnose the axle fatigue of light trucks with future applications to military ground vehicles. The load stress, the number of cycles of the load stress and previous damage are input to the model. Then, the system predicts the RUL of the axle based on the cumulative damage to the axle, which is given by the fuzzy model. The expert knowledge and linear damage model are used to generate the fuzzy rules and membership functions.

Ahmed et al. [2] designed a discrete hidden Markov model to detect manifold air leakage in the air intake system of gasoline engine and approximate the health status of inlet manifold. The manifold pressure, engine speed and throttle position are used as inputs to the model. They identified four states for different health conditions: a fault free stage, an intermediate fault stage 1, an intermediate fault stage 2 and a fault stage, quantified based as 0%, 4.5%, 9% and 18% of wide open throttle, respectively. Results of the experiment performed on a 1.3L production vehicle engine through On-Board Diagnostic version II (OBD-II) showed that the proposed model can be helpful for prognosis of air leaks.

Byttner et al. [5] presented the consensus self-organised method that aims to find and select related sensor data on each vehicle to be used in detecting faults that are not predefined. The model is generated and adopted on an on-board system while the vehicle is being used. They used the linear principle encoding analysis to reduce the volume of data transmitted from on-board systems to the server. Testing on real data for a cooling system of a city bus showed that their method has the potential to be used for self-discovery fault detection systems.

Zhang et al. [27] proposed the concept of connected vehicle diagnostics and prognostics (CVDP), which has been partially deployed in production at General Motors (GM). This approach aims to demonstrate that fleet-based cross-vehicle analysis can reduce trouble-shooting time by improving root-cause analysis. CVDP remotely and continuously collects vehicle engineering data and turns it into knowledge for the diagnostics and prognostics system. Moreover, CVDP also gathers data from vehicle assembly lines and repair workshops. Then, once the data is verified and validated, system faults are detected and RUL of various components are predicted. It has been reported that the battery monitoring system ECU has been programmed and implemented in production through OnStar [22] system to evaluate the benefits of the CDVP based on current-based and voltage-based algorithms.

Last [17] and Last et al. [18] presented data mining models to predict vehicle failures. Vehicle sensor readings and warranty failure data are used as inputs to single- and multi-target info-fuzzy network algorithms with minority oversampling and majority under-sampling techniques to issue the probability and the timing of as a case study. The data attribute in the model are: state-of-charge, battery age, off asleep amp hours, temperature, amp-hours during ignition off and travelled distance.

Instead of using classical Monte Carlo simulation methods, Abbas et al. [1] used a particle filtering-based approach to predict the failure mode in vehicle electrical power generation and storage systems. The advantages of this approach are that it needs less number of samples and is also capable of dealing with complex nonlinear and/or non-Gaussian cases. Their particle filtering-based approach has been implemented and tested using simulation data to determine the current level of lead-acid battery grid corrosion and determine the probability of the time-to-failure. The Arrhenius degradation model and estimation of internal resistance of battery based on measured voltage and current during cranking are two items required by the suggested method.

An engine oil quality estimation model based on component analysis and statistical analysis methods was introduced by Jun et al. [14, 15]. The model estimates the quality of the oil by analysing its degradation status. To design the model, various relations between engine mission profile data such as mileage, number of engine start-up, etc. and oil quality indicator were studied. As the model only requires the mission profile data, no sampling engine oil is needed. The main drawbacks of the introduced algorithm are that it only focuses on providing oil viscosity indicator and that there is a lack of guidance regarding when oil should be changed.

It has to be noted that as the number of electric and hybrid vehicles increased, PHM of lithium-ion batteries has attracted a lot of research interest in vehicle prognostics systems [23].

4   Challenges

From this brief literature review, there is some evidence that PHM systems are being deployed in vehicles, specifically in commercial vehicles, but very slowly despite the fact that their use could bring considerable cost savings. Some of the main challenges that we believe remain to be tackled are discussed in this section.

In recent years, the electronics control and software (ECS) systems in vehicles have become more complicated and this can bring three main challenges for the development and deployment of diagnostics and prognostics systems: unexpected new fault root in the interaction between the different components and/or sub-systems, infrequent and intermittent non-identified faults, which can be reported as "No Fault Found", high complexity of predicting the system RUL [27].

As many PHM systems have been developed relatively recently, it is difficult to accurately perform a sound cost-benefit analysis and to identify tangible benefits of implementing such PHM systems. Although increasing the sensitivity of a PHM system can reduce the probability of predicting a potential future fault or failure (true positive), it may also increase the possibility of trigging false alerts (false positive) when the system is in a reasonable good level of state of health. In contrast, if the sensitivity of the PHM system is not high, it is more likely that it will not be able to predict potential failures or faults (false negative). The possibility of giving false positive and/or false negative alerts seems to be one of the main criticisms of PHM systems.

PHM concepts were pioneered in the aerospace industry and then they have been applied in other sectors such as the automotive industry and particularly commercial vehicles. Although deploying PHM on commercial vehicles is creating an opportunity to get benefits with predictive maintenance systems, the accuracy of the system can be affected by the number of sensors that can be located in vehicles, which is significantly less than in aircraft.

PHM methods proposed in the literature often require more sensors with a high level of accuracy and/or computing power than is available on-board today's vehicles [5]. In addition, although most of the published prognostics studies state the intention to actually introduce a prognostic system into operation, the focus has been more on the fault detection and the prognostic system has been left for future work with no much evidence of this being realised yet. Moreover, a very limited number of research studies address the application of prognostic systems in maintenance management [3]. These issues can be resolved by efficient communication among theory developers, practitioners and manufacturers in the area of reliability and maintenance [13].

5   Conclusion

With PHM systems, maintenance work can be scheduled in advance of the failure. The maintenance and downtime therefore become significantly shorter with prognostics relative to diagnostics.

Currently, a large volume of data is being provided by the vehicle's electronic control units (ECU's) which can be extremely valuable to the process of vehicle health monitoring, but this is not yet widely or proactively used. Typically, each ECU is responsible for its own diagnostics and fault management, which is not beneficial for distributed functions. Moreover, system parameters should be monitored relative to each other. Therefore, an integrated and intelligent approach is appropriate to diagnose and predict system-wide failure in vehicles.

There has been considerable investment in telematics-based business solutions in the last few years. This has increased the pace of development and deployment of telematics-based PHM systems for commercial vehicles as telematics plays a key role in the PHM system. Moreover, in response to the demand for supplying more accurate and extensive data by fleet operators, the OEM's have started installing more advanced sensors in vehicles which can improve the accuracy and precision of future PHM systems.

Furthermore, predictive modelling has started to produce some benefits for fleet operators in various areas such as traffic, available parking spaces and weather. In the coming years, an even wider adoption of this approach could be used to build a better and more efficient fleet in terms of maintenance, routing and scheduling.

Acknowledgments. The research project is funded by the Technology Strategy Board and is being carried at Microlise Ltd in partnership with the University of Nottingham.

References

1. Abbas, M., Aldo, A.F., Marcos, E.O., Vachtsevanos, G.J.: An Intelligent Diagnostic/Prognostic Framework for Automotive Electrical Systems. In: 2007 IEEE Intelligent Vehicles Symposium, pp. 352–357 (2007)
2. Ahmed, Q., Iqbal, A., Taj, I., Ahmed, K.: Gasoline Engine Intake Manifold Leakage Diagnosis/Prognosis using Hidden Markov Model. Int. J. Innovative Comput. Inform. Control 8, 4661–4674 (2012)
3. Asmai, S.A., Hussin, B., Yusof, M.M.: A Framework of an Intelligent Maintenance Prognosis Tool. In: 2010 IEEE Second International Conference on Computer Research and Development, pp. 241–245 (2010)
4. Bevilacqua, M., Braglia, M.: The Analytic Hierarchy Process Applied to Maintenance Strategy Selection. Reliab. Eng. & Syst. Safe. 70(1), 71–83 (2000)
5. Byttner, S., Rögnvaldsson, T., Svensson, M.: Consensus Self-organized Models for Fault Detection (COSMO). Eng. Appl. Artif. Intel. 24(5), 833–839 (2011)
6. EC (European Community): Directive 85/347/EEC of European Parliament and Council of the European Union amending Directive 68/297/EEC on the standardization of provisions regarding the duty-free admission of fuel contained in the fuel tanks of commercial motor vehicles. Official Journal of the European Communities L183 (1985)
7. EC (European Community): Directive 2005/55/EC of the European Parliament and of the Council on the approximation of the laws of the Member States relating to the measures to be taken against the emission of gaseous and particulate pollutants from compression-ignition engines for use in vehicles, and the emission of gaseous pollutants from positive-ignition engines fuelled with natural gas or liquefied petroleum gas for use in vehicles. Official Journal of the European Union L275, 1–32 (2005)
8. Ferreiro, S., Arnaiz, A., Sierra, B., Irigoien, I.: Application of Bayesian Network in Prognostics for New Integrated Vehicle Health Management Concept. Expert Sys. Appl. 39, 6402–6418 (2012)
9. Garg, A., Deshmukh, S.G.: Maintenance Management: Literature Review and Directions. J. Qual. Maint. Eng. 12(3), 205–238 (2006)
10. Grantner, J., Bazuin, B., Dong, L., Alshawawreh, J.: Condition Based Maintenance for Light Trucks. In: 2010 IEEE International Conference on Systems Man and Cybernetics (2010)

11. Hooks, D.C., Dubuque, M.W., Simon, K.D.: System and Method for Analysing Different Scenarios for Operating and Designing Equipment. The Boeing Company, US Patent, US6532426B1 (2003)
12. Holmberg, K.: E-maintenance. Springer (2010)
13. Jardine, A.K.S., Lin, D., Banjevic, D.: A Review on Machinery Diagnostics and Prognostics Implementing Condition-based Maintenance. Mech. Syst. Signal Pr. 20(7), 1483–1510 (2006)
14. Jun, H.-B., Kiritsis, D., Gambera, M., Xirouchakis, P.: Predictive Algorithm to Determine the Suitable Time to Change Automotive Engine Oil. Comput. Ind. Eng. 51(4), 671–683 (2006)
15. Jun, H.-B., Conte, F.L., Kiritsis, D., Xirouchakis, P.: A Predictive Algorithm for Estimating the Quality of Vehicle Engine Oil. Int. J Ind. Eng.: Theory, Applications and Practice 15(4), 386–396 (2008)
16. Laman, F.C., Bose, C.S.C., Dasgupta, S.R.: Accelerated Failure Testing of Valve Regulated Lead-acid Batteries using Gas Studies. In: 1998 Twentieth International Telecommunications Energy Conference, pp. 74–78 (1998)
17. Last, M.: Vehicle Failure Prediction Using Warranty and Telematics Data. Learn. 29(3), 245–260 (2011)
18. Last, M., Sinaiski, A., Subramania, H.S.: Predictive Maintenance with Multi-target Classification Models. In: Nguyen, N.T., Le, M.T., Świątek, J. (eds.) ACIIDS 2010, Part II. LNCS (LNAI), vol. 5991, pp. 368–377. Springer, Heidelberg (2010)
19. Lebold, M., Thurston, M.: Open Standards for Condition-Based Maintenance and Prognostics Systems. In: 5th Annual Maintenance and Reliability Conference (2001)
20. Luo, J., Namburu, M., Pattipati, K., Qiao, L., Kawamoto, M., Chigusa, S.A.C.S.: Model-based Prognostic Techniques [maintenance applications]. In: 2003 AUTOTESTCON IEEE Systems Readiness Technology Conference, pp. 330–340 (2003)
21. Medina-Oliva, G., Weber, P., Iung, B.: PRM_based Patterns for Knowledge Formalisation of Industrial Systems to Support Maintenance Strategies Assessment. Reliab. Eng. Syst. Safe. 116, 38–56 (2013)
22. OnStar: OnStar (2013), https://www.onstar.com (retrieved June 5, 2013)
23. Rezvani, M., AbuAli, M., Lee, S., Lee, J., Ni, J.: A Comparative Analysis of Techniques for Electric Vehicle Battery Prognostics and Health Management (PHM). In: SAE International (2011)
24. Tinga, T.: Introduction: The Basics of Failure. In: Principles of Loads and Failure Mechanisms, pp. 3–10. Springer, London (2013)
25. Tran, V.T., Yang, B.-S., Tan, A.C.C.: Multi-step Ahead Direct Prediction for the Machine Condition Prognosis using Regression Trees and Neuro-fuzzy Systems. Expert Syst. Appl. 36(5), 9378–9387 (2009)
26. Vachtsevanos, G., Lewis, F., Roemer, M., Hess, A., Wu, B.: Intelligent Fault Diagnosis and Prognosis for Engineering Systems. John Wiley & Sons, Inc. (2006)
27. Zhang, Y., Gantt, G.W., Rychlinski, M.J., Edwards, R.M., Correia, J.J., Wolf, C.E.: Connected Vehicle Diagnostics and Prognostics, Concept, and Initial Practice. IEEE Transactions on Reliability 58(2), 286–294 (2009)

Computer Analysis of the Setting Force

Jakub Młyńczak

Silesian University of Technology, Faculty of Transport
Krasinskiego 8, 40-019 Katowice, Poland
jakub.mlynczak@polsl.pl

Abstract. The article presents the topic of computer analysis of setting force measurements in the railway switch drive-crossover system. Two algorithms for determining the setting force value have been discussed. The results presented are the effect of work on the implementation of a method for determining the setting force value in electronic measurement devices for common use.

Keywords: algorithm, setting force, electric railway drive, software.

1   Introduction

The setting force is the maximum force exerted by the setting slider of the drive to move the branch point, the derail or the swingnose crossing [3].

The measurement of force in the railway switch drive is aimed at determining whether the set force is correct. If the force is too weak to move the blades, they are partly moved. If the force is too strong, the railway switch drive may become damaged or it may work incorrectly or the crossover may change its position unintentionally. Such cases are undesirable and dangerous. The measurement and correct setting of the setting force is aimed at preventing this.

There is a problem with determining clearly at which time of the drive operation the setting force works. It may seem that this is the maximum force, which the drive exerts on the blade, but an analysis of forces operating within a railway switch that it is not always the case. The most systematic description of the setting force is presented by the German railway:

It is the mean from a one-second time period, which occurs 1 second after the slip of the overload clutch.

This definition is complete as it takes into account slight oscillations of the force occurring after the slip and averages them.

To measure forces operating in the drive on the point blades, a measuring shank of the measuring instrument should be inserted at the place of the pin coupling the setting slide of the drive with the setting rod of the point. The setting of the drive will result in the occurrence of force between the slide and the setting rod - its value will be indicated by the instrument. The measuring instrument should be equipped with the force registration option with a defined sampling frequency.

J. Mikulski (Ed.): TST 2013, CCIS 395, pp. 131–138, 2013.
© Springer-Verlag Berlin Heidelberg 2013

2   Analysis of Setting Force Measurements

A measurement is understood as a series of partial measurements, which can be expressed in the form of a sequence of results with an ordinal number assigned to each measurement, the measurement time and the force value. These results should be ordered chronologically and incrementally. Such a series of data can be depicted in the form of a graph. Fig. 1a presents the full railway switch operation cycle. In the beginning, the switch does not work, then it is switched with a setting force and the drive is switched off. Fig. 1b presents a graph of the measurement, which was performed during the setting force operation - at the time of the drive operation.

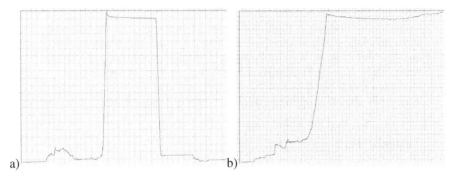

Fig. 1. A graph of force measurement results in the railway switch drive: a) from the time of switching the drive on to the time of switching it off, b) from the time switching the drive off to the completion of registration

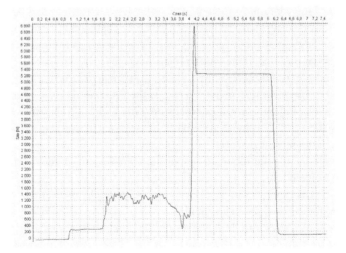

Fig. 2. A graph of force measurement results in the railway switch drive - a distinct slip of the slide at a time of approx. 4.1s

To be able to regard a measurement as correct, the continuity of partial measurements is required with a defined frequency and the possibility of defining clearly at what time the drive was at rest and at what time it was in the operating mode.

The moment the drive operation starts, a considerable increase in the force can be observed, which is depicted by the steep growing part of the graph presented in Fig. 2, between time values from 4 to 4.1 seconds. An increase in the force ends at the time of the clutch slip, in the drawing under analysis, it occurs at approximately 4.1 seconds and at a force approximately amounting to 6.8 kN.

3   Introduction to Algorithms

The task of the devised algorithms involves input data processing in a way allowing for obtaining the setting force value. The basic input data available include a table of partial force measurements at equal time intervals, which contain the following information:

- the number of each partial measurement (defined as N);
- partial measurement times;
- the value of force for the individual partial measurements (defined as A);
- the total number of partial measurements.

The data correctness is partly determined by the user and, in part, the verification is performed automatically while data are being loaded. The expected output data include the setting force value. The principles of operation of individual algorithms and sub-algorithms are discussed in a further part of the study. The optimisation of algorithms is a process which requires greater knowledge than their creation.

The notion of proper algorithm is understood as algorithms which are the direct object of considerations presented in the study.

The notion of sub-algorithm is understood as a significant element of the proper algorithm, which needs to be isolated because of its complexity. Sometimes sub-algorithms are used in more than one algorithm.

3.1   Data Processing before the Proper Algorithm Operation

Sub-algorithm of Data Correctness Verification
Before starting an analysis using algorithms, it should be decided whether a set of data should be analysed as correct. A correct set of data is considered to be the one, in which each partial measurement is correct (has a value) and the clutch slip point and the setting point value are positive values. The correctness of data continuity is verified automatically. If errors occur, no further data analysis can be performed.

Sub-algorithm of Data Value Correctness Verification
Situations, in which the clutch slip point and the setting force value are non-positive values, occur when the measuring instruments interpret the direction of the railway switch setting incorrectly or when this direction was negative (the measurement revealed negative values). This occurs when the arrow marked at the upper part of the

shank does not indicate the right part, while looking at the railway switch from the blade side. [4]

To obtain positive data, the user can start a sub-algorithm correcting these values.

The decision about data correctness is made by the user after becoming familiar with the data and the graph that depicts them, it is required as at this stage of data analysis, the programme does not have information about the value of the force at the clutch slip point and about the setting force value.

3.2   Data Processing after the Proper Algorithm Operation

After determining the clutch slip point by the proper algorithm, the value of setting force needs to be calculated. This is the task of sub-algorithm 0, which is used for calculating the mean value for the force from a one-second time period occurring a second after the clutch slip point.

3.3   Proper Algorithms

Algorithm 0

The principle of the operation of this algorithm is based on the theory that the clutch slip point is a moment, at which the highest force value occurs. The operation of the algorithm involves finding the moment, at which the maximum force occurs by comparing subsequent pairs of measurements and registering the higher one if it is higher than the "winner" from the previous pairs until all partial measurements are reviewed.

The setting force is calculated in accordance with sub-algorithm 0. A defect of this solution includes a lack of a correct result in cases, in which the force did not rise to its maximum value before the operation of the setting force or an increase with a higher value occurred at the time when the drive was turned off directly after changing the position of the switch. Simplicity is its greatest advantage.

Algorithm 1

In the case of this algorithm, to identify the clutch slip moment more accurately, the notion of mode was used. The mode is understood in this case as the value of force which occurred the largest number of times during measurements. It results from a graph analysis that such a situation takes place after the occurrence of the clutch slip and before turning off the drive - in the upper part of the graph. After analysing all cases, it can be concluded that both the clutch slip point and the maximum force and the mode value occur in the upper 50% of the range of the occurring forces, where the lowest value is considered to be the minimum force and its highest value is considered to be its maximum. To increase the precision of operation, the algorithm reduces all values smaller than 50% of the maximum to zero and next, it ignores this value while looking for the mode.

After finding the mode value, the algorithm begins to look for the maximum value before the occurrence of the $k/3$ of the repetition of the mode value where k is the total number of repetitions of this value. The $k/2$ point of the mode repetition is called the mode centre. This operation is aimed at eliminating a situation, in which the search for the local maximum begins outside the area of its occurrence, e.g. at the time of a violent increase in the force before the clutch slip.

After determining the local maximum in a selected area (from 0 to the time of occurrence of the k/2 mode repetition) using sub-algorithm 0, the programme calculates the setting force value. Just like for algorithm 0, the main defect of this solution is the fact that it is based on the theory that the force value at the clutch slip time is higher than the setting force. The greatest advantage of this algorithm, as compared to the previous one, includes the identification of the correct result also in cases when the occurrence of the total force maximum is not identical with the moment of the clutch slip occurrence. Attention should be paid to the fact that the data processing time is significantly longer due to the necessity of ordering the data to find the mode. To determine which value occurs most frequently, using as little memory as possible, the data should be sorted in ascending or descending order, where the same force values will be adjacent to each other. This requires from 1 to n! of additional runs of the programme over input data tables, where n is the number of partial measurements.

4   Procedures in Algorithms

This chapter describes procedures used for the operation of individual algorithms for the computer programme. A description of elements, which do not have a direct influence on the operation of the algorithm, such as the method of displaying data or their conversion, is not included. A data column is considered for all records, which constitute the input or output data. The notion of run is understood as a data column analysis, after which another run occurs or the operation of a function/procedure/ algorithm is ended. Records refer to subsequent numbers of partial measurements.

Algorithm 0
Algorithm 0 uses the following procedures to calculate the setting force value:

- MinMax
- Method0

The MinMax procedure detects the minimum and maximum used by the programme earlier for completion of the information bar while loading data.

The operation of the procedure involves an analysis of subsequent rows of the force value column. At the beginning, the first value in the column is assigned to the Min and Max variables. The programme moves to the next row and compares its value with the Max and Min values. If the value is higher than Max, it is recorded as Max. If the value is lower than Min, it is recorded as Min. Analysis of all rows one after the other renders the following values as the final result: the minimum (Min) and the maximum (Max) for the whole measurement period.

The Method0 procedure calculates the mean from 1-second time period occurring one second after the maximum. It establishes the beginning and end of a one-second time period, calculates the sum of forces during this period and calculates the arithmetic mean from this sum.

Algorithm 1

To calculate setting force values, Algorithm 1 triggers the following procedures:

- Cut;
- Bubble
- Mode
- Centre
- PunktPosl

The cut procedure is used for assigning the value of zero to force values lower than 50% of the maximum value of the measurements. It is aimed at facilitating work for the mode procedure. Values below this threshold do not affect the searched result and repetitions which may occur among them may be interpreted as mode values by the mode procedure, which would result in an incorrect interpretation of the graph. The procedure performs a logical test for each subsequent value of partial measurements to check if x is lower or equal to 50% of the maximum value. If a positive result is obtained, the value is changed to 0. If a negative result is obtained, the value remains unchanged.

The bubble procedure sorts input data using the bubble method to order them in a sequence from the lowest to the highest value. The same values are adjacent to each other.

The principle of the operation of this procedure is based on the mathematical assumption that out of two numbers, one is always smaller than or equal to the other one. The procedure compares a pair of numbers and if the second is greater than the first one, their places are switched. The fact of changing the place is recorded and the procedure moves on to the next pair of numbers, in which the first number is now the greater number from the previous pair. The procedure repeats the action for the entire data column. Next, it is checked if any change in the order has occurred. If a change has taken place, the procedure repeats the action from the first to the last row. No recorded changes mean that the second number was greater or equal to the previous one in each pair of numbers tested. This means that numbers were sorted and the procedure ends the work. Attention should be paid to the fact that sorted data do not correspond to the chronology of the measurements, they are working data which have been sorted only for the purpose of processing by the mode procedure.

The mode procedure is aimed at determining which fore value is the mode for a given measurement and when this force occurred. This procedure requires prior sorting of input data.

The adjacent numbers (which were previously sorted in ascending order) are compared one after another and the repetitions are counted. If the number of repetitions of a given number is greater than or equal to the number of repetitions for the previous number, this number is recorded as the current "winner". Analogically, if a greater number of repetitions occur later for another number, the "winner" changes. After reaching the end of the data column - the "winner" is considered to be the mode. If the same number of repetitions occurs for several different numbers, the higher number will be the mode, as it was analysed later.

The centre procedure is aimed at determining the place of the occurrence of n/2 repetitions of the mode value, where n is the total number of repetitions for the mode value. This action involves dividing the number of repetitions by two, rounding it off to a whole number and determining in which record the number of positive results will be n/2, by using a logical test whether x equal values of the dominant in the analysis of input data from before the bubble procedure (original ones).

The PunktPosl procedure works in a way similar to the MinMax procedure combined with the Method 0 procedure (find the maximum, calculate the arithmetic means from a one-second time period after its occurrence), the only difference being the fact that the search for the maximum does not end on the last record of the measurement, but on the record indicated by the Centre procedure.

5   Conclusion

Analysis of the operation of the individual algorithms on nearly 150 results of measurements allowed for formulating the following conclusions:

- The method of direct analysis of the results of measurements as described in algorithm 0 is burdened with considerable error due to the fact that the occurrence of the maximum force is not identical with the occurrence of the clutch slip. Moreover, this method does not analyse correctly measurements, in which a force value oscillation around the setting force value occurred. The verifiability of this method is approx. 70% and this value is too low.
- The result analysis method presented by algorithm 1 is more accurate than the previous one; in some cases, however (e.g. if the force does not rise above the setting force value before the clutch slip point), it does not bring satisfactory results. Its verifiability amounts to approx. 85%.
- The use of the mode notion for more accurate determination of the slip point is a good method; however, considering the necessity for implementing an algorithm to a computer environment, more time is needed for data processing and the complexity of the program increases. If the algorithm is implemented for a portable measuring instrument, which is not a PC, it may prove impossible in the form presented.
- On the basis of the development of the algorithms discussed, a theory can be put forward that it is possible to further improve their efficiency based on more complex mathematical operations (e.g. by using the notion of integral or by an attempt to approximate result measurements to the Gaussian curve). Such solutions, however, would be connected with an enormous increase in the complexity of the algorithm and in the computer performance required to calculate it.

Currently, work is being conducted on an algorithm, which will eliminate problems occurring in the algorithms discussed above.

References

1. Pełka, A.: Diagnozowanie urządzeń sterowania ruchem kolejowym na przykładzie napędu zwrotnicowego. Doctoral Dissertation. AGH, Kraków (2009)
2. Dobrzyniecki, P.: Komputerowa analiza siły nastawczej napędu zwrotnicowego. Engineer's thesis, Silesian School of Management in Katowice (2013)
3. Dokumentacja Techniczno - Ruchowa nr DTR-2006/EBISwitch 700 firmy Bombardier, Katowice (2006)
4. Dokumentacja Techniczno – Ruchowa nr PAMAR-MS/DTR/001 firmy Pamar, Jastrzębie Zdrój (2012)
5. Lüley, P., Franeková, M., Hudák, M.: Safety and functionality assessment of railway applications in terms of software. In: Mikulski, J. (ed.) TST 2012. CCIS, vol. 329, pp. 396–405. Springer, Heidelberg (2012)
6. Mikulski, J.: Using telematics in transport. In: Mikulski, J. (ed.) TST 2010. CCIS, vol. 104, pp. 175–182. Springer, Heidelberg (2010)
7. Mikulski, J.: Telematic Technologies in Transportation. In: Janecki, R., Sierpiński, G. (eds.) Contemporary Transportation Systems. Selected Theoretical and Practical Problems. New Culture of mobility, pp. 131–143. Publishing House of the Silesian University of Technology. Monograph no. 324, Gliwice (2011)
8. Gorczyca, P., Mikulski, J., Bialon, A.: Wireless local networks to record the railway traffic control equipment data. Advances in Electrical and Electronic Engineering 5(1-2), 128–131 (2011)
9. Rástočný, K., Nagy, P., Mikulski, J., et al.: Prvky zabezpečovacích systémov, EDIS, Žilina (2012)

Designing Safety Systems for an Electric Racing Car

Małgorzata Otrębska, Wojciech Skarka, Piotr Zamorski, and Karol Cichoński

Institute of Fundamentals of Machinery Design, Silesian University of Technology,
Konarskiego 18A, 44-100 Gliwice, Poland
{malgorzata.otrebska,wojciech.skarka}@polsl.pl,
piotr.zamorski@hotmail.com, karolcichonski89@gmail.com

Abstract. An electric vehicle MuSHELLka developed for the 2013 Shell Eco-marathon, has been equipped with active safety systems. Blind Spot Information System, Adaptive Cruise Control and Automatic Crash System. All those systems will ensure more safety to the driver and his competitors. Designs of submitted systems are based on real solutions,used nowadays in cars. Those systems adaptation to our vehicle and race needs was complicated. With the aid of special software PreScan from TASS, which is a computer simulator for advanced driver assistance systems, there were possibilities to design and test safety systems in the specified environment. It is an urban racetrack in Rotterdam, Holland. Also there were capabilities to specify sensors and their properties. The entirety of them together with Matlab/Simulink software have given anopportunity to build and verify selected safety systems.

Keywords: Advanced Driver Assistance System, Adaptive Cruise Control, Automatic Crash System, Blind Spot Information System, PreScan, Shell Eco-marathon.

1   Introduction

Developing Advanced Driver Assistance Systems in an electric vehicle MuSHELLka is important to ensure safety during the Shell Eco-marathon competition. Vehicles are moving each other very close, usually at different speeds. This could lead to a dangerous situation, which could pose at hreat of collision or accident. Applied front zone monitoring system, rear zone monitoring system and remote information system, have to prevent unexpected situations on the track. Official rules focus on safety. Each car must be equipped with rearview mirrors, horn and safety switch outside the vehicle. This elements are only part of the whole mandatory equipment, for example: safety belts, helmet. The provisions of the rules show that not only a result is important, but also a way to achieve it, asafe way.On the trackthere are simultaneously cars with different power trains, that cause differences in velocity.

Overtaking is an inherent element of the race. Each driver has on board rearview mirrors to know from wich side he/she will be overtaken. The horn is used to inform competitors about the intention of overtaking, so that they are aware and they could early see another car in mirrors. The rear zone monitoring system is integrated with

J. Mikulski (Ed.): TST 2013, CCIS 395, pp. 139–146, 2013.
© Springer-Verlag Berlin Heidelberg 2013

rearview mirrors. This system is responsible for constant monitoring and when it is necessary, for informing the driver about other cars or any obstacles. This solution is known as the Blind Spot information System and it is used to make driving safer.

Fig. 1. Vehicle MuSHELLka on the 2013 Shell Eco-marathon Race in Rotterdam, Holland

The front zone monitoring system works with the horn. It is responsible for enabling/disabling the horn and for sending information to the driver, that he/she should use it.This eliminates the risk of forgetting to usehorn, and thus the decision of the race referees. After determining an appropriate limit distance, the system reminds the driver about the sound signal.

The safety switch is required and is checked onsafety inspection. It is activated manually by the driver or the jury or staff. But when it is impossible, there will be a possibility to automatize this operation. It will be the same shock switch as in urban cars. An automatic power supply allows the system to send feedback to the team using a telemetric system, letting them to know and react very quickly.

The development of Advanced Driver Assistance System was carried outusing a special computer simulator, which is used to design and develop safety systems with a driver assistance system. It was the PreScan, from Tass company. The PreScan is a physics-based simulation platform that is used in the automotive industry for development of Advanced Driver Assistance Systems (ADAS) that are based on sensor technologies such as radar, laser/lidar, camera and GPS.

2   Concepts

The front zone monitoring system concept is based on Adaptive Cruise Control (ACC). The main aim of this system is to monitor thearea in front of the car. In urban vehicles radar is used as a sensor. However, in a concept electric vehicle, ultrasonic sensors are used. Because only the critical distance should be known, the velocity is not required. The output information from that system is a binary signal, which notifies driver to use horn.

Fig. 2. Concept based on ACC

An Automatic Collision NotificationSystem is based on an Automatic Crash System, which is used in cars. After a collision the system turns on exterior, interior lights and emergency lights, turns off the fuel pump and unlocks doors. Also this system is able to send information to the emergency service. The concept envisaged sending an alert to the team about the collision or about any other unexpected event on the racetrack. An alert will be send and after that the system is going to shutdown the engine automatically and to turn off the power.

A Blind Spot Information System – It is a system to monitor the rear zone of vehicle [11]. As in cars, this system works with mirrors and has a possibility to distinguish sides: left and right. The main aim of this system is to reduce the probability of unnoticed competitors. The driver is informed via special LEDs on the steering wheel.

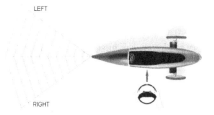

Fig. 3. Concept based on BLIS

3   Systems Design, Realization, Applied Sensors

According to the concept, three systems: ACC (Adaptive Cruise Control), ACS (Automatic Crash System) and BLIS (Blind Spot Information System)have been selected for implementation. The first step in systems designing was to determine the main objectives and assumptions of the project. Critical qualities for safety providing systems are: short response time, stability, reliability, immunity to interference, ease of use, low mass, small size.

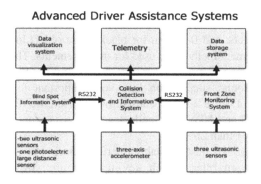

Fig. 4. ADAS integration and the method of communication

At this step of designing process it was very important to determine the level of integration and the method of communication. All safety systems send data to the same Data Visualization and Data Storage systems. That provides clarity, make systems easy to use and data easy to analyze. Communication between controllers is performed through the RS232 standard. All controllers have been designed with the use of 8-bit AVR Atmel microcontrollers [12].

3.1   BLIS

The most important step in designing this system was the selection of sensors. Key features of them were: high range, short response time, stability of work and ability to detect objects regardless of the material. Sensors must feature a small size and low power consumption, because the purpose of the vehicle in which they are mounted is anenergy-saving contest. Widely available sensors that meet these requirements are: ultrasonic sensors, photoelectric diffusive sensors and laser sensors. Laser sensors can be used only with thefirst class laser, because ahigher class can be dangerous for other participants [5].

The BLIS system utilises two ultrasonicHCSR-04 sensors and a diffusiveDatalogic S300 photoelectric sensor. The HC-SR04 ultrasonic sensor uses sonar to determine the distance from an object in the range of2cm – 400cm, with a resolution of 3mm. The sound wave that is used for measurements has a frequency of 40kHz [7].

Sensor characteristics determined during laboratory tests:

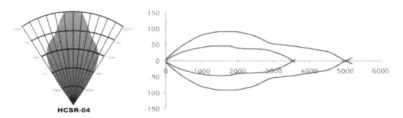

Fig. 5. HCSR-04 and Datalogic S300 sensors characteristics [8]

Datalogic S300 is an advanced photoelectric sensor with adetection range of 0-500cm for white objects, and 0-350cm for black matte object.Infrared radiation and triangulation measurement method are used for measurements. The sensor is equipped with mono-turn electronic trimmer that adjusts the sensitivity and the sensor operating distance. The background suppression is a very important feature,that allows to reduce the number of false alarms caused by interference from outside of the measuring range. PNP and NPN open collector is the sensor outputand themaximum response time is shorter than 2ms [8].

TheBLIS controller is based onahigh-performance, low-power Atmel AVR ATmega88-bit Microcontroller, which key features are: 8Kbytes flash program memory, 23 programmable I/O lines, 16MHz speed. The main task of the controller is to handle sensors and to transmit information about the detected threat to the visualization and storage data systems [9].

3.2   ACC

The ACC uses the same ultrasonic sensors as the BLIS system. Sensors are placed to form a single coherent zone of scanning space ahead of the vehicle. The controller is based on Atmel AVR8-bit ATmega 328Microcontroller with 20 MHz resonator.

BLIS and ACC detection zones are shown in the picture.

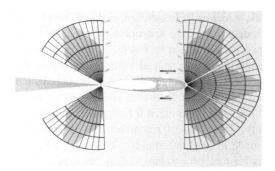

Fig. 6. BLIS and ACC detection

3.3   ACS

The ACS is based on measurements of acceleration. The main sensor is athree axisMMA7361L accelerometer. The MMA7361L is a low power, low profile capacitive micromachined accelerometer featuring signal conditioning, a 1-pole low pass filter, temperature compensation, self test, 0g-detect, which detects a linear freefall. The G-select allows to choose between two measuring ranges: ± 1.5gandsensitivity of800 mV/g, and ±6gprovidingsensitivityof 206 mV/g. The maximum response time is 0.5ms. Through the use of accelerometer, the system can detect collisions and determine the current position of the car [10].

The Controller is based on Atmel AVR8-bit ATmega2560 Microcontroller. In addition to the accelerometer handling it receives thedata from BLIS and ACC systems. Data are stored on anSD card and sent to the visualization and driver alert system. The visualization system consists of LED indicators located on the steering wheel, horn and of aspecially written mobile application that enables todisplay the most important driving parameters and transmits thedata to thedriver assistance teamusing the GSM network.

4   Virtual Prototyping of Suggested Systems

PreScan from TASS, which is a special software working with Matlab/Simulink, has been used for designing safety systems and computer simulations of dangerous situations. Virtual prototyping of suggested Advanced Driver Assistance Systems has provided several advantages. Research methodology consists of four steps (Fig.7) [6]:

- Building scenario
- Modeling sensors
- Adding control system
- Running experiment

The scenario building assumes the planning of real time actions. A special computer model of urban track was built and the model of vehicle was imported. The computer model of the racetrack, which is in Rotterdam, Holland, shows reality on a very high level. Each important detail, from the sensors point of view is maintained. A vehicle model can be equipped with different type sensors. Their parameters were earlier set up, after laboratory experiment on a special testing station. And then parameters were verified by the feedback from sensorsin the vehicle. The characteristic of a chosen sensor was mapped in the PreScan Software. This allows to verify them in different ways. And the system has been optimized for a specific race to provide the driver the highest level of safety. That kind of research helps in spare time and funds. The control system was made in Matlab/Simulink. This software enables users to design and verify algorithms for data processing. The use of PreScan with Matlab/Simulink provides a full adaptation of the system to expected and unexpected conditions. Tests allow to optimize the system and to eliminate possible errors that could adversely affect the actual security system.

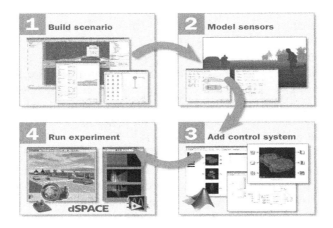

Fig. 7. Four steps of Advanced Driver Assistance Systems designing [6]

5   Conclusion

Results of Advanced Driver Assistance Systems development were satisfactory. The enlargement of safety systems, including advanced safety systems, was an excellent move. Now the MuSHELLka electric vehicle is very safe. What is important, not only driver's safety was increased,also safety on the racetrack. This is due to special research and tests, which were carried out during the whole year of preparation. The process of this system designing was not simple. It has taken a lot of time.

Fortunately, it was easier with thesupport from Tass and PreScan software. At the beginning, a prototype system with sensors was made. According to this design, it was possible to start the modelling process in PreScan software. This solution was helpful in developing the vehicle. The data from sensors, their characteristics and responses were taken and implicated in a computer simulator. This caused that at a very early stage of designing process, the team was able to know how it would work. Computer experimentswere made according to the physical layout, they were quick and recurrent. A test after test could be done. All relevant information collected in different conditions was saved. That helped in proper tuning of the system. After preliminary tests, safety systems have been built and installed into the car. During the designing the actual Advanced Driver Assistance Systems were verified by computer simulation. What is more, after wards special systems have been made, after tests which were made during the Shell Eco-marathon, a few things have left to improve for the next year. PreScan gives an opportunity to work on this during the next months.

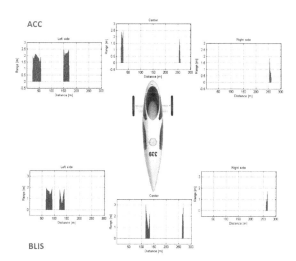

Fig. 8. Response of ADAS system to the situation on the track

References

1. Gietelink, O.J., Ploeg, J., De Schutter, B., Verhaegen, M.: Development of a driver information and warning system with vehicle hardware-in-the-loop simulations, Mechatronics. The Science of Intelligent Machines, A Journal of IFAC, the International Federation of Automatic Control 19(7), 1091–1104 (2009)
2. Skarka, W., Otrębska, M., Zamorski, P.: Simulation of dangerous operation incidents in designing advanced driver assistance systems. In: XII International Technical Systems Degradation Conference: Polskie Naukowo-Techniczne Towarzystwo Eksploatacyjne, Warszawa (2013)

3. Tutak, W.: Układy bezpieczeństwa czynnego w pojazdach samochodowych, Nie tylko me-chanik, Szkolenie z zakresu diagnostyki samochodowej, Politechnika Częstochowska (2010)
4. Zamorski, P.: Projekt i konstrukcja wybranego podukładu systemu zapewnienia bezpieczeństwa kierowcy pojazdu elektrycznego, Praca przejściowa, Instytut Podstaw Konstrukcji Maszyn, Politechnika Śląska, Gliwice (2013)
5. Cichoński, K.: System zapewnienia bezpieczeństwa wyścigowego pojazdu elektrycznego, Projekt inżynierski, Instytut Podstaw Konstrukcji Maszyn, Politechnika Śląska, Gliwice (2012)
6. Tass, Prescan, http://www.tass-safe.com/en/products/prescan (date of access June 12, 2013)
7. Data sheet "HCSR-04"
8. Data sheet "Datalogic S300"
9. Data sheet "ATmega8"
10. Data sheet "MMA7361L"
11. Wu, B.-F., Huang, H.-Y., Chen, C.-J., Chen, Y.-H., Chang, C.-W., Chen, Y.-L.: A vision-based blind spot warning system for daytime and nighttime driver assistance. Computers and Electrical Engineering 39, 846–862 (2013)
12. Rodríguez Flórez, S.A., Frémont, V., Bonnifait, P., Cherfaoui, V.: Multi-modal object de-tection and localization for high integrity driving assistance. Machine Vision and Applica-tions. Springer (December 2011)
13. Belbachir, A., Smal, J.C., Blosseville, J.M., Gruyer, D.: Simulation-Driven Validation of Advanced Driving-Assistance Systems. In: Transport Research Arena– Europe 2012, vol. 48, pp. 1205–1214 (2012)

Short-Term Traffic Flow Forecasting Method Based on the Data from Video Detectors Using a Neural Network

Teresa Pamuła

Silesian University of Technology, Faculty of Transport,
Krasińskiego 8, 40-019 Katowice, Poland
teresa.pamula@polsl.pl

Abstract. The paper presents the development of a short-term forecasting method for determining traffic flow values. The study is based on the data from two video detectors located at the ends of a transit road in the city of Gliwice. The data were recorded 24 h/day for a period of one year. Neural networks (NN) were used in the prediction models. The effects, of the size of a time window and the length of selected data registration, on the learning rate of the nets and on the quality of prediction were studied. Tests were performed using three classes of time series corresponding to: working days, Saturdays and Sundays. The aim of the study was to elaborate an accurate short-term predicting method, which can be used in traffic control systems especially incorporated into modules of Intelligent Transportation Systems (ITS).

Keywords: traffic flow prediction, neural network, time series.

1   Introduction

Forecasting of the traffic flow is an important part of transport planning, traffic management and intelligent transportation systems. In particular, short-term traffic forecasts can be utilized in real-time dynamic traffic control systems.

In recent years, a considerable effort is made to develop efficient traffic prediction methods, which is backed by a large number of publications in this field. A number of methods and techniques were developed for short-term traffic flow forecasting depending upon the type of acquired data and the potential end use of forecasts.

In [1] present an approach based on statistical analysis of historical data and simple heuristics. Two models of short-term forecasting have been developed. The first model uses a constant value as a forecast, while in the other model this value is linearly adjusted. [2] propose an aggregation model for forecasting. This aggregation model is elaborated using different fitting functions: the moving average (MA), exponential smoothing (ES), autoregressive MA (ARIMA) and simple neural network (NN) for evaluation of prediction values. In papers [3 - 5] authors used with success NN for forecasting. In [6] a novel fuzzy neural approach to prediction is proposed. This approach combines the capabilities of NN and fuzzy logic, which results in a

J. Mikulski (Ed.): TST 2013, CCIS 395, pp. 147–154, 2013.
© Springer-Verlag Berlin Heidelberg 2013

more accurate adaptation to real traffic data. In papers [8 - 11] models using 3 layer back-propagation neural networks proved to be efficient for classification and short-term forecasting of road traffic data.

This study is based on the data from video detectors located at the ends of a section of a transit road in Gliwice – Fig.1. The first video detector collected information about vehicles going to the centre of Gliwice and the second detector collected information about vehicles leaving Gliwice in the direction of the A4 motorway.

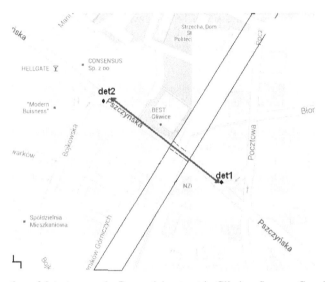

Fig. 1. Location of detectors on the Pszczyńska street in Gliwice. Source: Google Maps

The aim of the study was to examine the impact of the time windows length (20, 30 and 40 min) and days of the week on the quality of prediction. Combinations of window lengths and network structure layouts were tested to obtain the best forecasting solution.

2   Selecting Data for Prediction

Data for the traffic flow prediction were selected and processed as follows. The data were recorded 24 h/day for a period of one year from 1 June 2011 to 31 May 2012 and were initially divided into groups according to the classes of time series [10]. Part of the data was used to prepare training and test sequences.

The training set contained the data collected in July, September, November, January and March. To test the network we have used the data from randomly selected days of the remaining months. The length of the measurement period is 1/2 hour, in which travelling vehicles are counted, a new count is started every 5 minutes. This means that inputs provide traffic data to the network describing the mean traffic flow in the past 1/2 hour. The network output is a predicted value of traffic flow valid for the next 5 minutes.

3 Preparing the Training Sequences

Three different time windows were used during the analysis. The first window with a length of 20 minutes includes four measured values of traffic intensity for half an hour at 5 minute intervals. The second time window with a length of 30 min includes six measured values – Fig. 2 at intervals of 5 minutes and the third window has a length of 40 min, and 8 traffic data.

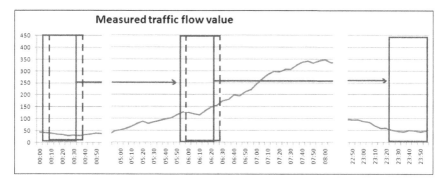

Fig. 2. Time window (30min)

For the 20 min time window the training sequence of test vectors consisted of 4 values of traffic flow intensity. Next, the fifth value was forecasted. For TW6 the training set has seven values and for TW8 it consists of nine values.

4 Neural Network Structure

A different structure of the neural network for each time window has been proposed. Networks have a different number of inputs and a different number of neurons in the hidden layers. For the time window of 20 minutes (containing 4 data items) we have adopted the structure of 4-10-1 (NN4); for the window of 30 minutes, the network structure is 6-18-1 (NN6), and for the time window of 40 min we have used the network structure 8-22-1 (NN8). The networks structure NN4 and NN8 is shown in Fig. 3.

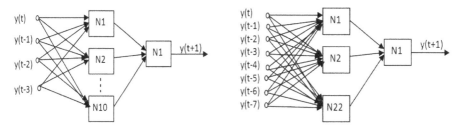

Fig. 3. The NN structure a) time window 4, b) time window 8

For each of the three classes of traffic time series (working days, Saturdays and Sundays) the same structures of neural networks were used. Depending on the group the learning sequence consisted of 3000 to 5000 vectors. For a group of Mon-Fri the training set was the longest, and the shortest was for the Saturdays and Sundays group.

The learning process terminates when the error mean square (RMS) value is between 0.02 and 0.03. The neural network learning rate is between 0.5 and 0.9 and momentum α=0,4 to 0,7. For all neural networks we have used a back-propagation learning method.

5   Research Results

The neural networks models have been evaluated. The research results are presented in tables and graphically interpreted on graphs. For NN4 the set of test vectors consists of 4 traffic flow intensity values. Next the 5th value was forecasted. For NN6 and NN8 test vectors have six and eight values, respectively.

5.1   Presentation of the Results on Graphs

The following graphs show the results of prediction for selected classes of time series. Predicted values were calculated using the NN8 model for different days. Those data were not part of the training sequence. Figure 4 shows the results of prediction for a working day – Tuesday (27 September 2011).

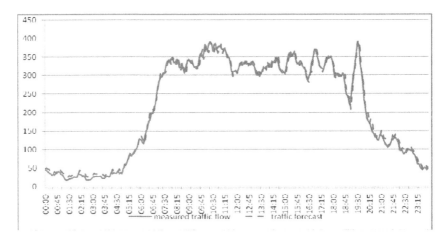

Fig. 4. The observed traffic flow and predictions result from the NN8 model for the working days class

The results of prediction for Saturday (25 February 2012) are shown in Fig. 5.

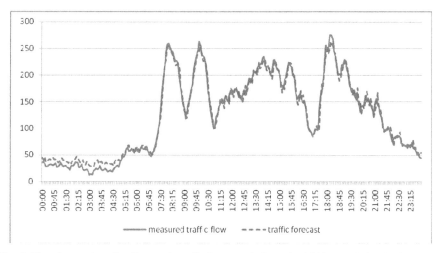

Fig. 5. The observed traffic flow and predictions result from the NN8 model for the Saturdays class

Figure 6 shows the results of prediction for Sunday (27 May 2012).

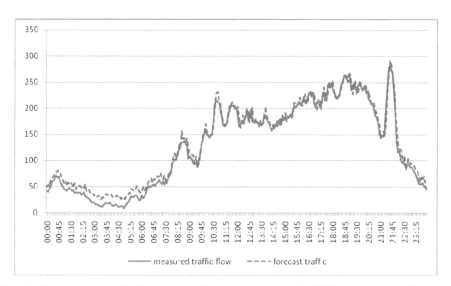

Fig. 6. The observed traffic flow and predictions result from the NN8 model for the Sundays class

The best results were obtained for the working days class. This can be explained by a greater repeatability of similar values of traffic flows intensity, particularly during the morning and afternoon peaks.

5.2   Comparison of Results

The neural networks models, after the training, have been evaluated. The results of predictions were analysed and compared taking into account the following error measures: root mean squared error (RMSE), mean absolute error (MAE) and the mean absolute percentage error (MAPE). Error values were evaluated according to the formulas:

$$RMSE = \sqrt{\frac{1}{N} \sum_{n=1}^{N} (y_n - y_f)^2} \tag{1}$$

$$MAE = \frac{1}{N} \sum_{n=1}^{N} |y_n - y_f| \tag{2}$$

$$MAPE = \frac{1}{N} \sum_{n=1}^{N} \frac{|y_n - y_f|}{y_n} \tag{3}$$

where N – total number of analysed data, y_n – measured values, y_f – the forecast value for the n-th measurement (y_n)

Prediction errors RMSE, MAE and MAPE were calculated for two detectors and groups associated with days of the week. The test data are not the part of the training vector set. Test results for detector 1 and detector 2 are shown in Table 1 and Table 2, respectively.

Table 1. The RMSE and MAPE errors of traffic flow predicting for detector 1

The time series class	Detector 1								
	RMSE			MAE			MAPE		
	NN4	NN6	NN8	NN4	NN6	NN8	NN4	NN6	NN8
Monday-Friday	11.01	11.50	**10.55**	**8.25**	8.68	8.45	0.07	**0.06**	0.09
Saturdays	11.09	11.28	**9.59**	8.99	9.30	**7.85**	**0.13**	0.14	0.14
Sundays	11.92	11.77	**11.68**	9.97	**9.62**	9.99	0.22	**0.15**	0.22

Analysing the data presented in Table 1, it may be observed that the lowest RMSE values were obtained for the network model NN8, independently of time series class. Regarding the two other values (MAE, MAPE) it is difficult to say which of the models is the best. Additionally the research results show that in order to properly forecast the traffic flow intensity, the time series prior to the forecast period should be less than 30 min.

Table 2. The RMSE and MAPE errors of traffic flow predicting for detector 2

The time series class	Detector 2								
	RMSE			MAE			MAPE		
	NN4	NN6	NN8	NN4	NN6	NN8	NN4	NN6	NN8
Monday-Friday	12.58	10.17	**9.58**	10.16	7.63	**7.37**	0.11	**0.06**	**0.06**
Saturdays	9.46	9.33	**8.95**	7.95	7.79	**7.50**	0.15	**0.14**	0.15
Sundays	8.17	9.19	**7.67**	6.05	6.87	**5.95**	**0.07**	0.10	0.10

Tests for detector 2 were made for the same day as in the case of detector 1. For both detectors similar prediction results were obtained.

6   Conclusion

In the study described in this paper, eighteen various neural networks have been used. The study was performed for the data from two detectors, for each of the three classes of time series. Each class was tested using three time windows. The best of NN models have been used to forecast these series.

The aim was to find the best model of short-term prediction of the traffic flow, which is an important part of urban traffic control planning. For both detectors, the best results were obtained for the time series of working days class and the network model NN8.

References

1. Chrobok, R., Kaumann, O., Wahle, J., Schreckenberg, M.: Different methods of traffic forecast based on real data. European Journal of Operational Research 155(3), 558–568 (2004)
2. Tan, M.-C., Wong, S.C., Xu, J.-M., Guan, Z.-R., Zhang, P.: An Aggregation Approach to Short-Term Traffic Flow Prediction. IEEE Transactions on Intelligent Transportation Systems 10, 60–69 (2009)
3. Vlahogianni, E.I., Karlaftis, M.G., Golias, J.C.: Optimized and meta-optimized neural networks for short-term traffic flow prediction: a genetic approach. Transportation Research Part C 13, 211–234 (2005)
4. Srinivasan, D., Choy, M.C., Cheu, R.L.: Neural networks for real-time traffic signal control. IEEE Trans. Intelligent Transportation Systems 7(3), 261–271 (2006)
5. Chen, H., Grant-Muller, S., Mussone, L., Montgomery, F.: A study of hybrid neural network approaches and the effects of missing data on traffic forecasting. Neural Computing and Applications 10, 277–286 (2001)
6. Quek, C., Pasquier, M., Boon, B., Lim, S.: POP-TRAFFIC A Novel Fuzzy Neural Approach to Road Traffic Analysis and Prediction. IEEE Transactions on Intelligent Transportation Systems 7(2), 133–146 (2006)

7. Karlaftis, M.G., Vlahogianni, E.I.: Statistical methods versus neural networks in transportation research: differences, similarities and some insights. Transportation Research, Part C. Emerging Technologies 19(3), 387–399 (2011)
8. Pamuła, T.: Traffic flow analysis based on the real data using neural networks. In: Mikulski, J. (ed.) TST 2012. CCIS, vol. 329, pp. 364–371. Springer, Heidelberg (2012)
9. Pamuła, T.: Road traffic parameters prediction in urban traffic management systems using neutal networks. Transport Problems 6(3), 123–129 (2011)
10. Pamuła, T.: Classification and prediction of traffic flow based on real data using neural networks. Archive of Transport 24(4), 519–522 (2012)
11. Pamuła, T.: Prognozowanie natężenia ruchu pojazdów na skrzyżowaniu za pomocą sieci neuronowej. Zeszyty Naukowe PŚl. nr 1862 Transp. z 74, 67–74 (2012)

Safety of Signalling Systems - Opinions and Reality

Karol Rástočný, Ľubomír Pekár, and Juraj Ždánsky

University of Žilina, Faculty of Electrical Engineering,
Department of Information and Control Systems, Univerzitná 1,
01026 Žilina, Slovakia
{karol.rastocny,lubomir.pekar,juraj.zdansky}@fel.uniza.sk

Abstract. Nowadays we witness a significant modernization of both railway tracks as well as signalling systems. The modernization is unarguably a right step towards the improvement to railway transport effectiveness and safety. The modernization of signalling devices is connected with the introduction of electronics, which requires a different approach in the development process of a signalling system, safety evaluation as well as in the case of its operation and maintenance. The introduction of electronics to interlocking systems calls for reconsideration of the old well-known "truths" about the signalling systems safety that are associated with conventional (i.e. mechanical, electromechanical or relay) signalling systems. Some of these arguments are still valid, some are applicable only in specific conditions or they should be revised and several of them are not valid anymore in the new perspective.

Keywords: safety, railway signalling system.

1 Introduction

Nowadays a massive building of ETCS is observed, which brings significant modernization not only of tracks, but also of signalling systems (SSs). The SSs modernization significantly contributes to increasing the efficiency and safety of railway transport. Building the ETCS is closely associated with the introduction of electronics to SSs and this fact requires also a different approach not only to development, but also to its operation and maintenance. The modernisation itself brings also the need to review the well-established "truths" about safety of railway transport, which are associated with traditional (mechanical, electromechanical, relay) signalling systems. Some arguments have a permanent validity, some need to be corrected and some have already lost their validity. For instance, the following arguments could be considered among them:

- „During the verification operation of SS a failure did not occur, thus SS is safe"
- „Signalling system has SIL ..."
- „Using time of the SS does not affect its safety, but only its reliability"
- „When it comes to safety, the price does not make any difference ..."

This paper presents the opinions of authors on the validity of some arguments stated below.

J. Mikulski (Ed.): TST 2013, CCIS 395, pp. 155–162, 2013.
© Springer-Verlag Berlin Heidelberg 2013

2 Argument: „During the Verification Operation of SS a Failure Did Not Occur, Thus SS is Safe"

Dependability and safety are indeed two different quality attributes of the SS, but interrelated, and it is undisputable that the factors of dependability (reliability, availability, maintainability) affect the safety of SS.

An Electronic Signalling System (ESS) is a generally implemented technique of composed protection against failure, for which the use of multi-channel architecture is typical. The reliability of individual components of ESS has a significant impact on the safety integrity level (SIL) of safety features of this implemented system. When evaluating the safety it must be proved that the ESS satisfies the requirements of the safety integrity against systematic failures and against random failures. The achievement of required SIL against systematic failures can be proved by testing; the achievement of required SIL against random failures of ESS is necessary to demonstrate also using quantitative methods (calculations) [3]. The necessity of quantitative methods using results from the values of tolerable hazard rate (THR) for each SIL (SIL - table in [3]). For instance, in the case of SIL4 requirement, the required value of mean time to a hazardous failure of the safety function is more than 10 000 years. If during the verification operation a failure is not recorded, or appropriately a hazardous failure of SS, it is a positive finding, but it cannot be a single and decisive argument for the evaluation of safety features of SS.

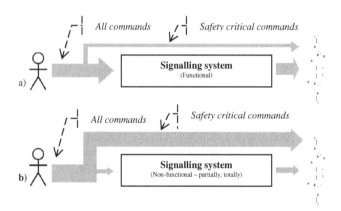

Fig. 1. Operator impact on the safety of railway transport – a model architecture

In principle, we should not be interested in the safety of SS, but in the safety of controlled (railway) transport process. SS is just a technical tool (technical measure), which allows us to achieve the required level of safety of the transport process [4].

From the perspective of the European standards the SS is rated as a control system with continuous operation, which means, that the safety of the transport process (controlled process) affects not only the integrity of the SS, but also its availability. This fact is shown in Fig. 1.

If the system is functional (Fig. 1 a)), and almost all commands of the operator are checked by the SS and if the command is not contrary to the safety of railway transport, the system will also perform it. If the command execution endangers the safety of railway transport, the SS will reject it. A very small part of the operator's commands (usually the safety-critical commands) is executed directly without checking by the signalling system and only the operator is responsible for their accuracy. Fig. 1 b) shows the situation, when the SS is non-functional or only partially functional. In this case to a large extent the operator is responsible for railway traffic control. Since the probability of operator's error is usually much greater than the probability of a hazardous failure of the SS, the availability of SS affects the safety of the controlled process.

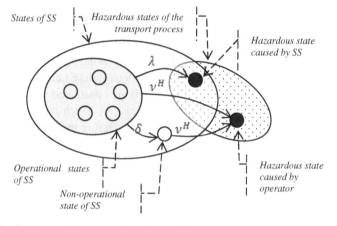

Fig. 2. Operator impact on the safety of railway transport – a state model

The SS state space (Fig. 2) can be divided into a set of functional states (failure-free state and failure states, which do not affect the current implemented safety functions) and a set of non-functional states between which two meaningfully important states should be also considered:

- a hazardous state of the SS, to which the signalling system is in the transition from functional states due to a failure of the system (transition λ), is a state that must be considered also a hazardous state of the controlled transport process;
- a pre-defined safe state, to which the SS is in the transition after a failure detection and negation (transition δ).

If the SS is in one of the functional states, the controlled transport process can get into a hazardous state only, if the operator is involved in the control of the transport process through commands that are not controlled by the SS itself (transition v^H) and the operator makes an error for the issuance of such safety-critical command.

A hazardous state of the controlled transport process could arise also when the SS is in a non-functional state and the transport process is directly controlled by the operator (is a continuous process).

3   Argument: „Using Time of the Signalling System Does Not Affect Its Safety, But only Its Reliability ...."

The reliability of SS also affects the useful life of the SS. In general, it is acceptable to assume that electronic components are not subject to aging and the occurrence of random failures of electronic components can be described by an exponential distribution (random failure rate is constant). It is a fact, that at the end of the useful life of electronic systems, the hardware failure rate increases due to aging of their mechanical parts (circuit boards, connectors ...).

Every SS must be subject to the processes of safety assessment. The SIL assessment against random failures must be in the sense of standards based on quantitative methods, and during the calculation of the hazardous failure rate of SS concrete values of the random failure rate of ESS components are considered. This means that the achieved results are valid only in that (time) range, in which the considered failure rates of individual components ESS are also valid. During the useful life of ESS the following conditions have to be applied:

$$\lambda_R(t) \leq \lambda_C(t),$$ (1)

$$\lambda_R^H(t) \leq \lambda_C^H(t).$$ (2)

where $\lambda_C(t)$ is the value of a random failure rate of SS considered by the safety assessment, $\lambda_R(t)$ is a real value of a random failure rate of SS, $\lambda_R^H(t)$ is a real value of a hazardous random failure rate of SS a $\lambda_C^H(t)$ is the calculated value of a hazardous random failure rate of SS [5]. This situation is shown in Fig. 3.

The ESS safety determination on preventive maintenance does not make sense, since electronic components are not subject to wear. In general, the useful life of ESS is approximately about 20 years.

The fact is that the external components (e. g. switch machines, signals ...) have a significant proportion of the failure rate of ESS. These are usually of the same construction as in classical SS, therefore, they are subject to mechanical wear and it is of great importance to take into account these elements, to think about their preventive maintenance. The situation is different in the case of internal components (logic of SS).

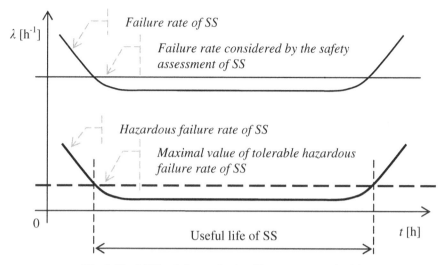

Fig. 3. Useful life of electronic signalling systems - principle

Nowadays, manufacturers attempt can be seen to build the logic of ESS based on standard commercially available electronic components. The development in the area of processor technologies and replacement of elements is so fast that it is questionable, whether the existing software (even if the software is not subject to physical wear) will be compatible with the new processor technologies. It is really assumed that after the end of the ESS useful life it will be necessary to replace the complete logic of the SS. This fact is contrary to the general expectation that the ESS will have a longer or comparable operational life than classical SS - because they are smarter!

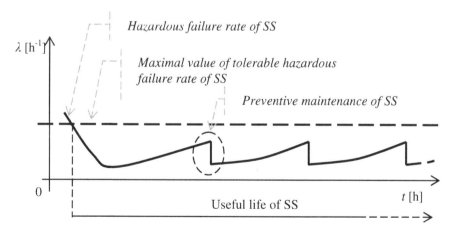

Fig. 4. Useful time of classical signalling system – principle

It is a normal effect that classical SS are in operation for more than 50 years. Such a long operational time is achieved through regular preventive maintenance that is aimed at replacing parts of the SS, which are subject to mechanical wear. It is also necessary to take into account the fact that for the technologically older (mechanical, electromechanical, relay) SS also different rules and procedures were applied in the safety assessment (valid for this period - to technological solutions, to existing views, to theoretical knowledge ...). The principle of operational life extension of classical SS is shown in Fig. 4.

4   Argument: „Signalling System Has SIL ...“

In principle, it is necessary to divide the functions of SS into (Fig. 4):

- control functions not affecting safety; terms of functions, the failure of which may cause operational problems, but it cannot endanger the traffic safety;
- control functions affecting safety; terms of functions, the failure of which may cause not only operational problems, but it can also endanger the safety of the train movement;
- protective functions; terms of functions, which are not subject to the control of train movement, but their task is to check the state of components not related to the control of train movement, but to check the implementation of conditions that increase the safety of passengers or service personnel (e.g. closing the door check).

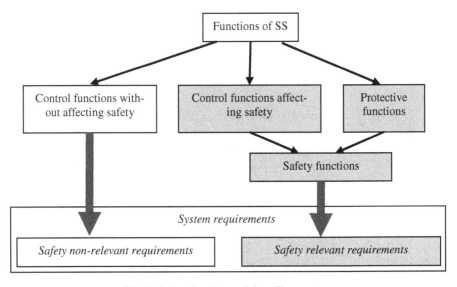

Fig. 5. Safety functions of signalling system

Protective functions and control functions affecting the safety are called safety functions. In accordance with [1], the THR must be determined for each safety function. The THR is determined on the basis of risk analysis (based on the knowledge of the risk associated with the presence of a hazard that the given safety function is reduced to a tolerable level). SS can include more safety functions, a different value of THR could be defined for each safety function [6].

If SS executes only one safety function with the hazardous failure rate λ_{F1}^H and SIL of SS is identifiable with a SIL safety function, it applies that

$$\lambda_{F1}^H = \lambda_{SS}^H, \tag{3}$$

where λ_{SS}^H is a hazardous failure rate of SS.

If SS executes more safety functions, the SIL of signalling system must not coincide (and generally does not coincide) with the SIL of the individual safety functions. In practice, also an incorrect argument can be seen that SIL of SS corresponds to the maximum value of SIL of the individual safety functions. It is not true. If SS executes for instance two independent safety functions - one safety function with the hazardous failure rate λ_{F1}^H and the second safety function with the hazardous failure rate λ_{F2}^H, it applies that

$$\lambda_{F1}^H + \lambda_{F2}^H < \lambda_{SS}^H. \tag{4}$$

It follows that the expression of SIL should always be associated with a particular safety function and not with a specific SS (this argument must not be valid, if SS executes one safety function). We can still claim about SS that it is developed (respectively that it is not developed) in accordance with the procedures and methods that correspond to a particular SIL according to [1 - 3].

5 Conclusion

In spite of the fact that in the area of safety philosophy for a long time no substantial change has occurred, a significant movement in the perception of the SS safety could be seen with the advent of electronics introduction. This is the movement from absolute to relative understanding of safety. Relativity is that we will accept a fact, that the safety of railway transport can be endangered due to the hazardous state (failure) of the SS. However, we require that the probability of the occurrence of hazardous state of the SS is not greater than the defined (required) tolerable value. The SS must perform this requirement during the whole time of its useful life.

Acknowledgements. This paper was written with the support of VEGA, the scientific grant agency. Grant No. VEGA-1/0388/12 "Quantitative Safety Integrity Level Evaluation of Control Systems in Railway Application".

References

1. EN 50 126: Railway applications - The specification and demonstration of Reliability, Availability, Maintainability and Safety (RAMS), Part 1, Part 2 (2007)
2. EN 50 128: Railway applications – Communication, signalling and processing systems – Software for railway control and protection systems (2011)

3. EN 50 129: Railway applications – Communication, signalling and processing systems – Safety-related electronic systems for signalling (2003)
4. Pekár, L., Rástocný, K.: Impact of human factor on the safety of traffic process. In: Proceeding of the Central European School of Doctoral Study, Krynica, pp. 37–41 (2012) ISBN 978-83-7351-507-9
5. Rástočný, K., Ilavsk, J.: What Is Concealed behind the Hazardous Failure Rate of a System? In: Mikulski, J. (ed.) TST 2011. CCIS, vol. 239, pp. 372–381. Springer, Heidelberg (2011)
6. Rástočný, K., Ždánsky, J., Nagy, P.: Some Specific Activities at the Railway Signalling System Development. In: Mikulski, J. (ed.) TST 2012. CCIS, vol. 329, pp. 349–355. Springer, Heidelberg (2012)
7. Rástočný, K., Nagy, P., Mikulski, J., et al.: Prvky zabezpečovacích systémov. EDIS, Žilina (2012)

Inertial Navigation: Improving Precision and Speed of Euler Angles Computing from MEMS Gyroscope Data

Vojtech Šimák, Dušan Nemec, Jozef Hrbček, and Aleš Janota

University of Žilina,
Univerzitna 8215/1, 01026 Žilina, Slovakia
{Vojtech.Simak,Jozef.Hrbcek,Ales.Janota}@fel.uniza.sk

Abstract. This paper deals with comparison of three different approaches of Euler angles computing from gyroscope output data. Methods are compared by their precision and computing time consumption. First method is based on infinitesimal rotation matrix. Second is based on transforming angular velocity to Euler angles derivations. The third method is based on quaternion rotation. Results of experiments are showing that the third approach seems to have the best results of all.

Keywords: gyroscope, euler angle, inertial navigation, MEMS, rotational matrix.

1   Introduction

The purpose of the inertial navigation in 3D space is to determine 6 independent variables: translation of an object in 3 axes and its rotation in 3 axes, relative to inertial frame of reference (i.e. such is neither rotating nor accelerating). In this paper will be described determination of rotation and the options of its expression and calculation from angular velocity measured by gyroscope. We will consider only Cartesian (orthonormal) right-hand coordinate system oriented by convention NED (North-East-Down, resp. resp. $x \rightarrow$ forward, $y \rightarrow$ right and $z \rightarrow$ down). This problematic is more detailed described in [3].

Note: Values given in coordinate system joined with measured object (system S´) will be marked with dash and values given relative to inertial frame of reference (system S) will be marked without dash. In this article we assume the term "rotation" as the rotation of object relative to coordinate system S, not rotation of coordinate system S' relative to the S (which is mathematically inverse).

2   Algorithms for Processing Data from 3-Axis Gyroscope

Gyroscope firmly joined with moving object $S´$ is measuring angular velocity as tri-component vector $\boldsymbol{\omega}' = [\omega'_x, \omega'_y, \omega'_z]$. These data are sampled with given sample frequency $f_{\text{sample}} = 1/\Delta T$. Sensor system has to process data sample by sample in

J. Mikulski (Ed.): TST 2013, CCIS 395, pp. 163–170, 2013.
© Springer-Verlag Berlin Heidelberg 2013

real-time (see Fig. 1). As mentioned above the outputs of algorithm are Euler angles α, β, γ, system should also provide utility of the transformation of vector from S to S' coordinate system.

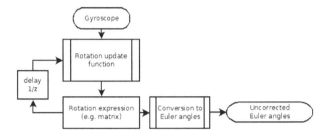

Fig. 1. Schematics expressing principle of real-time gyroscope data processing. If rotation is expressed primary by Euler angles, shown conversion block is not needed.

2.1 Algorithm Based on Rotation Matrix

First version of algorithm for processing measured angular velocity is utilizing matrix expression of rotation. Principle of this method is shown in Fig.2.

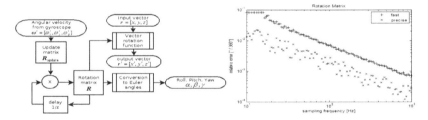

Fig. 2. Precise version of algorithm based on rotation matrix and relative error of fast and precise matrix-based algorithm

Previous rotation matrix R_{n-1} is multiplied by update matrix R_{update}:

$$R_n = R_{n-1} \cdot R_{\text{update}} \tag{1}$$

Update matrix defines rotation of object between 2 recent samples (ω'_{n-1} ; ω'_n) of angular velocity vector ω' with time span ΔT. It is possible to create the update matrix from angular velocity by two ways:

Precise Version
Let us assume that between two recent samples is angular velocity constant, so its direction defines rotation axis and magnitude multiplied by sample period ΔT defines the angle of rotation:

$$n = \frac{\omega'}{|\omega'|} = \frac{\omega'}{\sqrt{\omega_x'^2 + \omega_y'^2 + \omega_z'^2}} = [n_x, n_y, n_z]$$

(2)

$$\theta = |\omega'|.\Delta T.$$

Corresponding update matrix is:

$$R_{update} = \begin{bmatrix} c + n_x^2(1-c) & n_x n_y(1-c) - n_z s & n_x n_z(1-c) + n_y s \\ n_y n_x(1-c) + n_z s & c + n_y^2(1-c) & n_y n_z(1-c) - n_x s \\ n_z n_x(1-c) - n_y s & n_z n_y(1-c) + n_x s & c + n_z^2(1-c) \end{bmatrix}$$

(3)

where $c = \cos\theta$ and $s = \sin\theta$. If we use substitution:

$$u = 1 - c$$
$$u_x = n_x u \quad u_y = n_y u \quad u_z = n_z u$$
$$s_x = n_x s \quad s_y = n_y s \quad s_z = n_z s$$
$$r_{xx} = n_x u_x \quad r_{yy} = n_y u_y \quad r_{zz} = n_z u_z$$
$$r_{xy} = n_x u_y \quad r_{yz} = n_y u_z \quad r_{zx} = n_z u_x$$

(4)

we obtain:

$$R_{update} = \begin{bmatrix} c + r_{xx} & r_{xy} - u_z & r_{zx} + u_y \\ r_{xy} + u_z & c + r_{yy} & r_{yz} - u_x \\ r_{zx} - u_y & r_{yz} + u_x & c + r_{zz} \end{bmatrix}$$

(5)

Fast Version

In case of high sampling frequency, we can use infinitesimal rotation matrix based on first order approximation of trigonometric functions:

$$\lim_{x \to 0} \sin x = x \quad \lim_{x \to 0} \cos x = 1$$

(6)

Update matrix has form of infinitesimal rotational matrix:

$$R_{update} = \begin{bmatrix} 1 & -\omega_z' dT & \omega_y' dT \\ \omega_z' dT & 1 & -\omega_x' dT \\ -\omega_y' dT & \omega_x' dT & 1 \end{bmatrix}$$

(7)

Because of the linearity of equations (there is no need for calculation of trigonometric functions or normalization of axis vector) this is method fastest from all mentioned methods (it is about 3-times faster than precise version depending on used hardware). The main disadvantage is low accuracy, which constrains this algorithm for systems with high sampling frequency.

Fig. 2 compares fast and precise version by its relative error with respect to sampling frequency. As a test input for algorithms were used model of precession motion with perpendicular precession axis. Angular velocity of primary rotation and precession were $A = 1$ rad.s^{-1}. Angular velocity of object is than given by following:

$$\omega'_x = A \quad \omega'_y = A\sin(At) \quad \omega'_z = A\cos(At) \tag{8}$$

Initial pitch angle was $\beta_0 = 60°$. Fig. 2 also shows relative error of the least precise computed Euler angle after half turn ($t_{max} = \pi/A$).

Expression of rotation based on rotational matrices does not contain any singularities; therefore it is working with constant precision for every tilt. The advantage is also quick algorithm of vector transformation.

2.2   Algorithm Based on Euler Angles Rate Integration

This version uses relation between angular velocity ω' measured in coordinate system S' and time derivations of Euler angles:

$$\begin{bmatrix} \dot{\alpha} \\ \dot{\beta} \\ \dot{\gamma} \end{bmatrix} = \begin{bmatrix} 1 & \dfrac{\sin\alpha\sin\beta}{\cos\beta} & \dfrac{\cos\alpha\sin\beta}{\cos\beta} \\ 0 & \cos\alpha & -\sin\alpha \\ 0 & \dfrac{\sin\alpha}{\cos\beta} & \dfrac{\cos\alpha}{\cos\beta} \end{bmatrix} \cdot \begin{bmatrix} \omega'_x \\ \omega'_y \\ \omega'_z \end{bmatrix} \tag{9}$$

By integration of time derivations $\dot{\alpha}, \dot{\beta}, \dot{\gamma}$ we get resulting Euler angles. The principle is shown in Fig. 3.

There are two algorithms of numerical integration.

Step Integration

$$\alpha_n = \alpha_{n-1} + \dot{\alpha}_n \Delta T \tag{10}$$

Trapezoidal Integration

$$\alpha_n = \alpha_{n-1} + (\dot{\alpha}_{n-1} + \dot{\alpha}_n)\frac{\Delta T}{2} \tag{11}$$

Fig. 3 shows that step integration is in case of Euler angles integration little more precise.

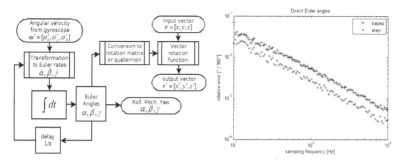

Fig. 3. Algorithm based on Euler angles rate integration and the relation between error and sampling frequency in algorithm based on direct Euler angles integration

The main disadvantage of this algorithm is singularity of expression (9) in case of $\cos \beta = 0$ called gimbal-lock, which is representing state, when x-axis is pointing downwards resp. upwards ($\beta = 90°$ resp. $\beta = -90°$). In surroundings of this singularity is rising numerical error. In case that position reaches this singularity, the information about 2 DoF is lost (see Fig. 4).

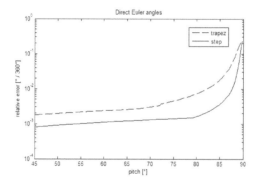

Fig. 4. Relation between error and initial pitch angle β_0 at $f_{sample} = 200$Hz of Euler angles based algorithm

Removing this error is possible by early conversion to another Euler convention which reaches singularity in other points (for example conversion to 1-2-1, 1-3-1, 2-3-1, 3-1-2, 3-1-3 or 3-2-3 conversion). After calculation of Euler angles in substitute convention, they are transformed back to the primary convention. Accuracy is then achieved in whole angle range. This is computation demanding non-linear operation described in [2].

2.3   Algorithm Based on Quaternion

Third possibility is to utilize primary expression of rotation using quaternion. Principle is expressed by Fig. 5:

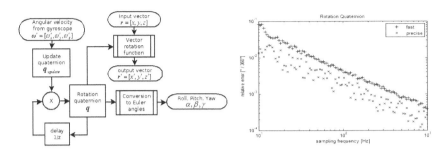

Fig. 5. Principle of quaternion-based algorithm and the comparison of fast and precise quaternion implementation by relative error after half turn relative to sampling frequency

Similar as rotational matrix, two variants of calculation are possible.

Precise Version

It is an analogy of precise matrix-based algorithm. The form of update quaternion is following:

$$
\begin{aligned}
\boldsymbol{q}_{\text{update}} &= -\left(n'_x \boldsymbol{i} + n'_y \boldsymbol{j} + n'_z \boldsymbol{k}\right)\sin\left(\frac{\omega' \Delta T}{2}\right) + \cos\left(\frac{\omega' \Delta T}{2}\right) \\
&= -\frac{\left(\omega'_x \boldsymbol{i} + \omega'_y \boldsymbol{j} + \omega'_z \boldsymbol{k}\right)}{\omega'}\sin\left(\frac{\omega' \Delta T}{2}\right) + \cos\left(\frac{\omega' \Delta T}{2}\right),
\end{aligned}
\tag{12}
$$

where $\omega' = |\boldsymbol{\omega}'| = \sqrt{\omega_x'^2 + \omega_y'^2 + \omega_z'^2}$.

Then it is valid:

$$
\boldsymbol{q}_n = \boldsymbol{q}_{\text{update}} \cdot \boldsymbol{q}_{n-1}
\tag{13}
$$

Faster Version

Neglecting higher order members, using approximations:

$$
\frac{\omega'_i}{\omega'}\sin\left(\frac{\omega' \Delta T}{2}\right) \approx \frac{\omega' \Delta T_i}{2} \qquad \cos\left(\frac{\omega' \Delta T}{2}\right) \approx 1
\tag{14}
$$

we obtain update quaternion in form:

$$
\boldsymbol{q}_{\text{update}} = \left(-\frac{\omega'_x dt}{2}\boldsymbol{i} - \frac{\omega'_y dt}{2}\boldsymbol{j} - \frac{\omega'_z dt}{2}\boldsymbol{k} + 1\right)
\tag{15}
$$

Then according to (13) is valid:

$$q_n = q_{update} \cdot q_{n-1}$$

$$\approx \left(-\frac{\omega'_x dt}{2} i - \frac{\omega'_y dt}{2} j - \frac{\omega'_z dt}{2} k + 1 \right) q_{n-1} \tag{16}$$

$$\approx q_{n-1} - \frac{dt}{2} \left(\omega'_x i + \omega'_y j + \omega'_z k \right) q_{n-1} = q_{n-1} + dq$$

which results in:

$$\frac{dq}{dt} = -\frac{1}{2} \left(\omega'_x i + \omega'_y j + \omega'_z k \right) q_{n-1} \tag{17}$$

Integration of quaternion derivation by time we get resulting rotation quaternion.

Table 1. Comparison of methods in terms of 8-bit AVR processor clock cycles

	Rotation matrix	*Euler angles*	*Arbitrary axis*	*Quaternion*
Redundancy	**	****	***	***
(count of variables)	9	3	4 (3)	4
Input data processing	*** +	***	*	****
(rotation update)	17230 (6034+)	14750	x	11462
Vector transformation	****	*	**	***
	2301	x	8063	4321
Transformation to rota-	*****	**	***	****
tional matrix	0	12930	6867	3536
Transformation to Euler	****	*****	**	***
angles	7820	0	13301	10673
Transformation to arbi-	***	*	*****	****
trary axis	5981	x	0	5424
Transformation to quater-	***	**	****	*****
nion	3370	13020	4050	0

Legend:
+	Multiplication of actual rotational matrix by infinitesimal matrix
x	Direct calculation doesn't exist, transformation to another type of expression is needed
*	Improper
**	Usable
***	Good
****	Excellent
*****	No demands on computing time

3   Summary

Advantages and disadvantages of mentioned expressions of rotations are shown in the table 1.

Mentioned cycle counts are average values from 1000 random inputs, using mathematical library optimized for AVR 8-bit microcontrollers. Algorithms are using software-implemented floating point arithmetic due to fact that AVR microcontrollers are not containing floating point unit (FPU). Utilization of 32-bit microcontroller with FPU reduces many times the count of needed clock cycles (in case of adding and multiplication of real numbers approx. 60 times depending on used processor).

From qualitative point of view is clear that quaternion and rotational matrix have similar properties. Selection of implementation depends mainly on demands on sensor system. When simultaneous Euler angles measuring and vector transformation is demanded, a combined system which is saving data in multiple forms is needed.

4   Conclusion

The resulting error of Euler angle calculation depends mainly on sample frequency. For device operating near 90° tilt the singularity of direct Euler angles integration is causing additional error and another way of rotation expression is needed (rotation matrix, quaternion). To obtain the best results it is necessary to consider balance between algorithm accuracy and its demands on computation time. In embedded systems the best results are obtained by using microprocessor with FPU for floating point calculations. The implementation of this computing is done in mobile robot – quad-rotor helicopter, other types of mobile robots are mentioned in [1].

Acknowledgments. The paper was elaborated with support of the Slovak grant agency VEGA, grant No. 1/0453/12 "Study of interactions of a motor vehicle, traffic flow and road".

References

1. Novák, P.: Mobilní roboty - pohony, senzory, řízení, p. 248. Nakladatelství BEN - technická literatura, Praha (2005)
2. Singla, P., Mortari, D., Junkins, J.L.: How to Avoid Singularity When Using Euler Angles? (2013), http://lairs.eng.buffalo.edu/pdffiles/pconf/C10.pdf (date of access: August 6, 2013)
3. Kvasnica, J.: a kol.: Mechanika. Academia Praha, Prague (2004)

Velocity Planning of an Electric Vehicle
Using an Evolutionary Algorithm

Mirosław Targosz, Michał Szumowski, Wojciech Skarka, and Piotr Przystałka

Silesian University of Technology, Faculty of Mechanical Engineering,
Konarskiego18 A, 44-100 Gliwice, Poland
{miroslaw.targosz,wojciech.skarka,piotr.przystalka}@polsl.pl,
michalszumowski@gmail.com

Abstract. This paper presents an approach to planning the driving velocity of an electric vehicle. As an object of study a prototype vehicle Mushellka has been chosen. It was built to take part in the Shell Eco-marathon competition. The competition took place in May 2012 and 2013. The paper presents the results of the determined optimum velocity for the street circuit in Rotterdam. Optimizations were performed using evolutionary algorithms. The objective function was to minimize the energy consumption. The calculations were performed in Matlab Simulink. The paper describes the mathematical modelling of the vehicle, the idea and the method of route planning, as well as the use of a prototype telematic system.

Keywords: velocity optimization, efficiency, electric vehicles, energy consumption.

1 Introduction

Determinants of the global market force a continuous improvement in the newly designed technical objects. Recently, the issue of optimal use of energy in transport has become of key importance. The energy efficiency and the optimum utilization of the engine belong to the most important technical problems in the automotive industry. Due to a highly non-linear performance of vehicles' engines, it is important that the engine shaft velocity and torque are placed in the areas of the highest efficiency.

The choice of the driving unit and of the range of gear ratios is optimized to provide relevant dynamic parameters of newly designed vehicles taking into account a high efficiency. However, covering a specific route in terms of optimal energy consumption depends on many factors, including velocity, mode of acceleration and braking, hill-climbing method etc.

In the literature descriptions of searching the optimum speed of passenger vehicles [1,6], trucks [2-4,10] and others [5] can be found, but very often parameters such as time of acceleration, time of deceleration are not subject to optimization neither is the velocity while turning [4,10].The optimization is also carried out in order to maximize velocity at the exit of a turn for racing cars [11].

J. Mikulski (Ed.): TST 2013, CCIS 395, pp. 171–177, 2013.
© Springer-Verlag Berlin Heidelberg 2013

This paper presents an approach to planning the optimal velocity of a prototype electric car. The following chapters describe a mathematical model of the vehicle and its tuning using a telematic system. The optimal velocity was obtained using an evolutionary algorithm. The construction of the chromosome has been described in details and the results of the optimization and verification have been presented.

2   Research Object

The research object is a lightweight wheeled vehicle Mushellka [7,9] with an electric drive. This vehicle has been designed and built at the Institute of Fundamentals of Machinery Design of the Silesian University of Technology. The vehicle took part in the European edition of the Shell Eco-marathon competition, which was held in Rotterdam in May 2012 and 2013. The competitions consist of driving the route of 16 km in no more than 39 minutes. After the ride the judges read the energy consumption (depending on class - liquid fuels, hydrogen, electricity) and carry out calculations in order to present the result as the number of kilometers per energy unit, e.g. km / l or km / kWh. The vehicle wins in a certain class that achieved the best results (most economical vehicle). These prestigious competitions are held for many years and have attracted crowds of students, scientists and industry personnel working on the idea of improving the energy efficiency. During these competitions a vehicle with the lowest weight and the least resistance is not enough to get the right result, of course, it is necessary to choose the right strategies to pass through each section of the track. Each team has the possibility to make only a few training runs on the track so it is not possible to select the optimal driving strategy experimentally. A number of simulations are performed with the use of a computer model.

The mathematical model takes into account all the components of the vehicle drag forces acting on the vehicle. A general equation of motion may be written as:

$$F_N - F_t - F_P - F_W = m\frac{dv}{dt} \tag{1}$$

Where:

F_N- driving force, F_t – rolling resistance, F_P – aerodynamic resistance, F_W – slope resistance, m – mass of the vehicle, v – velocity of the vehicle.

Particular components of the motion resistance were identified at specially designed test benches. The first is a test bench, which enables the study of the rolling resistance, the second allows to evaluate the efficiency of mechanical transmission [8]. The third allows to determine the mechanical characteristics of electric motors. The aerodynamic drag is known and it was estimated using CFD analysis, which has also been verified experimentally in the wind tunnel of the Institute of Aviation in

Warsaw. The research object is equipped with a telemetric module and data acquisition module [7] and it can collect the data like motor speed, vehicle speed, voltage and current supplied to the motor, temperature, GPS position; the vehicle also has an IMU (Inertial Measurement Unit). Measurement and data acquisition units will provide the necessary data about dynamics of the objects. Table 1 shows some of the identified vehicle parameters.

Table 1. Parameters of vehicle

Parameter		
Aerodynamic drag coefficient	cx	0,23
Frontal area	$A\ [m]$	0.296
Tyre rolling resistance coefficient	Crr	0.0014
Efficiency of transmission	η	95 %

Having modelled the object it will be possible to carry out a series of simulations of the system, taking into account different types of route and time. When the vehicle competes at races, the route parameters are known. We know the type of surface, the angle of route slope, the radius. The data is very precise, because the track is measured and there are no problems with the data interpretation. If we have built and identified a model of the object and route we can set various characteristics such as the energy consumption at different types of control and at different velocities during climbing and turning. A computer numerical model of the vehicle was programed in the Matlab-Simulink environment.

3   Telematic Driver Assistance System

The planning of an appropriate strategy of the race is very important. In motorsports, where all competing vehicles have similar performances, the optimal strategy is decisive as far as the final result is concerned. In the case of Shell Eco-marathon the strategy is even more important. The competition goes on a few days, preceded by tests. During this time competitors have the opportunity to find the optimal driving strategy.

Figure 1 shows the data flow between the racing car and the central computer using a telematic system [9]. The data such as velocity, energy consumption etc. is transferred by GSM network to the database.

The data is compared with the data obtained from computer simulations. If necessary, changes are made in the proposed strategy taking into account the driver's attention or a possible change of track. Weather conditions are very important, especially the wind force and direction. The operation of system in its current version consists of programming the optimum velocity of car in certain parts of the route, taking into account the most important parameters affecting the result.

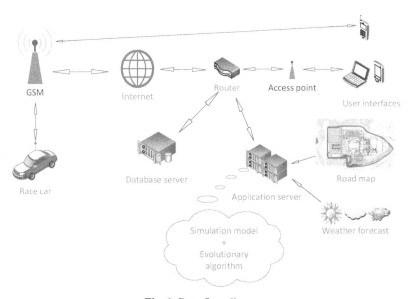

GSM

Internet

Router   Access point

User interfaces

Race car

Database server

Road map

Application server

Weather forecast

Simulation model
+
Evolutionary
algorithm

Fig. 1. Data flow diagram

4   Optimal Velocity Planning Method

The purpose of the Shell Eco Marathon race is to drive as far as possible with the use of the least amount of energy. In this race drivers have to go a certain amount of laps on the track at an average speed of 25 km/h with the minimal energy consumption. A factor indicating the number of kilometres that the vehicle travels per 1 kWh is a measure of the system efficiency. In this case the planning of the completion strategy can be reduced to the optimization task, in which the best possible trajectory of the linear velocity is sought. Therefore, the optimization of the strategy is based on the determination of the nominal velocity as a function of the distance. Taking into account these arguments the objective function can be defined as a meta-criterion:

$$f(\mathbf{cv}) = \sum_{i=1}^{3} w_i c_i = w_1 \frac{\alpha}{1+\varepsilon_{sim}^2} + w_2 \frac{|d_{cv} - d_{sim}|}{d_{cv}} + w_3 \frac{|t_{cv} - t_{sim}|}{t_{cv}} \tag{2}$$

where α is a scaling factor (in this study $\alpha = 10^6$), c_i and w_i indicate the i th criterion and its importance, ε_{sim} [km/kWh] is an estimator of the system efficiency calculated on the basis of the total energy consumption in the ride, d_{cv} and d_{sim} [m] are the reference path and the value of the covered distance obtained as a result of the simulation, t_{cv} and t_{sim} [s] represent the set limit value of the travel time and the travel time calculated on the basis of the simulation, $\mathbf{cv}$ is the velocity vector where cv_i [m/s] is defined for certain sections of the route (the size of this vector depends on the complexity of the route).

The first component of the objective function (2) is responsible for minimizing energy consumption. Two other components are penalty factors being the limitation that is imposed on the average velocity of the race car. Their goal is to ensure that the vehicle will drive an assumed way at the optimum time.

In this paper, the optimal solution (the minimum of the objective function) is searched using evolutionary algorithms [12,13]. Classical optimization methods (for example gradient-based techniques) cannot be adapted in this context mainly due to the discontinuity of the objective function (2).

5   Case Study

The use of an evolutionary algorithm to search for the optimum velocity of the vehicle at the route sections requires the definition of its basic features. In the present study, the optimization process was carried out using MATLAB® with Genetic Algorithm and Direct Search toolbox. Evolutionary algorithm parameters were chosen according to the guidelines suggested in the literature [12]. The fitness function was based on the meta-criterion (2), wherein the weights were defined using a trial and error procedure (w1=0.01, w2=0.99, w3=1) and other parameters such as set-point values were declared taking into consideration the characteristics of the race (dcv= 16300m, tcv = 2340s). Because of the preliminary results of simulation it was decided that the upper and lower limits of the reference value of the car velocity would equal to 0 and 11m/s, respectively. It was determined that individuals in the population would be composed of genes representing real numeric values. Genes in the chromosome correspond to the set-points of the velocity in such a way, that:

$$\mathbf{chr} = \mathbf{cv} = \begin{bmatrix} cv_1 & cv_2 & \cdots & cv_{24} \end{bmatrix} \tag{3}$$

The total length of the chromosome in this case depends on the number of specific sections of the route. The feasible population method was adapted to create a random well-dispersed initial population that satisfies all bounds. The ranking method was used to scale the fitness function and the uniform stochastic selection was employed to choose parents creating new individuals for the next generation. Reproduction was carried out applying the elite count method (the number of individuals equal to 2) and crossover as well as mutation operators. In the paper, the scattered crossover was executed with the probability of 0.8. The remaining individuals (other than elite and crossover children) were processed using a non-uniform mutation. The maximum number of generations was chosen as the criterion for stopping the algorithm. It was experimentally established that, the population size would equal to 200 and the maximum number of generations would equal to 500.

In the next step, an experimental simulation was conducted taking into account the optimization results. Figure 2 shows the results of simulations that were achieved for optimal velocities of the race car (red line marks turns on the route, blue line indicates the instantaneous speed of the vehicle). It can be seen in Figure 2, that there are three phases of the race. On the first lap the race car is accelerated to the average speed.

On the last lap the vehicle slows down to a complete halt. The middle plot in Figure 2 presents the laps between the first and the last. The simulation results showed that it is possible to obtain ε_{sim}= 455 km/kWh.

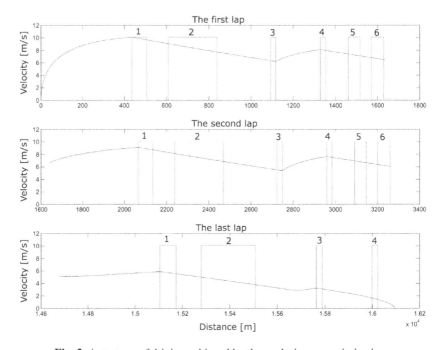

Fig. 2. A strategy of driving achieved by the evolutionary optimization

The best solution obtained during the optimization process was used to prepare an appropriate strategy for the driver that took part in the real world competition. During the Shell Eco-Marathon in 2012, the team from the Silesian University of Technology received the result of ε_{real}= 425 km/kWh. In the next year our team managed to improve the performance to a level ε_{real}= 455 km/kWh. Such a result confirms the correctness of the proposed approach.

6   Conclusion

This paper presents an approach to planning the driving speed of an electric vehicle. A prototype vehicle Mushellka for the Shell Eco-marathon competition was used as an object of the study. The competition took place in May 2012 and 2013. The paper presents the results of determination of the optimum speed for the street circuit in Rotterdam. Optimizations were performed using evolutionary algorithms. The objective function was to minimize the energy consumption. The calculations were performed in Matlab Simulink. The paper describes the mathematical modelling of the vehicle, the idea and method of route planning as well as the use of a prototype telematic system. A computer model of the vehicle can be used to optimize the parameters of the vehicle, and to verify the design and technology.

References

1. Dorri, M., Shamekhi, A.H.: Design and optimization of a new control strategy in a parallel hybrid electric vehicle in order to improve fuel economy. In: Proc. IMechE, Part D: J. Automobile Engineering, vol. 225
2. Fröberg, A., Hellström, E., Nielsen, L.: Explicit Fuel Optimal Speed Profiles for Heavy Trucks on a Set of Topographic Road Profiles
3. Hellström, E., Åslund, J., Nielsen, L.: Design of an efficient algorithm for fuel optimal look-ahead control, Control Engineering Practice (2010)
4. Hellström, E., Ivarsson, M., Aslund, J., Nielsen, L.: Look-ahead control for heavy trucks to minimize trip time and fuel consumption. Control Engineering Practice 17, 245–254 (2008)
5. Janssenswillen, J., Swinnen, R., Wolfs, S., Slaets, P.: Optimal Dynamic Predic-tive Cruise Control for differential driven electric vehicles. In: EVS26 International Battery, Hybrid and Fuel Cell Electric Vehicle Symposium
6. Li, S.E., Peng, H.: Strategies to Minimize Fuel Consumption of Passenger Cars during Car-Following Scenarios. In: 2011 American Control Conference, June 29-July 1 (2011)
7. Sternal, K., Cholewa, A., Skarka, W., Targosz, M.: Electric vehicle for the stu-dents' Shell Eco-marathon competition. Design of the car and telemetry system. In: Mikulski, J. (ed.) TST 2012. CCIS, vol. 329, pp. 26–33. Springer, Heidelberg (2012)
8. Targosz, M.: Test bench for efficiency evaluation of belt and chain transmissions. In: XII International Technical System Degradation Conferences, Liptowski, Mikulas, Slovakia, April 3-6 (2013)
9. Targosz, M., Skarka, W.: Synergia metod modelowania konstrukcji na przykładzie projek-tu Smart Power. Cz. 1. Mechanik 86(2) (2013)
10. van Keulen, T., de Jager, B., Foster, D., Steinbuch, M.: Velocity Trajectory Op-timization in Hybrid Electric Trucks
11. Velenis, E., Tsiotras, P.: Minimum Time vs Maximum Exit Velocity Path Opti-mization During Cornering
12. Deb, K.: Multi-objective optimization using evolutionary algorithms. Wiley (2009)
13. Rutkowski, L.: Methods and techniques of artificial intelligence. PWN, Warsaw (2005) (in Polish)

Efficiency Analysis of Train Monitoring System Applying the Changeable Block Distance Method

Andrzej Toruń[1] and Andrzej Lewiński[2]

[1] Railway Institute, Railway Traffic Control and Telecom Unit
04-275 Warszawa, J. Chłopickiego 50, Poland
atorun@ikolej.pl
[2] University of Technology and Humanities in Radom,
Faculty of Transport and Electrical Engineering,
26-600 Radom, Malczewskiego 29, Poland
a.lewinski@uthrad.pl

Abstract. The paper deals with efficiency analysis of railway line equipped with Changeable Block Distance Method (CDB) applying the different positioning methods (balises, GPS) and radio transmission (GSM-R) to the Dispatcher Centre with accordance to traditional Fixed Block Method (FDB) of train sequence control using insulated rail sections. For estimation the needs of such solution the Mass Service Model (based on Markov processes) has been elaborated to show which train traffic parameters assure the efficiency the CDB. The simulation model has been also presented to show how the queue of trains may be successfully unloaded in the stations using CDB method in comparison to FDB method. Both models require train traffic parameters related to real routes (sequence of several insulated rail sections with boundary stations) corresponding to typical time table including the different types of trains (truck, passenger and express trains).

Keywords: changeable block distance, train positioning, capacity, efficient analysis.

1 Introduction

The traditional methods of control the train succession connected with rail section or point detection of train have the technological limits disenabling the increasing of train efficiency. It is related to typical rule of train control corresponding to fixed block distance (FBD) rule (Fig. 1.a). It is mean that safe distance between trains is designed with respect to breaking way with the worst traction parameters of train in the route. it is mean that designed distance may not be shorter than the longest breaking way. It is a direct reason limiting the capacity of railway line with trains of diverted maximal speed (passenger and truck trains).

The increasing the capacity of railway line may be obtained using reduction of block distances between trains (Fig.1.b) or reduction the distance between trains by applying the Changeable Block Distance (CBD) rule (Fig. 1.c)

J. Mikulski (Ed.): TST 2013, CCIS 395, pp. 178–187, 2013.
© Springer-Verlag Berlin Heidelberg 2013

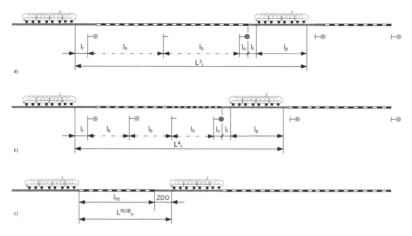

Fig. 1. The way of train succession with a) 3 stage block system b) 4 stage block system c) new method of train positioning 2

where:

$L^{3,4,ROB}{}_n$ – -is a succession distance for given variant of control

l_r –   is a distance related to delay of locomotive driver reaction,

l_b –   length of block distance, for 3 stage block system the minimal length of breaking way is assumed l_h defined for given railway line, for 4 stage block system the following condition must be satisfied $\frac{l_h}{2} \le l_b < l_h$, but in new CBD method is not fixed,

l_o –   protection distance after semaphore assumed as 15÷30m,

l_t –   distance connected with train after change of signals,

l_p –   length of trains,

l_{hz} –   breaking way of main train,

ZDO –   reserved safety margin distance.

In the paper the analysis of new method of train positioning has been presented allowing the implementation of CDB algorithm [5 - 8, 12, 13], without necessity of removing the existing railway control devices. This method may be applied to typical lines with traditional method of train control related to fixed block distance rule.

The original concept of proposed method is a qualification of train position using second, independent source of information from GNSS together with standard single block distance positioning and transmitting such information via public network to the Control Centre to update with respect to information detected from traditional systems (rail circuits, axe counters, etc.), estimation new end of train route and generation of back message to the centre [9 - 11].

To determine an influence the proposed positioning method for railway control process the authors suggest two arbitrary basic measures of efficiency estimated using computer aided methods and simulation experiments:

1. Tractability against interferences and failures related to immediately stop of train.
2. Capacity of railway line.

The comparison of such measures before and after implementation of proposed method give assumption that new method may increase the efficiency and capacity of railway line with guaranteed level of existing of safety. The choice of research methods allows to estimate both the railway line capacity and the probability of train stop.

2   Estimation of Influence of CBD Method for Fluency of Trains

The estimation of proposed CBD method for fluency of trains has been realized by determination of probability the event of train stop caused by proper reaction of train devices after receiving the emergency signals (faulty locomotive driver action or faulty devices action). For such evaluation the probabilistic analysis has done including Markov process models with following assumptions [1, 3, 4]:

–   The calls connected with permission of train drive incoming to the Control centre are determined and discrete,
–   The Markov process with finite number of states is homogenous, stationary (in common sense) and ergodic.

The general model of train control process with respect to Fixed Block Distance method is presented on Fig. 2. a), but the modification towards new CDB method (with the same description of states and intensities) is shown on the Fig. 2. b).

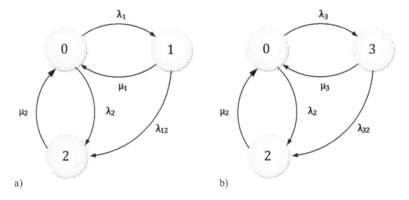

Fig. 2. The general model of train control process a) Fixed Block Distance, b) CBD method[2]

State 0 – state of correct system action – the locomotive driver works corresponding to last drive permission (last semaphore signal) up to next information about train movement,

State 1, 3 – the locomotive driver receives the drive permission (1- semaphore signal, 3- system telegram) and implements the action corresponding to safety drive with respect to semaphore signals,

State 2 – the train stops after emergency breaking system, the locomotive driver implements the procedure connected with train movement according to safety drive conditions (semaphore signals).

Corresponding to assumed Markov model the Fokker-Planc (Kolmogorov) equations are derived:

(1) – for model from Fig. 2 a).

$$
\begin{cases}
\dfrac{dP_0(t)}{dt} = -\lambda_1 \cdot P_0(t) + \mu_1 \cdot P_1(t) - \lambda_2 \cdot P_0(t) + \mu_2 \cdot P_2(t) \\[2mm]
\dfrac{dP_1(t)}{dt} = \lambda_1 \cdot P_0(t) - \lambda_{12} \cdot P_1(t) - \mu_1 \cdot P_1(t) \\[2mm]
\dfrac{dP_2(t)}{dt} = \lambda_{12} \cdot P_1(t) - \mu_2 \cdot P_2(t) + \lambda_2 \cdot P_0(t)
\end{cases}
\tag{1}
$$

$$
P_0(t) + P_1(t) + P_2(t) = 1
$$

where:

P_0, P_1, P_2 – probabilities of occurrence in the state 0, 1,2,

λ_1 –   intensity of events connected with departure of train to semaphore and receiving the information about next drive procedure λ_{12} – intensity of event connected with faulty reaction of locomotive driver or inproper action of SHP/CA system,

λ_2 –   intensity of events connected with RadioStop signal, implementation of service breaking (without driver) to total stop of train,

μ_1^{-1} –   time necessary for show the driver the information about next action – procedure of train driving with respect to safety conditions,

μ_2^{-1} –   time necessary for driver to next start after automatic stop of train.

(2) for model from Fig. 2 b).

$$
\begin{cases}
\dfrac{dP_0(t)}{dt} = \mu_3 \cdot P_3(t) - \lambda_3 \cdot P_0(t) - \lambda_2 \cdot P_0(t) + \mu_2 \cdot P_2(t) \\[2mm]
\dfrac{dP_2(t)}{dt} = \lambda_{32} \cdot P_3(t) - \mu_2 \cdot P_2(t) + \lambda_2 \cdot P_0(t) \\[2mm]
\dfrac{dP_3(t)}{dt} = \lambda_3 \cdot P_3(t) - \lambda_{32} \cdot P_3(t) - \mu_3 \cdot P_3(t)
\end{cases}
\tag{2}
$$

$$
P_0(t) + P_2(t) + P_3(t) = 1
$$

where:

P_0, P_2, P_3 – probabilities of occurrence in the state 0, 2, 3,

λ_2 –   intensity of events connected with receiving the RadioStop signal, implementation of service breaking (without driver) to total stop of train,

λ_3 –   intensity of events connected with up datedemend of ZNJ signal,

λ_{32} –   intensity of events connected with not receiving the information by RSW system,

μ_2^{-1}–   time necessary for driver to next start after automatic stop of train.

μ_3^{-1}–   time necessary for receiving the ZNJ signal and transfer to the locomotive driver, information about next action – driving procedure corresponding to safety conditions.

The linear equations (1) i (2) after Laplace transform have a form (3) and (4).

$$\begin{cases} s \cdot P_0 - 1 = \mu_1 \cdot P_1 - \lambda_1 \cdot P_0 - \lambda_2 \cdot P_0 + \mu_2 \cdot P_2 \\ s \cdot P_1 = \lambda_1 \cdot P_0 - \lambda_{12} \cdot P_1 - \mu_1 \cdot P_1 \\ s \cdot P_2 = \lambda_{12} \cdot P_1 + \lambda_2 \cdot P_0 - \mu_2 \cdot P_2 \end{cases} \tag{3}$$

$$\begin{cases} s \cdot P_0 - 1 = \mu_3 \cdot P_3 - \lambda_3 \cdot P_0 - \lambda_2 \cdot P_0 + \mu_2 \cdot P_2 \\ s \cdot P_2 = \lambda_{32} \cdot P_3 + \lambda_2 \cdot P_0 - \mu_2 \cdot P_2 \\ s \cdot P_3 = \lambda_3 \cdot P_3 - \lambda_{32} \cdot P_3 - \mu_3 \cdot P_3 \end{cases} \tag{4}$$

Using the Mathematica software we can estimate the boundary probabilities ($t \to \infty$) of occurrence in defined earlier states. The obtained values of P_2 are described by P_{2SOB} (5) i P_{2CBD} (6).

$$P_2 = P_2(t) \mid_{t \to \infty} = \frac{\lambda_1 \cdot \lambda_{12} + \lambda_2 \cdot (\lambda_{12} + \mu_1)}{(\lambda_{12} + \mu_1) \cdot (\lambda_2 + \mu_2) + \lambda_1 \cdot (\lambda_{12} + \mu_2)} \tag{5}$$

For values $\lambda_1 = 37.5$ [h⁻¹], $\mu_1 = 300$ [h⁻¹], $\lambda_3 = 120$ [h⁻¹], $\mu_3 = 720$ [h⁻¹], $\lambda_{32} = 0.001$ [h⁻¹], intensities λ_2 and λ_{12} assumed from statistic data from PKP PLK, and μ_2^{-1} assumed as a time necessary for train start after stop the obtained value is :

$$P_{2SOB} = 1.41 \cdot 10^{-5}$$

$$P_2 = P_2(t) \mid_{t \to \infty} = \frac{\lambda_3 \cdot \lambda_{32} + \lambda_2 \cdot (\lambda_{32} + \mu_3)}{\lambda_3 \cdot (\lambda_{32} + \mu_2) + \lambda_2 \cdot (\lambda_{32} + \mu_3) + \mu_2 \cdot (\lambda_{32} + \mu_3)} \tag{6}$$

For CDB such value is equal to:

$$P_{2CBD}=4.69 \cdot 10^{-6}$$

The verification of probabilities P2 estimated by analytical way has done using simulation in MATLAB&SIMULINK environment. The charts of P_{2FBD} and P_{2CBD} are presented on the Fig.3 and Fig.4. (The boundary values are equal $P_{2FBD}= 3.74 \cdot 10^{-5}$ for Fixed Block Distance method, and $P_{2CBD}= 2.53 \cdot 10^{-6}$ for CBD method).

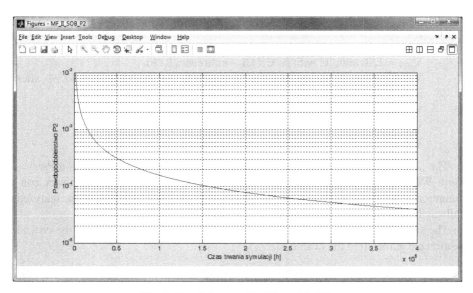

Fig. 3. Simulation result of P_{2FBD} (t) [13]

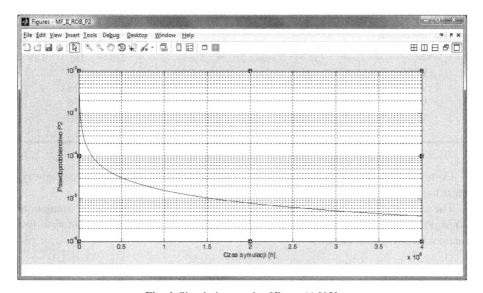

Fig. 4. Simulation result of P_{2CBD} (t) [13]

3   Estimation of CBD Method for Rail Line Capacity

For test of influence the proposed CDB method for train control efficiency the theoretical capacity of N_{max} is evaluated for real part of railway line.

In the experiment the basic assumption holds that for comparison the existing system with railway line devices (FBD) and additional positioning system for block distance indication are chosen. In addition the ETCS Level1 system with FBD increasing the speed to 160 km/h is analyzed. The analyzes are done for part (Psary – Góra Włodowska)   E-65 line No 4 (CMK).The following structure of train traffic is assumed:

- V_{max} = 220km\h, IC with ETCS L1 – optional, (10%),
- V_{max} = 160km\h, EuroCity, InterCity, (35% without fast train, 25% after reduction),
- V_{max} = 140km\h, Domestic Expresses, (30%),
- V_{max} = 120km\h, (Fast trains, non mass freight) (10%),
- V_{max} =   70km\h, mass freigth   – (25%),

The „theoretical drives of trains" simulations have done for even direction Psary – Góra Włodowska, using computer program SOT (designed for electric power consumption). Assuming the real route assures the very realistic drive time for analyzed railway line.

The simulation results of theoretical drives of trains the time of block the critical section are gathered in the (Table 1).

Table 1. The obtained times of drive through the critical section for different test variants using SOT program.[13]

The representative type of train	Test variant		
	I TFBD [s]	II TCBD [s]	III TFBD (ETCSL1) [s]
V200	xxx	xxx	102
V160	138	66	138
V140	156	66	156
V120	180	66	180
V70	312	66	312

Corresponding to obtained times of drive the capacity parameter for given railway regarding different test variant of train control is estimated (Table 2).

The capacity measures are verified using special software for train simulation SYM_POC. Fig 5 shows the window with graphical presentation of simulation for random mixed stream of trains.

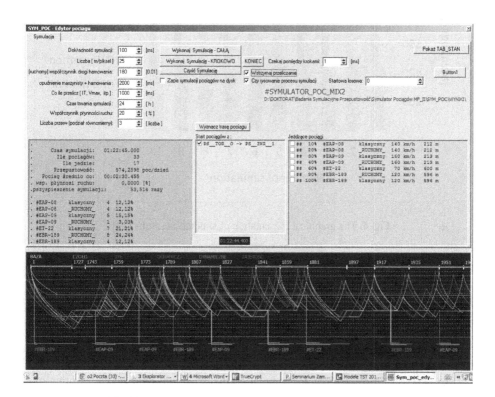

Fig. 5. The window of simulation program SYM_POC [13]

Table 2. The capacity estimation for assumed railway line [13]

Capacity line [train./day]	Test variant		
	FBD	CBD	FBD(ETCSL1)
Nmax	500.87	1047.27	500.87
Nr	397.52	1047.27	390.13

The results of simulation experiments the influence of CBD method for improvement of train capacity for given railway line are presented on Fig. 6.

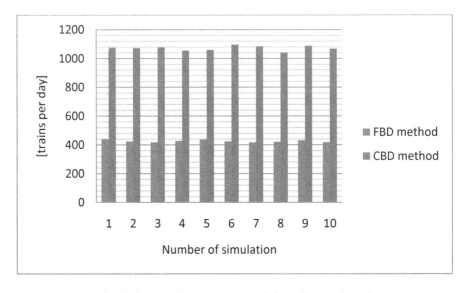

Fig. 6. The graphical presentation of simulation results [13]

4   Conclusion

The proposed method of train positioning implemented in the form of Changeable Block Distance (CBD) may significant improve the functionality and efficiency of train control in the railway line equipped in traditional line block devices.

The presented problem of increasing the efficiency shows that CBD method of train management gives the better results than existing typical solution such ETCS Level 1. The results of analytic and simulation investigations confirm the assumptions about Markov process modeling and are very helpful for future research works connected with implementation of CBD methods (some law regulations are necessary because the trains are controlled with respect to deck computer indications – the train with CBD application may pass the red signal but must assure the "electrical visibility" distance corresponding to safety breaking curve. In many papers [7 - 9, 11, 12] and especially in [13], the estimating the mean probability of CBD service based on Markov process shows the necessary conditions for implementation of presented method in polish railway environment. The simulations of CBD efficiency has been taken with respect to real PKP PLK S.A. line (Psary – Góra Włodowska) E-65 line No 4 (CMK), the positive results may be foundation for future experimental tests with trains equipped with CBD, GPS and GSM-R devices.

Presented CBD has no influence to the safety of control system corresponding to SIL-4 requirements according to PN-EN 50129 standard, the CBD may be treated as an overlay on the existing ATC and interlocking systems, it is fault may only switch on the CBD to the typical train control and monitoring and does not affect to existings procedures.

Implementation of such method has not influence to the number of train stops and safety because the proper reaction of emergency break devices (installed in locomotives) guarantee the fail-safe action after driver or device stop.

The future research works are connected with standardization of CBD procedures, laboratory and field tests of CBD experimental systems and extension of this method to the another railway applications.

References

1. Bester, L.: The Analysis of Integrated Safety System in Land Transport According to Unguarded Cross Level Systems, Ph D. dissertation, University of Technology and Humanities in Radom (October 2012)
2. Dąbrowa-Bajon, M.: Podstawy sterowania ruchem kolejowym. Oficyna Wydawnicza Politechniki Warszawskiej (2002)
3. Iosifescu, M.: Skończone procesy Markowa i ich zastosowania, wydanie 1. Wydawnictwo Naukowe PWN Warszawa (1988)
4. Kisilowski, J.: Podstawy technik pomiarowych. Skrypty naukowe WSTE, Warszawa (2005)
5. Lewiński, A., Bester, L.: Additional Warning System for Cross Level. In: Mikulski, J. (ed.) TST 2010. CCIS, vol. 104, pp. 226–231. Springer, Heidelberg (2010)
6. Lewiński, A., Perzyński, T., Toruń, A.: Funkcjonalność i bezpieczeństwo w systemach srk wykorzystujących zmienny odstęp blokowy, Logistyka 3/2012 (2012)
7. Lewiński, A., Perzyński, T., Toruń, A.: Modelowanie funkcjonalności i bezpieczeństwa systemów sterowania ruchem wyposażony w zmienny odstęp blokowy, Logistyka (March 2012)
8. Lewiński, A., Toruń, A.: Wpływ systemu sterowania realizującego zasadę ruchomego odstępu blokowego na przepustowość linii kolejowej, XVI Międzynarodowa Konferencja Naukowa TransComp – Komputerowe systemy wspomagania, nauki, przemysłu i transportu – U T-H Radom Zakopane (December 3-6, 2012)
9. Lewiński, A., Toruń, A.: The changeable block distance system analysis. In: Mikulski, J. (ed.) TST 2010. CCIS, vol. 104, pp. 67–74. Springer, Heidelberg (2010)
10. Lewiński, A., Toruń, A., Bester, L.: The Safety Analysis in the Open Transmission Standards in Railway Application. Archives of Transport System Telematics (4) (2011)
11. Lewiński, A., Toruń, A., Bester, L.: Methods of Implementation of the Open Transmission in Railway Control Systems (Sposoby realizacji transmisji otwartej w systemach sterowania ruchem kolejowym). Logistyka (March 2011)
12. Lewiński, A., Perzyński, T., Toruń, A.: The risk analysis as a basic designed methods of safety open network transmission applied in railway control systems. In: LogiTrans Conference, Szczyrk (2010) (in Polish)
13. Toruń A.: Metoda lokalizacji pociągu w procesie sterowania ruchem kolejowym. Rozprawa doktorska, Uniwersytet Technologiczno – Humanistyczny w Radomiu, Radom (2013)
14. Zabłocki, W.: Modelowanie systemów sterowania ruchem kolejowym. Prace Naukowe Politechniki Radomskiej, Transport 1(17) (2003)

Technical Infrastructure to Support Seamless Information Exchange in e-Navigation

Adam Weintrit

Gdynia Maritime University, The Faculty of Navigation 81-345 Gdynia, Poland
weintrit@am.gdynia.pl

Abstract. The International Maritime Organization (IMO) Correspondence Group on e-Navigation (the author is a member of this expert group since 2006) has reviewed the preliminary list of potential e-Navigation solutions and prioritized five potential main solutions, presented the finalized Cost Benefit and Risk Analysis, considered the further development of the detailed ship and shore architecture, giving an example of a technical infrastructure to support seamless information/data exchange in e-Navigation. In the paper author presents that technical infrastructure.

Keywords: e-Navigation, IMO, information exchange, transport telematics.

1   Introduction

The IMO Correspondence Group on e-Navigation has reviewed the preliminary list of potential e-Navigation solutions and has also considered additional potential e-Navigation solutions in order to address all identified gaps. The fact that a large number of solutions have been further reviewed the broadening of the scope reached a point where the process needed to be focused into a spearhead of prioritized solutions. The purpose is merely to describe a well defined and manageable starting point for the strategic implementation plan of e-Navigation. In light of this it has been necessary to integrate and prioritize the list of solutions given in NAV/58/WP6 rev.1 Annex 2 [5] (Preliminary List of Potential e-Navigation Solutions, which have nine main categories of solutions) to a maximum of five main practical solutions, covering shipboard and shore-based users. These solutions focus on workable and efficient transfer of marine information/data between ship and shore and vice-versa.

Accordingly, the IMO CG focused its attention on the following criteria [4]:

1. Seamless transfer of data between various equipment on board;
2. Seamless transfer of electronic information/data between ship and shore and vice-versa;
3. The work should be based on systems that are already in place (according to the already adopted IMO's e-Navigation strategy (MSC 85/26/Add.1, Annex 20) [2]) and development of potential futuristic carriage requirements should therefore be strictly limited;
4. CG should not concentrate on determining causes of marine casualties; and
5. List of potential e-Navigation solutions should be limited solely to achieve 1 and 2 above.

J. Mikulski (Ed.): TST 2013, CCIS 395, pp. 188–199, 2013.
© Springer-Verlag Berlin Heidelberg 2013

The IMO CG prioritized the following five main potential e-Navigation solutions, which are the basis for the Risk and Cost/Benefit Analyses [6]:

S1:   Improved, harmonized and user-friendly bridge design;
S2:   Means for standardized and automated reporting;
S3:   Improved reliability, resilience and integrity of bridge equipment and navigation information;
S4:   Integration and presentation of available information in graphical displays received via communication equipment; and
S9:   Improved Communication of VTS Service Portfolio.

The prioritized main potential e-Navigation solutions S2, S4 and S9 focus on efficient transfer of marine information/data between all appropriate users (ship-ship, ship-shore, shore-ship and shore-shore). Solutions S1 and S3 promote the workable and practical use of the information/data on board. The five prioritized potential solutions in combination ensure a holistic approach and interaction between the shipboard and shore-based users, which is at the core of e-Navigation.

The prioritization should not be seen as a reduction in the ambition level for e-Navigation. Remaining solutions will be assigned to a roadmap for future iterations of the e-Navigation Strategy Implementation Plan.

The solutions have served as the basis for the creation of Risk Control Options (RCOs) that were believed to be tangible and manageable in terms of quantifying the risk reducing effect and the related costs. The RCOs listed below demonstrate cost-effectiveness according to the IMO Formal Safety Assessment (FSA) criteria [7]:

RCO1:   Integration of navigation information and equipment including improved software quality assurance,
RCO2:   Bridge alert management,
RCO3:   Standardised mode(s) for navigation equipment,
RCO4:   Automated and standardised ship-shore reporting,
RCO5:   Improved reliability and resilience of PNT systems,
RCO6:   Improved shore-based services,
RCO7:   Bridge and workstation layout standardisation.

1.1   Development of the Concept of Maritime Service Portfolios

Maritime Service Portfolio (MSP) may be defined as an organized collection of operational and technical services provided from ashore to the mariner and other relevant stakeholders, in a given sea area, waterway, or port, as appropriate.

Maritime Service Portfolio is an example that could fit into Solution 9, which describes the Improved Communication of a VTS Service Portfolio. Maritime Service Portfolio could provide potential opportunities for digital information and communication service on board and ashore. MSPs will require a communication infrastructure capacity in order to provide information services.

In this respect, IMO CG agreed that MSPs should consider operations in the following areas:

1. port areas and approaches;
2. coastal waters and confined or restricted areas;
3. open sea and ocean areas;
4. areas with offshore and/or infrastructure developments;
5. Polar areas (Arctic and Antarctic);
6. other remote areas.

1.2   Development of the Detailed Ship and Shore Architecture

The IMO CG has received inputs on the further development of detailed ship and shore architecture. This development should be in accordance with the approved overarching e-Navigation architecture and the agreed recommendations of the FSA. It should further be noted that some maritime administrations are of the opinion that this development is premature at this time. However, additional e-Navigation solutions could also require adjustments on the detailed architecture.

Section 2 gives an example on technical e-Navigation infrastructure, based on the prioritized solutions S2, S4 and S9, which might fit in to the future detailed ship-shore architecture.

The IMO NAV Sub-Committee was invited in 2013 [4] to consider the possible use of the examples on technical e-Navigation infrastructure as the basis for the development of a more detailed ship-shore architecture, and provide comments as appropriate.

2   Basic Concepts

The IMO CG proposes the establishment of a technical infrastructure denoted the Maritime Cloud – a communication framework, where the identity of all registered Maritime Actors are registered in a Maritime Identity Registry, and all information services available at the individual actors are registered in a Maritime Service Portfolio Registry.

Obtaining a Maritime Identity will resemble applying for a call sign or a Maritime Mobile Service Identity (MMSI) number, and each actor will receive a digital certificate, which can be used to authenticate own information, and to establish a secure, encrypted communication link when sensitive or otherwise confidential information needs to communicated.

The Maritime Identity Registry will provide one or more Identity Brokers maintaining Identities, Attributes for identities and Certificates for identities. These Identities and their certificates will enable implementation of information security through public key infrastructures using security solutions well known in many other domains, e.g. the financial sector, this addresses security concerns such as Authenticity, Integrity and Confidentiality.

The Maritime Service Portfolio Registry will contain a service specification catalogue and a service instance catalogue. The specification of a service is located in the product specification part of the IHO S-100 GI Registry [1]. The Service Instance Catalogue is a register of provided services. The service instance catalogue links the

Service with the Service provider Identity and the Area / leg / junction / point where this service is offered as well as metadata for the provided service (e.g. quality, communication etc.) Service providers maintain their own information on provided services in the instance catalogue. Service consumers can make queries for available services in the instance catalogue.

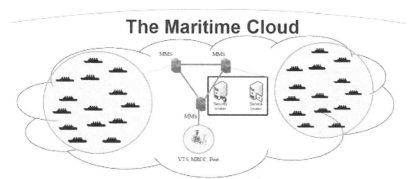

- *Actors connect regularly to a Maritime Messaging Server (MMS) inside the 'Maritime Cloud'. The network of MMS will maintain a geographical awareness of actors location at protocol level.*
- *The network of MMS will contain a distributed security- and service broker capability: A Maritime Identity Registry, and a Maritime Service Portfolio Reigstry*

Fig. 1. Actors connect regularly to a Maritime Messaging Server (MMS) inside the 'Maritime Cloud' [4], proposed by Danish Maritime Authority

The MMS server network inside the Maritime Cloud is envisaged to be operated as a distributed server network by one or more trusted third parties – could be as national or regional data centers - exchanging data at in a peer-to-peer network.

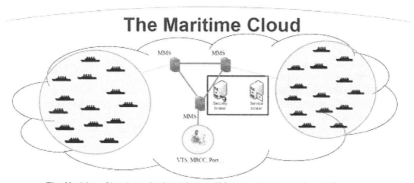

- *The Maritime Cloud can be based on well known, proven technologies*
- *Each Actor will reconnect to the MMS when changing datalink (roaming)*
- *Each actor may communicate directly with other actors, however the MMS network will implement a cache of messages (store and forward, priority queuing), for those actors that are temporarily inaccessible*

Fig. 2. The 'Maritime Cloud' based on proven technologies [4], proposed by Danish Maritime Authority

Actors will connect regularly to a Maritime Messaging Server (MMS) inside the Maritime Cloud. The network of MMS will at each connect update a geographical awareness of the position of each actor, at protocol level. Shore based or Satellite AIS information or other sources of tracking data could supplement the update rate of the geographical awareness of the MMS network, at protocol level.

The current (or historic) geographical position(s) of each actor could be made available as a basic system information service inside the Maritime Cloud, available only to those actors authorized by the actor himself, or authorized based on rules contained in a data distribution plan similar to that developed under the Long Range Identification and Tracking (LRIT) agreement.

In the Maritime Cloud, actors can communicate automatically and seamlessly, regardless of the choice of communication link. Actors connected via a TCP/IP communication link can communicate directly, including the ability of acknowledge of information/data tranfer. Actors temporarily disconnected, in a state of changing communication link, or not having a current TCP/IP based connection available, can be addressed via the MMS servers, which hold a priority queue of store and forward with acknowledge of delivery capabilities, for Maritime Information Messages (MIM) – a datacontainer for machine readable maritime information.

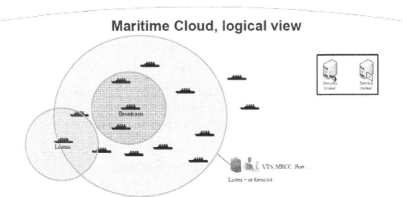

Maritime Cloud, logical view

* Actors can listen to an area – or a specific service
* Actors can Geocast to actors within a specified area
* Independent on technical implementation of communication link
* Automated quality assurance of utilized communication links and equipment

Fig. 3. The Maritime Cloud – logical view [4], proposed by Danish Maritime Authority

As an important concept, an actor can perform a Geocast to other actors, distributing a message to actors who listen to a certain geographical region or service, regardless of the communication link chosen by the individual actors.

The Almanac is an offline version of a public part of the Maritime Identity Registry and Maritime Service Portfolio Registry, which may be downloaded by actors. It will make available a 'whitepages / yellowpages phonebook' describing public, static attributes of actors, including public keys for use in establishing secure communication, and a directory of which different information services are available from which actors, in a particular area.

The ALMANAC

- Offline version of public part of 'Maritime Identity Registry' and 'Maritime Service Portfolio Registry '

- Can be downloaded as a 'white pages / yellow pages' phonebook – describes public, static information such as contact information and public keys for secure communication, and which information services each actor provides.

		SHIPS	Ports	MRCC	VTS	WEATHER
		- ENRICO III	- Aberdeen	- Reykjavik	- Brevik VTS	- Danish
		- EMA MAERSK	- Amsterdam	- Thorshavn	- Fejde VTS	Meterological
		- ESVAGT ALPHA	- ...	- ...	- ...	Institute
						- ...

Fig. 4. The Almanac - an offline version of a public part of the Maritime Identity Registry and Maritime Service Portfolio Registry [4], proposed by Danish Maritime Authority

Using this Almanac, the identity and contact information of other actors, such as name, location and callsign of a VTS centre, or name, IMO number, MMSI number callsign of a ship, is available together with a list of which services this particular actor provides.

The Almanac may function as an advanced phonebook for contact information via a multitude of communication channels, for instance providing a specific ships name, callsign, MMSI number for DSC calling or AIS messaging, e-mail address, phone number(s), INMARSAT terminal number or other contact information to a VTS centre, Port or MRCC – or vice versa.

Furthermore, the Almanac will enable a VTS centre to see which ships in it's area of responsibility support a certain automatic reporting service. A ship will be able to see which service providers can deliver Meteorological/Hydrographic data relevant to it's intended route. A ship will be able to see which information service are provided by a particular port. Even if the only service provided by a port is just a link to the ports own existing webpage - outside the Maritime Cloud - the registration in the Almanac will provide a single point of locating professional maritime information services.

2.1   S2: Meams for Automated Reporting

Automated reporting may be supported by this infrastructure. The Maritime Service Portfolio Registry may link to a service, describing the reporting requirements for entry to a particular port. Required reporting information may be delivered automatically to relevant actors.

Reporting may be performed from the ship – or by a trusted service provider ashore. That is a business decision of each vessel operator.

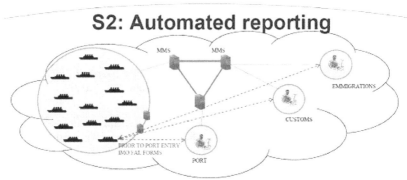

Fig. 5. S2: Automated reporting [4], proposed by Danish Maritime Authority

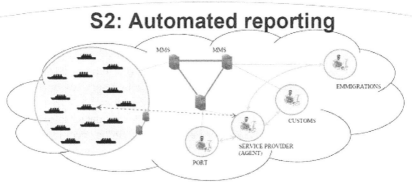

Fig. 6. S2: Automated reporting – via trusted service provider [4], proposed by Danish Maritime Authority

Reporting should be based on digital IMO FAL forms, or other harmonized reporting templates.

2.2   S4: Integration and Graphical Presentation

e-Navigation is about getting ships safely, securely and efficiently from berth to berth in an environmentally friendly way, using globally enhanced systems for navigation, communication and related services – with the human element in focus. The expectations for e-Navigation are given in MSC 85/26/Add.1 [3].

The promulgation of Maritime Safety Information relevant to ships without causing information overload by distributing irrelevant additional information, plays a key role to solution S4, related to the integration and presentation of available information in graphical displays, received via communication equipment.

MSI promulgation: Current solution

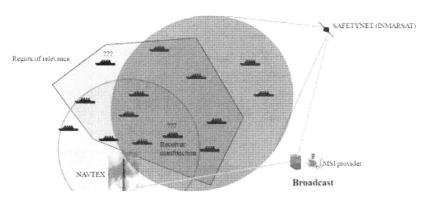

Fig. 7. Maritime Safety Information (MSI) promulgation: Current solution [4], proposed by Danish Maritime Authority

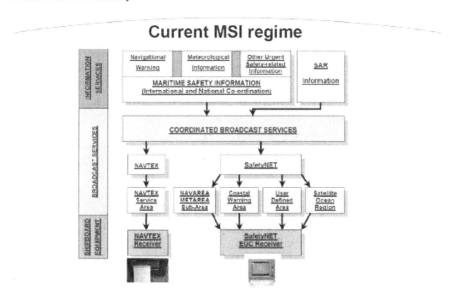

Fig. 8. Current MSI regime [4], proposed by Danish Maritime Authority

The current MSI promulgation regime applies NAVTEX and SafetyNet broadcast. The result is, that ships may be outside coverage (A4 area), the broadcast information may be irrelevant to many recipients, and the output on the bridge is typically on a dedicated display or printer – not a graphical representation. Worst of all – no one is likely to notice, that some recipients, for whom the information was indeed relevant, did not receive it, because their receiver was malfunctioning. The information flow cannot be fully quality assured.

S4: Maritime Cloud – MSI promulgation

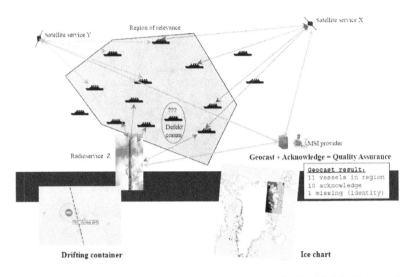

Fig. 9. S4: Maritime Cloud – MSI promulgation [4], proposed by Danish Maritime Authority

S4: MSI regime with Maritime Cloud

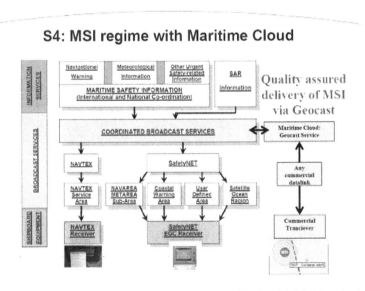

Fig. 10. S4: MSI regime with Maritime Cloud [4], proposed by Danish Maritime Authority

With the Maritime Cloud, only relevant recipients will receive the information regardless of the communication link chosen by the individual actor. No information overload, and the information can be graphically displayed. The lack of acknowledge will reveal that recipients did not receive the information - the communication service provider, the radio link and the onboard communication equipment can be quality assured. The need for radio inspection may change dramatically.

It might also be beneficiary to look into the traditional separation between MSI, Notice to Mariners and chart updates which are very much linked to the traditional ways of promulgating the information (often using old technology). A novel approach could be to handle what we call MSI and Preliminary and Temporary Notices to Mariners under one, since this encompasses temporary or dynamic information and bundle Permanent Notices to Mariners (NM) with ENC updates, since this encompasses less dynamic information.

2.3   S9: Improved VTS Communication

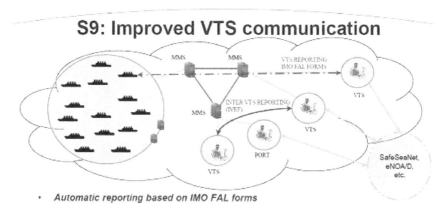

- *Automatic reporting based on IMO FAL forms*

- *Shore – shore Inter VTS reporting (IVEF) – or via existing systems (SafeSeaNet, eNOA/D, etc.) will reduce broadband communication cost for shipping*

Fig. 11. S9: Improved VTS Communication [4], proposed by Danish Maritime Authority

3   Other Examples of How Seamless Information Exchange Could Facilitate Future e-Navigation Solutions

The technical infrastructure under consideration may also facilitate the development of other advanced e-Navigation services, in the next iteration of the e-Navigation strategy. Examples are provided below.

A ship may automatically request berthing timeslots in a particular port, based on an estimated time of arrival. This may facilitate the ships own route optimization in terms of balancing speed / fuel efficiency.

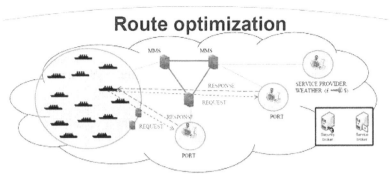

REQUEST: Estimated Time of Arrival – requesting timeslot for berthing

RESPONSE: Timeslot for berthing

Result: Basis for vessels own route optimization

Fig. 12. Route optimization [4], proposed by Danish Maritime Authority

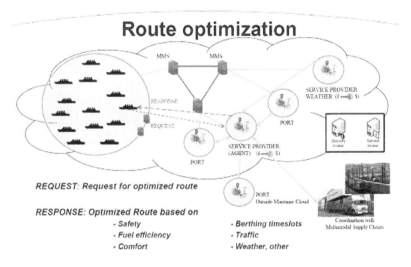

Fig. 13. Route optimization via trusted service provider (Agent) [4], proposed by Danish Maritime Authority

A ship could request an optimized route based on any number of parameters from a trusted service provider, based on safety, fuel efficiency, comfort, bearthing timeslots, traffic, weather and other. Having the frequently updated geographical awareness available in the Maritime Cloud may facilitate multimodal transport and supply chain optimization.

During a SAR operation, a MRCC could set up a data network amongst relevant selected actors, regardless of each actors choice of communication service provider.

Maritime Cloud: SAR data network

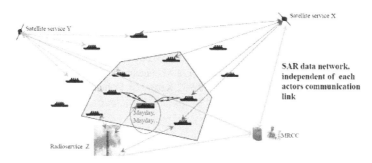

Fig. 14. Maritime Clouds: Search and Rescue (SAR) data network [4], proposed by Danish Maritime Authority

4   Conclusion

Paper based on the IMO document NAV 59/6 [4] gives examples on technical e-Navigation infrastructure, based on the prioritized solutions S2, S4 and S9, which might fit in to the future detailed ship-shore architecture or be the basis for the development of a more detailed ship-shore architecture.

References

1. IHO S-100. Universal Hydrographic Data Model. Edition 1.0.0. International Hydrographic Organization, Monaco (2010)
2. IMO, MSC 85/26.Add2 Annex 20. Report of the Maritime Safety Committee on its Eighty-Fifth Session. International Maritime Organization, London (2008)
3. IMO, MSC 85/26/Add.1 Report of the Maritime Safety Committee on its Eighty-Fifth Session. International Maritime Organization, London (2008)
4. IMO, NAV 59/6. Report from the Correspondence Group on e-Navigation to NAV 59. Submitted by Norway. International Maritime Organization, London (2013)
5. IMO, NAV 58/WP.6/Rev.1 Annex 2. e-Navigation - Report of the Working Group. International Maritime Organization, London (2012)
6. Weintrit, A.: Prioritized Main Potential Solutions for the e-Navigation Concept. TransNav, the International Journal on Marine Navigation and Safety of Sea Transportation 7(1), 27–38 (2013)
7. Weintrit, A.: Advances in e-Navigation Concept – Risk Control Options. Prace Naukowe Politechniki Warszawskiej, Zeszyt serii Transport, Warszawa (in print, 2013)

Telematics of Delivery Optimization Based on Cross Docking Concept in Poland

Katarzyna Bilińska – Reformat[1] and Anna Dewalska – Opitek[2]

[1] University of Economics, 1 Maja 50, 40-287 Katowice, Poland
kasiabr@ue.katowice.pl
[2] Silesian School of Management,
Krasinskiego 2, 40-952 Katowice, Poland
a.dewalska-opitek@swsz.katowice.pl

Abstract. Due to the increasing market competition, large retailers search for new methods to optimize and streamline deliveries based on telematics, which enable them to obtain a wide range of quality products while maintaining a high effectiveness, flexibility and efficiency of the supply chain. It is the cross docking that plays the key role in achieving the goal. The main idea of the concept is that goods are delivered to a warehouse and immediately prepared for further shipment, without stockpiling. The process requires an effective system of telematics. The theoretical deliberation on cross docking systems has been supplemented with a practical verification of its usefulness based on an example of a selected retail chain - Auchan Poland.

Keywords: cross docking, deliveries, large retailers.

1   Introduction

An increased competition is a characteristic feature of the contemporary market in which the retail companies operate. Its causes can be found in both the supply side of the market (increasing number of new retail outlets, the emergence of new chains, increase in online sales) and the demand side (decrease in consumption, and thus the volume of purchases caused by the economic crisis and progressive pauperisation of purchasers). To meet the challenges of competition, companies seek ways to optimize business operations, which are determined by the potential of the company and its economic power. Large-format retail chains, which are the subject of analysis in this study, seek to provide a wide range of quality products while maintaining a high effectiveness, flexibility and efficiency of the supply chain.

Retail chains in their procurement policies seek to exploit all the advantages resulting from the simultaneous centralization and decentralization of some functions of supply. Implementation of the first phase of the supply process (setting a purchasing policy, the choice of suppliers, negotiating) at the central level enables the sales network to achieve a scale effect and exceptionally favourable conditions of cooperation. Simultaneously with the centralization of strategic supply decisions, most networks

J. Mikulski (Ed.): TST 2013, CCIS 395, pp. 200–207, 2013.
© Springer-Verlag Berlin Heidelberg 2013

decentralize purchasing functions at the level of individual branches. This allows each branch to respond quickly to the actual demand occurring in its region and to adapt flexibly a size of an order to its actual needs [2]. In the past few years there have been significant changes in the implementation of the physical distribution of goods - direct deliveries of goods to retail outlets provided by manufacturers or dealers have been discontinued. Hyper-and supermarkets, and discount stores build and rent new central warehouses operating as a distribution centres known as cross docking (Cross Docking Distribution Centre) [3]. Due to a widespread use of cross docking telematic systems for supply logistics implemented by retail chains and increase in its role in the optimisation of supply (which is an important determinant of the success of a trading company in a competitive market), investigation of this subject seems to be important.

After developing an outline of a theoretical system of cross docking, a practical verification of its usefulness was conducted based on an example of a selected retail chain - Auchan Poland. A case study method was used. The studied case helped to draw conclusions regarding the use of cross docking system for a large-format retail chain. Also a possible further research on the optimisation of supply and implementation of new solutions in terms of supply to retail chains was identified.

2   Definition and Basic Functions of Cross Docking

Cross docking is a modern organizational structure of logistics, which is based on inter-docking [4].

The term may also be defined as a logistic concept, which integrates intermediate nodes into a transportation network [1]. The essence of the operation is to collect the goods from a number of points, or the contrary: to receive shipments from a particular point, in order to be able to deliver it later to one recipient (the first case) or to arrange distribution to various locations (the second solution). This process is characterized by the fact that the goods do not need to be stored in the warehouse. By eliminating the storage process, retail chains can significantly reduce costs of distribution, but it should be noted that cross docking requires accurate synchronization of all processes of goods receiving and delivering [2]. To make the process efficient, it should be telematics related.

There are three basic forms of cross-docking. These are: cross docking, direct docking and inter-docking.

The cross docking takes place at a rapid shipment of products ready to ship, between suppliers and customers. This warehousing strategy takes into account a fact associated with products handling which generates costs. It eliminates a phase of inventory storing in a warehouse. Cross docking reduces the expenditure on handling and storage, minimizes the amount of product downtime on the way from production to its final destination.

The direct handling reduces the handling and operational costs, and inventory. Therefore, this logistic method is used in various industries, mostly in food distribution. Initially, direct handling was performed only by the movement of goods directly from one truck to another. Currently, larger and more complex operations can be handled with this method. Distribution centres, with direct handling, use automated systems for temporary storage, sorting and consolidation of incoming materials for shipping.

However, the inter-docking is understood as re-loading the stock from the distribution centre's trucks to cars delivering the goods directly to the stores.

An example of a combined system of delivery to a retail chain is shown in figure1.

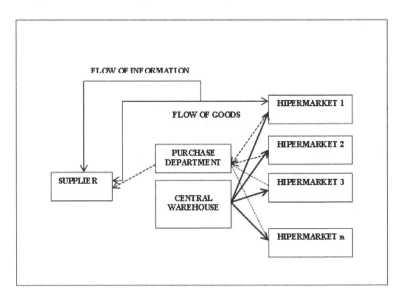

Fig. 1. System of delivery to a retail chain

Cross - docking is also referred to as an operational strategy in distribution centres, including the process of moving goods from the point of admission to the loading point, without the process of storage. The stock delivered to the warehouse is properly received, completed (according to orders) for many varying sets of range. The completed orders are loaded on trucks and transported to the appropriate facilities. A short time of the stock residence in the storage, from one to 24 hours, is a characteristic feature of this system. The cross – docking system enables large-format chains:

- full control over the logistics and security,
- high availability of goods,
- purchasing large parts of goods, which is the basis of negotiating lower prices,
- supplying various supermarkets and hypermarkets according to their needs, what reduces the cost of storage in the retail outlets,
- reducing the storage space to a minimum, what leads to an increase in the turnover,
- reducing the level of losses.

The basis of the cross – docking system is a close cooperation with suppliers. Sharing the information, a reliable communication and ensuring the quality and quantity of products received from suppliers determine the efficiency of the system. Therefore there is a need for information technology simplifying the procedures for orders placement and execution, which in turn leads to better management of physical distribution. Retail chains use an electronic exchange of information in their distribution centres, at the same time forcing suppliers to use such systems [6].

Procedures for cooperation between the entities of a given retail chain and the suppliers apply to both the direct and indirect process of supplying the store with durable goods and food products. In both cases, the retail chain's procurement is generated on the basis of sales (unit) or delivery (distribution centre). An order is usually automatically generated by a computer system. Before delivery, it is necessary to precisely determine the delivery time (hour), because most retailers use delivery notification. Failure in meeting the delivery date by the manufacturer is either a delivery rejection (failing) or a long wait of a driver for a free time block when the supply may possibly be discharged. The acceptance of the supplies of both goods and documents are subjected to a thorough control by the network staff. Any breach of the delivered documentation, goods, packaging, distribution of products, results in rejection of the delivered goods [6].

3   Practical Verification of the Use of Cross Docking System –Research Results

3.1   Research Methodology

Against the background of the presented theoretical considerations, the direct research results seem to be cognitively interesting, allowing for a practical verification of the cross docking system application in a selected retail chain in Poland. In February and March 2013 a qualitative research was conducted with the use of the case study method that allows an in-depth analysis of a particular phenomenon. As a means of obtaining information, a research technique of studying documents was used. The research object was a large-retailer Auchan Poland, and the subject was the use of cross docking system for logistics supply.

3.2   Auchan Polska as a Research Object

Auchan is an international group operating in 12 countries around the world. The Auchan shopping centres are located in France, Italy, Spain, Portugal, Poland, Hungary, Russia, Luxembourg, China, Taiwan, Ukraine and Romania. The Auchan company is an independent and not listed group, the owners of which are Mulliez Family Association and co-workers of the company under the Employee Share Ownership. The Auchan Group operates in five main business segments: Auchan hypermarkets, Simply supermarkets, Immochan shopping centres, Accord banking services and Auchan Direct innovation in e-commerce [6]. The company currently operates in 616 Auchan hypermarkets, 759 Simply supermarkets and 320 Immochan shopping centres in 12 countries. Auchan Shopping centres operate in accordance with the concept of "everything under one roof," what is characterized by the following parameters [7]:

- sales area from 8,500 to 18,000 m2,
- 45000 items in permanent sales - food and industrial goods,
- from 5000 to 25,000 customers per day,
- from 400 to 700 employees,
- from 30 to 170 shops in the a shopping centre,
- Auchan petrol station,
- car park from 1500 up to 5000 places.

The Auchan Group employs about 269 000 people, of whom 152 000 are share-holders of the company. The value of pre-tax income in 2011 amounted to 44.4 billion euro [7].

The history of the Auchan Group's expansion in Poland started in 1991, when the first branch of Auchan was opened. In May 1996, in Piaseczno near Warsaw, the first hypermarket was opened. At that time, it was the first large-format retail outlet that offered food and industrial products for every customer, without requiring special access cards. The Auchan hypermarket in Piaseczno operated on 8000 m2 of sales area, with 49 cashiers, and the first staff amounted for 549 employees [6].

Currently Auchan Poland has 22 hypermarkets and 50% of the shares in four shop-ping centres opened under the name of Auchan (Legnica, Wałbrzych, Racibórz and Zielona Góra), managed by the Schiever Poland company. The headquarters (main office) of Auchan Poland is in Piaseczno near Warsaw.

3.3   Cross Docking as a Form of Cooperation with the Suppliers of Auchan Poland

Auchan Poland procurement policy is based on centralization and decentralization of procurement decisions. Establishing the purchasing policy, choosing a supplier and negotiations take place at the central level, what makes it possible to achieve favour-able conditions for cooperation. Simultaneously with the centralization of strategic procurement decisions, the Auchan retail chain decentralizes purchasing functions at the level of its retail outlets. This strategy allows the sales departments in Auchan hypermarkets to respond quickly to the actual demand occurring in the region, and to adjust freely the size of the order to their actual needs.

The list of the Auchan hypermarkets direct suppliers is determined at the central level and is a strategic decision in the company's procurement policy. The operator is classified in the category of direct suppliers on the basis of five key criteria:

- the supplier's logistics base location in relation to the customer's base location (a shop in the Auchan retail chain),
- sales articles rotation of a given supplier and the range of sales,
- product quality,
- region of supplier's origin,
- pricing conditions included in a trade agreement between the manufacturer and the Auchan Poland.

Trade negotiations conducted by the Auchan Poland Purchasing Department with leading food and industrial products manufacturers allow for the agreements on the strategic cooperation between the parties, including the delivery of goods. The list of strategic suppliers for all three sectors in the Auchan Poland hypermarkets is presented in Table 1.

Table 1. Strategic suppliers of Auchan Polska

Suppliers of non-perishible foodstuffs	Suppliers of perishible foodstuffs	Suppliers of household-related goods
Carlsberg Polska Ltd.	Agros Nova Ltd. (Łowicz)	Amica Wronki Inc.
Coca-Cola HBC Polska Ltd.	Bakoma Ltd.	Candy Hoover Polska Ltd.
HJH Polska S.A.(Pudliszki)	Chłodnia Mazowsze	FagorMastercook Inc.
Kompania Piwowarska Inc.	Danone Ltd.	Firma Księgarska Olesiejuk Ltd.
McCormick Polska Inc. (KAMIS)	Drosed Inc. Siedlce	Florentyna ZPChr Sp.j.
Nestlé Polska Inc.	Marki Sokołów Inc.	Panasonic Polska
Pfeifer & Langen Polska Inc.	Mlekovita	Samsung Electronics Polska Ltd.
Procter and Gamble DS Polska Ltd.	S.M. Sudovia	Sony Polska
Unilever Polska Ltd.	Zakłady Mięsne SKIBA	Whirlpool Polska Inc.
Wawel Inc.	Zakłady Przetwórstwa Mięsnego Henryk Kania Inc.	Zelmer Inc.

Supplies of ordered goods delivered from manufacturers to hypermarkets of the Auchan retail chain are of a dual nature. Products are delivered via the chain warehouses, as well as directly to hypermarkets. Distribution points in the distribution channel, in the form of Auchan Central Warehouses located in Wolbórz and Wola Bykowska, and Refrigeration Platform in Grójec allow for appropriate distribution of supply and addressing it to the appropriate Auchan retail outlets. In the case of a direct delivery, shipments addressed to Auchan shops contain a smaller quantity of goods in order to supplement the current supply. Some goods e.g. a part of industrial goods are supplied directly from the manufacturers to a department of industrial goods receipt by the courier companies, however, cross docking is the main form of supply delivery [6].

As observed, the primary benefit for the Auchan Poland retail chain - the owner of a distribution centre - is receiving substantial trade discounts and the suppliers logistics fees - it is directly related to the reduction of costs for suppliers. The delivery of goods through a distribution centre allows shops to order products exactly when they are needed, instead of ordering once a week or less often, as in the case of direct deliveries. In addition, the company can achieve benefits associated with a reduction in inventory levels in shops, better product availability, etc. One of the main causes of excessive inventories, thereby unnecessarily frozen assets of the company, is the minimum amount of supplies required by some suppliers so that the direct deliveries were profitable for them. Centralization certainly eliminates this problem, and the transhipment warehouse is for Auchan Poland a relatively cheap alternative. As a result of centralization, not only was the level of inventories in the Auchan shops significantly reduced, but also the necessary financial capital [6].

It should be noted that the cross docking system has also some disadvantages. According to the Auchan Poland case study the cross docking is a fast service, therefore it requires an efficient organization not only at the point of forming shipments (central warehouse), but also in co-operation with suppliers and customers (so that the shipment was delivered to the point of completion on time, and then efficiently received). This means a noticeable increase in the cost of information technology and telecommunication solutions, training for employees. In addition, a large number of shipments and fast transhipment process may also lead to an increased risk of errors [6].

In conclusion, it can be observed that a cross-docking system of delivery requires an innovative approach, both in terms of technological solutions as well as of employees attitudes. By investing in modern ICT solutions and staff training, a retail chain can significantly reduce costs in the field of supplies storage and transport.

4   Conclusion

The cross docking as a way to optimise the supply is an important way to build a competitive advantage in the retail market, as it allows retail chains to maximize the availability of products for customers, while reducing the company's costs by buying cheaper goods from suppliers.

The applied research method - case study - helped to analyse a specific (individual) case. No matter how in-depth analysis of a given phenomenon, system or process, an individual case and qualitative nature of the information gathered make the general inference impossible. This points to a future area of research on the use of cross docking as a way to optimise a delivery - the use of quantitative methods of gathering information on a representative research sample will enable a statistical verification of the results.

In addition to the above considerations, there is a matter of benefits and possible drawbacks of this form of supplies for manufacturing companies, as well as the impact of cross-docking on the relationships between the manufacturers and retail chain, what sets the direction for further research in the future.

References

1. Li, Z., Hwee Sim, C., He, W., Chuan Chen, C.: A solution for Cross-docking Operations Planning, Scheduling and Coordination. J. Service Science and Manag. 5, 111–117 (2012)
2. Stephen, K., Boysen, N.: Cross-docking. J. Manag. Control 22, 129–130 (2011)
3. Tubis, A.: Organizacja dostaw do sieci handlowych. Współpraca producentów z dużymi detalistami. LogForum 2(1)(6), 5 (2006)
4. Rutkowski, K.: Logistyka dystrybucji. Specyfika. Tendencje rozwojowe. Dobre praktyki, pp. 55–56. SGH, Warszawa (2005)

5. Guzewski, T.: Cross-docking vs storage of goods, http://www.log24.pl (date of access: July 3, 2013)
6. Own materials of studied company
7. http://www.auchan.pl (date of access: July 3, 2013)
8. Mikulski, J.: Using Telematics in Transport. In: Mikulski, J. (ed.) TST 2010. CCIS, vol. 104, pp. 175–182. Springer, Heidelberg (2010)
9. Mikulski, J.: Telematic Technologies in Transportation. In: Janecki, R., Sierpiński, G. (eds.) Contemporary Transportation Systems. Selected Theoretical and Practical Problems. New Culture of Mobility, pp. 131–143. Publishing House of the Silesian University of Technology. Monograph no. 324, Gliwice (2011)

Role and Significance of Variable Message Signs in Traffic Management Systems

Dawid Brudny[1] and Stanisław Krawiec[2]

[1] APM Konior Piwowarczyk Konior Sp, z o.o.,
Barska 70, 43-300 Bielsko-Biała, Poland
dawid.brudny@apm.pl
[2] Silesian University of Technology, Faculty of Transport
Krasińskiego 8, 40-019 Katowice, Poland
stanislaw.krawiec@polsl.pl

Abstract. The article depicts the role of Variable Message Signs in traffic management systems. VMSs play a big role in improving the traffic safety, as they are an important source of information for the driver, thanks to their clarity and legibility. The fulfilment of formal and legal requirements regarding the VMS is an important aspect of their implementation. The article describes the principles of choosing and designing signs in regard to the traffic management projects, concepts and rules. The authors provided and compared examples of using those signs in Poland and in Austria.

Keywords: variable message signs, traffic management systems.

1   Introduction

Intelligent Transport Systems (ITS) are treated as advanced applications designed to ensure innovative solutions in the traffic management. Their other role is to inform the users about the current situation, thereby improving the situation on the road. The ITS connects many issues from the fields such as telecommunication, electronics, IT, transport engineering, in order to plan, design and manage transport systems.

Variable message signs are an important element of any traffic management system. Their goal is to warn travellers about the traffic events such as: traffic jams, accidents, road works, and to inform about the speed limit for the given section. The newest Polish document regarding the norms for Variable Message Signs is the work entitled "Technical Regulations of Variable Message Signs – 2011". This document contains the information regarding the rules of locating and positioning signs, dimensions of the displayed texts, requirements regarding the housing, and support constructions, technical and user properties of the signs. Another document in power is the PN-EN 12966-1+A1:2013 standard, which precisely describes the operation regulations and their compatibility evaluation methods. There is another document which regulates the use of VMSs, so called Appendix 1, "Detailed technical conditions for vertical signs and conditions of their placement on the road" to the

J. Mikulski (Ed.): TST 2013, CCIS 395, pp. 208–215, 2013.
© Springer-Verlag Berlin Heidelberg 2013

Regulation of the Minister of Infrastructure of 3 July 2003 in regard to detailed technical conditions for the signs and road signals and safety devices in traffic, as well as conditions needed to put them on the roads. This document contains information regarding the rules of locating and positioning signs, dimensions of the displayed texts, requirements regarding the housing, and support constructions, technical and user properties of the signs.

2   Traffic Management Systems in Poland

Poland is just at the beginning of the ITS implementation. Only a few Polish cities have built traffic management systems, i.e. Szczecin, Warszawa, Wrocław, Kraków. As for today, several cities are at the stage of settling the tenders for the ITS, or are implementing them. These are: Poznań, Bydgoszcz, Białystok, Kalisz, Lublin, Tri-City, Olsztyn, Rzeszów, Gliwice. Several other work on defining the parameters of the ITS infrastructure in a way that allows future integration of different systems (for example Katowice or Bielsko-Biała). The forecast for the next several years shows that many cities intend to invest in traffic management systems. The new EU budget for the 2014-2020 strongly supports it, as much of the funds are to be spent on innovative technologies that improve the traffic safety. Another important argument in regard to intelligent transport systems is the document entitled "The National Traffic Safety Improvement Programme 2013-2020", created by the National Traffic Safety Board (The Ministry of Transport, Construction and Maritime Economy). According to this document, the reason of threats for traffic participants is a too low level of intelligent transport systems implementation as a part of the traffic management (e.g. variable message signs, traffic control systems, information systems). The necessity of implementing intelligent transport systems in order to improve the users safety is one of conclusions.

The information given above clearly shows that Poland faces the necessity of developing the ITS, which means that we have a huge chance to lower the social costs, to improve safety, environmental protection and to obtain many other benefits that come from implementing such programmes. Still, one should pay attention when designing such projects, so they can be effective, as the ITS have an individual character. When creating an Intelligent Transport System three stages are necessary – planning, designing, and implementation, from which the first and the most important stage is planning. It consists mostly of such actions as the analysis of the use of existing road infrastructure, the identification of transport problems, conducting or updating traffic research, the analysis of possibility of expanding the existing road infrastructure. The last element of this stage should be the analysis of the existing economic benefits resulting from an ITS creation. Based on those data, one can start the process of designing a system and implementing it.

There is a document important in aiding investors (city, road administrators) when creating a technical specification for the ITS – the Directive of the European Parliament and of the Council 2010/40/EU of 7 July 2010 on the framework for the deployment of Intelligent Transport Systems in the field of road transport and for interfaces with other modes of transport. According to them the ITS should have the following parameters:

- efficiency,
- profitability,
- proportionality,
- supporting service continuity,
- ensuring interoperability,
- supporting backwards compatibility,
- promoting equal access,
- supporting maturity,
- ensuring the quality of describing time and place,
- facilitating the intermodality,
- respecting the coherence.

The ITS designed in such way should fulfil users expectations in 100%. Realization of such projects according to those tips will allow to standardize traffic management systems both in Poland and in the whole Europe. This can have an influence on the optimization of costs when integrating such systems into bigger agglomerations of several cities, or even nationwide.

3   Variable Message Signs in the Context of Traffic Safety Improvement

Poland is a country in which the network of state roads and highways is still insufficient for effective and safe travel. As of 11 November 2012 the total amount of built kilometres of the A and S class roads is about 2500, and 600 more is under construction. This means that the amount of kilometres given to use has quadrupled since 2003. According to the police statistics, the number of traffic accidents during the same time has dropped by 27.5%, the number of people killed in them has lowered by 35.7%, and the number of injured by 28.3%. Still, in comparison to other countries of the European Union, Poland is third to last when it comes to the fatal accidents per million citizens, before Lithuania and Romania. The European Union started an action programme to increase the traffic safety for years 2011-2020, the goal is to reduce the number of fatalities by half. It contains propositions of increasing vehicle safety and the infrastructure. Poland designed its own programme, called "The National Traffic Safety Programme 2013-2020". Its structure is based on five pillars:

- safe behaviour of traffic participants,
- safe road infrastructure,
- safe speed,
- safe vehicles,
- rescue and medical assistance system.

The main part of fatalities in car accidents due to the drivers behaviour comprises: a failure to give right of way, a failure to keep a safe distance, a speed inappropriate to traffic conditions, an incorrect overtaking, and an inappropriate behaviour regarding the pedestrians. Actions aimed at equipping the already existing roads with variable message signs can greatly affect the road safety. Test results and the analysis of traffic management systems in Germany can be an example here. They were conducted by the Straßenforschung Straßenverkehrstechnik BMVBW and are presented in the figure 1:

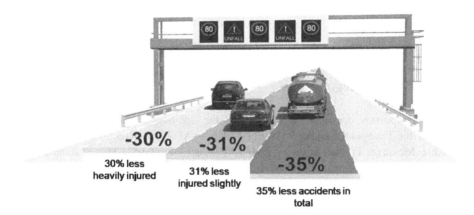

Fig. 1. The analysis of traffic management systems effect on the safety improvement in Germany

As the figure above shows, investments in variable message signs in Germany resulted in tangible benefits. The use of innovative solutions in the field of providing drivers with dynamic information resulted in lowering the number of heavily injured by 30%, 31% less was injured slightly, and there was 35% less accidents in total.

However, the installing of as many variable message signs as possible is not a solution itself. One cannot do that and wait for improvement in the statistics. The key to the success is conducting an analysis of the current situation in a selected area, and choosing proper signs, as well as creating an intelligent control system.

The expressway S-7 Kalsk (Pasłęk) – Miłomłyn can be used as an example. Six variable message signs were installed as a safety improvement system. The section is 36.5 km long and comprises three exits, VMSs were installed before each of them. A document, "The Project of a Control System of the Information Displayed on Variable Message Signs" was created based on the detailed technical specification and the construction works. It contains information regarding kinds of symbols displayed for each lane. Such a solution allows to inform drivers about the traffic conditions, restrictions, dangers, and a possibility to manage a stream of cars on the lane covered by the system. An important condition for the proper system work consists in sending the information to drivers in a way described by the following scheme:

What happened? – Where? – What to do?

The basis to take action by the system operator consists of the threat identification (what happened?), after which the information is sent to the system regarding the threat. In the case of discussed traffic control system, it is carried out by the dispatcher, based on the information received from police patrols, medical units, search units, from the Rescue Information Centre, or other sources. Next, the event is localized (where?), this information is also given by the reporting services. The last step consists in defining the consequences evoked by the event, and its influence on drivers and their surroundings. The final effect is the message addressed to the users by strictly described messages, displayed on proper variable message signs.

4   Variable Message Signs in Traffic Management Systems – Regulations

The most important document that regulates the use of variable message signs in Poland is the European Standard PN-EN 12966-1+A1:2013 "Road Vertical Signs – Variable Message Traffic Signs – Part 1: Product Standard". This standard was developed by the European Committee for Standardization on 15 March 2005 with later amendments on 3 October 2009. According to the CEN's internal regulations, this standard is in force in the following countries: Austria, Belgium, Bulgaria, Cyprus, Denmark, Estonia, Finland, France, Greece, Spain, Holland, Ireland, Island, Lithuania, Luxemburg, Latvia, Malta, Germany, Norway, Poland, Portugal, Czech Republic, Romania, Slovakia, Slovenia, Switzerland, Sweden, Hungary, Italy, and United Kingdom. It describes mainly the optical characteristics of variable message signs and their influence on the environment, which is relatively hostile. It is expected that VMSs, which task is to improve traffic safety, will function for 10 years. The standard presents parameters that must be tested on a testing module, and after that the manufacturer shall ensure that the final product, offered on the market, is fully consistent with the testing module. The optical characteristic contains information regarding the colour, luminance, beam width, uniformity, and the visible flickering.

An important elaboration that shows the road administrators the rules of using the variable message signs, is "The Technical Regulations of the Variable Message Signs – 2011". This document distinguishes three kinds of VMS:

- pictogram variable message signs,
- variable message text boards,
- variable message integrated boards.

Pictogram variable message signs are mainly signs from warning, mandatory, or prohibition groups. Those signs are made with a simplified background colour and symbols. They have black background, the symbols are white or yellow and the borders are usually red. In this this sign group an additional text line may be used to inform about the distance in kilometres to the event. For instance, the sign shows the A-33 symbol and 2 km underneath. Such configuration informs the driver that there is a traffic jam in 2 km. This gives the driver time to make a decision, whether to use an alternative route, if such exists. These signs can be created in two technologies:

pre-defined, in which one can display an earlier defined number of symbols, and freely programmable, which allows displaying unrestricted number of signs.

Variable text boards are used to display text messages. They are made mainly in monochromatic free programmable technology. During the process of designing one must remember that big text boards will need the use of a larger supporting structure, which can ultimately lead to a lesser efficiency of the investment measured by the benefits to cost ratio. The text boards should contain no more than three lines, as such amount is justified by the eye perception of the driver. Moreover, reading a 3 line message takes about 2 seconds. Using an expressway at the speed of 130 km/h means that when reading the message just once, the driver covers the distance of 72 m with no control of the road and the surroundings.

Integrated variable message boards are a compilation of the two boards mentioned above. The key principle of designing such sign type is placing on the right side a field dedicated for the sign, and on the left a field used for displaying text messages.

Preparing investments that take into consideration the use of variable message signs requires the road administrator to have a great knowledge in this field. The main document that regulates such solutions is the aforementioned PN-EN 12966-1+A1:2013 standard, which shall be complied with in Poland. The use of this standard during the preparation of the technical specification, and the enforcement of it towards the contractors, results in improvement in the quality and functionality of the constructed traffic management systems.

5   Examples of Variable Message Signs in Austria

Asfinag is the company that takes care of planning, building, administrating and toll collecting for the highways in Austria. It was established in 1982 and is owned only by the Republic of Austria; the total amount of roads it administers is 2,175 km. Its main tasks are to optimize the traffic flow, to improve safety on roads and to increase the roads availability. Since 2005 traffic control systems were implemented in 13 different sections of the highways in Austria, on a distance of 750 km. In Vienna, there is a National Traffic Management Centre, which takes mainly care of:

- the central management of traffic control systems,
- traffic and network management,
- traffic data analysis,
- monitoring of the current road situation,
- improving the traffic management systems,
- development of the on-road safety increasing strategies.

Apart from the tasks mentioned above, the Asfinag continues developing technical standards and guidance for designs. The tender procedures regulate, among other things, the amount of used road signs, they point out different stages of planning and building the traffic control system in Austria. The main elements that need to be taken into consideration by the Employer when preparing a tender specification for the system containing variable message signs, are:

- variable message signs must be readable far enough by the drivers, so they can adjust the driving manner in proper time. The VMS should be visible from 250 meters,
- important content that informs, i.e. about the danger on the road, must by readable from at least 150 metres, and additional signs form 75 metres,
- sign supporting structures must maintain the vertical gauge of no less than 4.5 metre, whereas the maximum height of the gauge should not exceed 5.50 metre,
- if, for some reason it is needed for the height gauge to be bigger than 5.50 metre, one must remember about the proper angle of the light beam emission, so that the sign readability remains unchanged,
- the line control signs should be put directly above the lane.

The figure 2 represents an example of defining the amount and types of the signs on the section covered by the traffic management system.

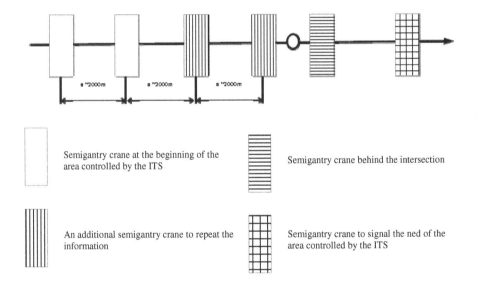

Fig. 2. Example of installation of variable message signs on the section of road covered by a traffic management system

Designing the location of variable message signs according to this scheme will give the driver a proper amount of information in proper time. The traffic participants are informed about the current situation on road, as well as about the best route on the section covered by this system. When entering, the driver is informed that he has entered an area controlled by an intelligent traffic management system. Then, after the suggested 2 km, he can read an information regarding the possible difficulties.

After the next 2 km the information is repeated, so the driver can take proper actions (for example, exit on the next junction, reduce the speed, change the driving lane). The final message is that the toll section is over.

Such actions allow a systematic reduction of fatalities on Austrian roads. When analysing fatalities statistics in the years 2001-2011, the number of fatalities was reduced by 47%, while in Poland, in a similar period, the number was lowered by 28%. Such information shows the legitimacy of implementing a properly thought traffic management system.

6   Conclusion

Variable Message Signs have an important influence on the safety improvement on roads. The intelligent choice of proper devices that fulfil the dreams of the European Union will also help in increasing the transport efficiency. However, until standards regulating the rules for designing, placing and selecting appropriate signs are not widely used in Poland, our ITS systems will be less effective than in other countries.

References

1. Adamski, A.: Intelligent Transport Systems: Control, Oversight and Management. AGH, Kraków (2003)
2. The Act of 27 July (2012) on Public Roads; Article 4 para 33-40, and Article 4a para 1-3 (2012)
3. Gaca, S., Suchorzewski, W., Tracz, M.: Traffic Engineering: Theory and Practice, Warsaw (2008)
4. Kornalewski, L., Szczepaniak, Z., Mitas, A.: The Technical Conditions for the VMS Variable Message Signs. IBDiM, Warsaw (2011)
5. PN-EN 12966-1+A1: Vertical Road Signs, Variable Message Road Information Signs (2013)
6. The Regulation of the Minister of Infrastructure of July 3, 2003: Appendix 1, Detailed Technical Conditions for Vertical Signs and Conditions of Their Placement on the Road (2003)
7. Gergel, M.: Traffic Management System on the A and S class roads in Austria. ASFINAG, Vienna (2011)
8. ASFINAG: The Standardization of the Display Modules and the Devices that Influence the Traffic, ASFINAG, Vienna (2007)
9. Sobczak, T., Ząbczyk, K.: Traffic Management System - Traffic Organization Project with the Use of the Variable Message Signs, the construction of the S17 Express Road, Kurów - Lublin - Piaski Section, GDDKiA Lublin
10. Jamroz, K., Krystek, R., Kustra, W.: The Conception of the Integrated Traffic Management System in the area of Gdańsk, Gdynia and Sopot, City Gdansk, Gdansk (2007)
11. Świątalski, P., Ryguła, A.: The S-7 Project of the Control System of the Displayed Message on the Variable Message Signs. Bielsko-Biała (2012)

Telematic Innovations in Transport Safety

Andrzej Bujak[1], Mirosław Smolarek[2], and Anna Orzeł[3]

[1] Gdańsk Banking School, Faculty of Finance and Management
Dolna Brama 8, 80-821 Gdańsk, Poland
andrzej.bujak@interia.pl
[2] Land Forces Military Academy, Command Institute
Czajkowskiego 109, 51-150 Wrocław, Poland
msmolarek@go2.pl
[3] Wrocław Banking School, Faculty of Finance and Management
Fabryczna 29-31, 53-609 Wrocław, Poland
aniaorzeł@poczta.onet.pl

Abstract. Contemporary world faces a rapid growth in the area of trade in goods, which increases the demand for safe and fast transportation of commodities. On one side the network of transport routes proliferates, but on the other hand they become more crowded, more dangerous, also distances of goods transport surge. Telematic innovations can be one of the solutions, which could increase the transport safety and reduce the costs of commodities supply. Telematics can back up the human element in the processes of transport management as well as it can influence directly the security of executors of logistic tasks related to the transport process.

Keywords: transport, telematic innovation, logistic supply processes, transportation safety.

1 Introduction

A rapid development of technology especially in the telecommunication, electronics and IT spheres supports the application of telematic solutions for intelligent transport systems (ITS), which use sophisticated know-how to bring together vehicles, people, infrastructure and the traffic environment. Some of the projects are designed for supporting vehicles operators in order to increase safety of travelling and transportation. Nowadays the automation of remote steering processes has been broadly applied to aviation, where autopilots disburden crew during the flight routines and support starting and landing. Automated appliances are progressively utilized in railroading to take control over a train even when a human factor fails. Also currently automated solutions are gradually introduced to road transport in order to increase the safety of road users, the security of transported commodities as well as effectiveness and cost efficiency of delivery. Technical progress in robotics and cybernetics together with employing satellite navigation allows scientists and inventors to construct telematic solutions, which can support drivers by their work, increase the transport safety and

J. Mikulski (Ed.): TST 2013, CCIS 395, pp. 216–223, 2013.
© Springer-Verlag Berlin Heidelberg 2013

security or even develop driverless vehicles. Research in this area is conducted all over the world. Some of the leading, sophisticated concepts are developed in Europe (SARTRE, HAVE it), in the United States (AHS, PATH) or in Japan (ITS Spot Services).

2   SARTRE - Safe Road Trains for the Environment

There is a large number of initiatives related to increasing the transport safety. One of the concepts is based on organizing "road trains". It is called also "platooning".

The idea of automated driving came back to 30-ties of 20th century, when at the 1939 World's Fairs in New York General Motors (GM) presented a concept of "driverless" vehicles moved under automated control [1]. In the following years scientists conducted research in this area, but a turning point for this concept was the introduction of computer technology and later on of satellite navigation. The USA, Japan as well as European countries undertook research in order to develop real solutions, which can have practical applications. In late 80-ties the first telematic research and development programmes such as a privately sponsored Pan-European project called Prometheus (Programme for a European Traffic of Highest Efficiency and Unprecedented Safety) or project DRIVE (Dedicated Road Infrastructure for Vehicle Safety in Europe) were launched by European Communities, which should prepare solutions for informing drivers better about road conditions. Additionally "intelligent" vehicles would interact with their surroundings [2]. Simultaneously a traffic safety programme was introduced in the USA (California) called Transportation Safety Research in the framework of Partners for Advanced Transit and Highways (PATH) related to the platooning concept. The idea of automated convoys is quite permissible and nowadays advanced research work is conducted on "road trains", which enable to "operate much closer together than it is possible under manual driving conditions, each lane can carry at least twice as much traffic as it can today" [3]. Especially now electronic and computer technologies allow to build such systems and some attempts to create such solutions are well under way.

The research proved that the telematic solutions related to platooning can increase drivers' safety as well as build up their comfort of working conditions. It is unnecessary to add that it is directly connected with the road traffic and transport safety. Moreover, aside from the above mentioned security benefits the grouping of vehicles in a platoon can triple the road capacity and save fuel by ca. ¼ [4]. Furthermore, a lesser fuel consumption directly influences the environment pollution by reducing the emission of exhaust gases.

The European Union tries to develop its own solutions in this area. One of the concepts of "road trains" is a project called SARTRE funded by the European Commission under the Framework Programme 7. SARTRE is conducted by seven European scientific institutes and companies led by Ricardo Company from the UK and VOLVO from Sweden. The programme will address the three keystones of transportation issues, environment, safety and traffic congestion while at the same time encouraging driver acceptance through the increased "driver comfort" [5].

The project goals are related to developing telematic and IT based communications and interactions between cars, which could organize themselves into platoons on highways. The concept based on creating electronically controlled and linked together automotive convoys in which the first vehicle as a leading unit (Lead Vehicle – LV) will be driven manually by a professional driver (a truck or a bus) and other trucks, busses or cars (Following Vehicles – FVs) could join such cavalcade semi-automatically.

During the movement in the "road train" the participating drivers will be relieved from their routine "driving" duties. During movement in such a column they could rest, eat, drink, read, listen to music or even sleep. The participating drivers could take responsibility for driving at every moment when he or she decides to leave the platoon and continue the journey on his or her own. The only obligation will be that the convoy leader will have to be a professional driver who can appropriately react to traffic conditions.

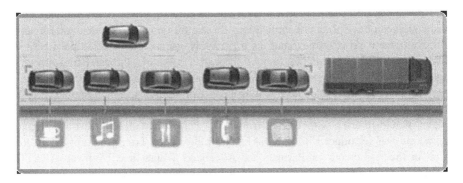

Fig. 1. SARTRE platooning concept [5]

All of the vehicles have to be equipped in a sophisticated car computer (so called Human - Machine Interface), a Vehicle to Vehicle communications node (V2V) for data exchange with the other vehicles. Several electronic control units have been used to control the vehicle's position in the platoon. Furthermore, sensors and actuators for automated control of the Following Vehicles are needed. To measure the position of the preceding vehicle others have to be equipped with with radars, laser sensors and cameras. However, at every moment the driver can put the vehicle in an override mode [7].

The objectives of research in the framework of SARTRE project were [5]:

1. To define a set of acceptable platooning strategies that will allow road trains to operate on public highways without changes to the road and roadside infrastructure;

2. To enhance, develop and integrate technologies for a prototype platooning system such that the defined strategies can be assessed under real world scenarios;

3. To demonstrate how the use of platoons can lead to environmental, safety and congestion improvements;
4. To illustrate how a new business model can be used to encourage the use of platoons with benefits to both lead vehicle operators and platoon subscribers.

In January 2011 the first successful test of SARTRE platooning was conducted in which a leading truck and a following car participated. But already in May 2012 the first "road train" consisting of a leading truck and four cars was effectively tested on a public highway in Spain. The convoy covered a distance of 200 km at the maximum speed of 85 km/h and 6 m spacing [6]. The project was defined for 36 months from September 2009 and ended in September 2012. SARTRE project proved platooning benefits and allowed to develop the technology, which can be used in the future.

3   HAVE IT - Highly Automated Vehicles for Intelligent Transport

SARTRE is not the only European solution, which could support drivers, reduce his/her workload, reduce human mistakes caused by tiredness, prevent accidents as well as to allow "green" driving. In February 2008 a three-year project called "HAVE it" (Highly Automated Vehicles for Intelligent Transport) was launched. Opposite to the platooning concept HAVE is a programme focused on individual drivers and on a simple vehicle. The development aim was to prepare a demonstrator for an "intelligent" vehicle, which could assist a driver by its work in an automatic or semiautomatic way depending on the traffic conditions and road situations. The technology will provide indications for the human operator. Moreover, he or she can delegate to an electronic "co-pilot" an autonomous driving in some specific road conditions such as driving in traffic congestions. The technology can temporary replace a human being during driving in traffic jams. The vehicle equipped with cameras, sensors, lidars, V2V communication equipment can conduct tasks such as automated queue assistance, or can help by avoiding roadworks. As the core of the system a telematic "co-pilot" analyses current traffic conditions and the status of the vehicle. The system calculates exact manoeuvres but the driver remains completely responsible for estimation of the situation and driving at any point in time. In this mode the driver is relieved from monotonous driving in traffic jams. He or she has to monitor the system carefully and can take over the complete driving tasks at any moment. Installed sensors can control automated breaking and acceleration of the vehicle.

The project consisted of four areas of research: an Automated Queue Assistance (demonstrated in a test truck), an Automated Road works Assistance, a Temporary Auto-Pilot (in a test car), and an Active Green Driving (in a test bus). The experiments showed that the designs equipped with innovative security instruments really supported the drivers in overloaded as well as under loaded circumstances. The reduction of fuel consumption and the increase in vehicles efficiency were a further benefit of the applied technology use.

4   Automated Highway System (AHS)

New transport concepts should be a combination of appropriate telematics-supported infrastructure, which interacts with vehicles stuffed with electronics to support or even to replace a driver. Probably the future is laid in driverless trucks concept, which could enhance reliability, effectiveness as well as reduce costs of the transport and prime costs of companies. One of the plausible future development is the Automated Highway System (AHS), which is also called Smart Road. The idea is that AHS is defined as „... a new relationship between vehicles and infrastructure. It refers to a set of designated lanes on a limited roadway, where specially equipped vehicles are operated under completely automatic control" [8]. The concept should use the current but electronically upgraded road infrastructure and develop solutions for fully automated driverless operation in terms of driving safety, efficiency as well as increase in comfort and safety of vehicles' operators. The main goal of the trail was to develop driverless vehicles in order to reduce the traffic intensity by decreasing distances between trucks, buses as well as cars and in this way by platooning to allocate more vehicles on the roads at the same time. Nonetheless, the system introduction needs a telematic upgrading of existing highways, which could "interact" with vehicles saturated with many sensors and appliances for power steering and automatic speed controls operated by an on-board computer. Communication between the vehicle and the "smart roads" will allow automated moving without interference of an operator. Sensors used in the AHS system will be developed for reading passive road indicators and markers, using a radar and inter-car communications systems in order to adjust a vehicle for road traffic conditions without any participation of a driving person. In the AHS concept vehicles will be platooned into convoys of eight to twenty-five units driving without human assistance just about one meter apart.

One of the most permissible development in the frame of AHS is the California Partners for Advanced Transit and Highways (PATH). The programme, launched in 1986, was a result of an agreement between the University of California's Institute of Transportation Studies and the California Department of Transportation. The goal of the program was to "...apply advanced technology to improve highway capacity and safety, and to reduce traffic congestion, air pollution, and energy consumption" [3]. In 1997 a public demonstration of the technology took place in San Diego (California). The platoon consisted of 8 cars, which were driving themselves at 6.5 meters spacing at the maximum speed of 96 km/h. The demonstration included splitting one of the cars, falling back and joining the platoon again [3].

Research work in the frame of PATH is still being continued, but after the first promising outcomes and demonstrations investments have been moved rather toward intelligent driverless vehicles than upgrading highways with telematic equipment.

5   ITS Spot Services

The designing of ITS solutions depends sometimes on specific conditions of a given country. In the case of Japan the population density, especially in the cities, results in traffic congestion, which is one of the most obstinate problems in the country. The reduction of traffic accidents is another area of interest. That is why Japan follows another path of development of telematic solutions for road and transport safety in comparison to Europe and the USA, which concentrated on safety and efficiency based on "driverless" systems. Nowadays the Japanese are leaders in the application of advanced communication and information technologies related to the reduction of traffic congestion and to enhancing the traffic flow.

The general concern of Japanese scientists and inventors is related to elimination of wasting time in traffic jams, which reduces the working capabilities. Another area of research is cutting down on the environment pollution by reducing the amount of exhaust gases produced by vehicles stuck in traffic jams.

The development of creating effective and safety driving concept is associated with a consortium called "ITS Japan", which consists of representatives from ITS-related organizations, industry and private business corporations as well as academic bodies, which work together with the four government ministries and agencies related to ITS [10]. The ITS Japan is responsible for promoting ITS R&D and deployment, linking ITS World Congress Asia-Pacific area, running Asia-Pacific ITS Forum Secretariat, liaison among ITS-related public and private organizations and academia, supporting ITS-related standardization activities [9]. A comprehensive plan for "intelligent traffic" development consists of development of solutions in the areas of advanced navigation systems, electronic toll collection systems, assistance appliances for safe driving, optimization of traffic management, increasing efficiency in road management, support for public transport, increasing efficiency of commercial vehicle operations, support for pedestrians and support for emergency vehicle operations [10].

In 2011 the Japanese launched the nationwide system "ITS Spot Services". The concept based on the interaction between a driver and "intelligent road" via high-speed and large-capacity communication called ITS spot and compatible car navigation device (OBU - on-board unit). Along Japanese highways approx. 1600 ITS spots have been installed, which collect the data about a vehicle: time, position, speed as well as acceleration, yaw angle etc. The data are transferred to road administrator's server, which consolidates and tabulates the collected information. Via the ITS spot the administrator can provide feedback to car drivers and pass the data to collaborative services such as telematic operators, logistic companies, etc.

The services provided for drivers can include a wide area of traffic information (e.g. traffic congestion data) for smart selecting routes by car navigation systems based on the current travel time data and traffic conditions (Dynamic Route Guidance). The driving safety support is anther application (reducing collision risk by alerting drivers in advance about traffic jams, obstacles ahead, providing road and traffic conditions by still pictures in real time, etc.). Further solutions include electronic toll collection and cashless payment, providing information about parking and rest areas, assuring Internet access (e.g. information about local sightseeing, restaurants, etc.) [11].

In the field of business the ITS Spot Services can be used for accurate planning of transport activities. For example one can predict the arrival time of delivery, shorten receiving or transhipment standby time, improve transport operation plans based on travelled routes and quite precisely estimated travel time.

Also public transport services profit from the ITS spot. The system "knows" the location of a bus and can calculate an estimated time of arrival. Furthermore, it can help to increase coordination of transfers between bus lines and shorten the waiting time. Information about the arrival time of a bus can be disseminate by the Internet or mobile phone network.

Support for public emergency services during disasters (e.g. earthquakes are quite common phenomenon in Japan) is another application of this technology. The system can help to ascertain the most convenient emergency routes for rescue teams or help by dissemination of information to drivers about suitability for driving [11]. What makes the Japanese ITS Spot Services development exclusive is the heavy involvement of the governmental institutions in the project and close cooperation with the industry. The governmental site is responsible for developing the road infrastructure, while electronics and car manufactures for designing ITS spot system compatible cars' on-board units [4]. It is predicted that with the introduction of a fully operable ITS spot system the market for such devices will rapidly grow in the next years.

The Japanese concept of communication between a road and a vehicle allows not only to spare time, reduce traffic congestion, increase traffic safety, reduce the number of car accidents, but thanks to an improved traffic flow also to reduce costs by a lower fuel consumption and the decrease of environmental pollution.

6   Conclusion

The increasing number of the world population and related road vehicles cause that the traffic congestions increase rapidly and traffic jams are an everyday element of human life. Crowded streets, roads and highways reduce transport effectiveness, increase costs of logistic operators and directly influence the traffic safety. The expansion of the road systems is not a solution. That is why sophisticated telematic and electronic technology has to be applied to support a solution of the dilemma. Attempts to develop a technology, which can support a driver and even to conduct driverless traffic on roads are quite advanced. Furthermore, proposed solutions such as AHS or SARTRE can bring more benefits than only an increase in the comfort of driving. Road trains can promote a safer transport. Electronic devices and computers react faster than a human being. The responsibility for a convoy safety is born by a professional, experienced driver. A reduced speed, very short distances between vehicles in a platoon allow a more efficient utilisation of road capacities and improve the traffic flow. Moreover, platooning will allow the reduction of costs, because the factors mentioned above such as shorter distances between trucks and a lower speed reduce the air resistance, which results in fuel savings of about 10-20%. But the most important thing is the increase in the safety of traffic participants, which is the most important factor of this kind of scientific work.

References

1. O'Toole, R.: Gridlock: Why We're Stuck in Traffic and What to Do About it?, p. 189. CATO Institute, Washington, DC
2. Wang, Y., Li, F.: Vehicular ad-hoc networks. In: Misra, M., Misra, S.C., Woungang, I. (eds.) Guide to Wireless Ad-Hoc Networks, pp. 503–504. Springer, London (2009)
3. Vehicle Platooning and Automated Highways, California PATH–Partners for Advanced Transit and Highways, `http://www.path.berkeley.edu/PATH/`
4. Basagni, S., Conti, M., et al.: Mobile Ad Hoc Networking: The Cutting Edge Directions, p. 45. John Wiley&Sons Inc., New Jersey (2013)
5. SARTRE - Safe Road Trains for the Environment, `http://www.sartre-project.eu` (date of access: July 17, 2013)
6. `https://www.media.volvocars.com/global/enhanced/en-gb/Media/Preview.aspx?mediaid=43899` (date of access: July 17, 2013)
7. Chan, E., et al.: Cooperative control of SARTRE automated platoon vehicles (2013), `http://www.sartre-project.eu/en/publications/Documents/ITSWC_2012_control.pdf` (date of access: July 17, 2013)
8. Cheon, S.: An Overview of Automated Highway Systems (AHS) and the Social and Institutional Challenges They Face, UCTC University of California Transportation Centre 2003, p. 3 (2013), `http://www.uctc.net/papers/624.pdf` (date of access: July 17, 2013)
9. `http://www.its-jp.org/english/what_its_e/its-japan-organization/` (date of access: July 17, 2013)
10. `http://www.mlit.go.jp/road/ITS/pdf/ITSinitiativesinJapan.pdf` (date of access: July 17, 2013)
11. Nishio, T.: Vehicle-Infrastructure Cooperative System and Probe Data in Japan (2013), `http://www.mlit.go.jp/road/ITS/j-html/news/event/20120515/documents/08.pdf` (date of access: July 17, 2013)
12. Mikulski, J.: Using telematics in transport. In: Mikulski, J. (ed.) TST 2010. CCIS, vol. 104, pp. 175–182. Springer, Heidelberg (2010)
13. Mikulski, J.: The possibility of using telematics in urban transportation. In: Mikulski, J. (ed.) TST 2011. CCIS, vol. 239, pp. 54–69. Springer, Heidelberg (2011)

Identification of Framework for Sustainable Development of Nautical Tourism on Inland Waterways in Croatia

Mihaela Skočibušić[1], Mato Brnardić[1], and Ema Brnardić[2]

[1] Faculty of Traffic and Transport Sciences, University of Zagreb,
Vukeliceva 4, 10000 Zagreb, Croatia
mihaela.bukljas@fpz.hr
[2] Croatian Chamber of Economy, County Chamber Sisak,
Kranjceviceva 16, 44000 Sisak, Croatia

Abstract. Development of nautical tourism on inland waterways and lakes has not been the subject of serious studies and analysis that could serve as a basis for further research or development potential of a structured and sustainable development of nautical tourism on inland waterways. The aim of this article is to identify and analyse the potential framework for sustainable development of nautical tourism on Croatian inland waterways with regard to infrastructural capacities as well as tourist offer and demand. The initial evaluation of the potential will be based on qualitative and quantitative indicators, and each of the proposed indicators will be elaborated. Authors will collect detailed information on infrastructure requirements of Croatian inland waterways with special emphasis on waterway infrastructure, access roads, accommodation and communications infrastructure, as well as support services that could contribute to the development of nautical tourism on Croatian rivers. Authors will propose a reference model for the development of nautical tourism based on existing relevant models.

Keywords: nautical tourism, infrastructure, indicators, GAP analysis, framework, sustainable development.

1   Introduction

In accordance with the development plans of the Croatian Government to promote integrated tourism growth, this paper is focused on exploring the potential for sustainable development of nautical tourism on the inland waterways of the Republic of Croatia. Potential of nautical tourism in the Croatian hinterland is poorly researched, where rivers and lakes are characterized by numerous existing and future tourist attractions such as [7]:

- Sisak - future nautical marina near Sisak Old Town, the Roman excavations in the city of Sisak;
- Zagreb - the possibility of nautical sports recreation on Lake Jarun and the Sava river;

J. Mikulski (Ed.): TST 2013, CCIS 395, pp. 224–233, 2013.
© Springer-Verlag Berlin Heidelberg 2013

- Plitvice Lakes National Park: Croatian most popular tourist eco-destination with UNESCO World Heritage status, which has received 1979.
- Lonja field, Krka and park Kopački rit - ecotourism.
- Rivers Kupa and Gacka - sport-fishing destination.
- River Dobra, bungalows, Cetina and Una - rafting and kayaking.

The result of this article is systematic and coordinated framework for future national and regional tourism development plans in the Croatian inland waterways, which would comply with "Nautical tourism development strategy for the period 2009-2019" which is primarily focused on the Adriatic coast and sustainable development of tourism along the Croatian coast and islands.

2   Identification of Framework for Sustainable Development of Nautical Tourism on Inland Waterways

Despite its capital tourism potential, rivers and lakes in the Republic of Croatia have not received nearly enough support at the national level as coastal tourism and nature parks. Possible tourism modalities for each attraction are eco-tourism, recreation on inland waters, camping, yahting, rafting, kayaking, fishing, etc. The division of registered tourist attractions from the categories above make an initial evaluation of the tourist potential of the Croatian inland waterways [4].

2.1   Key Factors and Potential Results

The overall objective framework for the development of nautical tourism in the Croatian inland waterways is to collect the necessary documentation and data on which structured development strategy can be formulated in the legislative and regulatory structure: Master plan for the development of nautical tourism on the Croatian inland waters, which is accompanied by an Action Plan for development of nautical tourism in the Croatian inland waterways defining specific tasks which will lead to the realization of the Master plan.

2.2   Assumptions and Risks

Assumptions and risks must be treated with all external influences that cause failure to the results and / or performance objectives despite all the planned activities. The main prerequisites for sustainable development of nautical tourism on inland waterways are:

- Existence of the political will of the Croatian government and relevant stakeholders for development of tourism and recreational activities in the Croatian inland waterways;
- Existence of a legal framework for the smooth development of recreational, tourism activities and safe navigation on Croatian inland waterways;
- Interest in investing in nautical tourism on inland waters by the private sector;

- Approval of the potential of nautical tourism on inland waters by all participants;
- Existence of basic infrastructure for the development of nautical tourism (waterway and other infrastructure).

The following risks are possible:

- The impact development of the tourist navigation on the environment;
- Uncertainties related to the construction of hydroelectric power plants and utilization of water potentials on inland waterways and their influence on the nautical tourism and recreational activities;
- The availability of financing;
- Availability of necessary information and documentation as construction, development projects would not be delayed due to administrative bottlenecks;
- Problems related to the field survey of rivers and lakes that need to be done to provide the necessary insight into the current situation and to identify possible locations for new development projects.

3   Model Analysis of Potential Nautical Tourism Development on Croatian Inland Waterways

Authors define the analysis model development potential of nautical tourism on inland waterways in through following six stages:

1) A detailed review of existing tourism activities on inland waterways and lakes in Croatia;
2) Reference model for the development of nautical tourism based on existing relevant models in Europe;
3) GAP analysis of nautical tourism in the inland waterways and lakes in Croatia;
4) Recommendations and guidelines for development of an appropriate legal framework which facilitates development of nautical tourism in the inland waterways and lakes in Croatia;
5) Development of policies and implementation strategies of nautical tourism on inland waterways and lakes in Croatia;
6) Action Plan for the development of nautical tourism on inland waterways and lakes in Croatia, with details of the scope and proposed initiative as well as supporting implementation plan.

3.1   Detailed Review of Existing Tourism Activities on Inland Waterways and Lakes in Croatia

The aim of this phase is to identify and analyze the potential of nautical tourism on Croatian inland waterways with respect to supply, demand and infrastructure capacities. The initial evaluation of the potentials for nautical tourism on inland waterways would be based on qualitative and quantitative indicators.

3.1.1 Methodology of Research

For each waterway or lake authors will identify tourist attractions / locations and classify them into one of the following categories:

1. Existing attractions: tourist attractions that are commercially exploited in the market advertising as a destination for foreign and local visitors;
2. Tourist attractions in preparation: tourist attractions, whose development plans have already been made, specific actions have been designed and therefor already secured financial resources;
3. Planned attractions: tourist attractions that are planned for the future but require further study before a decision on the implementation actions to be taken;
4. Potential attractions: tourist attractions that have been registered until this research and can not be classified into three previous categories, but show potential for the development of nautical tourism on the Croatian inland waterways.

As part of further research detailed information on infrastructure requirements will be collected on Croatian inland waterways and lakes with particular attention to navigable waterways infrastructure, access roads, accommodation and communications infrastructure, support services such as shops and gas stations, and any other relevant indicators that could contribute to the development of nautical tourism on inland waterways. Potential demand for nautical tourism in particular regions will define among others: current and potential "consumption" (nights, annual sales, revenue), capacity (number of targeted visitors, recorded number of visitors, origin of visitors, etc.), consumer characteristics of visitors (average spending per visitor, number of nights per visitor, etc.) [1].

3.1.2 Expected Results

Expected research results will generate a detailed review of potentials on Croatian inland waterways along with a description of the tourist attractions by their development status, current and potential tourist activities.

3.2   Reference Model for the Development of Nautical Tourism Based on Existing Relevant Models in Europe

With the aim registering existing trends and collection of best practices study on reference model nautical tourism on the waterways and lakes in Europe will be made with special emphasis on neighboring countries, such as Hungary [5]. Structured analysis of reference models in Europe will generate a detailed review of nautical tourism on European inland waterways, described on the basis of indicators of infrastructure, supply and demand.

3.2.1 Methodology of Research

Methodology of drafting a reference model consists of a detailed list of tourist attractions on the waterways and lakes in Europe. It is necessary to focus on tourist facilities which may be relevant for Croatia and which by its size are content to the existing situation in Croatia. The model should investigate real and perceived barriers to the development of nautical tourism, as well as mitigation measures that can reduce or remove the respective barriers. This methodology should also define existing administrative legal actors, national authorities responsible for the development of nautical tourism, as well as the relation between the private sector and national/regional tourism bodies. Generally, the analysis of the reference model can be regarded as an effective means of encouraging change and increasing competitive performance of the growing sector of nautical tourism on inland waterways and lakes.

3.2.2 Expected Results

Results will generate relevant overview of tourist attractions related to the nautical tourism on inland waterways and lakes in Europe and the detailed analysis of the relevant selected tourist attractions based on their characteristics, size and activity. Analysis of the reference model will provide an overview of modern and current trends in the field of nautical tourism on inland waterways and lakes, as well as the projection of future trends.

3.3   GAP Analysis of Nautical Tourism on the Inland Waterways and Lakes in Croatia

Using GAP analysis authors will identify the minimum requirements necessary for the successful development of nautical tourism on the inland waterways and lakes in Croatia. GAP analysis is a tool that is used to identify the difference between the current and desired future situation, so as to thereby evaluate the difference between two terms. GAP analysis indicates which preconditions are realized and which are not, and thus provides quantitative measure of time, financial and human resource investments necessary to achieve the desired situation.

3.3.1 Methodology of Research

GAP analysis will be carried out on the basis of results obtained in phase 1 and 2. GAP analysis should provide minimum requirements of every fairway and lake for the successful development of nautical tourism. GAP analysis will establish connection between demand and supply as well as infrastructure requirements which should definitely be ensured that the development of nautical tourism would be possible on inland waterways and lakes in Croatia. GAP analysis will compare the current state of existing nautical tourism on inland waterways with the potential / target state that are identified in the reference analysis.

3.3.2 Expected Results

GAP analysis will identify the need for sustainable development of nautical tourism in the inland waterways and lakes in Croatia and specify requirements using the instrument 4P marketing mix: product, price, distribution and sales, promotion. The practical result will be a set of all requirements necessary for sustainable long-term development of nautical tourism on the inland waterways and lakes in Croatia.

Appropriate marketing mix will provide insight into the current and desired future situation and make recommendations for the closure of the gap between current and target states of nautical tourism in inland waterways.

3.4   Relevant Legislation - Analysis and Recommendations

Relevant legislation will elaborate legal provision of nautical tourism, types of vessels that can provide services of nautical tourism, tourist types/services that are an integral part of the of nautical tourism, legal requirements of private and legal persons to provide services in the field of nautical tourism, cross-border procedures for vessels and passengers on international inland waterways or represent a natural boundary between Croatia and other countries. With the aim of stimulating development of nautical tourism on inland waterways authors will consider and provide a regulatory solution if it is possible to simplify, modify or improve the existing regulations.

3.4.1 Methodology of Research

In the analysis of the relevant legislative authors recommend to collect all the documentation in the form of laws, regulations, rules, regulations, etc. After finalizing the list of the relevant legislation the result will be report on the regulatory framework of nautical tourism on inland waters of the Croatian.

3.4.2 Expected Results

Preparation of the report on the regulatory framework of nautical tourism in the inland waters of the Croatian, as well as recommendations based on respective report, which relate to possible simplification, improvement or modification of legislation in order to foster development nautical tourism on inland waterways of the Republic of Croatia. The relevant report will contain legal determinants of nautical tourism on inland waterways - vessels, port authorities, regulatory framework for the tourism activities in the field of nautical tourism and detailed specification of cross border procedures for navigators on inland waterways.

3.5   Development of Policies and Implementation Strategies of Nautical Tourism on Inland Waterways and Lakes in Croatia

As part of this research SWOT analysis will be carried out to identify the strengths, weaknesses, opportunities and threats related to the nautical tourism on Croatian inland waterways and lakes [2]. Systematic development strategy will be developed and formulated in the form of regulatory Master plan for the development of nautical tourism on the Croatian inland waterways which will relate to [6]:

- National vision and strategy for the development of tourism in Croatia and contribution to wider economic state development;
- The level of targeted development of nautical tourism on inland waterways;
- Basic characteristics of nautical tourism on inland waterways, or the kind of activities that need to be developed;

-   Areas that could potentially be problematic for the development of nautical tourism;
-   Ecological consequences of nautical tourism on inland waterways and how they should be approached, in particular environmental consequences associated with the reallocation of land for tourism, preservation of natural parks and key environmental values navigable waterways (wetlands).

3.5.1 Methodology of Research

SWOT analysis should result in a policy framework for sustainable tourism on inland waterways. Table 1 provides a visual summary of the framework that should be accomplished.

Table 1. SWOT analysis and strategic options for sustainable development

	External: Opportunities (O-opportunities)	External: Threats (T-threats)
Internal: Strengths (S-strengths)	**SO** *"Maxi-Maxi" strategy* Strategies used by internal strengths to maximize aggravated achievement of identified opportunities	**ST** *"Maxi-Mini" strategy* Strategies used by internal strengths to minimize external threats which prevent realization of opportunities
Internal: Weaknesses (W-weaknesses)	**WO** *"Mini-Maxi" strategy* Strategies that minimize internal weaknesses so as to exploit provided opportunities	**WT** *"Mini-Mini" strategy* Strategies that minimize internal weaknesses while avoiding threats

3.5.2 Expected Results

Master plan for the development of nautical tourism on the Croatian inland waterways of the which also can be a strategic document and structural guide for sustainable development of nautical tourism.

3.6   Action Plan for the Development of Nautical Tourism in the Inland Waterways and Lakes in Croatia

Action plan for nautical tourism on the Croatian inland waterways will specify development activities and precise in detail short, medium and long-term implementation methods and conditions. Means of achieving the vision of nautical tourism inland waterways can be achieved by implementation strategy toward optimal marketing mix (product, selling price, distribution and sales, promotion).

3.6.1 Methodology of Research

Authors will develop logical matrix for (logframe) that will enable planning, management and evaluation of programs and projects related to the development of nautical tourism on inland waterways of the Republic of Croatia. Logical Framework Matrix will be developed for all three timelines (short / medium / long term) in accordance with the Table 2.

Table 2. Structure of the logframe matrix

Descriptive summary	**Objective** - a general description of the objectives (a reference to the Master Plan and Development strategy of nautical tourism)
Results	Which specific results can be expected from valid managing available funds described in the model 4P marketing mix?
Activities (projects)	What are the key activities to be undertaken in order to achieve results and successful project outcomes?
Costs	What are the key costs / resources: equipment, personnel, services, operating costs, etc.
Performance indicators	What are the indicators to achieve the objectives?
Means of Verification	What specific sources of information use to verify the respective indicators? What methods use to obtain data?
Assumptions and risks	What external conditions must be met for the project to achieve desired objectives?

3.6.2 Expected Results

Action Plan for nautical tourism on Croatian inland waterways which identifies specific development opportunities and provides a detailed short / medium / long-term conditions and methods of implementation in a way that provide detail information on:

1. Optimum management structure sector. In order to implement development activities they should be managed by the public sector and regulated by external actors from the private sector;
2. Optimum implementation structure. Issues related to the implementation of development strategies at the operational level, for example, the types of tourist attractions, the necessary infrastructure facilities, services, schedule of implementation, etc;
3. Optimal investment plan. Elaboration of several options involving the private sector with a clear specification of the relationship between public and private actors;
4. Identifying high-priority projects with current implementation potential.

3.7   Implementation of the Proposed Methodology

The proposed methodology found that there is a wide range of potential for nautical tourism, as one of the greatest shortcomings are inadequate piers for river vessels as well as their absence at key locations. This deficiency leads to the inability of utilization of the river potential, whose numerous tourist and nautical qualities are presented in the publication "Nautical and tourist guide of the Sava river basin." The design idea of setting typical piers on the river aims to lead to most acceptable solutions for improving the quality of infrastructure for sustainable development of nautical tourism throughout key partnership members of the "Economic regions in the Sava river basin" - ERUSRS, local governments, International Sava River Basin situated in Zagreb, water institutions, enterprises and other stakeholders. Expected effects of the proposed methodology implementation would be: increased number of active users of nautical tourism potential basin in terms of recreational and commercial shipping, fishing, rafting and other forms of nautical tourism, intensive connection of chambers of commerce member ERUSRS project, as well as their links with international and national organizations of the importance for resource management of the river basin, awareness in the region, importance and potential of the Sava as well as the need to preserve the environment.

4   Conclusion

In accordance with Croatian strategic and development plans the result of this article are identified, systematic and coordinated framework for future national and regional tourism development plans on the Croatian inland waterways. Authors proposed an overall objective framework for the development of nautical tourism on the Croatian inland waterways to collect and assess all necessary documentation and data throughout six stages: 1) A detailed review of existing tourism activities on inland waterways and lakes in Croatia, 2) Reference model for the development of nautical tourism based on existing relevant models in Europe, 3) GAP analysis of nautical tourism in the inland waterways and lakes in Croatia, 4) Recommendations and guidelines for development of an appropriate legal framework which facilitates development of nautical tourism in the inland waterways and lakes in Croatia, 5) Development of policies and implementation strategies of nautical tourism on inland waterways and lakes in Croatia, 6) Action Plan for the development of nautical tourism in the inland waterways and lakes in Croatia, with details of the scope of the proposed initiative and supporting appropriate implementation plan.

Identified framework in this paper is expected to initiate the development of nautical tourism on inland waterways in Croatia.

References

1. Pacific Consultants International Ltd.: Feasibility Study and Project Documentation for the Rehabilitation and Development of Transport and Navigation on the Sava River Waterway, Witteveen+Bos, The Netherlands, Zagreb (2009)
2. Bukljaš Skočibušić, M., Radačić, Ž., Jurčević, M.: Ekonomika prometa. Fakultet prometnih znanosti, Zagreb (2011)

3. Medium term development plan of inland waterways and ports of the Republic of Croatia (2009 - 2016), Ministry of Maritime Affairs, Transport and Infrastructure, Zagreb (2009)
4. Strategija razvoja nautičkog turizma Republike Hrvatke (2009– 2019), Ministry of Maritime Affairs, Transport and Infrastructure, Zagreb (2009)
5. Development strategy for inland waterway transport in the Republic of Croatia (2008-2018), Ministry of Maritime Affairs, Transport and Infrastructure, Zagreb (2009)
6. Brnardić, M.: Possibilities of introducing navigation on the Sava upstream from Sisak, Sava Newsflash, International Sava River Basin Commission, Zagreb (2013)
7. International Sava River Basin Commission: Sava – nautical and tourist guide, Croatian Chamber of Commerce, Zagreb (2011)

Selected Issues of Fractional Calculus in Modelling Accelerometers Used in Telematic Equipment

Radosław Cioć and Mirosław Luft

University of Technology and Humanities in Radom,
Faculty of Transport and Electrical Engineering,
26-600 Radom, Malczewskiego 29, Poland
{r.cioc,m.luft}@uthrad.pl

Abstract. The paper is inspired by developments of fractional calculus in different areas of science in recent years. The article shows simulation and laboratory studies on accelerometers applied in telematics (indicator devices, telecommunications equipment, driving profile monitoring, sensory telematics, etc.), which were modelled with fractional calculus. Measurement errors and comparison of classical and fractional models in terms of dynamic properties were examined.

Keywords: fractional calculus, accelerometer.

1 Introduction

Let a fractional derivative have the following form:

$$t_0 D_t^{(v)} f(t) = \lim_{\substack{h \to 0 \\ t-t_0=kh}} \left[\frac{1}{h^v} \sum_{i=0}^{k} a_i^{(v)} f(t - hi) \right] \begin{bmatrix} f(t) \\ f(t-h) \\ ... \\ f(t-kh) \end{bmatrix} \tag{1}$$

where:

$$a_i^{(v)} = \begin{cases} 1 & i = 0 \\ (-1)^i \dfrac{v(v-1)(v-2)...(v-i+1)}{i!} & i = 1,2,3,... \end{cases} \tag{2}$$

is defined as a backward difference of a discrete function and h is the function $f(t)$ increment defined over a specific range $[t_0, t]$:

$$h = \frac{t - t_0}{k} \tag{3}$$

J. Mikulski (Ed.): TST 2013, CCIS 395, pp. 234–242, 2013.
© Springer-Verlag Berlin Heidelberg 2013

On introducing the non-integer to the second order equation of the measuring transducer dynamic properties, the equation takes the form of:

$$\frac{d^2}{dt^2}w(t) + 2\zeta\omega_0 \frac{d^{(v_1)}}{dt^{(v_1)}}w(t) + \omega_0^2 w(t) = -\frac{d^2}{dt^2}x(t) \tag{4}$$

Generalizing equation (5) and considering that integer-order derivatives in the integral-derivative calculus are a special case of non-integer order derivatives, we can write:

$$
\begin{aligned}
A_2 \frac{d^{(v_2)}}{dt^{(v_2)}}w(t) + A_1 \frac{d^{(v_1)}}{dt^{(v_1)}}w(t) + A_0 \frac{d^{(v_0)}}{dt^{(v_0)}}w(t) = \\
B_2 \frac{d^{(u_2)}}{dt^{(u_2)}}x(t) + B_1 \frac{d^{(u_1)}}{dt^{(u_1)}}x(t) + B_0 \frac{d^{(u_0)}}{dt^{(u_0)}}x(t)
\end{aligned} \tag{5}
$$

where: u, v – are fractional order derivatives.

Hence equation (5) is a linear, differential equation of non-integer orders:

$$\sum_{i=0}^{n} {}_{t_0}A_i D_{t_0}^{(v_i)} w(t) = \sum_{j=0}^{m} {}_{t_0}B_j D_{t_0}^{(u_j)} x(t) \tag{6}$$

where:
$$A_i = const. \in R, \ i = 1, 2, ..., n-1, \ B_j = const. \in R,$$
$$j = 1, 2, ..., m, \ m \le n, \ m, n \in R, \ A_n = 1,$$

- $\ {}_{t_0}A_i D_{t_0}^{(v_i)} w(t)$, $\ {}_{t_0}B_j D_{t_0}^{(u_j)} x(t)$ – Riemann-Liouville or Grünwald-Letnikov's

  derivatives, $\ {}_{t_0}A_i D_{t_0}^{(v_i)} w(t)\Big|_{t=t_0}$, $\ {}_{t_0}B_j D_{t_0}^{(u_j)} x(t)\Big|_{t=t_0}$ – initial conditions,

- $w(t)$, $x(t)$ – functions for which Riemann-Liouville or Grünwald-Letnikov's derivatives exist.

Taking equation (6) into account, formula (5) in its matrix form can be written down as follows:

$$
\begin{bmatrix} A_2 & A_1 & A_0 \end{bmatrix}
\begin{bmatrix} D_t^{(v_2)} w(t) \\ D_t^{(v_1)} w(t) \\ D_t^{(v_0)} w(t) \end{bmatrix}
=
\begin{bmatrix} B_2 & B_1 & B_0 \end{bmatrix}
\begin{bmatrix} D_t^{(u_2)} x(t) \\ D_t^{(u_1)} x(t) \\ D_t^{(u_0)} x(t) \end{bmatrix}
\tag{7}
$$

Introducing coefficients $a_2^{v_i}$, $a_1^{v_i}$, $a_0^{v_i}$ and $b_2^{u_j}$, $b_1^{u_j}$, $b_0^{u_j}$ to equation (7), in view of the fact that: $a_0^{(v_i)} = 1$ for $i = 1, 2, ..., n$, $b_0^{(u_j)} = 1$ for $j = 1, 2, ..., m$ and

$$a_0 = \frac{A_n}{h^{v_n}} + \frac{A_{n-1}}{h^{v_{n-1}}} + ... + \frac{A_0}{h^{v_0}}, \quad b_0 = \frac{A_m}{h^{u_m}} + \frac{A_{m-1}}{h^{u_{m-1}}} + ... + \frac{A_0}{h^{u_0}}.$$

Considering that:

$$\begin{bmatrix} D_t^{(v_2)} w(t) \\ D_t^{(v_1)} w(t) \\ D_t^{(v_0)} w(t) \end{bmatrix} = \begin{bmatrix} \frac{1}{h^{v_2}} & 0 & 0 \\ 0 & \frac{1}{h^{v_1}} & 0 \\ 0 & 0 & \frac{1}{h^{v_0}} \end{bmatrix} \begin{bmatrix} a_0^{(v_2)} & a_1^{(v_2)} & a_2^{(v_2)} \\ a_0^{(v_1)} & a_1^{(v_1)} & a_2^{(v_1)} \\ a_0^{(v_0)} & a_1^{(v_0)} & a_2^{(v_0)} \end{bmatrix} \begin{bmatrix} w(2h) \\ w(h) \\ w(0h) \end{bmatrix} \quad (8a)$$

and:

$$\begin{bmatrix} D_t^{(u_2)} x(t) \\ D_t^{(u_1)} x(t) \\ D_t^{(u_0)} x(t) \end{bmatrix} = \begin{bmatrix} \frac{1}{h^{u_2}} & 0 & 0 \\ 0 & \frac{1}{h^{u_1}} & 0 \\ 0 & 0 & \frac{1}{h^{u_0}} \end{bmatrix} \begin{bmatrix} b_0^{(u_2)} & b_1^{(u_2)} & b_2^{(u_2)} \\ b_0^{(u_1)} & b_1^{(u_1)} & b_2^{(u_1)} \\ b_0^{(u_0)} & b_1^{(u_0)} & b_2^{(u_0)} \end{bmatrix} \begin{bmatrix} x(2h) \\ x(h) \\ x(0h) \end{bmatrix} \quad (8b)$$

a matrix equation is obtained:

$$[A_2 \ A_1 \ A_0] \begin{bmatrix} \frac{1}{h^{v_2}} & 0 & 0 \\ 0 & \frac{1}{h^{v_1}} & 0 \\ 0 & 0 & \frac{1}{h^{v_0}} \end{bmatrix} \begin{bmatrix} a_0^{(v_2)} & a_1^{(v_2)} & a_2^{(v_2)} \\ a_0^{(v_1)} & a_1^{(v_1)} & a_2^{(v_1)} \\ a_0^{(v_0)} & a_1^{(v_0)} & a_2^{(v_0)} \end{bmatrix} \begin{bmatrix} w(2h) \\ w(h) \\ w(0h) \end{bmatrix} = [a_2 \ a_1 \ a_0] \begin{bmatrix} w(2h) \\ w(h) \\ w(0h) \end{bmatrix} \quad (9a)$$

and:

$$[B_2 \ B_1 \ B_0] \begin{bmatrix} \frac{1}{h^{u_2}} & 0 & 0 \\ 0 & \frac{1}{h^{u_1}} & 0 \\ 0 & 0 & \frac{1}{h^{u_0}} \end{bmatrix} \begin{bmatrix} b_0^{(u_2)} & b_1^{(u_2)} & b_2^{(u_2)} \\ b_0^{(u_1)} & b_1^{(u_1)} & b_2^{(u_1)} \\ b_0^{(u_0)} & b_1^{(u_0)} & b_2^{(u_0)} \end{bmatrix} \begin{bmatrix} x(2h) \\ x(h) \\ x(0h) \end{bmatrix} = [b_2 \ b_1 \ b_0] \begin{bmatrix} x(2h) \\ x(h) \\ x(0h) \end{bmatrix} \quad (9b)$$

where:

$$\begin{bmatrix} A_2 \dfrac{1}{h^{v_1}} & A_1 \dfrac{1}{h^{v_1}} & A_0 \dfrac{1}{h^{v_0}} \end{bmatrix} \begin{bmatrix} a_0^{(v_2)} & a_1^{(v_2)} & a_2^{(v_2)} \\ a_0^{(v_1)} & a_1^{(v_1)} & a_2^{(v_1)} \\ a_0^{(v_0)} & a_1^{(v_0)} & a_2^{(v_0)} \end{bmatrix} = [a_2 \ a_1 \ a_0] \quad (10a)$$

and:

$$\begin{bmatrix} B_2 \dfrac{1}{h^{u_2}} & B_1 \dfrac{1}{h^{u_1}} & B_0 \dfrac{1}{h^{u_0}} \end{bmatrix} \begin{bmatrix} b_0^{(u_2)} & b_1^{(u_2)} & b_2^{(u_2)} \\ b_0^{(u_1)} & b_1^{(u_1)} & b_2^{(u_1)} \\ b_0^{(u_0)} & b_1^{(u_0)} & b_2^{(u_0)} \end{bmatrix} = \begin{bmatrix} b_2 & b_1 & b_0 \end{bmatrix} \qquad (10b)$$

Eventually, matrix equation (8) takes the form:

$$\begin{bmatrix} a_2 & a_1 & a_0 \end{bmatrix} \begin{bmatrix} w(2h) \\ w(h) \\ w(0h) \end{bmatrix} = \begin{bmatrix} b_2 & b_1 & b_0 \end{bmatrix} \begin{bmatrix} x(2h) \\ x(h) \\ x(0h) \end{bmatrix} \qquad (11)$$

The correctness of the presented method of reducing differential equation (5) to a form of matrix equation (11) was verified by determining logarithmic frequency characteristics of the oscillatory element of automatics and a measuring transducer for adopted fractional orders in equation (5) obtaining desired characteristics (characteristics overlapping).

It can be noticed here that for all adopted h increments, characteristics clearly overlap. This means that we should adopt h increments much lower than sampling frequencies.

2   Model of a Transducer Laboratory System for Acceleration Measurements

In order to identify the measuring transducer's dynamic properties, a measurement system depicted in Fig. 1 was built.

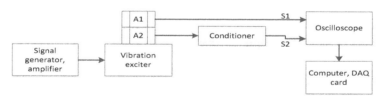

Fig. 1. Laboratory measurement system to test mechanical vibration transducers; A1 – reference accelerometer, A2 – tested accelerometer [Own study]

Simulations and laboratory tests were conducted for the measurement system with an accelerometer. Such a measurement system was built in the laboratory of the Faculty of Transport and Electrical Engineering, UTH in Radom. In order to determine the operator transmittance of the measuring transducer, the system was modelled, which consisted of two accelerometers, a conditioner and a μDAQ USB-26A16 card. An accelerometer of the DeltaTron type by Bruel&Kjaer, type 4507, having the sensitivity of 10.18mV/ms^{-2} was tested and the tested frequencies ranged from 0.4Hz to 6kHz. The conditioner's work ranged between 1Hz and 20kHz. The transducer was placed on an electrodynamic exciter. The reference accelerometer produced by VEB Metra (type KB12, sensitivity - 317mV/ms^{-2}) was aligned in one axis with the examined transducer.

The signal identified was a voltage-source signal from the end of the examined measurement track, the reference signal – the signal from the reference accelerometer which was a response to a sinusoidal function from a generator of 100Hz frequency.

The main purpose of the test conducted was identification of a mathematical model of a measuring transducer (6) on the basis of signals received from both transducers: the reference and the tested one. The identification method applied here was the ARX method comparing the tested signal to the reference signal and on the basis of the comparison discrete transmittance of the tested transducer was determined.

It was assumed that the sampling time in the ARX method is 10^{-4} s, for which the Nyquist criterion for sampling of frequency selection is the same as for the measurement card. Voltage-source signals were examined and then converted into acceleration.

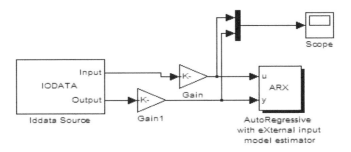

Fig. 2. Model of the measurement system for ARX identification of the tested transducer [Own study]

The ARX identification method (Fig. 2) allowed us to obtain a discrete transmittance of the tested transducer (measuring transducer model) in the following form:

$$G(z) = \frac{0.79196z^2 + 0.51435z}{z^2 - 0.6439z + 0.048034} \qquad (12)$$

As a result of the ARX identification method, the signal from the measuring transducer model and the characteristics from the reference transducer have the same amplitude and there is no phase shift between these signals (Fig. 3). The Figure allows us to notice that the error being the difference between the response of the obtained model (12) and the reference signal (prediction error) is in the order of 10^{-4}.

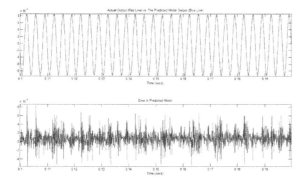

Fig. 3. The ARX identification method [5]

3   Measurement Error Analysis

As a result of conducted laboratory examinations relative and absolute measurement errors were determined. The determined measurement errors are direct errors – obtained from real signals collected by means of the μDAQ USB-26A16 measurement card. They are not of random character and are determined by the operator transmittance (or discrete transmittance) of the measuring transducer. Discrete transmittance of the measuring transducer (12) depends on the adopted method of its determination: i.e. on the ARX method, sensitivity and the measuring transducer parameters.

Figure 4 depicts a percentage characteristic of the relative error of the reference transducer and determined transducer model. The figure allows us to infer that the period of the entire measurement equals 0.05s. For the sampling period of 10^{-4} s we received 500 measurement samples. The high values of error peaks observed in the Figure result from determining the error for changeable characteristics over time during which they change their values from positive to negative ones.

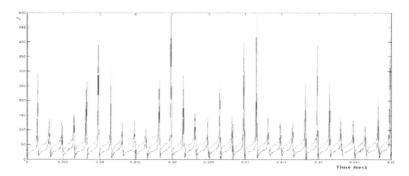

Fig. 4. Relative error characteristics for the reference transducer and the transducer model [5]

It was adopted that the measure of accuracy of the dynamic behaviour reproduction by the tested transducer and this transducer's model will be the median relative error. The median known also as a middle value is the value of a function in an orderly sequence, above and below which there is the same number of observations.

In the case tested (sinusoidal function of 300Hz frequency), the said median for the transducer's relative error was: 29.1945%; for the relative model of the transducer - 29.5564%.

The relative error for the transducer model has approximately the same values. The bigger the difference between frequencies of the tested performance and the performance at which identification was made, the bigger the difference between the relative error of the transducer and the relative error of the model is.

Table 1 includes relative error values for the transducer and its model at different frequencies.

Table 1. Relative error values for the transducer and its model [Own study]

Frequency [Hz]	Transducer's relative error [%]	Transducer model's relative error [%]
100	45.2213	30.8089
200	22.9227	30.2997
300	29.1945	29.5564
400	70.6078	28.3097
500	90.5626	26.0184

4   Comparison of Integer and Fractional Order Models of Accelerometers

In order to check, whether the model based on a fractional order equation describing dynamic properties of an object in a form of fractional orders reproduces the reference signal better than the "classical" model, on the basis of the transducer's transmittance model (12) obtained by the ARX method, a group of models was determined by means of non-integer order equations.

Tests started from one v_1 fractional order responsible for damping (equation (5)). The v_1 order derivative changes over its entire range of values from 0.94 to 1.08 by a 0.02 step (Fig. 5).

The above presented characteristics indicate (Fig. 5) that for the fractional order model of the transducer the linear range of processing expands, i.e. the phase shift in the range from around 1Hz upwards equals 0 at constant amplification, which equals approx. -2dB. In the classical model of the transducer the constant phase shift occurs up to the value of about 10Hz and the constant amplification of the amplitude which approximates that at the frequencies between 3.2Hz and 60Hz. In the case of the fractional model of the transducer the measurement frequency range at which the amplitude and phase are constant was expanded. The values of the median relative error for the transducer model of integer and non-integer order are presented in Table 2.

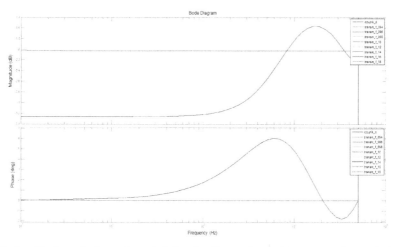

Fig. 5. Amplitude and phase characteristics for the $v_1=1$ non-integer notation and classical notation

Table 2. Values of median relative error for integer and non-integer order models [Own study]

Frequency [Hz]	Median relative error for the integer order model [%]	Median relative error for the non-integer order model [%]	Difference [%]
100	30.8089	20.8040	10.0049
200	30.2997	20.8041	9.4956
300	29.5564	20.8042	8.7522
400	28.3097	20.8039	7.5058
500	26.0184	20.8040	5.2144

Table 2 shows the values of the median relative error for integer and non-integer order models. The median relative error for the non-integer order transducer model is approximately constant for all examined frequencies and stands at 20.8%. In the case of the integer order transducer model the highest value of the median relative error was obtained for the lowest frequency of 100Hz, whereas the lowest value of the median relative error was obtained for the highest frequency, i.e. 500Hz. Analogical tests were conducted for the transducer of v_2 non -integer order.

5   Conclusion

The paper presents the use of a generalized method of describing dynamic properties of mechanical vibration transducers – accelerometers – based on non-integer order differential and fractional calculus, which allows to describe dynamic properties of a wide range of measuring transducers, i.e. of integer and non-integer orders.

Further research will be conducted to verify whether the model of dynamic properties of real accelerometers determined by means of non-integer derivative-integral equations conveys the dynamic performance of the real accelerometer over the entire processing range more accurately than modelling of the same accelerometer by means of integer order differential equations.

References

1. Luft, M., Szychta, E., Cioć, R., Pietruszczak, D.: Correction method of processing characteristics of the measuring transducer. In: Proceedings of the TRANSCOM 2011, pp. 83–86. Published by University of Zilina, Zilina (2011)
2. Luft, M., Szychta, E., Cioć, R., Pietruszczak, D.: Measuring transducer modelled by means of fractional calculus. In: Mikulski, J. (ed.) TST 2010. CCIS, vol. 104, pp. 286–295. Springer, Heidelberg (2010)
3. Ostalczyk, P.: Zarys rachunku różniczkowo-całkowego ułamkowych rzędów. Teoria i zastosowania w automatyce. Wydawnictwo Politechniki Łódzkiej, Łódź (2008) ISBN 978-83-7283-245-0
4. Pietruszczak, D.: Laboratory investigations of dynamic properties of accelerometers with fractional orders for application in telematics equipment. Archives of Transport System Telematics 5(2), 26–31 (2012) ISSN 1899-8208
5. Pietruszczak, D.: Analiza właściwości układów pomiarowych wielkości dynamicznych z wykorzystaniem rachunku różniczkowo-całkowego ułamkowych rzędów. Doctoral Thesis, Library of University of Technology and Humanities in Radom (2012) (in Polish)
6. Mikulski, J.: Using telematics in transport. In: Mikulski, J. (ed.) TST 2010. CCIS, vol. 104, pp. 175–182. Springer, Heidelberg (2010)
7. Gorczyca, P., Mikulski, J., Bialon, A.: Wireless local networks to record the railway traffic control equipment data. Advances in Electrical and Electronic Engineering 5(1-2), 128–131 (2011)

Diagnosing a Car Engine Fuel Injectors' Damage

Piotr Czech

Silesian University of Technology, Faculty of Transport,
Krasinskiego 8, 40-019 Katowice, Poland
piotr.czech@polsl.pl

Abstract. A combustion engine during operation generates vibration and acoustic phenomena. Vibroacoustic phenomena comprise information concerning the correctness of engine work and the condition of its each element. Many vibroacoustic phenomena sources occur in such engine, what causes a disruption of diagnostic information. All over the world attempts continue to use vibroacoustic phenomena to diagnose the condition of machines, also of combustion engines of motor vehicles. The development of methods for conversion of vibroacoustic signals and diagnostic signals allows expanding in the future the use of an on-board diagnostic system OBD in vehicles. The development of a complex diagnostic system is especially interesting, which would be able to diagnose the technical condition of particular elements of a car engine, using the information based on vibroacoustic signals. This article presents trials of using vibratory signals, generated by a four-cylinder combustion engine of 1.6 dm^3 capacity, for diagnostics of a fuel injector damage.

Keywords: internal combustion engines, artificial neural networks, diagnostics, on-board diagnostics.

1   Introduction

The task of injection system is to prepare fuel parameters in a way enabling a proper engine work, maintaining maximum environmental friendliness. This criterion connected with the emission of harmful substances is now the most important. Accurate discussion questions connected with the design and operation of combustion engines and injection systems can be found in [5, 15, 16].

As reported in literature for automotive services, many symptoms of incorrect engine operation is a result of bad injection system condition.

In the workshop practice the most frequent symptoms are:

- unstable work at slow running,
- increased toxic components emission in the exhaust,
- lower power of an engine,
- bad work of a catalytic converter system and lambda probe,
- difficult start
- failure indication by MIL lamp.

J. Mikulski (Ed.): TST 2013, CCIS 395, pp. 243–250, 2013.
© Springer-Verlag Berlin Heidelberg 2013

The time of fuel injector opening and fuel outflow expenditure from the injector after its opening has a direct influence on the injected fuel dose size. The time of injector opening is a direct consequence of each engine cycle duration. A static expenditure for each injector cannot differ more than 5%. The existence of disparities can be an effect of settled carbon formation, microcorrosion in the fuel outflow cross-section or injector discalibration in the case of its dry work (for example in gas installations, when injectors are not turned off and only a fuel pump is turned off).

A lack of fuel injection can result from of a lack of control impulse at the injector coil, a result of a clog or mechanically inefficient injector.

The injection obstruction is an effect of movement of sediments, which are formed during combustion or enter into the fuel during its production, storage, transport, distribution or use.

The majority of impurities settle during starting a heated engine, intensive engine work at high revolutions, or dry work of injector in the case of some solutions for engines powered by LPG gas.

Apart from injectors obstruction, sediments have adverse impacts causing abrasive and erosive wear of working surfaces of a needle valve, a pintle strangler and a pintle tip.

The workshop literature reports that an injector fault occurrence causes:

- lower fuel outflow,
- changed shape of fuel stream,
- changed size of sprayed fuel drops,
- poorer engine performance,
- smaller fuel consumption,
- shorter life of lambda probe and catalytic converter system,
- increase in toxic components in the exhaust,
- increase in operational costs,
- incorrect work of the whole fuel injection system.

Fuel injectors should be checked in respect of:

- leak tightness,
- correctness of fuel outflow,
- shape of sprayed fuel stream,
- size of fuel drop,
- fuel dose,
- coil activity.

2   Description of Experiment

The aim of the experiment was to detect damages in fuel inlets of internal combustion engine with the use of vibrations, which accompany it.

An internal combustion engine with spark ignition of 1.6 dm^3 capacity in Ford Focus was the object of tests.

Signals of engine head vibration were registered at the points near:

- intake valve, 1st cylinder,
- exhaust valve, 1st cylinder,
- exhaust valve, 4th cylinder,
- gearbox.

Measurements were taken for:

- 3rd gear,
- 4th gear,
- 5th gear,

at three engine speeds:

- 2000 rpm,
- 3000 rpm,
- 4000 rpm.

Each measurement was executed in two series, for the injector in running order and for the injector with a simulated damage.

In order to build damage descriptors for artificial neural networks from vibratory signals, bispectral distributions were designated [1, 12]:

$$BS(f_1, f_2) = \int\limits_{-\infty}^{+\infty}\int\limits_{-\infty}^{+\infty} C_3(\tau_1, \tau_2) e^{-j2\pi(f_1\tau_1 + f_2\tau_2)} d\tau_1 d\tau_2 \qquad (1)$$

A bispectral distribution is a function of frequencies f_1 and f_2 defined as a fast Fourier transform from the third-order cumulant. Examples of bispectral distributions are presented in Figure 1.

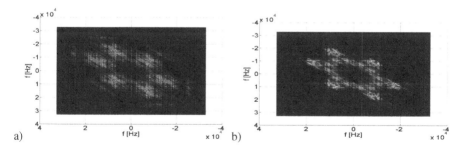

Fig. 1. Bispectral distribution for fuel inlet in good (a) and bad condition (b)

The diagnostic method proposed in this experiment was based on a diagonal matrix of bispectral vectors. Received frequency characteristics were divided into 1000 Hz, 3000 Hz or 5000 Hz ranges. The aim of this procedure was to check the influence of wide frequency characteristics bands on the diagnostic information. For each range a factor was marked, describing the character of amplitude. 36 amounts were used in the task. The factors included: crest factor, variability factor, clearance factor, impulse ratio, shape factor, skewness, mean absolute deviation, quarter deviation, arithmetic average, harmonic mean, geometric mean, central moments, quartiles, cumulant, root mean square, energy factor, peak to peak value, minimum, maximum, variance per cent variability factor.

In this experiment probabilistic neural networks (PNN) were used [6, 10, 13]. The influence of γ factor on the test error was studied in the tests. Experiments were conducted for 86 values of coefficient γ. An example of coefficient γ influence on the classification error value is presented in Figure 2.

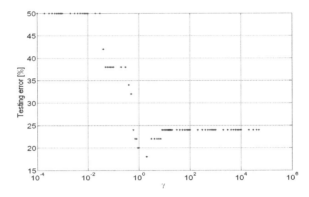

Fig. 2. The effect of coefficient γ on the correctness of the probabilistic neural network classification

Inputs for neural classifier consisted of vectors comprising marked factors in each of selected ranges. Altogether 432 pattern sets ("4 places of vibration" x "3 ways of bispectral matrix diagonal vector selection" x "36 factors") were created in the experiment.

3   Results of Experiment

A decision was made to check in the experiments the usefulness of an artificial neural network for diagnostics of the technical condition of a combustion engine fuel injection system.

The input data for the neural network constituted patterns built of information derived from vibratory signals measured at different points of the combustion engine and at the gearbox. The use of signals measured at different places aimed at showing the place influence on diagnostic results.

The first part of research consisted of a trial of building a diagnostic system showing the injection technical condition during a working car combustion engine at one rotational speed of the engine in one chosen gear.

In effect a neural classifier was built for 36 different parameters such as a rotational speed of the engine, gear number, place of vibration measurement and the way of division of bispectral vector diagonal matrix. For each classifier the best measure was used in patterns building process and the value of γ factor for neural network PNN, then the least fault values were received. The best obtained results are shown in Tables 1-4.

Table 1. The best achieved results – signals registered near the 1st cylinder exhaust valve

Engine rotational speed [rpm]	Selection method – wide spectrum bands [Hz]	Minimal value [%]		
		gear		
		3	4	5
2000	1000	0	0	0
2000	2000	0	0	0
2000	3000	2	0	4
3000	1000	50	50	50
3000	2000	50	50	50
3000	3000	50	50	50
4000	1000	0	0	0
4000	2000	0	0	0
4000	3000	0	0	0

Table 2. The best achieved results – signals registered near the 1st cylinder intake valve

Engine rotational speed [rpm]	Selection method – wide spectrum bands [Hz]	Minimal value [%]		
		gear		
		3	4	5
2000	1000	0	0	0
2000	2000	2	12	4
2000	3000	0	14	0
3000	1000	50	50	50
3000	2000	50	50	50
3000	3000	50	50	50
4000	1000	0	0	0
4000	2000	12	0	14
4000	3000	8	0	16

The experiments carried out show that properly working neural classifiers of PNN can be built.

Only for neural networks learning at data originating from vibratory signals registered at the rotational speed of engine equal to 3000 rpm, it was not possible to reach satisfactory results. It should be noted that assumptions of the experiment based on the diagnostic information originated from the examined object working at one rotational speed in the chosen gear.

Table 3. The best achieved results – signals registered near the 4th cylinder exhaust valve

| | | Minimal value [%] | | |
| | | gear | | |
Engine rotational speed [rpm]	Selection method – wide spectrum bands [Hz]	3	4	5
2000	1000	0	0	0
2000	2000	4	10	0
2000	3000	10	16	2
3000	1000	50	50	50
3000	2000	50	50	50
3000	3000	50	50	50
4000	1000	0	0	0
4000	2000	0	0	0
4000	3000	0	0	0

Table 4. The best achieved results – signals registered at the gearbox

| | | Minimal value [%] | | |
| | | gear | | |
Engine rotational speed [rpm]	Selection method – wide spectrum bands [Hz]	3	4	5
2000	1000	0	6	14
2000	2000	4	8	14
2000	3000	4	10	18
3000	1000	50	50	50
3000	2000	50	50	50
3000	3000	50	50	50
4000	1000	0	6	4
4000	2000	8	12	6
4000	3000	14	10	4

Because in this part of research the obtained results were good, in the next part a decision was made to check the ability of building a neural classifier PNN working irrespective of the chosen gear and rotational speed of the combustion engine.

Like in the previous experiment, the best measurements were determined and used in building patterns and factor γ values processed for a PNN neural network, the lowest failure values were reached. In effect, 12 neural classifiers were created, working at patterns received from vibratory signals registered at four measuring points and preprocessed using 3 variants of diagonal matrix of bispectral vector selection. The best obtained results are shown in Table 5.

Table 5. The best achieved results

| Selection method – wide spectrum bands [Hz] | Minimal value [%] | | | |
| | Signal registration place | | | |
	1st cylinder exhaust valve	1st cylinder intake valve	4th cylinder exhaust valve	gearbox
1000	17	17	17	17
2000	17	17	17	17
3000	17	17	17	17

Results achieved in this experiment, which allow a correct work of diagnostic system, were based on vibratory signals preprocessed using a bispectrum analysis. It may be noted that neural classifiers could not recognise an injector technical condition in the case of engine working at one of chosen rotational speeds, but irrespective of chosen gear. It is certainly caused by the lack of diagnostic information contained in patterns. That fact still requires closer verification and answering two questions. First, whether that is caused by a failure during registration of vibratory signals. Second, whether it results directly from the nature of changes in signals, from which it is not possible to differentiate classified conditions of fuel injectors.

4   Conclusion

Nowadays a car is the main means of transport for people and for goods movement. It is so easy to have a car that it can be found almost in every household. A large number of cars contribute to the environmental degradation. That is why global organizations and the biggest countries strive for introducing regulations aimed at limiting unfavourable trends caused by motorisation development all over the world.

Also in the world of science the work continues with the same aim. It should be noted that both types of work are carried out via designing and production of vehicles and also diagnostic systems as well as systems controlling their operation [2-4, 7, 9, 11, 14, 17, 18].

One of such actions lead to introduction of the duty of using an OBD system in cars [8]. This system operation could be expanded into diagnostics of particular engine elements condition, and also into the whole power transmission system based on vibroacoustic signals generated by these elements. The results obtained during experiments clearly confirm such possibility. Vibratory signals and parabolistic neural networks can become a basis of such diagnostic system.

References

1. Czech, P., Łazarz, B., Madej, H., Wojnar, G.: The use of bispectral analysis and SVM neural networks in the task of gearbox diagnosis. Scientific Journal VISNIK (9) (2009)
2. Czech, P., Madej, H.: Application of spectrum and spectrum histograms of vibration engine body for setting up the clearance model of the piston-cylinder assembly for RBF neural classifier. Eksploatacja i Niezawodność – Maintenance and Reliability (4) (2011)

3. Figlus, T.: Diagnosing the engine valve clearance, on the basis of the energy changes of the vibratory signal. Maintenance Problems 1 (2009)
4. Grega, R., Homišin, J., Kaššay, P., Krajňák, J.: The analyse of vibrations after changing shaft coupling in drive belt conveyer. Zeszyty Naukowe. Transport / Politechnika Śląska 72 (2011)
5. Heywood, J.B.: Internal combustion engines fundamentals. McGraw Hill Inc. (1988)
6. Korbicz, J., Kościelny, J., Kowalczuk, Z., Cholewa, W.: Fault diagnosis, Models, Artificial Intelligence, Applications. Springer (2004)
7. Czech, P.: Identification of Leakages in the Inlet System of an Internal Combustion Engine with the Use of Wigner-Ville Transform and RBF Neutal Networks. In: Mikulski, J. (ed.) TST 2012. CCIS, vol. 329, pp. 414–422. Springer, Heidelberg (2012)
8. Merkisz, J., Mazurek, S.: On-board diagnostics OBD in an automotive context. WKŁ, Warsaw (2007)
9. Młyńczak, J.: Analysis of intelligent transport systems (ITS) in public transport of Upper Silesia. In: Mikulski, J. (ed.) TST 2011. CCIS, vol. 239, pp. 164–171. Springer, Heidelberg (2011)
10. Osowski, S.: Neural networks for information processing. UW, Warsaw (2000)
11. Puškár, M., Bigoš, P., Puškárová, P.: Accurate measurements of output characteristics and detonations of motorbike high-speed racing engine and their optimization at actual atmospheric conditions and combusted mixture composition. Measurement 45 (2012)
12. Radkowski, S.: Diagnostics of gears using higher order spectral analysis techniques. In: 5th International Congress on Sound and Vibration, Adelaide, South Australia (1997)
13. Tadeusiewicz, R., Lula, P.: Introduction to neural networks. StatSoft, Cracow (2001)
14. Urbanský, M., Homišin, J., Krajňák, J.: Analysis of the causes of gaseous medium pressure changes in compression space of pneumatic coupling. Transactions of the Universities of Košice 2 (2011)
15. Wajand, J.A.: Piston internal combustion engines of average rotational speed and high-speed. WNT, Warsaw (2005)
16. Wendeker, M.: Steering of ignition in car engine. On-board diagnostic systems of car vehicles, Lublin (1999)
17. Węgrzyn, T., Piwnik, J.: Low alloy welding with micro-jet cooling. Archives of Metallurgy and Materials 2(57), 1 (2012)
18. Zuber, N., Ličen, H., Klašnja-Milićević, A.: Remote online condition monitoring of the bucket wheel excavator SR1300 – a case study, Facta Universitatis. Working and Living Environmental Protection 1(5) (2008)
19. Mikulski, J., Kwaśny, A.: Role of Telematics in Reducing the Negative Environmental Impact of Transport. In: Mikulski, J. (ed.) TST 2010. CCIS, vol. 104, pp. 11–29. Springer, Heidelberg (2010)
20. Mikulski, J.: Using telematics in transport. In: Mikulski, J. (ed.) TST 2010. CCIS, vol. 104, pp. 175–182. Springer, Heidelberg (2010)

Algorithm of Solving Collision Problem of Two Objects in Restricted Area

Mariusz Dramski and Marcin Mąka

Maritime University of Szczecin,
Wały Chrobrego 1-2, 70-500 Szczecin, Poland
{m.dramski,m.maka}@am.szczecin.pl

Abstract. The main task of navigation is to conduct an object from departure point to destination. It's natural that there is a need to consider all the limitations such coastlines, existing regulations etc. Safety requires also to observe all the dynamic objects which are able to change their position, course, speed etc. This paper presents the proposal of an algorithm of solving this problem for two or more moving objects in restricted area.

Keywords: navigation, collision problem, restricted area.

1   Introduction

The collision avoidance problem is one of the most important things in different types of traffic. In this paper an approach for navigation in restricted area is described. In [3] an algorithm for static situations was proposed. This time other moving objects are considered. The algorithm of solving collision problem can be also applied to other areas of transport.

First step in proposed solution is to transform the data from a format of digital map, to a graph containing all possible nodes to be reached and all the connections between them. This is realized using trapezoidal grid.

The second step is to find the optimal path using one of the algorithms such Bellman-Ford, Dijkstra or A*. Due to the computational complexity at O(n), the last one was chosen.

2   Trapezoidal Grid

The main advantage of data representation in the form of a grid (points, triangles, rectangles, trapezoids etc.) is that there is possible to determine the location of each point on the plane and consider other points or areas in relation to our point. In the case of grid the problem is reduced to determine the number of element containing considered point or it's edge, eventually corner, which are the borders of this element. The proposed algorithm can be shown at Fig. 1.

J. Mikulski (Ed.): TST 2013, CCIS 395, pp. 251–257, 2013.
© Springer-Verlag Berlin Heidelberg 2013

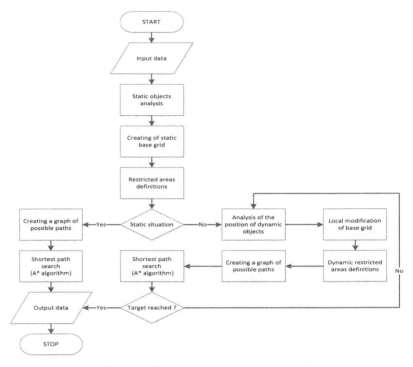

Fig. 1. An illustration of the proposed algorithm

As it can be seen the first problem is to determine whether the static or dynamic situation occurs. In the first case the solution is given in [3]. Comparing to the static situation some steps are repeated. The common ones are the analysis of all static objects, creating a base grid and determining the static restricted areas (coastlines, natural obstacles etc.).

In the dynamic situation there is a need to analyse all the objects with the ability to change their position, course, speed etc. It is necessary to do it at any time needed to conduct our object from the departure point to the destination. These tasks are:

- The analysis of the location of dynamic objects in the relation to the static ones,
- Local modification of the base grid, according to all moving objects in given moment,
- Determination of the dynamic restricted areas (existing only in given moments),

And at the end, there are two common steps:

- Creating the graph containing all the possible paths,
- Optimal path search.

All the steps (excluding the analysis of static restricted areas and the creation of base grid) are repeated periodically for each time period.

Input data is a set of ordered points representing subsequent objects present in the fragment of processed area.

The aim of the analysis of the static object is to verify the correctness of input data, determine the position of each object in the relation to other ones and the elimination of overlapped lines and nodes etc. [1].

The trapezoidal grid for static objects is created by conducting the straight vertical lines by the points which are the beginnings/ends of the vectors, representing the edges of each object.

The end of each section is the point of crossing the vertical lines with the vectors representing the edges. All the elements of grid have the trapezoid shapes (triangle in some particular cases) [2].

If the base of the processing is a navigational map, the restricted static areas are lands, areas excluded from maritime traffic, vessel wrecks, existing regulations etc. This procedure is deployed during the creation of a grid. Determining the restricted area is done on the base of the analysis of the vectors limited each element from top and bottom. The necessary condition to classify an area as restricted, is that two limited vectors belong to the same area and have opposite directions [2].

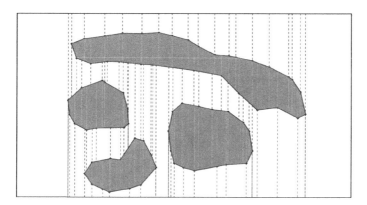

Fig. 2. Test area with trapezoidal grid and static restricted areas

If the dynamic situation is considered, there is a need of change of the grid structure in every successive time steps, depending on the current position of all moving objects in the area investigated. The algorithm described, proposes the local modification of base grid created for statical objects.

After the position of moving objects is given, all the elements containing them are found. Next, these elements are eliminated from the structure and replaced by new ones taking into account all the objects added.

In every time step the analysis of each created trapezoid is carried out. It is done in order to eliminate all the areas which are too narrow – there is no possibility of finding the safe path. Such areas become marked as restricted in the current moment. (Fig 3).

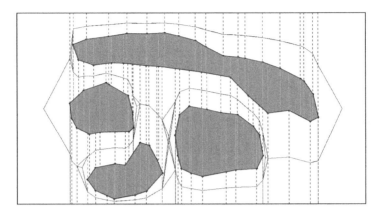

Fig. 3. Possible connections between trapezoids

If the length of vertical side of the trapezoid is less than some assumed limited value, but there still exists a possibility of safe path, only one node of the graph is placed, exactly in the middle of this side of trapezoid.

In the described version of the algorithm we assumed that the possible path can be conducted only through the adjacent elements of grid. There is no possibility to design a path omitting some areas or points.

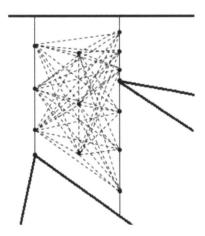

Fig. 4. Possible vertices connections

Because of the readability reason, Fig. 3 illustrates the grid containing up to 5 nodes and 8 connections in each element.

The graph of possible paths is redefined in every time step and depends on the current situation in the area investigated. Fig. 5 illustrates possible paths in one chosen randomly moment:

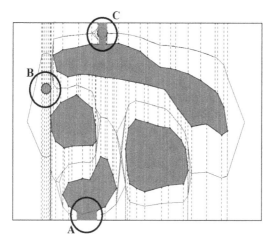

Fig. 5. Possible paths in one randomly chosen moment

A – restricted area – there is no possibility of find a safe path because of it's narrowness,
B – restricted area around the moving object (e.g. ship domain [6] etc.)
C – restricted area around the moving object with a connection with the narrowness of the possible path

At the example presented in Fig. 2,3 and 5, in the static situation, there were four restricted areas defined by 75 nodes and the same number of possible connections. The grid generated contains 141 trapezoids including 65 restricted and 76 allowed.

In the dynamic situation 35 time steps were considered. In the first 11 steps only one dynamic object was visible.

In the first 11 steps the number of the grid elements was constant with the total value of 168 trapezoids (80 restricted and 88 allowed). Later the total number of elements was changing in the interval of:

- from 98 to 111 restricted ones,
- from 83 to 96 allowed.

The average time of the execution of the algorithm was:

- from 23 [ms] to 26 [ms] for statical situations,
- from 78 [ms] to 148 [ms] for dynamical situations.

3   Optimal Path Search

There is a lot of popular algorithms solving the problem of the shortest path search in dynamic data structures. In [4] the analysis of each well known approach was carried out. The most often used method is Dijkstra algorithm proposed in 1959. The main advantage of this method was the least computational complexity in comparison to other ones. In 1968 P. Hart, N. Nilsson and B. Raphael proposed the extension of Dijkstra algorithm and called it A* [5]. Until now there are a different versions of this

approach including even the path search in the graphs changing it's structure dynamically. The A* algorithm has a computational complexity at the level O(n) which fact
makes it one of the fastest solutions of the considered problem. And this was the main
reason of choosing this method for the algorithm of avoiding collisions described in
this paper.

Figures 6, 7 and 8 illustrate the possible movement of the object taking into account a static restricted area and two other moving objects. The departure point is
situated on the left side of each picture in the middle line. The target is located in the
top-right corner of the area.

Fig. 6 presents the start moment for our object. There are no other moving objects
or obstacles. Only the static restricted area can be considered.

After 11 steps a first moving object appeared. At the Fig. 7 it can be observed that
the change of the path was made. Fig. 8 illustrates the situation with two moving
objects.

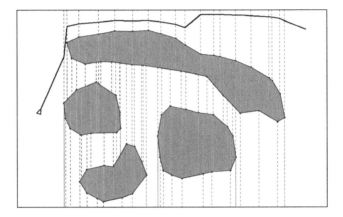

Fig. 6. The dynamic situation - step 1

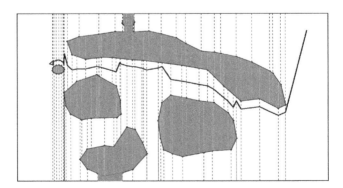

Fig. 7. The dynamic situation - step 12

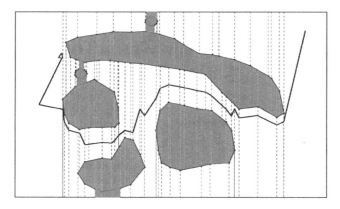

Fig. 8. The dynamic situation - step 21

4   Conclusion

An algorithm of solving the collision problem in navigation in restricted area was proposed. This is an extension of the approach described in [3] where only the static situation was considered.

As it can be observed in this paper, some other factors present in navigation weren't taken into account (such the dynamic of the ship, existing regulations etc.). This is the aim of further research and will be described in the nearest future. However, the proposed method can be applied in different areas of transport problems.

References

1. Mąka, M., Magaj, J.: Data extraction from an electronic S-57 standard chart for navigational decision systems. Scientific Journals Maritime University of Szczeci 30(102), 83–87 (2012)
2. Mąka, M.: The recurrent algorithm for area discretization using the trapezoidal mesh method. Scientific Journals Maritime University of Szczecin 29(101), 134–139 (2012)
3. Dramski, M., Mąka, M.: Selected shortest path in the graph algorithms with a use of trapezoidal grid in navigation in restricted area. Archives of Transport System Telematics (4), 3–7 (2012)
4. Dramski, M.: Shortest path problem in static navigation situations. Metody Informatyki Stosowanej, 173–180 (May 2011)
5. Hart, P.E., Nilsson, N.J., Raphael, B.: A Formal Basis for the Heuristic Determination of Minimum Cost Paths. IEEE Transactions on Systems Science and Cybernetics SSC 44(2), 100–107 (1968)
6. Pietrzykowski, Z., Uriasz, J.: The Ship Domain – A Criterion of Navigational Safety Assessment in an Open Sea Area. Journal of Navigation 62(1), 93–108 (2009)

Security of Digital Signature Schemes for Car-to-Car Communications within Intelligent Transportation Systems

Mária Franeková[1] and Peter Lüley[2]

[1] University of Žilina, Faculty of Electrical Engineering, Department of Control and Information Systems, Žilina, Slovak Republic
maria.franekova@fel.uniza.sk
[2] EVPÚ a.s., Trenčianska 19, 018 51 Nová Dubnica, Slovak Republic
luley@evpu.sk

Abstract. The paper deals with the problem of security mechanisms used in vehicular communication within intelligent transportation systems. The main part is orientated to a model of authentication and verification processors by using of OPNET Modeler with connection to OpenSSL on the basis of the digital signature scheme ECIES (Elliptic Curve Encryption Scheme). The results of time relations of ECDSA scheme digital signatures are described and mentioned according to lengths of cryptography keys for process of generation and verification of signatures with application for intelligent cars.

Keywords: intelligent transportation system, vehicular network, security, authorization, digital signature scheme, computational security, simulation.

1 Introduction

Recent development in the field of traffic telemetric and assistance systems can provide new possibilities in improving efficiency and road safety. The extent of these technologies is very wide – all kinds of the systems are already on the market or at least in development. During international ITS (Intelligent Transportation Systems) congresses and conferences, e. g. [1], [2], development teams inform about the conditions of development and use of the applications, e. g. an adaptive cruise control, the support of car driver at preservation of a secure distance from the car ahead, the development of navigation methods and others. Some systems offer the assistance with orientation to control, other provide information for car drivers to increase their comfort. To implement these systems it is necessary to ensure a reliable and secure wireless communication. Networks dealing with issues of traffic communication are called VANET (Vehicular Ad Hoc Networks). The purpose of such networks is to ensure the requested level of integrity, anonymity and authenticity services, while keeping the network delay below the level requested for safety-relevant (or irrelevant) application.

Currently there are several research groups worldwide involved in this kind of projects focusing also on verification of credibility of provided services in the

J. Mikulski (Ed.): TST 2013, CCIS 395, pp. 258–267, 2013.
© Springer-Verlag Berlin Heidelberg 2013

communication between vehicles VC (Vehicular Communications) for example CARLINK [3], SeVeCom [4], Car2Car [5], Safespot [6] and others.

Communication within intelligent transportation systems can be divided into communication between the cars, so-called C2C (Car-to-Car) or communication between the cars and the fixed stations RSU (Radio Station Unit), so-called C2I (Car-to-Infrastructure). For this type of communications a short-range communication DSRC (Dedicated Short Range Communications) is the best solution. This term is usually used to indicate a group of several standards – in particular 1609.2, IEEE 1609.3, IEEE 1609.4, IEEE 802.11p.

For the VANET network similar principles apply in the field of communication safety as for other wireless networks. The main safety requirements for communication between vehicles are [7]:

- authentication of the message and of its integrity – protection of the message against modification, a possibility of sender identification,
- undeniability of the message – a recipient cannot deny that he has sent the message,
- recency of the message – the recipient can be sure that the message is current and was generated within the specified interval,
- access control – decision which nodes in the network can execute assigned actions,
- confidentiality of the message – preservation of the message content from unauthorized parties.

C2C organization has been established by European car manufacturers and its goal is to implement secure functions in VANET network based on IPver6 (Internet Protocol version 6). From a value or customer benefit perspective, these applications can be roughly organized into three major categories [8]:

- safety-oriented applications,
- convenience-oriented applications
- commercial-oriented applications.

Safety-oriented applications actively monitor the nearby environment (the state of other cars or road conditions) via message exchanges between cars, so that applications are able to assist drivers in handling the upcoming events or potential danger. Some applications may automatically take appropriate actions (such as automatic braking) to avoid potential crashes, while others provide only advisory or warning information as configured by the driver. The examples of these applications are the following: Stopped or Slow Vehicle Advisor (SVA), Emergency Electronic Brake Light (EEBL), C2C Post Crash Notification (PCN), Road Hazard Condition Notification (RHCN), Cooperative Violation Warning (CCW) and others.

The main part of the paper is focused on the analysis of possibilities of the messages transfer between cars by using cryptographic digital signature schemes by its simulation in software modeling tool OPNET Modeler as well as on the verification of computing security of commercially available digital signature schemes.

2   Secure Principles of Vehicular Communications

The technology of digital signatures based on asymmetric cryptography using PKI (Public Key Infrastructure), which assumes the existence of a CAs (Certification Authorities), was enforced within the authorized communication between vehicles.

Each CA is responsible for the assigned region and manages the identification of all mobile nodes (vehicles) registered with it. To enable communication between nodes in different regions each CA provides certificates to other CAs. The principle of communication between the CA and individual nodes in the network is shown in Fig. 1. Each node is registered with only one CA and has a unique, long-term identification, pair of private and public keys and a long-term certificate. The list of node parameters and their validity is specified in the certificate issued by the CA after the node registration. For the communication security it is expected that each vehicle and each road unit is equipped with a hardware security module (HSM) [9]. Its purpose is to store and protect sensitive information and provide secure time base. Information stored in this module comprises mainly private keys to generate a digital signature on the basis of cryptography. In the case of risk all the information should be deleted. A module should also manage all cryptographic operations with a private key. The HSM is physically separated from the OBU (On-Board Unit) that performs public key operations. The HSM must have an API through which it can provide services to the other modules of the security architecture that run on the onboard unit (OBU).

Digital signatures are an essential tool to ensure a secure communication within currently developed ITS applications. A pseudo-anonymous authentication is used to ensure security and anonymity [7]. The principle of this authentication consists in the use of several public keys (which do not reveal the true identity of the node) and switching between them for a short time. Thus we achieve that messages signed by different keys are not connected.

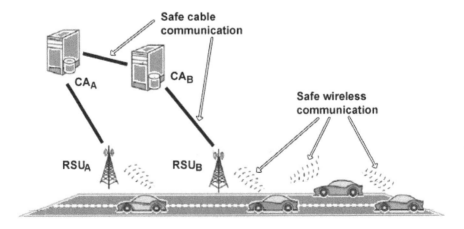

Fig. 1. Principle of communication between CA and the individual nodes in the network

3   Mathematical Principles of ECDSA Used in VANET Applications

Nowadays there exist several types of digital signatures based on asymmetric cryptography [10].

Most prospective algorithms for this purpose are as follows:

- RSA (Rivest Shamir Adleman) – extended in almost all cryptographic systems. The algorithm details are defined in RFC 3447 [11],
- DSA (Digital Signature Algorithm) – uses ElGamal algorithm [12],
- ECDSA (Elliptic Curve Digital Signature Algorithm) – DSA version using elliptic curves [13].

The most important parameters of digital signatures, which should be analysed in the framework of intelligent transport systems, are:

- the size of signature,
- the size of public key,
- the generation time of the signature,
- the verification time of the signature.

It should be noted that the realization of processes of particular phases of digital signature based on asymmetric cryptography is computationally difficult for the required safety, which for an authorized transmission of messages between multiple nodes in the road infrastructure can cause a delay in the received authorized message and consequently in the action to the occurred event. Therefore it is necessary to use computationally secure digital signature schemes that meet the computing speed requirements for signature generation and verification [14].

Calculation of individual operations of ECDSA algorithm is performed on the set of parameters known as system parameters (E, P, n, d). Calculation of these parameters is computationally difficult, but after the private key generation it is relatively easy to generate a public key. Nowadays hash function SHA-1 (Secure Hash Algorithm) is used with this algorithm, with a possibility to exchange for another hash function. Security of ECDSA standard is based on computational complexity of ECDLP (Elliptic Curve Discrete Logarithm Problem): for a specific elliptic curve E defined on the set of $E_p (a,b)$, and for points P, $Q \rightarrow E$ it determines integer d, where $0 \leq d \leq n\text{-}1$, where n is the order of point P and $Q = d*p$. The structure of the ECDSA algorithm for particular phases of digital signature is given in Table 1.

Based on published results of the SeVeCom project [4] in the framework of VANET network, with the use of modified digital signature schemes based on elliptic curves ECC (Elliptic Curve Cyptography), so-called integrated encryption scheme ECIES (Elliptic Curve Encryption Scheme) in the version with message authentication code HMAC-SHA1 (Hash-based Message Authentication Code) and with the encryption algorithm AES (Advanced Encryption Standard) in the CBC mode (Cipher Block Chaining) (Fig. 2) is assumed.

Table 1. Structure of digital signature ECDSA scheme

Generation of senders' keys	
Chose an elliptic curve E	Amount of points $E_P(a,b)$ should be divisible by a large prime number n
Chose a point $P \in E_P(a,b)$	Order of the point P is n
Chose d	d is a random integer in the $(1,n$-$1)$ range
Calculate Q	$Q=d*p$
Public key	$VK_a = \{E, P, n, Q\}$
Private key	$SK_a=\{d\}$
Generation of digital signature	
Chose k	k is a random integer in the $(1, n$-$1)$ range
Calculate $k.P$ and r	$k.P = (x_1,y_1)$; $r = x_1 mod\ n$, if $r = 0$, chose another k
Calculate s	$s = k^{-1}(H(M) + d*r\ )mod\ n$ $H(M)$ is has function SHA-1
Signature	(r, s)
Verification of digital signature	
Verification of $s´,r´$	$r´, s´$ are random integers in the range $(1,n$-$1)$
Calculate w	$w = (s´)^{-1}\ mod\ n$ and $H(M´)$
Calculate u_1, u_2	$u_1 = (H(M´).w)\ mod\ n$ $u_2 = r´.\ w\ mod\ n$
Calculate s	$u_1.P + u_2.Q = (x_0, y_0)$ $v = x_0\ mod\ n$
Test	$v=r$, where $M´, r´, s´$ are accepted versions M, r, s

4   Practical Implementation

The practical part of the work was realized in the OPNET Modeler software tool, which includes a wide range of options for modelling of various networks types [15]. Nowadays the OPNET Modeler does not include models for modelling the safety mechanisms by using certification authorities and digital signatures. The most relevant modelling capabilities of these mechanisms with already implemented models are IPsec or virtual private network (VPN). These models, however, are not sufficient to reliably replace the actual safety mechanisms used in the VANET network. Therefore models were created in the node editor and in the process editor. For communication between newly created models it was necessary to create a new type of packet.

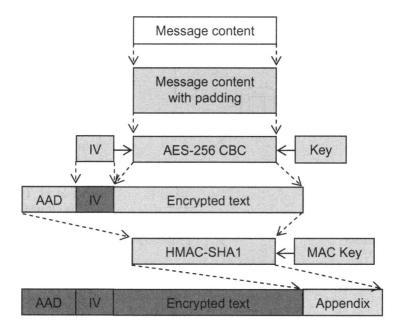

Fig. 2. ECIES integrated cryptographic scheme

For this purpose a software tool Packet Format Editor was used. This editor is in-cluded in the OPNET Modeler software package. The most effective solution for authentication of nodes in the network is a supplement to predefined models (for ex-ample *wlan_ station_mobile*) with an additional module – a cryptographic processor. This processor is designed to perform all operations related to authentication and verification of messages.

4.1   Model Realization in Process Editor

The cryptographic part of the model was complemented with a suitable block in the node editor. This block task is to control the full size of transferred data and therefore it must be located in the main direction of the block. In principle it is not important whether this block will perform all cryptographic operations or it will be divided to authentication and verification parts. The second option was used in this paper for a better illustration of this processor function. According to the authors' opinion the model called *wlan_wkstn_adv – mobile node* was the best candidate to create a safety-related model in the OPNET Modeler because of the possibility of various settings and because of the implementation of the node mobility [16]. Fig. 3 is showing the proposed location of safety nodes in the framework of the chosen model. *Authentica-tion processor* controls the full data flow from the source to the network and imple-ments safety operations (encryption and digital signatures). *Verification processor* on the other hand controls the data flow from the network to the node and implements verification of received messages. The location of these two processors is not completely correct from the theoretical point of view (they should be at the application level), but because of the full data flow control and because of the specific original design of the model this setup is the most effective.

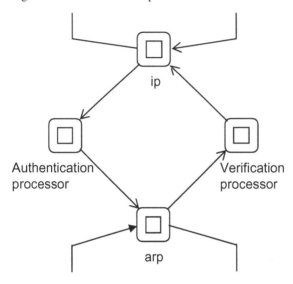

We created a hash code in the first part of authentication processor and then we signed this output by the algorithm of digital signature ECDSA (based on the process described in Table 1). The hash code is created in state 0 (st_0) and the digital signature in state 1 (st_1). State 0 is the default state and its output is the hash code and the return value *hmac_done*.

Fig. 3. Implementation of safety blocks in nodes editor

The *hmac_done* variable will be 1 at the moment of successful creation of hash code. After gaining this value the condition for transition to state 1 will be fulfilled. This state consequently signs the created hash code and creates output variables *signature* and *state*. The *signature* variable represents the signature attached to the message and variable *state* after gaining the value 1 fulfils the requirement for execution of MAC_PACKET_HANDLE function. This function will shift the message to the next levels (ARP, *wireless_lan_*MAC, *wlan_port*), which sends the message to the network. Verification is carried out in a similar manner. State 1 performs the same operation as for the authentication processor – it creates a hash code based on the received message. After the hash code creation the condition for transition to state 2 is fulfilled and the operation of signature verification can be executed. Input variables of this function are key (*eckey*), hash code (*digest*), the signature (*signature*). The output value of this function is variable *ret*. If the value is 1, the signature is considered correct and the transition is activated, which allows execution of action IP_PACKET_HANDLE. This function makes the message accessible for a lower level *(ip)*. If variable *ret* gains a different value, the DROP_PACKET action will be executed – the signature is not correct. This action will delete the invalid message. The authentication processor in the processor editor and the state diagram of verification processor are shown in Fig. 4a and Fig. 4b.

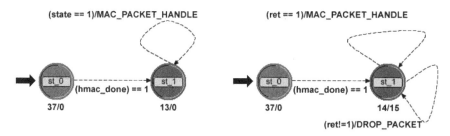

Fig. 4. Software implementation of authentication and verification processor for ECDSA scheme

4.2   Results of ECDSA Scheme Time Simulation

The OPNET Modeler software supports linking with libraries written in C or C ++. This linking allows the use of source code written in open-source OpenSSL [17]. The aim of the project was to create an open-source tool, which would have implemented all properties of Secure Sockets Layer (SSL v2/v3) and Transport Layer Security (TLS v1). Source codes *aes_cbc.c* and *hmac.c,* from the project which includes also features for verification of a hash code, were used to create a hash code. Features of source code called *ecdsa.h* were also used. This includes default parameters for generation of digital signatures. These parameters are linked to the output data from the previous state (HMAC output, keys). Libraries included in the installation folder of the OPNET Modeler must be used for the proper function of these subroutines. Link to these libraries should be made in "block header" not directly to the individual states. These subroutines are able to work also in a separate signing and verification part (with modifications) but also within a single unit. The key generation is realized by subroutine *ecdsap,* but there is a possibility to enter the key manually.

Examples of time relations of digital signatures creation and verification with prime elliptic curve (P) are shown in Fig. 5.

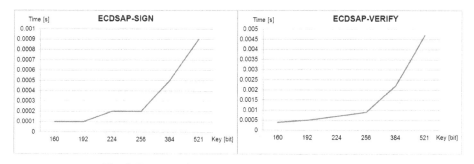

Fig. 5. Example of time relations of ECSA digital scheme

5   Conclusion

The future of our transportation system looks promising with the introduction of Intelligent Transportation System (ITS). ITS gives us the tools which could make our transportation systems safer. This paper surveys the state-of-the-art approaches, solutions, and technologies across a broad range of projects for the VANET communication systems with orientation to safety orientated applications using C2C and C2I platforms.

The possibilities of vehicles authentication within VANET networks were described in the paper. The analysis and modelling of safety features of VANET's cryptography protocols were carried out in the OPNET Modeler software tool with connection to OpenSSL library. A simple simulation of computation difficulty demonstration for chosen digital signatures was created. We assume that the capacity of calculation processor within the On Board Unit (OBU) of a vehicle will not be lower than the capacity of a 2.3GHz Intel Dual Core processor. We performed the calculations by a virtual device, which we created for this purpose using the VirtualBox software tool and an additional software, needed for the proper work of OpenSSL. In the future (up to year 2030) the equivalent lengths of keys (in bits) to assure the safety level within the ECDSA digital signature are recommended as 224-521 bits.

Acknowledgements. This work has been supported by the Educational Grant Agency of the Slovak Republic (KEGA) Number: 024ŽU-4/2012: Modernization of technology and education methods orientated to area of cryptography for safety critical applications.

References

1. Intelligent Transportation Congress, Stockholm, Sweden, September 21-25 (2009), http://www.safespot-eu.org/news/16th_its_world_congress2. html (date of access: July 17, 2013)
2. Intelligent Transportation Congress, Vienna, Austria, October 22–26 (2012), http://2012.itsworldcongress.com/ (date of access: July 17, 2013)
3. CARLINK: Wireless Traffic Service Platform for Linking Cars (2013), http://carlink.lcc.uma.es/ (date of access: July 17, 2013)
4. SeVeCom: Security Vehicle Communication (2013), http://www.sevecom.org/ (date of access: July 17, 2013)
5. Car2Car Communication Consortium (2013), http://www.car-2-car.org/ (date of access: July 17, 2013)
6. SAFESPOT Integrated Project: Cooperative vehicles and road infrastructure for road safety (2013), http://www.safespot-eu.org/ (date of access: July 17, 2013)
7. Papadimitratos, P., Levente, B., Holczer, T., Freudiger, J., Ma, Z., Kung, A., Hubaux, J.: Secure Vehicular Communication Systems: Design and Architecture. IEEE Communication Magazine (2008)
8. Emmelmann, M., Bochow, B., Christopher Kellum, C.: Intelligent Transportation System. Vehicular Communications. Wiley (2010) ISBN 9780470741542 (H/B)

9. Laurendeau, C., Barbeau, M.: Secure Anonymous Broadcasting in Vehicular Networks. In: IEEE Conference on Local Computer Networks, Washington, USA, pp. 661–668 (2007) ISBN 0-7695-3000-1
10. Vaudenay, S.: A Classical Introduction to Cryptography. Applications for Communication Security. Springer (2010) ISBN 0-387-25464-1
11. RFC 3447: Public-Key Cryptography Standards (PKCS) #1: RSA Cryptography Specifications Version 2 (2003)
12. FIPS 186-2: Digital Signature Standard, NIST (2000)
13. Enge, A.: Elliptic Curves and Their Applications to Cryptography – An Introduction. Kluwer Academic Publisher, Boston (2001) ISBN 0-387-25464-1
14. Franeková, M.: Mathematical Apparatus for Safety Evaluation of Cryptography and Safety Codes Used in Safety – Related Communication System. In: Mikulski, J. (ed.) TST 2011. CCIS, vol. 239, pp. 126–135. Springer, Heidelberg (2011)
15. OPNET technologies, INC. OONET Modeler 17.1 Documentation (2011)
16. Kopyčiar, T.: Safety Mechanisms of VANET Networks for Intelligent Transportation Applications, University of Žilina, Slovakia, Diploma work (2013) (in Slovak)
17. Beňuš, J., Franeková, M., Bubeníková, E.: Effectiveness of Digital Signature Schemes for Use in Vehicular Communication within Intelligent Transportation System. In: International Conference TRANSCOM 2013, July 24-26, pp. 17–20. University of Žilina, Slovakia (2013) ISBN 978-80-554-0692-3
18. Mikulski, J.: Using telematics in transport. In: Mikulski, J. (ed.) TST 2010. CCIS, vol. 104, pp. 175–182. Springer, Heidelberg (2010)
19. Mikulski, J.: The possibility of using telematics in urban transportation. In: Mikulski, J. (ed.) TST 2011. CCIS, vol. 239, pp. 54–69. Springer, Heidelberg (2011)

Selected Aspects of Traffic Signs Recognition: Visual versus RFID Approach

Paweł Forczmański and Krzysztof Małecki

West Pomeranian University of Technology, Dept. of Computer Science,
49 Żołnierska St., 71-210 Szczecin, Poland
{pforczmanski,kmalecki}@wi.zut.edu.pl

Abstract. Many scientific methods of traffic signs recognition involving digital image analysis have been proposed. Most of them are appearance-based approaches, employing template matching. In most cases they work on color images (or videos) and deal with all types of signs, regarding their shape and color. On the other hand, commercial systems, installed in higher-class cars, detect only the round speed limit signs and overtaking restrictions found all across Europe. The main disadvantage of visual recognition of traffic signs is associated with difficult conditions of image acquisition and hence problems with noise, blurring, scale and orientation changes should be solved. In the paper we present a classification of signs visual recognition methods and discuss their advantages and disadvantages. We compare them with an RFID approach.

Keywords: traffic sign recognition, RFID.

1 Introduction

One of the most interesting aspects that characterize evolution of transport system is the vehicular automation. It combines all the mechatronics and artificial intelligence to assist a vehicle's operator. Such elements introduced to vehicles may be labeled as intelligent or smart. After the introduction of integrated circuits, the complexity of automation technology increased. A vehicle using automation for specific tasks, e.g. navigation, may be referred to as semi-autonomous, while a vehicle relying solely on automation is consequently referred to as robotic or autonomous. It can be seen that manufacturers and researchers subsequently add a variety of automated functions to automobiles and other vehicles.

Nowadays, human is the one, who is responsible for the driving. Unfortunately, his/her perception can easily be disrupted. There is some research on the ability of drivers to perceive signs [15], which shows that even a driver focused on the way is not able to notice and remember all the passed signs. Even if the signs are visible for the driver, it is likely that they are obstructed by other objects, distorted due to bad weather conditions or the driver is distracted, for example, by a ringing phone of another passenger. Sometimes it happens that the driver has to think longer to recall a sign that has just been passed or which sign currently takes effect. As far as he could

J. Mikulski (Ed.): TST 2013, CCIS 395, pp. 268–274, 2013.
© Springer-Verlag Berlin Heidelberg 2013

remember anything at all, the whole process of remembering and recalling can reduce the comfort of travelling. It also have an influence on the road safety.

One of the examples of an intelligent system that help humans in above tasks is a Traffic Sign Recognition (TSR) technology. It enables a vehicle to recognize traffic signs put on the road e.g. "speed limit" or "do not overtake" or "pedestrian crossing". This is part of the features collectively called Advanced Driver Assistance System (ADAS).

The first TSR systems, which recognize speed limits, were developed in cooperation by Mobileye and Continental AG and appeared on the market in late 2008 on the redesigned BMW 7-Series, and the following year on the Mercedes-Benz S-Class. Unfortunately these systems only detect the round speed limit signs that are rather standardized in most of European countries (e.g.[1]).

More sophisticated systems add the detection of overtaking restrictions. One of exemplary systems was introduced in 2008 in cars made by Opel and used by other carmakers in their products (2011, Volkswagen; 2012, Volvo). This technology can read and identify the circular patterns and the numbers inside them. It is called Road Sign Information. The main constraint of above systems is a limited number of sign types that can be recognized and a low resistance to environmental conditions. The progress in research in this area implies that more advanced systems may be available in the near future [8]. It should be also noted, that the practical implementation of above systems is far behind the methods developed by researchers.

In this paper we compare methods based on visual recognition of traffic signs and RFID-based ones.

1.1   Visual Recognition of Traffic Signs

Despite a visible progress in this field, the traffic sign detection and recognition is still a challenging real-world problem of high industrial relevance. A detailed comparison of different state-of-the-art approaches based on computer vision methods can be found in [8] and [9]. The recognition of traffic signs can be divided into two subtasks: sign detection and sign classification (recognition). The first stage is mainly based on shape and color features, since traffic signs are standardized to some extent. The second stage uses different feature extractors (geometrical, like SIFT or LESH and color – dominant colors and low-frequency components of Discrete Cosine Transform) and classifiers (Adaboost, Support Vector Machine, Bayes, Artificial Neural Networks). Sometimes, the features are reduced using linear subspace methods, i.e. the Principal Component Analysis and Linear Discriminant Analysis. Some details related to the principles of selected visual recognition algorithms are provided in Table 1. As it can be seen, the accuracy (Acc.) varies from 70% to almost 100% and the speed of processing (Perf.) largely depends on the database volume and the performed tasks (detection, classification, verification) – many algorithms are able to work in real-time, which is crucial in real world conditions.

It should be noted, that traffic sign detection is a search problem in natural (outdoor) images. A useful detector must, therefore, be able to cope with rotation, different lighting conditions, perspective changes, occlusion and all kinds of weather conditions.

Table 1. Comparison of different visual traffic sign detection and recognition methods

Ref.	Main principles	Acc.	Err.	Perf.	Remarks
[1]	HSV, RANSAC, ANN	97%	1%	27 fps	Only speed limit signs
[2]	Adaboost, Bayes Classifier, LDA	N/A	6%	10 fps	Only one class of signs
[5]	Connected Components, Color/Shape, ANN	N/A	5%	5 fps	5 classes of signs
[6]	SIFT, Bag-of_Words, k-means	92%	2.5%	N/A	3 classes of signs
[7]	HSV, SIFT	99%	1%	N/A	Very small testing database (150 signs)
[10]	HSV, Contourlet Transform, LESH Features, SVM	97%	3%	N/A	Slow processing
[11]	PCA-SIFT, Adaboost	92%	8%	5 fps	Slow processing, large database
[12]	DCT, ANN, Naïve Bayes Classifer	93%	N/A	0.25 fps	Very slow speed, synthetic database (artificial distortions)
[14]	HSV, PCA	70-97%	N/A	N/A	Fast processing, low accuracy in case of distorted and occluded signs

On the other hand, humans are capable of detecting a large variety of existing road signs with close to perfect reliability in experimental setups. Therefore, the developed system should characterize high recognition accuracy and speed with possible lowest recognition error rate (Err.).

1.2   Solutions Based on RFID Technology

RFID (Radio-frequency identification) in general is a system which transmits the data from a transponder or a tag to its reader wirelessly using electromagnetic waves [16][17][18].

Logistics and transportation are major areas for RFID technology implementation. Shipping, freight and distribution centers use the RFID tracking technology. In the railroad industry, RFID tags mounted on locomotives and rolling stock identify the owner, identification number and type of equipment and its characteristics. In commercial aviation, RFID technology is being incorporated to support maintenance on commercial aircraft. RFID tags are used to identify baggage and cargo at several airports and airlines. Some countries are using RFID technology for vehicle registration and enforcement. RFID can help to detect and retrieve stolen cars. There are applications to increase driving comfort and to support inexperienced drivers [19], to improve the efficiency of road traffic [20], to alert the vehicle driver on the speed limit signboard at low speed area such as at school, university campus and curve area [21].

Important studies have been presented in [24] and concern an automatic adaptation of the longitudinal speed control of a vehicle to the circumstances of the road. The authors used a combination of three different sensor technologies: RFID tagging of traffic signals to convey their information to the car, Hall Effect sensors located in the vehicle's wheels for high accuracy measurement of the car speed and DGPS for precise positioning of the vehicle and control loop time. In [22] and later in [23] there was an introduction to the interesting solution for traffic sign recognition system based on RFID. The authors proposed a structure of a recognition system and a method for encoding tags with the value of traffic signs. Some interesting experiments were made.

2   Comparison

Fig. 1 shows a general idea of a traffic sign recognition using a variety of techniques.

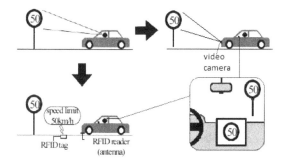

Fig. 1. General idea of a traffic sign recognition using a variety of techniques

There are several aspects that can be considered when we want to compare a visual recognition and an RFID-based identification of traffic signs. A compact presentation of the criteria used in this comparison is presented in Table 2 and in Table 3.

Table 2. Main features of visual and RFID-based traffic signs recognition

Feature	Visual	RFID
Infrastructure	Existing	New
Introduction time	Low	High
Cost of introduction	Low	High
Cost of usage	Low	Low
On-board device	Complex	Simple
Robustness	Low	Medium
Accuracy	High	High
Susceptibility to vandalism	Medium	Medium

One of the most important aspects comprises the way of introduction and its cost. While the visual recognition of signs can be introduced in a reasonably short time and its cost is spread onto all drivers (the cost of the device installed on-board), the RFID-based recognition needs more resources and a completely new infrastructure.

Table 3. Comparison of visual and RFID-based traffic signs recognition

The aspect	Visual	RFID
Type of traffic signs	Dependent on recognition algorithms	Dependent on how traffic signs are encoded
Recognition speed	Dependent on software and hardware	Dependent on software and hardware
Acts of vandalism	Signs can be removed, painted or turned	Tags can be removed
Distance from the traffic sign	Dependent on the camera sensitivity and quality of the traffic sign	Dependent on the kind of RFID technology
Visibility of the sign	Strategically important	Totally irrelevant

The introduction of RFID technology would require a small revolution. Assuming a slow and gradual implementation, surely it would take a few years. The budget for such an enterprise value comes close to half the cost of traditional traffic signs in such country as Poland. The investment so large in size may frighten, but its results, lower operating costs and improved safety on the road would be seen more and more with each year of use. The cost for drivers seems to be the same (they have to buy a traffic sign recognition system based on a video camera or RFID technology in the form of an external device or a solution integrated with the car).

On the other hand a system based on the RFID technology is able to display traffic signs for the entire section of the route on which they apply, notify the driver by beeps, warning against breaking the rules. Easy expansion of the system allows the implementation of many additional features.

Both systems are, unfortunately, rather vulnerable. The traditional traffic signs can be removed (as an act of vandalism or just for 'fun') or altered (painted or changed) in a quite easy way. On the other hand, small RFID markers may be damaged mechanically or also altered, yet it requires much more knowledge and much more resources.

3   Conclusion

In the paper we have presented a classification of signs visual recognition methods and discussed their advantages and disadvantages. We compared them with the RFID approach.

It is too early to talk about replacing the current traffic solutions by the RFID solutions. Rather, one should speak about the additional designation and infrastructure that could support the driver. It is worth noting that in the case of the system failure, the driver must be able to respond appropriately to the rules prevailing in a given stretch of road. Thus, for now, it is necessary to leave the current solutions and to introduce a new traffic signs systems, for example, based on the RFID technology.

References

1. Eichner, M.L., Breckon, T.P.: Integrated Speed Limit Detection and Recognition from Real-Time Video. In: Proc. IEEE Intelligent Vehicles Symposium, pp. 626–631. IEEE (2008)
2. Bahlmann, C., Zhu, Y., Ramesh, V., Pellkofer, M., Koehler, T.: A system for traffic sign detection, tracking, and recognition using color, shape, and motion information. In: Proceedings of the Intelligent Vehicles Symposium, pp. 255–260. IEEE (2005)
3. Kardkovacs, Z.T., Paroczi, Z., Varga, E., Siegler, A., Lucz, P.: Real-time traffic sign recognition system. In: 2011 2nd International Conference on Cognitive Infocommunications (CogInfoCom), pp. 1–5 (2011)
4. Hazelho, L., Ivo Creusen, I., van de Wouw, D., de With, P.H.N.: Large-scale classification of traffic signs under real-world conditions. In: Proc. SPIE 8304, Multimedia on Mobile Devices 2012; and Multimedia Content Access: Algorithms and Systems VI (2012)
5. Kus, M.C., Gokmen, M., Etaner-Uyar, S.: Traffic sign recognition using Scale Invariant Feature Transform and color classification. In: 23rd International Symposium on Computer and Information Sciences, ISCIS 2008, pp. 1–6 (2008)
6. Escalera, S., Baro, X., Pujol, O., Vitria, J., Radeva, P.: Traffic-Sign Recognition Systems. Springer Briefs in Computer Science. Springer, London (2011)
7. Mogelmose, A., Trivedi, M.M., Moeslund, T.B.: Vision-Based Traffic Sign Detection and Analysis for Intelligent Driver Assistance Systems: Perspectives and Survey. IEEE Transactions on Intelligent Transportation Systems 13(4), 1484–1497 (2012)
8. Zakir, U., Zafar, I., Edirisinghe, A.E.: Road Sign Detection and Recognition by using Local Energy Based Shape Histogram (LESH). International Journal of Image Processing 4(6), 566–582 (2011)
9. Ihara, A., Fujiyoshi, H., Takagi, M., Kumon, H., Tamatsu, Y.: Improved Matching Accuracy in Traffic Sign Recognition by Using Different Feature Subspaces. In: Machine Vision Applications 2009 (MVA 2009), vol. 3-26, pp. 130–133 (2009)
10. Yang, H., Liu, C., Liu, K., Huang, S.: Traffic Sign Recognition in disturbing Environments. In: Proc. of the 14 th Intl. Symp. on Methodologies for Intelligent Systems, pp. 28–31 (2003)
11. Fleyeh, H., Davami, E.: Eigen-based traffic sign recognition. Intelligent Transport Systems, IET 5(3), 190–196 (2011)
12. Johansson, G., Rumar, K.: Drivers and road signs: A preliminary investigation of the capacity of car drivers to get information from road signs. Ergonomics 9(1), 57–62 (1966)
13. Shepard, S.: RFID Radio Frequency Identification. McGraw-Hill Comp. Inc., USA (2005)
14. Bhuptani, M., Moradpour, S.: RFID Field Guide: Deploying Radio Frequency Identification Systems (2005)
15. Brown, D.: RFID Implementation. Book (2006)
16. Fuchs, S., Rass, S., Lamprecht, B., Kyamakya, K.: Context-Awareness and Collaborative Driving for Intelligent Vehicles and Smart Roads. In: 1st Int. Workshop on ITS for an Ubiquitous ROADS, pp. 1–6 (2007)
17. Al-Khateeb, K.A.S., Johari, J.A.Y., Al-Khateeb, W.F.: Dynamic Traffic Light Sequence Algorithm using RFID. Journal of Computer Science 4(7), 517–524 (2008)

18. Harmida, A.: In-Vehicle Signing System Using RFID, Project Report, UTeM, Malaysia (2011), http://library.utem.edu.my:8000/elmu/index.jsp?mod... (date of access: July 29, 2013)
19. Sato, Y., Makane, K.: Development and Evaluation of In-Vechicle Signing System Utilizing RFID Tags as Digital Traffic Signals. Int. J. ITS Res. 4, 53–58 (2006)
20. Hasan, Z., Morteza, T., Kianoush, S., Pegah, A.: Usage of ITS in the In-vehicle Signing System With RFID tags and Vehicle Routing and Road Traffic Simulation. In: Proc. of the 11th Int. IEEE Conf. on Intelligent Transportation Systems, Beijing, China, pp. 408–413 (2008)
21. Pérez, J., et al.: An RFID-based intelligent vehicle speed controller using active traffic signals. Sensors 10(6), 5872–5887 (2010)

How the Troposphere Affects Positioning Solution Using Satellite Navigation Systems

Jacek Januszewski

Gdynia Maritime University, al. Jana Pawla II 3
81–345 Gdynia, Poland
jacekjot@am.gdynia.pl

Abstract. The satellite navigation system (SNS) pseudorange measurements are affected by several random and systematic errors. The troposphere, neutral, the lowest part of the terrestrial atmosphere, is a non dispersive medium for radio waves below 15 GHz. It means for all SNS frequencies also. The troposphere causes the delay in both pseudorange and carrier-phase measurements. This delay is a function of the tropospheric refractive index, which depends on the local meteorological data. The user's position error caused by troposphere, is smaller than ionospheric error, but cannot be eliminated by measurements. It can only be approximated by a general calculation model. Several empirical models used for the mitigation of the tropospheric refraction where the meteorological surface data are taken into account are described in the paper. The role of the troposphere in the error budget for the SNS horizontal positioning performance, the detailed relations and equations concerning tropospheric delay are presented also.

Keywords: satellite navigation system, troposphere, tropospheric refraction, tropospheric delay.

1 Introduction

The satellite navigation systems (SNS) pseudorange and carrier phase measurements are affected by several random and systematic errors that each SNS user must take into account in position's calculation. Some of these errors can be estimated, thereby reducing their affect, and others must just be tolerated. In the case of SNS the errors are originated from satellite (ephemeris, clocks), signal propagation through the atmosphere (ionosphere, troposphere) and user's receiver (multipath, receiver). The effect of the atmosphere has become one of the major accuracy limiting factors for SNS positioning. The effect of ionosphere on SNS is described in [1, 2, 3, 4, 5].

Precise SNS applications are complicated by the tropospheric effect on the satellite signal. These signals are affected by the neutral atoms and the molecules in the troposphere. The combined effect of the electronically neutral atmosphere is denoted as tropospheric refraction, tropospheric path delay, or tropospheric delay of a signal from satellite to a user at the Earth's surface, called tropospheric delay in this paper.

J. Mikulski (Ed.): TST 2013, CCIS 395, pp. 275–283, 2013.
© Springer-Verlag Berlin Heidelberg 2013

2   Troposphere

The structure of the Earth's atmosphere can be described, for most practical purposes, as asset of concentric spherical shells with different physical and chemical properties. Various subdivisions are possible, but with respect to temperature we can distinct troposphere, stratosphere, mesosphere and thermosphere. The troposphere, non-ionised, the lowest layer of the atmosphere, the layer in which most of the common climatic variations occur, is directly in contact with the Earth's surface. Its height, depending on the observation point, varies from 7–8 km (the poles), 10–12 km (middle latitudes) to 14–17 km (equator) [4, 6].

The troposphere contains approximately 80% of the atmosphere's mass and 99% of its water vapour and aerosols. It consists of dry gases (N_2, O_2, Ar etc.) and water vapour. That's why the tropospheric delay can be divided into hydrostatic (dry) delay and non-hydrostatic (wet) delay. The dry component causes about 90% of the total tropospheric delay and can be predicted very accurately. The wet component, about 10%, is more difficult to predict due to uncertainties in the atmospheric distribution. Both components extend to different heights in the troposphere; the dry layer extends to a height of about 40 km, while the wet layer to a height of about 10 km [3].

The tropospheric delay is a function of the refractive index of the troposphere n and the height above Earth's surface, this index causes an excess satellite signal path delay and is dependent on the local temperature, pressure and relative humidity. Refractivity N, always greater than unity, $N = (n - 1) \cdot 10^6$, can be expressed as the sum of the refractivity of the dry gases N_d and the water vapour N_w [4]:

$$N_d = 77.64 \cdot \frac{P}{T} \quad N_w = 3.73 \cdot 10^5 \cdot \frac{e}{T^2} \tag{1}$$

where P is a total pressure and e is the partial pressure of the water vapour, both in millibars; and T is the temperature in Kelvin.

Signals from satellites at a low elevation angles travel a longer path through the troposphere than those at higher elevation angles. That's why the tropospheric delay is minimized at the user's zenith and maximized near the horizon. Because of this relation in some professional GPS receivers, e.g. Magnavox MX 200, one of the satellite selection criteria is the highest, i.e. the satellites with the highest angle are selected for position fix and/or for calculate the coefficients of dilution of precision.

The path length of a GPS satellite signal through troposphere is showed in the table 1. The calculations were made for different elevation angles, from interval $[0^O, 10^O]$ with step 1^O and from interval $[10^O, 90^O]$ with step 20° for three user's latitudes φ, at equator ($\varphi = 0^O$), at 55° (this value is the same that inclination orbit in GPS system) and at pole ($\varphi = 90^O$). It was assumed that troposphere height is at mentioned above latitudes, 17, 10 and 8 km respectively. Maximum (466 km) and minimum (10 km) of this path length is at equator for $h = 0^O$ and at latitude 55° for $h = 90^O$, respectively. In the case of other SNS the path length of a satellite signal depends on inclination orbit, but for the user at equator is the same, at poles almost the same.

With respect to signal propagation, the atmosphere is divided into the neutral atmosphere (non-ionized part) which comprises two parts, the troposphere with stratosphere and ionosphere. In this case the height of the tropospheric region is not clearly defined, it doesn't depend on the user's latitude and according to many authors its value is different, e.g. 40 km [3], 50 km [1, 7, 8, 9], and 70 km [10]. That's why the path length of a satellite signal in troposphere is significantly longer.

Table 1. The path length [km] of a GPS satellite signal through the troposphere for different user's latitudes φ and for different masking elevation angles h in the case of the subdivision of the atmosphere with respect to temperature

$h[^o]$	User's latitude $[^o]$			$h[^o]$	User's latitude $[^o]$		
	90	55	0		90	55	0
0	319	357	466	10	45	56	94
1	227	263	368	20	23	29	49
2	167	198	294	30	15	20	34
3	128	155	239	40	12	16	26
4	103	126	199	50	–	13	22
5	85	105	170	60	–	12	20
6	73	90	147	70	–	11	18
7	63	78	129	80	–	10.2	17.3
8	56	69	115	90	–	10	17
9	50	62	104				

3   Effects of Troposphere on Satellite Navigation Systems

As Medium Earth Orbits (MEO) with height about 20,000 km are used for constellations of all SNS, both current fully operational, May 2013, (GPS and GLONASS) and under construction (Galileo, BeiDou) and geostationary orbit (height about 36,000 km) is used in all Satellite Based Augmentation Systems (SBAS), both current operational (EGNOS, WAAS, MSAS) and under construction (SDCM, GAGAN), the signals transmitted from all satellites of these systems pass through the troposphere. The propagation media, e.g. troposphere, affect radio signals at all frequencies and cause refraction with a time delay of the arriving signals.

3.1   Tropospheric Delay

Unlike the ionosphere, the troposphere is a non-dispersive medium for frequencies under 15 GHz [2, 3, 8] or 30 GHz [6, 9], i.e. in both cases for all frequencies carrier of all mentioned above SNS and SBAS. The index n doesn't depend upon the frequency of the signal. As this index is larger than unity, the speed of propagation of SNS and SBAS signals is lower than that in free space and, therefore, the apparent range to a satellite appears larger. The phase and group velocities on all satellites frequencies, the measurements of code and carrier of all these frequencies experience a common delay [4]. The disadvantages is that an elimination of the tropospheric refraction by dual-frequency methods (simultaneous range measurements in the receiver), unlike ionospheric delay [3, 4, 5, 11] is not possible.

Path delay L due to tropospheric refraction can be presented as the sum of dry delay L_d and wet delay L_w. The refractivity profile and the tropospheric delay can be determined only if meteorological conditions (pressure, temperature and humidity along the propagation path of a signal) are known. Meanwhile the SNS users, transport users, in particular, rarely know these parameters. Therefore most of them base the estimation of tropospheric delay upon average meteorological conditions at their locations obtained from a model of the standard atmosphere for the day of the year and the user's latitude and altitude. Both the dry and wet component refractivities are dependent on the atmospheric conditions at the user's height above the reference ellipsoid.

The dry delay for the zenith direction using mathematical models can be predicted with an accuracy of a few millimetres from accurate surface pressure measurements. The models of wet delay based on meteorological data at the surface are less accurate, with typical error of 1-2 cm. Water vapour cannot be accurately predicted and modelled. When the satellite is not at zenith, a mapping function model is needed to determine how much greater a delay can be anticipated due to the larger path length of satellite signal through the troposphere [3]. For a satellite at zenith and for a satellite at any other arbitrary elevation angle the delay is called vertical (zenith) and slant, respectively. If estimated dry and wet zenith delays are $L_{z,d}$ and $L_{z,w}$, respectively, and tropospheric obliquity factor to scale the zenith delay is defined as a mapping function m(h) of the elevation angle h of the satellite, tropospheric delay L_h for the satellite at angle h is equal:

$$L_h = L_{z,d} \cdot m_d(h) + L_{z,w} \cdot m_w(h) \tag{2}$$

where $m_d(h)$ and $m_w(h)$ are separate mapping functions for the dry and wet components, respectively.

3.2   Corrections of Tropospheric Delays

Several mathematical models are known for the mitigation of the tropospheric refraction predicting quantity of wet and dry components using surface meteorological measurements or default meteorological data, both the models of mapping functions and the models of dry and wet zenith delays.

Nowadays existing mapping functions can be divided into two groups: the geodetic survey-oriented applications and the navigation-oriented applications, the latter, used in SNS, include both analytical models and more complex. The simplest model uses a common mapping functions, $m_d(h) = m_w(h) = m(h) = 1/(\sin h)$, ignoring differences in the atmosphere profiles of the dry gases and water vapour. If the delay $L_{z,d} = L_{z,w} = L_z$

is known the delay L_h is equal the product $L_z \cdot m(h)$. This model is consistent with a flat Earth, but is a poor approximation for low ($h \leq 15^o$) elevation satellites [3, 5]. More accurate models can be presented as follows [4, 12]:

Table 2. The tropospheric delay [m] at a masking elevation angle h from interval $[1^o, 15^o]$ if the delay of the zenith direction L_z is equal 2 m and 2.5 m

Model	L_z [m]	masking elevation angle h $[^o]$													
		1	2	3	4	5	6	7	8	9	10	11	12	13	14	15
The simplest	2	114.6	57.3	38.2	28.7	22.9	19.1	16.4	14.4	12.8	11.5	10.5	9.6	8.9	8.3	7.7
	2.5	143.2	71.6	47.8	35.8	28.7	23.9	20.5	18.0	16.0	14.4	13.1	12.0	11.1	10.3	9.6
More accurate	2	41.7	35.3	29.1	24.2	20.4	17.6	15.4	13.7	12.3	11.2	10.2	9.4	8.7	8.1	7.6
	2.5	52.1	44.1	36.3	30.2	25.5	22.0	19.3	17.1	15.4	14.0	12.8	11.8	10.9	10.2	9.5

Table 3. The tropospheric delay [m] at a masking elevation angle h from interval $[20^o, 90^o]$ if the delay of the zenith direction L_z is equal 2 m and 2.5 m

Model	L_z [m]	masking elevation angle h $[^o]$						
		20	30	40	50	60	70	80	90
the simplest and more accurate	2	5.8	4.0	3.1	2.6	2.3	2.1	2.0	2
	2.5	7.3	5.0	3.9	3.3	2.9	2.7	2.5	2.5

$$m(h) = \frac{1.001}{\sqrt{0.002001 + \sin^2 h}} \quad \text{or} \quad m(h) = \frac{1.001}{\sqrt{1 - ((\cos h)/1.001)^2}} \quad (3)$$

The tropospheric delay at an angle h is presented in the author's tables 2 and 3. As the delay L_z of zenith direction ($h = 90^o$) is in [6] equal 2 m, in [1] 2.3 m, in [3] 2.4 m, in [7] 2.5 m and in [13] from interval 2.0 - 2.5 m, it was assumed that this delay is equal 2 m and 2.5 m. The obliquity factor increases sharply as a satellite gets lower in the sky. At low elevation angles, the typical values are about two at 30°, four at 15°, six at 10°, and ten at 5° [4].

The calculations were made using two models, the simplest and more accurate, for different h, from interval $[1^o, 15^o]$ with step 1° and interval $[20^o, 90^o]$ with step 10°. The results confirm that the delay is for $h \geq 20^o$ for both models the same, but for $h \leq 15^o$ differs considerably. This delay is for the simplest model greater, the difference increases when angle h decreases. As the tables 2 and 3 showed that the delay is the biggest (at least 5.8 m for $L_z = 2$ m) for the angle $h \leq 20^o$ the knowledge of the number of satellites visible by receiver's antenna below 20° is substantial for each SNS user.

The percentage of satellites visible above given angle h for GPS, GLONASS and Galileo systems at different observer's latitudes [14, 15] is presented in the table 4 and at latitudes $50-60^o$ for elevation angle from interval $[1^o, 15^o]$ in the table 5. It was assumed that the number of satellites fully operational is GPS – 27, GLONASS – 24 and Galileo – 27. If the masking angle h is equal 0° it means that for all three systems 100% of satellite visible can be used in position determination, if this angle is equal 10° this percentage decreases to 80%, if $h_{min} = 20^O$ this is about 60% only, etc. The additional calculations showed that this distribution is almost the same for all SNS independently of theirs orbit's parameters, satellite constellations (number of satellites, in particular) and user's latitude. For the user it means that in the case e.g. of current GPS system (spatial segment consists of 31 satellites fully operational) if 15 satellites are at given moment visible above horizon (h = 0°) for h = 10° and h = 20° this number can decrease to 12 and 9 only, respectively.

Table 4. Percentage of GPS, GLONASS (GLO) and Galileo (GAL) satellites visible in open area above masking elevation angle h at different observer's latitudes (φ), l_m – weighted mean number of satellites visible above horizon (h = 0°)

Φ $[^O]$	System	l_m	Masking elevation angle h $[^O]$								
			0	10	20	30	40	50	60	70	80
0 – 10	GPS	10.7	100	80.8	59.3	39.0	24.4	15.2	8.3	3.6	1.0
	GLO	9.0	100	74.6	51.3	34.1	22.5	14.0	7.6	3.0	0.7
	GAL	11.1	100	81.2	60.0	40.2	25.4	15.9	8.6	3.6	0.9
20 – 30	GPS	9.9	100	78.8	61.9	47.0	33.8	21.2	10.5	4.3	1.0
	GLO	8.5	100	78.2	60.4	45.2	28.8	16.9	9.1	3.8	0.8
	GAL	10.2	100	78.6	61.5	47.0	34.3	21.9	11.2	4.9	1.2
50 – 60	GPS	10.4	100	75.9	56.6	41.8	30.5	20.4	12.6	6.5	2.4
	GLO	9.6	100	81.2	61.1	44.7	32.5	22.7	14.3	7.9	2.2
	GAL	10.9	100	77.0	57.3	42.8	31.0	21.7	13.5	7.1	2.3
70 – 80	GPS	10.9	100	81,9	63.8	41.9	23.7	11.9	2.9	–	–
	GLO	9.9	100	83.9	69.3	53.6	36.0	20.5	10.3	3.3	0.1
	GAL	11.2	100	83.6	66.1	45.7	26.8	14.0	4.2	0.1	–

As residual tropospheric delay does not depend on the signal frequency 1σ error caused by this delay is in the GPS typical UERE (User Equivalent Range Error) budget the same both in Standard Positioning Service (single frequency C/A code receiver) and Precise Positioning Service (dual frequency P/Y code receiver). The value of this error is 0.2 m [3, 16] it means less than in the case of satellite clock time or ephemeris considerably.

Next models of mapping functions are also simple, depending on elevation h only, but are example of separate functions for dry and wet delays. More sophisticated, but more complex models, both for dry and components, based on a truncated form of continued fraction depend on several coefficients. In different models these coefficients are empirically determined constants or functions of variable such as latitude, height, surface temperature and pressure, day of the year [3, 4, 5].

Table 5. Percentage of GPS, GLONASS (GLO) and Galileo (GAL) satellites visible in open area above masking elevation angle h at observer's latitudes 50–60°, above horizon (h = 0°) 100% of satellites are visible

Sys-tem	Masking elevation angle h [^{O}]													
	1	2	3	4	5	6	7	8	9	11	12	13	14	15
GPS	97.5	94.9	92.3	89.9	87.2	84.8	82.3	80.0	77.9	73.4	71.6	69.5	67.5	65.6
GLO	98.3	96.7	95.1	93.3	91.3	89.3	87.6	85.7	83.7	79.8	77.7	75.9	73.4	71.2
GAL	97.8	95.7	93.4	91.5	89.1	86.9	84.5	82.1	79.6	74.7	72.3	69.8	67.8	65.8

The traditional tropospheric delay models can be used to calculate the atmospheric delay at an arbitrary station based on the provided surface meteorological parameters and the rate of change with respect to height [17]. The most known models are:

- Hopfield model users real data covering the whole Earth and assumes the same functional model for both the wet and dry components. This model is based on a relationship between refractivity at height to that as surface. The relationship was derived empirically on the basis of extensive measurements.
- Saastamoinen model, the refractivity can alternatively be deduced from gas laws. In the first model tropospheric delay can be expressed as a function of zenith angle of satellite, atmospheric pressure, temperature and partial pressure of a water vapour. In the new model there are two additional correction terms.
- Goad and Goodman modified Hopfield model by assuming that the temperature decreases linearly with increasing height in the troposphere, but remains constant in the stratosphere.

For modelling the troposphere's dry and wet components of the delay without meteorological and sensors one accurate method was presented in [3]. Both components are considered as the function of height (above mean sea level) and five meteorological parameters (pressure, temperature, water vapour pressure, temperature lapse rate and water vapour lapse rate). User at latitude φ can calculate each of these parameters by interoperating values from the special tables. In the UNB3 model the global latitude is grouped in 15 degree increments [17].

In almost all SNS receivers the value of zenith delay and mapping functions can be approximated without the knowledge of meteorological data only. It means that the error of the length tropospheric path delay calculated for the satellite signal path can be for satellite at low elevation greater than for satellite at high elevation considerably. That's why in SNS receivers during position calculation the satellites at higher elevation must be taken into account first and satellites at low elevation passed over. The limit for the elimination of satellites at low elevation is masking angle which in the majority of SNS receivers can be selected by the user, in other receivers is constant, 5 degrees usually.

4   Conclusion

- to improve the SNS accuracy, a standard atmospheric model is normally used in the SNS data processing to provide an estimate of the tropospheric zenith delay at a site
- the traditional tropospheric delay models are not perfect for the real time navigation users, the users of all modes of transport also, however they are easy to use and applicable to different navigation positioning accuracies
- the tropospheric propagation delay is critical for precise position and baseline determination, can significantly degrade the SNS accuracy, in particular in the height component, because the tropospheric parameters are only poorly correlated over larger distances; an error of 1 cm in modelling the tropospheric zenith delay can result in a height error of around 3 cm
- tropospheric delays are significantly smaller than ionospheric delays under active solar conditions, vary much less over time, and affect code and carrier measurements identically. However the obliquity factors for the troposphere are much larger at low elevation angles than those for the ionosphere.

References

1. El-Rabbany, A.: Introduction to GPS the Global Positioning System. Artech House, Boston (2002)
2. Hofmann-Wellenhof, B., et al.: GNSS Global Navigation Satellite Systems GPS, GLONASS, Galileo & more. Springer, Wien (2008)
3. Kaplan, E.D., Hegarty, C.J.: Understanding GPS Principles and Applications. Artech House, Boston (2006)
4. Misra, P., Enge, P.: Global Positioning System Signals, Measurements, and Performance. Ganga-Jamuna Press, Lincoln (2006)
5. Seeber, G.: Satellite Geodesy. Walter de Gruyter, Berlin-New York (2003)
6. Samana, N.: Global Positioning Technologies and Performance. John Wiley & Sons, New Jersey (2008)
7. http://www.navleader.com (date of access: July 23, 2013)
8. http://www.tekmon.gr (date of access: July 23, 2013)
9. http://www.w3.uch.edu.tw (date of access: July 23, 2013)
10. http://www.cmmacs.ernet.in (date of access: July 23, 2013)
11. Januszewski, J.: How the Ionosphere Affects Positioning Solution Using Terrestrial and Satellite Navigation Systems? In: Mikulski, J. (ed.) TST 2012. CCIS, vol. 329, pp. 249–257. Springer, Heidelberg (2012)
12. Gleason, S., Gebre–Egziabher, D.: GNSS Applications and Methods. Artech House, Boston (2009)
13. Şanlioğlu, İ., Zeybek, M.: Investigation on GPS Heighting accuracy with use of tropospheric models in commercial GPS software for different height. FIG Working Week, Rome (2012)

14. Januszewski, J.: Position Accuracy of Satellite Navigation Systems in Restricted Area. In: 21st International Communications Satellites Systems Conference AIAA, paper 2417, Jokohama (2003)
15. Januszewski, J.: Geometry of Combined Constellations GPS and Galileo. In: European Navigation Conference Global Navigation Satellite Systems, Manchester (2006)
16. Prasad, R., Ruggieri, M.: Applied Satellite Navigation Using GPS, Galileo, and Augmentation Systems. Artech House, Boston (2005)
17. Song, S., et al.: Establishment of a new tropospheric delay correction model over China area. Science China Physics, Mechanics and Astronomy 54(12), 2271–2283 (2011)

Travel Demand and Transportation Supply Modelling for Agglomeration without Transportation Model

Grzegorz Karoń

Silesian University of Technology, Faculty of Transport,
Krasińskiego 8, 40-019 Katowice, Poland
grzegorz.karon@polsl.pl

Abstract. Travel demand and transportation supply modelling for conurbation area without transportation models has been presented in this article. Proposal of the methodology is based on four-stages modeling with trip-based travel-demand models. Methodology has been presented on example Upper-Silesian Conurbation in Poland.

Keywords: transportation modelling, travel demand, transportation supply, transportation survey, methodology of transport modelling, trip-based travel-demand models.

1 Introduction

The Upper-Silesian region is the conurbation type of agglomeration which is a cluster of many cities do not have a transportation model. This state is primarily due to orga-nizational problems (there is no managing authority for agglomeration) and problems of economic factors. The methodology in this article is based on four-stages modeling with trip-based travel-demand models. The models developed for the project of mod-ernization of tramway infrastructure in Upper-Silesian Conurbation have been pre-sented on the figures as example [5]. To carry out this project were performed certain of models presented in this article.

2 Assumptions of the Transportation Demand and Transportation Supply Models

The proposed methodology assumes that the transport model will be based on so-called *standard four-stage transportation model* with stages as sub-models: *trip generation model, trip distribution model, modal split model* and *traffic assignment model* (Fig. 1).

General form of four-stages transportation model can be written as follows (based on [1,6]):

$$T_{od}^{ishmk}(\boldsymbol{SE, TR, \beta}) = O_o^{\ ish} \cdot \mathrm{Pr}_o^i(d \mid sh) \cdot \mathrm{Pr}_o^i(m \mid shd) \cdot \mathrm{Pr}_o^i(k \mid shdm) \tag{1}$$

J. Mikulski (Ed.): TST 2013, CCIS 395, pp. 284–293, 2013.
© Springer-Verlag Berlin Heidelberg 2013

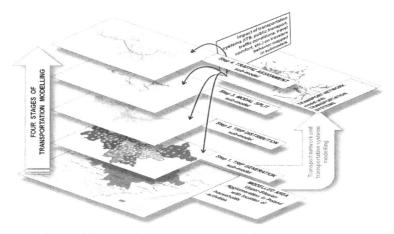

Fig. 1. Scheme of *four-stages transport modeling* – example [5]

where:

$T_{od}^{ishmk}(\boldsymbol{SE}, \boldsymbol{TR}, \boldsymbol{\beta})$ – number of users class i, who travelling between *TAZs* origin o and destination d, for purpose s in time period h by mode m use path k,

i – the user's class (category of socioeconomic characteristics),

o, d – the *TAZs* of trip o - origin and d - destination,

s – the trip purpose, or more properly the pair of purposes,

h – the time period in which trips are undertaken,

m – the mode, or sequence of modes, used during the trip,

k – the trip path – the series of links connecting centroids o and d over the network and representing the transportation service provided by mode m,

$\boldsymbol{SE}$ – vector of *socioeconomic variables* related to the *decision-makers* and the *activity system* with *variables of attraction of traffic generators* in zones,

$\boldsymbol{TR}$ – vector of *level-of-service attributes* of the transportation supply system,

$\boldsymbol{\beta}$ – vector of *coefficients and parameters*,

O_o^{ish} – the number of users in class i who, from origin zone o undertake a trip for purpose s in time period h,

$\Pr_o^i(d \,|\, sh)$ – probability, which gives the fraction of users i - class, who travelling between *TAZ's* origin o and destination d, for purpose s in time period h,

$\Pr_o^i(m \,|\, shd)$ – probability like $\Pr_o^i(d \,|\, sh)$ and users use mode m,

$\Pr_o^i(k \,|\, shdm)$ – probability like $\Pr_o^i(m \,|\, shd)$ and users use path k.

3   Study Area and Traffic Analysis Zones – TAZs

Agglomeration area is divided into *internal zones* and their number depend on a compromise between various criteria and municipal level – because *TAZs* system must be compatible with other administrative divisions, especially with census zones. *TAZs* should be homogenous (as it possible) in their land use (homogenous generators of trips by purpose) and population composition (income level, age etc.). *TAZ* boundaries should be compatibile with *cordons lines* and *screen lines* and shape of *TAZ* should allow an easy determination of their *centroid connestors*. *TAZs* system may be a hierarchical system where subzones are aggregated into zones.

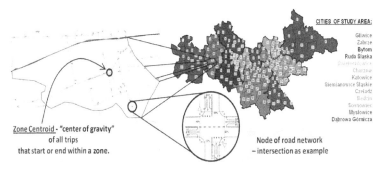

Fig. 2. Delimitation of the study area into Traffic Analysis Zones (TAZs) [5]

The Upper-Silesian Conurbation is divided into three level of traffic analysis zones (*TAZ*): 13 *macro TAZ* as zones with administrative boundaries of cities – municipal level, 185 *meso TAZ* as districts or quartes of cities, and planned to realise *micro TAZ* as quarters or smaller zones [5]. The area outside agglomeration is also divided into *external zones* at lesser level of detail. For Upper-Sielsian Conurbation there are 23 large outside zones – small cities around agglomeration without tramway sytem. Each *TAZ* is represented in model as if all its attributes and properties were concentrated in a single point – *zone controid*. Each *centroid* is attached to the transport network through *centroid connectors* representing the average *transport accessibility* (expressed by time or by distance or by costs) of joining the transport system for trips with origin or destination in zone (Fig. 2).

4   Surveys and Data Collection for Transport Model

Data set collected from surveys should contains:
-    *household syrvey* about trips made by all household members by all modes within agglomeration and leaving and arriving between agglomeration and external zones; survey should include socio-economic information e.g. income, car ownership, family size and structure, etc.; *travel diaries* need to be applied separately to each household member and collecting socio-economic information with trip rates by purpose (for origin-destination

matrices and other submodels and data for each trip incorporating precise *measures of level-of-service variables* for the reported chosen option and for the rest of the alternatives in each individual's choice set;

- *intercept survey* on points of *external, internal cordons* and *screen lines* with trips of users crossing the cordons nad screen lines; roadside interviews provide information about trips not registered in household surveys, i.e. external-external and external-internal trips in cordons; this data are also useful for validation;

- *traffic and passengers count* in selected points (on road sections, on stops, onboard public transport vehicles.

Colected data from mentioned above surveys correspond to *revealed-preference* information. This preference have limitations, especially for constructing good model for evaluation and forecasting, because of it may be so correlated in the survey-sample that it may be difficult to separate their effects in model estimation and therefore for forecasting purposes. Moreover *revealed-preference* information may be not useful for identification responses for policies which are entirely new, like completely new transportation mode, electronic road pricing (e.g. viaToll system in Poland) or new ITS systems (new ITS services [2, 3, 8, 9, 10]). The particular problem is with secondary qualitative variables like public-transport information services, security, etc. because these attributes cost money and problem is to find out, based on *revealed-preference* how much travellers value them before allocating resources among them.

Therefore another surveys so-called *stated-preferences* surveys are the quasi-experiment of real-life based on hypothetical situations and individuals users are asked about what they would choose to do (or how would they rank/rate certain options) in one or more hypothetical situations. The decision context may be a hypothetical or a real one: respondent may be asked to consider an actual travel or travel in the future. The alternatives offered are often hypothetical although one of them may be an existing – chosen mode of travel with its attributes. The respondents state their preferences towards each option by ranking them in order of attractiveness, rating them on scale of preferences strength or choosing the most preferred option from a pair or group of them.

With the syrveys problems the challenge is sample design. Problem is to identify *sampling strategies* (e.g. *multi-stage stratified random sampling heuristic* or *continous survey with up-to-date an existing data*) and *sample size* that allow relevant information and realiable and unbiased models without spending excessive resources on data collection. Statistical approach of estimate sample size with logical and less wasteful method reguire knowledge about the variable to be estimated, its coefficient of variation and desired accuracy of measurement together with the level of significance associated to it. It is desirable to use a combination of survey methods, including both *household survey* and *intercept survey*, to take advantage of the greater efficiences for different data objectives.

5   Trip Distribution Modelling

First stage of four-stages transport model is trip generation (production and atraction) model. Assuming *trip-based travel-demand model* one of the popular and basic models of trip generation are *linear regression* models (2) and (3):

$$O_o^{ish} = \sum_l \beta_l X_{lo}^i \qquad (2)$$

$$D_d^{ish} = \sum_n \beta_n X_{nd}^i \qquad (3)$$

where:

O_o^{ish} – the number of users in class i who undertake a trip from origin zone o ,

D_d^{ish} – the number of users in class i who ends his trips in destination zone d ,

X_{lo}^i – l-th socioeconomic variable for users class i in zone o (from **SE** vector),

X_{nd}^i – n-th variable of attraction of traffic generators in destination zone d ,

β_l , β_n – coefficients of linear regression (from $\boldsymbol{\beta}$ vector).

Impedance function (friction function), as a component of trip distribution model, is a function of generalized cost of travel C_{od}^{ish} – weighted sum of the monetary and non-monetary costs of a travel.

$$f\!\left(C_{od}^{ish}\right) = -\alpha C_{od}^{ish} e^{-\alpha C_{od}^{ish}} \qquad (4)$$

where:

α – parameter,

C_{od}^{ish} – generalized cost of travel.

Trip distribution is a model which results are origin-destination matrices separately for users class i, for each trip purpose s , for time period h . Origin-destination matrix can be determined from generalized gravity model (5).

$$T_{od}^{ish} = \gamma \cdot O_o^{ish} D_d^{ish} f\!\left(C_{od}^{ish}\right) \qquad (5)$$

where:

γ – parameter of "gravity".

And after simplifications gravity model can be written as formula (6).

$$T_{od}^{ish} = \frac{O_o^{ish} D_d^{ish} \cdot f\!\left(C_{od}^{ish}\right)}{\sum_{d'} \left(D_{d'}^{ish} \cdot f\!\left(C_{od'}^{ish}\right)\right)} \qquad (6)$$

where:

d' – all others destination zones except zone d being considered.

6   Transportation Network Modelling

For public transport systems (bus, tram, rail) and its transport networks the lines networks with stops and timetables/schedules must be modelled (see Fig. 3). Main characteristic of each section/link of road network is *volume delay function* (*VDF*) for current travel time. One of the most popular *VDF* is capacity restraint function (*C-R function*) so-colled *BPR-function* (*U.S. Bureau of Public Roads*) – see on Figure 4.

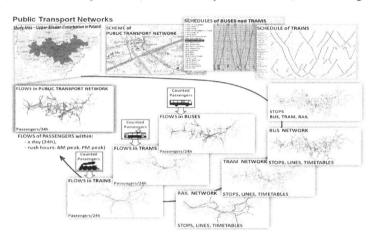

Fig. 3. Scheme of the public transportation systems modeling [4, 5]

The same problem of volume delay modelling is for nodes . There are at least four methotds of calculating current time for each turn in node and entire node. For fast calculating can be used function *Turns VDF*. In *Node VDF* method a *node delay* is calculated by *VDF* for saturation of the node (volume to capacity ratio). And then each *turn penalty* is the sum of *node delay* and the *turn-specific time* calculated by *VDF* for turn.   Impedance calculation precisely considers lane allocation and signal control are in *Intersection Capacity Analysis* (*ICA*) according to the HCM (*Highway*

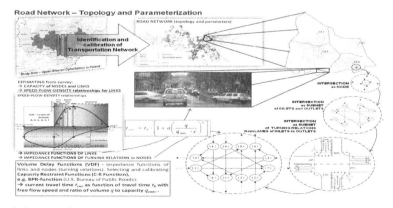

Fig. 4. Scheme of road transport network modeling for traffic flows of private cars [4, 5]

Capacity Manual). This method is more time consuming. Variants of this method is use it in traffic assignment procedure – *Assignment with ICA* – regular adjustment (iterative calculations) of the *turns VDFs* to the wait times and capacities calculated by *ICA*. The idea/scheme of described four methods for calculating *current time in loaded elements* of road network (sections/links and nodes) is shown on Figure 4.

7   Mode Choice (Modal Split) Modelling

The mode choice is model which share total demand matrix into the individual transport modes. This step of modelling uses *random utility models* with so-called *utility function* as follows (7):

$$U_m^i = V_m^i + \ln \mu_{P_{od}^i}^i(m) + \varepsilon_m^i \tag{7}$$

where:

U_m^i – perceived utility function of mode m assigned by users class i,

V_m^i – systematic utility – expected value of utility perceived by all users hav-
ing the same choice among users class i; this utility functions of mode choice models usually include *level-of-service* and *socioeconomic attributes*; *level-of-service* (*performance attributes*) describe the characteristics of the service offered by the specific mode, e.g. travel time (access/egress time, waiting time, in-vehicle time, etc.), monetary cost, service regularity, number of transfers, and so on; these attributes have negative coefficients because they usually represent disutilities for the user,

ε_m^i – random residual of alternative m for users class i,

$\mu_{P_{od}^i}^i(m)$ – level of membership $0 \le \mu_{P_{od}^i}^i(m) \le 1$ of alternative mode m in the choice set P_{od}^i of users i, where P_{od}^i is the generic choice set of alternatives modes m' for travelling between origin o and destination d.

With defined above utility function of mode m mode choice model can be described as logit model (8) or others logit models eg *single-level hierarchical logit model, multilevel hierarchical logit model, cross-nested logit model, generalized extreme value model.* All these models are useful in practice [7].

$$T_{od}^{ishm} = T_{od}^{ish} \frac{e^{\frac{U_m^i}{\theta}}}{\sum_{m' \in P_{od}^i} e^{\frac{U_{m'}^i}{\theta}}} \tag{8}$$

where:

θ – scale parameter of Gumbel distribution of ε_m^i for assumption that ε_m^i are independently and identically distributed as Gumbel random variables with zero mean, θ is proportional to the residuals' standard deviation.

8   Traffic Assignment Modelling

For public transport assignment ther are three main models in practice [7]: *transport system-based model*, *headway-based model* and *timetable-based model*. The *transport system-based model* is based on *all or nothing* methods, where each passenger choses the fastest route in the network without constraints caused by line routes and timetables. The *headway-based model* determines the transfer wait time at transfers stops from the mean value of headway of succeding line. This model is suitable for timetables with short headways and for forecasts (conceptual plannig) when timetable is still unknown. And the *timetable-based model* is suitable for public transport lines with timetables with long headways and necessity of timetables coordination for transfers. Area of Upper-Silesian Conurbation cover high population and industrial density area, suburbs and rural area. Because *timetable-based model* takes the accurate timetable into consideration it is therefore particulary suitable for rural areas of conurbation and for train network. For private transport assignment ther are variuos models in practice as follows [7]: *incremental assignment*, *equilibrium assignment* (with *LUCE* procedure for high convergence speed and *Lohse* procedure for learning precess of road-users about their last journey), *dynamic equilibrium assignment*, *assignment with ICA* (with continously re-calibration of *turn-specific VDF*), *stochastic assignment, dynamic stochastic assignment, TRIBUT assignment*.

The *incremenatl assignment* is a step procedure in which fractions of travel demand (o-d matrix) are assigned in steps. In each step, a fixed proportion of total demand is assigned, based on *all-or-nothing* assignment. After each step, link current travel times are recalculated based on link volumes and *VDF functions*. The *equilibrium assignment* The user equilibrium assignment is based on Wardrop's first principle, which states that *no driver can unilaterally reduce his travel costs by shifting to another path*. The state of eauilibrium is reached by multi-successive iteration with *incremental assignment* as starting assignment. If it is assumed that drivers have perfect knowledge about travel costs on a network and choose the best path according to Wardrop's first principle, this behavioural assumption leads to deterministic user equilibrium. The *stochastic assignment* takes account that route choice are peceived subjectively by the users, in some cases on the basis of incomplete inforamtion about journey time, real distance in congestion, costs and especially depends on the user's individual preferences. The *dynamic stochastic assignment* takes account individual time slices with volume and impedance separated for each such time slice, and temporary overload conditions in the netork are included. The *TRIBUT assignment* is used for modelling road tolls (e.g. viaToll system in Poland) by bicriterial procedure with criteria time and costs.

All assignment (for private and public transport) in practical modelling tools [7] are path-based, meaning that possible paths are calculated for each pair of o - d and loaded with demand share. Each path describes the local course of a translocation in the network model, which means, that all traversed network elements such as nodes, links, turns, connections, stops, line routes and schedules/timetables (for public transport) are known. Dynamic assignments of private transport procedures and public transport procedures create connections, and static procedures calculate path.

Path choice with utility function models can be described in assignment procedures as logit model. However *multinomial logit model* (8) is not appropriate for dense networks that have a lot of common path sections (alternative paths are interdependent), because there is not true independence axiom alternatives (*independence of irrelevant alternatives*), required in the theory of random utility. In such cases, can be use a modified multinomial logit model as *C-logit* (9).

$$\text{Pr}_{od}(k) = \frac{e^{-\frac{U_k^i}{\theta} - CF_k}}{\sum_{r \in P_{od}} e^{-\frac{U_r^i}{\theta} - CF_r}} \; ; \quad CF_k = \sum_{a \in k} w_{ak} \cdot \ln N_a \qquad (9)$$

where:

CF_k – *commonality factor* that reduces the systematic utility V_k^i of a path k according to its degree of overlap with other paths r in set of alternatives P_{od}^i,

a – section of path k ,

w_{ak} – weight of section a in path k ,

N_a – number of path between origin and destination using section a .

9   Conclusion

The *standard four-stage transportation model* with *trip-based travel-demand model* is one of the most popular model. This model assumes that the choices relating to each origin-destination trip are made independently of the choices for other trips within the same and other journeys. This assumption is made to simplify the modelling process, and is reasonable when most of the journeys in the modeling period consist of round trips (origin–destination–origin).

For transportation modelling in agglomerations more accurate, but more complex, are *trip-chaining travel-demand models* and *activity-based demand models*. Trip-chaining travel-demand models assume that the choice of an intermediate destination takes into account the preceding or following destinations on the trip chain and then the choice of transportation modes takes into account the whole sequence of trips in the chain. Activity-based demand models are aimed at relationships between the demand for travel and the organization of the different activities of a inhabitants.

These models are more complex than models described above because take into account the relationships between journeys made by the various members of the same household. Practical implementations in this case are microsimulation models, in which the decisions, activities, and trip-making of a large number of individual households and their members are explicitly represented [1, 6].

These models will be further modelled for Upper-Silesian Conurbation but scale of area (eg population over 1,8 million residents what is approx. 38,3 % of population of the Silesia Province), scale of public transport network (1331 bus stops, 194 bus and tram stops, 153 tram stop in 2009) [4] and costs of surveys are now the largest barriers for implemantation these models in Upper-Silesian Conurbation in practice.

References

1. Cascetta, E.: Transportation Systems Analysis, 2nd edn. Models and Applications. Springer, Heidelberg (2009)
2. Karoń, G., Mikulski, J.: Transportation Systems Modelling as Planning, Organisation and Management for Solutions Created with ITS. In: Mikulski, J. (ed.) TST 2011. CCIS, vol. 239, pp. 277–290. Springer, Heidelberg (2011)
3. Karoń, G., Mikulski, J.: Problems of ITS Architecture Development and ITS Implementation in Upper-Silesian Conurbation in Poland. In: Mikulski, J. (ed.) TST 2012. CCIS, vol. 329, pp. 183–198. Springer, Heidelberg (2012)
4. Karoń, G., Janecki, R., Sobota, A.: Traffic Modelling in Silesian Area – Public Transport Network Model. In: Zeszyty Naukowe Politechniki Śląskiej, Seria TRANSPORT z. 66. Nr kol. 1825, Gliwice, pp. 35–42 (2010)
5. Karoń, G., Janecki, R., Sobota, A., et al.: The investment program for the development of tramway infrastructure in 2008 – 2011. Traffic analysis. Silesian University of Technology, Katowice, Poland (2009)
6. Ortuzar, J., De, D., Willumsen, L.G.: Modelling Transport, 3rd edn. Wiley, New York (2009)
7. VISUM 12 – Fundamentals, PTV Planung Transport Verkehr AG, Karlsruhe, epubli GmbH, Berlin (2011)
8. Gorczyca, P., Mikulski, J., Bialon, A.: Wireless local networks to record the railway traffic control equipment data. Advances in Electrical and Electronic Engineering 5(1-2), 128–131 (2011)
9. Mikulski, J.: The possibility of using telematics in urban transportation. In: Mikulski, J. (ed.) TST 2011. CCIS, vol. 239, pp. 54–69. Springer, Heidelberg (2011)
10. Mikulski, J.: Telematic Technologies in Transportation. In: Janecki, R., Sierpiński, G. (eds.) Contemporary Transportation Systems. Selected Theoretical and Practical Problems. New Culture of Mobility, pp. 131–143. Publishing House of the Silesian University of Technology. Monograph no. 324, Gliwice (2011)

Proposal on a Riemannian Approach to Path Modeling in a Navigational Decision Support System

Piotr Kopacz

Gdynia Maritime University, Faculty of Navigation,
Al. Jana Pawla II 3, 81-345 Gdynia, Poland
kopi@nets.pl

Abstract. Author presents a Riemannian description of time-optimal path determining. The research objective is to develop a new computational model of space-time path based on the generalization of classic variational navigation problem and consider it on the Riemannian manifolds. Perturbation is structured by a constant or variable in space and/or time vector field. Author prepares the mathematical environment for a transparent method of navigational path computations, in particular 3-D and 2-D in the context of potential implementations in the software of the navigational decision support systems and their simulators. From geometric point of view author finds the deviation of geodesics under the action of a time-(in)dependent vector field. Author presents the corresponding example with rotational perturbation.

Keywords: navigation, path optimization, control problem, Riemannian geometry, telematics, decision support system, geodesic.

1 Introduction

Considering new generalized version of the classic navigation problem [12] creates a new class of non-trivial, theoretical issues in geometry [1, 6, 10] and practical aspects of research in for instance marine and air navigation through optimization [2, 3, 4, 7, 8, 11]. Mathematical solution, in particular the analysis of the brachistochrones with variable perturbation and generalized geodesics of the tested model, refers to its potential implementation in planning and monitoring of trajectories in modern navigational Geographic Information Systems (GIS), navigational aids and simulators. Automatic updating of the solution of navigation problem in real time with its graphical and analytical presentation on an electronic navigational chart that shows optimized various-criteria trajectories, gives a real possibility to increase navigational safety of the ship. It significantly facilitates the process of decision making, e.g. made by the ship's master, in the selection of the desired path, associated with the ship's movement, its optimization and monitoring in a modern, navigational Electronic Chart Display and Information System (ECDIS) and often necessary modification of ship's trajectory associated with the implementation of the originally adopted path.

J. Mikulski (Ed.): TST 2013, CCIS 395, pp. 294–302, 2013.
© Springer-Verlag Berlin Heidelberg 2013

The significance of discussed problem also indicates a serious mistake observed nowadays, resulting from simultaneous use of mathematical formulae from a variety of incompatible geometric global models in calculation methods used in navigational software, and even in the literature, and thus more frequent use of miscalculations of navigational parameters, generated by numerous navigational GIS by more and more mass user. Navigational calculations in the planning and monitoring of 2D and 3D trajectory based on the proposed description lead to algorithmically transparent information on the passage path so as to increase the safety of navigation.

2   Mathematical Description

Author considers the generalization of classic navigation problem [5, 12] on Riemannian manifolds. Throughout this paper manifolds and mappings are smooth and Einstein summation convention over repeated indices is assumed. Author follows the notations and theoretical assumptions applied in [9, 10].

Let a pair *(M, g)* be a Riemannian manifold where $g = g_{ij} dx^i \otimes dx^j$ is a Riemannian metric with non-degenerate, symmetric and positive definite matrix (g_{ij}), and M is an m-dimensional manifold with local coordinates (x^b), $1 \le b \le m$. Let the wind distribution on M be represented by a time-dependent vector field on M, i.e. by a projectable vector field ξ on $\mathbb{R} \times TM$ of the form

$$\xi = \frac{\partial}{\partial t} + \xi^i(t, x^j) \frac{\partial}{\partial x^i} . \tag{1}$$

To analyze the deformations of geodesics we consider the variational problem on $\mathbb{R} \times TM$ defined by the kinetic energy $\bar{T}$ in the form

$$\bar{T} = \frac{1}{2} g_{ij} y^i y^j \tag{2}$$

where $y^i = \dot{x}^i + \xi^i$.

The Euler-Lagrange equations of the mechanical system (2) are expressed in the form

$$\frac{\partial \bar{T}}{\partial x^k} - \frac{d}{dt} \left(\frac{\partial \bar{T}}{\partial \dot{x}^k} \right) = 0, \quad 1 \le k \le m \tag{3}$$

where

$$\bar{T} = \frac{1}{2} g_{ij} (\dot{x}^i + \xi^i)(\dot{x}^j + \xi^j) = \frac{1}{2} g_{ij} \dot{x}^i \dot{x}^j + g_{ij} \dot{x}^i \xi^j + \frac{1}{2} g_{ij} \xi^i \xi^j . \tag{4}$$

Let us denote

$$V = -g_{ij} \dot{x}^i \xi^j - \frac{1}{2} g_{ij} \xi^i \xi^j . \tag{5}$$

Thus

$$\bar{T} = T - V \tag{6}$$

where T is the kinetic energy of the unperturbed problem and V has the meaning of the potential energy caused by the wind. Computing (3) explicitly we obtain

$$\left(\frac{\partial g_{ij}}{\partial x^k}\xi^j + g_{ij}\frac{\partial \xi^j}{\partial x^k}\right)\dot{x}^i + \frac{1}{2}\frac{\partial}{\partial x^k}\left(g_{ij}\xi^i\xi^j\right) - \frac{\partial g_{kj}}{\partial x^i}\dot{x}^i\xi^j - g_{kj}\frac{\partial \xi^j}{\partial t} - g_{kj}\frac{\partial \xi^j}{\partial x^i}\dot{x}^i$$
$$- \Gamma_{kij}\dot{x}^i\dot{x}^j - g_{kj}\ddot{x}^j = 0 \tag{7}$$

where

$$F_k = \left(\frac{\partial g_{ij}}{\partial x^k}\xi^j + g_{ij}\frac{\partial \xi^j}{\partial x^k}\right)\dot{x}^i + \frac{1}{2}\frac{\partial}{\partial x^k}\left(g_{ij}\xi^i\xi^j\right) - \frac{\partial g_{kj}}{\partial x^i}\dot{x}^i\xi^j - g_{kj}\frac{\partial \xi^j}{\partial t} - g_{kj}\frac{\partial \xi^j}{\partial x^i}\dot{x}^i. \tag{8}$$

represents the force referred to the potential energy of perturbation and Γ_{ijk} are the standard Christoffel symbols of (g_{ij}). Author aims to find the deviation of geodesics via Zermelo navigation problem in Riemannian space under the force representing the action of the perturbing "wind" distribution modeled by the vector field on manifold M. Author considers a fibred manifold $\pi : \mathbb{R} \times M \to \mathbb{R}$ representing "sea" where π is the first canonical projection.

3 Shortest Path as Geodesic

Following [9, 10] author states the problem before perturbation which is defined in the general form

$$\Gamma_{kij}\dot{x}^i\dot{x}^j + g_{kj}\ddot{x}^j = 0. \tag{9}$$

Due to the potential real applications of presented model author lowers the time-space dimension down to 3 or 2. In case of dim $(\mathbb{R} \times M) = 3$ the metric g which determines the structure of the "sea" equals

$$g = g_{11}(x^1, x^2)dx^1 \otimes dx^1 + g_{12}(x^1, x^2)dx^1 \otimes dx^2 + g_{21}(x^1, x^2)dx^2 \otimes dx^1 +$$
$$g_{22}(x^1, x^2)dx^2 \otimes dx^2 . \tag{10}$$

Without loss of generality we consider here the model of Riemannian "sea" with the following type of metric

$$(g): \begin{cases} g_{11} = g_{11}(x^1, x^2) \\ g_{22} = g_{22}(x^2) \\ g_{12} = g_{21} = 0 \end{cases} \tag{11}$$

Then equation (9) gives the system of differential equations of second order

$$\begin{cases} g_{11}\ddot{x}^1 + \dfrac{1}{2}\dfrac{\partial g_{11}}{\partial x^1}(\dot{x}^1)^2 + \dfrac{\partial g_{11}}{\partial x^2}\dot{x}^1\dot{x}^2 = 0 \\ g_{22}\ddot{x}^2 - \dfrac{1}{2}\dfrac{\partial g_{11}}{\partial x^2}(\dot{x}^1)^2 + \dfrac{1}{2}\dfrac{\partial g_{22}}{\partial x^2}(\dot{x}^2)^2 = 0 \end{cases} \tag{12}$$

Author puts

$$(g): \begin{cases} g_{11} = x^1 \\ g_{22} = x^2 \\ g_{12} = g_{21} = 0 \end{cases} \tag{13}$$

Author considers in 3-dimensional case the particular components of the model "sea":

$$g = x^1 dx^1 \otimes dx^1 + x^2 dx^2 \otimes dx^2. \tag{14}$$

Then equation (12) takes the form

$$\begin{cases} 2x^1 \cdot \ddot{x}^1 + (\dot{x}^1)^2 = 0 \\ 2x^2 \cdot \ddot{x}^2 + (\dot{x})^2 = 0 \end{cases}. \tag{15}$$

Solving (15) author obtains the time-optimal path in considered geometric structure which fulfills the definition of its geodesic. The system before perturbation gives the components x^1, x^2 of the curve $\gamma(t)$

$$\begin{cases} x^1(t) = (C_1 \cdot t + C_2)^{\frac{2}{3}} \\ x^2(t) = (C_3 \cdot t + C_4)^{\frac{2}{3}} \end{cases} \qquad C_1, C_2, C_3, C_4 \in \mathbb{R}. \tag{16}$$

Thus, the geodesic path in $\mathbb{R}^3$ is parameterized as follows

$$\gamma(t) = \left(t, (C_1 \cdot t + C_2)^{\frac{2}{3}}, (C_3 \cdot t + C_4)^{\frac{2}{3}} \right). \tag{17}$$

For initial conditions assumed below the particular curve $\gamma(t)$ is presented graphically in Fig. 2 as dotted curve.

4   Perturbing the Geodesic Path with Rotational Vector Field

Author perturbs the geodesic path by a vector field on manifold M. The general form of the problem after perturbation yields

$$F_k - \Gamma_{kij}\dot{x}^i\dot{x}^j - g_{kj}\ddot{x}^j = 0, \tag{18}$$

where F_k, Γ_{ijk} states for the force (8) and Christoffel symbols of (g_{ij}), respectively.

In case of $\dim (\mathbb{R} \times M) = 3$ index $k \in \{1,2\}$ and the force $F = (F_1, F_2) = (F_1(x^1, x^2), F_2(x^1, x^2))$. Then the vector field ξ equals

$$\xi = \frac{\partial}{\partial t} + \xi^i(t, x^1, x^2)\frac{\partial}{\partial x^i} = \frac{\partial}{\partial t} + \xi^1(t, x^1, x^2)\frac{\partial}{\partial x^1} + \xi^2(t, x^1, x^2)\frac{\partial}{\partial x^2}. \tag{19}$$

From (18) author obtains the system of differential equations (20) in the navigation problem after perturbation

$$\begin{cases} F_1 - \Gamma_{111}(\dot{x}^1)^2 - (\Gamma_{112} + \Gamma_{121})\dot{x}^1\dot{x}^2 - \Gamma_{122}(\dot{x}^2)^2 - g_{11}\ddot{x}^1 - g_{12}\ddot{x}^2 = 0 \\ F_2 - \Gamma_{211}(\dot{x}^1)^2 - (\Gamma_{212} + \Gamma_{221})\dot{x}^1\dot{x}^2 - \Gamma_{222}(\dot{x}^2)^2 - g_{21}\ddot{x}^1 - g_{22}\ddot{x}^2 = 0 \end{cases}. \tag{20}$$

If we apply the Christoffel symbols Γ_{ijk}, the components of force F_1, F_2, order the equations in respect to the partial derivatives and consider the metric g with the assumptions $g_{12} = 0$ and $g_{21} = 0$, then the above system after perturbation yields

$$\begin{cases} g_{11}\ddot{x}^1 + \frac{1}{2}\frac{\partial g_{11}}{\partial x^1}(\dot{x}^1)^2 - \frac{1}{2}\frac{\partial g_{22}}{\partial x^1}(\dot{x}^2)^2 + \frac{\partial g_{11}}{\partial x^2}\dot{x}^1\dot{x}^2 + \left(g_{11}\frac{\partial \xi^1}{\partial x^2} + \frac{\partial g_{11}}{\partial x^2}\xi^1 - g_{22}\frac{\partial \xi^2}{\partial x^1} - \frac{\partial g_{22}}{\partial x^1}\xi^2\right)\dot{x}^2 - \frac{1}{2}\frac{\partial}{\partial x^1}(g_{11}\xi^1\xi^1 + g_{22}\xi^2\xi^2) \cdot \\ g_{22}\ddot{x}^2 - \frac{1}{2}\frac{\partial g_{11}}{\partial x^2}(\dot{x}^1)^2 + \frac{1}{2}\frac{\partial g_{22}}{\partial x^2}(\dot{x}^2)^2 + \frac{\partial g_{22}}{\partial x^1}\dot{x}^1\dot{x}^2 - \left(g_{11}\frac{\partial \xi^1}{\partial x^2} + \frac{\partial g_{11}}{\partial x^2}\xi^1 - g_{22}\frac{\partial \xi^2}{\partial x^1} - \frac{\partial g_{22}}{\partial x^1}\xi^2\right)\dot{x}^1 - \frac{1}{2}\frac{\partial}{\partial x^2}(g_{11}\xi^1\xi^1 + g_{22}\xi^2\xi^2) \cdot \end{cases} \tag{21}$$

Formula (21) lets to present the Zermelo navigation problem and provide the solution for arbitrary metric g and perturbing vector field ξ in case of $\dim (\mathbb{R} \times M) = 3$ with respect to the general assumptions considered in the paragraph 2. Then author obtains [9] the final system of equations in respect to (19) presented in (22)

$$\begin{cases} g_{11}\ddot{x}^1 + \frac{1}{2}\frac{\partial g_{11}}{\partial x^1}(\dot{x}^1)^2 + \frac{\partial g_{11}}{\partial x^2}\dot{x}^1\dot{x}^2 - \left(g_{22}\frac{\partial \xi^2}{\partial x^1} - \frac{\partial g_{11}}{\partial x^2}\xi^1 - g_{11}\frac{\partial \xi^1}{\partial x^2}\right)\dot{x}^2 - \frac{1}{2}\frac{\partial}{\partial x^1}(g_{11}\xi^1\xi^1 + g_{22}\xi^2\xi^2) + 2g_{11}\frac{\partial \xi^1}{\partial t} = 0 \\ g_{22}\ddot{x}^2 - \frac{1}{2}\frac{\partial g_{11}}{\partial x^2}(\dot{x}^1)^2 + \frac{1}{2}\frac{\partial g_{22}}{\partial x^2}(\dot{x}^2)^2 - \left(\frac{\partial g_{11}}{\partial x^2}\xi^1 + g_{11}\frac{\partial \xi^1}{\partial x^2} - g_{22}\frac{\partial \xi^2}{\partial x^1}\right)\dot{x}^1 - \frac{1}{2}\frac{\partial}{\partial x^2}(g_{11}\xi^1\xi^1 + g_{22}\xi^2\xi^2) + 2g_{22}\frac{\partial \xi^2}{\partial t} = 0 \end{cases} \tag{22}$$

The form of the particular final system is obtained after applying the particular metric (g_{11}, g_{22}) and perturbing vector field (ξ^1, ξ^2). In general, the vector field $\left(\frac{\partial}{\partial y^i}\right)_{1 \le i \le n}$ for wind distribution ξ is represented by $\xi = \xi^i(y)\left(\frac{\partial}{\partial y^i}\right)$. Hence

$$\text{"wind": } \xi(t, x^1, x^2) = \frac{\partial}{\partial t} + x^2\frac{\partial}{\partial x^1} - x^1\frac{\partial}{\partial x^2}. \tag{23}$$

Without loss of generality author chooses the rotational vector field of the components ξ^i as follows

$$(\xi): \begin{cases} \xi^1(t, x^1, x^2) = x^2 \\ \xi^2(t, x^1, x^2) = -x^1 \end{cases}. \tag{24}$$

The perturbing 3-D rotational vector field is presented graphically in Fig.1.

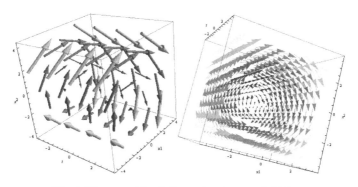

Fig. 1. The perturbing 3-D rotational vector field ξ

Applying chosen "sea" and "wind" components author obtains the final system of differential equations of the second order which represents the problem after rotational perturbation

$$\begin{cases} 2x^1 \cdot \ddot{x}^1 + (\dot{x}^1)^2 - 2x^1x^2 + 2(x^1 + x^2)\dot{x}^2 - (x^2)^2 = 0 \\ 2x^2 \cdot \ddot{x}^2 + (\dot{x}^2)^2 - 2x^1x^2 - 2(x^1 + x^2)\dot{x}^1 - (x^1)^2 = 0 \end{cases} \quad . \tag{25}$$

Solving above system yields the 3-dimensional curve $\tilde{\gamma}(t)$ representing the solution of the navigation problem after perturbation. As an exemplary particular example of the solution we assume the initial conditions $x^1(0) = 1$, $x^2(0) = 1$, $\dot{x}^1(0) = 1$, $\dot{x}^2(0) = 1$. Due to complexity of the system (25) here we obtain numerically the curve $\tilde{\gamma}(t)$ in $\mathbb{R}^3$ which is presented graphically as solid curve in Fig.2.

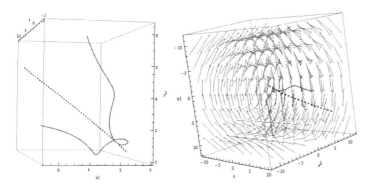

Fig. 2. Graphical presentation of 3-D solution of navigation problem with rotational vector field

Fig.2 also shows the whole situation for considered example. The curve after perturbation (solid curve) is a product of curve before the wind deformation (dotted curve), i.e. geodesic and the perturbing vector field (marked by arrows). Let us observe that if we lower the dimension down to two we obtain 2-D paths which are basically applied in the most of the computational models used in the marine and air navigational software. This may state for the mathematical basis of the author's concept of automatically updated various criteria–based 2-D or 3-D paths, i.e. parallel computations, which are presented on electronic charts in marine or air applications in the navigational decision support systems like Electronic Chart Display and Information System installed onboard the marine ships and in the simulators.

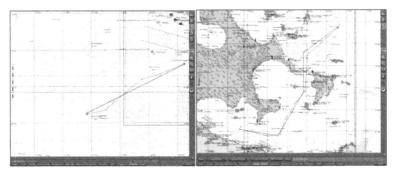

Fig. 3. Concept of automatically updated various criteria–based navigational 2-D paths presented on electronic chart in marine application of system GIS

The concept of presentation of automatically updated two various criteria–based navigational path son marine electronic chart used in real navigational simulator TransasNavi-Sailor 4000 is shown in Fig. 3. The two types of paths are generated here on the electronic navigational charts in the conformal Mercator projection due to different criteria. One represents the piecewise distance-optimal solution and the other the piecewise time-optimal solution under the vector perturbation between waypoints of the preplanned route. The initial (beginning of passage) and final (end of passage) positions are the same for both paths. However the behavior of the paths differs as the effect of perturbing fields. The author's concept considers the global parallel computations of the multi various criteria optimal paths which are automatically updated while ships is en route with the time-dependent perturbations. This takes into consideration available information on the position and dynamical data of the moving object, for example vessel, airplane, as well as updated perturbation data e.g. weather conditions modeled by the vector/tensor fields and the geometric (Riemannian) structure of the global or local model in which the computations are provided. More advanced research here refers to multicriteria optimization of monitored route which assumes the boundary conditions due to parallelly executed various criteria-based on the title proposal.

Finally the optimal path modification implied by anti-collision with moving obstacles as presented for instance in [11] may also be included in the complex solution of researched navigation problem coming initially and formally from [12]. The mathematical description referred to the proposal and solution for 3-D scenario with non-rotational perturbation has been presented in [9]. The optimal path due to considered criterion, if based on updated and reliable data e.g. modeled by an arbitrary vector field, may be followed by the moving object (ship, autonomous underwater vehicle (AUV), battery limited underwater glider) and optimize a control of navigated path.

5   Conclusion

The research develops a new computational model of space-time trajectory based on the generalization of classic navigation problem formalized initially in [12]. Author considers it on the Riemannian manifolds with perturbation in the form of a constant or variable in time and space vector field. Author aims to present a transparent method of path computations both locally and globally, its development in particular 2-D and 3-D case in the context of using the results in e-navigation, especially in the complex issue of the contemporary ship's trajectory planning, its real-time monitoring and multi-criteria optimization. From geometric point of view author finds the deviation of geodesics under the action of a time-(in)dependent vector field. Author obtains the final form of the system of partial differential equations (21) providing the solution of the navigation problem after perturbation under the force representing the action of the "wind" distribution modeled by the vector field on manifold M. In working example author applieds the 3-D rotational perturbation. Automation of the process for calculation of paths in real time significantly helps the decision making process for selecting the desired optimal trajectory based on assumed criteria, e.g. made by the captain of the ship. Mathematical solution to a given problem allows its potential implementation in the software of the navigational Geographic Information Systems, devices or simulators by providing transparent and algorithmic description of the boundary conditions of approximation.

A Riemannian approach can compose the fruitful connection between the theoretical and practical models of Zermelo problem. It can also be applied as a potential computational tool in modeling the practical aspects of air and marine navigation, in particular the optimization of complex process of route planning and monitoring. Further research might explore the geometric properties of the trajectories as the solutions of presented navigation problem depending on the type of perturbation and initial conditions.

References

1. Bao, D., Robles, C., Shen, Z.: Zermelo navigation on Riemannian manifolds. J. Differ. Geom. 66, 377–435 (2004)
2. Bijlsma, J.: Minimal-Fuel Route Computation for Aircraft with Pre-specified Flight Time. European Journal of Navigation 8(3), 26–30 (2010)
3. Bijlsma, J.: Optimal Aircraft Routing in General Wind Fields. J. Guid. Control Dynam. 32, 1025–1029 (2009)
4. Bijlsma, J.: Minimal-Time Route Computation for Ships with Pre-Specified Voyage Fuel Consumption. J. Navigation 61, 723–733 (2008)
5. Caratheodory, C.: Calculus of Variations and Partial Differential Equations of the first order. American Mathematical Society, Chelsea Publishing (1935/2008) (reprint)
6. Chern, S.S., Shen, Z.: Riemann-Finsler Geometry. Nankai Tracts in Mathematics, vol. 6. World Scientific (2005)
7. Jardin, M.R., Bryson, A.E.: Methods for Computing Minimum –Time Paths in Strong Winds. J. Guid. Control Dynam. 35, 165–171 (2012)

8. Jardin, M.R.: Neighboring optimal aircraft guidance in a general wind environment, Patent no US6600991, USA (2003)

9. Kopacz, P.: Simulation of Zermelo navigation on Riemannian manifolds for dim(R×M)=3, Navigational Problems: Marine Navigation and Safety of Sea Transportation, pp. 333–337. A Balkema Book, CRC Press, Taylor & Francis Group, Boca Raton – London - New York – Leiden (2013)

10. Palacek, R., Krupkova, O.: On the Zermelo problem in Riemannian manifolds. Balkan Journal of Geometry and Its Applications 17(2), 77–81 (2012)

11. Xu, C., Li, B., Teo, K., Chu, J.: On Zermelo's Navigation Problems with Moving Obstacles. In: Proceedings of the 5th International Conference on Optimization and Control with Applications (OCA 2012), Beijing, China, pp. 279–283 (2012)

12. Zermelo, E.: Uber das Navigationsproblembeiruhenderoderveranderlicher Windverteilung. Zeitschrift fur Angewandte Mathematik und Mechanik 11(2), 114–124 (1931)

Pedestrian Traffic Distribution Analysis Using Face Recognition Technology

Marcin Mikłasz[1], Piotr Olszewski[2], Adam Nowosielski[3], and Grzegorz Kawka[4]

[1] The West Pomeranian Business School, Faculty of Economics and Computer Science,
Żołnierska St. 53, 71-210 Szczecin, Poland
mmiklasz@zpsb.szczecin.pl
[2] Warsaw University of Technology, Faculty of Civil Engineering,
Al. Armii Ludowej 16, 00-637 Warszawa
p.olszewski@il.pw.edu.pl
[3] West Pomeranian University of Technology in Szczecin,
Faculty of Computer Science and Information Technology,
Żolnierska St. 52, 71-210 Szczecin, Poland
anowosielski@wi.zut.edu.pl
[4] P.H.U. Telsat,
J. Dabskiego 1a,72-300 Gryfice, Poland
telsat@gryfice.com.pl

Abstract. Pedestrian traffic distribution analysis in big public transport interchanges is aimed at improving transfer conditions, schedule optimization and route planning. Traditional survey of people flow is based on counting and interviewing of travellers. In the article, a new method of transport interchange analysis using image processing method is presented. In November 2009, Bemowo-Ratusz interchange in Warsaw has been subjected to detailed examination. The study was associated with the planned redevelopment. In parallel with the survey based on image processing methods, the traditional interview-based survey has been conducted in order to compare the results. Passenger transfer matrices obtained from optical analysis and traditional survey show good correlation. This proves the effectiveness and shows potential of image analysis methods for this kind of application.

Keywords: pedestrian traffic analysis, face recognition, face detection.

1 Introduction

Public transport schedule optimization and route planning are demanding tasks which require proper approach and good analysis. Of great importance here is pedestrian traffic distribution analysis in large public transport interchanges. The overall objective is improvement of passenger transfer conditions [7]. While traditional survey of people flow is based on counting and interviewing of travelers, a new method of transport interchange analysis using image processing method is presented in the article. The method bases on face recognition technology.

J. Mikulski (Ed.): TST 2013, CCIS 395, pp. 303–312, 2013.
© Springer-Verlag Berlin Heidelberg 2013

Biometric face recognition technologies contain automated methods and resources of verifying or recognizing the identity of a person on the basis of a face image [1]. For the task of pedestrian traffic distribution analysis people are recognized anonymously – they are registered at one location and recognized at another. There is no need of name or other privacy sensitive data storage.

Principles of face recognition systems have been described in the literature before [1], [8] with examples of typical applications. Basic structure of an automated face recognition system consists of four fundamental blocks [1]: face detector, feature extractor, database and classifier. Face detection aims to determine if the presented image contains faces and what are (if any present) their locations and sizes [2]. Extracted face images are processed in order to extract distinctive individual characteristics of a person (coding information content in a face image by a small number of coefficients). These features are then compared to those stored in the database in the classifier. Finally, result of identification is formulated. The reader can find valuable information regarding face recognition technology in numerous literature reviews which cover respectively: face detection [2], 3D face recognition [9] and recognition across pose [4], face recognition from single image per person [11], infrared face recognition [10] and others.

The rest of the article is structured as follows. Section 2 describes assumptions of the proposed approach. In Section 3 face recognition technology developed for pedestrian traffic analysis is presented. Section 4 includes comparative analysis of traditional and optical methods in the area of passenger volumes. Section 5 gives the comparison of the above methods in passenger transfers. The article ends with a summary.

2   Pedestrian Traffic Distribution Analysis – Assumptions

Figure 1 presents scheme of Bemowo-Ratusz interchange at the intersection of Górczewska Street and Powstańców Śląskich Street in Warsaw. This is an important public transport interchange and many people change the mode of transport there. In this area there are three bus stops (numbered 01, 02 and 04 in the figure) and two tram stops (numbered 05 and 06). There are in total 25 different bus and trams lines in both directions.

Fig. 1. Plan of Bemowo Ratusz public transport interchange

The Bemowo-Ratusz interchange has been subjected to detailed examination in November 2009. The study was associated with the planned redevelopment of tram lines. New method of transport interchange analysis using image processing method was introduced. Face recognition technology was utilized for pedestrian traffic distribution analysis. In parallel with the survey based on image processing methods, the traditional interview-based survey has been conducted in order to compare the results.

2.1   Tradition Survey of Bemowo-Ratusz Interchange

Tradition analysis of Bemowo-Ratusz interchange was based on surveys of passengers alighting, boarding and transferring between stops. The study was carried out on Thursday 19th November 2009. There were two survey periods: morning (7:00–10:00, 3 hours) and afternoon (14:00–17:00, 3 hours). In this survey, using classic interview-based method, the following measurements were taken:

- counting the number of people alighting from each vehicle,
- counting the number of people boarding each vehicle,
- interviewing people waiting at the platforms, i.e. only those boarding vehicles,
- measurement of the transfer times between stops.

Objective of the survey was primarily to obtain information whether a passenger changes the mode of transport or line at the interchange and between which platforms the transfer occurs. The team of interviewers comprised 21 people.

2.2   Optical Analysis of Bemowo-Ratusz Interchange

Optical analysis of Bemowo-Ratusz interchange was based on automatic counting and recognition of passengers who changed platforms or used public transport. Sony PMW-EX3 cameras were used for recording video. The video material was processed afterwards in order to find faces (detect people's faces). Then, on the basis of advanced methods of automatic face recognition, the same persons appearing on different platforms were recognized and time of their passage from platform to platform was calculated.

The study was conducted during the morning and evening rush hours: 7:30–10:30 and 14:00–17:00 on the 17th of November 2009. The team of surveyors/operators comprised 12 people. At each stop the crew of two cameramen recorded people entering and leaving the platform. The acquisition of video material required:

- assembling of appropriate hardware resources (cameras, platforms, fences, power supply);
- determination of camera locations;
- aiming each camera on the appropriate portion of the interchange to allow registration of all persons entering / leaving the platform;
- preparation of instructions, messages and notifications to participants;
- development and approval of a temporary traffic management scheme for the period of the survey.

3   Face Recognition Technology for Pedestrian Traffic Analysis

The use of face recognition technology for pedestrian traffic analysis requires transformation and processing of the whole raw video material registered by cameras at different locations. In the case of Bemowo-Ratusz interchange (on which case the whole method will be described further) the video material from 10 cameras was registered in FullHD quality (resolution of 1920x1080, 25 fps, no interlace). The data size was over 1 TB.

The first step was to detect and extract face images from a video stream. Two solutions were integrated here into cascade detector. In the first step well-known and widely used Viola Jones method [3] (implementation in OpenCV was used) processed video sequence in order to find faces. The results were verified by Verilook proprietary detector [12]. The second detector rejected many non-face regions, erroneously classified as faces by the Viola-Jones method. The main drawback, however, was the operation time of the Verilook approach. Hence the integration of both approaches into a serial solution. As a result, about 500 thousand separate images of faces from the morning session and about 570 thousand face images from the evening session were obtained. Depending on the platform, the number of registered faces during individual session ranged from about 40 thousand to about 70 thousand. It was approximately 30 GB of data.

The second step included processing and classification of extracted face images. Two task were conducted here. The first one was the standardization and quality examination of face images. The second was to cluster similar face images in consecutive image frames (the same person) in the appropriate classes. During classification stage the face representatives from the classes were selected. They were used for the following recognition stages. Images of poor quality, under or over exposed, blurred, occluded, highly rotated (almost profile pictures) usually were rejected since they are practically useless in identification process. The classification results were reviewed by the operator in software designed for this purpose.

Detection and classification stages allowed the extraction of individual persons from recordings. The calculated effectiveness exceeds 83% for the morning session and 79% for the evening session. The poorer performance in the evening session was affected by twilight and then night. The lighting conditions began to deteriorate significantly after 15:30. This means that 17% and 21% of travelers recorded in the video stream were not automatically detected and classified. In addition to the lighting conditions, the error was influenced by: omission of every third frame (which was employed in order to reduce the dimensionality), face occlusions (by other persons, faces or items of clothing e.g. scarf), incorrect eyes coordinates localization, non en-face faces, poor focus.

The output of the above step consisted of processed face images and their corresponding specifications recorded in databases (separate for each camera – location point). The total amount of data required in later stages occupied at this moment about 3 GB of storage space.

In the next step the feature vector representing the input faces image (the face representatives from each class) were obtained using holistic approaches (global approaches based on appearance) and using a combination of simple features [5]. The following simple feature extractors were considered [5]: scale, random, histogram, spectrumDFT and spectrumDCT. Three first extractors are based on rudimental image transformation. In two last cases, a feature vector is formulated from a set of selected spectral components obtained by performing orthogonal transformations on the input face image. In order to eliminate the significant effect of lighting the method of analyzing the local symmetry of the face image – the LIFE approach (Light Invariant Feature Extractor) – was also used. We provide a detailed description of the LIFE method in [6]. Adequate weight have been assigned to the feature vectors (determined on the basis of previous studies [5], [6]) giving their target combination. The resulting representation achieved the recognition rate of approximately 75% which should be considered a success for such large, dynamic and uncontrolled database.

The final stage of video processing was face recognition of individuals moving between stops. Appropriate associative matrices for databases obtained in the earlier stages have been constructed using the following principles: a person leaving one bus/tram stop was searched for at the other four stops. The searches were carried out within a 10-minute "time frame" for each database record.

Total time of processing video material amounted to 660 hours of computer work and about 130 hours of operator work. In the future, it is possible to optimize the processing of video through improvements of the individual steps and their connection into a fully automatic system. These actions will reduce the role and time commitment of operators.

4   Comparative Analysis of Traditional and Optical Methods – Passenger Volumes

The examination of Bemowo-Ratusz interchange has been carried out with face recognition based technique as well as using the traditional interview survey. Comparison of results obtained by two methods is presented and discussed below. The following facts should be noted:

1. The surveys were performed on different days of the week (study by image analysis on Tuesday and the study using traditional method on Thursday).
2. Number of people alighting at the interchange is very similar in both studies (4585 – image analysis, 4725 – traditional survey). See fig. 2 for details.
3. The time profile of the number of people alighting at the interchange is similar for both methods. See fig. 2 for details.
4. In the study using the traditional method, a higher number of people alighting at stops 01 and 06 was observed (in both morning and afternoon periods). For the image analysis method a higher number of people was observed at stops 02 and 04. However, these differences are not very significant. See fig. 3 for details.
5. The total number of people boarding public transport at the interchange calculated by the traditional method is higher by 1595 than calculated by image analysis (6534 in the traditional study and 4939 in the study by image analysis). See fig. 4 for details.
6. The time profile of the number of people boarding is similar for both methods – difference was observed at stop 01 in both periods and at stop 05 in the morning

session (a higher number of people by the traditional method was observed). See fig. 5 for details.

7. Both methods showed that more people boarded at the interchange in relation to people alighting.
8. Both methods showed that the busiest stops were bus stop 04 (alighting) and bus stop 01 (boarding). Compare fig. 3 and fig. 5.
9. The results of both studies largely coincide.

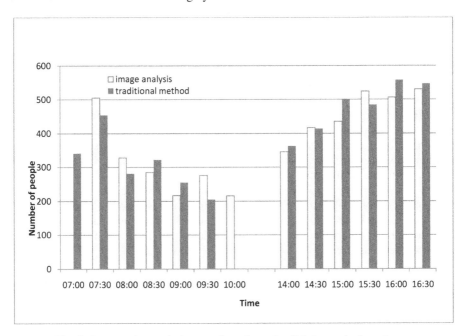

Fig. 2. Comparative analysis – number of people alighting at the interchange

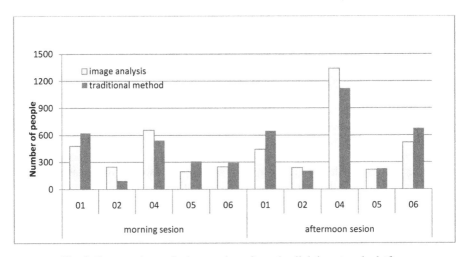

Fig. 3. Comparative analysis - number of people alighting at each platform

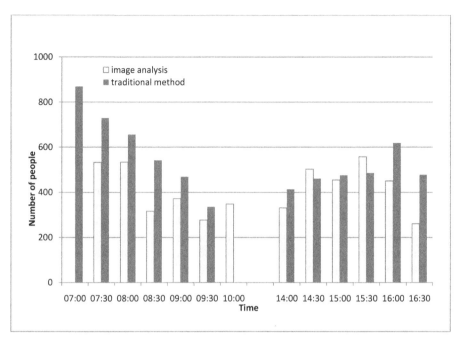

Fig. 4. Comparative analysis - number of people boarding at the interchange

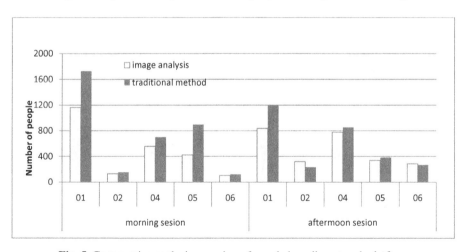

Fig. 5. Comparative analysis - number of people boarding at each platform

The method of image analysis allowed to count each registered person in the video stream. On the other hand this approach required more organizational work. The measurement process is subjected to a greater risk of distortion by an unexpected incident such as hardware failure, improper camera calibration, etc.

It is important that all the results obtained through the optical analysis can be verified by manual inspection. It is worth noting that the study by image analysis was an innovative one. It was a pilot study. Further improvements in face detection and face recognition methods are planned to address the main limitations of the proposed approach (reduction of the impact of directional lighting).

5   Comparative Analysis – Passenger Transfers

The main objective of both surveys was determination of the passenger transfer pattern at the interchange. With the traditional method, the numbers of transfers were obtained from the interviews, adjusted for the sampling rate which was determined at each stop and at each hour as the ratio of the number of interviews to the number of people boarding. The average percentage of passengers transferring at the interchange was 65% during the morning period and 60% during the afternoon period.

Figure 6 shows the pattern of transfers between the 5 bus/tram stops at the interchange obtained using the traditional method. The numbers are totals of both morning and afternoon survey periods. We can see that the heaviest transfers in both directions occur between tram stops (05, 06) and bus stops (01, 04).

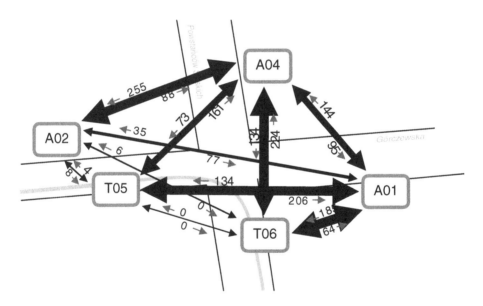

Fig. 6. Passenger transfer movements at the interchange (total of AM and PM periods)

The second set of transfer volumes was calculated from image analysis data. The actual numbers obtained by passenger face matching were adjusted up to account for the fact that 17% of passengers in the morning session and 21% in the evening session were not detected by image analysis system due to various reasons: face occlusion, poor illumination, etc. Since this detection error occurred at both platforms, the correction factor used was: 0.83*0.83 = 0.69 in the morning session and 0.79*0.79=0.62 in the evening session. The second correction was used to account for face matching error which based on pilot study results was about 25%. It means that 75% of faces were recognized and matched correctly. Thus, the correction factor used for transfers obtained by image analysis was 1/0.69/0.75 = 1.932 in the morning session and 1/0.62/0.75=2.151 in the evening session.

Table 1 shows the comparison of the total transfer volumes obtained by both methods for both survey periods. The numbers exclude same-platform transfers which were not recorded by image analysis method. The totals are close for the morning period – the difference is 12% which is very good considering that the surveys were done on different days. The difference is bigger for the afternoon survey period (about 22%). This can be explained by the fact that lighting conditions were getting worse after 16:00 hours in November – it was practically dark when the survey finished at 17:00. This significantly increased both detection and recognition errors.

Table 1. Comparison of transfer volumes obtained by both methods

Survey period	Total transfer volume obtained by method:		Volume ratio (3 to 2)	Correlation coefficient
	Interview	*Video*		
Morning	865	760	0.88	0.87
Afternoon	1128	877	0.78	0.91

Figure 7 shows the comparison of the individual inter-stop transfer volumes obtained by both methods. Although there is some scatter of points along the diagonal line, the results are generally in agreement: the same pairs of stops with the heaviest transfer volumes were identified by both methods. The coefficient of correlation between the two sets of results is 0.87 for the morning period and 0.91 for the afternoon.

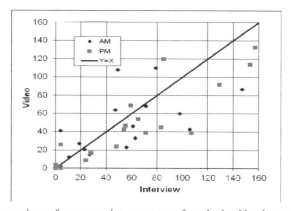

Fig. 7. Comparison of passenger inter-stop transfers obtained by the two methods

6   Conclusion

In conclusion, it is worth noting that the results of two types of pedestrian traffic distribution analysis (traditional one, interview-based and optical analysis) largely coincide and show good correlation. This proves the effectiveness and shows potential of image analysis methods for this kind of application.

Traditional approach allowed counting all persons appearing on stops. The method of image analysis counted only people entering or leaving the platform without calculating people transferring on the same platform. The method of image analysis appears to be more effective when counting people moving in large groups. Counting a group of people moving in different directions (boarding and alighting) using the traditional method is very difficult for busy bus stops and obviously erroneous.

Each method has its advantages and disadvantages. Each method has its own measurement errors that should be considered when creating an actual interchange passenger traffic movement model. It is worth noting the role of both types of research and their complementarity. Both studies provided valuable complementary information.

References

1. Kukharev, G., Kuzminski, A., Nowosielski, A.: Structure and Characteristics of Face Recognition Systems. Computing, Multimedia and Intelligent Techniques. Special issue on Live Biometrics and Security 1(1), 111–124 (2005)
2. Yang, M., Kriegman, D., Ahuja, N.: Detecting Faces in Images: A Survey. IEEE Transactions on Pattern Analysis and Machine Intelligence 24(1), 34–58 (2002)
3. Viola, P., Jones, M.J.: Robust Real-Time Face Detection. International Journal of Computer Vision 57(2), 137–154 (2004)
4. Zhang, X., Gao, Y.: Face recognition across pose: A review. Pattern Recognition 42, 2876–2896 (2009)
5. Kukharev, G., Forczmański, P., Nowosielski, A.: Wykorzystanie prostych ekstraktorów cech obrazu w programowo-sprzętowych systemach biometrycznych (Simple facial features extractors utilization in hardware-software biometric systems). Pomiary Automatyka Kontrola 7-bis206, 77–79 (2006)
6. Kukharev, G., Mikłasz, M., Sabuda, R., Kawka, G.: Metoda ekstrakcji cech orientowanych na sprzętową realizację w zadaniach rozpoznawania obrazów. Pomiary Automatyka Kontrola (8), 563–565 (2009)
7. Olszewski, P., Krukowski, P.: Quantitative assessment of public transport interchanges. In: 40th European Transport Conference, Glasgow (2012)
8. Zhao, W., Chellappa, R., Phillips, P.J., Rosenfeld, A.: Face Recognition: A Literature Survey. ACM Computing Surveys 35(4), 399–458 (2003)
9. Bowyer, K.W., Chang, K., Flynn, P.: A survey of approaches and challenges in 3D and multi-modal 3D + 2D face recognition. Computer Vision and Image Understanding 101(1), 1–15 (2006)
10. Kong, S.G., Heo, J., Abidi, B.R., Paik, J., Abidi, A.M.: Recent advances in visual and infrared face recognition - a review. Computer Vision and Image Understanding 97(1), 103–135 (2005)
11. Tan, X., Chen, S., Zhou, Z.-H., Zhang, F.: Face recognition from a single image per person: A survey. Pattern Recognition 39, 1725–1745 (2006)
12. http://www.neurotechnology.com/verilook.html (date of access: July 26, 2013)

Cost-Benefit-Based Implementation Strategy for Green Light Optimised Speed Advisory (GLOSA)

Wolfgang Niebel

German Aerospace Center (DLR), Institute of Transportation Systems,
Department of Traffic Management, Rutherfordstr. 2, 12489 Berlin, Germany
wolfgang.niebel@dlr.de

Abstract. GLOSA as a particular application of communicating vehicles and infrastructure has become a technically proved system. The paper shows that the implementation of the GLOSA functionality can generally be recommended from the economical point of view. This result is achieved by applying a simulation study combined with principles of a Cost-Benefit-Analysis to a real-world demonstration site in Braunschweig. However, constraints arise by the complexity of junction signalling and approach lanes.

Keywords: Transport economy and policy, Cost-benefit-analysis Strategies for transport telematics solutions implementation.

1 Introduction

This paper presents possible real-world strategies to implement the cooperative road telematics application GLOSA (Green Light Optimised Speed Advisory). Briefly described the vehicle receives via vehicle-to-infrastructure (V2I) communication the Signal Phase and Timing (SpaT) Data of the traffic signal it is approaching. Applying Advanced Driver Assistance Systems (ADAS) either the driver is informed about the resulting speed optimum or the conventional Automatic Cruise Control (ACC) is directly fed with the corresponding input. Within a few years, GLOSA has become a well-researched and developed technology in the ITS spectrum which aims to avoid or alleviate stops of vehicles at traffic signals in order to reduce fuel consumption, noise, and pollutant emissions, as well as to achieve gains in traffic efficiency.

A lot of studies investigated the possible effects by applying microscopic traffic simulation software. The thereto modelled networks and traffic parameters remain in most of the cases rather simple, e.g., ten uni-directional platooning cars on a single lane [1], or a uni-directional corridor including two traffic lights without any turns, oncoming or crossing traffic [2]. Even the comprehensive investigations in [3] concentrate on a short time period during the peak hour and give results only as an average of all 15 simulated junctions. Common criteria to measure the alterations are fuel consumption and delay or stop time. All sources conclude that the desired improvements can be realized but with a varying magnitude of impact depending on the

J. Mikulski (Ed.): TST 2013, CCIS 395, pp. 313–320, 2013.
© Springer-Verlag Berlin Heidelberg 2013

control parameters. While the maximum fuel gain reaches 30 % under perfect conditions [1], realistic values seem to be less than 10 % [2], [3]. But do these figures justify the necessary investments by public road authorities and vehicle owners also in an economical way? And if so, how and where to start with the technology rollout? The German national research project KOLINE went beyond the previous traffic-concentrated studies by adding a junction-related cost-benefit-analysis (CBA) [4] which integrates all different benefits, differentiates between junction types, and therefore supports stakeholders in deciding implementation strategies for the cooperative GLOSA system. Section 2 of this paper describes the traffic simulation and the CBA, followed by the generated CBA results in section 3. The arising implications and hints at further detailed studies to be conducted are contained in section 4.

2   Methodology

2.1   Network Parameters

The regarded road network as in Fig. 1 is situated in the north-east of the German city Braunschweig (Brunswick), which is inhabited by roughly 250,000 people. Within this network the speed limit is 50 km/h. Two out of the three succeeding traffic signal actuated intersections - nodes K61 and K47 - form part of the dual carriageway inner ring road. On work days these sections bear an average daily traffic (ADT) of more than 36,000 vehicles (sum of both directions according to the ADT definition). The western and eastern intersections, K61 resp. K46, both have their obvious superordinate stream in the east-west- and west-east-direction and perpendicular subordinate approaches. This layout results in a simple 2-phase fixed-time signal program with jointly signalised green times for all three turns of each respective approach. In contrast the middle intersection K47 at the merge of the ring road with the federal road B248 and another major road has remarkable traffic loads on almost all of its turn directions. This leads to a complex 4-phase fixed-time signal program where at each approach green time for left turns begins several seconds later than for the combined straight and right turns. These separately signalised left turns are assigned with dedicated lanes only within a relatively short range of approx. 50 m before the junction, meaning that left turning cars share most of the combined approach lanes together with straight and right turn traffic.

Thus, it will be distinguished between a *simple* and a *complex* junction. To get a better idea of the intersection layouts including their lane-turn-assignments they are depicted in Fig. 2 and Fig. 3.

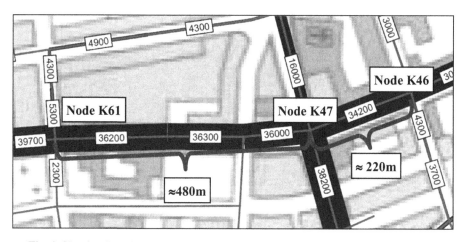

Fig. 1. Simulated road network with position of intersection nodes and ADT on its links

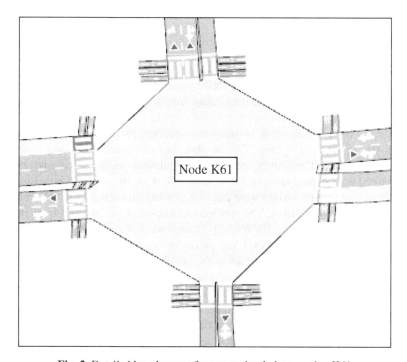

Fig. 2. Detailed lane layout of western simple intersection K61

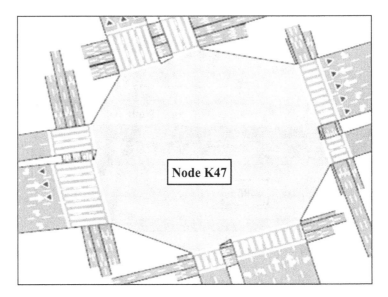

Fig. 3. Detailed lane layout of central complex intersection K47

2.2   Microscopic Traffic Simulation

The above described network was modelled with the microscopic simulation software AIMSUN 6.1.3 in time steps of 1 s (1 Hz). Implemented traffic load curves between 6 a.m. and 10 p.m. mirror the real ones taken from automatic counting systems. The model calibration on the parameter *network travel time* allowed a Root Mean Square Error (RMSE) of less than 10 % between the observed real values and the averaged values of the 16 simulation runs. This number was calculated according to the Student's t-distribution. The subsequent model validation on the parameter *tailback length* yielded an accepted error of 7.2 %. The NO_x, CO, HC, and PM pollutant emissions of cars, trucks, and busses were calculated using customised factors derived by the German handbook HBEFA. The applied fuel consumption factors are given in the German evaluation procedure BVWP [6]. Emissions of the climate gas CO_2 can directly be derived from these diesel and petrol numbers. Pollutant immission, noise emissions, and accidents were not part of the simulation due to the lack of embedded software algorithms.

The GLOSA functionality is coded outside the actual traffic simulation but acts as software-in-the-loop via an Application Programming Interface (API) by altering the desired speed of equipped vehicles within the 300 m proximity of a regarded junction. As a model simplification perfect message propagation conditions were assumed without further simulation of communication. The simulation software supported this V2I integration by providing the edible vehicle type attribute *penetration rate*. The respective control parameter of the scenarios T1 to T6 were set [0;5;15;25;35] %. Additionally, all scenarios comprised a signal program optimisation based on semi-aggregated traffic counts of 15 minute intervals and a consequential volume prediction. Scenarios T2 to T5 also incorporated the broadcast of estimated tailbacks to enhance the calculation accuracy of optimal speeds. These technical aspects are described in detail within [7] and [8].

2.3   Cost-Benefit-Analysis

Cost Determination. The investment costs per junction C_J comprise the communicating Road-Side Unit (RSU) at estimated $C_{RSU} = 10,000$ € and the optimisation software update at $C_{SW} = 3,000$ € for the evaluation period of 20 years. These prices base upon a real offer. The vehicle investment costs per On-Board Unit (OBU) can be assumed at $C_{OBU} = 500$ €, the usage duration equals the average vehicle life cycle of 10 years. The Application Unit (AU) being the ADAS/ACC is already existent and thus remains disregarded. The operation and maintenance costs of OBUs and RSUs seem to be negligible – the applied OBU LinkBird-MX of the KOLINE project for example consumes during normal operation only 3 W.

It is important to make further considerations, e.g., how many equipped junctions n_J a vehicle passes by during its trip, whether it is riding back and forth during a day (ADT/2), and how many different V2I functionalities are served by the OBU. Thereby only a fraction of these costs are assigned to one particular junction and functionality. In the KOLINE case we assumed that the penetration rate $R_{OBU} = [0;5;15;25;35]$ % and the number of functions nF_{OBU} are rising at the same rate, that is $\dfrac{R_{OBU}}{nF_{OBU}} = \text{const.} = \dfrac{5\%}{1} .. \dfrac{35\%}{7} = 0.05$. This assumption expresses the rising OBU attractiveness when more and more tasks can be executed with it.

The constant annual costs are calculated without discounting effects due to interest rates far below 3 %.

Benefit Derivation. Benefits - as difference of a criterion between the base line and a dedicated scenario - were computed for the criteria travel time, vehicle operation incl. fuel consumption, climate gas emission, and pollutant immissions basing on the simulated emissions and an external model. The original unit values were monetised according to the updated official German cost unit rates in [9] and afterwards summed up. The temporal extrapolation of the simulated average workday results first took into consideration the amount of 201 similar workdays per year. Further 101 days p.a. are workdays during school holidays, as well as Saturdays. The achievable benefits were linearly scaled down with the same factor the ADT decreases during these days. This rough and arguable approach was applied again to the remaining Sundays and public holidays.

Cost-Benefit-Figures. The annual benefits and costs can be put into relation either by their Benefit-Cost-Ratio (BCR) which should be greater than 1.0, or by their difference (Net Present Value NPV) which should be greater than zero to make the valuated project economically worth.

3   Results

3.1   Costs

The constant annual costs of scenario T1 with 0 % penetration rate amount to exceptional low 150 € per junction. The costs of scenarios T2 to T6 can be calculated under the aforementioned assumptions as can be seen in Fig. 4. It becomes clear, that the number of equipped junctions a vehicle is traversing on its journey plays a significant role. The complexity has no direct influence on the costs, but high ADT volumes normally yield more complex junctions in reverse.

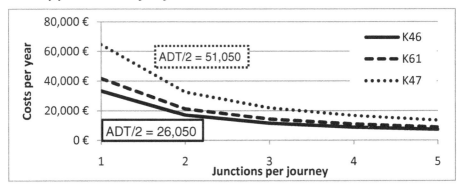

Fig. 4. Annual costs per junction

3.2   Benefits

The overall benefit of each junction can be seen in Fig. 5.

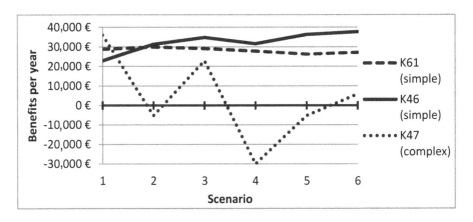

Fig. 5. Annual benefits per junction

It is notable that the complex junction K47 has negative benefits in some scenarios and a general decline of benefit with rising penetration rate. The highest benefit results from the pure signal program optimisation in scenario T1. This can be explained by the geometry of the approaching lanes (cf. sec. 2.1), where the separately signalised left turns share the combined approach lanes the first 250 m of the cooperate message broadcast radius together with straight and right turn traffic. Due to the shifted green time beginnings the optimal speed of some vehicles is lower than for others causing unwanted slow-downs of following vehicles. Thus the traffic flow of the status quo can become worse with the V2I application.

Both simple junctions do not face this problem and therefore have a positive benefit in all scenarios. Nevertheless, there is no continuous functional relation between the rate and benefit. The fall-back of scenario T4 remains unexplained.

At each junction scenario T6 at a penetration rate of 35 % and without the tailback broadcast is better than scenario T5 at the same rate but with the tailback incorporation. This can be explained by unsuitable algorithms.

3.3   Cost-Benefit-Figures

The following Table 1 incorporates only costs and benefits for the two simple junctions due to the negative effects of the complex junction. The BCR shows again the outstanding performance of scenario T1 without any communication units. But also the other scenarios perform well when the equipped vehicles traverse more than one cooperative junction per journey. In Braunschweig, e.g., the average number is 2.5. The NPV of scenario T1 is only achievable with a penetration rate of at least 35 % and six traversed junctions per journey.

Table 1. Benefit-Cost-Ratios and absolute net values (*in italic*) per scenario

Scenario	Number of traversed junctions n_j				
	1	2	3	4	5
T1			172 / 51,300 €		
T2	0,8	1,6	2,4	3,1	3,8
	-13,800 €	23,000 €	35,400 €	41,500 €	45,200 €
T3	0,9	1,7	2,5	3,2	4,0
	-11,100 €	25,700 €	38,100 €	44,200 €	47,900 €
T4	0,8	1,6	2,3	3,0	3,7
	-15,600 €	21,200 €	33,600 €	39,700 €	43,400 €
T5	0,8	1,6	2,4	3,2	3,9
	-12,500 €	24,300 €	36,700 €	42,800 €	46,500 €
T6	0,9	1,7	2,5	3,3	4,1
	-10,200 €	26,600 €	39,000 €	45,100 €	48,800 €

4   Conclusion

The introduction of the GLOSA functionality can generally be recommended from the economical point of view. As shown in sec. 3.2 constraints arise by the complexity of junction signalling and approach lanes. It must be ensured that differently signalised turn flows will not overlap and thereby influence each other in a negative way. As long as such effects cannot be excluded neither by the junction geometry nor by enhanced V2X technology GLOSA should be considered only for simple junctions. Further studies are needed for these extended V2I or V2V systems.

Since rising penetration rates seem to have only marginal positive effects, if at all, the speed of equipping the vehicle fleet is unimportant. In contrast, the number of traversed junctions per journey plays an important role. More investigations are needed which vehicle groups exceptionally often pass traffic signals, but it is likely that beside public transport busses commercial purpose vehicles like taxis or delivery vans are amongst them. They might also traverse a particular traffic signal more than twice a day and hence improve the Benefit-Cost-Rate further. Therefore, the market segment of commercial and fleet vehicles with a high kilometrage should be addressed first to be equipped with the GLOSA system.

Acknowledgement. The research within the KOLINE project received financial support from the German Federal Ministry of Economics and Technology (BMWi) according to a decision of the German Federal Parliament within the 3rd transport research framework "Mobility and Transport Technologies". The Institute of Transportation and Urban Engineering at TU Braunschweig was the leader of this project, of which in particular Dipl.-Ing. Ralf Kutzner contributed to the results' interpretation. Further project partners were the Institutfür Automation und Kommunikatione. V. Magdeburg (ifak), Institute of Control Engineering TU Braunschweig, Transver GmbH Munich, and Volkswagen AG Wolfsburg (VW).

References

1. Sanchez, M., Cano, J.-C.: Predicting Traffic lights to Improve Urban Traffic Fuel Consumption. In: Proceedings of 6th International Conference on ITS Telecommunications, pp. 331–336. IEEE (2006), doi:10.1109/ITST.2006.288906
2. Katsaros, K., Kernchen, R., Dianati, M., Rieck, D.: Performance study of a Green Light Optimized Speed Advisory (GLOSA) Application Using an Integrated Cooperative ITS Simulation Platform. In: 7th IEEE International Wireless Communications and Mobile Computing Conference (IWCMC), pp. 918–923. IEEE, New York (2011)
3. Tielert, T., Killat, M., Hartenstein, H., Luz, R., Hausberger, S., Benz, T.: The impact of traffic-light-to-vehicle communication on fuel consumption and emissions. In: Internet of Things (IOT 2010), pp. 1–8. IEEE (2010), doi:10.1109/IOT.2010.5678454
4. Niebel, W., Bley, O., Ebendt, R.: Evaluation of Microsimulated Traffic Light Optimisation Using V2I Technology. In: Mikulski, J. (ed.) TST 2012. CCIS, vol. 329, pp. 18–25. Springer, Heidelberg (2012)
5. Bundesministerium für Verkehr, Bau- und Wohnungswesen (publisher): Bundesverkehrswegeplan, Grundlagen für die Zukunft der Mobilität in Deutschland. Beschluss der Bundesregierung vom 2. Juli 2003, Berlin (2003)
6. Naumann, S., Bley, O.: A System for Traffic Light Control Optimisation and Automated Vehicle Guidance Using the V2X Communication Technology. Archives of Transport Systems Telematics (3), pp. 20–23 (2012)
7. Bley, O., Kutzner, R., Friedrich, B., Schüler, T.: Improvement in Traffic State Estimation at Signal Controlled Intersections by Merging Induction Loop Data with V2X Data. Archives of Transport Systems Telematics (3), pp. 3–7 (2012)
8. Bundesministerium für Verkehr, Bau und Stadtentwicklung BMVBS (publisher): Aktualisierung von Bewertungsansätzen für Wirtschaftlichkeitsuntersuchungen in der Bundesverkehrswegeplanung, Final Report. Essen, Freiburg, München (2009)

Analysis of Selected Dynamic Properties of Fractional Order Accelerometers for Application in Telematic Equipment

Daniel Pietruszczak and Elżbieta Szychta

University of Technology and Humanities in Radom,
Faculty of Transport and Electrical Engineering,
26-600 Radom, Malczewskiego 29, Poland
{d.pietruszczak,e.szychta}@uthrad.pl

Abstract. The paper presents simulation and laboratory studies on measuring transducers used in telematic equipment (railway vehicles diagnostic systems, suspension systems of motor vehicles, as motion sensors, etc.), which were modelled in classical differential equations as well as in fractional calculus.

Keywords: fractional calculus, measuring transducer.

1 Introduction

The aim of the paper is to investigate how accelerometer models based on fractional calculus convey their dynamic properties in comparison to models written in a form of differential equations of integer orders and in comparison to processing characteristics of their real equivalents/counterparts.

2 The Second Order Measuring Transducer

The second order measuring transducer for acceleration measurements (accelerometer), regarded as a representative group of measuring transducers, was investigated in simulations and in a laboratory.

An example of a measuring transducer of the second order is a mechanical transducer depicted in Figure 1.

Movement x of the base in relation to a stationary system of coordinates causes a movement of inert mass m, which can be divided into movement y_x in relation to the stationary system of coordinates and the movement in relation to the base y. The mass is hung on a spring, which coefficient of elasticity is k and which is fixed to a damper, with a damping coefficient of b. Movement y is converted into an electric signal and fed to the sensor's output. The use of piezoelectric elements is a typical conversion mechanism.

J. Mikulski (Ed.): TST 2013, CCIS 395, pp. 321–329, 2013.
© Springer-Verlag Berlin Heidelberg 2013

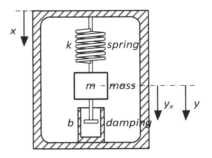

Fig. 1. Diagram of the accelerometer structure

Regardless of the mechanical structure of accelerometers and applied elements of mass movement conversion into an electric signal (piezoelectric, capacitive and piezoresistive accelerometers) their dynamic properties are modelled on the basis of a diagram shown in Fig. 1 and the following equation is derived:

$$\frac{d^2}{dt^2}y(t) + 2\zeta\omega_0\frac{d}{dt}y(t) + \omega_0^2 y(t) = 2\zeta\omega_0\frac{d}{dt}x(t) + \omega_0^2 x(t) \tag{1}$$

where: $\omega_0 = \sqrt{\dfrac{k_s}{m}}$ - circular frequency of free vibrations,

$\zeta = \dfrac{B_t}{2\sqrt{k_s m}}$ - degree of damping and $k = \dfrac{1}{k_s}$ - amplification factor.

Depending on selection of k_S, m and B_t, a transducer can serve for measuring displacements as a vibrometer assuming a low k_S and B_t and a high m, or accelerations as an accelerometer assuming a high k_S, a low m and B_t.

3   Quasi-fractional Model of the Measuring Transducer

Equation (1) describing the measuring transducer, can be expressed as a matrix equation:

$$\begin{bmatrix} a_2 & a_1 & a_0 \end{bmatrix}\begin{bmatrix} w_k \\ w_{k-1} \\ w_{k-2} \end{bmatrix} = \begin{bmatrix} b_2 & b_1 & b_0 \end{bmatrix}\begin{bmatrix} x_k \\ x_{k-1} \\ x_{k-2} \end{bmatrix} \tag{2}$$

Equation (2) can have the following derivative-integral expression:

$$A_2 \Delta_k^{(2)} w_k + A_1 \Delta_{k-1}^{(1)} + A_0 w_{k-2} = B_2 \Delta_k^{(2)} w_k + B_1 \Delta_k^{(1)} x_{k-1} + B_0 w_{k-2} \tag{3}$$

where $\Delta_k^{(n)}$ is the discrete function's reverse difference, defined as:

$$\Delta_k^{(n)} f(k) = \sum_{j=0}^{k} a_j^{(n)} f(k-j) \tag{4}$$

When (4) is taken into account, (3) has the matrix expression below:

$$\begin{bmatrix} a_2 & -a_1 - 2a_0 & a_2 + a_1 + a_0 \end{bmatrix} \begin{bmatrix} \Delta_k^{(2)} w_k \\ \Delta_k^{(1)} w_k \\ \Delta_k^{(0)} w_k \end{bmatrix} = \begin{bmatrix} b_0 & -b_1 - 2b_0 & b_2 + b_1 + b_0 \end{bmatrix} \begin{bmatrix} \Delta_k^{(2)} x_k \\ \Delta_k^{(1)} x_k \\ \Delta_k^{(0)} x_k \end{bmatrix} \tag{5}$$

where: $A_2 = a_2, A_1 = -a_1 - 2a_0, A_0 = a_2 + a_1 + a_0$
and: $B_2 = b_0 + b_1 + b_2, B_1 = -b_1 - 2b_0, B_0 = b_0$.

While comparing responses of the measuring transducer to the input sinusoidal signal, it was described by means of three models using the above method:

- a classic model (the transfer function of the measuring transducer model) described with operator transmittance (6). The operation of a transducer described by the equation was simulated for appropriately selected parameters: natural angular frequency and damping degree. Dynamic properties of the measuring transducer are described by an operator transmittance:

$$G(s) = \frac{1}{s^2 + 880s + 4.84 \cdot 10^6} \tag{6}$$

- a classic discrete model (a discrete transfer function of the measuring transducer model), derived from the operator transmittance model (6), described by means of a discrete transmittance (7):

$$G(z) = \frac{1.667 \cdot 10^{-15} z^2 + 6.666 \cdot 10^{-15} z + 1.667 \cdot 10^{-15}}{z^2 - 2z + 0.999} \tag{7}$$

Thus, the classic discrete model (7) was obtained by discretizing the classic model (6), the Zero-Order-Hold model with a sampling time: $T_p = 10^{-7}$ s, for which the Nyquist theorem of sampling frequency selection holds true.

– A quasi-fractional discrete model (a discrete transfer function of the fractional transducer model) is expressed with derivative integrals and described by a discrete transmittance (8):

$$G(z) = \frac{z^2}{1 \cdot 10^{14} z^2 - 2 \cdot 10^{14} z + 1 \cdot 10^{14}} \tag{8}$$

Discrete transmittance (8) is produced by implementation of the method of determining the quasi-fractional expression of the measuring transducer in MATLAB&Simulink. It can be noted that the measuring transducer model determined by the derivative-integral method presents the dynamic properties of the classically determined model (the diagrams of the models coincide). This confirms that integer-order differential and integral calculus is a special case of differential and integral calculus of non-integer orders.

Measuring transducer models (7) and (8) have been subject only to simulation testing and do not fully represent the real models. The simulations indicate that the quasi-fractional model (8) exhibits the same dynamic properties as the classic model (7). The time after which a model's description is independent of time – for the quasi-fractional model is the same as for the classic model.

Other examples of the transducer models: classic, discrete-classic and discrete-quasi-fractional are presented by transmittances (9), (10) and (11a)-(11c).

- Using the ARX identification method (AutoRegressive with EXternal input) described extensively in publications [1, 2, 3] and [6] the operator transmittance of the measure system described in Section 5:

$$G(s) = \frac{0.03215 s^2 + 1319.6 s + 1.338 \cdot 10^6}{s^2 + 4.678 \cdot 10^4 s + 2.309 \cdot 10^7} \tag{9}$$

– It was followed by a discrete transfer function. The discrete transfer function of the model was determined on the basis of the operator transmittance (9):

$$G(z) = \frac{0.03215 z^2 - 0.05368 z + 0,02163}{z^2 + 1.625 z + 0.6264} \tag{10}$$

A classic discrete model (10) was produced by discretizing the classic model by means of the 'Zero-Order-Hold' method with the sampling time $T_p = 10^{-4}$ s.

– A discrete transfer function of quasi-fractional models was determined with a method implemented in MATLAB&Simulink. For varying increment of h, quasi-fractional transducer models become discrete transmittances. For instance:

for $h = 10^{-7}$:
$$G_{f_1}(z) = \frac{3.228 z^2 - 6.443 z + 3.215}{100.5 z^2 - 200.5 z + 100} \tag{11a}$$

$$G_{f_2}(z) = \frac{3.347z^2 - 6.562z + 3.215}{104.7z^2 - 204.7z + 100} \tag{12b}$$

for $h = 10^{-6}$:

$$G_{f_3}(z) = \frac{4.548z^2 - 7.75z + 3.215}{104.7z^2 - 246.8z + 100} \tag{13c}$$

for $h = 10^{-5}$:

The model of real measurement system (9) in the form of a discrete transmittance (10) and models expressed by means of a differential and integral equation (11a)-(11c) were then compared. Both types of models were based on the classic model derived by the ARX identification method.

The simulations were carried out by ode3 integration method for a 100Hz sinusoidal input signal.

It can be observed that, for the adopted increment of h, the measure of differentiation accuracy, the diagrams clearly diverge. This means that other h increments, far lower than the sampling frequency, must be adopted.

4   Fractional Model of the Measuring Transducer

Riemann-Liouville or Grünwald-Letnikov's definition can be stated for non-integer order derivatives [4, 7]. Let the fractional derivative be:

$$_{t_0}D_t^{(v)} f(t) = \lim_{\substack{h \to 0 \\ t-t_0=kh}} \left[\frac{1}{h^v} \sum_{i=0}^{k} a_i^{(v)} f(t - hi) \right] \tag{12}$$

where:

$$a_i^{(v)} = \begin{cases} 1 & i = 0 \\ (-1)^i \dfrac{v(v-1)(v-2)...(v-i+1)}{i!} & i = 1,2,3,... \end{cases} \tag{13}$$

is defined as a reverse difference of the discrete function and h is the increment of $f(t)$ defined in the range $[t_0, t]$:

$$h = \frac{t - t_0}{k} \tag{14}$$

The introduction of a non-integer order to the measuring transducer's equation (1) converts it into:

$$\frac{d^2}{dt^2}w(t) + 2\zeta\omega_0 \frac{d^{(v_1)}}{dt^{(v_1)}}w(t) + \omega_0^2 w(t) = -\frac{d^2}{dt^2}x(t) \tag{15}$$

Generalizing (15) and considering that integer-order derivatives in the derivative-integral calculus are a special case of non-integer order derivatives, one can formulate:

$$A_2 \frac{d^{(v_2)}}{dt^{(v_2)}}w(t) + A_1 \frac{d^{(v_1)}}{dt^{(v_1)}}w(t) + A_0 \frac{d^{(v_0)}}{dt^{(v_0)}}w(t) =$$
$$B_2 \frac{d^{(u_2)}}{dt^{(u_2)}}x(t) + B_1 \frac{d^{(u_1)}}{dt^{(u_1)}}x(t) + B_0 \frac{d^{(u_0)}}{dt^{(u_0)}}x(t) \tag{16}$$

where: u, v – non-integer order derivatives.

Let (16) be a linear differential equation of non-integer orders:

$$\sum_{i=0}^{n} t_0 A_i D_{t_0}^{(v_i)} w(t) = \sum_{j=0}^{m} t_0 B_j D_{t_0}^{(u_j)} x(t) \tag{17}$$

where: $A_i = const. \in R,\ i = 1, 2, ..., n-1,\ B_j = const. \in R,$
$j = 1, 2, ..., m,\ m \leq n,\ m, n \in R,\ A_n = 1,$

$t_0 A_i D_{t_0}^{(v_i)} w(t),\ \ t_0 B_j D_{t_0}^{(u_j)} x(t)$ – Riemann-Liouville's or Grünwald-Letnikov's derivatives,

$t_0 A_i D_{t_0}^{(v_i)} w(t)\Big|_{t=t_0},\ \ t_0 B_j D_{t_0}^{(u_j)} x(t)\Big|_{t=t_0}$ – initial conditions,

$w(t)$, $x(t)$ – functions for which Riemann-Liouville's or Grünwald-Letnikov's derivatives exist.

The correctness of this method of differential equation (15) reducing to equation (16) was verified by determining logarithm frequency diagrams of transducers for the adopted non-integer orders in (16) and obtaining the desired diagram courses (overlapping of the diagrams).

It can be noted that the diagrams clearly overlap for all the adopted h increments. This means that h increments far lower than the sampling frequency should be assumed.

5   Model of a Laboratory System of an Acceleration Measuring Transducer

Signals received from accelerometers of different sensitivities were compared in the measuring system (Fig. 2). The sensitivity of accelerometer A1, which was adopted as a model, was approx. 30 times higher than that of the investigated accelerometer A2. Equations of dynamic properties describing the investigated accelerometer of integer and non-integer orders were determined by means of the ARX identification method on the basis of the data from accelerometers. The signals from so determined models were compared with the signal from the model accelerator. The relative errors of measurement were determined adopting the signal from the model accelerator as a reference value. The median of the series of 500 successive measurement samples was adopted as the error measure. Measurements were taken separately for the following frequencies of the vibration exciter: 100 Hz, 200 Hz, 300 Hz, 400 Hz and 500 Hz.

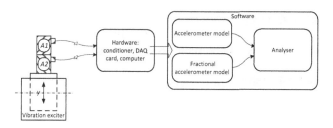

Fig. 2. Laboratory measuring system for mechanical vibration transducers testing: A1 – model accelerometer, A2 – investigated accelerometer [Own study]

Table 1 contains examples of investigation results. It shows measurement results of accelerations in the measuring system shown in Figure 2.

Table 1. Values of the relative error median for the transducer model of the integer and non-integer order [6]

Frequency [Hz]	Relative error median for the model of integer and non-integer order [%]	Relative error median for the non-integer order model [%]	Difference [%]
100	30.8089	20.8040	10.0049
200	30.2997	20.8041	9.4956
300	29.5564	20.8042	8.7522
400	28.3097	20.8039	7.5058
500	26.0184	20.8040	5.2144

Depending on investigated frequencies (Table 1) the accuracy of the accelerometer dynamic properties reproduction by the model ranges from approx. 5% to approx. 10%. These values can be increased by developing a more accurate model of non-integer orders.

In order to fully confirm preliminary investigations it is necessary to generalize the results obtained for the whole range of accelerometer processing (the widest possible range of frequencies) and for all types of accelerometers and of different sensitivities. Due to the pioneering character of investigations, the measurements must be taken with the utmost care and accuracy in order to minimize errors resulting from the inaccurate calibration. The equipment of high measurement accuracy usually used for accelerometer calibration is the best for this purpose.

6   Conclusion

The results of investigations proposed in this paper are to answer questions about legitimacy of modelling accelerometer dynamic properties by means of differential equations of non-integer orders, and in particular to answer the question: *Is the replacement of the "classic" modelling of dynamic properties by means of differential equations of integer orders with those of non-integer orders justified from the dynamic properties modelling accuracy point of view?*

The results obtained, although focused on investigations of the accelerometer dynamic properties modelling, will be significant for modelling dynamic properties of a very wide group of sensors and measuring transducers due to the typical notation of dynamic properties in a form of differential equations. As this method of modelling is commonly accepted not only for object but also phenomena modelling, it is assumed that the project research results will be useful while considering a general and widespread application of differential and integral calculus of non-integer orders for modelling physical phenomena. Confirmation of this hypothesis can be relevant for the development of accurate models of devices as well as for phenomena based on differential equations, especially in the case of models with a great number of variables, models reflecting fast-changing states or models describing dynamic properties of a new material functioning.

References

1. Luft, M., Szychta, E.z., Cioć, R., Pietruszczak, D.: Effect of fractional orders in differential equation describing damping in the measuring transducer. In: Mikulski, J. (ed.) TST 2011. CCIS, vol. 239, pp. 226–232. Springer, Heidelberg (2011)
2. Luft, M., Szychta, E., Cioć, R., Pietruszczak, D.: Correction method of processing characteristics of the measuring transducer. In: Proceedings of the TRANSCOM 2011, pp. 83–86. University of Zilina, Zilina (2011)
3. Luft, M., Szychta, E.z., Cioć, R., Pietruszczak, D.: Measuring transducer modelled by means of fractional calculus. In: Mikulski, J. (ed.) TST 2010. CCIS, vol. 104, pp. 286–295. Springer, Heidelberg (2010)
4. Ostalczyk, P.: Zarys rachunku różniczkowo-całkowego ułamkowych rzędów. Teoria i zastosowania w automatyce, Wydawnictwo Politechniki Łódzkiej, Łódź (2008) (in Polish) ISBN 978-83-7283-245-0

5. Pietruszczak, D.: Laboratory investigations of dynamic properties of accelerometers with fractional orders for application in telematics equipment. In: The 12th International Conference TST, Katowice-Ustroń, October 10-13 (2012) ISSN 1899-8208; Archives of Transport System Telematics 5(2), 26-31 (2012)
6. Pietruszczak, D.: Analiza właściwości układów pomiarowych wielkości dynamicznych z wykorzystaniem rachunku różniczkowo-całkowego ułamkowych rzędów, Doctoral Thesis, Library of University of Technology and Humanities in Radom (2012) (in Polish)
7. Podlubny, I.: Fractional Differential Equations. Academic Press, New York (1999)
8. Walter, P.L.: Selecting accelerometers for and assessing data from mechanical shock measurements. PCB Piezotronics Technical Note TN-24, USA (2008)
9. Gorczyca, P., Mikulski, J., Bialon, A.: Wireless local networks to record the railway traffic control equipment data. Advances in Electrical and Electronic Engineering 5(1-2), 128–131 (2011)
10. Mikulski, J.: Using Telematics in Transport. In: Mikulski, J. (ed.) TST 2010. CCIS, vol. 104, pp. 175–182. Springer, Heidelberg (2010)

exactEarthSatellite – AIS as One of the Most Advanced Shipping Monitoring Systems

Ryszard K. Miler[1] and Andrzej Bujak[2]

[1] Gdańsk Banking School, Faculty of Finance and Management,
Dolna Brama 8, 80-821 Gdańsk, Poland
rmiler@poczta.onet.pl
[2] Wrocław Banking School, Faculty of Finance and Management,
Fabryczna 29-31, 53-609 Wrocław, Poland
andrzej.bujak@interia.pl

Abstract. Maritime transport, due to its characteristics, global reach and an important role it plays in economical processes, is now an area of implementation of the newest and the most advanced solutions in shipping monitoring systems. Majority of these solutions are based on Automatic Identification System (AIS) signal transmission. exactAIS is a global vessel monitoring and tracking system based on world leading Satellite AIS (S-AIS) technology. This service enhances maritime domain awareness for government authorities and selected commercial organizations around the world, with superior detection capability, secure distribution of information and high quality of service. This paper is an attempt at providing a complex grasp of the benefits regarding the usage of exactEarth application on a level of the land-marine logistic supply chains.

Keywords: shipping monitoring systems, automatic identification system, satellite-AIS, exactEarth.

1 Introduction

The days of anonymity at sea has gone years ago. With LRIT [7] and satellite based AIS tracking the ship owner's office has had access to the precise location of its ships in real time over the world [8].

A scheme of building an effective shipping monitoring and control system has been already proved. It should consist at least of monitoring sensors and a fusion centre, data communications, ship-borne terminals and user terminals [3].

Automatic Identification System (AIS), which is one of the first shipping monitoring systems introduced, is a radio frequency (RF-based) communications system. The system has been designed primarily as a collision avoidance service for large Safety Of Life At Sea (SOLAS) class vessels [9]. As soon as AIS has been deployed successfully, it suffers from a major limitation. Due to the curvature of the Earth, its range is limited to approximately 50 nautical miles [2].

J. Mikulski (Ed.): TST 2013, CCIS 395, pp. 330–337, 2013.
© Springer-Verlag Berlin Heidelberg 2013

Maritime agencies and other customers wish to obtain a greater visibility of vessel traffic over a much broader area in order to enhance their operational effectiveness. A solution appeared through the exactEarth idea of collecting AIS signal transmissions from space [2].

2   exactEarthSatellite AIS

AIS, as an RF-based system, has been never designed for reception of signals from space, however exactEarthby deploying a constellation of microsatellites that orbit the Earth, extends the range of the original system. In addition Satellite AIS as a new system creates many new applications for competent maritime authorities. The visibility scope is significantly enhanced using microsatellites, the same time creating anincreased maritime situational awareness, which is now well beyond the 50 nautical mile range from shore as it was before. (Fig. 1)

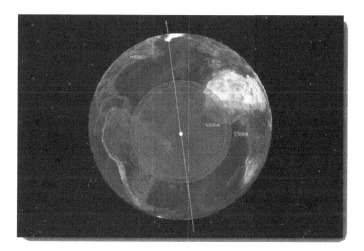

Fig. 1. The field of view from an AIS satellite at 650 km altitude (marked in purple) and 850 km altitude (highlighted in red)

As stated by the exactEarth company, satellites complete one orbit in approximately 100 minutes. From their vantage point 650 km above the Earth, the microsatellite covers up to 5,000 km surface in diameter. The satellites' objective is to collect AIS transmissions from all the ships that are within their field of view. [2]

In addition to complete global coverage, exactAIS detects many times more vessels than any other system, capturing thousands of distinct vessels in a single pass (see Fig.2). Utilizing a patented technology, the company is able to provide their customers with better information. It gives them greater opportunity to make better decisions for security, traffic management, environmental and safety applications [2].

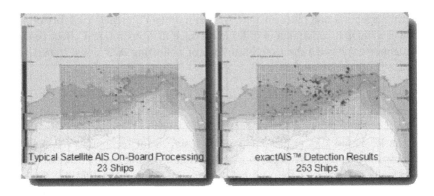

Fig. 2. The difference between standard and satellite exactAIS detection results (23v.253 ships)

Due to the fact the exactAIS® system uses a special AIS receiver and sophisticated patented technology to "de-collide" the signals it is possible extracting AIS messages from a much larger percentage of the ships in the same region than the standard AIS receivers [2]. At the same time maximum probability of ship detection in areas of high ship density is provided as well.

3   Benefits for the Competent Maritime Authorities and Customers

When it comes to understanding the global maritime traffic all customers can get a complete picture according to their needs. The system provides the best in class detection rate and meets the quality requirements of even the most demanding customers, ensuring that the data is delivered in a highly secure and timely way. exactAIS data is distributed to authorized users only. Organisations that meet the criteria of a "competent maritime authority", as defined by the International Maritime Organisation, are eligible to subscribe to the exactAIS service. [10]

There are several additional features of the exactAIS™ that can be utilized by customers: exactAIS Message Feed; exactAIS Viewer; exactAIS Archive; exactAIS Geospatial Web Services: Maritime Vessel Information on-demand; exactAIS Premium™ service.

exactAIS Message Feed provides the following AIS message content with all of the detected features listed below [2]:

- AIS position reports including ship ID (MMSI), GPS position, navigational status, course and speed;
- AIS static messages comprising ship name, ship type, IMO number, call sign, dimensions, destination and other important information;
- Aid to Navigation (AtoN) messages;
- Safety Text messages;
- Base station position reports and commands.

For customers who are interested in evaluating exactAIS® without integrating the data feed into their operational display systems, exactEarth provides a web-based viewing tool, called exactAIS Viewer™. exactAISViewer is a web-based application which enables customers to view all current vessel positions and plots them on a familiar set of GIS (Geographic Information System) map layers to enhance the viewing experience. Users can selectively filter the display to include only ships or areas of interest around the world (see Fig.3). The access to the system is provided by exactEarth through a web browser URL along with login credentials [2].

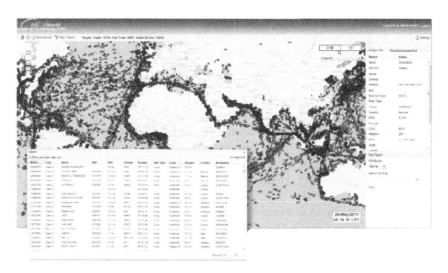

Fig. 3. A sample view from the exactAIS Viewer application (a global coverage)

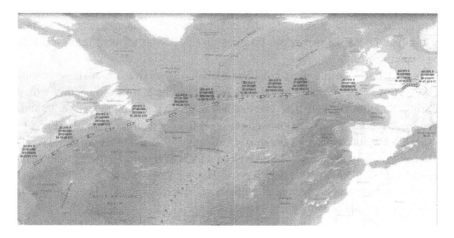

Fig. 4. The history of the MV Julius container ship traversing the Atlantic Ocean

According to the exactEarth announcements exactAIS Archive represents the most complete record of Satellite AIS vessel movements on a global scale. It is a direct result of the long and continuous operational capability of the exactEarth company [11].

With access to this archive all customers and competent maritime organisations can exploit the rich exactAIS database to gain an improved, comprehensive historical insight, general overview and knowledge of their maritime areas of interest (Fig.4).

It is easy to specify some of crucial benefits for users of this application [2]:

- with exactAIS Archive data it is easy to establish historical patterns of vessel behaviour, which helps for prosecution of illegal movements or actions, e.g. illegal discharging, encroachment into protected areas;
- exactAIS Archive data improves the ability to see vessel traffic patterns and seasonal traffic changes which provides critical information for planning and decision-making, e.g. allows authorities to establish the safest and fastest routes, prevents the risk of accident;
- archive data can help in anti-piracy operations by identifying suspicious vessel behaviours, delays on planned movement, time of arrival or deviations from the course;
- the exactAIS archive allows an in-depth analysis of Marine Protected Area violations improving environmental protection e.g. illegal ballast water exchange;
- archive data allows authorities to create improved ship modelling for behaviour prediction, reducing the risk of incident, costs and time in wider company scale.

exactAIS Geospatial Web Services deliver maritime vessel information, derived from Satellite and Terrestrial AIS sources, directly into customers geospatial platform of choice. exactEarth company offers a web services solution that allows instant access to exactAIS®data in an on-demand environment [2]. Image details shown in the Fig. 4 utilize the last known vessel information (LVI) with a global feed on the Ship View™ platform.

In order to provide the most complete global AIS service, exactAIS Premium™ service incorporates terrestrial-based AIS data. It means that in conjunction with exactEarth's Satellite constellation, customers can receive a comprehensive, complete and accurate record of all vessel movement regardless of their location [2]. (Fig. 6)

exactAIS Premium provides the most complete and adequate record of AIS vessel movements on a global scale. Thanks to exactAIS Premium application all data is delivered as a single integrated data service. Having access to this premium data service, all customers and competent maritime authorities can quickly integrate this data into their operational and analytical systems.

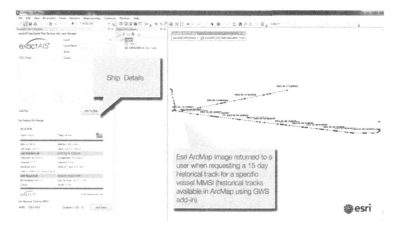

Fig. 5. A custom-add-in created specifically for Esri Arc-Map 10.1 users, showing the 30-day track for a specific vessel within the Esri platform

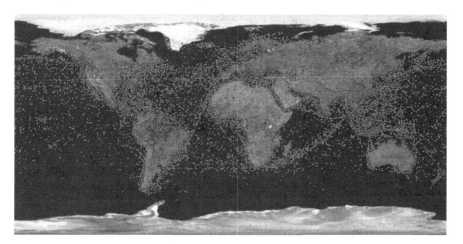

Fig. 6. An example of exactAIS Premium™ interface

Additionally, this way of access to the system can support customers in achieving some of the benefits [2]:

- elimination of the need to de-conflict AIS data from multiple sources of AIS information in the process of the integration of global AIS data;
- gathering better information for planning and decision-making e.g. impact analysis;
- improvement in ship routes modelling for behaviour prediction;
- modelling of seasonal traffic changes;
- prosecution for illegal movements or actions;
- support in safety analysis and accident prevention as well as anti-piracy operations;
- help in improvement to environmental protection;

According to the company statements exactAIS Premium data can easily be integrated into a variety of platforms for visualisation of ship tracks, including Esri Google Earth and the majority of applications for smartphones.

4   Conclusion

Taking control of the entire supply chain, from inbound logistics including sea-borne trade, over a complex distribution network of central warehouses, distribution warehouses and transportation terminals, to the final delivery at the customer's premises, requires a complex and real time view of the operation. [1]

Traditional supply chain execution systems fall short of tracking and tracing the order through all supply chain disciplines such as warehouse and transportation management (including shipment at sea). Once it leaves the warehouse, the order is in a disparate system. The aim of Supply Chain Shipment Monitoring (SCSM) is to bridge the gaps and to provide a global view of physical execution, including real-time monitoring, tracking and traceability.

Shipping monitoring systems (as exactAIS)can easily support SCSM and integrate unique identification standards for products (SGTIN), returnable assets (GRAI) and logistics units (SSCC) with data such as vessel position, estimated time of arrival (ETA) etc. This can improve substantially the ability of lot tracking and traceability [1].

exactAIS is a global vessel monitoring and tracking service based on the world leading Satellite AIS (S-AIS) detection technology. As it was proved S-AIS service delivered by the exactEarth company can enhance not only maritime domain awareness for government authorities and selected commercial organisations (called competent maritime authorities), but also can support all sea-born trade related logistic chains of supply around the world.

References

1. http://www.aptean.com/en/Solutions (date of access: July 23, 2013)
2. http://www.exactearth.com/products/exactais/
   (date of access: July 23, 2013)
3. Ma, K.: TCP Network Architecture. In: WASE International Conference on Technology Information Engineering, ICIE 2009, Shanghai, vol. 1. China Electric Power Press (2009)
4. Kościelski, M., Miler, R.K., Zieliński, M.: Automatic Identification System (AIS) as a Main Tool of NCAGS ADP Systems, ZeszytyNaukowe AMW (3) (170), Gdynia (2007)
5. Kościelski, M. , Miler, R.K. , Zieliński, M.: EMSA in the way to enhance safet yat EU seas, Zeszyty Naukowe AMW (2) (173), Gdynia (2008)
6. Miler, R.K.: Use of Vessel Monitoring Systems in Logistics Chain of Supply within EU Seas. In: Jaworski, J., Mytlewski, A. (eds.) Funkcjonowanie Systemów Logistycznych, CeDeWu, Warszawa, pp. 163–174 (2009)
7. The Long Range Identification and Tracking of Ships for more information see: R.K. Miler Use of Vessel Monitoring Systems in Logistics Chain of Supply within EU Seas, op.cit., pp. 163–174

8. Modern ships are equipped with much more systems – in addition to those already mentioned there are systems controlling the machinery, cargo systems, communication systems, voyage planning and navigation systems etc. .

9. Since 2004, the International Maritime Organization (IMO) has required AIS transponders to be aboard all vessels that exceed 300 gross tons. Over 60,000 ships worldwide have installed these transponders at a combined cost of several hundred million dollars, making AIS one of the most successful maritime technology deployments of all time. Additionally, AIS technology is increasingly being deployed in smaller vessels as well as Aids-To-Navigation (AtoN) and Search and Rescue (SAR) transponders

10. There are strict controls on the distribution of the data. For example, a competent maritime authority from a particular country is eligible to receive data on the following Class-A AIS-equipped vessels: all vessels within 1,000 nautical miles of that country's coastline, vessels carrying that country's flag, all vessels destined for ports in that country

11. exactEarth has been collecting operational AIS data from the exactAIS® servicesince July 2010. All of thisdata is stored in an archive at Toronto-based Data Processing Centre. Customers may now purchase this historical data, which includes all AIS messages processed by the exactAIS service dating from July 5, 2010 up to 30 days prior to the current date and time

12. The Ship View™ website was developed purely for illustrative purposes, showing how data can be used by different customers

13. Karoń, G., Mikulski, J.: Transportation Systems Modelling as Planning, Organisation and Management for Solutions Created with ITS. In: Mikulski, J. (ed.) TST 2011. CCIS, vol. 239, pp. 277–290. Springer, Heidelberg (2011)

14. Muzikářová, L., Franeková, M., Holečko, P., Hrnčiar, M.: Theory of information and signals, EDIS (2008)

Revision of the Modal Split of Traffic Model

Grzegorz Sierpiński

Silesian University of Technology, Faculty of Transport,
Krasińskiego 8, 40-019 Katowice, Poland
grzegorz.sierpinski@polsl.pl

Abstract. Knowledge about decision-making factors in mode choice is important during the transport processes designing. The traffic distribution modeling should be follow with agreement of sustainable development principles. The article describes the modal split of traffic model. Changes of function of utility was also proposed. Changes in the model are results of changes in the approach to the problem of transport in cities in directions to sustainable development.

Keywords: modal split, sustainable development, alternative transportation.

1   Introduction

In the most recent White Paper [31] the development tendencies of transportation systems in the EU until 2050 have been drafted. The discussion concerns the development of the modern transportation infrastructure, the environmental protection, the decrease of the demand for petroleum oil and its derivatives, the development of railways and of the widely understood sustainable transportation system, etc. The tendencies have been defined in different contexts, with the restriction expressed as: '(…) limitation mobility is not an option (…)'.

Taking into account the rules provided, among others, in the White Papers [30], [31], it necessary – in particular on the urbanised areas – to identify not only an current modal split of traffic but also of the real transportation needs of the travelling persons and they travel behaviours. It was as early as in the Bruntland Report that the concept of needs had been pointed out as one of the conditions of the correct approach to sustainable development[1].

A key element for the understanding of the transportation related behaviours and choices of the inhabitants is the statement that the main reason for a journey is its

---

[1] Definition of sustainable development (important also for transportation development) was described in the Brundtland Report [16]: '…sustainable development is the one corresponding to the needs of today's generation and not jeopardizing the capabilities of future generations, fulfilling the current and future needs. It is based on two fundamental assumptions: 1) firstly, one has to focus on the concept of needs and in particular the basic needs of the poorest, 2) when meeting the current and future needs one needs to take into account also the limited capability and must not ignore the limits set by the natural environment to the technological progress and to the social order…'

J. Mikulski (Ed.): TST 2013, CCIS 395, pp. 338–345, 2013.
© Springer-Verlag Berlin Heidelberg 2013

motivation; the motivation is determined as is also the source and the destination. Also the choice of the means of transportation is in many instances predetermined:

The modal split is the third stage of travel demand modeling (4 stage model). The choice of mode is influenced by various factors. The article includes a most popular modal split of traffic model and also different models. The proposition of extend this models was also described. Extend proposal is a result of research related with modal split and a few quality factors having influence for mode of transportation choice.

2   Multinomial Logit Model of Modal Split of Traffic

The choice of the mode of transportation depends on several factors - objective and subjective ones. Modeling the modal split requires the knowledge of the relationship between many variables, and the choice of the person traveling. This chapter presents the approach most commonly used for modeling the modal split.

The modal split of traffic models most common in the literature are mostly based on the logit model (e.g. [6, 7, 12, 14, 28, 31]), which is referred to the probability of choosing the mode of transportation, taking into account additional parameters. Such a model can take many forms. Equation (1) is the basic form [27], which applies to each in a some area means of transportation. An example of another approach is represented by equation (2) [6]. In this case, it is possible to separate the participation of non-pedestrian travels. It should be noted that this form of equation results from the specificity of the area and does not need to be universal. In the following discussion the focus is on the general form.

$$P_{it} = \frac{e^{\beta \cdot F_{it}}}{\sum_j e^{\beta \cdot F_{jt}}} \tag{1}$$

where:

P_{it} – probability of individual choosing mode i;
F_{it} – function of utility of mode i;
β – parameter for calibration
j – any type of mode;
t – particular travel between two zones.

$$P_{Veh\,t} = \xi_I + \xi_{II} \cdot \frac{e^{(\xi_{III} \cdot (L_t - \xi_{IV}))}}{\xi_V + e^{(\xi_{III} \cdot (L_t - \xi_{IV}))}} \tag{2}$$

where:

$P_{Veh\,t}$ – probability of individual choosing non-pedestrian trip in the traffic;
L_t – the distance between two concrete zones;
$\xi_I, ..., \xi_V$ – the parameters of the model.

By restricting model (1) to two modes of transportation, equation (3) can be written. Then, the graphical representation of the probability of selection of a transportation modes is shown in Figure 1.

$$P_{PTt} = \frac{e^{\beta \cdot F_{PTt}}}{e^{\beta \cdot F_{PTt}} + e^{\beta \cdot F_{PCt}}} \tag{3}$$

where:

P_{PTt} – probability of individual choosing public transport;
F_{it} – function of utility of mode i (PT – public transport, PC – personal car);
β – parameter for calibration
j – any type of mode;
t – particular travel between two zones.

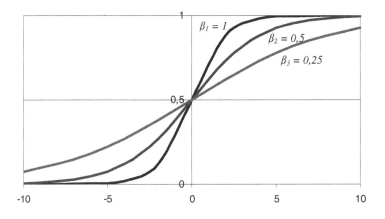

Fig. 1. A comparison of the logit function for three different values of calibration parameter [Own study]

In the case of equations (1) and (3) calculation must be preceded by an estimate of the function of utility for each type of area. Equation (4) contains the general elements taken into account in while determining the function of utility for personal cars and public urban transport [31]:

$$F_{PTt} = \xi_I \cdot x_{IVTt} + \xi_{II} \cdot x_{OVTt} + \xi_{III} \cdot x_{COSTt} + \xi_{IV} \cdot x_{WAITt} + \xi_V \cdot x_{XFERt}$$
$$F_{PCt} = \xi_I \cdot x_{IVTt} + \xi_{II} \cdot x_{OVTt} + \xi_{III} \cdot x_{COSTt} \tag{4}$$

where:

F_{PTt} – function of utility for public transport (in case of concrete travel t);
F_{PCt} – function of utility for personal cars(in case of concrete travel t);
x_{IVT} – in-vehicle time in minutes;
x_{OVT} – out of vehicle time in minutes;

x_{COST} – out of pocket cost (in money unit);
x_{WAIT} – wait time (time spent at bus or tram stop) in minutes;
x_{XFER} – number of transfers;
$\xi_I, ..., \xi_V$ – the parameters of the model.

3   Proposed Changes to the Model

Given actual travel behaviour, the limitation of the parameters defining the function of utility (4) is to be regarded as insufficient. The person traveling chooses the mode of transportation through the complex algorithm (though intuitive, and often subconscious). It seems reasonable to divide the factors having influence on the mode of transportation choice into more components. Equation (5) includes a proposal to include additional elements:

$$F_{i\,t} = \xi_I \cdot x_{TIME\,t} + \xi_{II} \cdot x_{DISTANCE\,t} + \xi_{III} \cdot x_{ACCESSIBILITY\,t} +$$
$$+ \xi_{IV} \cdot x_{ATMOSPHERIC\,t} + \xi_V \cdot x_{SUSTAINABLE\,t} + \xi_{VI} \cdot x_{COST\,t} + \qquad (5)$$
$$+ \xi_{VII} \cdot x_{PERSONAL\,t} + \xi_{VIII} \cdot x_{OTHERS\,t}$$

where:

F_{it} – function of utility of mode i (PUT – public urban transport[2], PC – personal car, R – railway, CP – carpooling, W – walking, B – bicycling, UB – urban bike etc.) - in case of concrete travel t;

x_{TIME} – sum of factors related with time (e.g. time necessary to pass to stop/railway station/car park and from bus-tram stop/railway station/car park to destination, waiting time for mean of transportation, travel time etc.);

$x_{DISTANCE}$ – sum of factors related with distance (e.g. distance source-destination, distance necessary to pass to stop/railway station/car park and from bus-tram stop/railway station/car park to destination etc.);

$x_{ACCESSIBILITY}$ – sum of factors related with accessibility (e.g. number of needed mode change, time of day – rush hours or not, place to car park near the destination etc.);

$x_{SUSTAINABLE}$ – sum of factors related with sustainable development (e.g. dedicated bus and bicycle lanes, priorities at the intersections, safe bicycle parks, urban bicycle system, other solutions from the domain of transportation telematics [11], [15], [20] include organizational changes[3]);

$x_{ATMOSPHERIC}$ – sum of factors related with atmospheric conditions (e.g. average number of sunny and wet days, temperature, average number of days with frost etc.);

---

[2] The detailed model should therefore allow for the more options of public urban transport, like e. g. travel by bus, tram, underground etc. [22].
[3] The selected initiatives are characterized in (e. g.): [1, 2, 7, 8-10, 17, 21-27, 29].

x_{COST} – sum of factors related with costs (e.g. cost of fuel, parking cost, tickets etc.);

$x_{PERSONAL}$ – sum of other personal factors (e.g. motivation, age, habits etc.);

x_{OTHERS} – sum of other factors (e.g. personal safety, convenience feeling etc.);

$\xi_I, ..., \xi_{VIII}$ – the parameters of the model.

In equation (5) the selected parameters can be divided into qualitative and quantitative variables. Qualitative variables in such a case may assume a logical value (0, 1), or have a certain weight assigned.

The choice made is an individual choice and therefore a subjective one. All of the factors in equation (5) depend on the travel behavior adopted in a given area, but also on the personal behavior of individuals (hence the variable $x_{PERSONAL}$). Research shows that, in most cases, the key factors for determining the choice of the mode of transportation are the total travel time and travel costs [24]. However, do not generalize this phenomenon, as the dependence on many specified factors can be noted depending on the other factors - such as weather conditions (Table 1).

Table 1. The correlation coefficients for selected features for the five selected European countries (with related to the modal split of traffic)

	Average temperature [°C]	Average rainfall per month [mm]	Average number of rainy days per year
France			
Personal Car	0,12	0,463	-0,221
Public Transport	-0,112	-0,327	0,341
Cycling	-0,476	-0,178	**0,633**
Walking	0,009	**-0,512**	-0,087
Holland			
Personal Car	0,505	**-0,787**	-0,323
Public Transport	-0,021	0,5	**0,612**
Cycling	**-0,597**	0,679	**-0,516**
Walking	0,03	**-0,528**	0,325
Norway			
Personal Car	0,206	0,262	0,477
Public Transport	-0,213	-0,222	-0,309
Cycling	0,089	-0,256	**-0,502**
Walking	-0,172	-0,103	-0,304
Spain			
Personal Car	**0,879**	-0,483	**-0,585**
Public Transport	-0,024	-0,324	-0,07
Cycling	-0,397	**0,837**	**0,897**
Walking	**-0,833**	**0,684**	0,511

Source: Own research based on information about modal split [5] and about atmospheric conditions [3] for 48 European cities from four countries.

The data show the occurrence relationships with varying degrees in various parts of Europe. In extreme cases, the correlation coefficient exceeded 0.75.

The motivation of travel is particularly important – passenger motivation categories included: home-work-home, home-education-home, home-other-home and non-home related.. Another share of travel by public urban transport will occur in the case of work-related travel and in the case of education-related one (e.g. [4], [13]). The age of the traveler is an important factor as well [19]. It should also be noted that, once prepared, the model should be calibrated in the following years through field studies, due to the ongoing socio-economic changes (e.g. [18]).

4   Conclusion

The model changes proposed in the paper, leading to the estimation of modal split, result from the dynamic development of modern technologies, including the direction of sustainability of transportation. It is also the consequence of the need to adapt the model to the travel behavior of travelers that is characterized by high complexity. The extension of the model taking into account the grouping of characteristics into eight categories makes the future transportation planning more possibly refer to sustainable development. The activities described should be preceded by extensive observations and searching point correlations in selected areas.

References

1. Autolib' Official Site, http://www.autolib.eu/ (date of accessMay 19, 2013)
2. Brzeziński, A., Masłowski, K., Piasecka, A.: Samochody wykorzystywane inaczej. Konferencja Naukowo Techniczna Miasto i Transport 2012. Innowacyjność Transportu – Oszczędzanie Energii. Politechnika Warszawska, 18 kwietnia (2012)
3. Climate & Temperature, http://www.climatemps.com/ (date of access May 19, 2013)
4. Commins, N., Nolan, A.: The determinants of mode of transport to work in the Greater Dublin Area. Transport Policy 18, 259–268 (2011)
5. European Platform on Mobility Management, http://www.epomm.eu (date of access May 19, 2013)
6. Karoń G., Janecki R., Sobota A., et al.: Program inwestycyjny rozwoju trakcji szynowej na lata 2008÷2011. Analiza ruchu. Praca naukowo-badawcza NB-67/RT5/2009
7. Macioszek, E.: Geometrical Determinants of Car Equivalents for Heavy Vehicles Crossing Circular Intersections. In: Mikulski, J. (ed.) TST 2012. CCIS, vol. 329, pp. 221–228. Springer, Heidelberg (2012)
8. Macioszek, E.: The Influence of Motorcycling and Cycling on Small One-Lane Roundabouts Capacity. In: Mikulski, J. (ed.) TST 2011. CCIS, vol. 239, pp. 291–298. Springer, Heidelberg (2011)
9. Manterys, T.: Badanie sprawności funkcjonowania wydzielonych drogowych pasów autobusowych w Krakowie w ciągu alei Trzech Wieszczów. Transport Miejski i Regionalny 7,8, 26–30 (2010)

10. Mathew, T.V., Krishna Rao, K.V.: Introduction to Transportation Engineering. Civil Engineering – Transportation Engineering. IIT Bombay, NPTEL Online, `http://www.cdeep.iitb.ac.in/nptel/Civil%20Engineering/` (date of access May 19, 2013)
11. Mikulski, J.: Telematic Technologies in Transportation. In: Janecki, R., Sierpiński, G. (eds.) Contemporary Transportation Systems. Selected Theoretical and Practical Problems. New Culture of Mobility, pp. 131–143. Publishing House of the Silesian University of Technology. Monograph no. 324, Gliwice (2011)
12. Modal Split, Lecture notes in Transportation Systems Engineering, Department of Civil Engineering, Indian Institute of Technology Bombay (August 2011), `http://www.civil.iitb.ac.in` (date of access May 20, 2013)
13. Müller, S., Tscharaktschiew, S., Haase, K.: Travel-to-school mode choice modelling and patterns of school choice in urban areas. Journal of Transport Geography 16, 342–357 (2008)
14. Ned Levine & Associates: A Spatial Statistics Program for the Analysis of Crime Incident Locations, The National Institute of Justice, Washington, DC (July 2010), `http://www.icpsr.umich.edu/CrimeStat/` (date of access May 19, 2013)
15. Nowacki, G. (ed.): Telematyka transportu drogowego. ITS Warszawa (2008)
16. Our Common Future. Report of the World Commission on Environment and Development, Transmitted to the General Assembly as an Annex to document A/42/427 – Development and International Co-operation: Environment, `http://www.un-documents.net/wced-ocf.htm` (date of access May 19, 2013)
17. Puławska S., Starowicz W.: Wykorzystanie wydzielonych drogowych pasów autobusowych w Krakowie przez pojazdy miejskiego transportu zbiorowego. Transport Miejski i Regionalny 7,8 (2010)
18. Scheiner, J.: Interrelations between travel mode choice and trip distance: trends in Germany 1976–2002. Journal of Transport Geography 18, 75–84 (2010)
19. Schmöcker, J.-D., Quddus, M.A., Noland, R.B., Bell, M.G.H.: Mode choice of older and disabled people: a case study of shopping trips in London. Journal of Transport Geography 16, 257–267 (2008)
20. Sierpiński, G., Celiński, I.: Use of GSM Technology as the Support to Manage the Modal Distribution in the Cities. In: Subic, A., Wellnitz, J., Leary, M., Koopmans, L.C. (eds.) Sustainable Automotive Technologies 2012, vol. 104, pp. 235–244. Springer, Heidelberg (2012)
21. Sierpiński, G.: Integration of activities as a method to the sustainable mobility. In: Janecki, R., Sierpiński, G. (eds.) Contemporary Transportation Systems. Selected theoretical and Practical Problems. New Culture of Mobility, pp. 93–102. Publishing House of the Silesian University of Technology. Monograph no. 324, Gliwice (2011)
22. Sierpiński, G.: Theoretical Model and Activities to Change the Modal Split of Traffic. In: Mikulski, J. (ed.) TST 2012. CCIS, vol. 329, pp. 45–51. Springer, Heidelberg (2012)
23. Sierpiński, G.: Travel behaviour and alternative modes of transportation. In: Mikulski, J. (ed.) TST 2011. CCIS, vol. 239, pp. 86–93. Springer, Heidelberg (2011)
24. Sierpiński, G.: Zachowania komunikacyjne osób podróżujących a wybór środka transportu w mieście. Prace Naukowe Politechniki Warszawskiej, Transport z. 84, Analiza i badania systemów transportowych i ich elementów, pp. 93–106. Politechnika Warszawska, Warszawa (2012)
25. Starowicz, W.: Zarządzanie mobilnością wyzwaniem polskich miast. Transport Miejski i Regionalny 1, 42–47 (2011)

26. Suchorzewski, W.: Opłaty za wjazd do obszarów śródmiejskich – sukcesy i porażki. In: Kaczmarek, M., Krych, A. (eds.) Skuteczne zmniejszenie zatłoczenia miast, Poznań – Rosnówko, pp. 195–206 (2009)
27. Transit Estimation and Mode Split, Urban Transportation Planning and Modeling, Iowa State University, Institute for Transportation, `http://www.ctre.iastate.edu/` (date of access May 19, 2013)
28. Transportation II Course, National Programme on Technology Enhanced Learning, `http://nptel.iitm.ac.in/courses/105104098/` (date of access May 19, 2013)
29. Velib' Official Site, `http://www.velib.paris.fr/` (date of access May 19, 2013)
30. White Paper: European transport policy for 2010: time to decide. COM, p. 370 (2001)
31. White Paper: Roadmap to a Single European Transport Area – Towards a competitive and resource efficient transport system. COM, p. 144 (2011)

Adjusting the Speed Characteristic of a Ship during a Voyage with Tropical Cyclone Avoidance

Bernard Wiśniewski, Piotr Medyna, and Jarosław Chomski

Maritime Academy in Szczecin,
Wały Chrobrego 1-2, 70-500 Szczecin, Poland
{b.wisniewski,p.medyna,j.chomski}@am.szczecin.pl

Abstract. One part of the m/v *Jawor's* voyage across the ocean is analyzed in this article. The performed calculations utilize selected speed characteristics and optimization algorithms. Various ranges of data referring to tropical cyclones are taken into consideration. The results are compared with actual parameters recorded on the ocean route.

Keywords: speed characteristic, ocean voyage, tropical cyclone.

1 Introduction

Speed characteristic is a particularly essential element in calculations of ship's weather-optimal route. If the speed characteristic is not adjusted, the ship misses the optimal position on the ocean as calculated and, consequently, encounters different weather conditions than expected, which in turn results in further divergence of the conditions taken for preliminary calculations from those actually encountered.

On the one hand, it hampers the process of seeking the optimal route and affects the efficiency of dynamic voyage planning, on the other hand it lowers the reliability of the tool applied, i.e. a program for sea-going ship routing, in the case it is used for the verification of routes already covered.

The latter possibility is of major importance for verification purposes, namely checking if in the actually recorded weather conditions the ship maintained contractual speeds, and met ETA as planned [4].

2 Methodology

The analysis was concerned with a major stretch of the ocean covered by a ship owned by the Polish Steamship Company, m/s Jawor, proceeding under ballast. According to log book entries the ship left Gibraltar and at 0700UTC on 15 September 2010 was in position 36°00'N/007°01'W, heading for position 36°54'N/065°00W (Fig.1.). The ship developed a speed of 14.5 knots in calm sea.

J. Mikulski (Ed.): TST 2013, CCIS 395, pp. 346–352, 2013.
© Springer-Verlag Berlin Heidelberg 2013

To calculate the ship's route we used a characteristic developed and adjusted for this vessel under ballast [3], Table 1. For a comparison, a speed characteristic SPOS (Ship Perfomance Optimisation System) for an averaged ship was used as default in that commercial system (Table 2.) [3, 5].

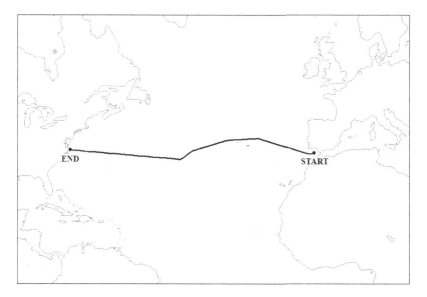

Fig. 1. The route of m/v Jawor 15 – 25 September, 2010

Calculations were made in the environment operating on the basis of directed graph theory. The weather data used were in the *grib* format (wind, sea) and came from NOAA forecasts. Besides, information on tropical cyclones Igor and Julia, prevailing on the ocean at the time was used (Figs 2 and 3) [2].

Table 1. Speed characteristic of the m/v Jawor under ballast, developed speed - % of speed in calm water

a)	Wind relative bearing					b)	Wave relative bearing				
Wind speed [kt]	0°	45°	90°	135°	180°	Wave height [m]	0°	45°	90°	135°	180°
0	100	100	100	100	100	0	100	100	100	100	100
10	96	97	99	101.5	102.5	2	97	98	99	101	102
20	91	94	98	103	105	4	85	88	92	95	98
30	85	90	97	104.5	107.5	6	70	74	79	83	88
40	78	85	95	106	110	8	52	58	64	69	76
50	70	79	93	107.5	112.5	10	38	43	50	56	63
60	63	74	91	109	114	12	28	33	38	44	49

Table 2. Speed characteristic SPOS default, developed speed - % of speed in calm water

a) Wind speed [kt]	Wind relative bearing					b) Wave height [m]	Wave relative bearing				
	0°	45°	90°	135°	180°		0°	45°	90°	135°	180°
0	100	100	100	100	100	0	100	100	100	100	100
10	100	100	100	100	100	2	98	98	100	100	100
20	98	99	100	100	101	4	90	90	95	100	100
30	95	97	98	100	101	6	85	85	90	90	95
40	85	90	95	100	102	8	65	70	80	85	90
50	80	85	90	95	102	10	0	0	0	0	0

The third of the cyclones moving over the Atlantic at the time, called Karl, moved between the Gulf of Mexico and the Caribbean Sea and did not affect the ship's route. The fourth cyclone – Lisa, appeared at longitude 030°W after the ship had crossed it, so it also did not have any impact on the calculations.

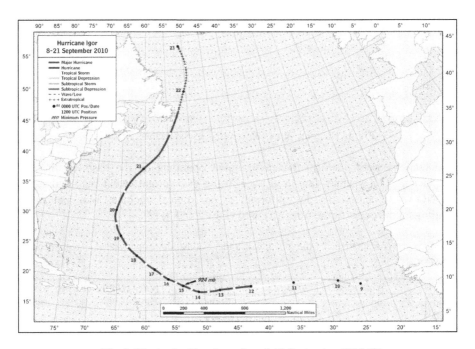

Fig. 2. The track of hurricane Igor 8-21 September 2010 [2]

The best-track data referring to hurricanes Igor and Julia were taken into account, that is data reflecting the behaviour of the hurricanes in a way most similar to the real one. Besides, the ship's route was calculated taking into account subsequent daily forecasts of hurricane movement, applying in this case the 1-2-3 rule for the determination of areas dangerous due to storm zones [1].

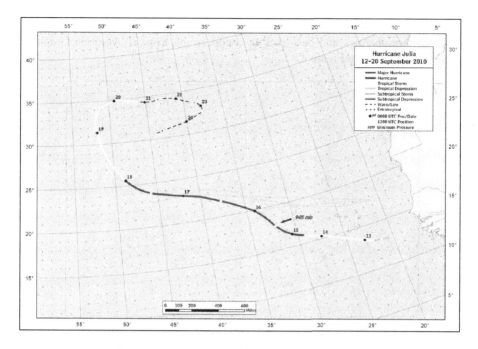

Fig. 3. The track of hurricane Julia 12-20 September 2010 [2]

3   Results

The actual route along which the m/v Jawor sailed is given in Figure 1. The time the vessel needed to cover that distance was 245 hours, or 10 days 5 hours. Calculations were also made for a route running across the same waypoints, using the speed characteristic developed for a ship under ballast and a default SPOS characteristic. The obtained times were, respectively: for the 'Jawor under ballast' characteristic longer by 2h 42', for the SPOS default characteristic shorter by 4h 12' than the actual time of the ship's voyage (Table 3).

The time calculated for the route actually covered by the m/v *Jawor*:

- for the speed characteristic ' Jawor under ballast': 247h 42', or 10d 3h 42'
- for SPOS default: 240h 48', or 10d 0h 48'

According to the entries in the ship's logbook the ship encountered winds reaching force 7°B twice, about 24h in total. Wind-induced waves 5 metres high were noted for a period of 20h. On a similar route calculated with the use of weather analyses and the characteristic 'Jawor under ballast', Hmax – 5.7m occurred over 164h of the voyage, 16h of sailing in waves 5+m, while for calculations based on 'SPOS default' the respective values were: Hmax – 5.9m over 165h of the voyage and 19h of sailing in waves 5+m. Longer time of the ship being in high waves can be noticed, and a higher value of maximum wave height for the route calculated with the use of speed characteristic 'SPOS default'.

Additionally, aimed to find the optimal route for the ship, calculations were made using weather analyses and best-track data concerning tropical cyclones. Graphical results are presented in Figure 4.

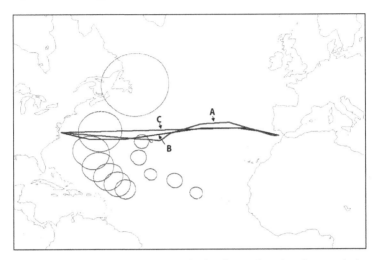

Fig. 4. A – real route of the m/v Jawor, B – calculated route based on best-track data and 'Jawor under ballast' characteristic, C- route based on best-track data and SPOS default characteristic. Circular figures show successive positions and ranges of the cyclones Igor (left) and Julia (right) at the voyage start and subsequent days, at 00300UTC.

The voyage length calculated on the basis of best-track data was respectively:

– for the speed characteristic 'Jawor under ballast': 240 h 12', or 10 days 0 h 12'
– for the speed characteristic SPOS default: 232 h 30', or 9 days 16 h 30'

The conditions along the route:
for the best-track data calculations, 'Jawor under ballast' characteristic
– Hmax – 6.3 m
– 18 h in 5+ m waves
  for the best-track data calculations, SPOS default characteristic
– Hmax – 7.2 m
– 24h in 5+ m waves.

The application of 'SPOS default' characteristic results in a slightly shorter calculated voyage length (that the vessel might not have reached anyway), but it brings the vessel into areas with more unfavourable wave conditions and longer presence in them.

Another variant of calculations consists in using analyses of wave and wind parameters and tropical cyclone related forecasts and advisory messages issued by the National Hurricane Center. The routes, composed of sections calculated for one day and additionally based on present weather reports are shown in Figure 5.

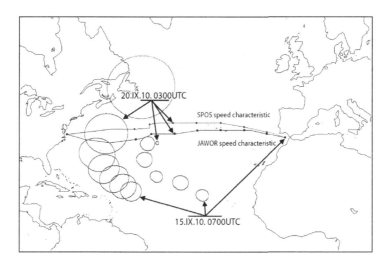

Fig. 5. Calculated voyage routes of the m/v Jawor based on uptodate reports on tropical cyclones, 1-2-3 rule, and various speed characteristics; ship and cyclone positions at the voyage start and at 0030UTC 20 Sept 2010 are marked

The voyage length calculated for tropical cyclone forecasts and using the 1-2-3 rule:

- based on the speed characteristic developed for the 'Jawor under ballast': 244 h 42', or 10 days 4h 42',
- based on mean SPOS default characteristic: 237 h 18', or 9 days 21h 18'.

Voyage length, distance and average speed of the m/v Jawor for various calculations variants are shown in Table 3 and Table 4.

Table 3. Voyage length of the m/v Jawor: various calculations variants

	real route	*along real route, Jawor characteristic*	*along real route, SPOS characteristic*	*accounting for best-track data, Jawor characteristic*	*accounting for best-track data, SPOS characteristic*	*1-2-3 rule, Jawor characteristic*	*1-2-3 rule, SPOS characteristic*
t	245h	247h 42'	240h 48'	240h 12'	232h 30'	244h 42'	237h 18'
$\Delta = $ t-t$_{real}$	-	**+2h 42'**	-4h 12'	**-4h 48'**	-12h 30'	**-0h 18'**	-7h 42'
V$_{average}$ [kt]	13.73	13.59	13.97	13.82	14	13.6	13.82

Table 4. Distances of the real route and variants of calculated routes

	real distance	distance for best-track data, Jawor characteristic	distance for best-track data, SPOS characteristic	distance for 1-2-3 rule & Jawor characteristic	distance for 1-2-3 rule & SPOS characteristic
Distance [Nm]	3365.2	3319.1	3254	3329	3280.3
Δ = distance – real distance	-	-46.1	-111.2	-36.2	-84.9

4   Conclusion

The application of speed characteristic that had been calculated and adjusted to m/v Jawor's ballast condition brought a slight difference (+1.1%) between the voyage length calculated after the actual sailing and the real voyage length. When the SPOS default characteristic was used, the difference was -1.7%, which implies that the ship's speed was overestimated. Additionally, in the case of SPOS default characteristic, the ship encountered higher waves and for longer time on the calculated route.

It turned out that the data on tropical cyclones for the first three days did not affect the calculation results, therefore the ship captain's choice of the route can be assessed as good one. The ship went off the orthodromic route at the right moment, and the further part of the route is similar to the one calculated by the computer program.

The use of SPOS characteristic, the 1-2-3 rule and cyclone reports resulted in more radical course alterations and higher waves encountered.

The above considerations show the importance of precise adjustment of ship's speed characteristic, particularly in bad weather conditions. Failure to adjust it will lead to a difference between calculated and actual position increasing in time.

References

1. Carr, M., Burkley, G.: Hurricane avoidance using the "34-knot wind radius" and "1-2-3" rules. Mariners Weather Log 43(2) (August 1999)
2. National Hurricane Center, http://www.nhc.noaa.gov/ (date of access July 19, 2013)
3. Wiśniewski, B.: The speed characteristics adaptation of Polish Steamship Company's dry bulk vessels to SPOS. Scientific Journals Maritime University of Szczecin 30(102), 143–149 (2012)
4. Wiśniewski, B., Korwin-Piotrowski, T., Wielgosz, M.: Navigational aspecsts of ship's voyage planning taking into account calculations of ETA (Estimated Time of Arival). Scientific Journals Maritime University of Szczecin nr 29(101), 182–187 (2012)
5. Wiśniewski, B., Wielgosz, M., Korwin-Piotrowski, T.: Procedury zintegrowanego plano-wania i programowania tras oceanicznych statków z wykorzystaniem systemu SPOS (Ship Performance Optimisation System). Wydawnictwo AM Szczecin (2012)

Security Increasing Trends in Intelligent Transportation Systems Utilising Modern Image Processing Methods

Emília Bubeníková, Mária Franeková, and Peter Holečko

University of Žilina 010 26 Žilina, Slovakia
{emilia.bubenikova,maria.franekova,peter.holecko}@fel.uniza.sk

Abstract. The paper is focused on a description of modern image processing methods in intelligent vehicles with emphasis on an LDWS (Lane Departure Warning System). The authors describe possible solutions for finding the horizontal road marking using a segmentation method based on a Hough's transformation. In practical realisation the image data have been recorded in the. AVI format using a camera located near the inner rear mirror of the vehicle. A Sobel's detector is used for the edge detection, which obtains a binary image containing pixels representing the borders of objects.

Keywords: intelligent transportation system, digital image processing, LDWS system, security focused applications, Hough's transformation, Sobel's detector.

1 Introduction

The programme to ensure the road safety for the period 2011-2020 established a number of areas that will be subject to the priority of innovation and technological progress in the EU [1]. Its main objective is to build a European strategy to accelerate research, development and use of intelligent integrated safety systems IISS (Intelligent Integrated Safety Systems) including advanced driver assistance systems ADAS (Advanced Driver Assistance Systems) in order to increase the road safety in Europe. The increasing number of accidents is the reason as well as the fact that contributions to attainable standard security measures already reached their limits.

Car manufacturers are developing new systems focused on minimisation of accidents occurrence. Collision warning and prevention of collisions are important components of ADAS systems, such as driving in the lane, adaptive cruise control, night vision, etc. These systems are often used as input image data obtained from cameras placed at appropriate locations such as car rear-view mirrors and windshield. Algorithms running in real time can warn the driver in time about an emerging dangerous situation and possibly subsequently react, for example by communication through the inter-VC (Vehicular Communications) [2].

LDWS systems are important representatives of ADAS systems. These are vehicle electronic systems based on computer vision methods [3], [8] that track the vehicle position in the lane and warn the driver if the vehicle deviates or is about to depart out

J. Mikulski (Ed.): TST 2013, CCIS 395, pp. 353–360, 2013.
© Springer-Verlag Berlin Heidelberg 2013

of the road. Many systems were originally developed for truck drivers, who are particularly susceptible to fatigue and sleepiness due to long driving hours.

2   Methods of Lines Detection in the Image

For a software implementation, we used the international standard ISO 17361:2007, which specifies the definition, classification, functions, human machine interface and test methods alerting against unintentional lane departure [4].

When a vehicle is travelling close to the centre of the lane, it is within the system's "no warning zone", the system does not issue any position warnings. The lane boundary is defined by lane road markings (Fig.1). Around the lane boundary there is an alert zone with the earliest and latest warning lines. If the vehicle leaves the safe zone and enters the alert zone, the system generates a warning to the driver. The LDWS does not take any automatic action to avoid the lane departure or to control the vehicle; therefore, drivers remain responsible for a safe operation of their vehicles.

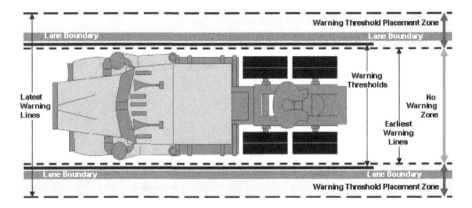

Fig. 1. LDWS warning thresholds and warning threshold placement zones

2.1   Line Detection via a Hough's Transformation

A Hough's transformation (HT) is a segmentation technique often used in cases, where objects have to be detected with a known shape of the boundary (line, circle and so on) [5], [6]. This method searches for the required shapes in a class of shapes using a polling procedure. The procedure is performed in a corresponding parametric space from which the candidate objects are obtained as local maxima in the accumulation space. It uses the principle that an infinite number of lines can pass a point, each in different direction. The transformation tries to identify one of these lines, which best fits the image data by crossing the most pixels. Its utilisation for lines searching using HT results from a normal line equation:

$$y = \frac{x.\cos\Theta}{\sin\Theta} + \frac{r}{\sin\Theta}, \tag{1}$$

where r represents the smallest distance of line (at point $X[x, y]$) from the beginning of coordinate system, Θ is the size of oriented angle from the positive x-axis to the half-line guided from the beginning of the coordinate system upright to the searched line (Fig.2). The use of a normal form of line equation has the advantage that it is independent of the axes orientation.

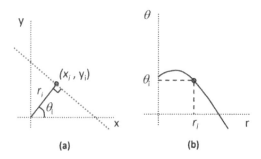

Fig. 2. Hough's transformation a) Cartesian image space, b) polar Hough-space

Coordinates of pixels x, y forming a line are used as the input data. The values of r and Θ are unknown. The coordinates of pixels are stepwise inserted into the equation and the set of r and Θ solutions forms a continuous curve in the Hough's space. The results are stored in a so called accumulator

2.2   The Line Search Algorithm

Image brightness values 0 and 1are the input to the algorithm. We are interested in points with brightness value logic 1.If we assume that the total number of such points is K and a line search algorithm (or line) is very simple and can be summarized in words:

1. We set the accumulator value to zero $A[\Theta_i, r_i]=0$ for all values of Θ_i, r_i,   i.e. $i=1,2, ..., M, j=1,2,..., N$.
2. For each pixel in the image (x_k, y_k) $k=1,2,..., K$, which brightness value is equal to 1and each value Θ_i, $i=1,2, ...M$ is calculated:$r_j = x_k \cos\Theta_i + y_k \sin\Theta_i$and we increase the contents of accumulator $A[\Theta_i, r_j]$ at the position (Θ_i, r_j), i.e. $A[\Theta_i, r_j]= A[\Theta_i, r_j]+1$.
3. After processing all the image pixels, the value in the accumulator $A[\Theta_i, r_j]$ determines the total number of points n_{ij}, that lie in the line with parameters (Θ_i, r_j). We find the maximum value in the accumulator and values Θ_i, r_j, where the maximum occurs, define the line, which contains the highest number of points.

The accuracy, i.e. the maximum deviation from the straight line is given by the fineness of space allocation, i.e. the number of cells M and N, which determine the dimensions of accumulator. The minimum and maximum values Θ and D are in the range $-90 \leq \Theta \leq 90$ and $-D \leq r \leq D$, where Θ is the size of oriented angle and D is the distance between opposite corners of the image.

In most cases before the very transformation a pre-processing method is used, which emphasises the edges of objects. Well known edge detectors can be used (Canny's, Sobel's) to obtain a binary image containing pixels representing the borders of objects.

The input parameter for line searching using the Hough's transformation is a colour section of the image being scanned. This colour image section is transformed from an RGB model into a greyscale image (YUV) according to the relation:

$$\begin{bmatrix} Y \\ U \\ V \end{bmatrix} = \begin{bmatrix} 0.299 & 0.587 & 0.144 \\ -0.147 & -0.289 & 0.436 \\ 0.615 & -0.515 & -0.100 \end{bmatrix} \cdot \begin{bmatrix} R \\ G \\ B \end{bmatrix}. \tag{2}$$

Next, the image is processed according to the calculated threshold by the edge operator. The authors utilised the Sobel's method to find edges in the image because of its satisfying results in a relatively short time [7].

2.3   Algorithm for Line Crossing Detection

The lane and the path of the vehicles are captured by cameras. Then from the video sequences the system estimates the vehicle position on the road and the lane width. Detection of line crossing in a software implementation works on the principle of seeking intersection of line segments. The position of found road marking lines(with HT) is cyclically compared to the segment, which has precisely defined values and represents the car in the image (Fig. 3).

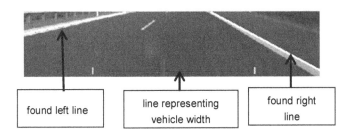

Fig. 3. Principle of line crossing detection

The intersection of two line segments on a plane can be determined in a general plane using the following mathematical analysis:

$$d(A,B,C) = x_A(y_B - y_C + y_A(x_C - x_B) + x_B y_C - y_B x_C), \tag{3}$$

where A, B, C are points of lines with coordinates $A[x_A, y_A]$, $B[x_B, y_B]$, $C[x_C, y_C]$.

Function $d(A,B,C)$ takes different signs according to the position in the half-plane defined by line BC. So if $d(A, P, Q).d(B, P, Q)<0$ line PQ separates the points A, B. If we examine the values:

$$s_A = d(A,P,Q), \quad s_p = d(P,A,B), \tag{4}$$

$$s_B = d(B,P,Q), \quad s_Q = d(Q,A,B).$$

If line segments AB, PQ do not have a common point then:

$$s_A.s_B > 0 \quad or \quad s_p.s_Q > 0. \tag{5}$$

That means they do not intersect and the line has not been crossed.

3   Software Implementation and Its Testing

The software implementation of a moving object (vehicle) detection on a road, with a focus on the detection of lane departure detection has been performed in MatlabR2010a using the Signal Processing Toolbox. The whole process of data processing was carried out in a number of logically related steps, which are based on a standard chain of image information processing (data acquisition, digitization, pre-processing, segmentation, object detection and description, understanding the content). The software implemented detection of road markings and crossing lines is schematically shown in Fig.4.

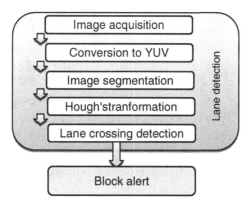

Fig. 4. Process of crossing lane detection system implementation and its links to block alert

The authors have chosen a segmentation method based on a Hough's transformation, which is a standard function of the software in which also the algorithm for line crossing detection from the captured colour video has been implemented.

The input data for the algorithm testing were recorded in advance and video sequences of the area in front of a car stored on a hard drive. The image data were first captured using a digital camera, with video recording function with 640x480 pixels resolution, which was placed under the windscreen in the interior mirror of a motor vehicle [6].

The algorithm sequentially reads individual video frames. Because the video recordings also contain data irrelevant for line crossing detection (horizon, outer area of vehicle's bonnet) each frame had to be cropped. The region of interest has been allocated as a road segment located in front of the vehicle and it was defined empirically with dimensions of 580x100 pixels.

The colour section of the image of interest is transformed to a greyscale and using an automatically determined threshold it is processed by the Sobel's edge detector. The output of edge operator application is a binary image.

HT functions (the principle is described above) are applied to the binary image. The output is a data structure containing positions of starting and ending points of lines, the distance of lines and the beginning of the coordinate system and the size of the oriented angle between the positive x-axis and the half-line guided from the beginning of the coordinate system upright to the searched line. If there are broken lines on the road, many lines are found. Fig.4 presents in red colour the lines found using HT. Their parameters are input to the algorithm for connection of similar lines, which compares the size of the oriented angle between all lines. The comparison finds several favourites, which angle orientation corresponds to the largest number of lines found at a defined adjustable toleration (default value is 5 degrees) and determines a single line.

The outputs are new lines parameters entering a so called poller. The poller's task is to determine validity of the line found from the last 10 frames. The poller ratio value (*n* out of 10) can be adjusted before the program start.

These data progress to the next processing using the algorithm for line crossing detection (the principle was mentioned earlier) and the fact is indicated by an optical information in a form of letter „A" (alert) on the image (Fig. 5).

Fig. 5. Display of alarm in image

To find optimal values of parameters of some input variables, like sensitivity of lines joining, votes ratio in the poller, alarm threshold setting, many combinations of input variables settings have been tested.

The correctness of detection has been validated based on the comparison of in advance determined frame numbers in which a subjectively determined line crossing has been determined in the examined .AVI record. Consequently these values were compared with the values determined on the same record using the designed algorithm. Three line crossings occurred in the selected testing record. For some ranges of testing input parameters the line crossing has not been detected at all or the detection was delayed by several tens of frames. Fig. 6 shows the comparison of subjectively determined values of video frames (red colour) and violet values of frames determined using the algorithm.

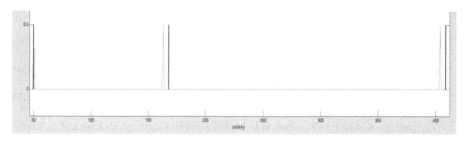

Fig. 6. Comparison of subjectively determined frames and frame values when an alarm has been triggered

4   Conclusion

For a practical utilisation of the algorithm it is desirable to detect line crossing and issue an alert in a visual form even before physical line crossing. Based on this requirement the input parameters values for a correct detection have been selected as follows:

- sensitivity of lines joining (values range 3-5),
- votes ratio in the poller (values range 4-6),
- alarm threshold setting (values range 10, 20).

These values were obtained as optimal based on a subjective line crossing comparison in frames numbered 50, 168, 409 and the designed algorithm, as it is shown in Fig. 6.

Currently the authors are working on an extension of line detection to detect temporary traffic signs, which on Slovak roads is realised using an orange colour. Temporary markings shall have priority over the original markings, and so their detection and recognition could be used to more precisely interpret the situation on the road.

Acknowledgments. This work has been supported by the European Regional Development Fund and the Ministry of Education of the Slovak Republic, ITMS 26220220089 "New methods of measurement of physical dynamic parameter and interactions of motor vehicles, traffic flow and road" and by the Educational Grant Agency of the Slovak Republic (KEGA) Number: 024ŽU-4/2012: Modernization of technology and education methods orientated towards the area of cryptography for safety critical applications.

References

1. European Strategies, `http://ec.europa.eu/transport/strategies/2011_white_paper_en.htm` (date of access: July 03, 2013)
2. Beňuš, J., Bubeníková, E., Franeková, M.: Effectiveness of digital signature schemes for use in vehicular communication within intelligent transportation system. In: TRANSCOM 2013, June 24-26, pp. 17–20 (2013) ISBN 978-80-554-0692-3
3. Hlaváč, V., Sedláček, M.: Signal and Image Processing (Zpracování signálu a obrazu), ČVUT Praha (2009)
4. ISO 17361: 2007, Intelligent transport systems – Lane departure warning systems – Performance requirements and test procedures (2007)
5. Hough, P.: Methodand Means for Recognizing Complex Patterns, U.S. Patent 3069654 (1962)
6. Zolotová, I., Karch, P.: Contribution to modification of Graph cut method and its implementation in the image segmentation. International Journal of Circuits, Systems and Signal Processing, 49–52 (2012) ISSN 19984464
7. Bubeníková, E., Muzikářová, Ľ., Halgaš, J.: Application of Image Processing in Intelligent Transport Systems. In: 11th IFAC/IEEE International Conference on Programmable Devices and Embedded Systems, Brno, pp. 53–56 (2012) ISBN 978-3-902823-21-2
8. Šimák, V., Hrbček, J., Pirník, R.: Traffic flow video-detection. In: International Conference SSKIVyšná Boca, p. 4 (February 2010) ISBN 978-80-227-3241-3
9. Mikulski, J.: Using telematics in transport. In: Mikulski, J. (ed.) TST 2010. CCIS, vol. 104, pp. 175–182. Springer, Heidelberg (2010)
10. Mikulski, J.: The possibility of using telematics in urban transportation. In: Mikulski, J. (ed.) TST 2011. CCIS, vol. 239, pp. 54–69. Springer, Heidelberg (2011)
11. Mikulski, J.: Telematic Technologies in Transportation. In: Janecki, R., Sierpiński, G. (eds.) Contemporary Transportation Systems. Selected Theoretical and Practical Problems. New Culture of mobility, pp. 131–143. Publishing House of the Silesian University of Technology. Monograph no. 324, Gliwice (2011)

Monitoring of Cargo in Logistic Systems of Transport and Storage

Andrzej Bujak[1] and Paweł Zając[2]

[1] Wrocław School of Banking, Faculty of Finance and Management,
29-31 Fabryczna St, 53-609 Wrocław, Poland
andrzej.bujak@interia.pl
[2] Wrocław University of Technology, Faculty of Mechanical Engineering,
5 Łukasiewicza St, 50- 371 Wrocław, Poland
pawel.zajac@pwr.wroc.pl

Abstract. The article addresses an automatic identification technology and its most common applications in cargo tracking systems. Based on the data acquired, capacities of individual technologies have been described and methods of implementing them in specific telematic systems discussed. The paper provides an algorithm for the choice of automatic identification technology under preset real conditions.

Keywords: optimisation of logistic system, energy consumption, bar codes.

1 Introduction

Cargo monitoring is a basic functional element of any modern logistic system, enabling efficient management of supply chains.

The following definition may be assumed [2]: "Monitoring is establishing the identity or the type of an object based on the properties read (code, PIN, biometric features) and finding a pattern corresponding to the property read in a database comprising all the objects entered into the system. By that means, one may identify goods marked with bar codes or RFID tags. When using biometrics, an individual code is established based on tests of the given property, e.g. a dermatoglyphic pattern, an iris pattern or a face image, followed by a search in a database containing patterns of individual codes registered in the system."

Academic publications usually place an explicit equation mark between monitoring and the "track-trace" process when dealing with units of pieces with different sizes managed in dispatching activities.

However, even though the aforementioned function is very useful, monitoring must also enable geographic positioning of cargo and identification of its status conditional on the function of temperature, pressure, humidity etc. Moreover, besides cargo monitoring, in contemporary logistic systems, there is also a demand for monitoring of persons (due to safety issues related to mass events or implants) and of animals.

J. Mikulski (Ed.): TST 2013, CCIS 395, pp. 361–369, 2013.
© Springer-Verlag Berlin Heidelberg 2013

Monitoring of certain physical parameters (e.g. a tank wall deformation) of such objects as power plants, planes or marine vessels enables their safe operation.

Monitoring thus understood constitutes a very broad field for consideration, since one may think of position and condition monitoring of cargo/persons during transport, reloading works, any type of cargo handling operations, warehousing or storage. Each of these stages involves a need for inspection and supervision resulting from the necessity to take appropriate care for the cargo/people. Hence the following notions may appear in the discourse: cargo tracking and track & trace systems, traceability, cargo status control, automatic identification as well as a number of auxiliary technologies, such as barcodes, RFID, radio communications, GPS/GPRS, GSM, databases and database management systems etc.

The main premises for implementation of a vehicle, object or cargo identification technologies include rapid and reliable data acquisition and storage. In the business practice, this is referred to as the Automatic Data Capture (ADC) and is most frequently based on barcodes and Electronic Data Interchange (EDI) substituting hardcopy documents with electronic messages [2].

Depending on individual needs, various ADC techniques are applied in practice, and they may be classified under the following 6 groups [4]:

- optical, including barcodes,
- magnetic,
- electromagnetic, including data reading and radio signal modulation (RFID),
- biometric,
- tactile,
- smart cards.

Besides the aforementioned solutions applied in cargo monitoring systems, one may also use active tags of:

- shock and tilt,
- time and temperature,
- freshness,

as well as GSP and GPRS technology based telematic systems.

The choice of an appropriate technology of automatic identification, transfer and storage of data concerning objects as well as their encoding seems to be an issue fairly difficult to handle for a manager. This paper addresses algorithms proposed to enable the choice of a suitable monitoring technology depending on the field of activity.

2   Problem Analysis

The cost-effectiveness of using tags has been analysed with regard to shock and tilt tags, since about 50% of all reasons for cargo damage are related to the hazards they indicate. The following assumptions have been made for the sake of the analysis:

- transport scale – 120 thousand units of palleted cargo per annum,
- base (without cargo status monitoring) percentage of cargo damage on the level of 0.16% of the cargo transported per annum,
- value of an average unit load – PLN 1.5 thousand,
- average price of a single tag – PLN 0.79.

Furthermore, in accordance with the principles of tag application it has been assumed that the choice of tags is correct and that every second case requires using both shock and tilt tag, leading to an average cost of tags per single cargo at the amount of PLN 11.80.

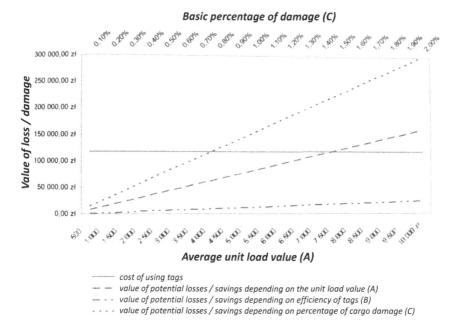

Fig. 1. Annual cost-effectiveness analysis of cargo status monitoring tags based on the example of shock and tilt tags

Three analyses illustrated in Fig. 1 have been conducted for the foregoing assumptions:

A. The cost of using tags has been compared with the value of potential losses (and hence the potential savings) depending on the average value of the unit loads transported. This analysis has implied that using tags for cheap shipments is by no means economically sound. The tags are simply too expensive. For the assumed damage percentage (i.e. 0.16%), the value of losses is higher than the cost of using tags with reference to all the cargo transported only when the value of a single shipment comes to PLN 7.5. Consequently, one may assume that a full efficiency of tags, i.e. elimination of all possible defects, would only lead to savings being attained on transport of unit loads with the value exceeding PLN 0.75.

B. Savings may be attained when using tags depending on their functional efficiency understood as the tag activation (assumed to be certain) once a nonconformity has been registered and, more importantly, saving the cargo from being damaged. However, the tag activation itself is no guarantee of the damage avoidance, still it makes it possible to document the manner of cargo handling which may constitute grounds for compensation claims. The results obtained in this case have implied that using tags brings no savings, although it significantly contributes to reducing the loss values. However, the expenses incurred to apply the tags with all the cargo transported (at their average value on the level of PLN 1.5) will not even return when they are one hundred per cent efficient.
C. The case shows changes to the loss value depending on different base levels of the cargo damage percentage against the tag application costs. And again, 100% efficiency of tags has been assumed.

The analysis has proved that at the damage percentage of around 1.2% (about 7÷8 times more than under average conditions), the value of losses and so the value of potential savings exceeds the tag application costs in all the cargo transported. Consequently, not until the damaged share of unit loads with the average value of PLN 1.5 comes to the above level may the tags bring some tangible savings. However, one should also imagine a situation of an enterprise recording 120 cases of damage, and that of entire unit loads, per 10 thousand unit loads shipped. Such a number and scale of damage is rather unusual, and should certainly not be envisaged [5].

3   Algorithm for the Choice of Suitable Cargo Monitoring Technology under Preset Real Conditions

Having analysed individual cargo monitoring technologies, one may come up with criteria according to which an algorithm for their choice can be developed. The fundamental breakdown in this respect assumes the options of point-based, continuous and whole vehicle monitoring.

Point-based monitoring involves identification of shipments by a man using barcode readers or checking whether a preset shock or tilt value has been exceeded at the given tag.

Continuous monitoring is only possible within a warehouse, but it is more effective when it comes to theft prevention (alarm gates) and additional services such as automatic recording of shipments by passing them through registration gates integrated with the given warehouse management system.

Monitoring of whole vehicles is only possible after packed and appropriately marked packages have left the warehouse. Besides vehicle position monitoring, it is also possible to record numerous other useful parameters and send them to the parties directly interested in the given shipment on an ongoing basis.

A mixed monitoring mode combines at least two technologies ensuring monitoring continuity at all stages of the logistics chain.

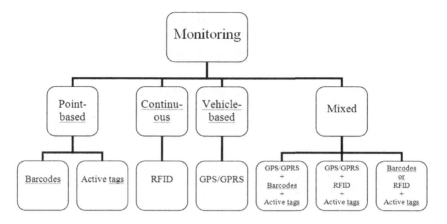

Fig. 2. Breakdown of monitoring systems

3.1 Choice of a Suitable Barcode

Barcodes may be categorised according to the amount of information they contain. As the need be, a barcode may only enable a reference to a database where more information on the product is stored (e.g. storage location), which is the case of line codes, or it may be a database itself as in two dimensional barcodes. The number of digits or characters forming the code has changed in time, and the most common barcode used nowadays is the GS1-128, which ensures sufficiently large amount of data being encoded (128 alphanumeric characters) whereas the costs of its implementation do not differ significantly from other line codes. As far as two-dimensional barcodes are concerned, there is no clear market leader, and depending on the region of the world, companies tend to apply various solutions.

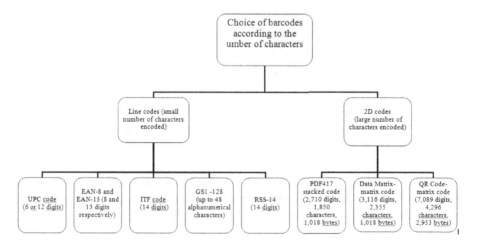

Fig. 3. Choice of barcodes according to the number of characters

Two-dimensional barcodes are characterised by a certain advantage compared to line codes, since they are better secured, and owing to small dimensions, they may be used to mark very small items. There are also the RSS-14 reduced size line barcodes providing an alternative to small 2D barcodes. However, they do not require any new equipment to be purchased when a company has already been using line code technologies and scanners. The same applies to complex codes which may be scanned using the same laser and video devices. In this case, the line code constitutes a pattern for a 2D element searching which enhances the scanning process. The diagram provided in Fig. 3 can be used for the sake of a barcode type selection.

3.2   Choice of RFID Tags

Passive tags are most commonly used in logistics owing to their small dimensions and costs. A sample chip manufactured by Hitachi is 0.05 on 0.05 mm in size, and its thickness enables it to be placed on a sheet of paper. The second type of tags, namely the semi-passive ones, feature a battery powering the microchip only, which enables acquisition of such data as temperature of the goods transported, for instance. Batteries of active tags power both the chip and the antenna.

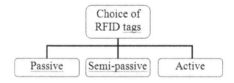

Fig. 4. Choice of RFID tags

The main feature of the RFID technology is a wide range as well as the application of a reading method which does not require the device to be visible. This type of tags enables tracking of the product movement. Goods in packages marked with RFID tags may be registered many times as they move from location to location, both within an enterprise and along the entire supply chain.

Therefore, while analysing the costs related to the RFID technology, one should enquire about the value by which the flow capacity of the given warehouse is to increase, and hence that of the supply chain as well, once the system has been implemented. The answer may be obtained by examining each case separately.

As a matter of fact, the actual limitation is currently the cost. The amount to be invested in the carrier is approx. EUR 0.20 which may rise considerably on large quantities of goods being handled to become an important encumbrance, incomparably larger than with a "traditional" barcode the fabrication of which costs but a small fraction of a eurocent.

3.3   Choice of a Suitable Active Tag

Application of active tags is economically sound only when handling valuable shipments. Bearing in mind the analysis discussed in section 3, it should be concluded that using these tags for goods of moderate value is simply unprofitable. Benefits may only be involved in monitoring of random unit loads in order to increase the quality of cargo management processes while handling and transporting goods. It should be emphasised that the cargo status monitoring is conducted on an ongoing basis and the actual tag application outcome is whether it becomes activated or not, this leading to a lack of information about the stage of the logistic chain at which the minimum or maximum temperature is exceeded, a shock takes place or the cargo tilts.

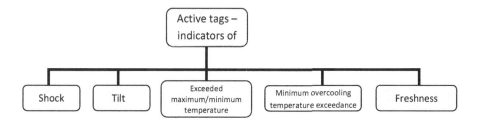

Fig. 5. Types of active tags

It must also be added that, compared to entire GPS/GPRS systems, active tags are a cheaper solution but they do not offer the same multitude of solutions and on-line access to all parameters, and not merely the selected ones. However, a considerable advantage of tags is the ability to monitor cargo at each stage of the logistics chain.

3.4   Choice of the GPS/GPRS Monitoring System

Cargo monitoring systems based on application of the GPS and GPRS technologies are the most expensive solutions discussed in this paper, but they ensure the most comprehensive spectrum of options of real and instant acquisition of information concerning the cargo transported or the whole vehicle. Unlike with barcodes and the RFID technology, they do not identify specific products and storage locations. Compared to tags, they immediately deliver data on the change of product parameters working automatically, providing information on the time, place and extent of exceeding the chosen parameter, and all handled without man's interference or a possibility that the data have been tampered with. Hence it is the single most efficient of discussed solutions in terms of application in bulk cargo transport and whole vehicle monitoring.

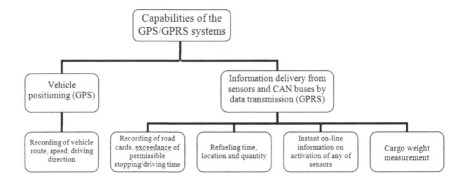

Fig. 6. Capabilities of the GPS/GPRS systems

4   Conclusion

Under the current conditions of the transport market, the carrier assessment criteria are not only the shipment delivery time and cost but also its condition. Hence the increasing interest in the cargo monitoring systems being observed. When handing a shipment over to a carrier or a logistic company, one has specific requirements concerning appropriate quality and conditions in which the cargo is to be shipped. The choice of monitoring technology primarily depends on the scope of services covering the cargo/the vehicle (machine)/the person.

1. Basic functions of product identification are fulfilled by means of barcodes whose structure depends on the amount of data stored (1D codes can hold less information than 2D codes). In combination with a database, line barcodes may provide information on the product position, whereas two-dimensional codes, owing to their increased information storage capacity on a small area, may themselves function as a database travelling together with the cargo (e.g. in a bill of lading). Also technologies of direct application of codes on various products (on the product wall) are becoming more and more popular.

2. Transponders (RFID) enable remote identification of shipments by means of an antenna, without the necessity of scanning as with barcodes. The cargo identification process is much faster, and hence the data transfer capacity between reloading points increases. There are various types of RFID tags available, and their prices differ as well. And even though this technology is more expensive than barcodes, it offers a wider scope of application. The capacity to repeatedly record IDs as they move from one to another location enables shipment tracking not only inside the factory, but also during distribution as well as in reloading points, warehouses and destinations, namely in the course of the entire cargo transport process.

3. Active tags provide an on-line information on the conditions in which the shipment is transported, e.g. the indicators of shock and tilt, time and temperature as well as freshness. A definite advantage of these identifiers is the cargo monitoring at each stage of the logistics chain without the necessity of ensuring the infrastructure mentioned in items 1 and 2 of the Conclusions. The information supplied lacks the

function of location, and hence one must presume certain things. There is also no information on the time when damage occurred, therefore it is impossible to conclude at what stage the defined transport regimes were violated.

4. The most technically advanced solutions are provided by GPS/GPRS systems. They transfer plenty of parameters such as those concerning the vehicle location, fuel level or the cargo weight. Their primary area of application is monitoring of vehicles, whereas by installing additional sensors, coders, transponders or active tags, their functionality may be considerably expanded with selected functions (e.g. tyre pressure detection). All the information acquired may be observed in real time using a computer. A certain shortcoming of such systems is the fact that they do not monitor individual shipments separately but only watch over the given parameter characteristic of the entire cargo space. What they also do not monitor is the cargo status during its loading and unloading as well as at the storage site when it has reached the destination point.

References

1. Active Labels for Impact & Tilt,
   http://www.shocklog.com (date of access July 17, 2013)
2. Cardco – plastic cards, http://www.kartyplastikowe.cardco.home.pl/
   (date of access July 17, 2013)
3. Vehicle monitoring centre, http://www.cma.com.pl/ (date of access July 17, 2013)
4. Durski, W., Redmer, A.: Monitorowanie stanu ładunków podczas transportu. Logistyka 3 (2008)
5. Kwaśniowski, S., Zając, P. (eds.): Automatyczna identyfikacja w systemach logistycznych. OWPW, Wrocław (2004)
6. Lisińska-Kuśnierz, M., Ucherek, M.: Opakowania aktywne i inteligentne. WNPTTŻ, Kraków (2003)
7. Code 16K Barcode Generator,
   http://www.racoindustries.com/barcodegenerator/
   (date of access July 17, 2013)
8. Cold Chain Technologies, http://www.coldchaintech.com (date of access July 17, 2013)
9. Damage Prevention Specialists,
   http://www.shockwatch.com.au/swlables.htm
   (date of access July 17, 2013)
10. DataMatrix, http://www.datamatrix.pl/budowa.php (date of access July 17, 2013)
11. DirectPartMarking – 2D BarCode, http://www.industrialvision.co.th (date of access July 17, 2013)
12. EAN Barcodes and Ecom, http://barcodes.gs1us.org (date of access July 17, 2013)
13. Fresh Check Indicator, http://www.lifelinestechnology.com/ (date of access July 17, 2013)
14. GS1 Polska ILiM, Etykieta logistyczna GS1 w Europie, http://www.gs1pl.org
   (date of access July 17, 2013)
15. Software Dungeon Gates, software-dungeon.co.uk (date of access July 17, 2013)
16. Teleartom Sp. z o.o, http://www.teleartom.com.pl/ (date of access July 17, 2013)
17. UID World, http://www.uidworld.com/Images/uid_direct_part.jpg
   (date of access: July 17, 2013)

Vision Method for Rope Angle Swing Measurement for Overhead Travelling Cranes – Validation Approach

Paweł Hyla and Janusz Szpytko

AGH University of Science and Technology,
A. Mickiewicza Av. 30, 30-059 Krakow, Poland
{hyla,szpytko}@agh.edu.pl

Abstract. Cranes operation process focused on goods fixed to an elastic rope requires elimination of possible negative phenomena such as load deflection from equilibrium. Modern trends in practice depend on minimizing the negative effects of payload swinging. This paper presents a method for measuring the swing angle of steel ropes. In the article, the authors attention has been focused on issues related to the possibility of using a "smart camera" device in the contactless sensor architecture for geometric parameters measurement. The second part of the paper was focused on the described method accuracy validation. For this purpose, a contact sensor built on a rotary encoder base was used. The obtained results provide a basis for further research on the described method improvement.

Keywords: sway sensor, image analysis, overhead traveling crane.

1   Introduction

The cranes, which belong to the group of Large Rail-Mounted Handling Devices (LRMHD) [1], play a significant role in handling the goods or supporting important technological operations in heavy industry. At present, in a variety of automated manufacturing processes higher and higher requirements are imposed on the safety, efficiency and reliability of crane operations [2, 3, 4]. That challenge is connected with the necessity of optimizing, organizing and synchronizing all the transportation operations performed by LRMHD devices. The contemporary automation level of the crane operations involves implementing in the crane control system solutions enabling precise positioning of the payload, with reduction of their unwanted sway during moving the cargo from the starting point to its destination [5]. The discussed proposal can be realized by controlling efficiently the speed of all crane mechanisms motion to reduce or even to eliminate interacting dynamical forces, combined with sudden accelerations [1, 4]. However, it is important that the transport task must be accomplished as fast as possible, too.

The research problem connected with an anti-sway problem [6, 7] has been extensively researched over the past decades. In general, proposed and described solutions can be classified as open and closed-loop control systems [4]. Close loop

J. Mikulski (Ed.): TST 2013, CCIS 395, pp. 370–377, 2013.
© Springer-Verlag Berlin Heidelberg 2013

sway angle control methods are strongly connected with the necessity of measuring the angle of a swinging rope under dynamic effect of the suspended cargo in real time. This solution requires the use of a special, reliable [8] physical sensor for measuring rope angles in a reference system. In turn, open-loop methods are described as preventive methods. The anti-swing parameters usually are calculated on the base of a mathematical model of a swinging mass suspended on a weightless strand (mathematical pendulum). In fact the final anti-sway system setpoints depend on the boundary conditions, usually connected with the crane rope length and the payload mass [6, 7, 9]. The open-loop methods have also some disadvantages (neglecting a not full robustness against system uncertainties, parameters variation, system nonlinearities and disturbances resulting for example from external phenomena such as wind). Some authors believe that an effective anti-sway system in an open loop architecture especially for a crane cannot be described like a single pendulum model and propose a much more complicated double-pendulum model [10, 11, 12].

The paper presents a concept of contactless vision method based on telematics [13, 14] for measurement of an angle of a swinging rope with suspended payload for a material handling device. The authors attention was focused on the method usability and on accuracy estimation. The tests were conducted on a scaled physical model of an overhead traveling crane with the maximum hoisting capacity of 150 kg. A contactless angle measurement method with the use of image analysis technique was carried out in real time but only in one plane.

2   Image Analysis in Contactless Strand Swing Measurement

Among the six major human senses like vision, hearing, smell, taste, touch, and non-touch feelings ability, vision is probably the one that can deliver a lot of information [15] about surroundings, where a human being is actually present. Additionally, the captured data must be processed in a short period of time, closely related to real time. However, a large amount of possessed information is linked with necessary sufficient own brain power for fast and reliable information processing in real time. Thus, a device with a video stream gathering possibility and image analysis functionality seems to be a natural substitute of human vision ability provided that the vision ability is connected with sufficient computer power for image analysing.

The vision system has evolved together with a new approach to image processing issues. A new quality achieved through a combined image acquired with processing by the camera itself shows a new kind of embedded vision system device for which a new term – a smart camera – starts to be used [16, 17, 18, 19]. The ultimate purpose of a smart camera is to mimic human eyes and brain functionally and simultaneously interpret what the camera "sees", through embedded so-called artificial intelligence functionalities. The EOS (*Embedded Operating System*) constitutes the main feature of smart cameras [20]. A characteristic feature of the EOS is a unique composition of kernel, shell and the file system of mother OS (*Operating System*). Additionally, the EOS has got attached drivers and services, which complete the software structure.

Through a unique composition, tailored for the specific hardware, the embedded system becomes an integral part of a specific device. Usually, embedded systems do not have an open architecture that allows to add and install a new equipment [21].

2.1 Vision Method with a Smart Camera for Swinging Strand Angle Extraction

A hardware architecture containing a smart camera solution has been adapted for a non-contact measurement [22, 23] of the strand swing, using image analysis techniques. For this purpose an XCI V3 Sony smart camera has been suspended under the trolley hoist mechanism (Fig. 1) in such a way that the field of camera view covers all ropes scrolling through a pulley block mounted next to the crane's hook.

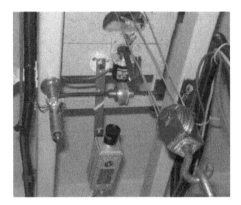

Fig. 1. Sony XCI V3 smart camera suspended under the crane hoist mechanism

Figure 1 presents not processed screen shots captured by the smart camera. For supervising smart camera actions a dedicated and embedded system was compiled, containing a fully operational NI Vision Builder AI software [24]. The algorithm was divided to four phases.

In the first phase the images were taken by the smart camera. All images were acquired in the grey scale with 640 x 480 pixels size. An example of four unprocessed images captured by the system is presented in Figures 2 to 5. Next, the image was shrunk to the region with definite dimensions of h x w pixels (so-called ROI) [25]. Then the formed Region of Interest in the second phase was subject to binarization with a suitable range of threshold (assigning to each pixel the value of 0 or 1). This step enables to isolate the rope edges from each image for the angle extraction, independently of the environmental background and of natural lighting level changes. The preliminary image is processed according to the following equations (1-3):

$$\text{ImgSource} \equiv \{s_{\mu,v}\}_{h \times w}. \qquad s_{\mu,v} \in \langle 0,255 \rangle \qquad (1)$$

where:

s   - image source,
h   - image height,
w   - image width.

based on the binarization threshold value we can achieve:

$$\text{ImgDestination} \equiv \left\{bin_{\mu,v}\right\}_{h\times w}. \qquad bin_{\mu,v} \in \langle 0,1 \rangle \qquad (2)$$

in which:

$$bin_{\mu,v} = \left\{ \begin{array}{c} 1 \quad \left(s_{\mu,v} \geq p_b\right) \wedge \left(s_{\mu,v} \leq p_{b+1}\right) \\ else \end{array} \right\}. \qquad (3)$$

where:

bin - binarization,
p_b - binarization threshold.

An example of equations (1-3) in relation to a single horizontal line of captured image is presented in Figure 2.

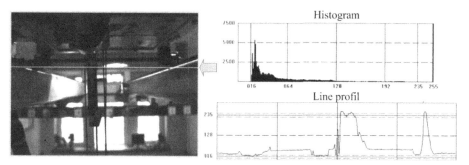

Fig. 2. Image histogram with a profile of single horizontal line (the data are represented on a scale from 0-255)

Finally, in the last phase, the algorithm has an ability to distribute measured values directly into the automated control system, through a dedicated application connection (in this case it is an NI Distribution Manager System) that enables the data exchange between other host computers inside the same workgroup, to which the smart camera was connected.

The applicability of described method of contactless strand angle measurement depends on the closed-loop control system adaptation possibility. Thus, there is a need to determine the sampling rate of the presented measuring system. The time for each stage realization was estimated based on five hundred loops. The obtained results are presented in Table 1.

Table 1. Non-contact vision system for strand angle extraction - time consumption

	$t_{average}$ [ms]	$\sigma*$	t_{min} [ms]	t_{max} [ms]
Step 1: Image acquiring	5.380	1.886	4.000	12.000
Step 2: ROI creating	2.958	0.199	2.654	3.453
Step 3: Threshold image	2.080	0.523	1.000	3.000
Step 4: Edge finding	10.354	0.989	9.363	13.263
Step 5: Geometry measure	10.636	0.924	9.678	13.896
Step 6: Variable sharing	31.329	1.775	27.339	36.526
Total time	**62.737**	-	**54.034**	**82.138**

* Standard deviation.

3   Non-contact Vision Method for Strand Swing Amplitude Measurement – Method Accuracy Verification

In the implementation of a closed-loop control system not only the sampling rate is important, but also the measurement accuracy. To verify the measurements obtained with the vision system help, the sway angle was obtained using a contact technique, too. The contact sensor assembly with a rotary encoder with 2000 pulse per rotation resolution and 10 cm leveller with punched holes (enabling a slide on the rope), was mounted directly on the steel strand. The described sensor was mounted directly on the rope [26].

The detailed data acquisition system for a swing sensor solution is presented in Figure 3.

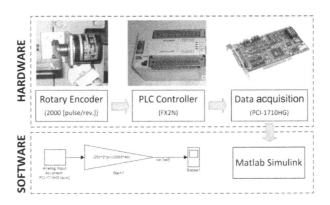

Fig. 3. Data acquisition system for rope sway angle extraction with a rotary encoder

3.1   Experiment Description

The rope length of the overhead travelling crane physical model was fixed as 0.1 m, additionally the rope payload was assumed to be 100 kg. After that, using both the encoder contact swing sensor and the non-contact vision measure system a swing angle was recorded independently for each sensor. The obtained data was synchronized in time and presented on two graphs. The first graph (Fig. 4), presents the data obtained with the encoder sensor help and the second one (Fig. 5) presents the data acquired from the vision system.

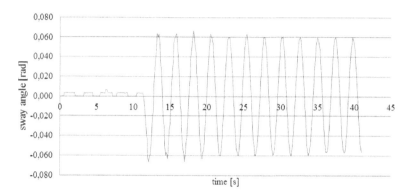

Fig. 4. Characteristics of the rope angle sway measure in the contact technique (rotary encoder with a leveller)

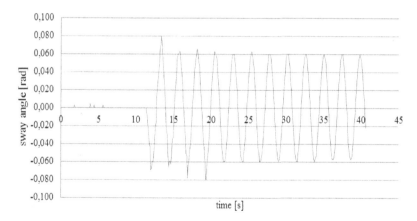

Fig. 5. Characteristics of the rope angle sway measure in the non-contact technique (smart camera)

Analysing Figure 4 and 5 it is possible to conclude that the sensor built on the encoder base (in the contact technique) is more sensitive than the non-contact vision sensor (comparing the first 10 seconds of both diagrams). Further consideration of the diagrams enable noticing a difference in measurement of 0.02 rad, which in the angular measure constitutes $1°14'$. In percentage terms, this result represents nearly 12% of the total maximum rope swing. Although the obtained results are satisfactory, there is still a need for further research to get a better performance.

4   Conclusion

The paper focuses the attention on one of several issues connected with a real problem related to the need of precise movement of suspended load from a starting point to a destination point, according to a designed trajectory without or with minimum payload sway. The problem occurs especially in the handling heavy and large-size loads in steel and heavy industry, but it is not limited to only this type of cargo transportation.

The presented contactless sensor allows to use closed-loop control systems to prevent excessive sway of the suspended load during transport. In practice, it is an important step in the positioning accuracy, safety and reliability of the goods handling process by all material handling devices, in which the payload is moved using steel ropes or chains. However, the described sensor as a part of a bigger closed-loop control system has a chance to play a particular role in an anti-sway solution in the future. The main advantage of presented solution consists in a non-contact measurement and in the method universality. The adaptation to different crane types with all kinds of ropes with different diameters was achieved only through the image analysis software modification. However, at the moment the main unsolved disadvantages are related with a high sensitivity of the described method to all kinds extraneous disturbances connected with electromagnetic interference, especially connected with visible radiation. The impossibility to use the presented non-contact vision sensor in darkness is the second important fault.

Acknowledgment. The research project is financed from the Polish Science budget in the year 2013.

References

1. Szpytko, J.: Kształtowanie procesu eksploatacji środków transportu bliskiego. Biblioteka Problemów Eksploatacji, ITE, Kraków - Radom (2004)
2. Smoczek, J., Szpytko, J.: A mechatronics approach in intelligent control systems of the overhead traveling cranes prototyping. Information Technology and Control 37(2), 154–158 (2008)
3. Szpytko, J., Wozniak, D.A.: To keep operational potential of transport device e-based on reliability indicators. In: European Safety and Reliability Conference ESREL, Stavanger, Norway, pp. 2377–2384 (2007)
4. Hyla, P.: The crane control systems: A survey. In: Proc. of the 17th International Conference of Methods and Models in Automation and Robotics MMAR 2012, Międzyzdroje, August 27-30, pp. 505–509 (2012)

5. Smoczek, J., Szpytko, J., Hyla, P.: Non-collision path planning of a payload in crane operating space. Solid State Phenomena, Mechatronic Systems and Materials IV 198, 559–564 (2013)
6. Smoczek, J., Szpytko, J.: Fuzzy logic approach to the gain scheduling crane control system. In: Proc. of 15th IFAC International Conference on Methods and Models in Automation and Robotics MMAR, pp. 261–266 (2010)
7. Smoczek, J., Szpytko, J.: Design of gain scheduling anti-sway crane controller using genetic fuzzy system. In: Proc. of IFAC 17th International Conference on Methods and Models in Automation and Robotics MMAR, pp. 573–578 (2012)
8. Smalko, Z., Szpytko, J.: Safety in engineering practice. In: 17th European Safety and Reliability Conf. ESREL, Valencia, Spain, pp. 1231–1237 (2009)
9. Smoczek, J.: Intelligent crane control systems. ITE, Kraków-Radom (2011)
10. Kenison, M., Singhose, W.: Input shaper design for double-pendulum planar gantry cranes. In: Conference on Control Applications, pp. 1–6 (1999)
11. Neupert, J., Heinze, T., Sawodny, O., Schneider, K.: Observer design for boom cranes with double-pendulum effect. In: 18th IEEE International Conference on Control Applications, Part of 2009 IEEE Multi-conference on Systems and Control, Saint Petersburg, Russia, pp. 1545–1550 (2009)
12. Khalil, H.K.: Nonlinear systems. Prentice Hall, Upper Saddle River (2002)
13. Mikulski, J. (ed.): Advances in transport systems telematics. Wydawnictwa Komunikacji i Łączności, Warszawa (2008)
14. Szpytko, J., Kocerba, A., Tekielak, M.: Telematic based transport device tracking and supervision system. In: Dolgui, A., Morel, G., Pereria, C.E. (eds.) Preprints INCOM 2006: 12th IFAC/ IFIP/ IFORS/ IEEE/ IMS Symposium on Information Control Problems in Manufacturing, pp. 99–104. Ecole Nationale Superieure des Mines, Saint Etienne (2006)
15. Shi, Y.: Real, F. D.: Smart Cameras: Fundamentals and Classification. In: Belbachir, A.N. (ed.) Smart Cameras. Springer (2010)
16. Belbachir, A.N. (ed.): Smart Cameras. Springer (2009)
17. Hornberg, A. (ed.): Handbook of Machine Vision. Wiley-Vch Verlag, Darmstadt (2006)
18. Wang, L., Xi, J. (eds.): Smart Devices and Machines for Advanced Manufacturing. Springer, London (2008)
19. Broers, H., Caarls, W., Jonker, P., Kleihorst, R.: Architecture study for smart cameras. In: Proc. EOS Conference on Industrial Imaging and Machine Vision European Optical Society, Munich, Germany, pp. 39–49 (2005)
20. Ganssle, J.: Embedded systems world class design. Elsevier, Burlington (2008)
21. Szpytko, J., Hyla, P.: Estimation of the intelligent camera computing power for the real-time image preprocessing. Journal of KONES 18(4), 503–509 (2011)
22. Pahk, H.J., Ahn, W.J.: A new method of noncontact measurement for 3D micro pattern in semiconductor wafer: implementing a new optical probe. International Journal of Machine Tools and Manufacture 41(13-14), 2031–2037 (2001)
23. Soloman, S. (ed.): Sensors Handbook. McGraw-Hill Professional, New York (2009)
24. Szpytko, J., Hyla, P.: Badania położenia zawieszonego na linie ładunku w procesie przemieszczania suwnicą pomostową. Logistyka 6, 3671–3680 (2011)
25. Storch, B., Wierucka, I.: Optyczne pomiary zarysów powtarzalnych z wykorzystaniem technik przetwarzania obrazu. Acta Mechanica et Automatica 1(2), 59–62 (2007)
26. Kocerba, A., Szpytko, J.: Metoda pomiaru kąta wychylenia ładunku zawieszonego na linie w suwnicach pomostowych. Logistyka 2, 1–9 (2008)

Possibility to Control and Adjust the Suspensions of Vehicles

Łukasz Konieczny, Rafał Burdzik, and Tomasz Figlus

Silesian University of Technology,
Faculty of Transport Krasińskiego 8, 40-019 Katowice, Poland
lukasz.konieczny@polsl.pl

Abstract. The use of passive spring and damping elements with fixed unchangeable characteristics of the suspensions of vehicles suspension is a compromise in terms of the characteristics of these components selection criterion for the sake of safety and comfort. In these embodiments, it is impossible to adjust the parameters of the suspension. The use of spring and damping elements with controlled characteristics for semiactive, active and adaptive suspension to adjust the suspension for specific road conditions and driving style. The paper presents a comparison of passive solutions based on traditional mechanical components and hydropneumatic suspension and active adoption used in vehicles, comparing the characteristics of spring and damping elements used in these solutions.

Keywords: active vehicle suspension, hydropneumatic suspension.

1   Introduction

The passive spring and damping elements used in the vehicle suspensions with constant characteristics are the compromise solutions if we talk about the safety and the comfort of travelling and the price. These suspensions are not able to cope with the growing requirements and practically, their possibilities to develop are to lower their mass and reaching the required durability. Currently, the development tendencies concerning the suspension systems of vehicles apply to semi-active suspension systems, active and adaptive ones which enable to adjust the suspension parameters to the specific road conditions and the driving style. The possibilities to regulate the spring-damping elements characteristics call the necessity to create the steering rules in case of these suspensions for the given criteria, such as comfort driving or sports driving [4-8]. Using these solutions is connected with fulfilling the energetic requirements which for the passenger car are between 7kW (active hydropneumatic suspension) and 20 kW (fully active suspension).

Figure 1 shows types of used suspensions in vehicles. In passive 'conventional' suspensions the elements characteristics both the spring and damping are constant and not regulated. In case of the adaptation and semi active suspensions it is possible to switch the characteristics of the chosen component during the travel. For the semi

J. Mikulski (Ed.): TST 2013, CCIS 395, pp. 378–383, 2013.
© Springer-Verlag Berlin Heidelberg 2013

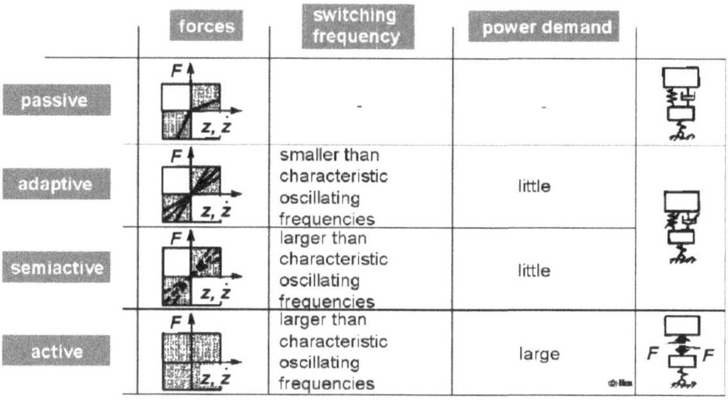

	forces	switching frequency	power demand	
passive		-	-	
adaptive		smaller than characteristic oscillating frequencies	little	
semiactive		larger than characteristic oscillating frequencies	little	
active		larger than characteristic oscillating frequencies	large	

Fig. 1. Comparison of solutions of the passenger car suspension [1]

active suspensions the frequency of switching is higher from the characteristic frequencies of a wheel and the car body. In the adaptation and semi active systems there is a need for energy to steer the engines and the electronics. In case of active suspensions the executive elements may generate forces which is connected with the use of additional outside source of energy.

2   The Spring Elements of Suspensions – Comparison

In mechanic suspension together with the load increase, the static deflection of the spring element goes up, and in case of full burden, the range of accessible wheel stroke while banging is significantly reduced (it is one of the dominant defect of the suspension of this type). The full range of spring deflection is the sum of the static deflection and the dynamic deflection (figure 2). The properties of spring elements are strongly correlated to materials and production technologies. This elements shouldn't be repaired or welded, even by novel methods [10,11].

In case of hydro-pneumatic suspension or pneumatic one, the static deflection is not dependant on the burden, the full range of spring burden is equal to the dynamic deflection. There is not such a situation when we have both the reduction of the wheel stroke range while banging and the increase of static burden, which enables to use gas spring with low stiffness factor in comparison to the stiffness factors of the spring elements used in mechanic suspensions and obtaining the suspension which assures the high comfort of travelling.

For different solutions of the suspension, the self vibration frequency of the sprung mass may increase or decrease with the increase of the static burden. In the mechanic suspension the frequency decreases, in hydro-pneumatic increases and in pneumatic stays constant (figure 3).

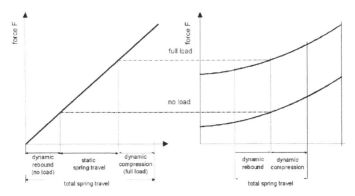

Fig. 2. The spring deflection of the mechanic suspension and the pneumatic or hydro-pneumatic ones [1]

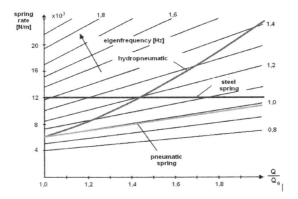

Fig. 3. Comparison the properties of the mechanic, pneumatic and hydro-pneumatic suspension

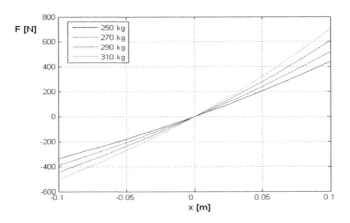

Fig. 4. Dynamic force vs. displacement characteristics for different static load in hydropneumatic strut (Citroen BX front strut)

In case of hydro-pneumatic suspensions it is beneficiary to increase the progression of the gas spring characteristics (with the constant mass of the gas) for the increase of the static burden of a vehicle (figure 4).

The further generations of the hydro-pneumatic suspensions, like Activia, thanks to the motor operated valves makes it possible to increase the gas volume (additional hydro-pneumatic sphere) for a given axle, increasing or decreasing in this way the suspension stiffness.

3   Damping Elements – Comparison

In case of using damping elements, currently mainly in the vehicle suspensions we use the hydraulic damper. In the typical passive hydraulic damper it is possible to gain required damping characteristics by proper shaping of the canal geometry and using the valves. In figure 5, we present the exemplary characteristics of hydraulic two-tube damper [3].

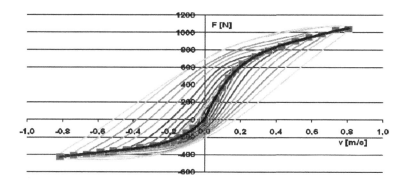

Fig. 5. Characteristic of the two-tube damper (Fiat Seicento)

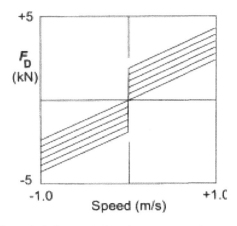

Fig. 6. Theoretical characteristics of electrorheological damper [2]

In case of dampers with regulated characteristics, the solutions with motor operated valves regulating the discharge are used (CDC Continuous Damping Control, ADS Adaptive Damping System, CES Continuously Controlled Electronic Suspension and with the intelligent liquids - Magnetoreological and Electrorheological).

Depending on the solution, the selection of damp characteristics parameters can be calculated from the frequency from several hundred Hz and steered with the frequency of several dozen Hz. The exemplary characteristic of damping the damper with the regulated characteristic is presented in figure 6.

4   Conclusion

Summarizing, the development tendencies in the structure of the passenger car suspensions are focused on the use of the spring-damping elements with the possibility to regulate their characteristics, practically in the real time and the use of fully active solutions which enable to generate forces in the suspension system. Used steering algorithms optimize the parameters of suspension settings on the basis of the analysis of numbers of the recorded values (the vertical acceleration of the car body and particular wheels, the direction and the speed of the vehicle etc.) in the automatic cog, often enabling the driver to choose the settings in the comfort drive of sports drive.

References

1. Wolff, H.: Untersuchung und Optimierung des Federungsverhaltens von Rettungswagen unter besonderer Berücksichtigung von Reibungseinflüssen Rheinisch-Westfälische Technische Hochschule Aachen (1975)
2. Dixon, J.C.: The Shock Absorber Handbook, 2nd edn. Professional Engineering Publishing Ltd. (2007)
3. Konieczny, Ł., Burdzik, R., Warczek, J.: Determinations of shock absorber dumping characteristics taking stroke value into consideration account. Diagnostyka 3, 51–54 (2010)
4. Konieczny, Ł.: Wyznaczanie charakterystyk tłumienia kolumny hydropneumatycznej z uwzględnieniem wybranych parametrów, Silesian University of Technology Scientific Papers, s. Transport 69, 85–89 (2010) (in Polish)
5. Burdzik, R., Konieczny, Ł., Łazarz, B.: Influence of damping characteristics changes on vehicles vibration research. In: 19th International Congress on Sound and Vibration (ICSV19), Conference Proceedings, pp. 657 (2012)
6. Burdzik, R.: Monitoring system of vibration propagation in vehicles and method of analysing vibration modes. In: Mikulski, J. (ed.) TST 2012. CCIS, vol. 329, pp. 406–413. Springer, Heidelberg (2012)
7. Michalski, R., Wierzbicki, S.: An analysis of degradation of vehicles in operation. Maintenance and Reliability 1(37), 30–32 (2008)
8. Tuma, J., Simek, J., Skuta, J., et al.: Active vibration control of hydrodynamic journal bearings. Vibration Problems ICOVP, Springer Proceedings in Physics 139, 425–431 (2011)

9. Adamiec, J., Grabowski, A., Lisiecki, A.: Joining of an Ni-Al alloy by means of laser beam welding, Laser Technology VII: Applications of Lasers. In: Proceedings of the Society of Photo-Optical Instrumentation Engineers (SPIE), vol. 5229, pp. 215–218 (2003)
10. Węgrzyn, T., Wieszała, R.: Main alloy elements in covered electrodes in terms of the amount of oxygen in weld metal deposits (WMD). Metalurgija 51(2), 183–186 (2012)
11. Folęga, P., Siwiec, G.: Numerical analysis of selected materials for flexsplines. Archives of Metallurgy and Materials 57(1), 185–191 (2012)
12. Muzikářová, L., Franeková, M., Holečko, P., Hrnčiar, M.: Theory of information and signals. In: English, EDIS (2008) ISBN 978-80-8070-992-1
13. Mikulski, J., Kwaśny, A.: Role of telematics in reducing the negative environmental impact of transport. In: Mikulski, J. (ed.) TST 2010. CCIS, vol. 104, pp. 11–29. Springer, Heidelberg (2010)
14. Mikulski, J.: Using telematics in transport. In: Mikulski, J. (ed.) TST 2010. CCIS, vol. 104, pp. 175–182. Springer, Heidelberg (2010)

Intelligent Approach to Valve Clearance Diagnostic in Cars

Piotr Czech

Silesian University of Technology, Faculty of Transport,
Krasinskiego 8, 40-019 Katowice, Poland
piotr.czech@polsl.pl

Abstract. In many research centres all over the world work is nowadays being carried out aimed at compiling a method for diagnostic of machines technical condition. Non-destructive methods, including methods using vibroacoustic phenomena, have a special meaning. As we can read in the literature, vibroacoustic signals generated during the work of technical objects have necessary information connected with the technical condition of those objects. An appropriate transformation of registered signals is the main problem. This paper suggests using a discrete wavelet transform and energy and entropy, which provide the basis for a diagnostic system of valve clearance in a car combustion engine. Research aimed at building a diagnostic system using neural networks was conducted. This approach to diagnosis of the technical condition of combustion engine elements gives a possibility for the future enlargement of an on-board diagnostic system OBD, which is being used nowadays.

Keywords: internal combustion engines, artificial neural networks, diagnostics, on-board diagnostics.

1   Introduction

According to the literature a repair of engine timing system is very expensive and time-consuming for garages. For example, some of valve damages become serious errors of all engines, and only the regeneration can be economically unreasonable.

The timing system of a combustion engine is responsible for controlling the beginning and the end of fresh fuel inflow and of the exhaust outflow. It should be fully synchronized with pistons movement, which depends on the crankshaft position. The movement of inflow and outflow valves is caused by the camshaft rotation, which is powered by the engine crankshaft.

The timing system has to provide also the flow field for the fuel aimed at supporting a correct speed of flow. The flow field depends on sizes of valve seats, valve heads, valve spindles and changes its own value during the valve lift.

To improve cylinders filling, the lift and inflow valve diameter increase. It should be noticed that valves having a smaller diameter go under a smaller deformation and they are longer hermetic.

J. Mikulski (Ed.): TST 2013, CCIS 395, pp. 384–391, 2013.
© Springer-Verlag Berlin Heidelberg 2013

Discussions of detailed solutions used in timing systems design can be found in [13, 14], but [4] describes directly the inflow process.

The main valve features:

- good thermal conduction,
- resistance to work in severe conditions,
- corrosion resistance,
- abrasion resistance.

Automotive literature presents causes of valve damages:

- thermal overload or mechanical overload (plastic strain of valve head, structure changes of the valve material, thermal corrosion of doping, corrosion pits of valve faces, surface cracks, valve spindle breaking off, doping burnout),
- interferences during valve transmission labour (camshaft mover damage, defective valve spindle fastening, eccentric pressure valve rocker arm, too tight valve slide bar, too loose valve slide bar, lack of valve rotation during its work, too intensive rotation during its work),
- valves closing errors (too big valve clearance, too small valve clearance, valve seat deformation),
- defective valve material selection,
- defective valve installation (misalignment of valve seat and valve slide bar), incorrect valve clearance, valve marking),
- defects of design (defective valve plate configuration, defective valve spindle foot),
- executive defects (overheat during forging, stelliting defects, thermal treatment defects, surface chroming defects, valve stem end quenching defects, defective fibre alignment),
- material defects (inclusions and material pollution, surface defects, material structure defects).

The most frequent reason of valve damage are:

- thermal or mechanic overload: 38%,
- executive defects: 22%,
- timing system defects: 10%,
- material defects: 9%,
- defective installation and operation: 8%
- design defects: 7%
- other: 6%

To avoid valve damages, instructions for car mechanics are:

- valve clearance has to be set precisely,
- control times have to be set correctly,
- after the vee-belt or chain exchange, the belt stretcher should be also exchanged,
- after the cylinder head treatment, valve returning position should be checked,
- valve spring should be correctly mounted during building,

- new washers should be used under valve seat,
- new key valve spring should be used,
- guide shoe and valve face have to be collateral,
- only elements suggested by the carmaker should be used,
- while engine fitting, every foreign matter has to be removed from the combustion chamber and from the fuel system.

2   Description of Experiment

An eight-valve combustion engine of Fiat Punto, of 1.2 dm^3 capacity, was the object of research.

In those experiments the main aim was to diagnose malfunctions of the timing system, consisting in an incorrect valve clearance. An increase in valve clearance up to 0.8 mm and a decrease of up to 0.06 mm were simulated in relation to a normal clearance, which is 0.45 mm. A change of clearance obtained by a change of thickness of the regulation plates for the exhaust valve.

Vibroacoustic signals were registered during road tests. Acceleration of vibrations was measured:

- in vertical direction on the 1st cylinder,
- in horizontal direction on the 1st cylinder,
- in horizontal direction on the 4th cylinder,
- on the clutch,
- on the gearbox,
- on the main transmission.

Additionally the acoustic pressure was registered in the engine chamber. Tests were conducted for:

- gear 1-5,
- rotational speeds of engine: 1500 rpm, 2000 rpm, 3000 rpm, 4000 rpm.

Registered vibroacoustic signals were initially processed with the use of discrete wavelet transform (DWT). The discrete wavelet transform of the signal $x(t)$ is marked as scalar products $x(t)$ and a sequence of basic functions $\psi(t)$:

$$DWT = \int_{-\infty}^{+\infty} \psi(t) \cdot x(t)\, dt \qquad (1)$$

The signal approximation is achieved on a given level – a_J, and a detail sum on the next levels – d_j, as a result of multi-level signal decomposition:

$$x(t) = a_J(t) + \sum_{j=1}^{J} d_j(t) \qquad (2)$$

Together with the increase in signal decomposition level the participation of details decreases, which causes that with the decrease of resolution, the contents of details in signal approximation decrease.

In order to describe the character of changes in a decomposed vibroacoustic signal, with the use of discrete wavelet analysis, two methods of conduct were chosen. The first assumes the use of signal entropy as a measure, which characterises changes in signal $x_j(t)$. It can be calculated with the use of relationship:

$$E_{Sh} = -\sum_{j} x_j^2(t) \cdot \log\left(x_j^2(t)\right)$$ (3)

The value of entropy is the measure of disorder and of grade of randomness and may be treated as the measure of the amount of information.

The second method of conduct assumes the use of signal energy to describe the changes occurring in a vibroacoustic signal. It was assumed here, that according to a definition of discrete wavelet transform, the total energy of signal before decomposition is equal to the sum of approximation energy and further details. Total energy of signal after decomposition on defined number of levels was assumed as 100% and calculated what percentage of that energy is the approximation signal and further details.

On the basis of such two methods of conduct, two types of models used in the process of neural networks teaching and testing were applied.

In the process of models building it was essential to determine on how many levels the basic signal will be arranged and what basic wavelet will be used. The usefulness of 52 basic wavelets was checked in the tests. The wavelets from the following families were used: discrete meyer, reverse biorthogonal, symlets, coiflets, biorthogonal, daubechies, haar. In conducted experiments the usefulness of created sets of models for successive 10 levels of decomposition was checked (Table 1).

Table 1. Sets of models

Selected levels of decomposition	Number of inputs of neural network
1	2
1-2	3
1-3	4
1-4	5
1-5	6
1-6	7
1-7	8
1-8	9
1-9	10
1-10	11

For the studies carried out, artificial neural networks of probabilistic neural networks type were applied [9, 11]. The artificial neural networks of PNN type are used as the neural classifiers dividing the set of data into a determined number of output categories. While using such network type, proper smoothening coefficient γ should be selected. In the experiments the performance of the network for 86 various values of γ coefficient was checked.

3   Results of Experiment

In the first part of the experiment the possibility of two conditions was checked – engine work correctness and occurrence of incorrect valve clearance. All neural networks built in this part of research had two outputs.

Probabilistic neural networks (PNN) were taught on data coming from vibroacoustic signals registered in a specific way (out of 7 ways), for engine working in one gear (out of 5 gears), at a given speed (out of 4 speeds). Each of them was tested for models using energy or entropy of signal arranged in 10 different versions of the number of decomposition levels. In total, the functioning of 2800 versions of classifiers were tested, and each of them was tested for various parameters of coefficient γ.

In order to determine the best basic wavelet to build descriptors, such arrangement of the number of cases was used, in which, with the use of given basic wavelet, the classifiers were characterised with the minimum error value. The best wavelet would be this, for which the number of cases was 1400 ("7 places of vibroacoustic signals measurement" x "5 gears" x "4 engine rotation speeds" x "10 signal decomposition levels"). It would equal to a situation where independently of the signal measurement method and of the chosen number of decomposition levels used to build models, the classifier would show the minimum error with the use of given basic wavelet. In the experiment, however, such situation did not occur. The number of cases for which, with the use of given wavelet in the process of model building, the classifier reached the minimum value is shown in Figure 1.

Based on the obtained results, it cannot be clearly said about main superiority of wavelet above others in respect of those results. A similar situation occurs while trying to say, which wavelet is completely not suitable to the pattern building process. Results show that depending on the examined variant, classifiers taught at patterns reached by using the same wavelet had different effect (Fig.2).

Results do not show also a clearly bigger usefulness in building patterns of energy process than of signal entropy (and inversely).

Analysing together all examined variants (Fig. 1) it can be said, that the best parameters of building patterns using discrete wavelet transform (DWT) are:

- base wavelet: discrete meyer,
- chosen decomposition levels: 1-10.

Because the first part of research ended with very good results, in the next part the possibility of diagnosing three conditions, such as correct engine work, increase in and decrease of valve clearance was checked. For this research, all neural networks had three ways.

Similar as in the first part the usefulness of each base wavelet in the pattern building process was checked. 2800 groups of classifiers were created similarly to those from the first part of the research.

Examples of results are shown in Figures 3 and 4 – chosen as in the first part of research.

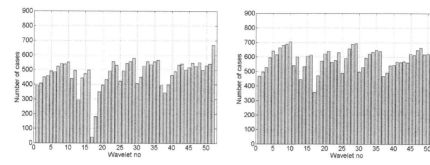

Fig. 1. Arrangement of number of cases in which the classification errors were minimum – models: energy (on the left), entropy (on the right)

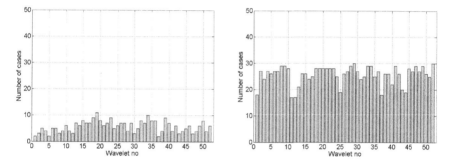

Fig. 2. Arrangement of number of cases in which the classification errors were minimum – models: energy, acoustic pressure, 5 gear (on the left), entropy, acoustic pressure, 5 gear (on the right)

Analysing particular results it can be noted, that the usefulness of each wavelet in the pattern building process was at the similar level for the corresponding data variants in the first and second part of the research (recognized two or three classes).

Also for this part of research, a clear definition of the best and the worst base wavelet was impossible, apart from the chosen way of signal registration or preliminary data conversion.

Based on the obtained total results (Fig. 3), it can be said that the best variant of a pattern building system using a discrete wavelet transform is to take:

– base wavelet: discrete meyer,
– signal decomposition levels: 1-10.

It should be noted that the choice is the same as in the first part of the research.

As the experiments aimed at diagnosing two and three classes for majority of examined pattern building variants the best taught PNN neural networks were characterized by faultless or almost faultless working.

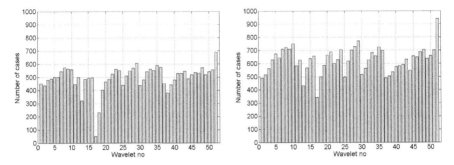

Fig. 3. Arrangement of number of cases in which the classification errors were minimum – models: energy (on the left), entropy (on the right)

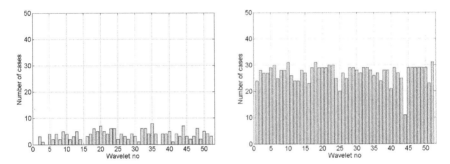

Fig. 4. Arrangement of number of cases in which the classification errors were minimum – models: energy, acoustic pressure, 5 gear (on the left), entropy, acoustic pressure, 5 gear (on the right)

4   Conclusion

The possibility of diagnosing a whole vehicle and its component elements is a necessary task, but very difficult to perform. Those diagnostic methods seem to be especially useful, which enable detection of damages at an early stage. Also the way of research conducting is very important, which provides a non-destructive diagnosis. Examples of using those methods can be found in the literature [1, 2, 5, 16].

Besides methods of object condition diagnosing, the literature widely shows issues connected with designing and producing [3, 12, 15] and monitoring the correctness of these objects work [6-8, 10].

It should to be noted that only obtaining desirable results for designing, producing, controlling and diagnosing phase can give a guarantee for long and failure-free time of machine work.

The present article was focused on the phase connected with the diagnosis of the technical condition of chosen combustion car engine elements. In the future results obtained in this research can increase the functionality of an OBD on-board system used nowadays in cars.

References

1. Czech, P., Madej, H.: Application of spectrum and spectrum histograms of vibration engine body for setting up the clearance model of the piston-cylinder assembly for RBF neural classifier. Eksploatacja i Niezawodność – Maintenance and Reliability (4) (2011)
2. Figlus, T.: Diagnosing the engine valve clearance, on the basis of the energy changes of the vibratory signal. Maintenance Problems 1 (2009)
3. Grega, R., Homišin, J., Kaššay, P., Krajňák, J.: The analyse of vibrations after changing shaft coupling in drive belt conveyer. Zeszyty Naukowe. Transport / Politechnika Śląska, z. 72 (2011)
4. Heywood, J.B.: Internal combustion engines fundamentals. McGraw Hill Inc. (1988)
5. Korbicz, J., Kościelny, J., Kowalczuk, Z., Cholewa, W.: Fault diagnosis, Models, Artificial Intelligence, Applications. Springer (2004)
6. Czech, P.: Identification of Leakages in the Inlet System of an Internal Combustion Engine with the Use of Wigner-Ville Transform and RBF Neutal Networks. In: Mikulski, J. (ed.) TST 2012. CCIS, vol. 329, pp. 414–422. Springer, Heidelberg (2012)
7. Merkisz, J.: Mazurek, St.: On-board diagnostics OBD in an automotive context. WKŁ, Warsaw (2007)
8. Młyńczak, J.: Analysis of intelligent transport systems (ITS) in public transport of upper Silesia. In: Mikulski, J. (ed.) TST 2011. CCIS, vol. 239, pp. 164–171. Springer, Heidelberg (2011)
9. Osowski, S.: Neural networks for information processing. UW, Warsaw (2000)
10. Puškár, M., Bigoš, P., Puškárová, P.: Accurate measurements of output characteristics and detonations of motorbike high-speed racing engine and their optimization at actual atmospheric conditions and combusted mixture composition. Measurement 45 (2012)
11. Tadeusiewicz, R., Lula, P.: Introduction to neural networks. StatSoft, Cracow (2001)
12. Urbanský, M., Homišin, J., Krajňák, J.: Analysis of the causes of gaseous medium pressure changes in compression space of pneumatic coupling. Transactions of the Universities of Košice 2 (2011)
13. Wajand, J.A.: Piston internal combustion engines of average rotational speed and high-speed. WNT, Warsaw (2005)
14. Wendeker, M.: Steering of ignition in car engine. On-board diagnostic systems of car vehicles, Lublin (1999)
15. Węgrzyn, T., Piwnik, J.: Low alloy welding with micro-jet cooling. Archives of Metallurgy and Materials, z. 2, t. 57, nr 1 (2012)
16. Zuber, N., Ličen, H., Klašnja-Milićević, A.: Remote online condition monitoring of the bucket wheel excavator SR1300 – a case study. Facta Universitatis, Series: Working and Living Environmental Protection 1(5) (2008)
17. Mikulski, J., Kwaśny, A.: Role of telematics in reducing the negative environmental impact of transport. In: Mikulski, J. (ed.) TST 2010. CCIS, vol. 104, pp. 11–29. Springer, Heidelberg (2010)
18. Mikulski, J.: Using telematics in transport. In: Mikulski, J. (ed.) TST 2010. CCIS, vol. 104, pp. 175–182. Springer, Heidelberg (2010)

Conception of National System of Monitoring Dangerous Goods Vehicles

Gabriel Nowacki[1], Anna Niedzicka[2], and Małgorzata Walendzik[2]

[1] Military University of Technology, Cybernetics Faculty,
Gen. Sylwestra Kaliskiego 2, 00-908 Warsaw 49, Poland
gnowacki@wat.edu.pl
[2] Motor Transport Institute, Transport Management &Telematics Centre,
Jagiellońska 80, 03-301 Warsaw, Poland
{anna.niedzicka,malgorzata.walendzik}@its.waw.pl

Abstract. The paper refers to problems on dangerous goods transport. Realization of the planned tasks may significantly contribute to improving safety of people and environment and developing methods to minimise damages and costs, improving the exchange of information between centres of production, carriers, receivers and emergency centres and determine methods of cooperation at the place of a breakdown.

Keywords: model, demonstrator, NSMDGV, terminal.

1 Introduction

Hazardous material is a material or object which, according to ADR is not be accepted for carriage by road, or is approved for such carriage under the conditions laid down in those provisions [10].

There are nine classes of dangerous goods as follows:

- Class 1. Explosive substances and articles;
- Class 2. Gases, including compressed, liquefied and dissolved under pressure gases and vapours (Flammable gases e.g. butane, propane acetylene. Non-flammable and non-toxic, likely to cause asphyxiation e.g. nitrogen, CO_2 or oxidizers e.g. oxygen. Toxic e.g. Chlorine, Phosgene);
- Class 3. Flammable liquids:
- Class 4.1. Flammable solids, self-reactive substances and solid desensitized explosives;
- Class 4.2. Substances liable to spontaneous combustion;
- Class 4.3. Substances which, in contact with water, emit flammable gases;
- Class 5.1. Oxidizing substances;
- Class 5.2. Organic peroxides;
- Class 6.1. Toxic substances;
- Class 6.2. Infectious substances;

J. Mikulski (Ed.): TST 2013, CCIS 395, pp. 392–399, 2013.
© Springer-Verlag Berlin Heidelberg 2013

- Class 7. Radioactive material;
- Class 8. Corrosive substances;
- Class 9. Miscellaneous dangerous substances and articles.

The largest amounts transported concern liquid materials (Tab. 1, 2).

Table 1. Percentage share of the dangerous goods transported [1, 3 - 5]

Class	Share	Percentage
Class 1	Explosive substances and articles	0.95%
Class 2	Gases, including compressed, liquefied and vapours	25.17%
Class 3	Flammable liquids	66.19%
Class 4.1	Flammable solids, self-reactive substances	1.50%
Class 8	Corrosive substances	1.62%
Class 9	Miscellaneous dangerous substances and articles	2.93%
Rest	Class 4.2, 4.3, 5.1, 5.2, 6.1, 6.2, 7	1,64%

Table 2. Percentage share arranged according to the form of transport [1 - 5]

Transport means	Percentage
Tankers	79%
Containers	20%
Goods in bulks	1%

To make a right choice of packaging for the transport of dangerous goods, some materials classified as hazardous classes ADR, may be included in the so-called packing groups according to the degree of danger they present. In most cases, the degree of risk is assessed on a three-stage scale packing group: substances presenting high danger, substances presenting medium danger, substances presenting low danger.

2   Organization of Carriage of Dangerous Goods

2.1   Responsibility of Dangerous Goods in Poland

Road transport of dangerous goods, means any movement of dangerous goods by the vehicle on public road or other generally accessible roads, including stops required during the transportation and activities related to this haulage [6].

Road transport of dangerous goods is a complex process, which is why many sectors are responsible for its implementation [6 - 9]:

The minister responsible for transport, supervises the transport of dangerous goods and the entity executing tasks associated with this transport with the exception of the armed forces vehicles,

- Minister of National Defence, supervises the transport of dangerous goods by the transport means belonging to the armed forces,
- Minister responsible for the economy, deals with the matters of technical conditions and testing of packaging of dangerous goods,

- Minister responsible for health, deals with the matters of the conditions of carriage of infectious substances,
- Provincial Inspector of Road Transport - in the matters of the road transport safety inspections of hazardous materials,
- President of the National Atomic Energy Agency, on in the matters concerning conditions of carriage of radioactive material.

2.2   Control Services of Dangerous Goods

The participant of carriage of dangerous goods is required to send a copy of the annual report on its activities in the carriage of dangerous goods and related activities, hereinafter referred to as "annual report" before the February 28 of each year following the year covered by the report, to the voivodship road transport inspector appropriate for the seat or place of residence for the participant of dangerous goods carriage.

If, a serious accident or breakdown occurred in connection with the carriage of dangerous goods, within the meaning of ADR, the transport participant, within 14 days from the day of the event, is to submit the report:

- to the appropriate, for the place of the event, Regional Road Transport Inspector - in the case of road transport of dangerous goods,
- Head of the Armed Forces Support Inspectorate - in the case of transport of dangerous goods by the transport means belonging to the armed forces or means of transport, for which the armed forces are responsible.

Information about a serious incident or accident in the carriage of dangerous goods is transferred to the Minister responsible for transport by these authorities, immediately upon receipt by them of the accident report [6 - 8].

The inspection of the transport of dangerous goods is conducted by:

1) Road Transport Inspectorate officer – on the roads, parking lots and at the place of business of the participant in the carriage of dangerous goods,
2) Police officers - on the roads and parking lots,
3) Border Guard officers - on the roads and parking lots,
4) Customs officers - on Polish territory,
5) Military Police Soldiers – with respect to the carriage of dangerous goods performed by the armed forces.

In carrying out inspection, the officers work together, to the extent necessary, with the authorized representatives of:

1) Nuclear regulatory bodies - on the conditions of carriage of radioactive material,
2) Transport Technical Supervision - on the conditions of carriage of dangerous goods,
3) Inspectorate for Armed Forces Support and the Military Technical Inspection – on the carriage of dangerous goods performed by the armed forces,
4) Inspection of Environmental Protection – on the matters relating to compliance with environmental regulations.

Road Transport Chief Inspector reports serious or repeated infringements, jeopardizing the safety of the transport of dangerous goods, carried out by the vehicle or company from another Member State of the European Union, to the competent authorities of the Member State of the European Union, in which the vehicle or the company is registered.

According to the competence possessed, the Road Transport Chief Inspector, provides the Minister responsible for transport matters the information, before March 31 of each calendar year, on penalties imposed for violations relating to the carriage of dangerous goods and the number of checks on the transport of dangerous goods, observed breaches of regulations, relating to the carriage of dangerous goods.

Road Transport Chief Inspector conveys to the European Commission each calendar year, and not later than 12 months from the end of this year, a report on the inspection of road transport of dangerous goods which contains the following information:

1) If possible, the actual or estimated volume of dangerous goods by transported by road (in the tons transported or in ton-kilometres);
2) The number of checks carried out;
3) The number of vehicles checked at registration location (vehicles registered in this country, in other EU Member States or other countries);
4) The number and types of infringements.

2.3   Problems of Dangerous Goods Monitoring

Road transport of goods within the EU, including Poland is growing constantly, as is evidenced by the data presented in Tab. 3.

Table 3. Road transport - transport of goods [11]

Year	Goods weight
2000	1 006 705 000 ton
2005	1 079 761 000 ton
2009	1 339 473 000 ton
2010	1 551 841 000 ton
2011	1 596 209 000 ton

According to the of Central Statistical Office (CSO), about 10 percent of cargo transported by trucks on the Polish roads are dangerous goods. In 2011, it was 159.6 million tons of dangerous goods, often representing lethal threat. In Poland, 90% of dangerous goods are transported by road, and only 10% by rail (20.1 million). 159.6 million tons per year, is 438 thousand tons a day - to carry the load on standard semi-trailers with a capacity of 18 tons, it takes 24.26 thousand trucks per day.

According to the Road Transport Inspection data, in 2011, inspectors checked more than 16 thousand vehicles carrying hazardous materials. The most common violations consisted of bypassing restrictions on drivers' driving times and mandatory rest periods, lack of fire-fighting equipment in vehicles, poor labelling of goods and lack of required transport certificates and documents.

Similar data can be found in the report of the Supreme Audit Office (SAO). Irregularities lead to a situation in which entrepreneurs, advisors for the safety matters and drivers are not adequately prepared to organize and carry out transport of dangerous goods. Hazardous materials are transported in Poland often during peak traffic hours, near public buildings and green areas. There are more and more frequent accidents and crashes involving their transport. Provincial governors and Marshals are not aware of the potential risks, and the persons directly responsible for the transport of these materials are poorly prepared for that.

Every day on the Polish roads, one can meet thousands of trucks carrying explosives, corrosive, or radioactive materials. They drive virtually unattended.

Dangerous goods (flammable, explosive, corrosive, and even radioactive) are carried in Poland often during peak traffic hours, near schools, hospitals or nature reserves. Improper handling of them can result in death, the huge material losses and environmental contamination.

Under the ADR agreement, [10] in the case of vehicles carrying dangerous goods at high risk, there should be monitoring devices used for dangerous goods (telemetry systems, tracking devices for movement of goods), effectively prevent the theft of vehicles and cargo.

In addition, following the tragic events of September 11, 2001 in New York, and March 11, 2004 in Madrid, the EU directive was adopted, which drew attention to the possibility of terrorist attacks, including the use of dangerous goods, which are subject to the obligation of monitoring (tracking).

Therefore, to ensure the monitoring of dangerous goods in Poland, it is necessary to design and implement a national dangerous goods monitoring system.

3   Characteristics of NSMDGV

3.1   Structure of System

A consortium composed Motor Transport Institute, Institute of Communications, Roads and Bridges Research Institute, intends to carry out the following tasks:

1. Analysis of legislative, international, EU and national documents on the transport of dangerous goods.
2. Analysis of operating and implemented ITS solutions in the EU countries and Poland, associated with the process of monitoring dangerous goods.
3. Analysis of the functional, communication and physical (transport layer) structure of the systems monitoring vehicles carrying dangerous goods.
4. Identifying the needs for interoperability, reliability, security, and mobility of the ITS solutions at different user levels.
5. Identification of monitoring systems for vehicles carrying dangerous goods in the world and the EU.
6. Developing a model of the national monitoring system for vehicles carrying dangerous goods - NSMDGV (Fig. 1).

7. Developing technical specifications for the demonstrator of the national monitoring system for vehicles carrying dangerous goods - NSMDGV.
8. Producing the national monitoring system demonstrator for vehicles carrying dangerous goods - NSMDGV.

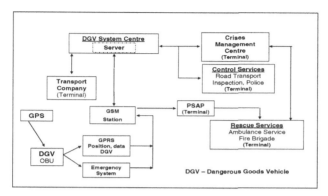

Fig. 1. Scheme of NSMDGV

The final effect of project will be model and demonstrator of the National Monitoring System of Dangerous Goods Vehicles consists of following elements:

- demonstrator of system centre,
- five demonstrators of OBU for DGV,
- five demonstrators of terminals for Crises Management Centre, Control Services, PSAP, Rescue Services and Transport Company,
- demonstrator of innovation sensor for detecting chemical and gases threats.

Demonstrator of System Centre will be perform as a form of communications server with interface, that provides:

- communications with objects,
- random configuration of objects,
- monitoring of objects on map,
- configuration of alarm state of objects,
- creating of standard rotes.
- Demonstrator of OBU for DGV can provide some functions as follows:
- localization of DGV,
- communications to System Centre,
- identification and configuration of OBU,
- data collection from sensors, meters and logical inputs.

Demonstrator of terminal will be perform as a form of client applications connected to communications server. The applications provide as follows:

- monitoring of actual positions of objects on map,
- configuration of alarm state of objects,
- creating of standard rotes.

3.2   Technical Characteristics of System

The use of GPS and GSM technology, supported by a specialized software package enables the location of vehicles on the Polish territory as well as the entire Europe. This solution not only enables the precise location of the vehicle, but allows:

- monitoring the cargo, its physical and chemical state, which substantially affect the safety of those involved in transport as well as members of the public
- localising the vehicle transporting dangerous goods and other vehicles on the road,
- more efficient management of the fleet of transport companies, which has a direct impact on reducing the cost of transport,
- remote immobilisation of the vehicle, in case of e.g. theft,
- acquisition of a vehicle operating data,
- acquisition of the prevailing meteorological data from the vehicle,
- maintaining constant communication, vehicle – base, and sending messages,
- in the event of a breakdown or disaster automatic notification of the appropriate crisis management centre and emergency services,
- selection of the optimal and economical routes (defining route and maximum deviation from it for safety reasons such as traffic, weather conditions and surface condition).

The accidents of transport dangerous goods are caused mainly by changes in the tankers and containers environment during transportation (such as temperature, humidity, pressure, etc.) or a mixture of goods caused by a chemical reaction and lead to combustion, explosion, toxic gas leaks and so on. Therefore, it has great significance of improving the security of road tankers and container in the real-time state can be monitored during whole the transportation of dangerous goods. Early and accurate detection, characterization and warning of a chemical and gas event are critical to an effective response. To achieve these objectives, an integrated system of sensors is needed and a supporting information technology network.

Demonstrator of NSMDGV should be in line with all specifications (environmental, physical and electromagnetic compatibility) determined by EU directives and standards defined by CEN, ISO and ETSI. The main of tem are following:

- Council Directive 73/23/EEC of 19 February 1973 on the harmonization of the laws of Member States relating to electrical equipment designed for use within certain voltage limits;
- Council Directive 89/336/EEC of 3 May 1989 on the approximation of the laws of the Member States relating to electromagnetic compatibility;
- Directive 1999/5/EC of the European Parliament and of the Council of 9 March 1999 on radio equipment and telecommunications terminal equipment and the mutual recognition of their conformity;
- PN-ETS 300 135:1997/A1:1999. Radio Equipment and Systems. Angle-modulated Citizens' Band radio equipment. Technical characteristics and methods of measurement;
- PN-ETS 300 673;2005. Radio Equipment and Systems RES. Electromagnetic Compability (EMS);

- PN-ETSI EN 300 433-2 V1.1.1:2003. PN-ETSI EN 301 489-1 V1.6.1:2006. PN-ETSI EN 301 489-13 V1.2.1:2003. Electromagnetic compatibility (EMC) and Radio Spectrum Matters;
- PN-EN 60950-1:2007/A1:2011. Information technology equipment – Safety.

4   Conclusion

The project refers to the model and the demonstrator of the national monitoring system for the vehicles carrying dangerous goods - NSMDGV.

Developing the model and the implementation of the national monitoring system demonstrator for the vehicles carrying dangerous goods - NSMDGV can significantly contribute to:

- improving the safety of people and the environment,
- developing methods to minimize the damages and costs,
- improving the exchange of information between the centres of production, transport, collection and rescue,
- developing methods of cooperation at the breakdown site.

References

1. Grzegorczyk, K., Hancyk, B., Buchcar, R.: Dangerous Goods in Road Transport. ADR 2007-2009. BUCH-CAR. Błonie (2007)
2. Grzegorczyk, K., Buchar, R.: Dangerous Goods. Transport in practise. ADR 2011-2013. BUCHCH-CAR (1) (2011)
3. Grzegorczyk, K.: Changes in Dangerous Goods Transport. Dangerous Goods (Towary Niebezpieczne) (1) (2011)
4. Grzegorczyk, K.: Transport of Dangerous Goods. Dangerous Goods (Towary Niebezpieczne) (3) (2011)
5. Różycki, M.: Safety Transport of Dangerous Goods. PPHU Moritz Marek Różycki (2009)
6. The act from 15 November 2011. OJ. 2011, No 227, pos. 1367 (2011)
7. The act from 15 November 1984. Transport Law. OJ. 2000, No 50, pos. 601 (2000)
8. The act from 29 November 2000. Atomic Law. OJ. 2007, No 42, pos. 276 (2007)
9. The act from 21 December 2000 refers Technical Inspection. OJ. 2000, No 122, pos. 1321 (2000)
10. The European Agreement concerning the International Carriage of Dangerous Goods by Road, ADR (January 1, 2013),
    http://www.unece.org/trans/danger/publi/adr/adr_e.html
11. The statistics of Central Statistical Office from 23 July 2012. Concise Statistical Yearbook of Poland, Warsaw (2012)
12. Mikulski, J., Kwaśny, A.: Role of telematics in reducing the negative environmental impact of transport. In: Mikulski, J. (ed.) TST 2010. CCIS, vol. 104, pp. 11–29. Springer, Heidelberg (2010)

Practical Aspects of Applying Telematics
in XXI Century Metropolises Management

Ewa Wolniewicz-Warska and Paweł Olczak

Kapsch Telematic Services Sp. z o.o., Poland
{Ewa.WolniewiczWarska,Pawel.Olczak}@kapsch.net

Abstract. By 2025, urban residents will be 63% of the world population, as reported by the latest forecast. The issue of implementation of effective communications solutions is seen as one of the major challenges for the municipalities in the twenty-first century. These solutions are designed to encourage the development of public transport, to facilitate the administration of private transport and help protect the city's infrastructure and environment. The implementation of intelligent urban transport systems brings tangible benefits to agglomeration: it increases safety, improves communication, helps to reduce air pollution and to reduce damage to roads and pavements, and also brings the financial impact on urban investments. In particular, the article discusses the ecological value of telematics applications in the metropolises. On the background data on environmental pollution in cities, and on the legal background in this area the potential of intelligent traffic management systems is presented.

Keywords: ITS, urban solutions, low emission zones, low traffic zones, limited access zones, traffic management, city tolling, congestion charges, noise.

1   Introduction

Undoubtedly, urbanization in developing countries is one of the greatest changes within this century. According to the specialists it is projected that between the years 2000 and 2030 developing countries will triple their build-up urban area from 200,000 square kilometres to 600,000 square kilometres. These added 400,000 square kilometres, constructed in just 30 years, equal the world's built-up area in 2000.[1]

Taking it into consideration, managing mobility for today's urban centres and city access routes has recently become a really important challenge that all developed cities have to face. Currently, it is absolutely necessary to balance the mix of transportation and parking needs for residents and businesses, commuters and visitors, while retaining the vibrance and individuality that every urban centre possesses.

To assist traffic management, electronic telematic systems can be used to automatically detect and direct the flow of people and their vehicles. Such systems can be used for demand management, traffic surveillance, traffic information, journey time or as an effective means to monitor and deter environmental conditions, such as

---

[1] The World Bank, Eco2 Cities – Ecological cities as economic cities.

J. Mikulski (Ed.): TST 2013, CCIS 395, pp. 400–409, 2013.
© Springer-Verlag Berlin Heidelberg 2013

harmful pollution (e.g., CO_2, PM_{10}, ozone, etc.) and noise emission. In other words, carefully applied intelligent transport solutions make the transport system not only much safer, more secure and efficient, but also have the power to highly reduce a negative environmental impact (as the transport sector is one of the main starting points for a successful air quality management).

Increased urban traffic challenges city's administrations in numerous ways. The strong urbanisation process brings a massive increase in both the demand for transport and energy consumption. High levels of pollution are mainly a problem faced by large and mega-cities, where the concentration of pollutants often exceeds the standards set by the World Health Organisation (WHO) three- to fourfold. Cumulative, long-term exposure to elevated levels of small and fine particulates is associated with reduced lung function, increased frequency of respiratory disease and reduced life expectancy. Most of the long-term studies of such health impacts in large urban populations, to date, have been conducted in the US and Europe. In developing as well as developed cities, short-term exposures to increased fine particulate concentrations have also been studied, and associated with increased rates of daily mortality and hospital admissions, mostly as a result of chronic respiratory and cardiovascular conditions.

Car traffic is a source of pollution and energy consumption, hence lowering the quality of life and upsetting energy balances. First cities that implemented congestion charging systems were London, Singapore and Stockholm. To give an example: The Stockholm congestion pricing system was implemented on a permanent basis on 1 August 2007, after a seven-month trial period. The primary purpose of the congestion tax was to reduce traffic congestion and improve the environmental situation in central Stockholm. It did work in both of these areas. The Italian zones, however, did not get the same international attention so far and are often innocently being downgraded to the status of tourist traps while in fact working efficiently towards full compliance with the European Commission's directive 2008/50/EC. This directive defines and regulates ambient air quality targets in order to avoid, reduce and protect from the negative impacts on human health and the environment as a whole (e.g. concentration of PM_{10} must not exceed 50 µg/m³ on more than 35 days in a year) [1].

In Poland, according to GUS (Central Statistical Office) data [11] from the beginning of 2011 60.7% of the population lives in 908 cities. It should also be noted that the vast majority of jobs are located in urban areas as well as offices, central agencies, commercial centers, educational and cultural institutions. So it is highly expected that Polish cities infrastructure is facing a need for further rapid increase of traffic, both: local inhabitants, as well as residents of a suburban neighborhood and tourists.

The level of interest in intelligent transportation systems in Poland is growing, but simultaneously there is no real progress of law adaptation to enable its further growth. For example, many European cities, for more than ten years, have been using technology which enables to charge for the entrance to city centers or to toll the most polluted vehicles. Unfortunately, in Poland, the law on public roads still does not allow for such a solution.

2   Policy

As each city has its unique traffic patterns and characteristics, so too are the strategies implemented to keep traffic flowing and to motivate drivers to modify their travelling habits. The truth is that nowadays society demands equitable access to community services and adequate mobility by all modes. However, the absence of an equitable pricing regime for public transport versus cars and personal convenience and flexibility afforded by the motor vehicle, encourages excessive car use. However, it is absolutely necessary to remember that cars are low occupancy vehicles that in peak hours do not pay their way taking into account the extra congestion, pollution and crashes they cause. What's more it is also a barrier to enhanced public transport use [18].

Telematics technologies can assist in implementing traffic restraint schemes that are most suitable for a specific urban areas such as e.g. the application of road use charges and vehicle access management. The properly selected and designed solutions reflect the objectives of the policy makers and the specific priorities of the locality. By determining an optimal mix of policy, charging strategy and technology Kapsch is able to offer a solution tailored to the requirements of that particular urban area and one that is flexible to changing conditions, including future demands such as integration with a regional or nationwide charging network. However, it is necessary to remember that the implementation of technical vehicle inspection requires numerous difficult decisions to be adopted on both a local and national level.

2.1   Italy as an Example

The first LTZs have been implemented in Italy in 1992 with the common aim of reducing congestion and pollution, thus making city centres more pleasant for residents and visitors alike. Italy had, back then, been one of the first countries to realize and use the potential of a new evolving technology, namely Internet Protocol (IP) cameras for identifying vehicles' license plate numbers on-the-fly. Each zone has its own regulations decided by the commune's province, whereas the majority of these zones are based on the principle that only vehicles with valid permits (which could depend on the vehicle's emission class, residence, etc.) are allowed to enter. In total, there exist several hundreds of such limited access zones throughout Italy, whereas the major part of these zones is installed in very small communes. In addition to the permit scheme, a complete driving ban has been introduced within a lot of LTZs as well. How well the common goal of getting rid of the vehicles and particulate matter within the LTZs is achieved, strongly correlates with the enforcement scheme, which again splits the zones up into two parts: those with electronic enforcement equipment and those without (cf. Section "Enforcement"). This paper will – after identifying common impacts and the diversity of Italian LTZs –present the impacts of Bologna's electronically enforced charged zone which has been implemented by Kapsch TrafficCom AG and can be seen as one of the pioneers in terms of electronically enforced charged zones.

2.2   Enforcement

Congestion charging systems as well as limited traffic zones require the utilization of an enforcement scheme. Such an enforcement scheme has the responsibility of ensuring that drivers respect the regulations that are in place. In case of a LTZ, the enforcement scheme, typically, has to identify vehicles without valid permit that are entering the zone. These so-called violators, then, usually have to pay a penalty for violating against the regulation. If an insufficient enforcement scheme is applied or enforcement is completely neglected, the violation rate typically grows and the LTZ's positive effects on environment and quality of life vanish.

In manually enforced LTZs, specifically entitled personnel (often police officers) have to be physically located next to the street and check whether vehicles entering or having entered the LTZs have a valid permit. The major drawbacks of manual enforcement are that it is inefficient and expensive, whereas expenses grow proportional to the size of the zone (and the thereby required larger amount of personnel). In electronically enforced LTZs, electronic enforcement equipment is installed at all entrances to the LTZ. The most basic installation, as it is most widely deployed throughout Italian electronically enforced LTZs, consists of Automatic Number Plate Recognition (ANPR) cameras only. These ANPR cameras take images of the vehicles' rear license plates (in other countries, sometimes front license plate images or additional images of the drivers are required) and compare the extracted license plate numbers with valid permits in order to determine whether a vehicle is allowed to enter. In case of an infringement, an invoice is sent to the vehicle's owner.

2.3   Technology

Automatic Number Plate Recognition (ANPR) cameras are the core component of electronically enforced LTZs. Their job is to automatically register any vehicle passage and identify the characters of the passing vehicle's license plate. For certain LTZ schemes such as accurate time-based charging, however, it makes sense to not rely on ANPR cameras due to their limited identification performance; e.g. under adverse lightning or weather conditions, broken license plates, etc. Subsequently, for specific LTZ schemes, equipping vehicles with so-called on-board units (OBUs) is favourable. These OBUs are communicating with road-side mounted transceivers via the Dedicated Short Range Communication (DSRC) protocol at 5.8 GHz which has been jointly standardized by ISO and CEN specifically for the purposes of traffic telematics. The communication performance of DSRC is world-wide unbeaten achieving performance rates over 99.9 % while ANPR may reach values around 95 to 98 % with the assistance of expensive manual verification in the Back Office (i.e. by operators correcting license plate numbers that have been misread by the ANPR cameras). The figure 1 shows a typical installation of a Kapsch TrafficCom AG ANPR camera within an Italian LTZ.

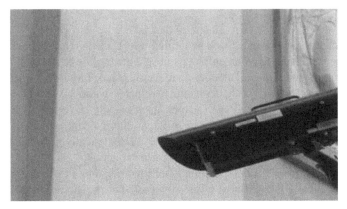

Fig. 1. Typical pole installation with a Kapsch TrafficCom AG ANPR camera in an Italian LTZ

It must also be noted that beside roadside and/or in-vehicle sensors, every electronically enforced LTZ will also require a Back Office System (BOS) which has additional tasks such as manual verification of license plates, rating of transactions, invoicing, etc. The complexity of a BOS varies enormously and mainly depends on the following two items:

- Utilized scheme of the LTZ: Identifying violators only (e.g. typical Italian limited traffic zone) signifies less effort than identifying every vehicle (e.g. passage-based or time-based charging schemes).
- Utilized technology: ANPR cameras require manual verification of misread license plates. DSRC reduces the need for manual verification as – independent of the utilized scheme – only violators have to be identified by ANPR cameras as all other vehicles are identified through the installed OBUs anyway.

3   Impacts of Limited Traffic Zones (LTZs)

LTZs represent a traffic management measure on the demand side and are consequently based on the principle of regulating traffic before it is being generated. Such traffic demand management measures have the aim of encouraging drivers to change their typical behaviour by switching to alternative modes of transport. Thereby, the traffic amount of vehicles entering a LTZ is drastically reduced leading to decreased travel and stop times. Other measures such as the creation of new P&R (park and ride) facilities, improved public transport, car sharing schemes or introduction of "green waves" are typical traffic supply management measures and provide people with alternatives to their private cars.

The reductions achieved by LTZs on the traffic amount have several positive impacts on the citizens' quality of life:

- Vehicle-related pollutants: An overall decrease of vehicle related pollutants such as CO_2, NO_X, PM_{10} or $PM_{2.5}$ is achieved. The table below provides an overview of achieved reductions after the implementation of electronically enforced charging schemes.

- Traffic-related noise: Noise typically decreases with reduced traffic; statistics, however, are only available from Stockholm where changes of -1 to -4 dBa were observed [4].

- Traffic safety: Studies from London and Stockholm generally approve a coordinated effect on road safety as the positive effect of reduced traffic is greater than then negative effect of increased speeds. [4 - 6]

Table 1. Changes to emissions of CO2, NOX and PM10 in electronically enforced charging schemes[3, 5 - 7]

Implementation	CO_2	NO_X	PM_{10}
Stockholm	-13%	-8.5%	-13%
London Central Zone	-16.4%	-13.4%	-15.5%
London Western Extension Zone	-11%	-12%	-12.2%
Milan	-9%	-11%	-19%

All of the above mentioned items have major effects on the public health. There have been studies all over the world, proving that there is a strong correlation between mortality and exposure to fine particles. Urban outdoor air pollution from small particles is estimated by WHO to cause about 1,3 million deaths globally per year [19]. Examples include the Harvard Six Cities Study and its more recent follow-up study evidencing a statistically significant 14% increase in all-cause mortality, 26% increase in cardiovascular mortality and 37% increase in lung cancer mortality–all for a 10 $\mu g/m^3$ annual increase of $PM_{2.5}$ [8]. Similar results have been achieved in a WHO survey studying pollutants' impact on health in 13 major Italian cities; e.g. 8220 cases of death per year are attributable to PM_{10} concentrations over 20 $\mu g/m^3$in Italian cities [9].

The implementation of LTZs results also in traffic-related improvements which are strongly linked to reduction of vehicle-related pollutants. This, subsequently, leads to a significant decrease of mortality and not only improves public health but the whole city's quality of life.

3.1 Analysis

It has to be noted that for the upcoming analysis this paper focuses on Italy's larger LTZs only (a total of 228 zones) and thereby ignores several hundred manually enforced small zones which are in operation in many of Italy's communes but are of no direct relevance for the reduction of pollution in cities. As displayed in Figure 2, out of the 228 considered LTZs, 70% are electronically enforced and thereof 26% are low emission zones. These low emission zones have either permits or access restrictions linked to the vehicles' emission class. For instance, a typical scenario is that older

vehicles with a low European emission standard (e.g. EURO 1, 2 and 3) are not allowed to enter the city during the winter months due to high particular matter emission levels.

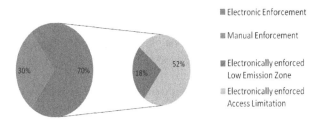

Fig. 2. Fragmentation of Italy's large limited traffic zones

Including the electronically enforced zones, there are 7 Italian LTZs which have
implemented day pass ticket schemes similar to the well known London congestion
charge scheme (these zones are further on referred to as charged traffic zones). The
day pass ticket schemes allow vehicle owners to buy tickets which are valid for one
single day and permit them to drive into the zone, whereas the day pass tickets must
be seen as addition to the scheme available for residents and frequent users who can
buy permits on a yearly basis. Besides the high number of charged traffic zones in
Italy, it is even more important to highlight that the Italian implementations do work
as efficiently as experienced in other countries. One city that proves Italian cities'
achievement is the city of Bologna, which has introduced an electronically enforced
charged traffic zone in 2006. Table 2 shows the traffic reductions of vehicles entering
the charged traffic zone before and after the implementation of the charged traffic
zone in Bologna.

Table 2. Reduction of vehicles entering the LTZ in Bologna from 2004 to 2006 [2]

	07:00 – 20:00	00:00 – 24:00
Working days	-22.7%	-24%
Sat	-27.8%	-26.2%
Sun	-35.5%	-30.9%

As discussed in Section "Impacts of limited traffic zones", reduced traffic also
leads to a decrease of vehicle-related pollutants. The city of Bologna's initial aim was
to reduce the amount of PM10 by 3 % by implementing the charged traffic zone. Results of the PM10 measuring station at the border of the charged traffic zone in Bologna show that the level of PM10 has decreased by approximately 10 μg/m³ (equal to
22 %) since the system's implementation in 2006. Thereby, the city's desired reduction of 3 % has been exceeded by far. These changes are displayed in Figure 3 and
affirm the results observed in other European charged traffic zones such as London or
Milan.

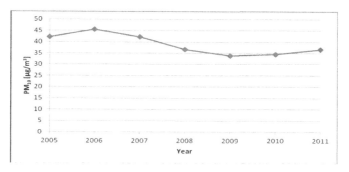

Fig. 3. Yearly changes to PM10 at measuring station "Porta San Felice" at the border of the charged traffic zone in Bologna from 2005 to 2011 [10]

Taking into account that the measuring station is not located within the charged traffic zone but at the border, reductions of PM_{10} within the zone can be expected to be even higher. The small increases during the last two years are a result of colder winters with more snowfall than in the years before. This can also be observed in Figure 4, where PM_{10} peaks during the winter months are more distinctive during 2011 and 2010 compared to 2009 while the other months show very similar patterns with low variance.

Figure 4 displays the changes to PM_{10} at the same measuring station throughout 2011, 2010 and 2009. It can be noticed that the particular matter emission levels are much higher during the winter months, justifying the measure of some Italian cities which decided to ban older vehicles with a low European emission standard (e.g. EURO 1, 2and 3) in winter months.

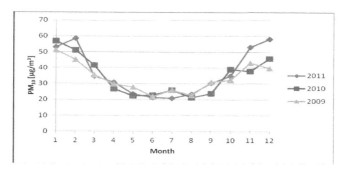

Fig. 4. Monthly changes to PM10at measuring station "Porta San Felice" at the border of the charged traffic zone in Bologna in 2009, 2010 and 2011 [10]

Looking at the emissions of NO_2 at the same measuring station in Bologna (see Figure 5), it can be seen that emissions have been rising until 2006 when the charged traffic zone was implemented. Since then, NO_2 emissions have been steadily decreasing from 70 to 50 $\mu g/m^3$ (equal to -28.5 %).

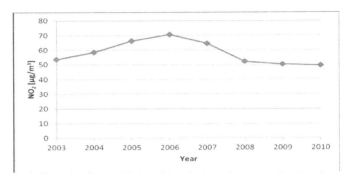

Fig. 5. Changes to NO2 at measuring station "Porta San Felice" at the border of the charged traffic zone in Bologna from 2003 to 2010 [10]

There is not sufficient data available regarding CO2 and PM2.5 for the charged traffic zone in Bologna. Corresponding to the observed impacts in other charged traffic zones and the similar results within Bologna, it can be assumed that reductions for these pollutants are also similar and therefore in the range of -10 to -25%. Bologna's achievements through the implementation of its charged traffic zone have also been acknowledged by the European Commission's expert group on ITS for Urban areas who included Bologna's charged traffic zone in its collection of best practice examples for traffic and access management.

4   Conclusion

Looking at the achievements of Polish cities in the field of innovative transportation solutions implementation, one can have an impression that all those projects have single, or even closed character and do not fully benefit from the potential of ITS based on an integrated architecture and a coherent strategy at the local, regional or even national level.

ITS is not only a source of additional income for local governments, but also a very effective and relatively low capital-consuming tool for shaping transport policy. European policymakers seem to realize that for many years. Unfortunately, in Poland, despite the increasing awareness of ITS solutions on many levels still encounter problems. It is believed that once again Poland misses an incredible opportunity to solve the problem with jammed roads, to improve the quality of life in cities, to improve safety and air quality, and strengthen the competitiveness of different urban areas and its touristic attractiveness.

A very interesting discussion for a long time takes place in Warsaw, where it was recently decided to extend charged parking zone. The decision, which apparently should gladden the inhabitants of selected districts / streets, has proved to be a problem at the moment when it became apparent that in order to adjust the selected streets to collect parking fees there is a need to significantly reduce the number of available parking places.

There is also one more controversy: the city transport policy (in ex. the increase of ticket prices) which in no way encourages the use of public transport. As a result, on the one hand, the authorities of Warsaw limited number of public parking places and promote public transport. Maybe in this case, instead of expanding charged parking zones it would be worth considering the introduction of congestion charging to the center, as it is in Bologna, London or Stockholm?

In addition to legal issues there are also some political ones: how to convince users to such solutions, or how to undertake hard decisions on the eve of the next election, how to effectively include ITS into municipal transport or development strategy? It all really depends only on the determination and vision of the city presented by the decision makers.

References

1. EC. Directive 2008/50/EC on ambient air quality and cleaner air for Europe (2008)
2. CURACAO. Deliverable D3: Case Study Results Report (2009)
3. SLB Analysis. The Stockholm trial: Effects on air quality and health (2006)
4. Stockholms stad. Facts and results from the Stockholm trials (2006)
5. Transport for London. Fourth annual report (2006)
6. Transport for London. Sixth annual report (2008)
7. di Milano, C.: Monitoraggio Ecopass: Indicatori sintetici (2009)
8. Lepeule, J.: Chronic exposure to fine particles and mortality: An extended follow-up of the Harvard six cities study from 1974 to 2009 (2012)
9. World Health Organization. Health impact of PM10and Ozone in 13 Italian cities (2006)
10. Agencia Regionale Prevenzione e Ambiente (ARPA) dell'Emilia-Romagna (2012), Data extract via web service available at: http://www.arpa.emr.it (date of access: June 02, 2012)
11. http://stat.gov.pl (date of access: August 07, 2013)
12. Kapsch TrafficCom AG, Thomas Siegl, Dietrich Leihs, Adriano Trapuzzano; Eco Traffic Management in Cities (2012)
13. Eco2 Cities – Ecological cities as economic cities, The World Bank (2010)
14. World Health Organisation – Regional Office for Europe – Air quality guidelines for Europe, 2nd edn. European Series, no. 91, Copenhagen (2000)
15. World Health Organisation – Regional Office for Europe – Health impact assessment of air pollution in the eight major Italian cities, Rome (2002)
16. World Health Organisation – Regional Office for Europe – Health aspects of air pollution: results from the systematic review of health aspects of air pollution in Europe, Copenhagen, EUR/04/5046025 (2004)
17. http://kapsch.net (date of access: August 07, 2013)
18. Intelligent Transport Systems Sustainable Transport: A Sourcebook for Policy makers in Developing Cities
19. Harvard School of Public Health, The Global Economic Burden of Non-communicable Diseases (January 2012)

Quality and Quantity Improvement for Current RDS-TMC

Petr Bureš

Czech Technical University in Prague, Faculty of Transportation Sciences,
Konviktska 20, 110 00 Praha 1, Czech Republic
bures@fd.cvut.cz

Abstract. The main objective of this paper is to present a project that aims to
increase quality and capacity of existing legacy systems based on RDS-TMC
and to discuss how it can be achieved and what the potential increase is. For
this, we will adapt withdrawn standard ALERT Plus, that is optimized for delivery of status oriented traffic information with lower latency. We will describe
how it can be implemented in coexistence with standard ALERT-C service on
the same broadcast channel, with the same data (i.e. location tables) and show
potential benefits of such service in environments with lots of traffic flow messages. At the end of the paper argue the business case for such system to show
that this improvement has a potential.

Keywords: traffic information, high density, distribution, transmission.

1   Introduction

This paper outlines the goals of the research and development project Turbo TMC.
The project is aimed on enhancing the quality of traffic information by introducing
monitoring and testing solutions for parties involved in TTI value chain and also on
enhancing the quantity of TTI by utilizing protocol ALERT plus in addition to
ALERT C for TTI distribution. In the first part of this paper we describe our proposed
solution for quality enhancement and in the second part we will deal with the solution
to achieve better throughput of standard RDS delivery channel. We will also discuss
limitation of this approach and its business opportunities.

1.1   RDS-TMC in the Frame of ALERT-C and ALERT-Plus

RDS or Radio Data System allows transmission of digital information over analog
(VHF FM) channel [1, 4, 6, 7]. RDS services are carried over by so called RDS
groups. Standard defines 32 possible group types, TMC service is conveyed by 2
group types, 3A (TMC service information) and 8A (actual traffic messages).

TMC or Traffic Message Channel allows silent delivery of live traffic information
suitable for processing by a navigation system, which then offers the driver the proposal for alternative routes to avoid traffic incidents. TMC defines structure traffic

J. Mikulski (Ed.): TST 2013, CCIS 395, pp. 410–417, 2013.
© Springer-Verlag Berlin Heidelberg 2013

information. It introduces set of rules and tables that are used together to encode and to decode traffic information at traffic center and navigation device.

Two methodologies have been distinguished in time being. The universal, free to all, event oriented TMC service called ALERT-C. The value added service, generally a paid-for service, with event and status-oriented messages, called ALERT-Plus.

ALERT-C

In ALERT-C (Advice and Problem Location for European Road Traffic, Version C) [6] each traffic incident encoded as a TMC message consists of an event code and a location code in addition to expected incident duration, extent and other details.

Event codes table contains a list of up to 2048 event phrases. Some phrases describe individual situations such as a crash, while others cover combinations of events such as a crash causing long delays. Location codes table represents simplification of road network, assigns numerical codes to locations (typically major junctions) on the road. Location tables are then integrated in the maps provided by in-vehicle navigation system. Event code and location code tables, which allow real interpretation of TMC message, are never broadcast over RDS. It is always delivered into device by other means.

ALERT-Plus

In ALERT-Plus both possible services (ALERT-C with ALERT-Plus) exists [7], allowing operation of a universal service as well as an added value RDS-TMC service on the same transmitter. A service provider is thus able to offer the universal service, and to propose in parallel to his clients more sophisticated information such as travel times, level of services, in much more efficient way.

The ALERT-Plus broadcasting protocol provides an information coding technique which allows the recipient to recover the broadcast information in its entirety. The transmitted messages contain dynamic data (statuses) which can only be interpreted with reference to static data (locations, also referred as collections). To facilitate broadcasting, locations are grouped together in addresses called collections. Both transmitter and receiver must be aware of all elements.

1.2   Why to Monitor Quality of Traffic Information Service?

Public services have a tendency to decay over time. The system efficiency is solely evaluated and almost never periodically assessed. This is caused by the business environment at public authorities, where it is much easier to get funds for setting up a system than for its continuous service [8]. This is most true in the situation where more parties are involved in the system, like it is in traffic information distribution, especially over RDS-TMC.

Problem is, that set of standards for RDS-TMC does not specify in detail how to handle and interpret traffic information received over the RDS-TMC. Direct consequence of this is that every navigation system vendor invests a lot of money into "tuning" their device to handle received messages in "best" way, as a black box [3].

The result of this tuning and customization is often not as good as it could be, sometimes vendor even overlook some crucial facts, because of limited understanding and almost no possibility of real testing. Organizations responsible for generation of traffic information start to realize this problem and to mitigate it, for example Austria started in 2010 to give conformity statements to navigation devices that properly interpret traffic information. Also other providers started to look at this problem, started testing behavior of navigation devices under specified conditions more extensively [1,5] and some published their results.

1.3   Why to Enhance Quantity of Traffic Information in the Service?

As RDS provides very limited capacity for amount of data, 1184 bits per second including 40% the overhead, TMC must be very space efficient. As it was said RDS is managed in so called groups, since each group size is 104 bits then we have circa 11 groups per second. For data relating to dynamically changing situations, the appropriate RDS-TMC groups are repeated in quick succession. Typically a 3 TMC group / second are transmitted. In order to minimize errors immediate repetition is used (group 8A must be received exactly same 2 or 3 times).

In the standard [6] maximum number of messages to be transmitted is 300. The maximum of 300 hundred messages is computed for mixed service where single (status oriented) and double (event oriented) group messages are equally distributed and 5 minutes of repetition is considered enough. It may be sufficient for rural areas, but if the service shall inform about the status of each important road segment in the area, then this number becomes a limitation.

Modern techniques of data collection (using fleets) are able to cover large areas and therefore to generate very many status messages (likely going to thousands). Therefore we need to find a way how to convey more information through RDS-TMC, using same infrastructure (location tables), without seriously compromising the RDS transmitting itself.

2   Monitoring of Quality of RDS-TMC

There could be two approaches to the monitoring of quality of RDS-TMC. The actuality and preciseness of provided traffic information and technical quality related to encoding and decoding of traffic information. First approach is very demanding to resources, since to properly judge correctness of provided information the evaluator has to have knowledge about actual traffic status in the area, which is hard to get. Second approach, the one we decided for in the project Monitor and TurboTMC, is to evaluate technical quality of coding and provision of TTI (a proper use of technical means in order to get effective service). It also includes a TMC interpretation quality and it takes place in navigation devices and evaluates if handling of messages and presentation to the user meets requirements expected by users and service providers.

2.1   Technical Quality Coding and Provision of TTI

Technical quality of RDS encoded information, i.e. a proper use of technical means (parameters of RDS transmission and coding of messages) in order to get effective service are important due to their direct influence on their processing and interpretation in navigation devices. These issues have to be quantified and then can be expressed as indicators.

Indicators of RDS Related Availability of the Service and Its Optimal Usage

The indicators of the service availability optimal usage are mainly inferred from parameters mentioned in related technical standards [6, 7] and handbooks. These indicators influence all other quality indicators.

Table 1. RDS-TMC quality tests - indicators [own work]

Code	Description	Priority
T0.1	TMC service availability in RDS stream	High
T0.2	RDS group error rate	High
T0.3	Optimal use of RDS channel by TMC service (25%)	Middle
T1.1	Number of immediate repetition of RDS groups	Low
T1.2	TMC message sizes	Low
T1.3	3A group detail – comparison to reality	Middle
T2.1	Number of actual TMC messages	Middle

For example, the simpler messages the better utilization of the RDS-TMC channel. Many messages conveys additional data, that makes messages bigger, but does not add to its information content – this problem can be solved by analysis and further training of service operators. This shows next table, where percentage of 2 group messages have been dramatically reduced (by 50%) after such training.

Table 2. TMC message size during 2 consecutive measurements

TMC message size	Before consultation		After consultation	
	messages	Percent	messages	Percent
1 group	0	**0,00%**	476	**58,33%**
2 groups	12415	**76,10%**	175	**21,45%**
3 groups	2291	14,04%	81	9,93%
4 groups	1556	9,54%	76	9,31%
5 groups	53	0,32%	8	0,98%

Indicators of TMC Message Quality

Indicators of TMC message quality are inferred from European standards and handbooks and best practices documents. They are also based on common sense of using the RDS channel efficiently and on getting maximum of actionable information, i.e. such information one can take an action upon.

Table 3. Message quality tests - indicators [own work]

Code	Description	Priority
T3.1	Number of orphan TMC messages	Middle
T3.2	Average repetition of each TMC message	Middle
T3.3	Time from last reception of each TMC message	High
T3.4	Number of cancellation messages related to current messages	Middle
T4.1	**Invalid, superfluous or vague information in a message**	**High**
T4.2	**Use of quantifier with values 0/1**	**High**
T4.3	Control code analysis (label 1)	Middle
T4.4	Use of supplementary information (label 6)	Middle
T4.5	Use of secondary event (label 9)	Middle
T4.6	Use of other labels in multi group messages	Middle

These individual message quality indicators do not have do not have exactly set limits for meeting the requirements and some of them can be defined in several ways, but all of them show parameters important for the final customer, the driver and his perception of the quality of service. It is important to mention here, that all of these indicators have been implemented into a test suite; however they are not performed automatically, because they often need a human supervision.

2.2   TMC Interpretation Quality

Navigation system vendors are faced with difficult situation. TMC standard allows many possible interpretations. They do not have qualified experts in TMC, it is just an extra feature. They often to don't have possibility to test their TMC implementation and TMC service implementation is different in every country.

This situation leads to a fact that each navigation device handles TMC service in different way. While service providers expect that all navigation systems will behave in the same way upon reception of same message.

Table 4. TMC interpretation - indicators [own work]

Code	Description	Priority
T5.1	Tuning of TMC service – manual / automatic / search	High
T5.2	Possibility to set up / save preferred TMC service	Middle
T5.3	Reception of TMC messages just from one service	High
T6.1	Typical message processing visualization and handling i.e.: explicit duration, long incidents, supplementary information, explicit cancellation, quantifiers, vague phrases, linear/area messages.	Middle

TMC interpretation quality is a complex issue that can be solved only by rigorous testing (by testing equipment) on navigation vendor's side with help of a typical messages of given service provider and best practices of how to interpret and handle these messages. The project TurboTMC plans to provide both.

Fig. 1. Example of different interpretation of long (extent = 7) TMC messages

3 Enhancing the Quantity of TMC Service

The ALERT-Plus protocol is a great platform for multiplying the throughput of information through the RDS channel. Its structure is given by RDS-TMC containers. By event description they are alike to progressive protocol TPEG [2].

However the standards defining ALERT-Plus solution were never published as full European or international standards and after short period of existence were withdrawn without any practical implementation. The project TurboTMC aims to bridge the gap between the withdrawn standards and current use of TMC services, which are more and more often used to carry status oriented messages in an ordinary ALERT-C environment.

3.1 Comparison between ALERT-C and ALERT-Plus

In ALERT-C service providers are expected to ensure that the number of RDS-TMC messages that they have transmitted which have not been specifically cancelled, or will have automatically expired, does not exceed the 300 maximum. This number is deduced using assumptions summarized in table 1, (5 minutes of repetition for every message, 2 groups immediate repetition, 1.5 average message size). However, as the last column in the table 1 shows, repetition time can be much longer (10 minutes) if not the right gap is used and messages are not as small as they should be, so if more additional information is used.

In ALERT-Plus, one message (104 bits) could carry 5 or 7 status information (see figure 2). This can be 5 successive travel times on predefined segmented link or 7 parking information related to 7 different car parks. Since ALERT-Plus allows only single group messages, we get 7:1 or 5:1 quantity enhancement ratio. If all other parameters of the RDS-TMC service remains (gaps, repetition) we could have 5-7 more information in the service.

Table 5. Repetition time for every message in the service given different service parameters and average message sizes

number of messages	300	300	300	300	**300**	300	300
immediate repetition	3	3	3	2	**2**	2	2
average message size	1	1,5	2	1	**1,5**	2	3
8A groups per second	2,96	2,96	2,96	2,96	**2,96**	2,96	2,96
Repetition time [min]	**5,08**	**7,61**	**10,15**	**3,38**	**5,08**	**6,77**	**10,15**

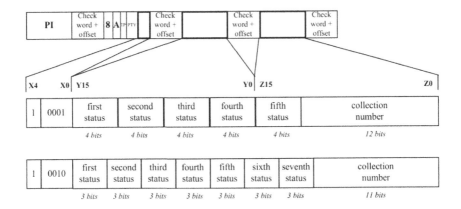

Fig. 2. ALERT-Plus RDS-TMC user message structure [7]

The collection number represents a meta location table that usually describes set of predefined locations from enhanced / modified ALERT-C location table. These sets could contain overlapping locations, because of strong regionalization of the service.

If we still want to support ALERT-C we could have 10-20% of TMC reserved to it, rest 80-90% would be used by ALERT-Plus, if we also count 25% collection overlap, we could get: 20% * 300 = 60 ALERT-C messages, 80% * 300 = 240 ALERT-Plus messages, that means **240*7*0.75 = 1260** unique travel times in 5 minutes time frame. Together it amounts to 60+756 = 1320 mixed ALERT-C/Plus messages.

3.2   Problems to Be Solved

Since the ALERT-Plus standard is similar to ALETR-C in its hindrances it still uses tables that must be installed in the terminal and in the encoding system for processing messages: location tables, collection tables, code conversion tables. Location tables are defined in separate standard and are different from ALERT-C location tables. This could be a severe hindrance, however see a solution with use of enhancements to RDS-TMC standard in 2012 that allows to logically splitting one long segment into several smaller segments more suitable for ALERT-Plus service. So that a standard, already implemented location table could be used. Just collection tables, code conversion tables would need to be distributed and this does not involve serious effort of map producer to implement table to the map.

4   Conclusion

In this paper we discussed need for monitoring of RDS-TMC quality at different parts of TTI distribution value chain. We have shown what features could be monitored and evaluated in RDS-TMC data stream, individual TMC messages and in navigation device processing algorithms. On one example we have shown how dramatically could raise the service quality if it is being monitored.

Also the reason for higher quantity of RDS-TMC messages was mentioned together with its solution. By using ALERT-Plus the provider could have both the public and private service on one radio frequency with dramatic increase of information throughput (from 300 max to 1320 avg).

All of these issues are being addressed in the project TurboTMC.

Acknowledgements. The authors acknowledge the financial support provided by the Technology Agency of the Czech Republic through project TurboTMC (TA03031386).

References

1. Bures, P., Vlcinsky, J.: Monitoring of Live Traffic Information in the Czech Republic. In: Mikulski, J. (ed.) TST 2011. CCIS, vol. 239, pp. 9–16. Springer, Heidelberg (2011)
2. Bures, P.: The architecture of traffic and travel information system based on protocol TPEG. Presented at the Proceedings of the 2009 Euro American Conference on Telematics and Information Systems: New Opportunities to Increase Digital Citizenship, Prague, Czech Republic (2009)
3. Bělinová, Z., Bureš, P., Jesty, P.: Intelligent Transport System architecture Different Approaches and Future Trends. In: Düh, J., Hufnagl, H., Juritsch, E., Pfliegl, R., Schimany, H.-K., Schönegger, H. (eds.) Data and Mobility. AISC, vol. 81, pp. 115–125. Springer, Heidelberg (2010)
4. Zelinka, T., Svitek, M.: Adaptive communications solutions in complex transport telematics systems. In: Proceedings of the 12th WSEAS International Conference on Communications - New Aspects of Communications, Greece. Recent advances in electrical engineering, pp. 206–212 (2008)
5. Bouchner, P., Novotny, S., Jirina, M.: Identification of driver's drowsiness using driving information and EEG. Neural Network World 20(6), 773–791 (2010)
6. EN ISO 14819-1.: Intelligent transport systems — Traffic and travel information: Part 1: Coding protocol for Radio Data System – Traffic Message Channel (RDS-TMC) – RDS-TMC using ALERT-C. ISO copyright office, Geneva (2011)
7. ENV 12313-4.: Traffic and Traveler Information (TTI) - TTI Messages via Traffic Message Coding: Part 4: Coding Protocol for Radio Data System - Traffic Message Channel (RDS-TMC) - RDS-TMC using ALERT Plus with ALERT C. European Committee for Standardization, Brussels (1998)
8. Belinova, Z., Bures, P., Barta, D.: Evolving ITS Architecture - the Czech Experience. In: Mikulski, J. (ed.) TST 2011. CCIS, vol. 239, pp. 94–101. Springer, Heidelberg (2011)

Concept of On-Board Comfort Vibration Monitoring System for Vehicles

Rafał Burdzik, Łukasz Konieczny, and Tomasz Figlus

Silesian University of Technology, Faculty of Transport
Krasińskiego 8, 40-019 Katowice, Poland
rafal.burdzik@polsl.pl

Abstract. Ride comfort is extremely difficult to determine because of the variations in individual sensitivity to vibration. Vibration can cause a variety of diseases or at least unpleasant feeling states. The impact of this phenomenon is subjective and depends on human perception. The vibration perception depends on values, time and frequency band of the vibration. Exposure to vibration and the human perception are strongly connected with comfort or discomfort feeling on the driver and passengers. For identification the mapping of vibration measuring in multiple points is very useful. Under the studies in question, active experiments were undertaken featuring measurements of vibration accelerations in a vertical direction perpendicular to the horizontal surface of vehicle in selected points located in carbody. The analytical experiment on application of neural networks in the identification of pressure level in tires of a vehicle based on vibration signals was conducted. Based on the results the concept of onboard comfort vibration monitoring system for vehicles was developed.

Keywords: vibration monitoring system, comfort, neural network.

1   Introduction

Human vibration perception in transport is strongly correlated with comfort and safety. The consequences of the impact of vibration on humans are all kinds of adverse effects in the body, resulting from the exposure to vibration. Range and process behavior of these changes depends largely on where they penetrate into the body. The division of human perception of vibrations determines the subjective and psychosomatic responses as well as disturbances in the system functioning. As regards the location where vibrations penetrate the human organism, one may speak of general and local vibrations [1-3]. The range of impacts vibrations exert on a vehicle driver is very broad, starting from the feeling of discomfort to safety hazards caused by vibrations at resonant frequencies of specific organs, thus affecting the driver's responses. Vibration signal can be used as source of technical state condition of machine [4-7].The ongoing development of the automotive industry is not only about improving vehicle subunits but also about using new structural materials manufactured by state-of-the-art metallurgical technologies and application of new technologies for joining vehicle components [8-13].

J. Mikulski (Ed.): TST 2013, CCIS 395, pp. 418–425, 2013.
© Springer-Verlag Berlin Heidelberg 2013

2   Research on Vehicle Vibration

To develop the project of on-board comfort vibration monitoring system for vehicles the large scope of research has to be conducted. The active research experiments were conducted on real passenger car (Fig. 2). The vehicle was excited to vibration by special kinematic excitation machine. The vibration sensors were placed in chosen location on vehicle construction. The vibration of suspension elements and floor panel were recorded. The research method and measurement points localization has been depicted in Fig. 1.

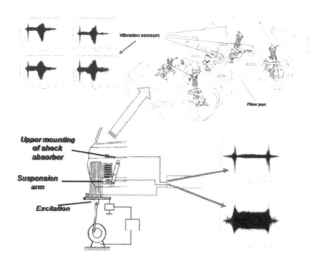

Fig. 1. The research method and measurement points

Fig. 2. The object of the research and example of position of vibration sensor

3   Floor Panel Vibration Surface

The obtained result are signals with splot of stationary and nonstationary vibrations (Fig. 3) [14].

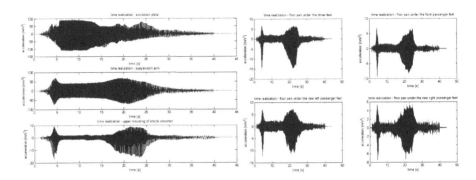

Fig. 3. Recorded signals (excitation plate, suspension arm, upper mounting of shock absorber, floor pan: under driver feet, front passenger, rear left, rear right)

There has been proposed the model of the surface of the vehicle floor panel vibrations based on several statistical estimators of the vibration signal. It is assumed to enable representation of several signal characteristics in the form of a set of surfaces in a geometrical distribution of vibrations. The methodology of determination of the surface estimates for characteristics of the vehicle vibrations comfort entails determination of a set of global signal measures at specific geometrical points and determination of a surface approximating the distribution of these values on the floor panel. Some of the exemplary vibration mapping determining on the studies conducted was that of an experimental modal analysis. The vibration surfaces thus established have been illustrated in the following figure 4.

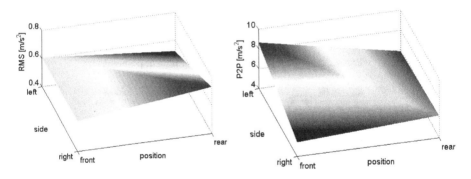

Fig. 4. Global vibration surface estimates as functions (left- value of X_{RMS}, right- Peak-to-Peak)

4 Application of VSA and Neural Networks in the Identification of Damping Properties

For the vibration comfort of automotive vehicles the damping properties are very important. The suspension system determining the vibration transfer from road roughness to carbody. The vibration isolation efficiency depends on shock absorbers characteristics. There was proposed and developed the system for monitoring and diagnosing of shock absorbers. The registered vibration signals are processing by the Vibroacoustic Signals Analyzer (VSA) program using CWT (Continues Wavelet Transformation). It is a self-designed program for the signal processed with friendly-user interface, which was described in [15]. The results of VSA are vectors of technical conditions as estimators of resonances of unsprung and sprung masses. This vector is input function of the programmed neural network classifier. Algorithm of vibration monitoring and diagnosing system of damping properties shows in figures 5 and 6.

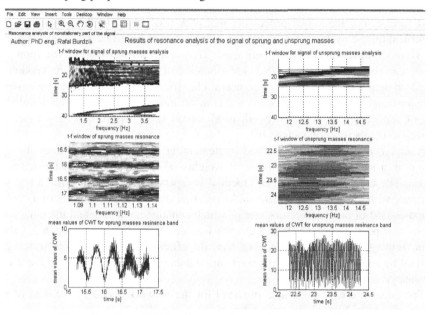

Fig. 5. Interface of VSA – CWT analysis and resonances windows

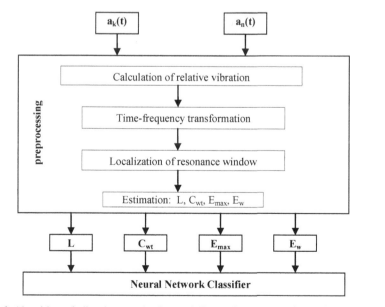

Fig. 6. Algorithm of vibration monitoring and diagnosing system of damping properties

5   Application of VSA and Neural Networks in the Identification of Pressure Level in Tires

The pressure level in tires is very important for the driving safety and comfort. It can determine values of vibration transfer to car body and pressure forces of wheels and road surface. For the signal processing the VSA was used. For the neural network identification the system of tires pressure level chosen time realization measures of the vibration in resonances area were used. The vector of estimators of vibration signal is obtained as the result of VSA. Identification of pressure level in tires module is based on neural network theory. The neural classification system can be applied as a decision-making module in the on-board comfort monitoring system. The simulating test of application of neural network in abnormal tire pressure detection based on vibration signals was conducted [16].

Neural networks are programmed implementing automatically trainings through assigning a sample task. Adaptation of weights takes place in successive teaching cycles. The most commonly applied method is supervised by learning with a teacher. Learning with a teacher takes place under external supervision. Examples of a correct action consist of pairs of vectors, one of which contains input data and the other contains the expected output values. For each teaching pair, the error function is calculated. Having exhausted the teaching data, the efficiency of the network training is verified by its testing based on the verification data of similar properties to the teaching data [17].

The paper presents the results obtained for the network tested by the data of the expected values. Identified pressure levels are grouped in 3 classes (value suggested by the producer, lower and higher). Numerous types and architectures of neural networks were tested. As the criteria of network efficiency value of 80% of the correct classified of pressure level in complete testing matrix was determined. The output data were rounded to a logical 1 or 0 with the specified accuracy. The network properties and testing results have been depicted in Table 1.

Table 1. Neural Network 1

Type of Neural Network	feed-forward backpropagation network
Number of layers	3
Number of neurons in I layer	4
Activation function in I layer	LOGSIG Logarithmic sigmoid transfer function
Number of neurons in II layer	6
Activation function in II layer	PURELIN Linear transfer function
Number of neurons in III layer	3
Activation function in III layer (output)	TANSIG Hyperbolic tangent sigmoid function

The results of the network 1 testing are presented in Table 2. In the Table with the results of testing the lighter color cells are signalizing the correct identification, the darker cells are signalizing the incorrect classification.

Table 2. Matrix of the outputs after test for Neural Network 1

	Values of the pressure in tires [bar]										
	0,6	0,8	1,0	1,2	1,4	1,6	1,8	2,0	2,2	2,4	2,6
Lower value	1	1	1	1	1	1	1	0	0	0	0
Values suggested by the producer	0	0	0	0	0	0	0	1	1 (0)	1 (0)	0
Higher value	0	0	0	0	0	0	0	0	0 (1)	0 (1)	1

6   Concept of On-board Comfort Vibration Monitoring System for Vehicles

The conception of the on-board comfort vibration monitoring system for vehicles was proposed. The system has parameters for monitoring and control [18-22]. It is designed as 3-modular system integrated with VSA. First module is registering the floor panel vibration for surface and mapping of vibration transferred to human organism in multiple geometrical points distribution of vibrations. Second module is for the monitoring of the damping properties of the suspension. The last module is for the identification of pressure level in tires.

The obtain results of the developed system will be compare with some references measures correlated to the comfort feeling and safety of vehicle driving.

The architectures of the conception of the on-board comfort vibration monitoring system for vehicles has been depicted in Fig. 7.

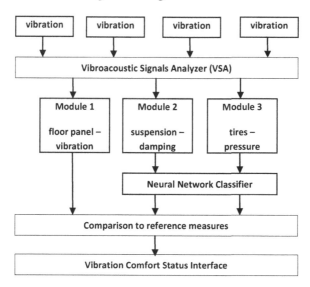

Fig. 7. Architectures of the conception of the on-board comfort vibration monitoring system for vehicles

7   Conclusion

The conception of the on-board comfort vibration monitoring system for vehicles is based on the results of experimental research and analytical studies on neural network application for classification. It is complex system of 3 independent modules. Possibilities of monitoring of the vibrations of suspension and carbody (floor panel) enables suspension diagnosing and vibration exposure of passengers. The module for tires pressure level identification allows signalization of abnormal pressure and prevent from vibration comfort worsen.

References

1. Wyllie, I.H., Griffin, M.J.: Discomfort from sinusoidal oscillation in the pitch and fore-and-aft axes at frequencies between 0.2 and 1.6Hz. Journal of Sound and Vibration 324 (2009)
2. Burdzik, R., Konieczny, Ł., Łazarz, B.: Influence of damping characteristics changes on vehicles vibration research. In: 19th International Congress on Sound and Vibration (ICSV19), Conference Proceedings, p. 657 (2012)
3. Burdzik, R., Doleček, R.: Research of vibration distribution in vehicle constructive. Perner's Contacts VII, 416-425 (2012)
4. Tuma, J.: Gearbox noise and vibration prediction and control. International Journal of Acoustics and Vibration 14, 99–108 (2009)
5. Jasiński, M., Radkowski, S.: Use of bispectral-based fault detection method in the vibroacoustic diagnosis of the gearbox. Engineering Asset Lifecycle Management, 651–660 (2010)
6. Michalski, R., Wierzbicki, S.: An analysis of degradation of vehicles in operation. Maintenance and Reliability 1(37), 30–32 (2008)
7. Grządziela, A.: Modelling of propeller shaft dynamics at pulse load. Polish Maritime Research 15(4), 52–58 (2008)
8. Blacha, L., Siwiec, G., Oleksiak, B.: Loss of aluminium during the process of Ti-Al-V alloy smelting in a vacuum induction melting (VIM) furnace. Metalurgija 52(3), 301–304 (2013)
9. Mencik, J.: Determination of parameters of visco-elastic materials by instrumented indentation. Chem. Listy 104, 275–278 (2010)
10. Kaźmierczak-Bałata, A., Bodzenta, J., Trefon-Radziejewska, D.: Determination of thermal-diffusivity dependence on temperature of transparent samples by thermal wave method. International Journal of Thermophysics 31(1), 180–186 (2010)
11. Folęga, P., Siwiec, G.: Numerical analysis of selected materials for flexsplines. Archives of Metallurgy and Materials 57(1), 185–191 (2012)
12. Węgrzyn, T., Wieszała, R.: Significant alloy elements in welded steel structures of car body. Archives of Materials and Metallurgy 57(1), 45–52 (2012)
13. Dobrzański, L.A., Bonek, M., Hajduczek, E., Klimpel, A., Lisiecki, A.: Application of high power diode laser (hpdl) for alloying of X40CRMOV5-1 steel surface layer by tungsten carbides. Journal of Materials Processing Technology 155/156, 1956–1963 (2004)
14. Burdzik, R.: Material vibration propagation in floor pan. Archives of Materials Science and Engineering, AMSE 59(1), 22–27 (2013)

15. Burdzik, R.: Monitoring system of vibration propagation in vehicles and method of analysing vibration modes. In: Mikulski, J. (ed.) TST 2012. CCIS, vol. 329, pp. 406–413. Springer, Heidelberg (2012)
16. Burdzik, R., Peruń, G., Warczek, J.: Application of Neural Networks in the Identification of Pressure Level in Tires of a Vehicle Based on Vibration Signals. In: 5th International Congress on Technical Diagnostics 2012, vol. 135 (2012)
17. Tadeusiewicz, R.: Sieci neuronowe, Warszawa (1993)
18. Batko, W., Cioch, W., Jamro, E.: Monitoring system for grinding machine of turbine-engine blades. Journal of Polish CIMAC 2(2), 13–18 (2007)
19. Farana, R., Wagnerova, R.: Sliding mode controls of complex control systems. In: Singhal, R.K., Singh, B.P. (eds.) Mine Planning and Equipment Selection, pp. 11–17 (2001)
20. Muzikářová, L., Franeková, M., Holečko, P., Hrnčiar, M.: Theory of information and signals. In: EDIS (2008)
21. Mikulski, J., Kwaśny, A.: Role of telematics in reducing the negative environmental impact of transport. In: Mikulski, J. (ed.) TST 2010. CCIS, vol. 104, pp. 11–29. Springer, Heidelberg (2010)
22. Mikulski, J.: Using telematics in transport. In: Mikulski, J. (ed.) TST 2010. CCIS, vol. 104, pp. 175–182. Springer, Heidelberg (2010)

Some Problems of Functional Analysis of Electronic Toll Collection System (ViaToll)

Zbigniew Kasprzyk and Mirosław Siergiejczyk

Warsaw University of Technology, Faculty of Transport
Koszykowa 75, 00-662 Warsaw, Poland
{zka,msi}@wt.pw.edu.pl

Abstract. The article presents the issues of transport telematics systems. Presented toll collection systems, which are used in Poland. Particular attention was paid to the electronic toll collection system, which utilizes transponder OBU mounted on the vehicle. Through its use is not required to stop the vehicle in order to pay the tolls. Analysis of the situation occurring now makes it necessary to make a functional analysis of electronic toll collection systems.

Keywords: transport telematics, toll collection systems, electronic devices.

1 Introduction

The issue of transport telematics appeared in Polish literature in the mid-nineties. Even then, attempts were made to determine the extent of the conceptual and the area of transport telematics applications [1 - 2], which is defined as a field of knowledge and technical activities integrating information technology with telecommunications as applied to the needs of the transport systems.

Motorway telematics combines the use of intelligent transport systems on motorways in order to significantly increase travel and transportation security, increased reliability of transport, improve the use of road infrastructure and achieve better economic performance by reducing environmental degradation. Transport telematics systems are particularly useful in the following areas:

- control and monitoring of the use of motor vehicles,
- fleet management,
- toll collection vehicles
- information on the methods and conditions of travel.

An important system in the area of telematics is highway toll collection system. Autonomous decision on driver's of choosing route of travel, determines the payment of tolls on toll roads or the continuing traveling without paying the legal tolls. This decision starts, in the structure of the motorway telematics processing, the collection of the information used for further applications for the intelligent transportation on highways and toll roads. The proper functioning of the toll collection system contributes significantly to the increase in travel safety. The toll motorway sections during the entire transport process follows a two-way transmission of data (information).

J. Mikulski (Ed.): TST 2013, CCIS 395, pp. 426–432, 2013.
© Springer-Verlag Berlin Heidelberg 2013

This is necessary due to the nature of the installed devices and their use. These devices communicate each other by the way of question and answer using actuators and sensors. In addition to the flow of information on the layout of a telematics system, the data are distributed partly outside the system to GSM, GPS and the Internet. This is to contact the user with a charging system before you travel and monitoring of vehicle tracking user in order to determine its position, and determine the moment since entering the paid section. Toll collection system is significantly involved in the supply and processing of information within the telematics motorway.

2   Electronic Toll Collection System (ViaToll)

Figure 1 shows the types of electronic toll collection systems used in the world.

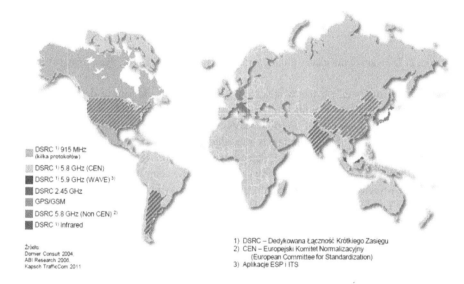

Fig. 1. Electronic toll collection systems used in the world [4]

According to the law on main public roads [3], all users of motor vehicles are obligated to pay a fee for toll roads. The introducing, since the 1st of July 2011, the National Toll Collection System has enabled the payment of tolls electronically for users of vehicles with a maximum mass exceeding 3.5 tones. Users of other types of vehicles still have to use the manual toll collection systems. Therefore, on the toll roads, there are two basic types of toll systems: manual toll system and an electronic toll collection system.

In Poland, within the framework of ViaToll electronic toll collection system in the 5.8 GHz DSRC technology (CEN) (Figure 1) was introduced. DSRC technology is used as a tool for automatic toll collection for passing a toll motorways, expressways and selected roads. This is done with the cooperation of sensors placed on gateways and transponders in the vehicle for which the fee is charged for the journey. The principle of DSRC technology functioning is as follows (Figure 2).

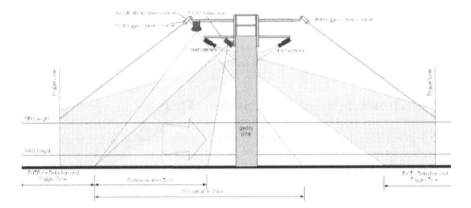

Fig. 2. Diagram of the gantry pillar operating in the 5.8 GHz DSRC technology [4]

Transponder mounted on the windscreen, at the time of entering a detection zone, sends a signal to the sensor with information about the vehicle (radio at 5.8 GHz microwave frequency at speeds of up to 500 kb/s). The laser scanner classifies the type of vehicle. Additionally vehicle journey is recorded by CCTV cameras installed on the control gantry. Similarly, an exit point detection zone is recorded by CCTV installed on the gantry. The data recorded by the gantry are sent to the central tolling, where after the processing of vehicle parameters data, the settlement of payment takes place.

Electronic Toll Collection System in Poland operates as an open system or a closed system, depending on the type of the motorway.

Closed toll system always has a point of entry to the toll road and the point of exit from the toll road. In this system, the user has no possibility to exit from the toll road between the point of entry and the point of exit. Depending on traffic volume, Toll Plazas consist of a belt entry or exit lanes located on Toll Stations. In a closed system toll roads the payment is carried out basing on the distance traveled by the vehicle and the vehicle category. The length of the the toll road section, covered by the distance, is based on the information contained in the transponder, which is read by the detector DSRC located on the gantry.

Open toll system has Toll Plazas with exit lanes, where payment is made for the journey. The number of lanes in each direction, in an open system, is defined in such a way that ensured the maximum throughput of the system. All entry and exit lanes are controlled by an automatic toll collection system in the form of an Electronic Toll Collection System with the system manual (mixed system). In an open system toll road the payment is made basing of the current section of the toll road without taking into account the distance traveled by the vehicle and on the vehicle category. The most toll roads in Poland actually operates and in the coming years will operate in an open system.

3   Functional Analysis of the Electronic Toll Collection System

In analyzing the functional elements of a gantry carrying out their functions in the 5.8 GHz DSRC system (Figure 2), we can conclude that the relationship in terms of reliability can be illustrated as shown in Figure 3.

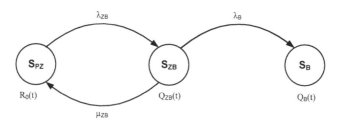

Fig. 3. Relations in the DSRC system using transponder and CCTV cameras

Symbols in Figure 3:

$R_0(t)$ – probability function of the system staying in complete capability,

$Q_{ZB}(t)$ – probability function of the system staying in a state of emergency safety,

$Q_B(t)$ – probability function of the system staying in a state of safety failure,

λ_{ZB} – intensity go from complete capability to the state of emergency safety,

λ_B – intensity go from emergency safety to the state of safety failure,

μ_{ZB} – intensity go from emergency safety to the state of complete capability.

State of complete capability S_{PZ} is a state in which all components are functioning properly performing the function of gantry payment. State of emergency safety S_{ZB1} is a state in which the fault is one of the equipment on the gantry. State of safety failure S_B is a state in which the elements of the gantry are faulty and there is no possibility to take the   electronic toll from the users of the toll road.

The system shown in Figure 3 can be described by the following equations Kolmogorov-Chapman:

$$R_0'(t) = -\lambda_{ZB} \cdot R_0(t) + \mu_{ZB} \cdot Q_{ZB}(t)$$
$$Q_{ZB}'(t) = \lambda_{ZB} \cdot R_0(t) - \mu_{ZB} \cdot Q_{ZB}(t) - \lambda_B \cdot Q_{ZB}(t) \tag{1}$$
$$Q_B'(t) = \lambda_B \cdot Q_{ZB}(t)$$

Assuming the initial conditions:

$$R_0(0) = 1$$
$$Q_{ZB}(0) = Q_B(0) = 0 \tag{2}$$

and applying the Laplace transform to give the following equations:

$$s \cdot R_0^*(s) - 1 = -\lambda_{ZB} \cdot R_0^*(s) + \mu_{ZB} \cdot Q_{ZB1}^*(s)$$
$$s \cdot Q_{ZB}^*(s) = \lambda_{ZB} \cdot R_0^*(s) - \mu_{ZB} \cdot Q_{ZB}^*(s) - \lambda_B \cdot Q_{ZB}^*(s) \qquad (3)$$
$$Q_B^*(s) = \lambda_B \cdot Q_{ZB}^*(s)$$

Using the reverse transformation, were obtained:

$$R_0(t) = \frac{\exp\left[-\frac{t \cdot (\lambda_B + \lambda_{ZB} + \mu_{ZB})}{2}\right] \cdot \left[\begin{array}{l} \lambda_B \cdot \sinh\left[\frac{t \cdot \sqrt{A}}{2}\right] - \lambda_{ZB} \cdot \sinh\left[\frac{t \cdot \sqrt{A}}{2}\right] + \\ \mu_{ZB} \cdot \sinh\left[\frac{t \cdot \sqrt{A}}{2}\right] + \cosh\left[\frac{t \cdot \sqrt{A}}{2}\right] \cdot \sqrt{A} \end{array}\right]}{\sqrt{A}} \qquad (4)$$

$$Q_{ZB}(t) = \frac{2 \cdot \lambda_{ZB} \cdot \exp\left[-\frac{t \cdot (\lambda_B + \lambda_{ZB} + \mu_{ZB})}{2}\right] \cdot \sinh\left(\frac{t \cdot \sqrt{B}}{2}\right)}{\sqrt{B}} \qquad (5)$$

$$Q_B(t) = \frac{2 \cdot \lambda_B \cdot \lambda_{ZB} \cdot \exp\left[-\frac{t \cdot (\lambda_B + \lambda_{ZB} + \mu_{ZB})}{2}\right] \cdot \sinh\left(\frac{t \cdot \sqrt{B}}{2}\right)}{\sqrt{B}} \qquad (6)$$

where:

$$A = \left(4 \cdot \left(\frac{\lambda_B}{2} + \frac{\lambda_{ZB}}{2} + \frac{\mu_{ZB}}{2}\right)^2 - 4 \cdot \lambda_B \cdot \lambda_{ZB}\right)$$

$$B = \left(\lambda_B^2 - 2 \cdot \lambda_B \cdot \lambda_{ZB} + 2 \cdot \lambda_B \cdot \mu_{ZB} + \lambda_{ZB}^2 + 2 \cdot \lambda_{ZB} \cdot \mu_{ZB} + \mu_{ZB}^2\right)$$

The obtained relations allow to determine the probabilities of staying DSRC system in states of complete capability R_0, emergency safety Q_{ZB} and safety failure Q_B.

Computer simulation method makes it possible to determine the impact of changes in indicators of reliability of system components on the reliability of the system under test. Adopted the following values for the system analyzed:

– research time one year:

$$t = 8760 \text{ [h]},$$

– intensity go from complete capability for the state of emergency safety:

$$\lambda_{ZB} = 0{,}000005 = 5 \cdot 10^{-6} \left[\frac{1}{h} \right]$$

– intensity go from emergency safety for the state of safety failure:

$$\lambda_{ZB} = 0{,}000003 = 3 \cdot 10^{-6} \left[\frac{1}{h} \right]$$

Intensity go from emergency safety to the state of complete capability μ_{ZB} is the inverse of the exponential distribution repair time t_{ZB} :

$$\mu_{ZB} = \frac{1}{t_{ZB}} \left[\frac{1}{h} \right] \tag{7}$$

Probability stay in complete capability as a function of intensity repair of the analyzed system shown in Figure 4.

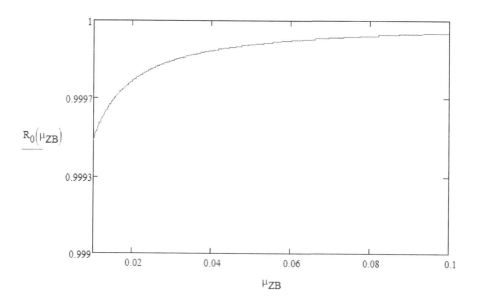

Fig. 4. Dependence of probability stay in complete capability R_0 as a function of intensity repair of the analyzed system

Functional analysis of the electronic toll collection system allowed the determination of probabilities DSRC system staying in different states. Determination and analysis of the probabilities of these relationships as a function of repair system revealed that:

- the value of the probability of the system staying in complete capability R_0 is the maximum for the minimum of time t_{ZB},
- function $R_0 = f(\mu_{ZB})$ is an increasing function and has a non-linear character.

4   Conclusion

This paper presents the types of electronic toll collection systems in Poland and the world. The analysis of functional and reliability gantry electronic toll collection system in the 5.8 GHz DSRC technology was made. Assuming three analyzed states reliability of electronic toll collection system and the transition between them, there were determined the equations, allowing the determination of the probability of the system staying in those states. Determined relations enabled to define the influence of the intensity of the effect of possible repairs on the value of the probability of the system staying in complete capability.

References

1. Wawrzyński, W.: Transport telematics - conceptual scope and field of application. Overview of Communication (11) (1997)
2. Wawrzyński, W.: Place of telematics in the discipline of transport. Department of Transportation PW, Warsaw (2003)
3. Act of 7 November 2008 amending the Act on public roads and other laws, the consolidated text Dz.U. 2008 nr 218 poz. 1391
4. http://www.word.opole.pl/data/newsFiles/prezentacja_etc_dla_o wrbrd_-_wyci_g.pdf (date of access: August 07, 2013)
5. Kołowrocki, K., Soszyńska-Budny, J.: Reliability and safety of complex technical systems and processes. Springer, London (2011)
6. Paś, J., Duer, S.: Determination of the impact indicators of electromagnetic interferences on computer information systems. Neural Computing & Applications (2012), doi:10.1007/s00521-012-1165-1
7. Rosiński, A.: Design of the electronic protection systems with utilization of the method of analysis of reliability structures. In: Proceedings of the Nineteenth International Conference on Systems Engineering, ICSEng 2008, Las Vegas, USA, pp. 421–426 (2008)
8. Siergiejczyk, M., Paś, J., Rosiński, A.: Application of closed circuit television for highway telematics. In: Mikulski, J. (ed.) TST 2012. CCIS, vol. 329, pp. 159–165. Springer, Heidelberg (2012)

Experimental and Simulation Research on Car Acceleration and Braking on Snow-Covered Roads

Krzysztof Kędziora[1] and Konrad J. Waluś[2]

[1] Prof. Dr. Jan Sehn Institute of Forensic Research in Cracow
31-033 Krakow, Poland
kkedziora@ies.krakow.pl
[2] Poznan University of Technology
60-965 Poznan, Poland
konrad.walus@put.poznan.pl

Abstract. This paper presents the results of experimental investigations of the acceleration and deceleration of a passenger car equipped with summer and winter tires. The research was carried out on a paved section of road, covered with snow, with a variable longitudinal gradient (grade line). This road section seen from above, has the shape of an arc of large initial radius, which then passes into a straight section of road. Vehicle motion parameters were recorded, inter alia, with the use of the built-in measurement equipment DATRON. Geometric surface features were measured using a surveying instrument – TPS. Information about the average value of vertical alignment at each point of the roadway, over the entire length of the test section, allowed compensation of gravitational acceleration effect on the characteristics of the acceleration and deceleration, obtained in the tests.

Keywords: acceleration, deceleration, tires, winter conditions.

1 Introduction

The main problem in accident reconstruction is to determine the coefficient of adhesion of the tire to road surface before and after the traffic crash. The optimal technique for determining the rate deceleration trials are provided on-site, using the same, as in this case, type of vehicle, tires, in similar weather conditions. In the case of these attempts failure experts use a theoretical method for determining the properties of anti-skid surface. It is based on the determination of the adhesion coefficient from tables in the literature. A suitable factor is selected by an expert on the basis of several well-known parameters such as the type of surface (asphalt, concrete, cobblestones, etc.), weather conditions (surface dry, wet, icy), type of vehicle (passenger, van, truck), presence or absence of ABS. In most common cases such procedure is sufficient to analyze the event. The problem occurs when the road surface is unusual [1], or if the conditions depend on the influence of other parameters, such as temperature or density. In some cases it is not possible to carry out a reliable deceleration test on the scene, because at the time of the reconstruction, the surface properties are

J. Mikulski (Ed.): TST 2013, CCIS 395, pp. 433–440, 2013.
© Springer-Verlag Berlin Heidelberg 2013

completely different than at the time of the accident. An example of surface for which adhesion is subject to frequent and large fluctuations, is a snowy surface, on which experimental studies discussed in this article were conducted.

2 Analysis of Existing Research

Analyses of tire adhesion to the snowy surface were carried out in the past by many authors. For example, authors of paper [3] conducted an intensive analysis of stopping cars with tires all year round, probably not equipped with ABS (because the presence of optimality-skid devices for vehicles in this work is not mentioned), the initial velocity within the range of 25-54 km/h. Tests were performed on almost all road surfaces encountered in the winter, in the temperature ranging from -42°C to -4°C. Examples of the deceleration, calculated on the basis of adhesion factors listed in [3], for some winter conditions, are summarized in Table 1 (in parentheses are temperatures of the deceleration intensity linearly dependent).

Table 1. Summary of the deceleration [3]

Description	Deceleration $[m/s^2]$
Ice not destroyed by chains or spikes that looked like glass	0.53-1.86 (t_0-t_{-25})
Thick layer of black ice, not destroyed by blocked tires, sliding hard to notice by an average driver	1.18-2.55 $(t_{-5}-t_{-40})$
A thin layer of black ice, partially destroyed by blocked slipping tires, hard to notice by an average driver	1.67-4.81 $(t_{-3}-t_{-30})$
A continuous layer of snow compacted to form an icy surface	1.18-3.83
Packed snow and ice covered with a layer of fresh snow and frozen fog 3-100 mm thick, not ridden by vehicles	1.77-4.41 $(t_{-10}-t_{-40})$
Packed snow and ice covered with a layer of old, rough, crusty snow with thickness of 100-200 mm, not ridden by vehicles	4.22-4.41 $(t_{-15}-t_{-40})$
The snow which fell directly into the street, compacted by vehicles, but not forming a dense layer of snow and ice	2.35-3.63 (low temperature effect.)
The snow which fell directly into the street, not affected by vehicles	1.47-4.12 (t_0-t_{-10})

Values of deceleration arise from [4], within the ranges of values given in Table 1. Based on some research, carried out at a temperature of -6° C using a car fitted with all-season tires, and probably without the ABS system (the fact of the presence of skid-optimization devices is not mentioned for vehicles used in this work), values of deceleration (acceleration and speed) are summarized in Table 2.

Table 2. Summary of the deceleration values [4]

Surface	Braking [m/s²]	Accelerating [m/s²]
Compacted snow	3.43	1.96
Smooth ice	0.88	0.78

Research of a passenger car braking process intensity carried out under winter conditions, equipped with different types of tires and with an ABS system switched on and off are shown in [2]. Deceleration values, calculated from [2] are summarized in Table 3 (for research on icy pavement) and 4 (on the snow surface).

Table 3. Summary of braking deceleration on the icy surface [2]

Tire type	ABS	Surface temperature [°C]	Ambient temperature [°C]	Braking deceleration [m/s²]
winter	yes	-5.4	-5.9	2.65-1.47
	no			2.06-1.47
summer	yes	-5.2	-3.1	1.96-1.28
	no			1.57-1.47
all-season	yes	-3.6	0.0	1.86-1.18
	no			1.57-1.18
winter	yes	-1.9	2.0	1.47-0.98
	no			0.98

Table 4. Summary of deceleration values on a snow-covered surface [2]

Tire type	ABS	Surface temperature [°C]	Ambient temperature [°C]	Braking deceleration [m/s²]
winter	yes	-2.2	-3.0	2.16-2.06
	no			2.55
winter	yes	-5.0	-5.9	2.75-2.65
	no			3.14-2.94
winter	yes	-0.8	-1.2	2.35
	no			2.84-2.75
all-season	yes	-0.8	-1.2	1.57-1.47
	no			2.06-1.57

It follows from results listed in Table 3 that at icy surface higher deceleration values were obtained when the car was braking with ABS enabled. On the contrary for experiments carried out on snow-covered roads, lower deceleration values were obtained. Based on the findings, summarized in Table 4, a clear trend can be seen to obtain higher values of deceleration during braking with an ABS system turned off, regardless of the type of tires fitted. In [5] there are two ways depicted to explain this phenomenon. First of all – in the case of braking on a thin layer of snow (up to 10 mm) partially blocked wheels of the car tear off this layer, leading to contact between tires and a wet road surface, which promotes an increase in deceleration. Secondly – in front of locked tires snow is piling up, which also increases the movement resistance of the vehicle. Both effects do not occur in the case of a vehicle fitted with an ABS braking system.

3   Own Research

All references based on which statements in section 2 of this article are made relate to research carried out in the 90's and earlier. It could be postulated that braking effectiveness of a "modern" car, equipped with a modern ABS system and new tires should be noticeably higher than in the presented research. To verify this hypothesis a cycle of acceleration and braking experiments under winter conditions were conducted for a selected passenger car. The experiments were carried out using a SKODA OCTAVIA II Tour Combi 1.6, with front axle driven wheels. The vehicle was equipped with ABS and traction control system activated during acceleration. Two sets of 195/65 R15 tires were used interchangeably for tests:

- summer tires: Continental ContiEcoContact 3,
- winter tires: Kleber Krisalp HP2.

The study was conducted during the ongoing snowfall, on a surface covered with a thick, uniform snow layer, which was previously compacted as a result of traffic. It had a temperature of -4.6 °C. Ambient temperature was -3.0 °C. Geometric characteristics of the surface were determined using geodetic instrument – TPS. Results of geodetic measurements are shown in Figures 1 and 2.

During the experiments the car was moving slightly uphill. On the basis of the shape of vertical alignment and equation of its linear approximation, shown in Figure 2, it can be concluded that the angle of inclination of the surface on the entire segment length was virtually constant, and the average value was about 1.45° (or about 2.53%), as calculated (1).

$$\alpha = a\tan(0{,}0253) \cong 1{,}45^{o}$$

$$y_{x=0} = 0{,}0253 \cdot 0 - 7{,}3892 \cong -7{,}39$$
$$y_{x=356} = 0{,}0253 \cdot 356 - 7{,}3892 \cong 1{,}62 \tag{1}$$
$$\frac{y_{x=356} - y_{x=0}}{356} \cdot 100 \cong 2{,}53\%$$

Acceleration values obtained in the tests were adjusted by the designated angle of the test section, based on formula (2).

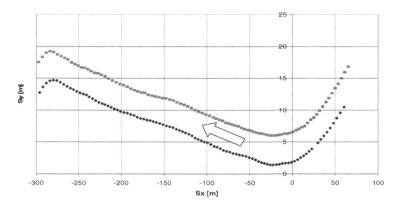

Fig. 1. Viewpoints that lie on the edges of the test section in plain view, whose coordinates were measured using TPS, the arrow shows the direction of movement of the car at the time of experiments

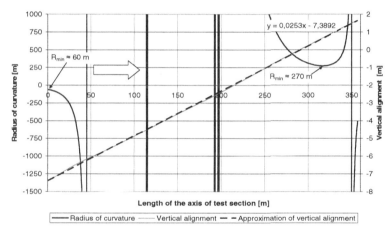

Fig. 2. Characteristics of radius of curvature and vertical alignment test zone as a function of the length of the axis, the arrow shows the direction of the car during experiments

$$a_{cor\_\alpha} = a_m \cdot \cos \alpha + g \cdot \sin \alpha \qquad (2)$$

where:
a_m – measured acceleration value,
$g = 9.81$ [m/s^2] – gravitational acceleration.

As it is apparent from Figure 1, only the beginning of the test section was substantially curved: the minimum value of the curvature radius of this part of the section was about 60 m. The central part was running along a route similar to the rectilinear path, and at the end there was a bend with a curvature radius of about 270 m.

Given that both at the start and end of the test track the car was driven at a very low speed, the need to perform turning manoeuvres was benign, resulting in the formation of the horizontal path, which did not affect significantly the obtained longitudinal acceleration values of the vehicle.

The range of car braking process studies included a heavy vehicle's acceleration from a standing start to a speed of about 50 km/h, and braking from that speed to a stop. In all tests the vehicle was loaded with three people (driver and two passengers in the rear) with a weight of about 80 kg each. On the seat next to the driver part of the measuring apparatus was built over. A Datron measuring system was built on the vehicle for tests, which included, inter alia, two V1 optical heads (at the front and rear of the vehicle) and an AEP data acquisition unit.

The car was driven by an experienced race driver.

The value of the average acceleration as a function of acceleration path was a measure of the acceleration intensity, expressed by formula (3).

$$\overline{a}_{accelarating\,(v,s)} = \frac{v_{max}^2}{2s_{accelerating}} \tag{3}$$

An average delay by stopping track was taken as a measure of car braking intensity (4) and the Mean Fully Developed Deceleration (MFDD), which is an average value of deceleration during a full delay occurrence. Its calculations covered the range of 80% to 10% of the initial velocity, identified with a maximum speed achieved (5).

$$\overline{a}_{braking\,(v,s)} = \frac{v_{max}^2}{2s_{braking}} \tag{4}$$

$$MFDD = \frac{0,8v_{max}^2 - 0,1v_{max}^2}{2(s_{0,1v_{max}} - s_{0,8v_{max}})} \tag{5}$$

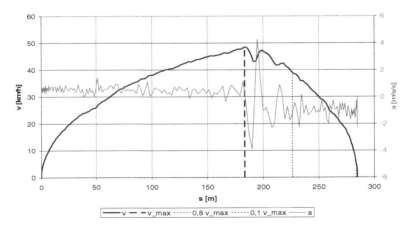

Fig. 3. Sample characteristics of acceleration and speed as a function of the distance for experimental studies

After the studies the measurement data were exported to MS Excel in which characteristic of velocity and acceleration were plotted as a function of distance (Figure 3). Geodetic data, derived from the tachymeter after numerical processing were imported to the PC-CRASH software, which allowed for the execution of dynamic computer simulation and visualization, corresponding to the research made (Figure 4).

Fig. 4. Research surface imported to the PC-Crash with the car SKODA OCTAVIA

4   Analysis of Test Results

Results of research are shown in Table 5 as the arithmetic mean values of MFDD and a(v,s), determined separately for each performed sample of acceleration and deceleration. In addition, Table 5 includes a designated speed and the total distance by the vehicle during the test. Data from the two measuring heads V1 were taken for averaging. The uncertainty determined for both types of deceleration was expressed by the standard deviation recorded in Table 5 in brackets.

Table 5. Results of studies on an inclined road surface

Tires	Trials number	$a_{acc}(s)$ $[m/s^2]$	$a_{brak}(s)$ $[m/s^2]$	MFDD $[m/s^2]$	V_{max} $[km/h]$	s_{calk} $[m]$
winter	8	0.52 (0.02)	-0.99 (0.04)	-1.00 (0.04)	50.9 (0.9)	291 (7)
summer	9	1.17 (0.07)	-2.54 (0.09)	-2.67 (0.1)	52.5 (0.7)	133 (5)

Values of acceleration and deceleration corrected by road deviation angle according to formula 2, are shown in Table 6.

Table 6. Results of studies corrected by the angle of the road surface inclination

Tires	$a_{acc}(s)$ $[m/s^2]$	$a_{brak}(s)$ $[m/s^2]$	MFDD $[m/s^2]$
summer	0.77	-0.74	-0.75
winter	1.42	-2.3	-2.42

On the basis of data contained in Table 6, given the standard deviations recorded in Table 5, it can be concluded that the absolute value of the acceleration obtained by a car, equipped with summer tires, during acceleration and deceleration time was the same. It should be noted that the conditions for traction during acceleration of the car were much worse than during braking. Only the front wheels of the test car were driven, which at the time of acceleration in the forward direction are always unloaded. However, in the process of braking, braking forces are transmitted to the ground through all four wheels of the vehicle. This means that the tested tires were capable of carrying a higher acceleration than braking forces. It should be noted that values obtained in the range of 0.75-0.77 m/s^2 are about 0.5-1.2 m/s^2 lower than the deceleration of a car with summer tires, as published in the literature, at least in the previous studies (Table 3). The reason for this is difficult to explain. Perhaps over the last years the summer tires are more specialized by manufacturers to drive in summer conditions, so that their anti-slipping properties on snow-covered roads were significantly worse.

Deceleration of the car equipped with winter tires (Table 6) does not differ from the data presented in the literature, summarized in Tables 1, 3 and 4. As expected, the acceleration obtained by the car during the speed increasing was significantly lower (by approximately 1 m/s^2) than the braking deceleration.

5   Conclusion

Acceleration values during speeding up and during braking presented in this article can be complementary to the data resulting from the existing literature. In order to increase further the dynamic range information of the car in winter conditions, it is advisable to carry out further experimental studies. It should be borne in mind that during subsequent studies, even when using the same research set (i.e., vehicle, tires, driver, test equipment, space studies) a considerable scatter of the data may occur, associated with a lack of reproducibility of the road surface while driving in winter conditions.

References

1. Christoffersen, S.R., Jarzombek, M.J., Wallingford, J.G., Greenlees, W., Minihan, T.P.: Deceleration Factors on Off-Road Surfaces Applicable for Accident Reconstruction. SAE Technical Paper Series, 950139 (1995)
2. Eddie, R.: Ice, ABS, and Temperature. SAE Technical Paper Series, 940726 (1994)
3. Martin, D.P., Schaefer, G.F.: Tire-Road Friction in Winter Conditions for Accident Reconstruction. SAE Technical Paper Series, 960657 (1996)
4. Navin, F., Macnabb, M., Nicolletti, C.: Vehicle Traction Experiments on Snow and Ice. SAE Technical Paper Series, 960652 (1996)
5. Unarski, J., Wach, W., Zębala, J.: Wartości współczynnika tarcia wróżnych szczególnych okolicznościach. Paragraf na Drodze 10(2000), 32–40 (2000)

Evaluation of Possibilities of a Motor Vehicle Technical Condition Assessment after an Accident Repair in the Aspect of Road Traffic Safety

Jerzy Kisilowski[1] and Jarosław Zalewski[2]

[1] Kazimierz Pulaski University of Technology and Humanities,
Faculty of Transport and Electrical Engineering
26-600 Radom, Poland
kisilow@kisilowscy.waw.pl
[2] Warsaw University of Technology, Faculty of Administration and Social Sciences
00-661 Warsaw, Poland
j.zalewski@ans.pw.edu.pl

Abstract. The paper presents analyses of the modification possibilities of the method of allowing a further use of motor vehicles repaired after accidents. An overall assessment of the process of communication fault clearing was prepared in terms of the selected aspects of a vehicle technical condition.

The focus was on the possibility of taking into account two elements at the stage of assessing the suitability of a vehicle for further use. The first is the assessment of mass, the examination of the influence of mass is the second aspect.

Keywords: car damage repair, stochastic technical stability, road accident.

1 Introduction

The paper presents considerations on the possibility of extending the scope of evaluating the technical condition of a motor vehicle, which was repaired after an accident, in terms of further use. The idea of post-accident repairs is to restore the state of the vehicle before the accident, or at least close to it. A roadworthy vehicle is assumed to meet the requirements of road transport safety. However, existing procedures do not seem to be complete in view of the absence of any guidelines concerning possible deviations after a repair from the nominal state of a vehicle.

Deliberations were conducted to answer the question of what elements could the process of communication fault clearing be complemented, regarding the admission of a repaired motor vehicle for roadworthiness.

2 Characteristics of a Process of Car Damage Repair

Following a road accident both inspection and description of the accident scene are accomplished, however the main components of such description are [6]:

J. Mikulski (Ed.): TST 2013, CCIS 395, pp. 441–449, 2013.
© Springer-Verlag Berlin Heidelberg 2013

a) an inspection protocol of the accident scene, in which general information about the accident (geometry, nature and legal status of the road, road surface conditions, weather conditions and visibility) should be included, and the analysis of the evidence from the scene (characteristic trails of vehicles involved, the trajectories of the wheel tracks in the adopted coordinate system, description of the changes between the state after the accident and the moment of protocol preparation);

b) a sketch of the accident scene prepared in scale and with the wheel trails mapped on it along with the location of debris, liquids, etc.;

c) a photographic documentation containing an overview and the detailed records of accident fragments, photogrammetric documentation which allows mapping the distance on the basis of captured images, detailed photographic records of both vehicles and infrastructure elements involved in the collision.

In further steps, in addition to inspection and description, a reconstruction of an accident is carried out. All collected materials along with the evidence from the scene [5] comprise the basis on which an expert opinion can be elaborated [1] for certain procedures enabling the completion of the whole process.

One of the elements of a car damage repair is an assessment of a degree of damages to a vehicle involved and directing it for repair or, on the basis of the opinion concerning a total damage, transferring it for disposal.

In the case of a vehicle directed for repair on the basis of examination by an expert, the valuation of an insurance company, the protocol and report from the accident reconstruction, the damaged vehicle is transferred to a workshop, where the scope of activities performed depends on the extent of damages and the overall deformation of a vehicle body. It seems, however, that if the degree of damages to the vehicle was so large that its body shape was reshaped, its mass – inertia parameters were also disturbed. Therefore, it seems necessary to control vehicles undergoing the accident repairs, which would allow a clear statement of their roadworthiness.

The disturbance of mass – inertia parameters may lead to a more rapid wear of certain elements in the vehicle chassis, which in turn can cause instability of such vehicle motion. Taking into account the degree of damages to the vehicle after an accident and the extent of repairs, it seems important to introduce an additional inspection of the repaired vehicle in respect of evaluation of both the centre of mass location and the moments of inertia, as well as the examination of motion stability on the basis of specific manoeuvres performing, such as a double lane change.

Conducting such analyses on real objects is expensive and logistically difficult, but with accurate mathematical models of vehicles, they can be carried out using the virtual environment reflecting real situations, especially in the examination of stability.

A further part of the paper is devoted to analysis concerning selected aspects of disturbances of the mass – inertia parameters and stability of a vehicle, which was repaired after an accident.

3   Selected Aspects of Mass – Inertia Parameters of a Motor Vehicle

The results of a collision are changes in mass – inertia parameters, which can affect the further use of a vehicle. It seems that the control of the basic points in a vehicle body itself, which is often not carried out because of the additional costs related to the car damage repair [2], cannot provide a complete assessment of the distribution of mass and moments of inertia in a vehicle. Examining the distance between the characteristic points in a vehicle body comes down to the analysis of its shape, or geometry, only.

The evaluation only on the basis of a vehicle appearance after the repair cannot give a complete answer in the analysed matter. It is impossible, with distance measurements, to validate the mass distribution and the moments of inertia in a repaired vehicle. Therefore, it seems important to determine the location of the centre of mass in such a vehicle against the condition before the accident.

The analysis concerning the changes of the centre of mass location in a vehicle body as a result of the collision was carried out, among others, in [7] and [8]. Calculations in [7] were performed for both cars involved in the previously simulated collision. Certain simplifying assumptions were adopted:

- the vehicle body is represented by a set of cuboid like blocks;
- a uniform distribution of mass in all elements was assumed;
- the centres of mass of every block, into which the vehicle body was divided are at the intersection of their diagonals, if the solid is represented by a cuboid with a rectangular base. For cuboids with the right triangular base it was assumed, that in the overview the centre of mass is located at a distance of one third of the length of each leg, while in a side view – at the middle of its height;
- wheels were included in the mass of a vehicle;
- the origin of the coordinate system, against which the measurements were made, was placed in the right front corner of the vehicle on a road level surface;
- the percentage participation of mass of each cuboidal element in the total mass of a vehicle was assumed as the ratio of its surface to the surface of the whole vehicle in the overview projection.

An example of a vehicle body division into cuboidal elements before and after a collision is shown in Figures 1 – 3.

According to the dimensions shown in Fig. 1, the vehicle was divided into two blocks. Fig. 2 shows the height of solids assumed in order to calculate the location of the centre of mass along the vertical axis..

In Fig. 3 a projection of a vehicle in the x-y plane is shown with a measured depth of deformations resulting from the collision. The body was divided into six blocks and their masses and positions assumed as intended. The block comprising the engine compartment retains the size and shape, and hence the mass.

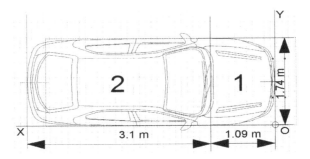

Fig. 1. Division of a vehicle body before the collision into two blocks, the x-y plane projection [Own study]

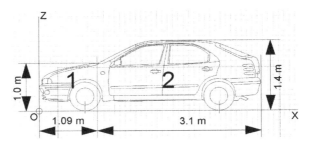

Fig. 2. Division of a vehicle body before the collision into two blocks, the x-z plane projection [Own study]

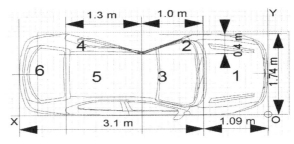

Fig. 3. Division of a vehicle body after the collision into six blocks, the *x-y* plane projection [Own study]

Paper [8] analysed changes of mass – inertia parameters of a vehicle model after a collision, where an uneven weight distribution was adopted including the location of major items, such as the engine, gearbox, seats, etc., in a vehicle.

From the considerations above two observations can be made. The first relates to the method of assuming the mass distribution in a vehicle model, which may significantly influence the results of calculating the centre of mass. The uneven mass distribution can provide these closer to reality than for a vehicle being treated as a solid of a uniform mass distribution. Such accuracy should be taken into account when determining the centre of mass, for example, to examine the stability of a vehicle model.

As the second observation it must be noted that so far analyses of changes in mass – inertia parameters of a vehicle after the accident, not after the post-accident repair, were carried out. Thus, the most important issue seems to be answering the question, to what extent and by what order of magnitude the centre of mass and the mass moments of inertia of a repaired vehicle may differ from the nominal parameters. This is even more important because not every vehicle is repaired in authorised workshops, which means a variety of remedial technologies and materials used.

No works concerning the analysis of disturbed location of the centre of mass for different classes of vehicles before and after the collision as well as after the repair were found. In paper [11] a two-dimensional motion of a vehicle with a dislocated centre of mass and a disturbed moment of inertia around the vertical axis, as a result of an accident, was analysed. A plane motion of the vehicle was considered. In [3] the effect of various locations of the centre of mass in a curvilinear motion of the vehicle was presented. In [4] typical accident damages in a vehicle as well as the methods and techniques for their repair were shown.

In [9] it was stated that the dislocation of the centre of mass in a vehicle as a result of the front impact crash at a velocity of 50km/h may reach about 0.6m. The crash at the relative velocity of 100km/h could disturb the centre of mass by about 0.75m.

Paper [10] presents the results of analysis concerning the influence of the centre of mass location along the longitudinal plane of a vehicle on its steerability. The load in the form of additional weights was realised for three cases:

-   loading the front passenger compartment with 100kg;
-   loading the middle of a passenger compartment with 150kg;
-   loading the rear of a vehicle with 150kg placed in the trunk.

As a result of these additional weights the distance of the centre of mass from the front axle equalled 1.167m, 1.240m and 1.435m, respectively.

4   The Issue of a Motor Vehicle Stability

Considerations conducted in chapter 3 may be applied in the second element of the car damage repair, which allows a more complete assessment of vehicle roadworthiness after repair. That element is the examination of a vehicle motion under specified driving conditions with external disturbances acting on a mechanical system, in this case a motor vehicle. In a series of works a concept of vehicle stability is limited to elements related to motion mechanics, sometimes using disturbances acting constantly (e.g., a constant value lateral force, derived from a blow of wind). Attempts were also made to examine the stability of mathematical models of vehicles using, e.g. a Lapunov, Lagrange or technical stability definition.

Such research, however, does not provide full capabilities of analysis, since the above mentioned definitions of stability have limitations, especially when considering the nature of disturbances acting on the object.

The definition of stochastic technical stability gives the most complete possible assessment of a motor vehicle mathematical model among the popular definitions, because its main advantage is the ability to analyse the motion of a model with random disturbances acting on it. These disturbances can originate from e.g. unevenness of a road surface in the case of examination of a motor vehicle mathematical model, or unevenness of a track in the examination of a rail vehicle. Results of such analyses can be related to the results of the real technical objects.

The examination of stochastic technical stability was carried out for mathematical models of a rail vehicle [12] and a motor vehicle [7]. In [12] the results of stochastic technical stability examination for a rail wheelset are shown. Using the presented definition areas Ω and ω were defined for the transverse vibrations of a wheelset.

The area of feasible solutions Ω was identified as the maximum clearance between the rim of the wheel and the rail and determined l_y. The research was conducted for transverse vibrations of an eleven degrees of freedom wheelset with disturbances originating from the geometric unevenness of the track, gauge changes and the rail head profile changes [13].

A stochastic technical stability was also used in the examination of a mathematical model of a motor vehicle traveling on an uneven road surface [7]. A computer simulation of a vehicle motion, while performing a double lane change manoeuvre, was used. Mass – inertia parameters of the vehicle were disturbed as a result of an accident and a repair. For such a model with disturbed parameters the results of examination were compared with the results for the vehicle with the nominal body geometry. The task is shown in Fig. 4, where the area of feasible solutions Ω is defined (Fig. 5). Trajectories of solutions for both cases were analysed. Quantitative results were obtained using the analysis of the λ Kolmogorov-Smirnov probability test The study was conducted at the level of significance of $\alpha = 0,05$. The probability of vehicle finding itself in an extreme location on the road tripled for the vehicle with disturbed parameters. In [7] the possibility of using the stochastic technical stability examination for non-linear mathematical models of a vehicle was presented as well.

Both in the examination of a vehicle and in the rail mathematical model a method of dividing the area of feasible solutions into a set of classes was used, and then the probability of finding a solution in the given class was examined. This method is versatile because of the possibility to choose the areas of feasible solutions.

Research on a stochastic technical stability of a vehicle model were conducted in two ranges. First, the trajectories and frequencies of occurrence of a deviation from an initial position were compared. The research was conducted for the trajectories after swerving to avoid an obstacle and then returning to the previous lane.

As shown in Fig. 4 and 5 the area, in which the trajectory can lie, was divided into 10 equal intervals, and therefore it was possible to determine whether in the road sections [s, s + ds] and [s', s' + ds'] the trajectories exit beyond this area. For so adopted conditions the trajectories after clearing the obstacles remain in the area Ω, which was adopted as two lanes of the total width equal to about 5 m, the minimum lane width in accordance with [14]. As shown in Fig. 5 it was assumed that the motion is stable when the centre of mass of a particular vehicle model does not exceed the specified distance from the centre line of the road dividing the two lanes.

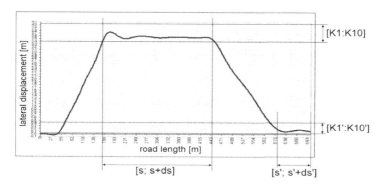

Fig. 4. The set of feasible solutions in the state area E [7]

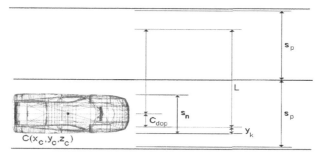

Fig. 5. Conditions for the vehicle to remain in the lane during a manoeuvre of avoiding an obstacle [7]

In the work [7] it was also assumed that the car bypassing the barrier at a speed of 100 km/h should fit in the lane about 4 m wide. This follows from the research on the vehicle's centre of mass trajectory, so the vehicle width should be taken into account. At a disturbed motion, when the centre of mass of the model exceeds the accepted range of 4 m (an icy surface), the outer wheels can be dangerously close to the edge of the road or stay in contact with the shoulder, which could cause a collision or an accident.

The second part of the results analysis in [7] is related to the remaining of the trajectory in certain road intervals. For all the compared results in certain classes, the differences between the frequencies of occurrence are up to 0.6 between the values for a disturbed and an undisturbed vehicle motion.

The terms of the vehicle stability as a real object are presented in ISO 8855:1991 or PN-ISO 8855:1999 "Road vehicles. Dynamics and behaviour while driving. Terminology", p. 6.2 "Equilibrium and stability."

In this standard the steady state condition of a vehicle is specified, in which the sum of applied external forces and moments, as well as inertial forces and moments balancing them, forms a constant set. The transition has been described as other state conditions than those described above.

Stability definitions given according to the standard were compared in [7] to the stability defined for a mathematical model under different assumptions and criteria, as well as the adopted motion disturbances originating from the road unevenness.

5   Conclusion

For further analyses, the approach described above can be used. A disturbance of the vehicle body centre of mass can contribute to instability of motion, as shown in [7]. The disturbance of the centre of mass in the body of a sports vehicle mathematical model taken into account in [7] was assumed to have been caused by an improper repair after the accident. It was shown that a collision at a speed high enough can cause substantial deformations of the body, and hence, lead to changes in the mass distribution and abnormal mass – inertia parameters. This element, checking the whole structure of vehicles, should be included in the process of car damage repair, at least when the structural part of the body including the passenger compartment or the chassis fixings was damaged. As for the items related to the disturbances in the body geometry, the determination of the extent to which those caused by collisions are eliminated during the repairs seems to be an important aspect.

Indication of the relationship between technical stability stochastic mathematical models of cars and stability developed in ISO 8855:1991 for the actual vehicle may allow the verification of the suitability of the repaired vehicle to operation. The ability to conduct computer simulations of the dynamics of vehicle models greatly simplifies the feasibility of this element and reduces costs. It is also possible to reference the results of simulation to the definition of the actual used cars. This allows the simulation results obtained, under certain conditions and with certain criteria, to refer to the results of real technical objects. This allows the verification of the experimental studies.

Computer simulations can be performed on different models and for different manoeuvres. An analysis using the examination of stochastic technical stability of different mathematical models of vehicles is possible, in various traffic conditions and for different manoeuvres. Hence, it is possible to conclude whether the vehicle after the accident repair will have mass – inertia parameters disturbed little enough to not pose a threat in road traffic.

References

1. Kończykowski, W.: Odtwarzanie i analiza wypadku drogowego. Info-Ekspert, Warszawa (1994)
2. Wrona, J., Wrona, R.: Wybrane zagadnienia wpływu napraw powypadkowych nadwozi na bezpieczeństwo drogowe, Eksploatacja i Niezawodność. Maintenance and Reliability 4 (2008)
3. Lozia, Z., Simiński, P., Zdanowicz, P.: Wpływ położenia środka masy na zachowanie się pojazdu w ruchu krzywoliniowym, Czasopismo Techniczne, Wydawnictwo Politechniki Krakowskiej, Kraków (2008)
4. Livesey, W.A., Robinson, A.: The repair of vehicle bodies, 5th edn. Elsevier (2006)

5. Franck, D., Franck, H.: Mathematical method for accident reconstruction. A forensic engineering perspective. CRC Press, Boca Raton (2010)
6. Prochowski, L., Unarski, J., Wach, W., Wicher, J.: Podstawy rekonstrukcji wypadków drogowych. WKŁ, Warszawa (2008)
7. Zalewski, J.: Modelling of the influence of car body disturbances on the stability of motion of road vehicle. Doctoral Thesis, Warsaw (2011)
8. Wicher, J., Stawicki, R.: Modelowanie zderzenia samochodów. Zeszyty Naukowe Instytutu Pojazdów, PW, SIMR 1(31) (1999)
9. Wicher, J.: Bezpieczeństwo samochodów i ruchu drogowego. WKŁ, Warszawa (2003)
10. Janczur, R., Świder, P.: Wpływ położenia środka masy na sterowność samochodu – wyniki badań, IV konferencja naukowo-techniczna, Kielce (2004)
11. Minamoto, H., Takezono, S.: Two-dimensional motion of vehicles damaged due to collision. Vehicle System Dynamics 34(4) (2000)
12. Kardas-Cinal, E.: Badanie stateczności stochastycznej modelu matematycznego pojazdu szynowego. Rozprawa doktorska. Politechnika Warszawska, Warszawa (1994)
13. Kisilowski, J., Kardas-Cinal, E.: Some Problems Related to Investigation of Wheelset Model Stability, Warszawa, Dynamical Problems in Mechanical Systems, PAN IPPT (1991)
14. Regulation of the Ministry of Transport and Maritime Economy of March 2, (Journal of Laws No. 43, item 430) (1999)

Importance of Cloud-Based Maritime Fleet Management Software

Jolanta Joszczuk–Januszewska

Gdynia Maritime University, al. Jana Pawla II 3
81345 Gdynia, Poland
jolajj@am.gdynia.pl

Abstract. Fleet management is the management of a company's transportation fleet. Fleet management includes commercial motor vehicles such as cars, ships, vans and trucks, as well as rail cars. Fleet management also refers to the management of ships while at sea. Maritime fleet management contracts are normally given to fleet management companies that handle aspects like crewing, maintenance, and day-to-day operations. Maritime fleet management software as a tool of Information Technology (IT) enables people to accomplish a series of specific tasks in the management of any or all aspects relating to a company's fleet of ships. Based on examples it can be explained importance of cloud-based maritime fleet management software solution which is presented in this paper. Also is described the framework of solution based on cloud computing (CC) in the shipping industry, allowing software as a service (SaaS) which is considered be the part of the nomenclature of CC.

Keywords: maritime fleet management software, cloud computing, software as a service.

1 Introduction

Fleet management software is computer software that enables people to accomplish a series of specific tasks in the management of any or all aspects relating to a fleet of motor vehicles (cars, truck, ships, trains) operated by a company, government, or other organisation. Fleet management software as directly related to fleet management has become increasingly necessary in later years.

Maritime fleet management software is an Information Technology (IT) tool that is used to simplify administrative and operational tasks of ship and fleet management by providing support in areas such as: maintenance planning and control, compliance management (vessel and crew, operational processes), crew management, document management, reporting procedures, analysing key operational data, cost and process optimization.

Another important function of maritime fleet management software is to transfer and replicate data between the office and the individual ships of the fleet. This ensures that the respective databases on shore and on board remain synchronized and that all involved personnel working with the same information.

J. Mikulski (Ed.): TST 2013, CCIS 395, pp. 450–458, 2013.
© Springer-Verlag Berlin Heidelberg 2013

Based on examples it can be explained importance of cloud-based maritime fleet management software solution which is presented in this paper [1]. Also is described the framework of solution based on cloud computing (CC) in the shipping industry, allowing software as a service (SaaS) which is considered to be the part of the nomenclature of CC [2].

2   Cloud Computing in the Maritime Fleet Management

Growth and popularity surround CC within the business world, but shipping industry is far more complex than the average office set up [3], [4]. So is it a concept that works for shipping?

CC is an evolving paradigm. Cloud technology itself has been defined by the U. S. National Institute of Standards and Technology (NIST) and this definition characterizes important aspects of CC and is intended to serve as a means for broad comparisons of cloud services and deployment strategies, and to provide a baseline for discussion from what is CC to how to best use cloud technology [5].

The NIST's definition of CC identifies five essential characteristics:

- on-demand self-service. A consumer can unilaterally provision computing capabilities, such as server time and network storage, as needed automatically without requiring human interaction with each service provider.
- broad network access. Capabilities are available over the network and accessed through standard mechanisms that promote use by heterogeneous thin or thick client platforms (e.g. mobile phones, tablets, laptops and workstations).
- resource pooling. The provider's computing resources are pooled to serve multiple consumers using a multi-tenant model, with different physical and virtual resources dynamically assigned and reassigned according to consumer demand.
- rapid elasticity. Capabilities can be elastically provisioned and released, in some cases automatically, to scale rapidly outward and inward commensurate with demand. To the consumer, the capabilities available for provisioning often appear unlimited and can be appropriated in any quantity at any time.
- measured service. Cloud systems automatically control and optimize resource use by leveraging a metering capability at some level of abstraction appropriate to the type of service (e.g. storage, processing, bandwidth and active user accounts). Resource usage can be monitored, controlled, and reported, providing transparency for both the provider and consumer of the utilized service.

NIST has explained that CC has also service model – Software as a Service (SaaS) through which applications are provided in the cloud.

This indicates CC as a concept that works for shipping. This is exactly what we need in fleet management when managing ship to shore data synchronisation [6],[7].

3   Importance of Mespas R5 Software Solution

MESPAS is the world's leading fleet management software provider based on cloud computing. MESPAS is located in Switzerland. The mespas R5 software solution covers all major functionalities in terms of technical fleet management: asset management, procurement, and crew management [6],[8].

For example, with mespas R5 Asset Management we can achieve cost-efficient operations and a reliable performance of the fleet. The crews can efficiently plan and execute the technical maintenance of the vessels, and office staff are given an accurate, immediate overview of past, current and future tasks across the fleet.

Asset Management helps ensure that all aspects of fleet management are in compliance with regulations and requirements. Planned maintenance takes place on time, and vessels are kept on schedule and in top condition. The solution significantly reduces the life-cycle costs of equipment and machinery.

Mespas R5 Asset Management is a user-friendly and smart planned maintenance software. It is linked to the MESPAS central database, giving users the added benefit of working with a comprehensive and up-to-date set of data.

Data quality is of great importance in order to run reports, to compare and benchmark.

Importance of mespas cloud solution involved from comparison to traditinal/inhouse-installed software is given in the Table 1.

Table 1. MESPAS cloud solution versus in-house-installed software [6]

MESPAS cloud solution		Traditional / inhouse-installed software
SOFTWARE		
All must-have modules available; easy-to-use to ensure running of software with no or little training.	Products / Module	Typically, considerable training is needed until users are familiar with system.
Feedback from many users reflected in software, all clients benefit from improvements automatically.	Experience	No cross-industry experience reflected in software.
DATA		
Data specialists implement master data according to stringent rules and industry requirements. All data are entered once only – no data duplication, ensuring highest data quality and comparability.	Data quality	Company must define and enforce own standards and regulations. No industry comparisons; comparability restricted to own company; often not even vessel-to-vessel comparisons available.

Table 1. (*continued*)

OPERATIONS		
Implementation & deployment of software within few weeks, no need for time-consuming setup of in-house IT infrastructure (evaluation, acquisition, setup).	Speed of deployment	Deployment can be started only when in-house IT infrastructure (evaluation, acquisition, setup, maintenance) is up and running.
No client-based staff needed to manage synchronization; synchronization can be automated. Assured reliability of synchronization process and data quality.	Synchronization ship-shore	Reliability of synchronization process not guaranteed; typically time-consuming process.
Sophisticated reporting tool available to general real-time reports (standard or customized) for single vessels or across fleet.	Reporting	Very limited reporting; comparisons restricted to data on same server; manual intervention and processing before data can be used for reporting.
Ongoing support via web, telephone or e-mail.	Support	Extensive in-house support needed in terms of IT, software and business know-how.
Planned maintenance system (PMS) is type-approved by DET NORSKE VERITAS (DNV) and Germanischer Lloyd (GL), allowing to change from continuous machinery survey to planned maintenance. MESPAS supports compliance with Machinery Planned Maintenance System (MPMS) requirements of classification societies.	Certification / Classification	Certification is a prerequisite, any reputable competitor will be certified.

IT & SYSTEM ADMINISTRATION		
Clients do not need dedicated IT staff; during implementation a project manager is advisable.	Personnel	Dedicated system administrator, IT staff to manage dedicated IT infrastructure.
With MESPAS, clients need no software-specific IT know-how.	Know-how	IT specialists required; diligent know-how transfer must be ensured with any personnel change.

4   Solution Proposed by iFleet Systems Company

iFleet Systems Company is a Microsoft Software developer and cloud integration services provider specialising in vessel management systems and software for the shipping industry [9]. Its primary focus is to enhance fleet management and operations by providing cost effective and reliable vessel management systems using its unique capabilities and ship to shore data synchronization. Using the latest proven technologies such as cloud computing it can develop, manage and integrate ship IT systems and fleet management software on board vessels and shore based operations.

4.1   Development

iFleet Systems Company has developed a suite of specialist IT data management systems for the maritime industry. It help companies manage the flow of information between their ships and offices, improving their data handling, document management and reporting systems [9].

Cloud Computing as Hosted Services. In marketing, cloud computing is mostly used to sell hosted services in the sense of Application Service Provisioning that run client server software on a remote location. End users access cloud-based applications through a web browser or a light-weight desktop or mobile application while the business software and user's data are stored on servers at a remote location.

The cloud hosted solutions iFleet develop are built using a secure development lifecycle. Its success is to provide bespoke systems that fit the customer's needs rather than a packaged solution that contains hidden on going additional expense.

Business Intelligence Reporting. Once an organisation has analysed its mission, identified all its stakeholders, and defined its goals, it needs a way to measure progress toward those goals. Key Performance Indicators (KPIs) and Key Risk Indicators (KRIs) are these measurements and iFleet Systems Company will allow to warehouse clean data to build KPIs and KRIs that are reliable and reflect the organisation's goals.

iFleet Company can develop and design KPIs and KRIs which can be delivered to senior management via a wide array of media applications. Once collated the data is used to produce KPIs and KRIs that allow the fleet to be monitored.

4.2   Cloud Integration

Connecting the business systems together can be a major technical hurdle. Different systems using separate data formats and incompatible architectures have traditionally proved a challenge to integrate.

Often, these systems are buried deep inside corporate networks without connectivity – exacerbating the problem. The cloud can provide the solution [9].

Using Microsoft's state-of-the-art cloud computing platform; seamlessly joining the dots without impacting system operation makes connecting and publishing the IT systems more responsive and streamlined.

Using a Scalable Cloud Platform to Integrate Backend Systems. Integrating multiple systems together, based on different technologies and different architectures in a secure way can be expensive and technically challenging. Microsoft's Windows Azure AppFabric delivers the solution.

This integration allows the systems to be seamlessly integrated with security included without any additional software and hardware requirements. It provides a cost effective solution to link together on-premises services and applications located anywhere in the world. It also provides the ability to publish these services to the cloud, allowing seamless connectivity to customers, partners and suppliers.

iFleet Cloud Integration Services. The following list identifies the essential services [9]:

- **Security integration**
  Using online data protection practices and policies that have been developed over 15 years the security behind the delivery of the Microsoft Cloud Services exceeds those normally found in most shipping organizations.

  The cloud hosted solutions are built using a secure development lifecycle that ensures security and privacy is incorporated into services by design, from software development to service operations. This approach results in 5 different layers of security – data, application, host, network and physical.

- **Communications**
  Using the latest Microsoft services to provide messaging, document management and data access, iFleet Systems Company specializes in deploying mission critical communications such as email, instant messaging, document management and telephony into the cloud. When utilising the cloud hosted solutions the customers retain all rights, title and interest in the Microsoft data stores.

- **Data backup**
  iFleet Systems Company provides a cloud based data backup service that is combined with the strictest and toughest of security measures.

  Daily backups are performed without the need for human intervention, and only the work done that day needs to be backed up as the rest is already saved from the initial backup.

  Should the worst happen and you experience a disaster that wipes out all of your data in the office or remote laptops, data recovery from the remote server is equally as quick and simple to restore; and what's more, this restoration can be done anywhere in the world at any time.

  The benefits of online data backup are vast, and with cost effective rates, iFleet Systems really are the perfect solution for the data storage.

- **Data synchronisation between systems in disparate locations**
  Synchronising data between different systems in different locations can prove difficult. Microsoft's SQL Data Sync and SQL Azure provide the solution. They allow data to be continually and seamlessly replicated between systems for a fraction of the cost of competing technologies.

Because they're based in the cloud, there are no expensive licenses or hardware to buy and development times can be slashed.

- **Cloud Email, Messaging and Document Management**

Microsoft desktop productivity tools are the clear market leader. Until now, if we wanted the backend components to Office such as Exchange and SharePoint, we had to install and run them yourselves. Instant messaging and web conferencing typically had to be procured and deployed separately and the users were forced to use desktop versions of the Office suite.

Using cloud-based productivity tools means we can radically reduce our IT delivery costs by moving away from an upfront cost plus maintenance to a single, low, per user per month cost.

5   Marineopsys with Cloud-Based Complete Fleet Management Software Suite

Marineopsys fleet management software solution is specially designed for the maritime industry [10]. Marineopsys automates maintenance, supply chain, chartering, operations, crewing, accounting and reporting – in a single, integrated and powerful business management software solution. This solution is built on two main platforms: SaaS and Cloudsuite framework.

5.1   Software as a Service – SaaS

Marineopsys solution is available as SaaS solution which is one of the most important recent innovations in terms of deploying and using software. Simply put, SaaS means delivering software over the Internet, which is used to provide, support and run the system. SaaS is considered to be the part of the nomenclature of CC as service model.

With this comprehensive SaaS solution, companies can start using fleet management solution with ease. SaaS solution will have minimal initial adoption costs compared to the high adoption costs of client server based systems. The implementation time will also be significantly reduced saving time and money to the customers [7].

The customers can start using the system without worrying about procuring hardware and hiring IT personnel to maintain the infrastructure. This will reduce the operational costs of using a fleet management system. The customers will need a web browser only and will take care of all IT jobs like maintaining, monitoring and backing up valuable data. The access to the system will be fully secure through Secure Sockets Layer (SSL) connection.

5.2   Cloudsuite Framework

Marineopsys solution is built on in house developed Cloudsuite framework specially designed for cloud computing. The framework is designed for rapid application development thereby facilitating very quick application customization based on customer requirements. The architecture is scalable to support different databases like MySQL, Oracle, SQL Server.

Developing a new application on this framework can reduce up to 60% of effort compared to traditional ways. This will ensure a faster turnaround time for change requests. The framework also ensures security at all the layers thereby storing data with highest integrity and supports scaling the application to provide better performance as the client base increases.

6   Conclusion

Based on examples presented in paper implementing cloud-based maritime fleet management software gains importance now. It is a business necessity.

MESPAS is the world's leading fleet management software system provider based on cloud computing, and the fastest growing software as a service company in the maritime industry [11].

With SaaS, we're not talking about a new technology. The SaaS concept is based on the idea to provide, support and run software via the Internet. So companies starting to employ SaaS will not have to change technology; they'll just make use of a new way of accessing computing. Then the importance of SaaS on a global basis.

For example, in December 2012, the Singapore-based company Union Marine Management Services has signed a contract with MESPAS to implement mespas R5 on its fleet of bulk carriers and vehicle carriers [6]. Union Marine Management Services can focus on ramping up its core business operations, while MESPAS provides the cloud computing software working tools. Furthermore MESPAS is in charge of system implementation services such as database population and system configuration.

Importance of iFleet Systems Company solution is connected with:

- Specialist software development for the shipping industry, adding value while reducing costs.
- Quickly and cost-effectively extend IT systems across the fleet and shore based operations.

Marineopsys reduces the cost of implementing and operating a fleet management software solution by one-third with its cloud solution. We will not need to procure expensive hardware and hire IT resources to implement and maintain our system.

References

1. Franclin Jr., C., Chee, B.J.S.: Cloud Computing. CRC Press Inc., Taylor & Francis Group, Boca Raton (2010)
2. Babcock, C.: Management Strategies for the Cloud Revolution. McGraw-Hill, New York (2010)
3. Mell, P., Grance, T.: The NIST Definition of Cloud Computing. National Institute of Standards and Technology, Information Technology Laboratory (2011)
4. Business Software Alliance. BSA Global Cloud Computing Scorecard (2013)
5. Cisco Global Cloud Index. Forecast and Methodology, 2010-2015 (2011)

6. MESPAS, `http://www.mespas.com/` (date of access: July 18, 2013)
7. Thoma, C.: Software as a Service - revolutionizing fleet management. Digital Ship 12(1), 40–42 (2011)
8. Thoma, C.: Fleet management on the basis of cloud software. Ship & Offshore (3), 76–77 (2011)
9. iFleet Systems, `http://www.ifleetsystems.com/` (date of access: July 18, 2013)
10. Marineopsys, `http://www.marineopsys.com/` (date of access: July 18, 2013)
11. Joszczuk–Januszewska, J.: The Benefits of Cloud Computing in the Maritime Transport. In: Mikulski, J. (ed.) TST 2012. CCIS, vol. 329, pp. 258–266. Springer, Heidelberg (2012)

Fuzzy Algorithm for Highway
Speed Harmonisation in VISSIM

Milan Koukol and Ondřej Přibyl

Czech Technical University in Prague, Faculty of Transportation Sciences,
Konviktská 20, 110 00 Prague 1, Czech Republic
{koukol,pribylo}@fd.cvut.cz

Abstract. In this paper is demonstrated, how a fuzzy control system can be implemented and verified directly in a microsimulation tool from the company PTV, VISSIM. A new fuzzy algorithm for speed harmonisation is developed and its implementation is explained in details. The main advantage of this solution is in the direct implementation of the control algorithm in the microsimulation tool without the need to deal with an API and external software. Additionally, the configuration and optimisation of the control algorithm is performed quickly in the tool and directly responds to the microsimulation results. This has an impact on the time to implement such a solution as well as the overall cost, since a single resource able to work with the microsimulation tool can do the work and no programming experience are required.

Keywords: highway management systems, fuzzy control system, microsimulation, VISSIM.

1   Introduction

Highway management systems have become very popular in the recent years. In the Czech Republic, we have been facing first applications of such systems and the demand is increasing. This is also due to the fact, that many international studies demonstrate their impact on road safety as well as ecology and economy. Some results from a study summarizing results from many international projects include [1]. Similar evaluation is in progress also for the systems in the Czech Republic. In this paper we focus on design of a speed harmonisation system and demonstrate how such a system can be implemented and verified directly in a microsimulation tool from company PTV, VISSIM and add-on module VAP. The proposed approach is however adoptable for any fuzzy traffic control. Additionally, the configuration and optimisation of the control algorithm is performed quickly in the tool and directly responds to the microsimulation results.

A real problem from the Prague city ring is presented in this paper. A new fuzzy algorithm to speed harmonisation is developed and compared to the existing solution based on decision trees. The results are presented and the improvements by using a fuzzy control system are discussed. After additional testing and verification, such control algorithm shall be implemented on the Prague city ring.

J. Mikulski (Ed.): TST 2013, CCIS 395, pp. 459–467, 2013.
© Springer-Verlag Berlin Heidelberg 2013

2   Speed Harmonisation

In this chapter, we provide a short overview of the different speed harmonization algorithms. A nice description of the current experiences with speed harmonization was provided in MARZ [2]. It was prepared by the transport ministry in Germany and provides a complete overview and recommendations for implementation of highway management systems. It covers all different areas needed for successful implementation of such systems, starting with the definition of terms, different physical control layers, data preprocessing algorithms, as well as control algorithms and requirements on the actuators. It has been used for several implementations in Germany, a country with most advanced highway management system in Europa. The speed harmonization algorithm described here is based on a decision tree and uses speed (km/h), traffic density (veh/km) and traffic volume (veh/h). The decisions within the MARZ algorithm are based on the fundamental diagram and include hysteresis.

Natural improvement of the above mentioned algorithms based on decision trees are methods based on so-called fuzzy decision trees [3]. In the Czech Republic, only one implementation of a speed harmonization algorithm is in use since 2010. The Prague ring with 40km of roads in both direction and traffic volume of up to 60000 veh/day [4] is equipped with 18 resp. 16 gantries with variable speed limits (for the different directions respectively). The Speed harmonization algorithm implemented here was prepared as a part of the research grant INEP and is described in [5]. It is a modular system based on the principles of MARZ algorithms. The algorithm was however before implementation adopted based on results of extensive simulation. Different control algorithms as well as different setting of their parameters were evaluated using microsimulation tool VISSIM. Within the speed harmonization module, the speed limit is controlled by means of variable message signs (VMS). The decision on the optimal speed limit restriction is based on traffic flow data obtained from the road cross sections with induction loop. The table below shows the conditions at which the speed limit restriction is switched on or off.

Table 1. The decision tree for the speed harmonization within project INEP [5]

Speed limit displayed at VMS	$Q_{pcu}(i)$ or $(S(i) and D(i))$			$Q_{pcu}(i)$ or $(S(i) and D(i))$		
120	$\geq Q_{pcu}^{on120}$			$< Q_{pcu}^{off120}$		
100	$\geq Q_{pcu}^{on100}$			$< Q_{pcu}^{off100}$		
80	$\geq Q_{pcu}^{on80}$	$\leq S^{on80}$	$\geq D^{on80}$	$< Q_{pcu}^{off80}$	$> S^{off80}$	$< D^{off80}$
60		$\leq S^{on60}$	$\geq D^{on60}$		$> S^{off60}$	$< D^{off60}$

This decision tree algorithm with particular switching values obtained from simulation results was evaluated on the Prague city ring where it has been in use. The following chapter describes its enhancement discussed above, a fuzzy decision tree (FDT). The main results are presented in the following chapter.

2.1   Fuzzy Decision Tree of the Speed Harmonisation

The proposed fuzzy decision tree uses three input variables: traffic volume (veh/h), speed (km/h) and traffic density (veh/km). The volume has four linguistic variables very small, small, medium and high. The speed has two linguistic variables medium and slow and the last input density has two linguistic variables medium and low. The input membership functions are provided for clarity in Fig.1. The parameters of the membership functions were set on the base of existing expert knowledge.

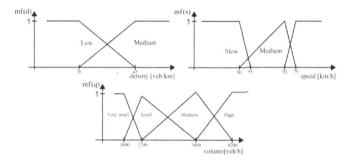

Fig. 1. The membership functions of the input variables - volume, density, speed

Our FDT has one output variable - *desired speed* (km/h) - with six linguistic variables (very very slow, very slow, slow, medium, fast and very fast) as depicted in Fig.2. Similarly to the membership functions on the input variables, they were designed using expert knowledge.

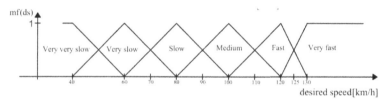

Fig. 2. The membership functions of the output variable desired speed

The rule base together with the database containing the different inference mechanism is commonly known as the fuzzy knowledge base. Each fuzzy rule consists of two parts; an antecedent (between the IF and THEN) and a consequent (following THEN). The fuzzy rules are provided in the following table, where one lane corresponds to one fuzzy rule.

Table 2. Table providing the fuzzy rules

If	Q very small			Then	DS veryfast
If	Q small			Then	DS fast
If	Q medium			Then	DS medium
If	Q high			Then	DS slow
If	S medium	And	D medium	Then	DS slow
If	S slow	And	D low	Then	DS very slow

3   Implementation of the Fuzzy Control Algorithms in PTV VISSIM

This section describes the design of the fuzzy control system (also called fuzzy inference system - FIS) for a highway system. An overview of a fuzzy control system within the scope of highway control system is illustrated in Fig.3. In this paper, we selected the PTV VISSIM [6] software to help us in the project because of its usage at the Faculty of Transportation Sciences (Czech Technical University). For traffic control system design and development, the VAP language (Vehicle Actuated Programming) was used.VAP [7] is a simple programming language embedded as an add-on module to VISSIM. In order to make programming easier, PTV implemented a graphical user interface to design and edit VAP – based control directly and in a user friendly way. This interface is called Visualization VAP (VisVAP) [8] and can be used for example for intersection control design, speed harmonisation, ramp metering and others. VisVAP is a Graphical User Interface which broadens the possibilities of VAP language use for design of traffic control systems. VisVAP application can be defined as "a tool" for a comfortable design and editing of a program for traffic control system. The main reason we decided to use VisVAP is the fact that there is no procedure for design of a fuzzy based traffic control for speed harmonization in Vis-VAP at the moment.

The micro-simulation model in VISSIM application is depicted in the upper part of the Fig.3. The bottom part depicts the control strategy (system). The Control strategy requires vehicular detectors to provide accurate information of the prevailing traffic

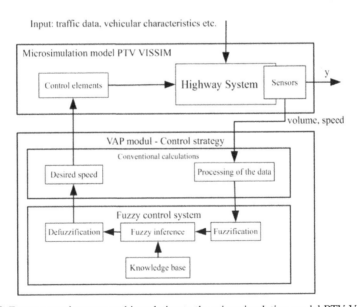

Fig. 3. Fuzzy control system and its relation to the microsimulation model PTV VISSIM

conditions in real-time. This information (volume, speed) is used as an input data for the control system. The control strategy input data (measured values) must be processed (processing of the data) before entering the fuzzy control system. Those processed data enter the fuzzy control system. This paper focuses on and deals with the fuzzy control system in detail. At the end of this paper we also show how to convert the crisp values calculated by the fuzzy control system into values (desired speed) shown at the VMS. The process step "Desired speed" converts the output of the system to the speed limits transmitted to the VMS.

3.1   The Base Elements of VisVAP for the Fuzzy Algorithm Construction

Any VisVAP flow chart of the fuzzy control system consists of some basic elements [8]. Please note that we are not providing all of the available elements, but only those needed for the design of a fuzzy control system.

Table 3. VisVAP elements

Symbol	Element	Description
Start	Terminus	Defines the start and the end of the program logic
mf_q := 0	Statement	Used for commands and assignments
(alpha < q) & (q < beta)	Condition	Used for logical conditions

All above mentioned elements were used to implement the fuzzy control system. Parameterization of chosen membership function and crisp value calculation in defuzzification process seem to be the key element in such control system design. For a better overview of fuzzy logic and its advantages please refer to [9].

3.2   Fuzzification, Inference Engine and Defuzzification in VisVAP

In this section, the steps used in aFIS (fuzzy inference system) are described [10]. The important steps for designing (identification) of a fuzzy system are described in chapter. The following steps aim to focus on the particular issues described above and provide description on how to implement them using VisVAP.

Computing a Degree of Membership

First, the degree of membership is calculated for the input variables. Given the inputs (crisp values) their membership values are computed. This process is called 'input fuzzification'. In the next step, the degree of membership is calculated for the all input value. The proposed system uses triangular type of membership functions. This decision was based on the computational efficiency of proposed shapes (see for example discussion in [11]) and an easier parameterization. The following equation and Fig 4 demonstrates parameterization of a triangular membership function. All parameters α, β and γ, that is referred to in the flow chart and in expressions must be defined in the parameters table (VisVAP). The following diagram is an excerpt from VisVAP demonstrating of calculation the membership function for the triangular function. We used only two elements, the Condition and the Statement.

$$\Lambda(q, \alpha, \beta, \gamma) = \begin{cases} 0 & q < \alpha \\ (q - \alpha)/(\beta - \alpha) & \alpha \le q \le \beta \\ (\gamma - q)/(\gamma - \beta) & \beta \le q \le \gamma \\ 0 & q > \gamma \end{cases} \tag{1}$$

Rule Evaluation and Consequent

Next, the weight for a rule antecedent is computed. The minimum of all rule's degree of membership is applied in our model. The implementation in VisVAP is demonstrated in Fig.5. The resulting value is considered to be a weight of the rule (also called firing strength) and is applied to the consequent membership function of the desired speed. Fig.5 describes the fifth rule from the table 2.

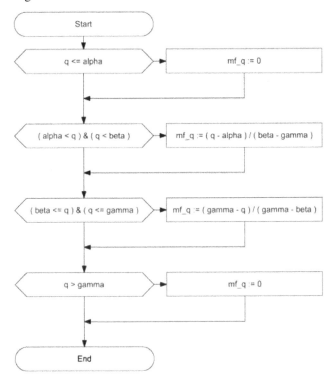

Fig. 4. VisVAP flow chart of the triangular function (mf = membership function)

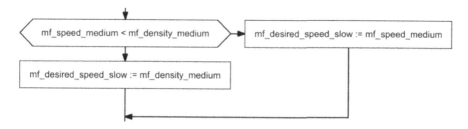

Fig. 5. Example of the rule evaluation in VisVAP(mf = membership function)

Defuzzification

The process of transforming a fuzzy set into a specific numeric value (desired speed) is called defuzzication, where the membership function of output set is determined (given) by the union of cut-of membership functions (applies for Mamdani's type of FIS – [10]). We use the centroid (see the equation 2), which returns the center of the area under the fuzzy set obtained in previous step. This method is the most common choice in applications for its simple structure of min/max operations. The calculations are shown below Fig.6.

$$ds^* = \frac{\sum_{j=1}^{m} ds\_x_j * mf(ds_j)}{\sum_{j=1}^{m} mf(ds_j)} \tag{2}$$

desired_speed := (mf_desired_speed_fast_y_1 * ds_x_1 + mf_desired_speed_fast_y_2 * ds_x_2) / (mf_desired_speed_fast_y_1 + mf_desired_speed_fast_y_2)

Fig. 6. Example of the defuzzification process in VisVAP

Integration of the main and secondary communication of the fuzzy engine into the control program core is the final step. Basically it is nothing more, than a basic system which can be expanded or easily modified. For instance it is possible to apply data smoothing and trend prognosis. Furthermore it is possible to apply various methods of fuzzification and defuzzication with discrete expression.

The desired speed limit must be computed based on the defuzzified crisp output values. Here, the decision on the speed limit to be shown at the VMS is made according to the rules set shown in table 4.

Table 4. Conversion of crisp values to desired speed limit shown at the VMS

Condition	Speed limit displayed at VMS
Crisp value ds $\geq$ 125	No further speed limit restriction
110 $\geq$ Crisp value ds < 125	120
90 $\geq$ Crisp value ds < 110	100
70 $\geq$ Crisp value ds < 90	80
Crisp value ds < 70	60

One issue not mentioned earlier within this paper is a hysteresis. For practical implementation it is not recommended to keep switching the output speed restriction for example every computing period. It would certainly not lead to harmonization of traffic. For this reason, an artificial hysteresis was introduced and implemented in a way that a new speed cannot be changed back to its original value in less than two following iterations. On the other hand, the speed limit can be further more restricted within this interval. In other words, the transition 100-80-100 (km/h) is not allowed, however a transition 100-80-60 (km/h) is a valid one.

4   Conclusion

In this paper, an approach to implement a fuzzy control system directly within a microsimulation tool VISSIM was presented. It provides a detailed overview so that everybody can evaluate control strategies without detailed knowledge of programming languages or the need to purchase an additional API. Based on own experience, in real world projects a significant amount of time and effort can be saved compared to standard programming, especially since this task is typically not the main scope of such a project, but only a need to demonstrate its results. To simplify such evaluation is really an important issue nowadays, so we believe that the described implementation approach can be very useful and can bring more advanced control strategies into use. This article has clearly shown the potential of VisVAP software in design of an advanced control system. The designed system can be applied to many different applications. Next, this approach will be used and evaluated in larger projects, where different highway management strategies (including road line traffic control) will be compared and enhanced using a microsimulation tool. This is the objective of a research project TA2-0522 (SIRID - Development of a new generation of a highway control and test system) from the Technological Agency of the Czech Republic. The authors would like to acknowledge this possibility and the cooperation of the entire research team participating on this project.In SIRID, an advanced algorithm for a highway speed harmonisation will be developed as an improvement of the existing solution using more advanced algorithmic and different input variables. The new algorithm will be directly evaluated and compared to the existing algorithms.

References

1. Přibyl, O., Michaelsen, M.: Universal highway management system and its impact on safety. Presented at the Network of National ITS Associations Workshops, Prague (2009)
2. Bundesanstalt für Straßenwessen, Merkblattfür die Ausstattung von Verkehrsrechnerzentralen und Unterzentralen (MARZ), Bundesministerium für Verkehr Bau- und Wohnungswesen, Ausgabe (1999)
3. Ramya, R., Anandanatarajan, R., Priya, R., Arul Selvan, G.: Applications of fuzzy logic and artificial neural network for solving real world problem. In: IEEE-International Conference on Advances in Engineering, Science And Management (ICAESM 2012) (2012)
4. Road and Motorway Directorate of the Czech Republic, http://www.rsd.cz/ (date of access: July 26, 2013)

5. Šůstek, M., Přibyl, O., Wosyka, J.: Systém identifikace nehod a zvýšení propustností liniových komunikací. Závěrečná zpráva 2009.Projekt VaV CG944-033-120 (2010)
6. VISSIM 5.40-01 - User Manual, Karlsruhe: PTV Planung Transport Verkehr AG (2011)
7. VAP 2.16 Interface, User Manual, Karlsruhe: PTV Planung Transport Verkehr AG (2012)
8. VisVAP 2.16 User Manual, Karlsruhe: PTV Planung Transport Verkehr AG (2006)
9. Babuška, R.: Fuzzy Modeling for Control, 1st edn. Springer (1998) 978-0792381549
10. Jura, P.: Basics of the fuzzy logic for control and modeling. Brno University of Technology, Brno (2003) 80-214-2261-0
11. Kosko, B., Mitaim, S.: The shape of fuzzy sets in adaptive function approximation. IEEE Transactions on Fuzzy Systems 9, 637–656 (2001) (1063-6703)

Airport Traffic Simulation Using Petri Nets

Jacek Skorupski

Warsaw University of Technology, Faculty of Transport, Warsaw, Poland
`jsk@wt.pw.edu.pl`

Abstract. Airport traffic consists of aircraft performing landing, takeoff and taxi procedures. It is controlled by air traffic controller (ATC). To safely perform this task he/she uses traffic surveillance equipment and voice communication systems to issue control clearances. One of the most important indicators of this process efficiency is practical airport capacity, which refers to the number of aircraft handled and delays which occurred at the same time. This paper presents the concept of airport traffic modelling using coloured, timed, stochastic Petri nets. By the example of the airport with one runway and simultaneous takeoff and landing operations, the applicability of such models in analysis of air traffic processes is shown. Simulation experiments, in which CPN Tools package was used, showed the impact of the initial formation of landing aircraft stream on airside capacity of the airport. They also showed the possibility of its increase by changes in the organisation of takeoff and landing processes.

Keywords: air traffic control, traffic processes modelling, Petri nets, airport capacity.

1 Introduction

The efficient interaction of all elements of airport is necessary to achieve a high level of safety, which in addition to the speed of movement is one of the fundamental factors of competitiveness of air transport. Particularly important processes in this complex system are traffic processes, including takeoffs and landings on runways, taxiing after landing and taxiing before takeoff which are held on taxiways. Numerous attempts are taken to develop effective models of airport elements. They use various methods of mathematical modelling. These include, among others: dynamical programming, fuzzy sets, queuing models, hierarchical Bayesian models.

A new concept of airport traffic modelling using coloured, timed, stochastic Petri nets is presented in the following sections. Petri nets are a convenient tool for analysis of traffic processes in transport. However, they are rarely used in airport capacity analysis. The few examples include [1,4]. The general approach to the use of coloured Petri nets in modelling of aircraft operations can be found in [2].

In this paper it was assumed that the planes report for take-off and landing according to the flight plan previously submitted, but disturbed by random factors. Such disruptions can occur at any stage (taxi, takeoff, approach, final approach, landing). In addition, this study examines the approach procedure with many details. For instance

J. Mikulski (Ed.): TST 2013, CCIS 395, pp. 468–475, 2013.
© Springer-Verlag Berlin Heidelberg 2013

the procedural separations at fourth and at the second mile before the runway threshold is taken into account. Also the go-around procedure is included in the model.

The paper is completed with the example of utilisation of the model for determination of average operational delay, at given traffic procedures, and dependent on the traffic volume. Two cases were examined. In one of them traffic flow was characterised by a random time distance between consecutive aircraft inputs to the system. The other case provides initial, partial arrangement of landing aircraft flow.

The results were obtained using the CPN Tools 3.4 package [5,10]. A single simulation run corresponds to 30 takeoff operations and 30 landing operations, which is adequate to study traffic activities in real airport of assumed size and configuration. To determine the airside capacity of the airport - in different simulation runs the aircraft input rate was iteratively changed, so that it was possible to observe the dependence of traffic volume and mean operational delay. The whole study consisted of 100 individual simulation runs, for which the input intensity covered entire relevant area.

2   Airport Traffic Model

In this paper active elements of the transport system are studied, dealt dynamically, during the realization of their task - that is, the traffic processes. Infrastructure and organization are limitations to this process and must be, to some extent considered during its modelling. It is assumed that the purpose of the modelling is the airport's airside capacity. The search for opportunities to increase capacity, as well as its precise estimation is one of the most important elements of the Single European Sky concept [9].

2.1   Methodology

The air traffic process includes the organizational rules, regulations and standards, to ensure the safety of all traffic participants. In this process, there are time periods in which aircraft move in a planned manner, in accordance with standard procedures. These fragments of the traffic process are characterized by its duration. The process is dynamic, but in those time periods there are no events influencing the level of safety, and procedures such as changing speed or direction are planned, in accordance with the constraints resulting from characteristics of infrastructure components and tailored to the exploitation characteristics of vehicles.

Between these fragments there are traffic events which are extracted whereas the scope of the analysis. In this case these events are defined as having an impact on safety of traffic.

The above mentioned events may have the nature of conditions, which logical value can be evaluated. In this case they are represented by a Boolean *true* or *false*. They may also have a nature of a certain process, mostly short-term. In this case, the event will be represented by its type, but also by duration.

This approach to the traffic process allows the use of Petri nets for modelling it [7]. Stable traffic situations correspond to places in the net, traffic events – to transitions. Tokens in places can be identified as traffic participants or states of environment.

The following methodology of air traffic processes analysis in terms of Petri net elements was adopted:

(a) The set of places P corresponds to traffic situations, in which a plane can be found during normal traffic.

(b) The set of transitions T corresponds to the set of events (actions) that change the traffic situation, particularly affecting the safety of manoeuvres.

(c) The input function I defines the traffic situations that determine occurrence of certain events, output function O defines what event (action) must occur to change the status of the analyzed system, and the inhibitor function H specifies the traffic situations that must not exist to certain events can occur.

(d) The initial marking M_0 defines the traffic situation in which we begin the analysis, and the current marking M describes the current state of the system.

2.2   The Object of Modelling

In this study the modelled system is an airport with one runway. There is one taxiway leading to runway threshold that is used by all aircraft. If it is impossible to perform the takeoff procedure immediately after finishing taxiing – aircraft wait at the end of taxiway before entering the runway. The takeoff sequence results from the order of reaching the waiting point on the FIFO rule.

In the case of a landing procedure, the scope of analysis includes final approach, starting from the fourth mile from runway threshold, up to aircraft exit into the taxiway. Runway occupancy time is dependent on the type of aircraft. It was assumed that in the modelled system there are three categories of aircraft. For each of them runway is equipped with a dedicated rapid exit taxiway. Should it be impossible to maintain the necessary separation at the second mile from the runway threshold, model provides the execution of missed landing procedure.

2.3   Petri Net for Airport Traffic Modelling

The model presented in this paper, was developed based on the Petri net, satisfying a number of conditions, which are necessary for the proper mapping of the essential elements of the system. Such a net must be: coloured, timed, stochastic and with priorities. Airport traffic model can therefore be written as [8]:

$$S_{AT} = \{P, T, I, O, H, M_0, \tau, X, \Gamma, C, G, E, R, r_0, B\} \tag{1}$$

where:

P – set of places,

T – set of transitions, $T \cap P = \emptyset$,

I, O, H, are functions respectively of input, output and inhibitors:

$I, O, H: T \rightarrow B(P)$, where $B(P)$ is the multiset over the set P, and functions I, O, H are determined for transition $t \in T$ as:

$t^+ = \{p \in P: I(t,p) > 0\}$ – input set of transition t,

$t^- = \{p \in P: O(t,p) > 0\}$ – output set of transition t,

$t^o = \{p \in P: H(t,p) > 0\}$ – inhibition set of transition t,

$M_0: P \rightarrow \mathbb{Z}_+ \times R$ – initial marking,

$\tau: T \times P \rightarrow \mathbb{R}_+$ – delay function, specifying static delay $\tau(t)$ of transition t,

$X: T \times P \rightarrow \mathbb{R}_+$ –random time of realisation of traffic event (transition) t,

Γ – nonempty, finite set of colours,

C – function determining tokens that can be stored in a given place: $C: P \rightarrow \Gamma$,

G – function defining the conditions that must be satisfied for the transition, before it can be fired,

E – function describing the so-called weight of arcs,

R – set of timestamps (also called time points) $R \subseteq \mathbb{R}$,

r_0 – initial time, $r \in R$.

$B: T \rightarrow \mathbb{R}_+$ – function determining the priority of transition t.

3   The Model of Takeoff and Landing

The structure of Petri net modelling takeoff process and preceding it taxiing for take-off process is shown in Figure 1. We can distinguish 13 places and 10 transitions here. We will accept the following designations of places:

$$P = \{p_1, p_2, ..., p_{13}\} \qquad (2)$$

where: p_1 – „generator", p_2 – „ac after loading", p_3 – „ac may taxi to RWY", p_4 – „ac ready for takeoff", p_5 – „ac may line-up the RWY", p_6 – „ac at RWY threshold", p_7 – „begin of takeoff", p_8 – „end of phase I", p_9 – „airborne", p_{10} – „out", p_{11} – „RWY occupied", p_{12} – „RWY free", p_{13} – „may line-up".

The following designations of transitions were adopted in the model:

$$T = \{t_1, t_2, ..., t_{10}\} \qquad (3)$$

where: t_1 – „takeoff input", t_2 – „clearance for taxiing", t_3 – „taxiing", t_4 – „clearance for RWY line-up", t_5 – „runway line-up", t_6 – „clearance for takeoff", t_7 – „takeoff phase I", t_8 – „detachment", t_9 – „procedural turn", t_{10} – „destination".

The structure of Petri net which is modelling the landing process from the fourth mile from the runway threshold to exit into one of the taxiways is shown in Figure 2.

In this model one can distinguish 11 places and 10 transitions. We will adopt the following designations of places:

$$P = \{p_{11}, p_{12}, ..., p_{21}\} \qquad (4)$$

where: p_{11} – „RWY occupied", p_{12} – „RWY free", p_{13} – „may line-up", p_{14} – „generator init", p_{15} – „initialise", p_{16} – „4th mile", p_{17} – „4th mile - separation", p_{18} – „2nd mile", p_{19} – „2nd mile - separation", p_{20} – „touchdown", p_{21} – „exit in TX".

In addition, the following transitions designations were adopted in the model:

$$T = \{t_{11}, t_{12}, ..., t_{17}\} \tag{5}$$

where: t_{11} – „generator", t_{12} – „landing input", t_{13} – „approach", t_{14} – „overshoot", t_{15} – „final landing", t_{16} – „braking", t_{17} – „destination".

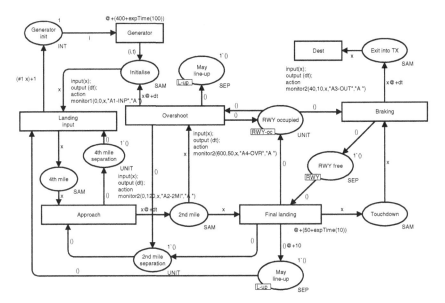

Fig. 1. Model of takeoff process at the airport with one runway

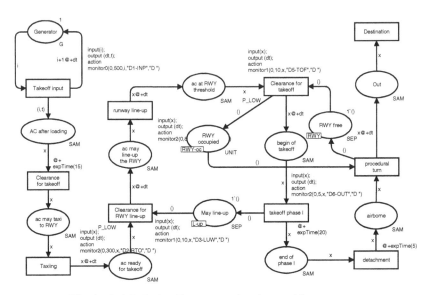

Fig. 2. Model of landing process at the airport with one runway

4   Simulation Analysis of Airport Traffic

The presented model can be used to analyse various issues related to airport operations. These are among others:

- research of the efficiency of use of existing infrastructure at the existing traffic volume and structure,
- analysis of the possibility of increasing traffic at the airport, with simultaneous control of quality indicators,
- study of the effects of the planned modernisation, such as changes in equipment, extension of runways, taxiways and fast runway exits,
- airport's airside capacity analysis, both in existing traffic and equipment as well as in case of changes (failure or upgrade).

4.1   Simulation Experiments

Simulation experiments were performed iteratively. In each iteration the input stream intensity was increased until the saturated traffic was achieved. The study began with input stream mean intensity of:

- in experiment 1 – 12 aircraft per hour, both arriving and departing,
- in experiment 2 – 20 arriving aircraft per hour and 12 departing aircraft per hour.

Simulation with the use of CPN Tools package was provided by the successive events method, with the rhythm of event changes determined by the timestamps $r \in R$ (see formula (1)). This package performs the simulation in step-by-step mode, which allows observation of the progress of traffic process, and if necessary change the parameters characterising the system. Thanks to available automatic replication, it is possible to perform many simulation runs for different initial markings or different input parameters. This latter feature was used in this study to repeat the simulation process with different characteristics of aircraft input stream.

4.2   Results of Simulation Experiments

The result of a single simulation run is a pair of values that specify the traffic volume and operational delay. In the first experiment the average input intensity of landing and takeoff aircraft was the same. Results of this experiment for 100 completed simulation runs are given in Figure 3a. Each point is the result of simulation using CPN Tools of 30 landing and 30 taking off planes.

As an airside capacity of the airport, the traffic volume for which the probability that the average delay is greater than the accepted value (10 minutes) is bigger than 0,5 was adopted [6]. In this example it reached 18 takeoff and landing operations per hour.

For the second simulation experiment it was assumed that landing aircraft are initially formed into a stream, in which spacing between aircraft is practically constant and close to the value of separation on approach to landing, which is equal two minutes. Additionally, in a study it was assumed that the flow of taking off aircraft starts about 40 minutes after the beginning of the series of landings. The results are presented in Figure 3b. They show a significant increase in capacity of the airport, despite the continued unfavourable composition of the traffic (50% of landings and 50% of takeoffs, which report randomly with high intensity).

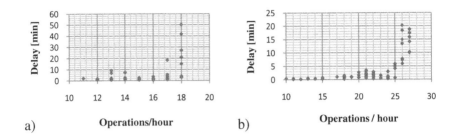

Fig. 3. Results of experiments: a) without initial forming of traffic streams, b) landing traffic spacing – 2 minutes, takeoff traffic postponed by 40 minutes

The increase in capacity is significant – about 50%. Traffic volume at which saturation occurs and also rapid increase in the average delay is 27 operations per hour. The initial arrangement of arriving aircraft stream is very beneficial, as it allows increasing the number of landing operations performed per unit of time. But on the other hand the close packing of landing aircraft makes taking off planes to wait for completion of the entire series of 30 simulated landings. In this case there is no practical ability to perform any takeoffs in the gaps between landings. The waiting time of departing aircraft is larger in this case than in experiment 1. However increase in capacity is possible, thanks to changes in the departing aircraft stream. The highest value of capacity occurs when departing aircraft stream begins reporting readiness to taxi after completion of a little over half of the landings. Figure 3b shows the results for that particular situation – the series of takeoffs begins 40 minutes after the beginning of a series of landings. If they begin simultaneously resulting airport capacity is lower. The same occurs when it begins later. In these cases, the increase in capacity is about 20%.

5   Conclusion

This paper presents an integrated model of taking off and landing processes built using coloured, timed, stochastic Petri nets. As shown by simulation experiments conducted using CPN Tools package, this model allows for easy and efficient obtaining reliable results. As the toolbox permits to study the occurrence graph of model execution, verification of the formal correctness of developed models was also performed.

The results of simulation experiments lead to some interesting conclusions. Air traffic control services in approach area tend to implement the controller support systems that allow the formation of landing stream in order to increase its internal density, of course in accordance to the separation rules. This allows for greater number of operations per unit time, thereby increasing the capacity of the airport. It is the reasonable attitude, but as shown by simulation experiments, only when the number of taking off aircraft is small. Otherwise, the necessity of waiting for finishing the series of landings causes significant delays in departures, and capacity decreases. The most preferred solution is to control the flow of taking off aircraft in such a way, that initial moment of their reporting to ATC is planned after completing about half of the landings. Obtained in this way increase in total capacity reaches 50% of the value calculated for the landing stream without forming. Any larger displacement of taking off stream reduces the delay, but also reduces the total number of operations per unit time. Similarly smaller displacement increases the waiting time without increasing the number of operations. In both cases, no increase in capacity is achieved.

References

1. Davidrajuh, R., Lin, B.: Exploring airport traffic capability using Petri net based model. Expert Systems with Applications 38(9), 10923–10931 (2011)
2. Everdij, M., Blom, H.: Modelling hybrid state Markov processes through dynamically and stochastically coloured Petri Nets, Distributed Control and Stochastic Analysis of Hybrid Systems Supporting Safety Critical Real-Time Systems Design (HYBRIDGE Project), EU IST Programme (2004)
3. Lower, M., Magott, J., Skorupski, J.: Air Traffic Incidents Analysis with the Use of Fuzzy Sets. In: Rutkowski, L., Korytkowski, M., Scherer, R., Tadeusiewicz, R., Zadeh, L.A., Zurada, J.M. (eds.) ICAISC 2013, Part I. LNCS (LNAI), vol. 7894, pp. 306–317. Springer, Heidelberg (2013)
4. Oberheid, H., Söffker, D.: Cooperative Arrival Management in Air Traffic Control - A Coloured Petri Net Model of Sequence Planning. In: van Hee, K.M., Valk, R. (eds.) PETRI NETS 2008. LNCS, vol. 5062, pp. 348–367. Springer, Heidelberg (2008)
5. Vinter Ratzer, A., et al.: CPN Tools for Editing, Simulating, and Analysing Coloured Petri Nets. In: van der Aalst, W.M.P., Best, E. (eds.) ICATPN 2003. LNCS, vol. 2679, pp. 450–462. Springer, Heidelberg (2003)
6. Skorupski, J.: Method of determining airport capacity for different systems of air traffic organisation. Ph.D. thesis. Warsaw University of Technology (1997)
7. Skorupski, J.: Method of analysis of the relation between serious incident and accident in air traffic. In: Berenguer, C. (ed.) Advances in Safety, Reliability and Risk Management, pp. 2393–2401. CRC Press/Taylor & Francis, London (2011)
8. Skorupski, J.: Traffic Incidents as a Tool for Improvement of Transport Safety. In: Weintrit, A. (ed.) Navigational Problems – Marine Navigation and Safety of Sea Transportation, pp. 101–108. CRC Press/Taylor & Francis/Balkema, Leiden (2013)
9. Tobaruela, G.: Capacity Estimation for the Single European Sky. In: 5th International Conference on Research in Air Transportation, San Francisco, USA (2012)
10. Westergaard, M., Kristensen, L.M.: The Access/CPN Framework: A Tool for Interacting with the CPN Tools Simulator. In: Franceschinis, G., Wolf, K. (eds.) PETRI NETS 2009. LNCS, vol. 5606, pp. 313–322. Springer, Heidelberg (2009)

Single Window for Maritime Safety Information

Ryszard Wawruch

Gdynia Maritime University, Morska 81-87,
81-225 Gdynia, Poland
wawruch@am.gdynia.pl

Abstract. Paper presents remarks on the legal aspects connected with and technical infrastructure needed for broadcasting from shore to ship of maritime safety information (MSI) and transmission of the same kind of information from ship to shore. It includes the idea and scope of MSI, collecting, processing and broadcasting of this information by shore stations, the reception and display on board ship and transmission from ship to other vessels and competent authorities on shore. The infrastructure contains major items needed to: the formatting of MSI into an S-100 compatible format, the creating a single window for MSI and the transmission of safety related information from shore stations and ships. Maritime Assistance Service (MAS) is suggested as a contact point for collecting and dissemination of MSI.

Keywords: E-navigation, single window, maritime safety information.

1 Introduction

Maritime Safety Information (MSI) means information essential for the safety of navigation, protection of maritime environment and prevention of accidents at sea. According to the Circular 1288 "Amendments to the Resolution A.706(17): World-Wide Navigational Warning Service" (MSC.1/Circ.1288) issued by the Maritime Safety Committee (MSC) of the International Maritime Organisation (IMO) MSI covers a large scope of information including information about acts of piracy, tsunamis and other natural phenomena, health advisory information as recommended by the World Health Organisation (WHO) and security related information. Minimal requirements for its contents and principle of dissemination are defined in the international regulations established by IMO (conventions, codes and recommendations).

Now, there is a particularly high expectation to improve the processing and dissemination of MSI and its integration within bridge systems and shore systems [1].

2 Legal Basis

Requirements regarding MSI are included in the following conventions, codes and resolutions of the International Maritime Organisation (IMO):

J. Mikulski (Ed.): TST 2013, CCIS 395, pp. 476–485, 2013.
© Springer-Verlag Berlin Heidelberg 2013

1. International Convention for the Safety of Life at Sea (SOLAS Convention), 1974, as amended [3]:
   - Regulation V/4 (Navigational warnings) and Resolution A.706(17): World-Wide Navigational Warning Service;
   - Regulation V/5 (Meteorological services and warnings) and Resolution A.528(13): Recommendation on weather routeing;
   - Regulation V/9 (Hydrographic services);
   - Regulation V/11 (Ship Reporting System – SRS) and Resolution A.851(20): General principles for ship reporting systems and ship reporting requirements, including guidelines for reporting incidents involving dangerous goods, harmful substances and/or marine pollutants;
   - Regulation V/12 (Vessel Traffic Service – VTS);
   - Regulation V/31 (Danger messages);
   - Regulation V/32 (Information required in danger messages);
   - Regulation VII/6 (Reporting of incidents involving dangerous goods);
   - Regulation VIII/12 (Accidents to nuclear ships);
   - Regulation XI/3 (Obligations of Contracting Governments with respect to security);
   - Regulation XI/4 (Requirements for Companies and ships);
   - Regulation XI/6 (Ship security alert system);
   - Regulation XI/7 (Threats to ships); and
   - Regulation XI/9 (Control and compliance measures).
2. International Convention for the Prevention of Pollution from Ships (MARPOL Convention), 1973, as modified by the Protocol of 1978 relating thereto, as amended:
   - Article 8 (Reports on incidents involving the discharge or possible discharge of harmful substances); and
   - Protocol I (Provisions concerning reports on incidents involving the discharge or possible discharge of harmful substances (in application of article 8)).
3. International Convention relating to Intervention on the High Seas in Cases of Oil Pollution Casualties, 1969 (Intervention Convention) Article III (a) and (f) (Consultations and notifications).
4. International Convention on Oil Pollution Preparedness, Response and Co-operation, 1990 (OPRC Convention) Articles 4 and 5.
5. International Code for the Safe Carriage of Packaged Irradiated Nuclear Fuel, Plutonium and High-Level Radioactive Wastes on Board Ships (INF Code), Paragraphs 29 and 30.

According to these international regulations, each government and ship shall:

1. Government:
   - Take all steps necessary to ensure that, when intelligence of any dangers is received from whatever reliable source, it shall be promptly brought to the knowledge of those concerned;
   - Carry out meteorological arrangements:

- For transmission and reception of weather messages to and from ships, using the appropriate shore-based facilities for terrestrial and space radio-communications services;
- For examination, dissemination and exchange of ship's messages in the manner most suitable for the purpose of aiding navigation;
- To warn ships of gales, storms and tropical cyclones by the issue of information in text and, as far as practicable, graphic form;
- To issue and transmit, at least twice daily, in text and, as far as practicable, graphic form including charts transmitted by facsimile or in digital form for reconstitution on board the ship's by data processing system, weather information suitable for shipping containing hydro-meteorological data, meteorological analysis and prognosis, warnings and forecasts of weather, waves and ice; and
- To prepare and issue such publications as may be necessary for the efficient conduct of meteorological work at sea and to arrange, if practicable, for the publication and making available of daily weather charts for the information of departing ships;

- Make hydrographic and nautical information and its upgrading available on a world-wide scale as timely, reliably, and unambiguously as possible;
- Promulgate notices to mariners in order that nautical charts and publications on board ships are kept, as far as possible, up to date, and to provide data management arrangements to support these services;
- Ensure that vessel traffic services established on its territory or on its request by IMO outside its territorial waters broadcast in proper manner information indispensable for efficient work of the following services: information, maritime assistance and traffic organisation; and
- Ensure the provision of security level information to port facilities within its territory, and to ships operating in its territorial waters or having communicated an intention to enter its territorial sea and provide a point of contact through which such ships can request advice or assistance and to which such ships can report any security concerns about other ships, movements or communications.

2. Ship:
- Communicate by all means at its disposal to ships in the vicinity and to the competent authorities, the information about met dangerous ice, a dangerous derelict, or any other direct danger to navigation, or a tropical storm, or encounters sub-freezing air temperatures associated with gale force winds causing severe ice accretion on superstructures, or winds of force 10 or above on the Beaufort scale for which no storm warning has been received;
- Report the particulars of an incident involving the loss or likely loss overboard of dangerous goods in packaged form or in solid form in bulk into the sea, without delay and to the fullest extent possible to the nearest coastal state;
- Participate in ship reporting systems (SRS) and transmit required reports (sailing plan, position report, deviation report, final report, etc.);

- Transmit results of the ship's weather observation at the main standard times for surface synoptic observations (i.e. at least four time daily and at more frequent intervals when in the vicinity of a tropical cyclone, or of a suspected tropical cyclone), using ship's terrestrial or space radiocommunication facilities;
- Receive MSI transmitted by shore stations and other vessels;
- Transmit required security related information to the officers duly authorized by the government of the port of call; and
- Be fitted with security alert system which after activation shall initiate and transmit a ship-to-shore security alert identifying the ship, its location and indicating that the security of the ship is under threat or it has been compromised.

In order to make transmission and receiving of the MSI possible governments and ships shall [3]:

1. Government - undertake to make available, as it deems practical and necessary, appropriate shore-based facilities for following space and terrestrial radiocommunication services to cover the various sea areas:
   - Radiocommunication service utilizing geostationary and polar orbiting satellites in the Maritime Mobile-Satellite Service; and
   - The maritime mobile service in the bands: 415 - 535 kHz, 1605 - 4000 kHz, 4000 - 27500 kHz and 156 - 174 MHz.
2. Ship - be equipped with radiocommunication facilities as required by the chapter IV of the SOLAS Convention.

3   Information Transmitted and Institutions and Organisations Participating in the Exchange of MSI

MSI comprises wide scope of information: navigational, hydrographical, meteorological, traffic related, ship and port security related, etc. It is collected and transmitted by ships and many shore institutions and services in different formats using various means of broadcasting. Particular types of MSI may be transmitted from shore by: ship's flag state administration, coastal state administration, hydrographic office, NAVAREA and METAREA co-ordinators, different governmental and private meteorological services, Maritime Assistance Service (MAS), Maritime Rescue Coordination Centre (MRCC), counter-piracy service, coastal and harbour VTS, security port service, port authority, harbour master's office, etc. It may be broadcasted using voice communication (preferable in English), or in digital form for reconstitution on board the ships by data processing system (e.g. NAVTEX) and in graphic form including charts transmitted by facsimile.

SOLAS Convention defines information required in danger messages transmitted by ships only. The form in which they are sent is not obligatory. They may be transmitted by terrestrial and space radiocommunication services either in plain language (preferably English) or by means of the International Code of Signals. The following information is required in particular types of these messages [3]:

1. Message regarding ice, derelicts and other direct dangers to navigation:
   - The kind of ice, derelict or danger observed and its position; and
   - The date and time (Universal Co-ordinated Time) when the danger was last observed.
2. Message about tropical cyclones (storms):
   - A statement that a tropical cyclone has been encountered;
   - The date and time (Universal Co-ordinated Time) and position of ship when the observation was taken; and
   - As much of the following information as is practicable:
     - Barometric pressure, preferably corrected and its change during the past three hours;
     - True wind direction and force on the Beaufort scale;
     - Description of the sea state (smooth, moderate, rough, high); and
     - Description of the swell (slight, moderate, heavy), the true direction from which it comes and period or length (short, average, long).
3. Message regarding winds of force 10 or above on the Beaufort scale – data like for the tropical storm but excluding the details concerning sea and swell.
4. Message about sub-freezing air temperatures associated with gale force winds causing severe ice accretion on superstructures:
   - The date and time (Universal Co-ordinated Time) and position of ship when the observation was taken;
   - Air temperature and sea temperature (if practicable); and
   - Wind force and direction.

Additionally, convention presents samples of such messages, e.g. [3]:

"TTT DERELICT. OBSERVED DERELICT ALOMOST SUBMERGED IN 4006N, 1243 W, AT 1630 UTC.APR 21"

The text below presents sample of MSI received as navigational warning by NAVTEX on 18th of May 2013:

"ZCZC MA99
171330 UTC APR 13
NORWEGIAN NAV WARNING 195 /2013
MARINERS ARE KINDLY REQUESTED TO TAKE PART IN A SURVEY CONCERNING THE QUALITY OF MSI BROADCAST VIA SAFETYNET AND NAVTEX. THE PURPOSE OF THE SURVEY IS TO IMPROVE THE SERVICE. TWO SHORT QUESTIONNAIRES ARE AVAILABLE AS BELOW:
1. NAVIGATIONAL WARNINGS:
WWW.SURVEYMONKEY.COM/S/IHO-SURVEY
2. METEO INFO AND WARNINGS:
WWW.JCOMM.INFO/MMMS
NNNN"

Fig. 1 presents, as sample, information about cyclone received from Wilkens Weather Technologies as forecast for Aaron Studwell on 13rd of May 2013 at 1800 UTC [6].

There are not any other international standards regarding collecting, dissemination and broadcasting of the MSI except International Hydrographic Office (IHO) Geospatial Standard S-100 for Hydrographic Data.

S-100 is a framework standard intended to allow development of data models and associated product specifications for a variety of data sources, products, and customers. This includes new spatial models to support imagery and gridded data, 3-D and time-varying data (x, y, z, and time), and new applications that go beyond the scope of traditional hydrography. S-100 comprises multiple components that are aligned with the ISO 19100 series of geospatial standards [5].

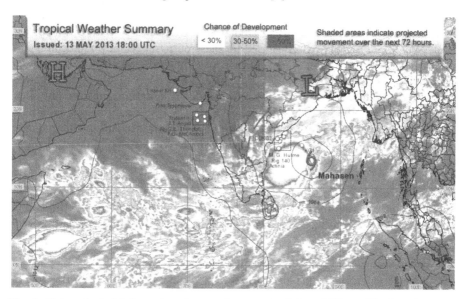

Fig. 1. Meteorological information about cyclone received from Wilkens Weather Technologies as forecast for Aaron Studwell on 13rd of May 2013 at 1800 UTC [6]. Bay of Bengal: At 1800UTC Monday, Tropical Cyclone Mahasen was located near 12.9N 85.4E and moving to the northwest at 9kts. Maximum sustained winds are 50kts. Please refer to the latest bulletin for information on this system. Arabian Sea: There are no suspect areas at this time. Elsewhere, tropical cyclone development is not expected through Friday.

4   Single Window for MSI

The main tasks of the maritime administration and shore institutions and organizations responsible for broadcasting of MSI to ships are:

1. Collecting, exchange and processing of hydrographic, meteorological, nautical and safety and security related information delivered in different format and using different methods of transmission by ships (including danger messages) and many

shore stakeholders like hydrographic office, meteorological service, services responsible for national and maritime security, VTS, MRCC, MAS, etc.
2. Broadcasting of the MSI in different manner to ships.

A single window for MSI shall facilitate the exchange of information between all above mentioned stakeholders and integrate computerized flow management systems. Standard S-100 mentioned in chapter 3 shall be used to convey and share MSI and do to that the infrastructure shall base on its format. It will help to modernize the World Wide Navigation Warning System (WWNWS), and in consequence the functional requirement of the Global Maritime Distress and Safety System (GMDSS) introduced by IMO approximately twenty years ago and dealing with the MSI transmissions and receiving. The infrastructure shall utilise present communication systems as required by chapter IV of the SOLAS Convention. Additionally it shall have the capacity to introduce of new communication systems for broadcasting and addressed transmission using Digital Selective Calling (DSC) of MSI. Now SafetyNet, NAVTEX and NBDP is used for these purposes but new radiocommunication technology like INMARSAT Fleet Broad Band, digital HF, NAVDAT and VDE may be considered. NAVDAT is already a solution available by the International Telecommunication Union (ITU) to broadcast digital information, but other radio systems identified by ITU compatible with GMDSS requirements should be tested and added to the infrastructure if relevant. The infrastructure should integrate the formatting of MSI under S-100 format, a single window for MSI and a transmission network to broadcast MSI to ships. Exchange protocols between the single window for MSI and ships should be developed. To enhance MSI into digital messages, it is necessary to format MSI into a comprehensible language in order to secure the interoperability of data and the integration, automation, exchange and interconnection of the systems [2]. An international MSI exchange standard is necessary to [2]:

1. Develop within IHO and World Meteorological Organisation (WMO) a nautical and meteorological information S-100 format in order to achieve the formatting of MSI.
2. Modernize MSI transmission from shore to ships (actually based on telex messages).
3. Integrate and display MSI on bridge systems.
4. Transmit and share data between onshore services involved in the collection and in the processing of the MSI and those interested by the knowledge of the nautical situation.

MSI under S-100 format transmitted to a ship must be integrated and display in automatic manner on ship's navigational bridge monitor.

It should be possible for a ship to feed back a competent authority onshore. The single window for MSI should integrate standard messages from ships to consolidate a general overview of safety information [2].

5   Maritime Assistance Service (MAS) as a Point of Contact for MSI

Maritime Assistance Services (MAS) are introduced according to recommendations of the IMO Resolution A.950(23) adopted on 5th of December 2003 in order to help the ships in danger other than danger to the human life at sea. It means the circumstances of a ship's operation that involve MAS are not those requiring rescue of persons at sea. Assistance of MAS may be needed when the ship [4]:

1. Is involved in an incident (e.g., loss of cargo, accidental discharge of oil, etc.) that does not impair its seakeeping ability but nevertheless has to be reported.
2. According to its master's assessment, is in need of assistance but not in a distress situation requiring the rescue of persons on board.
3. Is found to be in a distress situation and those on board have already been rescued, with the possible exception of those who have remained aboard or have been placed on board to attempt to deal with the ship's situation.

If, however, in an evolving situation, the persons on board find themselves in distress, the involvement of the MRCC and not the MAS will have priority [4].

The establishment of MAS does not necessarily entail the setting up of a new organization. The functions of the MAS could, at the discretion of the maritime administration, be discharged by an existing organization, preferably an MRCC, or alternatively a harbour master's office, a coast guard operations centre, VTS centre or another body. The allocation of MAS functions to an MRCC could be an advantageous and effective solution but would require the MRCC personnel to be well trained in distinguishing between circumstances causing a ship to find itself in a distress situation and circumstances placing a ship in a difficult situation but not in distress as defined in the SAR Convention and procedures arising there from. The MRCC concept entails co-ordination of search and rescue operations. By contrast, MAS, within the scope of the described resolution, is responsible for receiving and transmitting communications and monitoring the situation only [4].

Other effective solution is allocation of MAS functions to a VTS which cooperates with MRCC in the event of commencing a search and rescue operation and is a point of contact for ships operating in its area.

First of all MAS is a contact point. According to the IMO recommendation it shall perform following functions [4]:

1. Receiving reports, consultations and notifications provided for by the relevant IMO instruments in the event of an incident involving a ship.
2. Monitoring the ship's situation if a report discloses an incident that may give rise to a situation where the ship is in need of assistance.
3. Serving as the point of contact between the master and the coastal state if the ship's situation requires exchanges of information between the ship and the coastal state other than a distress situation that could lead to a search and rescue operation.

4. Serving as the point of contact between those involved in a marine salvage operation undertaken by private facilities at the request of the company and the coastal state if this state considers that it should monitor the conduct of the operation.

National instructions and procedures shall indicate to the organization performing the MAS functions at a minimum [4]:

1. The authority or organization to which it transmits the information obtained from a ship.
2. The authority or organization from which it receives instructions concerning its action and the particulars to be transmitted to the ship.

Nevertheless, as soon as information indicates that the ship's situation might subsequently require a rescue operation, the MRCC if the MAS function is not discharged by it, must be informed so that it can make preparations to respond if necessary.

MAS should be operational on a 24-hour basis. It should be possible for the English language to be used in communication between a ship in need of assistance and MAS. MAS should be authorized by its respective government to exchange with each other information concerning reports received and situations involving ships which may be in need of assistance.

Due to the described functions dedicated to the MAS, it may be designated as a point of contact for collecting and dissemination of the MSI.

6   Conclusion

The single window for MSI infrastructure shall meet present and revised conventional requirements for means and methods of communication between ships and between ship and shore and fulfil following requirements defined by the IMO Working Group on e-navigation as so called e-navigation solution [3]:

- S1: Improved, harmonized and user-friendly bridge design;
- S2: Means for standardized and automated reporting;
- S3: Improved reliability, resilience and integrity of bridge equipment and navigation information;
- S4: Integration and presentation of available information in graphical displays received via communication equipment; and
- S9: Improved communication of VTS portfolio.

Designation of the Maritime Assistance Service (MAS) as a point of contact for radiocommunication between ships and shore will simplify MSI infrastructure and facilitate the introducing of one common standard for exchange of information. The open question which has to be solved is usefulness of the IHO Geospatial Standard S-100 for Hydrographic Data for exchange of health advisory information according to the recommendation of the World Health Organisation (WHO).

VTS should comprise at least an information service and may also include others such as a navigational assistance service or a traffic organization service or both of them. Transmission of the VTS traffic picture could help navigator to have a better overview of the surrounding traffic. Mandatory reporting from ships to VTS and centre of the ship reporting system (SRS) could be automated into standard messages to be process to a single window. Due to that, the allocation of MAS functions to a VTS centre could be an advantageous and effective solution.

Present concept of the technical infrastructure of a single window for MSI considered by the IMO Working Group on e-navigation is presented in Fig. 2. It does not take into consideration security related information and health advisory information. Information delivered by hydrographical and meteorological services is disseminated outside the single window.

According to the concept presented in this paper all kind of the Maritime Safety Information may be exchanged through single window.

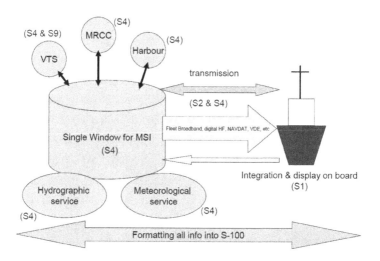

Fig. 2. General arrangement of the technical infrastructure of a single window for MSI [2]

References

1. Development of an e-navigation strategy implementation plan, Report from the Correspondence Group on e-navigation to NAV 59, NAV 59/6, IMO, London (2013)
2. Development of an e-navigation strategy implementation plan, Single Window for Maritime Safety Information. Submitted by France, IMO, London (2013)
3. International Convention for the Safety of Life at Sea (SOLAS), 1974, as amended, IMO, London (2009)
4. Resolution, A.: 950(23) Maritime Assistance Services (MAS), IMO, London (2003)
5. The IHO S-100 Standard and e-Navigation Information. Concept Exploration with Ship Reporting Data and Product Specification, E-NAV10/INF/7, IMO, London (2012)
6. http://www.wilkensweather.com/ (date of access: July 18, 2013)

Author Index